Chandrasekar Vuppalapati

Artificial Intelligence and Data Science in Agriculture

Also of interest

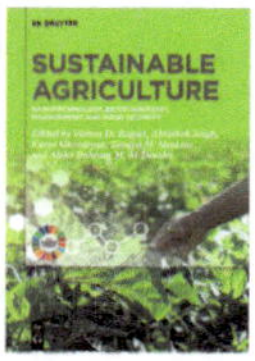

Sustainable Agriculture.
Nanotechnology, Biotechnology, Management and Food Security
Vishnu D. Rajput, Abhishek Singh, Karen Ghazaryan, Tatiana M. Minkina, Abdel Rahman M. Al-Tawaha (Eds.), 2025
ISBN 978-3-11-136197-0 e-ISBN (PDF) 978-3-11-136975-4
e-ISBN (EPUB) 978-3-11-136994-5

Food Biotechnology.
Food Processing, Gene Editing and Safety
Oluwatosin Ademola Ijabadeniyi, Christiana Eleojo Aruwa, Titilayo Adenike Ajayeoba (Eds.), 2025
ISBN 978-3-11-144121-4, e-ISBN (PDF) 978-3-11-144123-8,
e-ISBN (EPUB) 978-3-11-144157-3

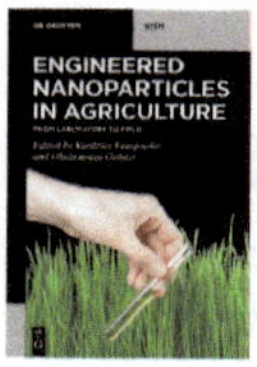

Engineered Nanoparticles in Agriculture.
From Laboratory to Field
Vasileios Fotopoulos, Gholamreza Gohari (Eds.), 2023
ISBN 978-1-5015-2315-1, e-ISBN (PDF) 978-1-5015-2322-9,
e-ISBN (EPUB) 978-1-5015-1552-1

Soft Computing and Optimization Techniques for Sustainable Agriculture
Debesh Mishra, Suchismita Satapathy, Prasenjit Chatterjee, 2022
ISBN 978-3-11-074495-8, e-ISBN (PDF) 978-3-11-074536-8,
e-ISBN (EPUB) 978-3-11-074537-5

Machine Learning for Sustainable Development
Kamal Kant Hiran, Deepak Khazanchi, Ajay Kumar Vyas, Sanjeevikumar Padmanaban (Eds.), 2021
ISBN 978-3-11-070248-4, e-ISBN (PDF) 978-3-11-070251-4,
e-ISBN (EPUB) 978-3-11-070258-3

Chandrasekar Vuppalapati

Artificial Intelligence and Data Science in Agriculture

Specialty Crops and Climate Change Modeling

DE GRUYTER

Author
Chandrasekar Vuppalapati
Computer Engineering Department
San Jose State University
One Washington Square
Engineering Building Room 284
San Jose, CA 95192-0180
USA
chandrasekar.vuppalapati@sjsu.edu

ISBN 978-3-11-143841-2
ISBN 978-3-11-143889-4 (PDF)
ISBN 978-3-11-143945-7 (EPUB)
DOI https://doi.org/10.1515/9783111438894

Library of Congress Control Number: 2024946885

Bibliographic information published by the Deutsche Nationalbibliothek
The Deutsche Nationalbibliothek lists this publication in the Deutsche Nationalbibliografie; detailed bibliographic data are available on the internet at http://dnb.dnb.de.

De Gruyter and Walter de Gruyter GmbH are part of De Gruyter Brill.
www.degruyterbrill.com

Questions about General Product Safety Regulation:
productsafety@degruyterbrill.com

Cover illustration: structuresxx/iStock/Getty Images Plus
Printing: CPI books GmbH, Leck

FSC www.fsc.org MIX Papier | Fördert gute Waldnutzung FSC® C083411

The author dedicates his works, book, and efforts of this book to his late father Murahari Rao Vuppalapati, who had inspired him to write the book and guided the author's pursuits of life, and to his loving mother Hanumayamma Vuppalapati, who was the inspiration to develop company and dairy products for the betterment of humanity and future generations.

Acknowledgments

The author is deeply indebted to the love, support, and encouragement of his wife, Anitha Ilapakurti, and the active support of his daughters, Sriya Vuppalapati and Shruti Vuppalapati, who helped draft the first version of the manuscript.

The author is deeply thankful to the support of his elder brother, Rajasekar Vuppalapati, and the joyful support of his younger brother, Jaya Shankar Vuppalapati. Additionally, the author is also very thankful to his elder sisters, Padmavati Vuppalapati and Sridevi Vuppalapati.

The author sincerely thanks Santosh Kedari and his team in India for conducting field studies and surveys for dairy, agriculture, and specialty crop analytics and bringing the market feedback for the betterment of services.

The author is deeply indebted to Sharat Kedari, who helped in setting Cloud and machine learning (ML) algorithms and developed economic, climate, and specialty crops ML models. In addition, the author is thankful for the support, hard work, and dedication of Vanaja Satish who helped to develop specialty crop ML models, climate change models, and climate projections models. Finally, the author is sincerely and deeply thankful to Sandhya Vissapragada for her contributions in data science and in creating machine learning and climate change models on Microsoft Azure and Google Cloud and developed climate change, economic, and deployment models.

 | https://doi.org/10.1515/9783111438894-202

Preface

Specialty crops are fruits and vegetables, tree nuts, dried fruits, horticulture, and nursery crops including floriculture. They made up 18.44% of the $433.569 billion in cash receipts from agriculture in the United States in 2021. In 2020, they were 21.47% of the $363.464 billion. Specialty crops are getting more attention across the country as shown in the 2018 farm bill (Agricultural Act of the 2018 Farm Bill (P.L. 115–334)) with more provisions that deal with specialty crop issues, reflecting their growing importance in the global economy. The US population is changing fast, and this has increased the demand for specialty crops and created new market opportunities for US farmers. This can be seen from the retail advertising dollars. On the supply side, the specialty crops have many benefits for farmers, such as adding value to their crops, being more resilient to climate change, and using fewer resources while keeping yields.

Specialty crops enhance the competitiveness and diversity of the US agriculture sector. The federal government supports the development and marketing of specialty crops through a grant program that aims to improve their outcomes. Many states have a strong stake in the specialty crop industry, as it provides economic and employment opportunities for farmers and processors.

Some examples of states that rely heavily on specialty crops are California, Florida, Wisconsin, Idaho, and Georgia. California is the leading producer of specialty crops in USA, both in quantity and variety, with over 400 different crops grown. Some of these crops, such as almonds, pistachios, artichokes, and broccoli, are almost exclusively grown in California. Florida, the second-largest producer, is famous for its oranges, but also grows about 300 other commodities, earning the title of Specialty Crop State. Nursery and vegetable crops each generate billions of dollars in value for Florida. Specialty crops are also an important component of the Midwest region's rural economy, with an estimated value of $1.8 billion. Wisconsin, for instance, produces about $5.3 billion in economic activity and 24,800 jobs from specialty crop processing each year. Idaho is known for its specialty crops of potatoes and onions, which are the main drivers of its agricultural economy. Georgia's top specialty crops include blueberries, watermelon, bell peppers, sweet corn, cucumbers, cabbage, onions, and pecans, which play a significant role in the state's economy.

Specialty crops also contribute to the food security of USA, as one-third of the food Americans eat is directly or indirectly derived from honeybee pollination. Honeybees are vital pollinators for many specialty crops, especially in Georgia, where they ensure the successful production of crops worth approximately $1.5 billion.

At the global level, the total market addressable (TAM) for specialty crops estimated at $1.6 trillion in the year 2022 is projected to reach a revised size of $1.8 trillion by 2026, growing at a cumulative annual growth rate (CAGR) of 3.8%. The major geographies and countries that can play an important role include North America (USA and Canada), Asia (Japan and China), Europe (France, Germany, Italy, UK, Spain, Russia), Asia-Pacific (Australia, India, South Korea), Latin America (Argentina, Brazil, Mexico, rest of Latin America), Middle East, and Africa. In essence, every continent has high stakes vested in specialty crops.

Growing specialty crops, however, has its own difficulties. Specialty crops are generally more vulnerable to weather stressors and need more careful management than traditional row crops. Specialty crop growers face risk from unexpected weather events and disasters, losses from pests and disease, uncertainty about government regulation or credit conditions, uncertainty in price and the ability to find buyers, and uncertainty related to human factors such as labor access that may affect their businesses. While these risks affect all farmers, the characteristics of specialty crop production and their associated markets often lead to higher levels of risk. For example, many specialty crops are sold in thinner markets than conventional crops, where the market involves a very small number of buyers or sellers. This means there is less information available to set prices that reflect actual supply and demand factors, making it harder for producers to predict cash flows. Thinner markets make it more difficult for government and insurance providers to offer products that protect against price risk based on sound principles. This also can make it impossible to establish hedging options such as futures markets.

This book presents specialty crops statistical models that estimate crop yields based on historical weather data and uses weather simulations from climate models to create scenarios of how yields, and yield variability, might change under climate change in the year 2100. The book also creates sustainability, risk, and insurance pricing models and helps farmers through market value chain. An economic model then converted those changes in yield into changes in crop production and crop prices under two scenarios: one in which farmers can adapt to changes in yield by changing their planting behavior (i.e., switching crops, crop acreage, and management) and the other in which they cannot. The study contrasted climate scenarios resulting from different projections of greenhouse gas emissions levels with a hypothetical future with climate similar to that of the past several decades.

The book aims to equip present and future software engineering teams, agriculture students, economists, and macroeconomists with the skills and tools to use advanced data science, artificial intelligence, climate patterns, and economic models effectively to create software features that help to secure specialty crops economic viability through enhanced productivity for the long term and ensure sufficient food for the planet and the future generations. The book also covers:

- Yield models,
- Pricing models,
- Sustainability models, and
- Climate projections and forecasting models.

Finally, it is our fiduciary responsibility to help farmers who are feeding us, despite suffering. The book aims to help software engineers, data scientists, and agricultural economists work together and create applications that benefit small-scale specialty crops farmers and offer practical guidance for improving and maintaining small farms.

Contents

Section I: **Introduction**

Chapter 1
Introduction

This chapter covers:
- What is artificial intelligence (AI)?
- Machine learning (ML)
- Generative AI
- Time series
- Data pipeline
- Agricultural machine learning use cases
  - Field fresh tomatoes retail prices and post-harvest cost components
- Polynomial regression
- Univariate and multivariate time series
  - America's most beloved imported fruits: avocados' imports

This chapter explores artificial intelligence (AI), focusing on techniques like deep learning and generative AI. Additionally, we introduce the concept of time series analysis and develop detailed models for both univariate and multivariate avocado imports. Furthermore, we delve into the processing of regression techniques, highlighting their importance in modern data analysis. Lastly, we explore the linkage between field fresh tomatoes retail prices and post-harvest components, such as transportation and storage, providing valuable insights into this complex industry.

Artificial intelligence (AI) stands as a pivotal technology in our digital age, significantly influencing the economy through its growing application across various fields [1]. A key factor behind the rising popularity and adoption of AI is its software's capacity to learn from real-world experiences and enhance its performance over time. This adaptability allows AI to be utilized in diverse areas, from manufacturing cutting-edge high-tech equipment to offering personalized recommendations. Furthermore, AI has facilitated the development of innovative business models by analyzing data patterns and creating products tailored to meet specific customer needs.

The field of agriculture, which has been a crucial and ancient profession, can benefit from the use of AI applications to enhance productivity and sustainability, especially for small-scale farmers. To learn more about the use of AI in agriculture, you can refer to my books on the topics of machine learning (ML) and AI in agricultural economics, and AI and heuristics for enhanced food security.

Specialty crops are a valuable global industry, worth $1.9 trillion, and are undergoing a digital, data-driven, and intelligent transformation to meet increasing demand and overcome various challenges and disruptive forces [2]. The demand for food is increasing while the supply side [3] faces limitations such as reduced harvested land, limited farming inputs, and scarce or limited availability of water, fertilizers, and human resources. As the world's population grows, AI will become more critical in meeting the demand for agricultural production and addressing the challenges that arise.

To address the upcoming demands, challenges, and disruptive forces that will affect the agricultural industry, digital transformation is essential. This transformation must be infused with augmented intelligence, powered by advanced technologies such as AI and ML. It is important to note that agriculture represents the next frontier for AI and ML [4, 5], with AI playing a crucial role in macro-economics. By enhancing human capabilities, AI can enhance agricultural productivity across a range of domains such as crop monitoring, macro-economic forecasting, robotics, and predictive analytics. In the near future, we may even witness the entire food production process, from planting to delivery, being carried out without human intervention [6].

The agricultural industry presents a wealth of opportunities for the harvest of data disruptive technological wave (AI/ML), positioning it as one of the most promising sectors for these innovative technologies. Through the use of advanced algorithms and predictive models, AI-ML can facilitate more efficient and effective crop management, allowing for greater precision and accuracy in a variety of agricultural processes. This can result in increased yields, improved resource utilization, and reduced waste, among other benefits. As such, there is a growing interest in exploring the potential of AI-ML within the discipline of agriculture, emphasis toward leveraging these technologies to drive sustainable and profitable outcomes.

AI is a vast and multifaceted field that can be defined differently depending on the context and implied use cases [7]. Despite the lack of a single comprehensive definition, it is evident that the field of AI encompasses a wide range of perspectives and applications. To learn more about AI, please refer to my other books on the topic.

The origins of the concept of AI can be traced back to Alan Turing, who first pondered the possibility of "thinking machines" that could reason like humans in 1950 [8]. Shortly thereafter, John McCarthy introduced the term ""artificial intelligence" to refer to machines that could think independently, suggesting that the threshold would be reached when "a computer can perform tasks that are commonly thought to require intelligence when performed by a human being."

Other researchers have outlined a helpful taxonomy for defining AI systems, which includes the following categories [9, 10]:
- Thinking like humans can be achieved through intellectual designs.
- Making inferences and optimizations is very similar to a human's approach.
- Acting like humans, which encompasses language capabilities such as speech to text or text to speech.
- Acting wisely similar to human beings, involves the use of self-learning cognitive agents and with adaptability as core of the agent's DNA.

The field of digital science has introduced the groundbreaking concept of AI. AI refers to intellect demonstrated by silicon processing units (CPU and GPUs), as opposed to the innate biological synapse-driven cognition exhibited by living beings. According to Gartner Market Research, AI uses complex mathematical intuition derived from digital logic gate assemblies to interpret events, automate decisions, and take actions. Figure 1 illustrates the combined design of AI. This innovative technology possesses the capability to revolutionize various industries and transform the way we live and succeed.

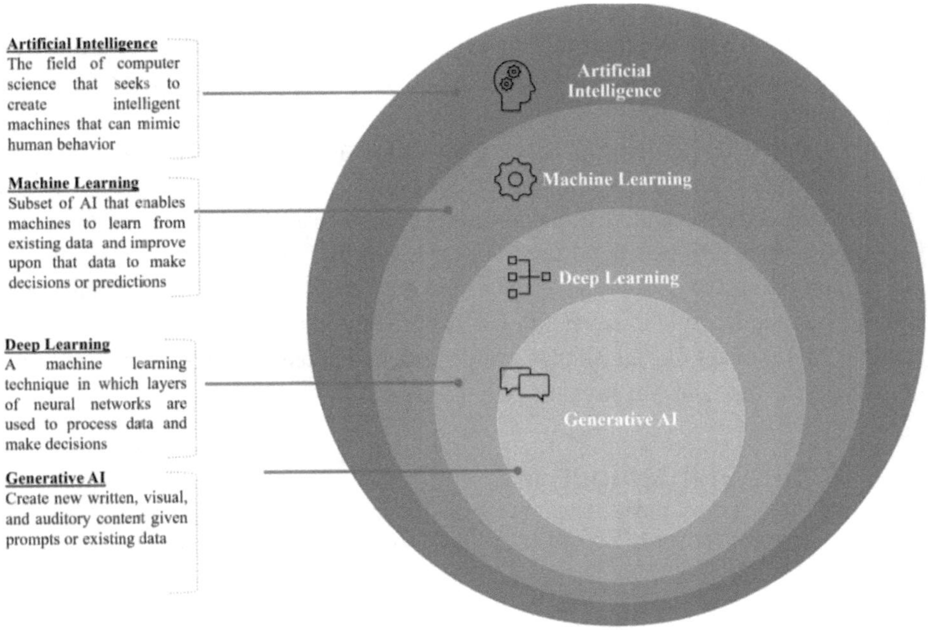

Figure 1: Artificial intelligence.

Brief history

The manmade intellect has a rich and extensive history that spans multiple decades. The earliest work on AI began in the 1950s and 1960s, when researchers delved into the possibility of creating machines with human-like "thinking" abilities. During this era, AI research primarily focused on "symbolic" AI, where researchers created symbolic representations of knowledge to solve problems.

The 1970s and 1980s marked a shift in AI research toward "subsymbolic" AI, which uses statistical methods and mathematical models to solve problems. This change was brought on by the complexity and difficulty of scaling symbolic AI and the development of new computer hardware, enabling quick processing of vast amounts of data.

With the progress of AI research in the 1990s and 2000s, new subfields emerged, including ML, which developed techniques that allowed machines to learn from data without explicit instruction. Another significant subfield that emulated the human biological approach was the development of networks that represented human neurons. By the 2000s, machines were capable of learning without explicit instructions and began to mimic the human brain. In summary, we have discovered pathways that enable machines to surpass human intelligence without incurring the cost of learning that humans experience!

In recent years, during the 2010s and 2020s, generative large language and small language models have emerged, driving the field of AI forward. These models could be used on any language-based task, thanks to their state-of-the-art reasoning and knowledge capabilities.

AI has made significant progress since the 1950s and continues to evolve rapidly. By using advanced techniques to mimic and predict human behavior (Figure 2), AI enables machines to perform cognitive functions like perception, reasoning, learning, and problem-solving, unlocking new opportunities across various fields.

A comprehensive AI solution, often called an "intelligent system" or "smart technology," can acquire human-level knowledge through machine reading and computer vision. It then utilizes this knowledge to automate and accelerate tasks that were traditionally performed solely by humans [11].

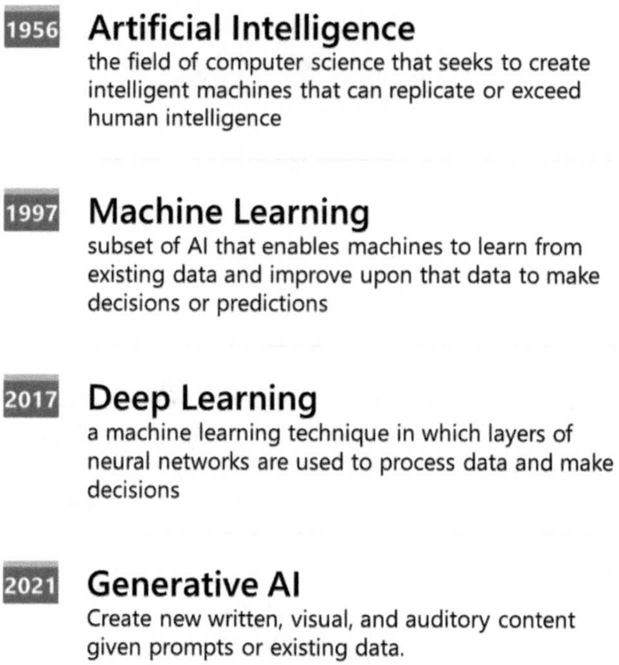

Figure 2: AI history.

India's $1 trillion climate challenge: Meeting 2030 targets [11]

In December 2021, the Union Environment Ministry informed the Rajya Sabha that India would need an estimated $1 trillion by 2030 to achieve its national climate change targets, which were announced at the Glasgow Climate Change Conference (COP26) but are not yet part of the nationally determined contributions (NDCs). India's current NDCs, submitted in 2015 under the Paris Agreement, include three unchanged targets: reducing GDP emissions intensity by 33–35% from 2005 levels, achieving 40% cumulative electric power installed capacity from nonfossil fuel sources, and creating an additional carbon sink of 2.5–3 billion tonnes of CO_2 equivalent by 2030. Balancing climate change efforts with sustainable development and poverty eradication, India estimates that around $1 trillion in climate financing will be required by 2030 to meet these expanded goals [11, 12].

Machine learning (ML)

Machine learning (ML), a subset of AI, improves machine performance through statistical methods and experience rather than explicit programming. These algorithms can identify patterns, make predictions, detect anomalies, and provide recommendations by processing data. A key advantage of ML is its ability to automatically adjust and improve in response to new data, a feature traditionally managed by rule-based systems. This book will specifically explore supervised learning, using statistical techniques to develop ML applications for specialty crops.

The adaptation gap:

Following China, India is the largest producer of coal in the world [13]. As its primary energy source, 57% of India's energy supply is accredited to coal usage – which may be compared to the global average of 24% – and the country consumes 12.5% of the world's coal. In 2021, India's primary energy consumption surged with coal increasing by 16% and 8% above its 2019 level. Likewise, all fuels –with the exception of nuclear and hydro – experiencing consumption growth leading to a 10% annual increase in primary energy consumption from 32 to 35 EJ in 2021. The combined share of energy consumption from oil, gas, and coal remained at 90%, similar to prepandemic levels [13].

In 2022, India has allotted 4.9% of its GDP toward adaptation efforts regarding CO_2 emission-based climate change. The country's projected GDP allocation for the year 2030 is 5.4%, assuming an 8% rate of economic growth.

Many nations lack the resources to close the gap between what's needed and what's being spent on adaptation. For India, by 2030, this gap will cumulatively exceed $1 trillion, affecting public health, agriculture, and water resources. As climate change worsens, crop yields continue to decline [15]. It is unfortunate; however, this trend will continue, despite humanity's efforts to mitigate climate change.

Mother nature [16]

Hydropower in California is both affordable and environmental friendly, but its production is highly dependent on drought conditions, affecting electricity costs and air quality [16]. Increased hydropower leads to cleaner electricity, reduced reliance on fossil fuels, fewer blackout risks during heat waves, and lower greenhouse gas emissions. However, droughts and heat waves worsen air quality in low-income areas, as natural gas combustion releases harmful pollutants, causing health issues like asthma and heart problems for nearby residents [16].

According to a recent study [16], reductions in hydropower output can lead to an increase in natural gas burning as a means of maintaining electricity generation. This highlights the interdependence of different energy sources and the need for a diversified energy mix to ensure reliable and sustainable power generation. Moreover, the study highlights the significant impact of drought on energy systems, which can exacerbate the risk of chronic pollution exposure. By understanding and mitigating these risks, stakeholders can work toward promoting more resilient and sustainable energy systems.

The agricultural industry is rapidly integrating AI and ML to monitor livestock health, including vital signs, daily activity levels, and food intake [5]. The Cow Necklace [17, 18], a Class 10 wearable veterinary sensor that records a cow's vital signs and enables farmers to monitor milk productivity and improve the animal's general health, is one notable instance of this technology.

Monitoring food intake and overall health can serve an essential role in meeting carbon engineering objectives, in addition to the advantages of increased animal health. Countries such as India, for example, aim to create additional carbon sinks, such as forests and tree cover, to the tune of 2.5 and 3 billion tons of CO_2 eq of by 2030 [11]. In this context, innovative companies that use AI and ML to monitor and improve the health of livestock are well-positioned to significantly advance sustainability initiatives. It is noteworthy that such companies have already been acknowledged for their quality; some of them were recognized with Fast Company's Best Designs[1] of 2023 award, joining other well-known winners[2] in this field.

1 Fast Company is a celebrated business media brand known for its exceptional coverage of innovation in technology, leadership, and transformative ideas. It aims to inspire progressive business leaders to think expansively, lead with purpose, and shape the future of business. https://www.fastcompany.com/about-us

2 Cow Necklace Hanumayamma Innovations and Technologies. Inc., a 2023 Fast Company Honoree: https://www.fastcompany.com/90933745/established-excellence-5-14-years-in-business-innovation-by-design-2023

Hanumayamma Innovations and Technologies Inc. is a Delaware-based corporation founded in 2010. We are a US-based corporation with leading products in agriculture analytics, dairy analytics, specialty crops sensors and analytics, wearable veterinary sensor (class 10) for animal husbandry, and data analytics (DnA) platform made exclusively for farmers worldwide. Our analytics platform and sensors help farmers around the world with practical suggestions on yield analytics, sustainability, extreme weather, and food security. https://www.hanuinnotech.com/

Deep learning (DL)

Deep learning (DL) is a network-based learning method. In Figure 3, the neural network then employs these parameters to make predictions for new outcomes. In this process, we're going to use both the preparing set (D_i^{train}) and the examination set (D_i^{test}). The neural networks are trained using standard supervised learning across all tasks. The overall goal is to measure the model's performance, with parameters ϕ, in predicting the outcome variable, Y, for new data.

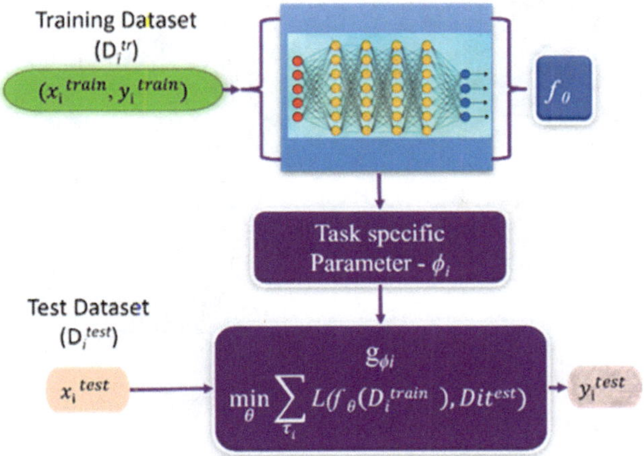

Figure 3: Deep learning.

Generative AI (large language model)

Generative AI is a fascinating subfield of AI dedicated to developing systems that can create new examples, such as images, text, or speech, that mimic a given dataset. It includes areas like natural language generation and large language models. Generative AI (Figure 4) aims to build algorithms that understand a dataset's probability distribution to produce similar new examples, with models divided into generative types like GPT-3 and DALL-E, and discriminative types like deep neural networks for classification tasks.

Generative AI is an advanced branch of AI that enhances other AI domains by using models to extract key features from data and learn underlying probability distributions to generate new examples. This technology has significant potential in fields like computer vision, natural language processing (NLP), speech recognition, and transcription. A notable breakthrough in this area is the generative pretrained transformer (GPT), which uses an autoregressive language model and DL to create human-like text. These models are pretrained on vast amounts of text and predict the most likely next word based on the input, providing a flexible text-in/text-out interface. ChatGPT models are some of the industrial uses. Historically, NLP models performed text classification. Nevertheless, GPT models perform natural language generation.

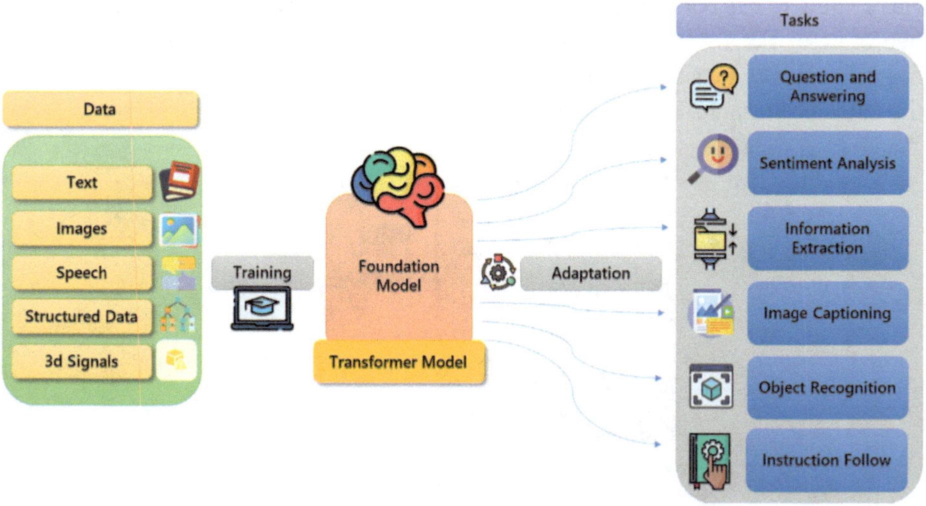

Figure 4: Foundation model.

During my tenure working on various industrial AI implementations, I have architected and developed numerous generative AI use cases, particularly in the fields of marketing with multi-touch attribution (MTA) and marketing mix modeling (MMM). Initially, MTA and MMM were applied predominantly to quantitative numerical data, but the advent of generative AI has enabled the inclusion of large text corpora in these use cases. Here are some illustrative examples:

- **T-Mobile retail stores:** Conducted MTA to incentivize sales promotions and establish a feedback loop for customer success interaction metrics.
- **T-Mobile wholesale analytics:** Executed MTA and MMM to identify trends, channel marketing funds toward event promotions, and make investment decisions for overall budget allocation.
- **Deloitte auditor use case:** Performed email campaign analysis to gauge customer sentiment and streamline the sales confirmation process using ML models.
- **Shell corporate marketing:** Analyzed traffic patterns, in-station buying behaviors, and customer campaign data to identify prospective email campaign clusters for promoting new product introductions.
- **Cisco-managed services:** Integrated customer feedback from multichannel interactions to prevent truck rolls, thereby achieving cost objectives.
- **Cisco stadium vision**: Conducted customer acquisition cluster modeling on event databases, multichannel interactions, and social media integration.

These examples highlight the transformative impact of generative AI on various marketing and operational strategies.

Foundation models

The future of AI lies in flexible, reusable models that can be applied to any industry or domain task. Foundation models, in particular, have been instrumental in driving the latest breakthroughs in AI systems since their introduction in 2018. These models capture general patterns and structures of data and have revolutionized how AI systems are constructed.

A foundation model, as depicted in Figure 4, is an ML model trained on massive amounts of unlabeled information, making it adaptable to a broad range of tasks. By unifying different tasks and modalities into one, these models eliminate the need to train multiple models and integrate them together, replacing task-specific models. For instance, a large language foundation model, due to its extensive training, can be readily used for a variety of NLP tasks without the need for further customization.

Foundation models utilize self-supervised learning and transfer learning to apply information learned in one situation to another situation or task. However, the training process for these models can be complex and resource-intensive due to their size and data requirements. The scale of these models plays a significant role in the training process.

Data pipeline

ML models rely on technologies that gather data from various sources, with data pipelines[3] serving as the backbone of this process by extracting, transforming, and storing data in target systems. These pipelines perform all necessary procedures to convert raw data into a usable format for end-users, such as data analysts and scientists. In this book, we have utilized data pipelines to obtain yield, pricing, and climate models.

Building and maintaining a data pipeline is a laborious task, but it is essential for ML models that rely on data. Data pipelines guarantee that the facts are consistent, precise, and current, enabling models to provide reliable and trustworthy results. In this book, we have used data pipelines to get yield, pricing, and climate models.

- Step 1: Download average refrigerator prices from Regional Refrigerated Truck Rates by Distance (Figure 5).
- Step 2: Based on region and distance, prepare time series of truck rates.

The graph (Figure 5) shows the "Rate Per Mile" trend from 2000 to around 2017, starting at about 1.5 and gradually increasing to around 2.5 by 2005, with periodic fluctuations. From 2005 to 2010, the rate rises significantly with volatility, peaking at nearly 3.5 around 2010. Post-2010, the trend remains volatile with sharp peaks and troughs,

3 Data pipeline: https://docs.databricks.com/getting-started/data-pipeline-get-started.html

maintaining an upward trajectory and stabilizing between 3.0 and 3.5 by 2017, reflecting the inflationary aspects of transporting goods in the USA and aiding in the analysis of pricing models.

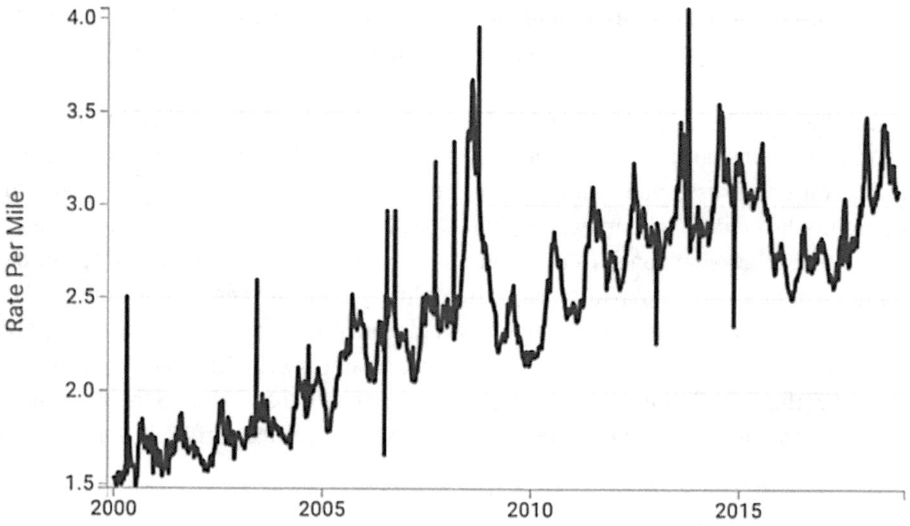

Figure 5: Refrigerated truck rates.

The graph (Figure 6) provides a breakdown of various commodities by their weight in 10,000-pound units, categorized by their origin. *Potatoes* are the highest in volume, exceeding 18 million pounds, primarily sourced from *Idaho and Colorado. Apples* follow, with significant contributions from *Washington and California-central. Onions (dry), tomatoes, and seedless watermelons* each range between 8 and 12 million pounds, with *Mexico and California-central* being major contributors. Other notable commodities include *iceberg lettuce and strawberries*, predominantly sourced from *California-central and Mexico.* Commodities like cantaloupe, plum-type tomatoes, oranges, and corn (sweet) fall between 2 and 6 million pounds, with contributions from regions like Florida, Arizona, and Georgia among others.

Data pipeline: average weekly regional refrigerated truck rates by distance (Florida, California, Sinaloa, Mexico, and Baja California, Mexico)

Refrigerated trucks play a crucial role in transporting fresh produce during the agricultural season, ensuring access to fresh food. Their demand significantly increases during harvest periods. Spring and summer present challenges such as tightened capacity,

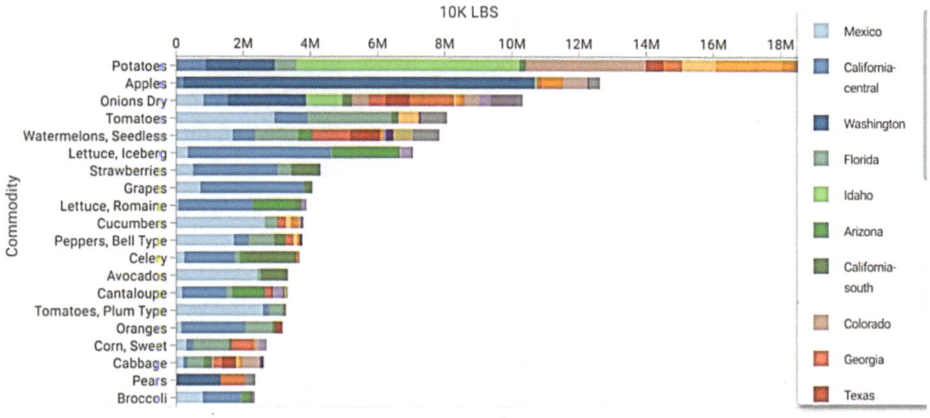

Figure 6: Top 20 commodities and district by volume.

higher rates, and scheduling difficulties for shippers using refrigerated trucks in the USA. The earliest harvests begin in South America and Mexico, with produce reaching the USA by February, primarily through air shipments to Philadelphia. From there, the distribution moves from the Southeast to southern Texas, the Rio Grande Valley, and southern California by late March, and continues northward as temperatures rise [19].

Exogenous variable: US–Mexico border produce

The rising demand for produce along the US–Mexico border impacts the frequency of US-bound truck traffic and the prices of fruits and vegetables in American stores [20]. This emphasizes the importance of efficient and reliable transportation logistics for fresh produce in both the economy and daily life. Timely and cost-effective transport by carriers helps reduce pricing pressures and provides consumers with better access to high-quality produce. Given the critical role of fresh produce transportation in the economy, industry participants must focus on optimizing logistics. Minimizing supply chain disruptions is essential to maintaining the flow of fresh produce.

Author
Chandrasekar Vuppalapati

Software code for this model:
Average_Weekly_Regional_Refrigerated_Truck_Rates_by_Distance.ipynb (Jupyter Notebook Code)

Commodity pricing is significantly affected by refrigerated truck rates due to their linked demand. This book offers a model for extracting refrigerated truck rates for distances exceeding 2,500 miles (4,023 km) in California. Since the implementation of NAFTA in 1994, the Canadian dollar to US dollar exchange rate and the Mexican Peso to US dollar exchange rate have become important factors influencing truck and specialty crop rates, with the truck rate variable being used in subsequent pricing models.

Source	Name
USDA	Refrigerated truck rates data

Step 1: USDA truck data

Collect the data from refrigerated truck rates file in CSV format.

```
import pandas as pd
# Read the data into a DataFrame
data = pd.read_csv('Average_Weekly_Regional_Refrigerated_Truck_Rates_by_Distance.csv')
#Convert the 'date' column to datetime format
data['date'] = pd.to datetime(data['date'], format='%m/%d/%Y')
```

Output:
Prepared date index column.

Step 2: Prepare California region truck rates

Prepare California region 2,500+ miles truck rates per hour. Extract date and time.

```
#Extract year and month from the 'date' column
data['year'] = data['date'].dt.year
data['month'] = data['date'].dt.month
```

```
#Filter the data for CALIFORNIA region with shipment distance 2500+ miles
california_data = data[(data['region'] == 'CALIFORNIA') & (data['shipment_distance'] == '2500+
miles')]

# Calculate the monthly average cost for CALIFORNIA region with shipment distance 2500+ miles
california_avg_cost=california_data.groupby(['year', 'month'])['regional_rates'].mean().reset_index()
```

Output:

	year	month	regional_rates
0	2000	1	1.105125
1	2000	2	1.034036
2	2000	3	1.094955
3	2000	4	1.233148
4	2000	5	1.328710

Step 3: Prepare Florida region truck rates

Prepare Florida region 2,500+ miles truck rates per hour.

```
# Filter the data for FLORIDA region with shipment distance 0 miles-500 miles
florida_data = data[(data['region'] == 'FLORIDA') & (data['shipment_distance'] == '0-500 miles')]

# Calculate the monthly average cost for FLORIDA region with shipment distance 0 miles-500 miles
florida_avg_cost = florida_data.groupby(['year', 'month'])['regional_rates'].mean().reset_index()
```

Output:

	year	month	regional_rates
0	2000	1	1.105125
1	2000	2	1.034036
2	2000	3	1.094955
3	2000	4	1.233148
4	2000	5	1.328710

The average

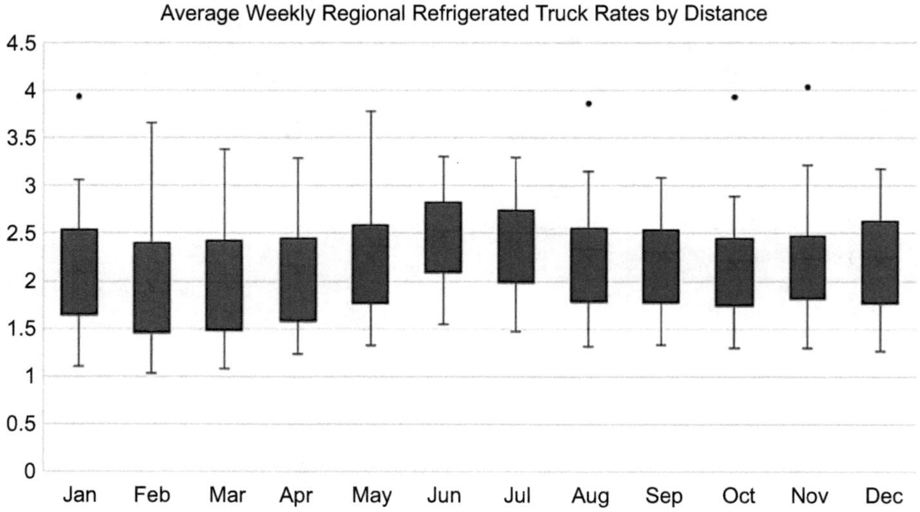

With most recent rates for the year 2022 as follows:

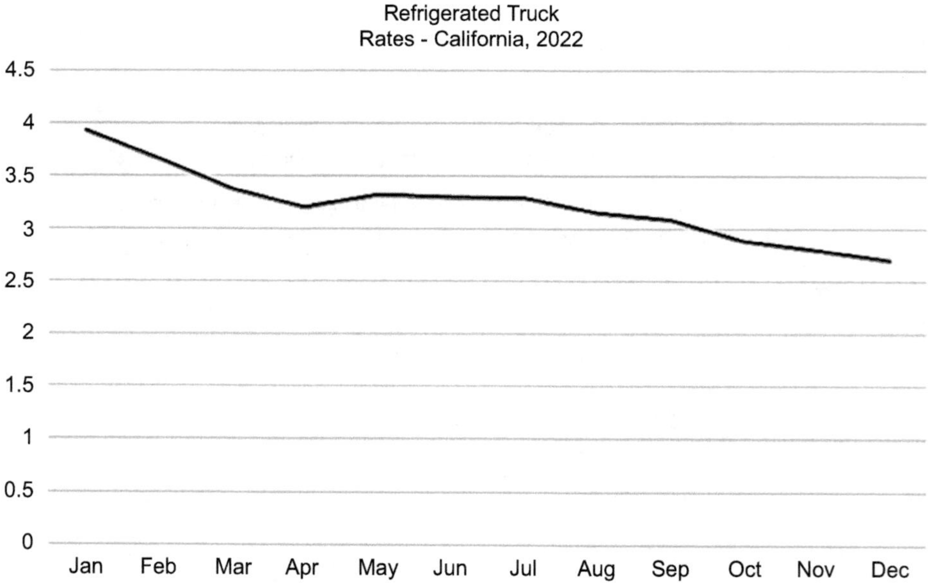

In the spring, spot market freight volume typically increases by about 30%, impacting various transportation modes. This surge in demand often results in higher rates for carriers, including those in refrigerated, dry-van, less-than-truckload services, and railroads. To maintain profitability, carriers may seek rate hikes. By understanding these seasonal trends, carriers can better prepare for the increased business during spring. Consequently, they can adjust their pricing strategies accordingly [19].

Supervised learning

Supervised learning is a fundamental ML method where an algorithm learns from training data and human feedback to link input features with output labels. By using human-labeled data, the machine identifies patterns between inputs and outputs [10]. For instance, supervised learning in a regression model demonstrated that factors like diesel prices, regional trucking rates, inflation, and CO_2 impact the US average retail price of tomatoes. This method is versatile and used in predictive modeling, classification, and recommendation systems. It finds applications across various industries, including finance, manufacturing, mining, marketing, agriculture, and e-commerce.

Advancing agriculture at an appropriate rate is essential for the growth of both the industrial sector and other areas of the economy. Without such progress, agriculture could become a significant obstacle, restricting overall economic development.

Author
Chandrasekar Vuppalapati

Supervised learning algorithms consist of linear, logistic, random forest, and gradient boosting techniques, among others. To learn more about these algorithms, please refer to my books.

Precipitation and ML variable

Water is essential for agriculture [22] and integrating precipitation with macro-economic variables in model development enhances the understanding of food grain production. Including rainfall in these models provides decision-makers with crucial insights into its impact on crop yields and total production. This information is valuable for various sectors, enabling informed decisions, proactive risk management, and supporting environmental, social, and corporate governance objectives.

Sustainability targets and banking

Central banks, as financial regulators, possess various policy tools that can shape investment decisions and resource allocation to meet sustainability goals. By effectively managing these tools, they can promote sustainable economic growth and development while mitigating [14] economic risks and enhancing financial system stability. Thus, central banks have a crucial responsibility to use their policy instruments wisely to achieve long-term sustainability objectives.

Regression models

Linear regression is a statistical method for modeling the relationship between a scalar dependent variable (y) and one or more independent variables (X), with simple linear regression involving just one independent variable. This technique is especially intuitive when both the dependent and independent variables are numeric and is widely effective across various industries [23, 24]. By expressing the dependent variable as a linear combination of the independent variables, linear regression aids decision-makers in making informed choices and proactively managing potential risks.

With its clear and understandable output, linear regression is a popular and widely used modeling technique that has proven to be effective in solving complex problems. By establishing the relationship between variables, linear regression enables organizations to make better decisions and achieve better results:

$$x = w_0 + w_1 a_1 + w_2 a_2 + \ldots + wkak \tag{1}$$

where (x) represents the dependent variable, ($a_1, a_2, \ldots, a_k$) are the attribute values, and ($w_0, w_1, \ldots, w_k$) are the weights.

Metrics for regression models

When it comes to regression models, the system of measurement returned is typically considered to estimate the amount of error. A well-fitted classifier is one where the deviation between studied and anticipated values is small. However, analyzing the relationship of the remainders can reveal potential bias in the model. By analyzing the residuals, decision-makers can obtain crucial insights into the model's accuracy and reliability.

Overall, considering the residuals of a regression model is essential in deeper comprehension of its performance and identifying any potential sources of bias. The following systems of measurement are typically employed as important performance indicators of regression models [25, 26]:

- The mean absolute error (MAE) measures prediction accuracy; lower scores mean better performance.
- The root mean squared error (RMSE) calculates error magnitude; higher values indicate larger errors [27, 28].
- The relative absolute error (RAE) measures relative prediction error using mean absolute difference.
- Mean zero one error (MZOE) shows perdiction accuracy; 1for incorrect, 0 for correct.
- Coefficient of determination, or R2, assesses model fit; ranges from 0 (no fit) to 1 (perfect fit).

For more about logistic regression, random forest trees, gradient boosting regressors [29, 30, 31, 32], please refer to my books in this area.

Florida tomatoes

ML model: field fresh tomatoes retail prices and post-harvest cost components: storage, packing, shipping, and transportation

Transporting goods typically prioritizes delivery time, safety, and cost. However, fresh produce like Florida tomatoes requires additional considerations, as they can be harvested either ripe or green. To ensure green tomatoes ripen properly, they are often transported to storage facilities and treated with *ethylene gas* to expedite the ripening process [32, 33].

In addition to the costs of transportation, senders must also consider the costs of storing and ripening tomatoes. These costs include the *price of CO_2, energy, CPI, and ethylene propylene. Furthermore, refrigerated trucks are often necessary to ensure that the tomatoes remain fresh during transport*, adding an additional layer of cost. (Please see Figure 7 for an illustration of refrigerated truck rates.)

The USA consistently has higher shipment figures compared to imports on all dates. On 07/01/2023, both imports and US figures peaked with 26,381 and 38,177 units, respectively. There is a noticeable fluctuation in the numbers across different dates, with some dates in 2023 showing a slight increase compared to the same period in 2022.

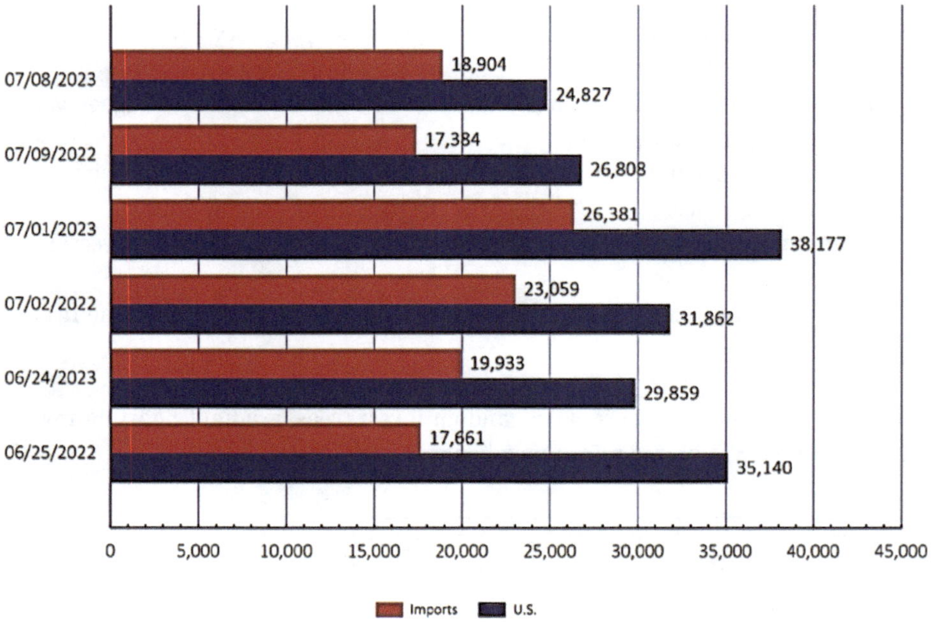

Figure 7: Shipments.

Overall, transporting fresh produce like tomatoes requires careful consideration of several factors, including ripening processes, storage costs, and transportation expenses. By understanding these factors, senders can make informed decisions and ensure that their goods arrive fresh, safe, and on time.

The stated rates cover spot market sales per load, including brokers' fees for single-destination truckload shipments (Figure 10). Additional fees for terminal market deliveries, multi-pickup, and multi-drop shipments are excluded unless specified. These rates are for common loads in 48–53 foot refrigerated trailers, destined for 10 cities including Atlanta, Baltimore, Boston, Chicago, Dallas, Los Angeles, Miami, New York, Philadelphia, and Seattle [34].

Understanding transportation fares and the factors that impact them is crucial for shippers and receivers when making informed decisions about their transportation needs. It is essential to carefully consider these factors, including the size of the load, the destination city, and any additional fees that may apply.

By doing so, organizations can ensure that their goods arrive at their destination safely and cost-effectively. This knowledge can help shippers and receivers negotiate rates with carriers, plan routes effectively, and optimize their logistics operations.

Overall, taking a strategic approach to transportation rates and logistics can lead to significant cost savings and a more efficient supply chain. By staying informed and up to date on market trends and factors that impact transportation rates, organizations can make informed decisions and gain a competitive advantage in their industry.

Source: 40,000-pound fresh produce shipments [34].

Software code for this model:
FinalReleaseMLTomatoesRetailPrices_FuelCost_RefrigeratorTruckRatesModel.ipynb
(Jupyter Notebook Code)

Experiment sources

The following table has experiment sources.

Data source	Name
USDA	Retail prices of fresh and processed vegetables for tomatoes under trade and prices by category.
FRED	Tomatoes average price (APU0000712311), US diesel sales price (GASDESM, CPIAUCSL, and producer prices by industry[4]: agricultural, construction, mining machinery maintenance).

Step 1: Load libraries

Load Python core libraries, scikit-learn, and Matplotlib.

```
"""
Created on Thu Dec 29 20:36:05 2022

@author:chvuppal
"""
```

4 Commercial machinery repair and maintenance: https://fred.stlouisfed.org/series/PCU8113108113105

```
import http.client
import argparse
import os
import pandas as pd
import numpy as np
import pandas as pd
import csv
import requests
import functools as ft
from datetime import date
from sklearn.preprocessing import MinMaxScaler
from sklearn.model_selection import train_test_split
from sklearn.linear_model import LinearRegression
from sklearn.metrics import r2_score
from sklearn import metrics
from sklearn.impute import SimpleImputer
import matplotlib.pyplot as plt
import eli5
import plotly.graph_objects as go
import seaborn as sns; sns.set()
```

Step 2: Feature: global prices (PNGASUSUSDM)

Global benchmark prices are set by top exporters in US dollars. Download and load the feature from the FRED data source.

```
# PNGASUSUSDM

dfPNGASUSUSDM = pd.read_csv('PNGASUSUSDM.csv')
dfPNGASUSUSDM
```

```
dfPNGASUSUSDM=dfPNGASUSUSDM.set_index('date')
dfPNGASUSUSDM
```

```
dfPNGASUSUSDM.plot()
```

Output:

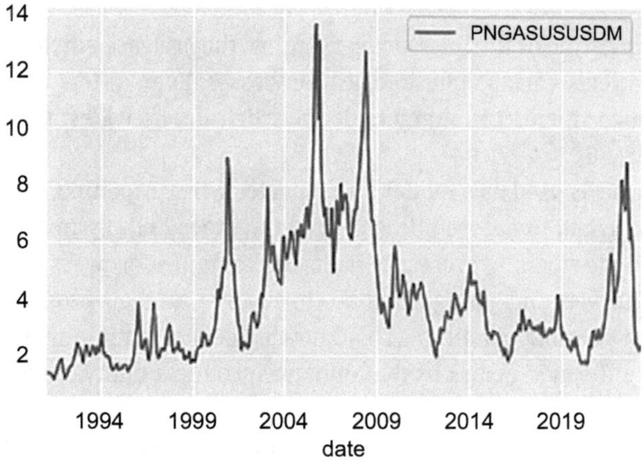

Step 3: Feature: consumer price index (CPIAUCSL)

CPIAUCSL is a price index.

```
dfCPIAUCSL = pd.read_csv('CPIAUCSL.csv')
dfCPIAUCSL
```

```
dfCPIAUCSL=dfCPIAUCSL.set_index('date')
```

```
dfCPIAUCSL.plot()
```

Output:

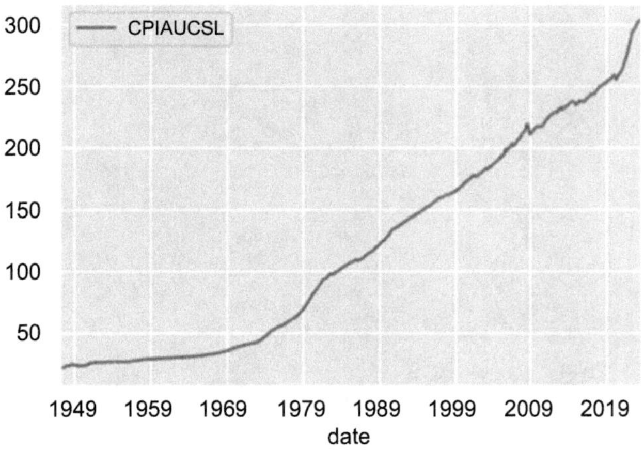

Step 4: Feature: producer price index by commodity ethylene propylene (WPU07110224)

Tomatoes can be harvested either ripe or unripe. During ripening, they release ethylene gas, a natural hormone that affects various physiological processes. Even at low concentrations, ethylene can induce ripening in many fruits, highlighting its widespread impact across plant species [35, 36].

In fact, ethylene biosynthesis is used as a model for climacteric fruit ripening. It is this gas production that turns green tomatoes into ripe, red tomatoes [33]. By understanding the role of ethylene in the ripening process of fruits like tomatoes, growers and producers can optimize their harvest and storage methods to ensure that their produce reaches consumers in the best possible condition. This knowledge is essential for the agricultural industry to make informed decisions that enhance product quality, safety, and taste.

Overall, understanding the impact of ethylene gas on fruit ripening is an essential component of the agricultural industry and can lead to better outcomes for growers, producers, and consumers alike.

```
# PolymersofEthylene
dfPolymersofEthylene = pd.read_csv('WPU07110224.csv')
dfPolymersofEthylene
```

```
dfPolymersofEthylene=dfPolymersofEthylene.set_index('date')
```

```
dfPolymersofEthylene.plot()
```

Output:

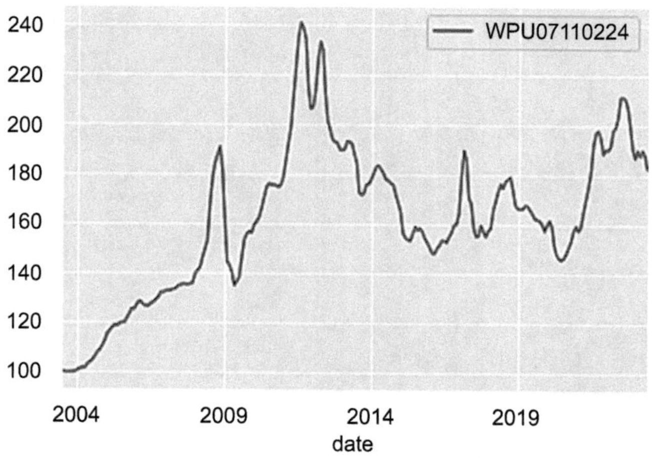

Green and unripe tomatoes are treated with ethylene gas to accelerate ripening and turn them red, mimicking their natural ethylene production [37]. Ethylene is a natural hormone found in fruits and vegetables that is responsible for their ripening process. As fruits and vegetables ripen, they release more ethylene, which speeds up the ripening process and can cause them to spoil faster. Ethylene absorbents extend fruit and vegetable shelf life by removing ethylene. By doing so, the rate of ripening is slowed down, and the fruits and vegetables can stay fresh for a longer time. This can be especially useful for farmers and grocery stores that need to transport and store large quantities of produce for longer periods without spoilage [38, 39].

Step 5: Feature: US diesel sales price (GASDESM)

Diesel prices.

```
# dfUSDieselSalesPrice

dfUSDieselSalesPrice = Read CSV File ('GASDESM.csv')
dfUSDieselSalesPrice['date'] = pd.to_datetime(dfUSDieselSalesPrice['DATE'])
dfUSDieselSalesPrice.rename(columns = {'GASDESM':'USDieselSalesPrice'}, inplace = True)
dfUSDieselSalesPrice.drop('DATE', inplace=True, axis=1)
dfUSDieselSalesPrice=dfUSDieselSalesPrice.set_index('date')
dfUSDieselSalesPrice.plot()
```

Output:

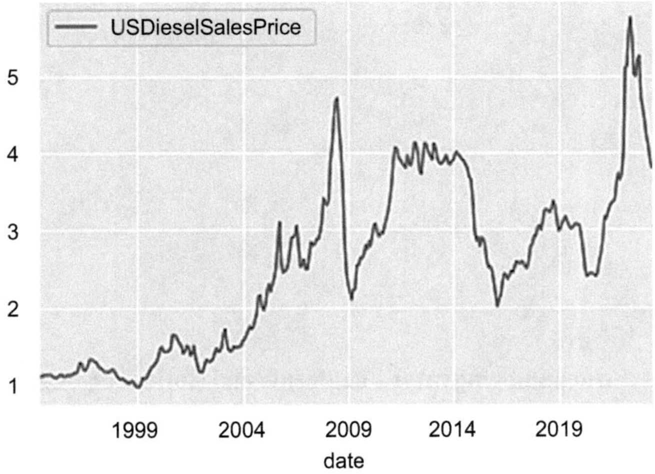

Step 6: Feature: industrial CO_2(PCU3251203251204)

Cherry tomatoes' shelf life is extended by modified packaging air and CO_2 pretreatment [40] and delaying ripening [41]. The use of CO_2 pretreatment and cold storage is a favorable procedure for extending the retail time of cherry tomatoes and maintaining their quality during distribution. By leveraging this technique, growers and producers can reduce waste, improve profitability, and provide consumers with fresh, high-quality produce.

```
#PCU3251203251204
dfPCU3251203251204 = pd.read_csv('PCU3251203251204.csv')
dfPCU3251203251204['date'] = pd.to_datetime(dfPCU3251203251204['DATE'])
dfPCU3251203251204
```

```
dfPCU3251203251204.rename(columns = {'PCU3251203251204':'CO2Price'}, inplace = True)
```

```
dfPCU3251203251204.drop('DATE', inplace=True, axis=1)
```

```
dfPCU3251203251204=dfPCU3251203251204.set_index('date')
```

```
dfPCU3251203251204.plot()
```

Output:

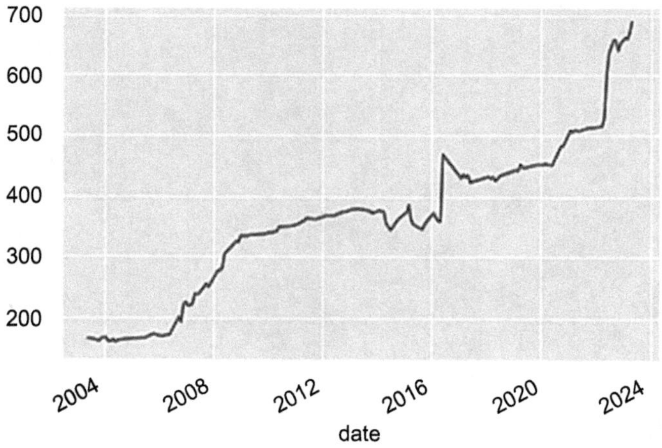

Step 6: Feature: refrigerator truck shipping rates – California and Florida regional rates

Truck shipping rates.

```
# Read the data into a DataFrame
refrigeratedTruckRatesbyDistance =
pd.read_csv('Florida_Refrigerated_Truck_Rates_by_Distance.csv')

refrigeratedTruckRatesbyDistance
```

```
refrigeratedTruckRatesbyDistance['day']='01'
```

```
refrigeratedTruckRatesbyDistance['date'] =
pd.to_datetime(dict(year=refrigeratedTruckRatesbyDistance.year,
                    month=refrigeratedTruckRatesbyDistance.month,
                    day=refrigeratedTruckRatesbyDistance.day))
```

```
refrigeratedTruckRatesbyDistance.drop(['Unnamed: 0', 'year', 'month', 'day'], inplace=True, axis=1)

refrigeratedTruckRatesbyDistance=refrigeratedTruckRatesbyDistance.set_index('date')
refrigeratedTruckRatesbyDistance
```

Output:

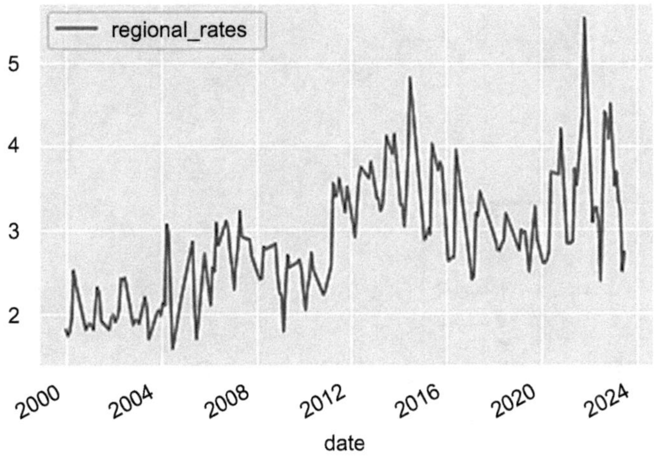

Step 7: Combined DataFrame and perform data analysis

Combine all features into one data frame with the date as the index.

```
dfList1 = [ dfPCU3251203251204,refrigeratedTruckRatesbyDistance, dfAveragePriceTomatoes, dfUSDies
elSalesPrice,dfCPIAUCSL,dfPNGASUSUSDM,dfPolymersofEthylene]
combined_df
```

Output:

date							
2003-06-01	.	2.084848	1.398	1.424	183.100	5.829048	100.000
2003-07-01	165.9	1.704545	1.460	1.435	183.700	5.027273	99.700
2003-11-01	161.7	2.010732	1.480	1.482	185.000	4.491667	99.600
2003-12-01	166.3	2.045455	1.533	1.490	185.500	6.140000	99.800
2004-01-01	166.7	1.985795	1.472	1.551	186.300	6.150526	100.400
...	...	...	...	...	...	...	...
2022-12-01	652.144	4.500000	2.228	4.714	298.990	5.746818	190.607
2023-02-01	661.379	3.513258	1.990	4.413	301.648	2.438000	190.142
2023-03-01	658.730	3.683712	1.932	4.211	301.808	2.409130	187.903
2023-04-01	669.615	3.342803	1.874	4.099	302.918	2.195500	190.068
2023-05-01	688.066	3.210227	1.798	3.915	303.294	2.315217	188.092

144 rows × 7 columns

Next, check for nulls.

```
combined_df.isna().any()
```

Output:

```
CO2Price                       False
regional_rates                 False
AverageRetailTomatoPrices      False
USDieselSalesPrice             False
CPIAUCSL                       False
PNGASUSUSDM                    False
PPIEthylenePropylene           False
dtype: bool
```

Average retail tomato price has strings “.”. Replace them with nulls and re-run null analysis.

```
combined_df['AverageRetailTomatoPrices']=combined_df['AverageRetailTomatoPrices'].replace
('.', np.NaN)
```

```
combined_df.isna().any()
```

Output:

```
CO2Price                      True
regional_rates               False
AverageRetailTomatoPrices     True
USDieselSalesPrice           False
CPIAUCSL                     False
PNGASUSUSDM                  False
PPIEthylenePropylene         False
dtype: bool
```

Step 8: Apply imputation strategy to fix nulls

Combine all features into one data frame with the date as the index.

```
combined_df = combined_df.fillna(method='ffill').fillna(method='bfill'
combined_df.isna().any()
```

Output:

```
CO2Price                     False
regional_rates               False
AverageRetailTomatoPrices    False
USDieselSalesPrice           False
CPIAUCSL                     False
PNGASUSUSDM                  False
PPIEthylenePropylene         False
dtype: bool
```

Finally, check the data frame for signatures before developing regressive algorithms.

```
combined_df['AverageRetailTomatoPrices'] = combined_df['AverageRetailTomatoPrices'].astype(float)
combined_df['PPIEthylenePropylene'] = combined_df['PPIEthylenePropylene'].astype(float)
combined_df['CO2Price'] = combined_df['CO2Price'].astype(float)
#combined_df['GASREGM'] = combined_df['GASREGM'].astype(float)
```

Combined DataFrame output. All columns are numerical and can be regressed.

Step 9: Correlation analysis

Correlation analysis provides a glimpse into how each feature influence the predictor one – “AverageRetailTomatoPrices”

```
combined_df[[ 'CO2Price','AverageRetailTomatoPrices','USDieselSalesPrice','regional_rates','CPIAUCSL',
'PPIEthylenePropylene']].corr()
sns.heatmap(combined_df.corr());
```

Output:

	CO2Price	AverageRetailTomatoPrices	USDieselSalesPrice	regional_rates	CPIAUCSL	PPIEthylenePropylene
CO2Price	1.000000	0.449541	0.622047	0.523904	0.971907	0.693617
AverageRetailTomatoPrices	0.449541	1.000000	0.108703	0.131599	0.480053	0.103694
USDieselSalesPrice	0.622047	0.108703	1.000000	0.541917	0.636200	0.784216
regional_rates	0.523904	0.131599	0.541917	1.000000	0.557206	0.567500
CPIAUCSL	0.971907	0.480053	0.636200	0.557206	1.000000	0.635105
PPIEthylenePropylene	0.693617	0.103694	0.784216	0.567500	0.635105	1.000000

The correlation analysis indicates that CO_2 price (44.951%), diesel prices (10.87%), regional refrigerator truck rates (13.159%), CPI (48%), and producer prices of ethylene propylene (10.369%) are positively correlated with average retail tomato prices.

Similarly, CO_2 price (62.204%), average retail tomato prices (10.870%), regional refrigerator truck rates (54.197%), CPI (63.62%), and producer prices of ethylene propylene (78.426%) are all positively correlated with US diesel prices.

These findings suggest that both energy and transportation have a significant impact on retail tomato prices. By taking these factors into consideration, growers and producers can make informed decisions regarding their operations and pricing strategies. Understanding the correlation between these variables can help organizations optimize their supply chain and improve their profitability in the tomato market.

The prices of oil and related products have great correlation to petrochemical prices, with feedstock costs representing the largest dividend of petrochemical production costs, surpassing fixed costs, power, and transportation. During the COVID-19 outbreak in the year 2020, petrochemical products such as ethylene, propylene, and benzene experienced a sharp decline in price, reaching their lowest levels in recent years. Fortunately, prices were able to recover following the pandemic. In 2022, petrochemical prices reached their highest levels in recent years, impacting the industry and its consumers [42]. Staying informed about these trends allows businesses to make informed decisions and develop strategies to navigate changing market conditions.

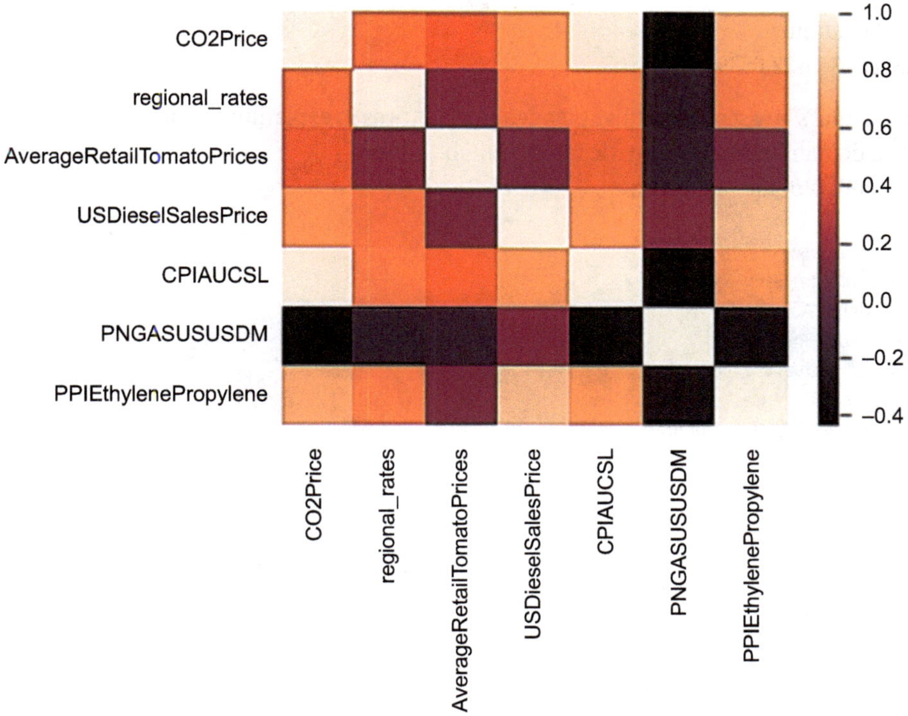

Step 10: Regression models: linear regressor

Regression analysis provides the relationship between the feature Y variables and a list of independent variables.

```
X =combined_df[['CO2Price',
'USDieselSalesPrice', 'regional_rates', 'CPIAUCSL', 'PPIEthylenePropylene']]

y= combined_df['AverageRetailTomataPrices']

X_train,X_test,y_train,y_test = train_test_split(X,y,test_size=0.2,random_state=0)

regressor = LinearRegression()
regressor.fit(X_train,y_train)

y_pred = regressor.predict(X_test)
y_pred

r2_score(y_test,y_pred)dtype:bool
```

Model output:
0.326572 or 32.657%

The model's low scores highlight inadequate features in explaining retail tomato prices; next, demand-side and climatic factors will be added.

Let's plot the regressor:

```
plt.scatter(y_test,y_pred)
plt.xlabel('Actual')
plt.ylabel("Predicted")
plt.title('Actual vs Predicted')
#overlay the regression line
z = np.polyfit(y_test, y_pred, 1)
p = np.poly 1d(z)
plt.plot(y_test,p(y_test), color='b')
plt.show()
```

Output:

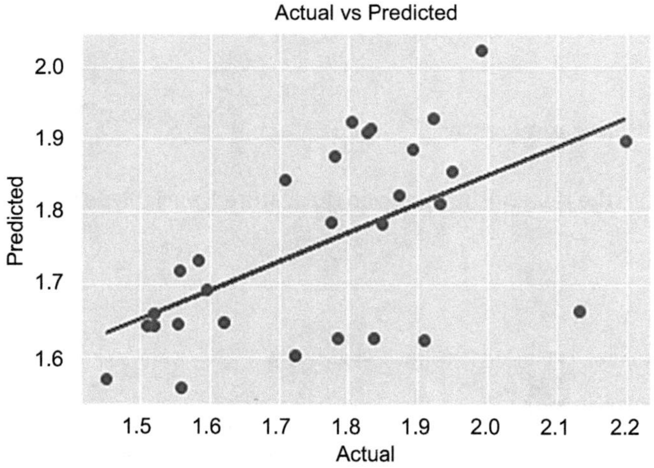

Model interpretability:

```
eli5.explain_weights(regressor, feature_names = list(X.columns))
```

Output: Top y features include CPI, CO_2, ethylene, and transportation costs. However, the model has high BIAS.

y top features

Weight?	Feature
+1.028	<BIAS>
+0.004	CPIAUCSL
+0.000	CO2Price
-0.002	PPIEthylenePropylene
-0.007	regional_rates
-0.048	USDieselSalesPrice

Step 11: Regression models: random forest regressor

Random forest uses multiple decision trees to classify data, enhance accuracy, and prevent over-fitting through subsampling and averaging. To avoid overly large trees that consume too much memory, parameters like max_depth and min_samples_leaf can be adjusted; in this analysis, setting max_depth to three improved performance and controlled tree complexity.

```
X =combined_df[[
'CO2Price', 'USDieselSalesPrice', 'regional_rates', 'CPIAUCSL', 'PPIEthylenePropylene']]

y= combined_df['AverageRetailTomatoPrices']

X_train,X_test,y_train,y_test = train_test_split(X,y,test_size = 0.2,random_state=0)

regr = RandomForestRegressor(max_depth=3,random_state=0)
regr.fit(X_train,y_train)
regr.score(X_test,y_test)
```

Output:
0.48641 or 48.641%

Step 12: Regression models: gradient boosting regressor

This technique incrementally builds a model, optimizing differentiable loss functions by fitting regression trees to the loss function's negative gradient.

```
from sklearn.ensemble import GradientBoostingRegressor

gbr = GradientBoostingRegressor(random_state=0)

X =combined_df[[
'USDieselSalesPrice', 'regional_rates', 'CPIAUCSL', 'PPIEthylenePropylene', 'CO2Price']]

y= combined_df['AverageRetailTomatoPrices']

X_train,X_test,y_train,y_test = train_test_split(X,y,test_size=0.2,random_state=0)

gbr.fit(X_train,y_train)
gbr.score(X_test,y_test)
```

Output:
0.65843 or 65.843%

The following provides explainability:
Output:

Weight	Feature
0.4864 ± 0.5178	CPIAUCSL
0.1771 ± 0.3408	CO2Price
0.1229 ± 0.4717	USDieselSalesPrice
0.1166 ± 0.3787	PPIEthylenePropylene
0.0969 ± 0.4663	regional_rates

CPI, CO_2, diesel, ethylene, and regional rates all impact the retail price of tomatoes.

California–Florida truck routes tomatoes

ML model: CA–FL routes: field fresh tomatoes retail prices and post-harvest cost components: Storage, packing, shipping, and transportation

Improving the accuracy of models predicting tomato transportation is challenging due to the complex logistics of the industry. The US imports tomatoes from Canada and Mexico, with varied export schedules that overlap with domestic production periods in California and Florida. [43]. By taking these factors into account and continuously refining our models, we can better understand and predict the retail cost of fresh tomatoes.

Country	Places	Open field	Protected condition
USA	California	May to November	Throughout the Year‡
	Florida	October to June	
	Other states of the U.S.	July to September	
Mexico	Sinaloa, Mexico	December to April	Throughout the Year†
	Baja California, Mexico	May to December	
Canada		July to September	Throughout the year except extreme cold months that is January and February

‡For entire USA † For entire Mexico

Source: Timeline of tomato shipping in North America countries (USA, Canada, and Mexico) from open field production and protected conditions (shade house, greenhouse, and tunnels). (Source: information derived from https://www.ers.usda.gov/calendar

The price of transport needs to be derived from both Florida and California on during the respective months to map with retail prices. Till step 6 the same as previous model.

Step 6: Feature: refrigerator truck shipping rates – Florida (October to June) month rates

Download truck dashboard from USDA.

```
# Read the data into a DataFrame
flrefrigeratedTruckRatesbyDistance=flrefrigeratedTruckRatesbyDistance.reset_index()
flrefrigeratedTruckRatesbyDistance
```

```
flDecOnly= flrefrigeratedTruckRatesbyDistance['date'].dt.month.between(12,12)
df_flDecOnly = flrefrigeratedTruckRatesbyDistance.loc[flDecOnly]
df_flDecOnly
```

Output:

	date	regional_rates
7	2000-12-01	1.863636
16	2001-12-01	1.954545
25	2002-12-01	1.931818
34	2003-12-01	2.045455
54	2006-12-01	2.727273
69	2008-12-01	2.454545
78	2009-12-01	2.534091
86	2010-12-01	2.272727
170	2022-12-01	4.500000

```
flJanThroughApr = flrefrigeratedTruckRatesbyDistance['date'].dt.month.between(1,4)
df_flJanThroughApr = flrefrigeratedTruckRatesbyDistance.loc[flJanThroughApr]
df_flJanThroughApr
```

Output:

	date	regional_rates
0	2000-01-01	1.818182
1	2000-02-01	1.745455
2	2000-03-01	1.795455
3	2000-04-01	1.954545
8	2001-01-01	1.890909
...	...	...
162	2022-03-01	3.079545
163	2022-04-01	3.248106
171	2023-02-01	3.513258
172	2023-03-01	3.683712
173	2023-04-01	3.342803

73 rows × 2 columns

Step 7: Feature: refrigerator truck shipping rates – California (May to November) month rates

Load California from May through November.

```
caMayThroughNov = carefrigeratedTruckRatesbyDistance['date'].dt.month.between(5,11)
df_caMayThroughNov = carefrigeratedTruckRatesbyDistance.loc[caMayThroughNov]
df_caMayThroughNov
```

Output:

	date	regional_rates
4	2000-05-01	3.277063
5	2000-06-01	3.119369
6	2000-07-01	2.969876
7	2000-08-01	3.078679
8	2000-09-01	3.012669
...	...	...
232	2022-10-01	15.400150
233	2022-11-01	15.366667
239	2023-05-01	14.044444
240	2023-06-01	14.583333
241	2023-07-01	12.444444

144 rows × 2 columns

Step 8: Merge data frames California (May to November) and Florida (October to June) rates

The concat() function in pandas is a way to combine two tables of data, either by adding columns or rows from one table to another. It does all the hard work of putting the tables together, like fitting the pieces of a puzzle. It can also help you keep only the parts of the tables that are the same or different, depending on what you need.

```
frames = [df_flJanThroughApr, df_caMayThroughNov,df_flDecOnly]

result = pd.concat(frames)
display(result)
refrigeratedTruckRatesbyDistance = result.copy()
refrigeratedTruckRatesbyDistance=refrigeratedTruckRatesbyDistance.set_index('date')
refrigeratedTruckRatesbyDistance
```

Output:

	regional_rates
date	
2000-01-01	1.818182
2000-02-01	1.745455
2000-03-01	1.795455
2000-04-01	1.954545
2001-01-01	1.890909
...	...
2006-12-01	2.727273
2008-12-01	2.454545
2009-12-01	2.534091
2010-12-01	2.272727
2022-12-01	4.500000

226 rows × 1 columns

```
refrigeratedTruckRatesbyDistance=refrigeratedTruckRatesbyDistance.sort_index()
refrigeratedTruckRatesbyDistance.plot()
```

Output:

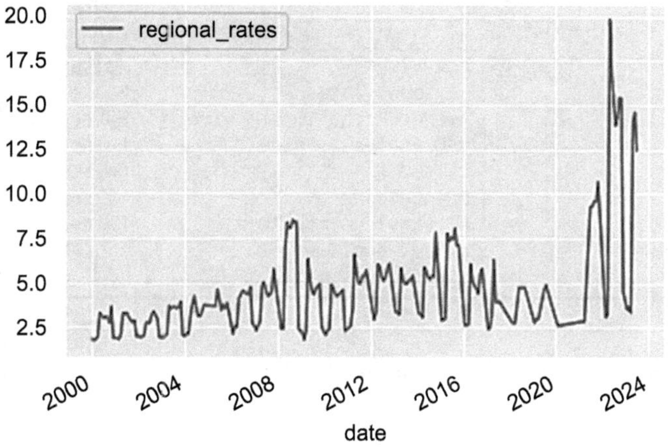

Step 9: Combined DataFrame and perform data analysis

Combine all features into one data frame with the date as the index.

```
dfList1 = [ dfPCU3251203251204, refrigeratedTruckRatesbyDistance, dfAveragePriceTomatoes,
dfUSDieselSalesPrice,dfCPIAUCSL,dfPNGASUSUSDM,dfPolymersofEthylene]
combined_df = ft.reduce(lambda left,right: pd.merge(left, right, on="date"), dfList1)
combined_df
```

Output:

date							
2003-06-01	.	2.084848	1.398	1.424	183.100	5.829048	100.000
2003-07-01	165.9	1.704545	1.460	1.435	183.700	5.027273	99.700
2003-11-01	161.7	2.010732	1.480	1.482	185.000	4.491667	99.600
2003-12-01	166.3	2.045455	1.533	1.490	185.500	6.140000	99.800
2004-01-01	166.7	1.985795	1.472	1.551	186.300	6.150526	100.400
...	...	...	...	...	...	...	...
2022-12-01	652.144	4.500000	2.228	4.714	298.990	5.746818	190.607
2023-02-01	661.379	3.513258	1.990	4.413	301.648	2.438000	190.142
2023-03-01	658.730	3.683712	1.932	4.211	301.808	2.409130	187.903
2023-04-01	669.615	3.342803	1.874	4.099	302.918	2.195500	190.068
2023-05-01	688.066	3.210227	1.798	3.915	303.294	2.315217	188.092

144 rows × 7 columns

Next, check for nulls.

```
combined_df.isna().any()
```

Output:

```
CO2Price                      False
regional_rates                False
AverageRetailTomatoPrices     False
USDieselSalesPrice            False
CPIAUCSL                      False
PNGASUSUSDM                   False
PPIEthylenePropylene          False
dtype: bool
```

Average retail tomato price has strings ".". Replace them with nulls and re-run the null analysis.

```
combined_df['AverageRetailTomatoPrices']=combined_df['AverageRetailTomatoPrices'].replace
('.', np.NaN)
combined_df.isna().any()
```

Output:

```
CO2Price                      True
regional_rates               False
AverageRetailTomatoPrices     True
USDieselSalesPrice           False
CPIAUCSL                     False
PNGASUSUSDM                  False
PPIEthylenePropylene         False
dtype: bool
```

Step 10: Apply imputation strategy to fix nulls

Combine all features into one data frame with the date as the index.

```
combined_df = combined_df.fillna(method='ffill').fillna(method='bfill')combined_df.isna().any()
combined_df.isna().any()
```

Output:

```
CO2Price                       False
regional_rates                 False
AverageRetailTomatoPrices      False
USDieselSalesPrice             False
CPIAUCSL                       False
PNGASUSUSDM                    False
PPIEthylenePropylene           False
dtype: bool
```

Finally, check the data frame for signature before developing regressive algorithms.

```
combined_df['AverageRetailTomatoPrices'] = combined_df['AverageRetailTomatoPrices'].astype(float)
combined_df['PPIEthylenePropylene'] = combined_df['PPIEthylenePropylene'].astype(float)
combined_df['CO2Price'] = combined_df['CO2Price'].astype(float)
#combined_df['GASREGM'] = combined_df['GASREGM'].astype(float)
```

Output:

```
<class 'pandas.core.frame.DataFrame'>
DatetimeIndex: 144 entries, 2003-06-01 to 2023-05-01
Data columns (total 7 columns):
 #   Column                     Non-Null Count  Dtype
---  ------                     --------------  -----
 0   CO2Price                   144 non-null    float64
 1   regional_rates             144 non-null    float64
 2   AverageRetailTomatoPrices  144 non-null    float64
 3   USDieselSalesPrice         144 non-null    float64
 4   CPIAUCSL                   144 non-null    float64
 5   PNGASUSUSDM                144 non-null    float64
 6   PPIEthylenePropylene       144 non-null    float64
dtypes: float64(7)
memory usage: 9.0 KB
```

All columns are numerical and can be regressed.

Step 11: Correlation analysis

Correlation analysis provides a glimpse into how each feature influences the predictor one – 'AverageRetailTomatoPrices'.

```
combined_df[['CO2Price','AverageRetailTomatoPrices','USDieselSalesPrice','regional_rates','CPIAUCSL',
'PPIEthylenePropylene']].corr()
```

```
sns.heatmap(combined_df.corr());
```

Output:

	CO2Price	AverageRetailTomatoPrices	USDieselSalesPrice	regional_rates	CPIAUCSL	PPIEthylenePropylene
CO2Price	1.000000	0.478190	0.621874	0.481956	0.967981	0.719389
AverageRetailTomatoPrices	0.478190	1.000000	0.135883	0.120987	0.513726	0.139897
USDieselSalesPrice	0.621874	0.135883	1.000000	0.561919	0.648326	0.780303
regional_rates	0.481956	0.120987	0.561919	1.000000	0.515740	0.407406
CPIAUCSL	0.967981	0.513726	0.648326	0.515740	1.000000	0.663427
PPIEthylenePropylene	0.719389	0.139897	0.780303	0.407406	0.663427	1.000000

As it can be seen, CO_2 price (47.819% ~~44.951%~~), diesel prices (13.586% ~~10.87%~~), regional refrigerator truck rates (12.09% ~~13.159%~~), CPI (51.37% ~~48%~~), and producer prices of ethylene propylene (13.987% ~~10.369%~~) are positively correlated with average retail tomato prices. Similarly, CO_2 price (62.204%), average retail tomato prices (13.58% ~~10.870%~~), regional refrigerator truck rates (56.19% ~~54.197%~~), CPI (64.63% ~~63.62%~~), and producer prices of ethylene propylene (78.00% ~~78.426%~~) are all positively correlated with US deisel prices. Both energy and transportation show to have an immense influence on retail tomato prices.

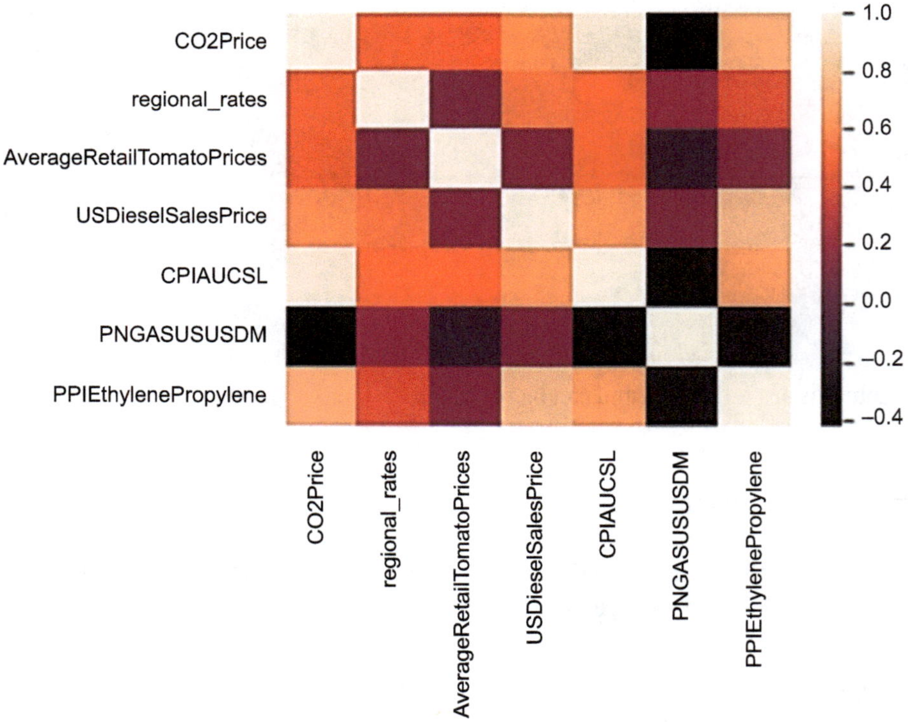

Step 12: Regression models: linear regressor

Regression analysis provides relationship between feature Y variables and list of independent variables.

```
X =combined_df[['CO2Price',
'USDieselSalesPrice', 'regional_rates', 'CPIAUCSL', 'PPIEthylenePropylene']]
y= combined_df['AverageRetailTomatoPrices']

X_train,X_test,y_train,y_test=train_test_split(X,y,test_size=0.2,random_state=0)
regressor = LinearRegression()
regressor.fit(X_train,y_train)
y_pred = regressor.predict(X_test)
y_pred
r2_score(y_test,y_pred)dtype: bool
```

Output:
0.3981 or 39.817%

The model has low scores. What it tells us is that all features included in the regression do not have full explainability for the average retail costs of fresh tomatoes. Of course, we've used only transportation, shipping, and storage components that are on the supply side of the demand. In a subsequent chapter, I will include the demand side of the variables plus climatic variables to develop the model.

```
plt.scatter(y_test,y_pred)
plt.xlabel('Actual')
plt.ylabel("Predicted")
plt.title('Actual vs Predicted')
#overlay the regression line
z = np.polyfit(y_test, y_pred, 1)
p = np.polyld(z)
plt.plot(y_test,p(y_test), color='b')
plt.show()
```

Output:

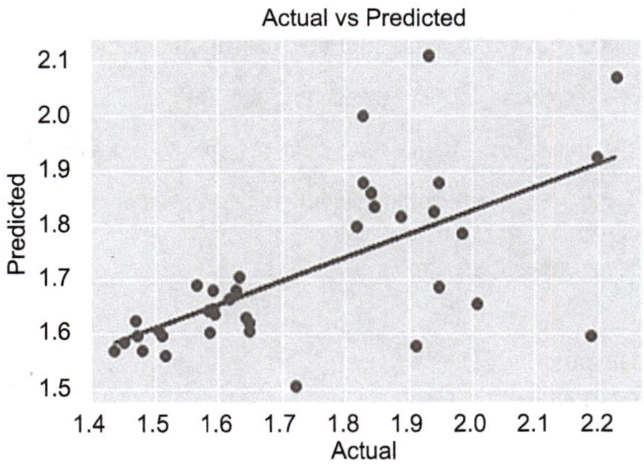

```
eli5.explain_weights(gbr,feature_names=
list(X.columns))
```

Output: Top *y* features include CPI, CO_2, ethylene, and transportation costs. However, the model has high BIAS.

y top features

Weight?	Feature
+0.661	<BIAS>
+0.006	CPIAUCSL
+0.000	CO2Price
-0.002	PPIEthylenePropylene
-0.012	regional_rates
-0.018	USDieselSalesPrice

Step 11: Multi-tree (RF) regression model

Multi-tree regression model is a method that creates multiple decision trees to predict outcomes from data. It works by using different parts of the data to create each tree, and then it combines the results to make more accurate predictions. However, when using the default settings, the trees can become too big and use too much memory, which can cause problems for some datasets. To solve this issue, we can adjust settings like "max_depth" and "min_samples_leaf" to control the size and complexity of the trees. In this particular case, the "max_depth" was set to 3 to make sure the trees weren't too big, and the analysis was more efficient.

```
X =combined_df[[
'CO2Price', 'USDieselSalesPrice', 'regional_rates', 'CPIAUCSL', 'PPIEthylenePropylene']]

y= combined_df['AverageRetailTomatoPrices']

X_train,X_test,y_train,y_test = train_test_split(X,y,test_size=0.2,random_state=0)

regr = RandomForestRegressor(max_depth=3,random_state=0)
regr.fit(X_train,y_train)
regr.score(X_test,y_test)
```

Output:
0.51844 or 51.844%

Step 12: Regression models: gradient-boosted ensemble regression

Gradient-boosted ensemble regression builds a precise model step-by-step, starting with a simple model and adding complexity to improve accuracy. By focusing on areas where the initial model underperforms and fitting regression trees at each stage, it enhances predictions and overall model performance for any problem with a measurable outcome.

```
from sklearn.ensemble importGradientBoostingRegressor

gbr = GradientBoostingRegressor(random_state=0)

X =combined_df[[
'USDieselSalesPrice', 'regional_rates', 'CPIAUCSL', 'PPIEthylene', 'CO2Price']]

y= combined_df['AverageRetailTomatoPrices']

X_train,X_test,y_train,y_test = train_test_split(X,y,test_size=0.2,random_state=0)

gbr.fit(X_train,y_train)
gbr.score(X_test,y_test)
```

Output:
0.57679 or 57.679%

Explainability:

```
eli5.explain_weights(gbr,feature_names=
list(X.columns))
```

Output:
CPI,CO_2, diesel, ethylene, and regional rates all impact the retail price of tomatoes.

Weight	Feature
0.5004 ± 0.5171	CPIAUCSL
0.1889 ± 0.4356	regional_rates
0.1307 ± 0.4501	USDieselSalesPrice
0.1212 ± 0.4652	PPIEthylenePropylene
0.0588 ± 0.2533	CO2Price

Temporal data analysis

Temporal data analysis, or time series analysis, helps us comprehend how data changes over time. It is essential because most datasets have a time component, and understanding these changes can yield valuable insights. A time series can be broken down into trend, seasonality, and randomness. The trend shows the overall direction of the data, seasonality identifies repeating patterns, and randomness accounts for unpredictable noise. By analyzing these elements, we can uncover deeper patterns, make accurate predictions, and inform decision-making across various fields.

$$Y_t = m_t + s_t + \varepsilon_t \tag{2}$$

where m_t is the trend, s_t stands for seasonality, and ε_t stands for the random variable.

Three characteristics lead to the following time series behavior.

- White noise is a type of time series data that has no overall trend or repeating patterns. It is essentially just random noise that is present in the data. White noise is called "white" because it contains all frequencies in equal amounts, like white light contains all colors. This type of data is sometimes used as a benchmark for comparing other time series data to see if there are any meaningful patterns or trends in the data. Since white noise does not have any underlying patterns, any patterns that are found in other datasets can be attributed to something other than just randomness (Figure 8).

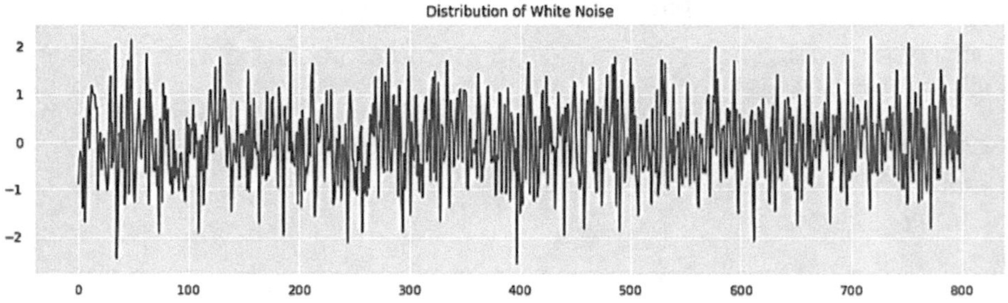

Figure 8: White noise.

- A time series that has a trend, but no seasonality means that the data is changing in a consistent direction over time, but there are no repeating patterns that happen at specific times of the year. For example, if we were looking at sales data for a product that was increasing in sales every year, but there were no differences in sales between different seasons or months, then we would say that the data has a trend but no seasonality. Understanding whether a time series has trends, seasonality, or both is important for making predictions and understanding the underlying patterns in the data. We focus on the trend in the time series to understand data changes and predict future sales (a good example is production and import of fresh avocados in the USA [47] (table g3)); see Figure 9.

As it can be seen, US imports of avocados have increased substantially due to various factors including, limited US production, foreign products that are better and cheaper, transportation, and marketing factors [47]. Avocado import trend could be better explained using power and polynomial regressor (order 6).

$$Y_{\text{fresh avocados import}} = 0.148x^{2.4684}$$

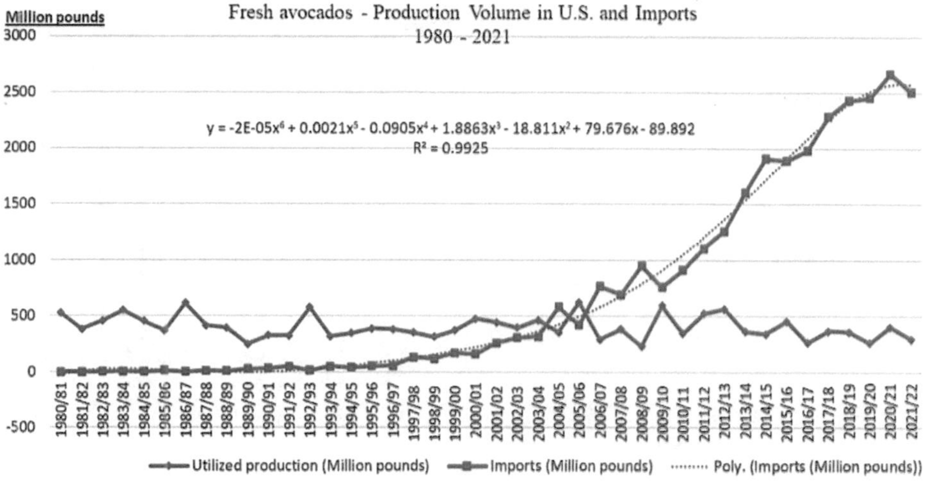

Figure 9: Fresh avocados.

Fresh avacados	Equation	R^2 Value
Exponential	$y = 2.9495e^{0.1828x}$	$R^2 = 0.8565$
Linear	$y = 63.476x - 671.03$	$R^2 = 0.7922$
Logarithmic	$y = 674.2\ln(x) - 1196.8$	$R^2 = 0.4567$
Nonlinear (poly)	$y = -2E{-}05x^6 + 0.0021x^5 - 0.0905x^4 + 1.8863x^3 - 18.811x^2 + 79.676x - 89.892$	$R^2 = 0.9925$
Power	$y = 0.148x^{2.4684}$	$R^2 = 0.9677$

Since the early 2000s, US avocado consumption (Figure 9) has tripled to over 8 pounds per person by 2021. Despite averaging 400 million pounds of annual production, domestic output has declined since 2011, leading to increased imports to meet year-round demand [47] (Figure 10).

- This has seasonality and no trend (refrigerator truck rates exhibit seasonality and no trend) – refrigerated truck rates in the US trucking industry experience seasonal fluctuations, with tighter capacity, higher rates, and more scheduling constraints in spring and summer [19]. June and July shipping rates tend to be higher (Figure 11).
- A time series exhibiting both trend and seasonality indicates that the data consistently changes in a particular direction over time while also displaying recurring patterns at specific times of the year (Figure 12).

Kansas State's wheat yield per area harvested between the years 1982 and 2020 shows both trend and seasonality, which means that the amount of wheat produced each year is changing in a consistent direction over time, and that there are also repeating patterns that happen drought years. Understanding these trends and patterns is important for farmers and policymakers who need to make decisions about when to plant, harvest, and sell crops. By analyzing the data, they can predict when to expect high or low yields and adjust their strategies according to maximize their profits and minimize their losses [48].

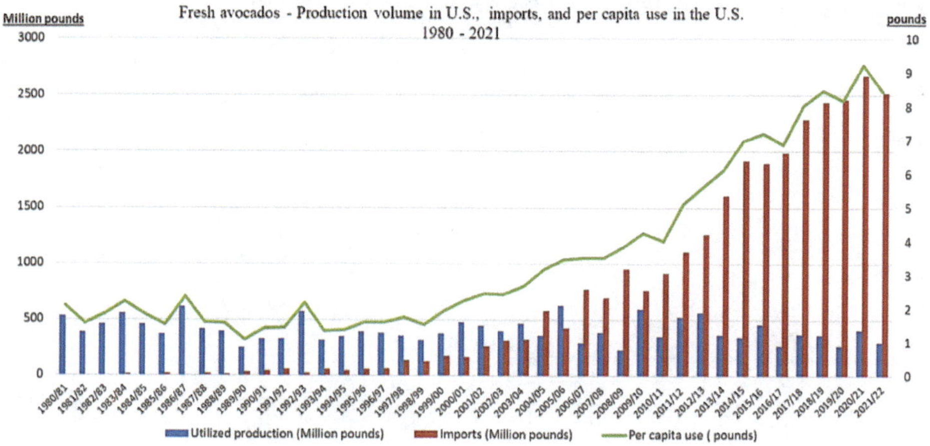

Figure 10: Avocados imports.

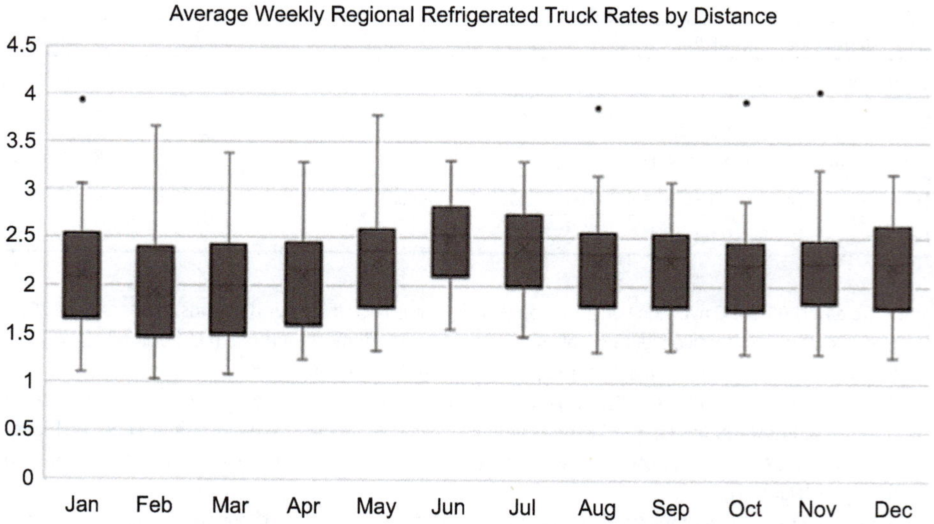

Figure 11: US refrigerator truck rates.

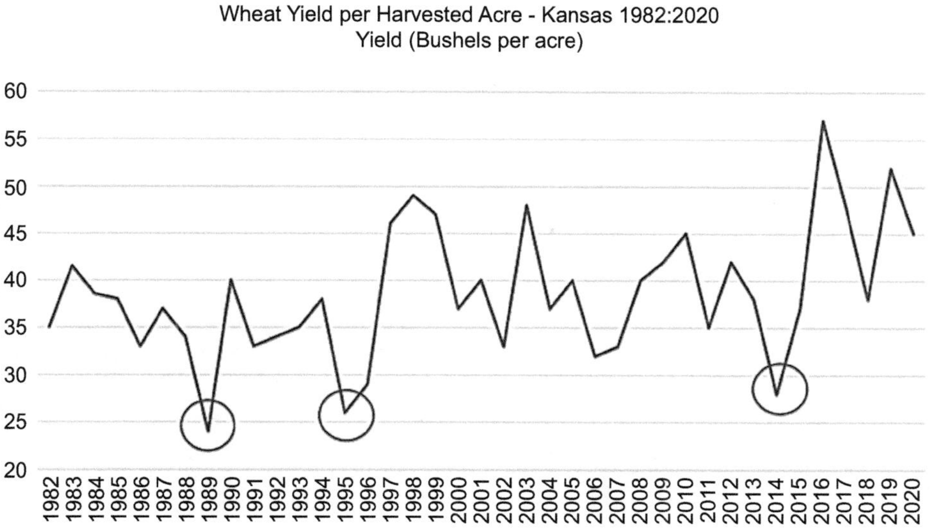

Figure 12: Wheat yield.

Time series data refers to information that varies over a period. It can be divided into two categories: stationary and nonstationary. Nonstationary data has statistical means, variances, and covariances that change over time. This type of data can exhibit trends, cycles, random walks, or a combination of these behaviors, which makes it difficult to accurately predict and model. To build accurate predictive models and extract maximum information from time series data, it must be transformed into stationary data. Stationary data has consistent statistical properties over time, which makes it more predictable and easier to model.

The process of transforming nonstationary data into stationary data involves standard data processing checks such as inspecting data, checking for nulls, and creating a dataset for time series processing. By following these steps (Figure 13) and ensuring that our time series data is stationary, we can build accurate predictive models that provide valuable insights into trends and patterns over time. The following diagram illustrates the process of transforming nonstationary data into stationary data, including exploratory data analysis [48].

Single-variable temporal data

Single-variable temporal data, or univariate time series, involves time and one other variable representing the field to be forecasted. It focuses on a single field that changes over time and is often used in forecasting to predict future values based on past trends.

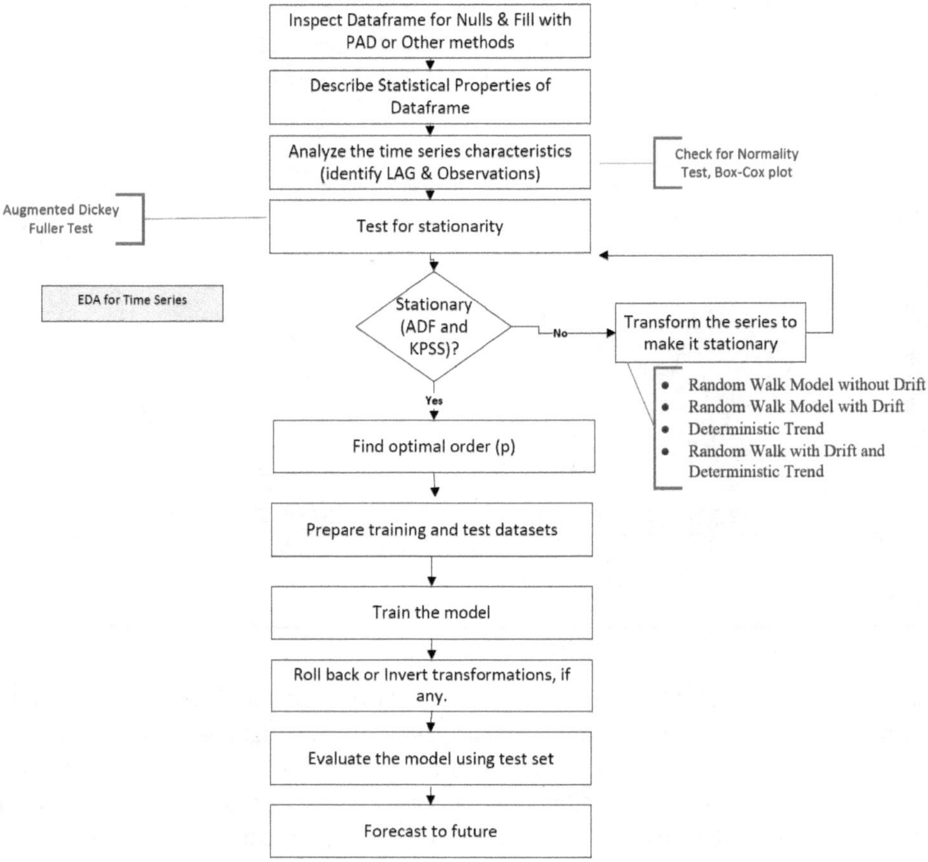

Figure 13: Time series flow chart.

By analyzing this data, patterns and relationships can be discerned, allowing for the development of accurate predictive models.

Multivariate time series

Multivariate time series data includes multiple variables, one of which represents time and others that represent different parameters. These relationships are analyzed using K-equations, with each equation corresponding to a lag of another series. The exogenous series, denoted as X, is illustrated in equations (3) and (4). The primary aim of analyzing multivariate time series is to understand how a series is affected by its own past values and those of other variables. By studying these relationships and lags, we can gain insights into the series' behavior and trends, enabling accurate predictions and informed decision-making. For more information on related topics like autocorrelation, partial autocorrelation function [50, 51], and stationarity checks [52], refer to my other books.

$$y_{1,t} = f(y_{1,t-1} \ldots, y_{k,t-1}, \ldots y_{1,t-p} \ldots y_{k,t-p}, \ldots X_{t-1} X_{t-2} \ldots\ldots\ldots) \quad (2)$$

$$y_{k,t} = f(y_{1,t-1} \ldots, y_{k,t-1}, \ldots y_{1,t-p} \ldots y_{k,t-p}, \ldots X_{t-1} X_{t-2} \ldots\ldots\ldots) \quad (3)$$

Forecasting models

ARIMA is a type of model used to predict time series data. It combines three components – autoregression, moving average, and integration – to produce predictions. Auto ARIMA is a more advanced version of ARIMA that uses an advanced search to find the best parameters. This helps to make the predictions more accurate by finding the best metric parameters, such as the Akaike knowledge criterion.

Vector autoregression (VAR) is another statistical model used to analyze time series data. It is used when we have multiple variables that change over time and allow us to capture the relationships between these variables. A VAR model uses lagged values of multiple time series variables as predictors. In other words, it looks at how the values of multiple variables in the past can help predict the values of these variables in the future. By using VAR models in our analyses, we can gain deeper insights into the patterns and trends of time series data and make more accurate predictions of future outcomes [53].

Prophet forecasting

Prophet forecasting is a powerful tool that can be used to make predictions about time series data. It works by using an additive model to capture nonlinear trends, seasonal effects, and holiday effects. This approach is particularly useful for temporal data that exhibits glaring recurring arrangements and multiple flavors of chronological information. It's designed to be easy to use and fully automated, meaning that users can simply input their time series data and generate a forecast. It is also robust to missing data and can handle outliers effectively. Businesses can use Prophet to forecast sales, capacity, and other important metrics. By utilizing Prophet, businesses can gain valuable insights into their historical records and derive more accurate estimates about future movements and patterns.

Mexico avocados

Model final release avocados imports Prophet model notebook file

Univariate time series model: America's most beloved imported fruits: avocados imports

The share of imported fruits and vegetables in US consumption has grown significantly over the past few decades, with imports accounting for 34% of fresh fruit consumption and 25% of vegetable consumption. This trend has been driven by trade, which has made produce available outside of the traditional US growing season and provided access to a wider variety of produce.

Over the past decade, the US fruit trade grew by $8.9 billion, reaching $18.9 billion in 2021, with avocados, bananas, and fresh grapes comprising 40.6% of all fruit imports [54]. This increase highlights the importance of global trade in meeting consumer demand and the need for stringent food safety and quality standards [55]. The fruit and tree nuts yearbook tables dataset, spanning from 1980/81 to 2023, provides insights into the supply and utilization of fresh avocados, revealing both trends and seasonality in the data.

Step 1: Data load

To begin analyzing the dataset, we need to load and summarize the data. We will be using a tool called Prophet, which requires the data to be in Pandas DataFrames. Pandas is a Python library used for data manipulation and analysis.

```
from sklearn.metrics import mean_absolute_error
from prophet import Prophet
df = pd.read_csv(r"FreshAvocadosImports.csv",index_col=0)
#summarize shape
print(df.shape)
#show first few rows
print(df.head())
```

Output:

```
(42, 1)
   Fresh avocados import (Million pounds)
Year
1980       1.9
```

```
1981    1.5
1982    3.4
1983    7.3
1984    3.7
```

After loading the dataset into a Pandas DataFrame, we can run an example to get a better understanding of the data.

Step 2: Load and plot dataset

To better understand a temporal data, we need to plot the data. Plotting the data allows us to visually identify any trends, seasonal patterns, outliers, and other characteristics that may not be immediately apparent from just looking at the numbers.

```
from pandas import read_csv
from matplotlib import pyplot
#plot the time series
df.plot()
pyplot.show()
```

Output:

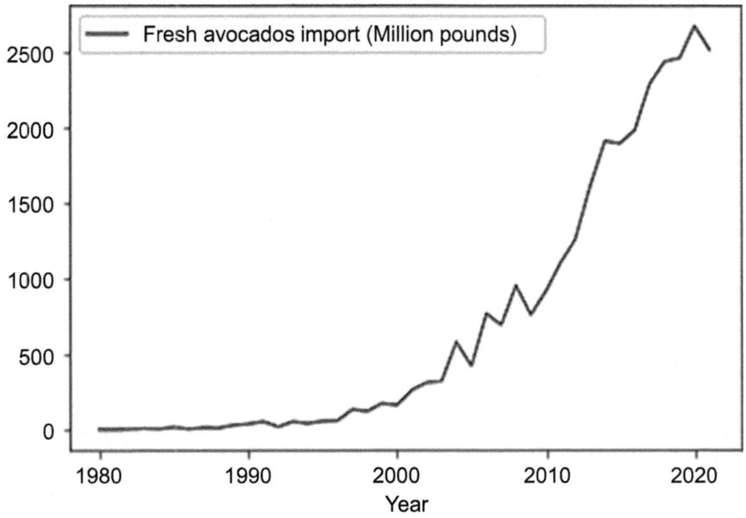

Step 3: Avocados import with prophet

To use Prophet for forecasting, define and configure a Prophet() object, ensuring your dataset is formatted as a Pandas DataFrame with 'ds' for date-times and 'y' for observations. Fit the object to your dataset using the fit() function to train the model, enabling it to predict future trends and support informed decision-making.

```
df["ds"]=pd.to_datetime(df["Year"])
df.rename(columns={"Fresh avocados import (Million pounds)": "y"}, inplace = True)
df.isna().any()
df.drop('Year',inplace=True, axis=1)
df.info()
```

Output:

```
<class 'pandas.core.frame.DataFrame'>
RangeIndex: 42 entries, 0 to 41
Data columns (total 2 columns):
 #   Column  Non-Null Count  Dtype
---  ------  --------------  -----
 0   y       42 non-null      float64
 1   ds      42 non-null      datetime64[ns]
dtypes: datetime64[ns](1), float64(1)
memory usage: 800.0 bytes
```

```
# define the model
model = Prophet()
# fit the model
model.fit(df)
```

Output: <prophet.forecaster.Prophet at 0x7f7844b92940>

Step 4: Make an in-sample forecast

Forecasting using historical data, known as an "in-sample forecast," helps evaluate a model's performance and its ability to generalize by predicting on data used during training. To generate a forecast, we use the predict() function with a DataFrame containing date-times in a 'ds' column, enabling us to assess the model's accuracy and effectiveness for future predictions.

```
# define the period for which we want a prediction
future = list()
for i in range(1, 5):
  year = str(2005+i)
  future.append([year])
  print(future)

future = pd.DataFrame(future)
future ['ds'] = pd.to_datetime(future['ds'],format='%Y')
future
```

Output:

	ds
0	2006-01-01
1	2007-01-01
2	2008-01-01
3	2009-01-01

Step 5: Predict

After creating a "forecast" DataFrame, use the predict() function to generate predictions, resulting in a DataFrame with key columns like 'ds' (forecast date), 'yhat' (predicted value), 'yhat_lower' (lower bound estimate), and 'yhat_upper' (upper bound estimate). These bounds highlight the forecast's uncertainty, with a wider range indicating greater uncertainty, helping us assess prediction reliability and decide if further measures are needed to reduce uncertainty.

```
# use the model to make a forecast
forecast = model.predict(future)
# summarize the forecast
print (forecast[['ds', 'yhat', 'yhat_lower', 'yhat_upper']].head())
# plot forecast
model.plot(forecast)
pyplot.show()
```

Output:

```
ds          yhat  yhat_lower   yhat_upper
0 2006-01-01  1034.886937  534.495263  1532.092600
1 2007-01-01  1103.267727  588.661728  1606.952177
2 2008-01-01  1179.912626  698.630640  1712.550443
3 2009-01-01  1228.700249  727.445885  1734.597993
```

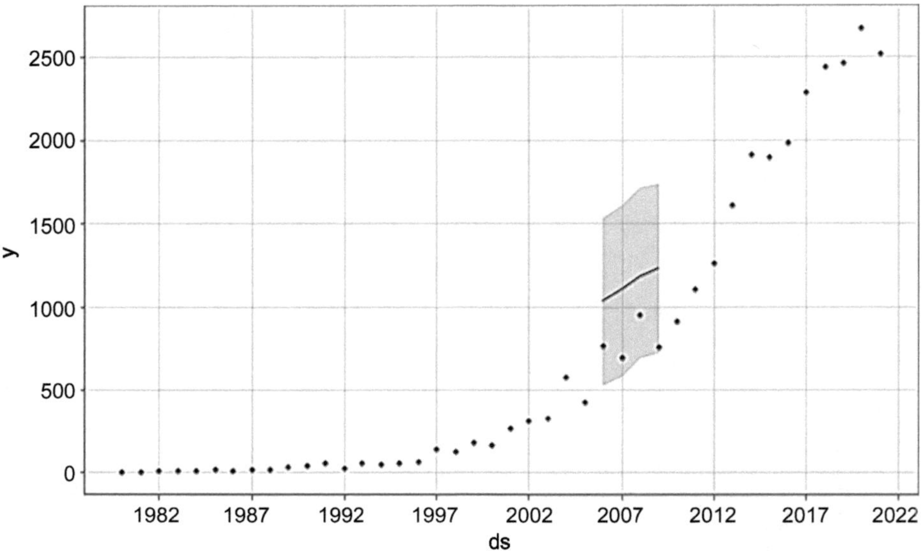

Step 6: Model accuracies: MAE

Generate predictions by passing the "forecast" DataFrame to the predict() function, resulting in a DataFrame with key columns such as 'ds' (forecast date), 'yhat' (predicted value), 'yhat_lower' (lower bound), and 'yhat_upper' (upper bound). These bounds indicate the forecast's uncertainty, with a wider range suggesting more uncertainty, aiding in the assessment of prediction reliability and the need for additional measures.

```
combined_df = pd.merge(df[['ds','y']],forecast[['ds', 'yhat', 'yhat_lower', 'yhat_upper']][-5:], on='ds') combined df
```

```
from sklearn.metrics import mean_absolute_error, mean_absolute_percentage_error

#Check MAE value
MAE = mean_absolute_error(combined_df['y'], combined_df['yhat'])
print(f'The MAE for the baseline model is {MAE}')
```

Output:

	ds	y	yhat	yhat_lower	yhat_upper
0	2006-01-01	769.099287	1034.886937	534.495263	1532.092600
1	2007-01-01	694.098532	1103.267727	588.661728	1606.952177
2	2008-01-01	951.809311	1179.912626	698.630640	1712.550443
3	2009-01-01	760.616158	1228.700249	727.445885	1734.597993

The MAE for the baseline model is 342.7860626489213 or 342.786 million pounds.

Step 7: COVID-19 import spike

The corona virus pandemic and increased at-home cooking have significantly boosted US sales of Mexican avocados, with Mexican-sourced avocados selling a record 2.1 billion pounds this fiscal year and projecting 2.3 billion pounds for 2021 [56]. This surge, driven by avocados' popularity as a versatile and healthy ingredient, is expected to continue as more Americans embrace home cooking and seek nutritious options.

Mexican avocado imports boom during pandemic has not caught by univariate model!

In 2021, the USA imported $3.0 billion worth of avocados, with 92% of the value and 89% of the volume coming from Mexico.

In 2020, Mexico exported $3.2 billion worth of avocados, with 79% going to the USA, and around 80% from Michoacán sent to the USA in both 2020 and 2021, ensuring a year-round supply through complementary growing seasons and emphasizing the importance of cross-border trade for both economies [57].

Re-running the model for COVID-19 pandemic year has increased model errors. It's expected as model has no signals to tam the explositives of COVID-19-induced spikes. As can be seen above time series gifnal, the model under catching imports boom (Figure 14).

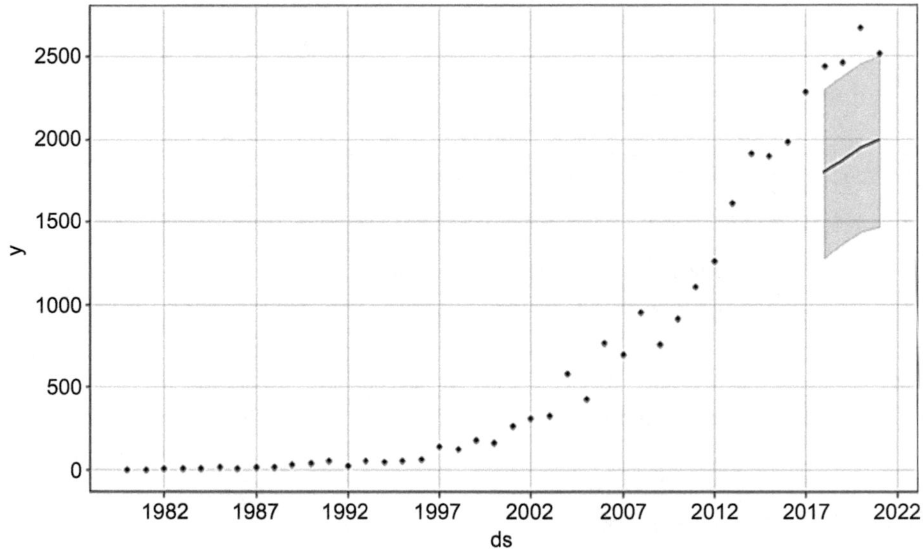

Figure 7: Avocado imports.

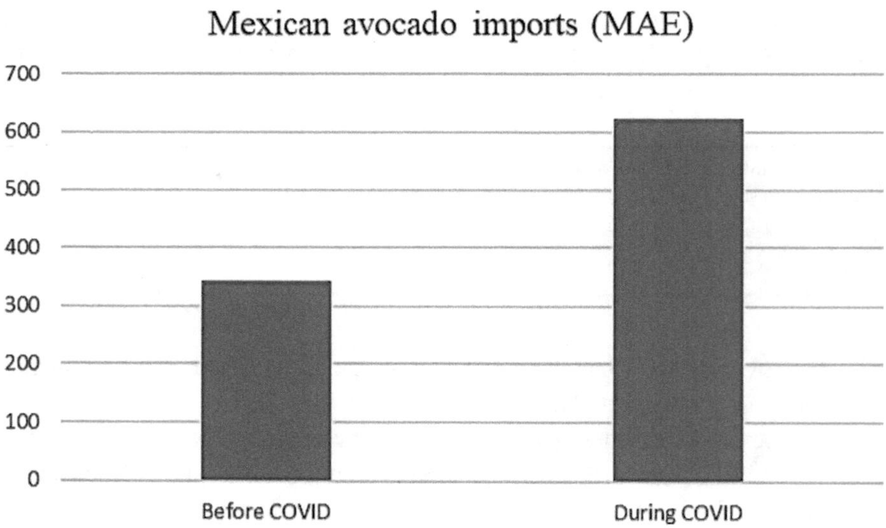


```
combined_df = pd.merge(df[['ds', 'y']],forecast[['ds', 'yhat', 'yhat_lower', 'yhat_upper']][-5:], on='ds') combined df
```

```
from sklearn.metrics import mean_absolute_error, mean_absolute_percentage_error

#Check MAE value
MAE = mean_absolute_error(combined_df['y'], combined_df['yhat'])
print(f'The MAE for the baseline model is {MAE}')
```

	ds	y	yhat	yhat_lower	yhat_upper
0	2018-01-01	2436.528067	1797.260667	1277.860179	2297.166560
1	2019-01-01	2461.458457	1865.717086	1362.521003	2377.643474
2	2020-01-01	2674.415826	1942.402534	1433.902202	2454.544033
3	2021-01-01	2516.509580	1991.207799	1463.904729	2501.413511

Step 8: Estimate

An out-of-sample forecast extends the forecast period beyond the training data to evaluate a model's ability to predict unseen values, providing crucial insights into its generalization, accuracy, and reliability for making informed decisions.

```
# define the period for which we want a prediction
future = list()
for i in range(1, 10):
    year = str(2019+i)
    future.append([year])
    print(future)

future = pd.DataFrame(future)
future
```

```
future.columns = ['ds']
```

```
future['ds'] = pd.to_datetime(future['ds'], format='%Y')
```

```
# use the model to make a forecast
forecast = model.predict(future)
```

```
# summarize the forecast
print(forecast[['ds', 'yhat', 'yhat_lower', 'yhat_upper']])
# plot forecast
model.plot(forecast)
pyplot.show()
```

Output:

	ds	yhat	yhat_lower	yhat_upper
0	2020-01-01	1942.402534	1439.981408	2380.672036
1	2021-01-01	1991.207799	1479.311773	2497.984907
2	2022-01-01	2051.429850	1508.334175	2514.693066
3	2023-01-01	2119.886270	1647.445623	2608.811627
4	2024-01-01	2196.571718	1684.553586	2679.726310
5	2025-01-01	2245.376983	1731.313672	2752.775831
6	2026-01-01	2305.599034	1785.132976	2824.769616
7	2027-01-01	2374.055453	1863.138400	2864.169116
8	2028-01-01	2450.740902	1956.438125	2958.873801

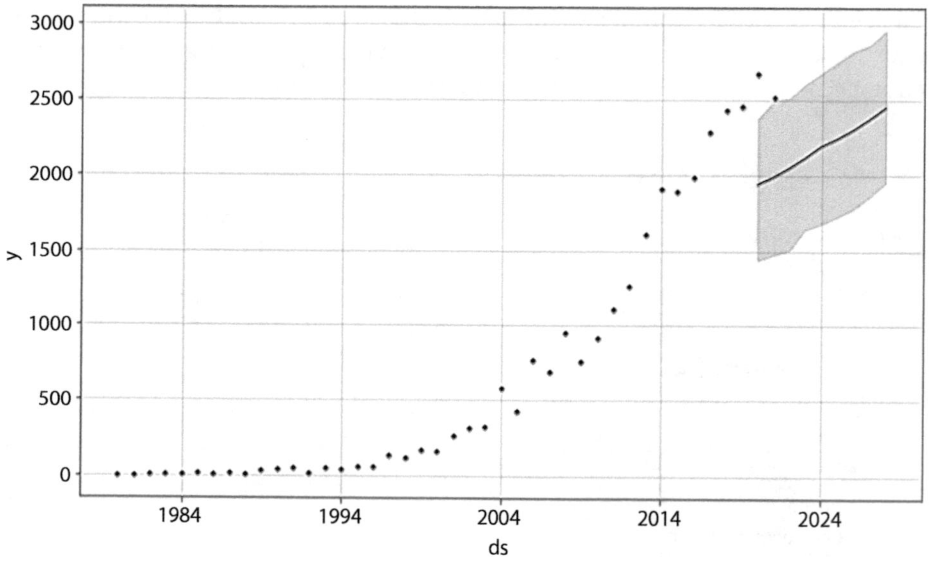

If there are no drastic geopolitical or economic changes in the next five years, the model suggests that avocado imports from Mexico will continue to rise, maintaining an upward trend.

Summary

Univariate models are effective at capturing trends and providing forecasting capabilities. However, they may require additional information or signals, such as detecting COVID-19 spikes, to make accurate predictions. This is where multivariate models come in handy. Multivariate models require all future feature values to accurately forecast outcomes, which involves imputing future datasets. In the next section, we will delve into the various imputation strategies used in multivariate models.

Mexico avocados

Final release avocados imports Prophet model notebook.

Multivariate time series model: America's most beloved imported fruits: avocados imports

The import of avocados is subject to a multitude of factors, including agricultural yields in the USA and Mexico, input costs, labor costs, fertilizer costs, exchange rates, transportation costs, imports from other countries, and consumer taste preferences in the USA. In essence, micro- and geopolitical factors, tariffs, commerce, and climate/weather all come into play, making it a complex and multifaceted process [60].

To address this complexity, many real-world pricing, optimization, yield, and cost models rely on multivariate modeling techniques. These models take into account multiple variables and their interrelationships to provide a more accurate and complete insight into the factors that influence avocado import.

Step 1: Data load

Prepare data.

```
from sklearn.metrics import mean_absolute_error
from prophet import Prophet
```

```
df = pd.read_csv(r"FinalFreshAvocadosImportswithMXNandProd.csv",index_col=0)
# summarize shape
print(df.shape)
# show first few rows
print(df.head())
```

Output:

```
(28, 3)
  Fresh avocados import (Million pounds) Utilized production  DEXMXUS
date
1/1/94     40.954000     348.0 3.385302
1/1/95     56.008000     389.0 6.446705
1/1/96     58.830000     382.0 7.600435
1/1/97     133.724000    354.0 7.917675
1/1/98     121.662108    316.6 9.152085
```

The initial output of the example displays a dataset spanning 28 years with four columns: date, avocado imports in millions of pounds, the Mexican pesos to US dollar spot exchange rate, and US avocado production [60]. Reviewing the first five rows helps in understanding the dataset's structure, which is essential for selecting appropriate analysis and forecasting methods.

Step 2: View temporal data

Plotting temporal data allows us to quickly generate visualizations of the data and gain insights into its behavior over time. By plotting the data, we can better understand its characteristics and make more informed decisions about how to analyze and forecast it.

```
from pandas import read_csv
from matplotlib import pyplot
# plot the time series
df["Fresh avocados import (Million pounds)"].plot()
pyplot.show()
```

Output:

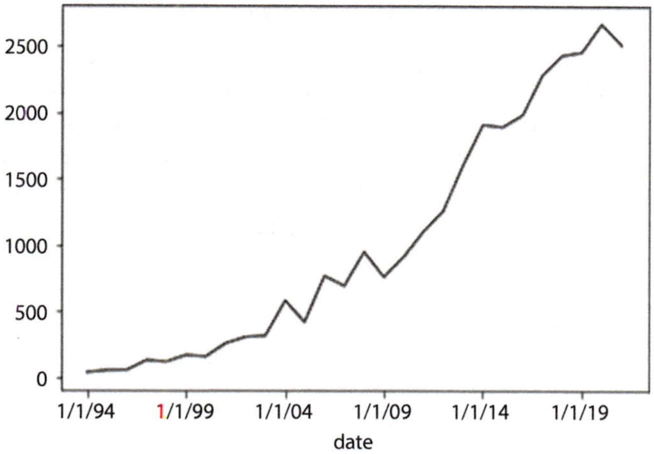


```
df["Utilized production"].plot()
pyplot.show()
```

Output

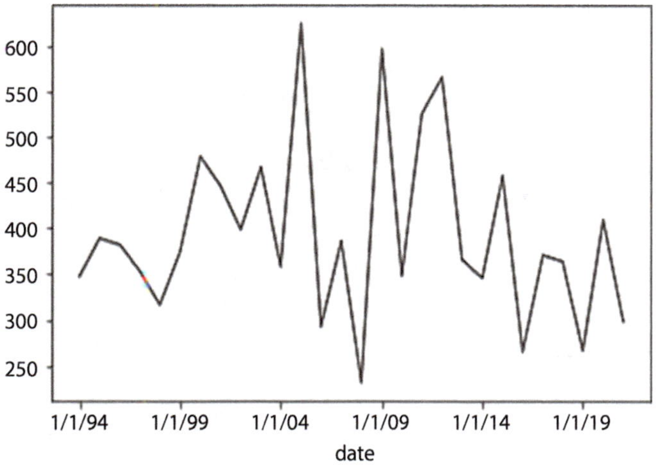

For the 2009/2010 growing year, the production of Mexican Hass avocados was expected to increase by 5.6% from the previous year, with a forecast of 1.18 million metric tons. This growth is mainly attributed to favorable weather conditions throughout the growing year in Michoacán, the state where 92% of the total Mexican avocado production is grown. Because of the high international demand for Mexican Hass avocados, there was also a 4% increase in production area (measured in hectares) in the 2009/2010 season compared to the previous year. Another contributing factor to the increase in production is Michoacán's commitment to implementing Phytosanitary programs to control pests.

Notably, the production of Mexican Hass avocados exhibits a polynomial trend of order 6, indicating a complex and nuanced relationship between the various factors that impact production. This underscores the importance of leveraging sophisticated modeling techniques to gain a deeper understanding of the factors driving production and to inform effective strategies for meeting growing demand.

```
df["DEXMXUS"].plot()
pyplot.show()
```

Output:

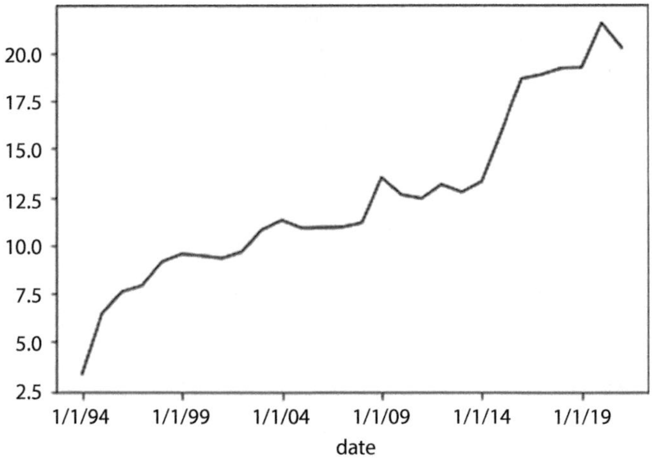

Step 3: Avocados import with prophet

Run temporal data.

```
df["ds"] = pd.to_datetime(df["date"])
df.rename(columns = {"Fresh avocados import (Million pounds)": "y" }, inplace = True)
df.drop('date', inplace=True, axis=1)
```

```
Prophetdf=df.copy()
```

```
n_obs = int(Prophetdf.shape[0] * 0.9)
Prophetdf_train, Prophetdf_test = Prophetdf[0:n_obs],Prophetdf[n_obs:]
print(Prophetdf_train.shape,Prophetdf_test.shape)
```

Output:
(25, 4) (3, 4)

```
Prophetdf_train.head()
```

```
col_list =list( Prophetdf.columns)
col_list
```

```
remove_items = ['ds','y' ]
for i in remove_items:
  col_list.remove(i)
```

```
Prophet_cols = col_list
```

Output:
Get Prophet columns. ['Utilized production', 'DEXMXUS']

```
# define the model
multi_model = Prophet(interval_width = 0.95)
```

```
multi_model.fit(Prophetdf_train)
```

Output:
<prophet.forecaster.Prophet at 0x7ff46f6f79b0>

Step 4: Prepare future data

Call make future data frame to prepare the future DataFrame.

```
future = multi_model.make_future_dataframe(periods = Prophetdf_test.shape[0],freq='YS',
include_history=True)
future.tail(15)
```

```
for col in Prophet_cols:
  future[col]=Prophetdf[col]
future.info()
```

Step 5: Predict

Once our dataset and Prophet model are prepared, the predict() function generates a forecast, returning a DataFrame with key columns for the forecast date ('ds'), predicted value ('yhat'), and uncertainty bounds ('yhat_lower' and 'yhat_upper').

```
forecastProphet = multi_model.predict(future)
forecastProphet = multi_model.predict(future)
forecastProphet[['ds','yhat', 'yhat_lower','yhat_upper']].tail()
```

Output:

	ds	yhat	yhat_lower	yhat_upper
23	2017-01-01	1941.441706	1508.146607	2399.403223
24	2018-01-01	2042.393334	1599.625234	2508.553528
25	2019-01-01	2133.481823	1698.281344	2573.256774
26	2020-01-01	2214.719287	1800.233984	2659.205372
27	2021-01-01	2336.653507	1860.703152	2781.003652

```
fig1 = multi_model.plot(forecastProphet);
```

Output:

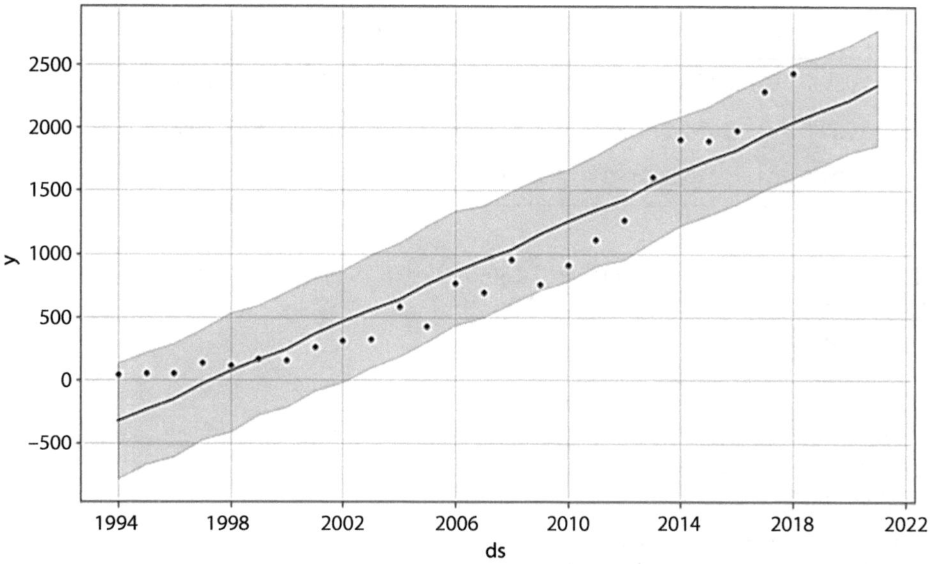

Step 6: Model accuracies: MAE

To evaluate prediction model accuracy, we use error metrics like mean-squared error and root mean square error for emphasizing larger errors, mean absolute error for equal error treatment, and the F1 score for binary classification scenarios where trend direction is more important than exact values.

```
combined_df = pd.merge(df[['ds','y']],forecast[['ds', 'yhat', 'yhat_lower', 'yhat_upper']][-5:], on='ds') combined_df
```

```
from sklearn.metrics import mean_absolute_error, mean_absolute_percentage_error

#Check MAE value
MAE = mean_absolute_error(combined_df['y'], combined_df['yhat'])
print(f'The MAE for the baseline model is {MAE}')
```

Output:

	ds	y	yhat	yhat_lower	yhat_upper
0	2019-01-01	2461.458457	2133.481823	1698.281344	2573.256774
1	2020-01-01	2674.415826	2214.719287	1800.233984	2659.205372
2	2021-01-01	2516.509580	2336.653507	1860.703152	2781.003652

The MAE for the baseline model is 322.5097486100229 or 322.4097 million pounds.

Plot the data:

```
import seaborn as sns
plt.rcParams.update({'figure.figsize': (15, 3), 'figure.dpi': 300})
fig, ax = plt.subplots()

sns.lineplot(data = combined_df, x = 'ds', y = 'y', label = 'Original')
sns.lineplot(data= combined_df, x = 'ds', y = 'yhat', label = 'Forecast')
plt.grid(linestyle = ,-', linewidth = 0.3)

plt.legend(["Original","forecast"])
```

Output:

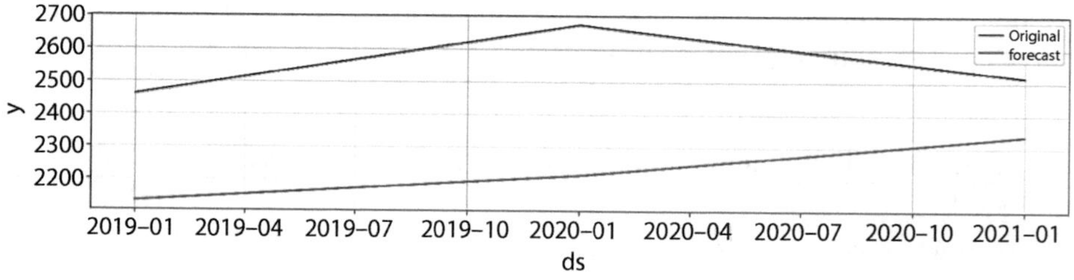

View complete dataset:

```
combined_prophet_fulldf = pd.merge(Prophetdf[['ds','y']],forecastProphet[['ds', 'yhat', 'yhat_lower', 'yhat_upper']], on='ds')
combined_prophet_fulldf
```

```
#Check MAE value
MAE_fulldf = mean_absolute_error(Prophetdf['y'], combined_prophet_fulldf['yhat'])
print(f'The MAE for the baseline model is {MAE_fulldf}')
```

```
fig, ax = plt.subplots()

sns.lineplot(data = Prophetdf, x = 'ds', y = 'y',label = 'Original')
sns.lineplot(data= combined_prophet_fulldf, x = 'ds', y = 'yhat', label = 'Forecast')
plt.grid(linestyle = ,-', linewidth = 0.3)

plt.legend(["Original","forecast"])
```

Output: Instead of taking the test DataFrame, take the entire DataFrame

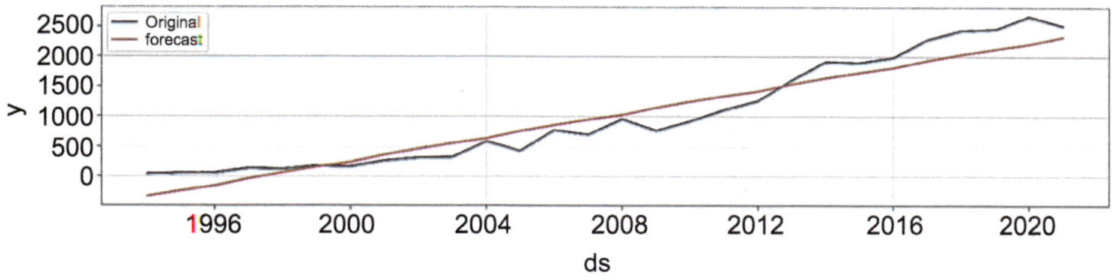

Let's plot the performance for the entire dataset: The MAE for the baseline model is 212.496925827295.

Forecasting dataset preparation: what-if modeling

After developing a forecasting model, the next step involves preparing future datasets and addressing any missing data, with one approach being the "what-if" model, which allows business users to explore hypothetical scenarios and outcomes, thereby gaining insights for informed decision-making and strategy optimization.

Step 1: Prepare and load what-if dataset

First, let's load the what-if dataset. This data is completely scenario-driven data:

```
futurewhatifdf=pd.read_csv(r"Whatif.csv",index_col=0)
# summarize shape
print(futurewhatifdf.shape)
# show first few rows
print(futurewhatifdf.head())
```

```
futurewhatifdf=futurewhatifdf.reset_index()
```

```
futurewhatifdf
```

Output:

	date	Utilized production	DEXMXUS
0	1/1/22	280.2	19.992
1	1/1/23	191.0	29.909
2	1/1/24	161.0	40.002
3	1/1/25	600.9	2.990
4	1/1/26	304.0	7.990
5	1/1/27	190.9	2.990
6	1/1/28	280.2	19.992
7	1/1/29	161.0	29.909
8	1/1/30	191.0	7.990

Step 2: Setup time column

``Convery date to reqyured ds coikunb.

```
futurewhatifdf.rename(columns = {"date": "ds" }, inplace = True)
futurewhatifdf.info()
futurewhatifdf["ds"] = pd.to_datetime(futurewhatifdf["ds"])
```

Output:

```
<class 'pandas.core.frame.DataFrame'>
RangeIndex: 9 entries, 0 to 8
Data columns (total 3 columns):
 #   Column               Non-Null Count  Dtype
---  ------               --------------  -----
 0   ds                   9 non-null      datetime64[ns]
 1   Utilized production  9 non-null      float64
 2   DEXMXUS              9 non-null      float64
dtypes: datetime64[ns](1), float64(2)
memory usage: 344.0 bytes
```

Step 3: Predict

Call predict on what-if data.

```
#forecastProphet = multi_model.predict(futurewhatifdf)
forecastProphet = multi_model.predict(futurewhatifdf)
```

```
forecastProphet[['ds', 'yhat', 'yhat_lower','yhat_upper']].tail()
```

What-if:

	ds	yhat	yhat_lower	yhat_upper
4	2026-01-01	2832.816935	2375.000018	3281.971852
5	2027-01-01	2923.905424	2468.854231	3398.077209
6	2028-01-01	3005.142889	2530.981191	3421.457557
7	2029-01-01	3127.077108	2669.122755	3587.848332

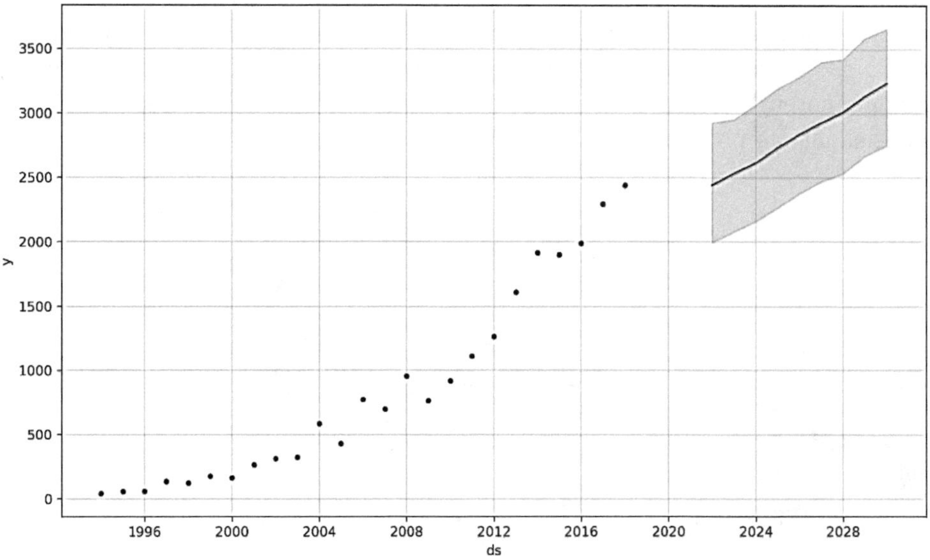

"What-if" modeling is a scenario-based approach that is less science-driven and more intuition-driven, in my view. This method involves exploring hypothetical scenarios and exceptional pathways to underscore the workings of the model and inform decision-making processes.

While “what-if” modeling can be a useful tool for gaining insights and exploring possibilities, a more reliable way to prepare future datasets for forecasting is through trend engineering of independent features. This involves techniques like linear interpolation, spline interpolation, and trend engineering, which are more data-driven and less reliant on subjective inputs. By leveraging these approaches, organizations can obtain more accurate and reliable predictions, allowing them to make educated business decisions and optimize their strategies for success.

Additional ML experiments

Commercial machinery repair and maintenance feature

Agriculture is a demanding field that requires intensive labor. While mechanization [58, 59] has been widely adopted in planting and harvesting, with planting operations like forming planting beds, applying fertilizer, precision planting seeds, and using weed control chemicals done simultaneously, the use of machines has played a pivotal role. However, given the widespread adoption of machines in agriculture, it is vital to underscore the function of *maintenance agricultural* and mining machinery [58]. Impact of these services on industry is questioned. (Hint: To explore this topic further, consider re-running the model with the new feature PCU8113108113105.) By incorporating additional features and variables into the analysis, organizations can acquire a more thorough insight of the factors that impact the industry and inform effective decision-making processes.

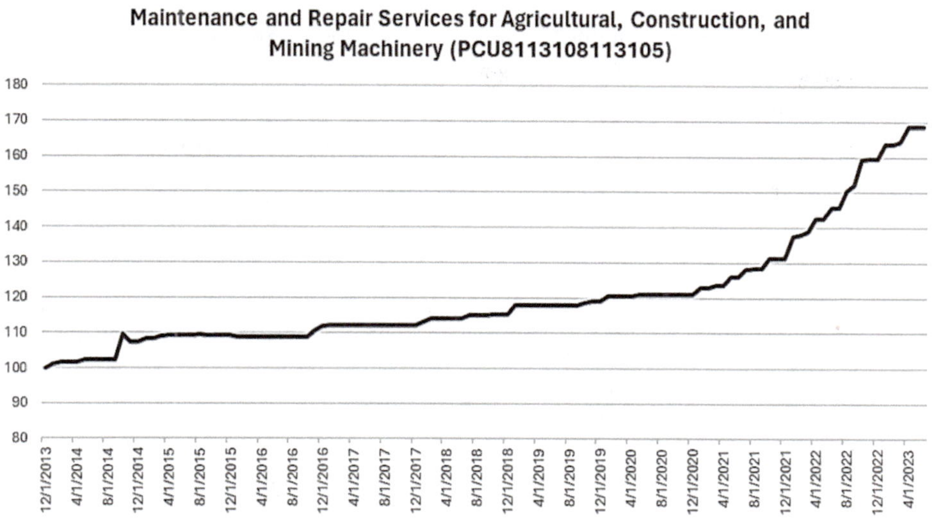

Data: Producer price index[5] for machine maintenance.

US trucking industry

In the US trucking industry, shipping demand, especially for refrigerated trucks carrying perishable goods, increases during spring and summer due to the fresh produce season and additional imports from Mexico and South America.

5 PCU8113108113105: https://fred.stlouisfed.org/series/PCU8113108113105

The produce season begins in the Southeast, southern Texas, and the Rio Grande Valley, then moves to southern California by late March and continues northward as temperatures rise, increasing nationwide demand for trucking services. Understanding the fresh produce season's impact on the trucking industry enables organizations to better prepare for its associated challenges and opportunities.

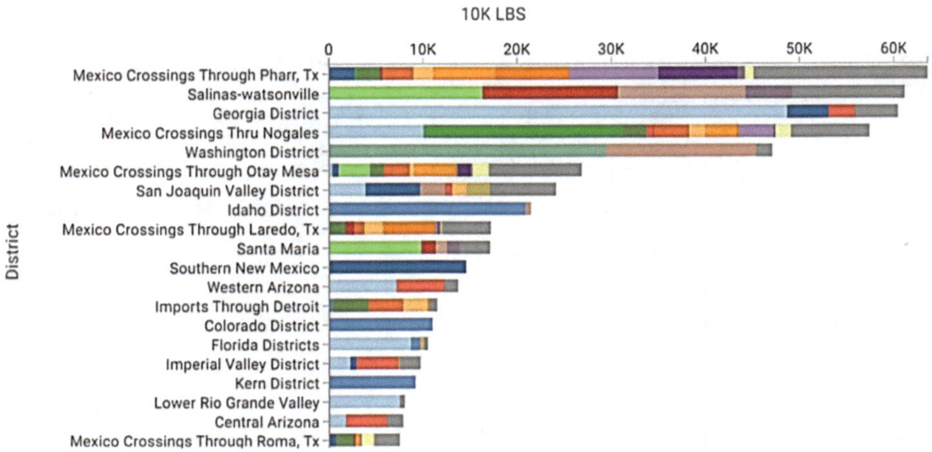

Source: USDA 30-day rolling data: top 20 commodities and districts.

Re-run the ML model with Mexico district crossings through Phart-Texas and Laredo-Texas.

After finishing this chapter, you will have a thorough understanding of several important concepts in computer science, including AI, ML, DL, and generative AI. You will also learn about different types of learning and how to model time series data.

You will be able to evaluate performance metrics for different techniques used in classification, regression, and time series analysis. Specifically, you will have expertise in modeling both univariate and multivariate time series models for specialty crops, such as avocados and fresh tomatoes, using regressive and time series models.

Chapter 2
Specialty (high-value and niche) crops

This chapter covers:
- High-value crops
- Market value and potential
- Workforce openings
- Critical industry needs
- Market value chain
- Specialty crops pricing forecast framework
- ML models
  - Maine and New Hampshire strawberries pricing model
- Crops pricing behavior
- Bell curve modeling
- Contractual processing

The chapter talks about specialty crops that are not commonly grown but are very important for generating money for the government and farmers. These specialty crops are important because they offer new opportunities for businesses and markets. To understand this industry better, the chapter introduces a model that shows how these specialty crops go from being grown to being sold in stores. This model helps us understand how prices are set for these crops. To make these prices more accurate, the chapter discusses a new technology that uses advanced statistical techniques to predict prices for strawberries in Maine and New Hampshire. This helps farmers and processors make better decisions and make more money. Overall, this chapter underscores the economic importance of specialty crops and illustrates how science and technology can improve decision-making and profitability in the industry.

Meeting the growing demand for fruit and vegetables in a healthy, balanced diet poses significant challenges for domestic production regions in many countries. Supply chains are experiencing significant transformations driven by a multitude of factors, including consumer demand for healthy food choices and local produce, environmental shifts and resource scarcity, labor availability and costs, evolving macroeconomic conditions and international food policies, sustainability initiatives, and the growth of local protections. As a result, there is a pressing need for innovative approaches to ensure that the supply of these highly nutritious foods can keep up with demand while also meeting sustainability goals.

The chapter talks about a type of farming called "specialty crop cultivation." This involves growing things like fruits, vegetables, flowers, herbs, and spices. These crops are important because they can help us have a healthy and balanced diet. However, they do not get as much attention as other crops like corn and soybeans. In fact, in the USA in 2020, only 2% of the land that was used for farming was used for growing fruits and vegetables, while over 50% was used for growing crops like corn and soybeans. This shows that we need to pay more attention to specialty crops if we want to have a diverse and healthy diet (Figure 1).

This gap is also reflected in risk insurance programs, where specialty crops receive less support than commodity crops. To address this issue, a comprehensive model is needed to enable and cultivate specialty crops. For more information on this topic, please see the author's book [61]. By leveraging cutting-edge technologies and innovative approaches, we can improve the sustainability and resilience of specialty crop cultivation, ensuring a more equitable and nutritious food system for all [62, 63].

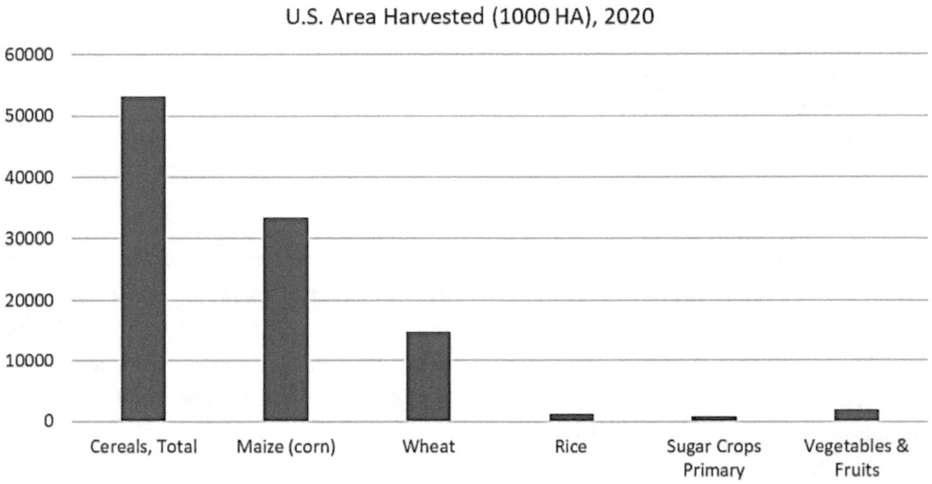

Figure 1: US area harvested.

Specialty crops, though occupying a small portion of global harvested land, are essential for enhancing farmers' incomes and boosting national economic output. In 2020, fruit and vegetable production reached $1.1 trillion, contributing to a total crop value of $1.7 trillion within an agricultural sector valued at $4.14 trillion, a significant rise from 1991 when these values were $221.11 billion and $709.46 billion, respectively (FAO 2020).

The numbers speak for themselves: specialty crops, even though they occupy a small portion of the cropped area, generate a much higher value output than other crops. By placing priority on cultivating specialty crops and investing in innovative solutions to support this sector, we can create more sustainable and equitable food systems while also boosting economic growth and promoting the livelihoods of farmers (refer to Figures 2 and 3 for more information).

Specialty crops hold immense potential for growth, even with limited land. As the area dedicated to horticulture continues to increase, the output generated by specialty crops rises significantly, leading to a substantial increase in revenue. This trend has already had a positive impact on small farmers in countries such as China and India,

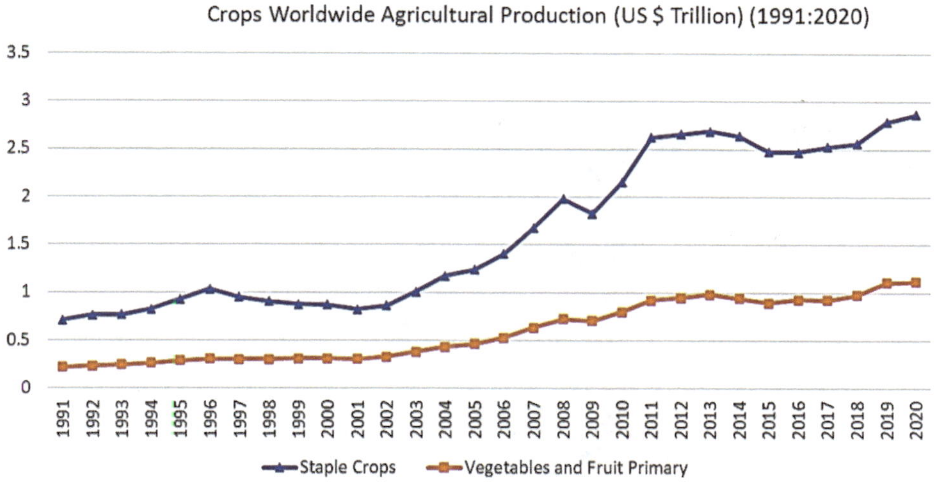

Figure 2: Crops worldwide agricultural production.

lifting many out of poverty. For example, coffee cultivation in Indonesia has been a major factor in bringing the country out of poverty [63].

Efforts are being made to promote the fiscal, economic, and social sustainability of small-marginal specialty crop developers and the rural and suburban communities that depend on them. Integrated management policies are being introduced, with a focus on risk management and easy access to markets, to enhance the coverage of specialty crops. These initiatives aim to create a more supportive environment for specialty crop development and contribute to the well-being of local communities. The US Federal Risk Agency (RMA) is expanding programs to cover more crops and counties, increasing coverage limits, and pursuing new forms of coverage such as Micro Farm Insurance. Additionally, the Production and Revenue History pilot program is being expanded to include fresh fruits and vegetables on the East Coast. These efforts will help ensure that specialty crop producers have the support they need to thrive and contribute to a more balanced and fair food system [64].

It is paramount to prioritize the cultivation of specialty crops to meet the nutritional requirements of individuals and foster healthier societies in the future. However, the current outlook is concerning, as the cultivation of specialty crops only meets the minimum per capita nutrition target of four hundred grams per day for 55% of the global population residing in countries where this is feasible, according to the guidelines set by the World Health Organization (WHO). Additionally, there are several areas around the world where access to fresh produce is scarce, as highlighted in [65].

Because of the increasing global population, a rising need for fruits and vegetables is forecasted in the direction of increase. Without improvements in yield productivity, the world is at risk of becoming a society with low nutrients and insufficient fresh produce. By prioritizing the cultivation of specialty crops and investing in innovative

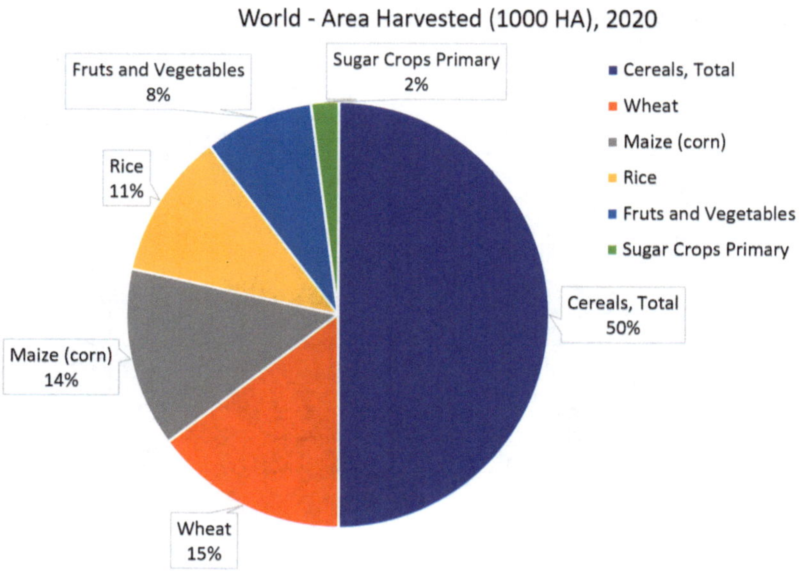

Figure 3: World area harvested.

solutions, we can guarantee that upcoming generations have access to the nourishing foods essential for their growth and well-being to thrive [66].

The study of specialty crops is both pragmatic and futuristic, as it contributes significantly to economic value and cash receipts. As temperatures rise and extreme weather events become more frequent, many food production systems are becoming increasingly threatened. This highlights the importance of the high-value growth industry of specialty crops, particularly in terms of safeguarding food production despite the threat of climate change [67].

As the threat to production systems of food grows, it is important to consider which foods consumers may have to cut back on or abandon entirely. By studying food security and specialty crops, we can gain a comprehensive view of the challenges and opportunities facing the food system in the years to come. This knowledge can inform policies and practices that support sustainable and equitable food production, ensuring that future generations have access to the nutritious foods they need to thrive [67, 68].

The USDA's extensive catalog of specialty crops encompasses a diverse range of products, including nursery and greenhouse cultivations such as flowers, foliage, Christmas trees, and shrubs. Although wine and related products are not explicitly mentioned, the USDA has provided aid to wine producer groups in the past (Figures 3 and 4).

By clarifying the definition of specialty crops and supporting their cultivation, the USDA is helping to create more sustainable and equitable food systems. Through

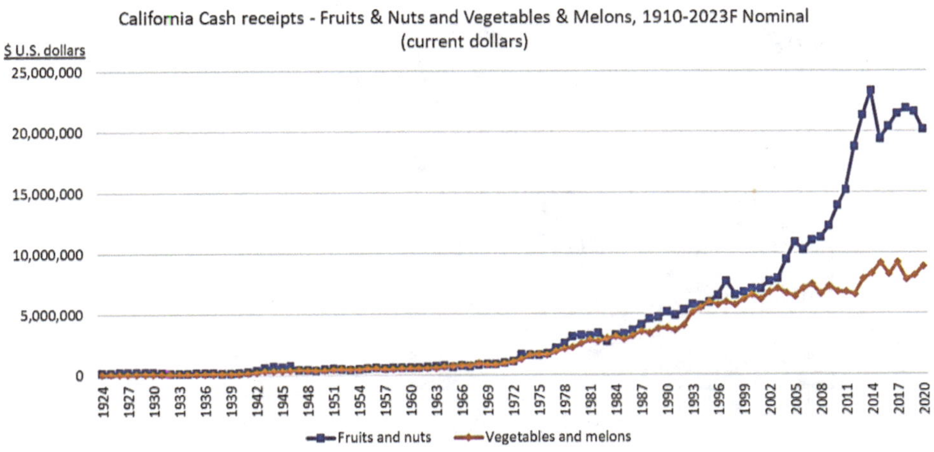

Figure 4: California cash receipts.

innovative solutions, such as machine learning (ML) and artificial intelligence (AI), we can further enhance the productivity and resilience of specialty crop cultivation, ensuring a more nutritious and abundant food supply for all.

Specialty crops ML models are designed to identify potential declines or increases in fruit and vegetable production in current production areas. These models can also help identify opportunities to produce fruits and vegetables in new areas of the world under future climate scenarios. Conducting multi-model simulations, including multi-crop and statistical models, is essential for studying specialty crops.

In this book, I will cover important specialty crops such as tomatoes, pistachios, strawberries, oranges, lettuce, potatoes, onions, and garlic. These crops were selected based on their importance to nutrition, economic significance, and data availability. By exploring these crops in detail, we can gain a deeper understanding of their unique challenges and opportunities for cultivation and develop innovative solutions to support sustainable and equitable food systems [69].

Access and affordability of fruits and vegetables are crucial for food nutrition and security (Figure 5). Retail prices of the most and least expensive fruits and vegetables show that potatoes are the most affordable vegetable for all sections of society. Despite their affordability, potatoes can be used in a variety of delicious ways, such as French fries and mashed potatoes, making them a versatile and tempting ingredient for many meals. By prioritizing the cultivation and affordability of a diverse range of fruits and vegetables, we can ensure that all members of society have access to nutritious foods they need to thrive.

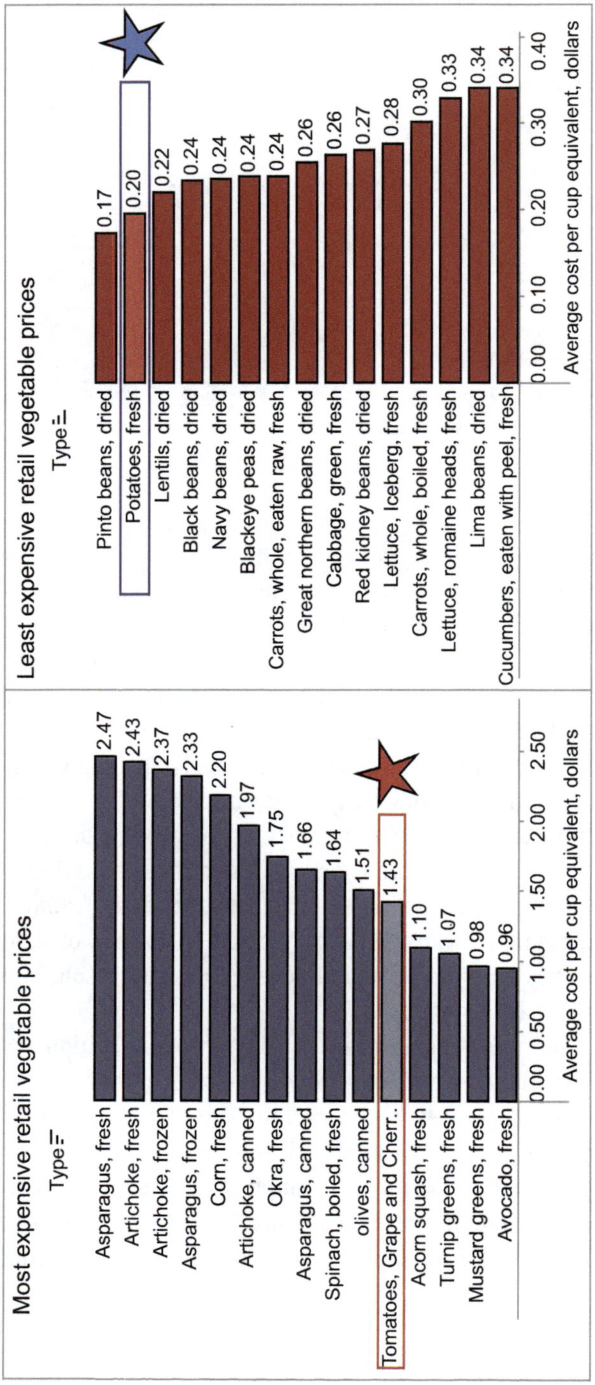

Figure 5: Vegetable prices.

Tomatoes – most expensive retail prices. Potat oes – least expensive retail prices.

Tomatoes offer a great food security to the world!

Studying the climate impact [70] on tomato production is crucial for ensuring access and affordability, which are essential pillars of food security. Additionally, economic significance is another important criterion, which is assessed in terms of cash receipts by the state. By considering both the economic and nutritional importance of tomatoes, we can develop policies and practices that support sustainable and equitable tomato production and guarantee that this food continues to prosper in the face of climate change.

Commodity		Cash receipts (CR) rank	US receipts (USD)
Grapes	Fruits and tree nuts	15	$6.069 billion
Potatoes	Vegetables	17	$4.034 billion
Strawberries	Fruits and tree nuts	18	$3,194 billion
Pistachios	Fruits and tree nuts	21	$3.194 billion
Tomatoes	Vegetables	26	$1.652 billion

Potato and tomato are the top five entries to US cash receipts (Figure 6).

Rank	Commodity	State receipts	Share of State receipts	Cumulative share of State receipts	U.S. receipts	Share of U.S. receipts by commodity
		$1,000	Percent	Percent	$1,000	Percent
10	Hay	8,628,163	2.0	79.3	8,628,163	100.0
15	Grapes	5,530,652	1.3	86.2	5,530,652	100.0
16	Almonds	5,028,320	1.2	87.3	5,028,320	100.0
17	**Potatoes**	**3,676,246**	**0.8**	**88.2**	**3,676,246**	**100.0**
18	Strawberries	3,422,240	0.8	89.0	3,422,240	100.0
20	Apples	3,032,674	0.7	90.4	3,032,674	100.0
21	**Pistachios**	2,910,600	0.7	91.1	2,910,600	100.0
22	Lettuce	2,680,150	0.6	91.7	2,680,150	100.0
23	Sorghum	2,151,321	0.5	92.2	2,151,321	100.0
24	Sugar beets	1,776,753	0.4	92.6	1,776,753	100.0
25	**Oranges**	1,611,752	0.4	92.9	1,611,752	100.0
26	**Tomatoes**	1,505,500	0.3	93.3	1,505,500	100.0
27	Sugarcane for sugar and seed	1,464,925	0.3	93.6	1,464,925	100.0
28	Peanuts	1,416,607	0.3	93.9	1,416,607	100.0
29	Dry beans	1,247,282	0.3	94.2	1,247,282	100.0
30	Blueberries	1,100,320	0.3	94.5	1,100,320	100.0
32	**Onions**	1,037,388	0.2	95.0	1,037,388	100.0

Figure 6: Share of US receipts by commodity.

★ Top five entries with cash receipts.

Third criterion is the additional importance of selected vegetables, fruits, and tree nuts in terms of their relevance in shaping the future healthier societies:

- For centuries, potatoes have been regarded as lifesavers in various cultures and societies, and they continue to hold a crucial position in our lives to this day. It is no surprise that French fries and Indian potato samosas are the most popular party foods and a favorite among children worldwide, owing to their universal appeal. Potatoes have become a symbol of cultural unification in our societies, bringing people together and transcending boundaries.
- According to the USDA's long-term projections, it is anticipated that potatoes will constitute 24% of the total value of vegetable farms by 2032, reflecting a 2% increase from 2022. This highlights the significance of potatoes as a crucial food item for the future. While there is a projected 9% growth in potato production, the value is expected to rise by 10% during the 2022–2032 period. However, it is essential to note that this projection assumes average weather and sufficient water supplies, which may be challenging to maintain due to the harsh realities of climate change, extreme weather conditions, water shortages, and population growth.
- Tomatoes are an essential component of popular dishes such as pizza, pasta, Indian curries, and healthy salad bowls, rendering these dishes incomplete without them. Tomatoes for processing play a critical role in the food processing and allied industries, which are the backbone of the pizza business, fast food chains, traditional cuisine, and healthy food choices. Inadequate tomato supplies can have a detrimental impact on our well-being and quality of life. It is no surprise that, in 2021, 64% of processed vegetables are composed of tomatoes, given their foundational role in our daily lives [71].
- Horticultural products is the largest category and shows a consistent upward trend. The pistachio and tree nut industry are also slated to grow by 2032, from $37 billion to $142 billion by 2032 (Figure 7). In 2020–2022, there is a noticeable increase in the total export value from around $140 billion to $160 billion. The projection (2025–2032) shows a gradual and steady increase in total export value, reaching close to $200 billion by 2032. By prioritizing sustainable and equitable cultivation of specialty crops and investing in innovative solutions, we can ensure a nutritious and abundant food supply for future generations [71].

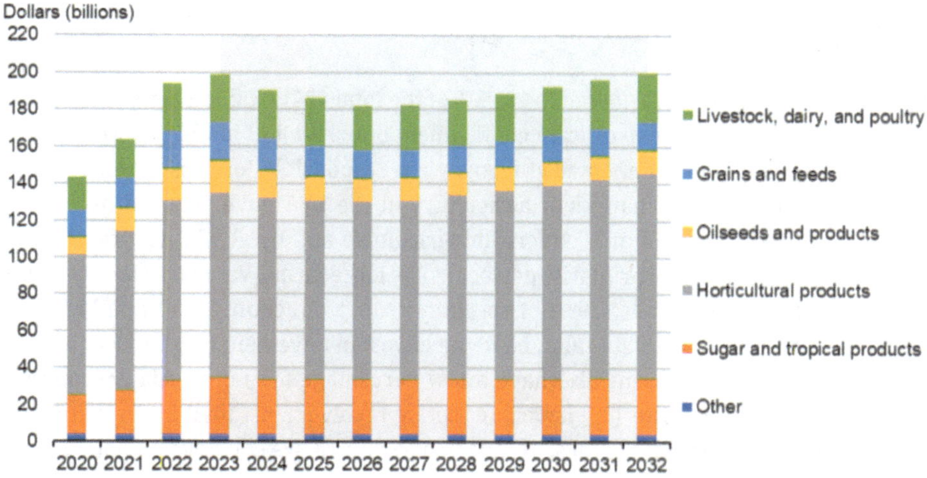

Figure 7: Projections.

The primary objective of this book is to achieve food resilience by exploring innovative solutions and strategies for sustainable and equitable food production, distribution, and consumption. By prioritizing food resilience, we can ensure that everyone has access to the nutritious foods they require to flourish while simultaneously safeguarding our planet for future generations.

Cropland is a fundamental component of global agricultural production, with approximately 10% dedicated to permanent crops, spanning an area of approximately 0.166 billion hectares. These permanent crops show a pivotal role in sustaining surging order pro high-quality agricultural products and supporting sustainable economic development.

Furthermore, irrigation constitutes a crucial land management practice in agriculture, with 21% of cropland equipped with irrigation systems. By prioritizing sustainable and efficient irrigation practices, we can ensure that crops receive the necessary water to flourish while also conserving this valuable resource for future generations. This is particularly crucial given the mounting water scarcity in many regions of the world and the need to balance agricultural production with environmental sustainability.

In essence, the efficient management of cropland and irrigation resources is vital in achieving sustainable agricultural practices that promote economic development, environmental sustainability, and food security. By leveraging scientific knowledge and advanced technologies, stakeholders can attain sustainable and profitable agricultural practices that benefit both producers and consumers while preserving the natural resources that underpin agricultural production (refer to Reference [64] for more information).

Employment opportunities

Specialty crops, which contributed to 19.95% of the total $241.0 billion agricultural cash receipts in 2021 [72], offer significant employment opportunities at the grassroots level. Historically, small and family-owned farms were responsible for most specialty crop farming. However, the dynamics of agriculture in the USA have changed over time, reflecting the transformation of American agriculture and rural life. As a result, specialty crop farming is now primarily performed by large farms. Very large family farms have the highest percentage (29%) of specialty crop production. Small family farms, both with lower and moderate sales, have the lowest involvement (9% and 8%, respectively). Mid-size family farms also have a low percentage (8%) of specialty crop production. Large family farms [71] have a moderate involvement (14%) in specialty crop production. By understanding these trends in agriculture, we can develop policies and practices that support sustainable and equitable specialty crop production while also creating opportunities for small and family-owned farms [72].

	Small-family farms (lower sales)	Small-family farms (moderate sales)	Mid-size-family farms	Large-family farms	Very Large-family farms
			(percent)		
Specialty crops	9	8	8	14	29

The 2017 population count revealed the following details: The majority of family farms are small family farms, with a total of 1,798,439 farms. Mid-size family farms are significantly fewer, with 108,304 farms. Large and very large family farms are the least numerous, with 52,592 farms. This distribution indicates that the agricultural sector is predominantly composed of small family farms, which make up the vast majority of the total number of family farms. Mid-size and large/very large family farms represent a smaller fraction of the total number of family farms [71]. By recognizing the significance of family-owned farms and supporting their growth and sustainability, we can ensure that the agricultural sector remains a pivotal part of our economy while also promoting local food systems and environmental conservation.

Type [71]	Number	
Small family farms	1,798,439	
Mid-size family farms	108,304	
Large and very large family farms	52,592	

Small family farm producers are more likely to be female, age 65 or older, and identify as Hispanic or of a race other than white or Asian. They may have served in the military, work off the farm, and are often new or beginning farmers (having farmed for 10 years or less). In contrast, mid-size and large-scale family farm producers share many demographic characteristics. The majority farm as their primary occupation and do not work off the farm. Fewer have served in the military, and a low percentage are new or beginning farmers. By understanding the diverse backgrounds and needs of family farm producers, we can develop policies and programs that support their success and promote a vibrant and sustainable agricultural sector [71].

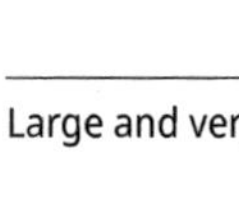

Ninety-six percent of US farms are family owned.

The dynamics of specialty crop farming differ in other parts of the world, where small farms are the major cultivators. In China and India, for example, the bulk of the countryside inhabitants depend on fruits, vegetables, and other specialty crop farming. The same applies to tomatoes, which are grown for both fresh market produce and processing into paste for industrial use. Fresh tomatoes from Florida are a major export, with Florida producing over 50% of the US market needs. This type of cultivation is labor-intensive and provides significant employment opportunities for farmers and allied industries such as storage, packing, and transportation. In contrast, tomatoes for paste are primarily grown in California and involve a highly mechanized process, with only 2,350 selected farmers providing tomatoes for paste (see Figure 8). By understanding these regional differences and the different needs of farmers and industries, we can

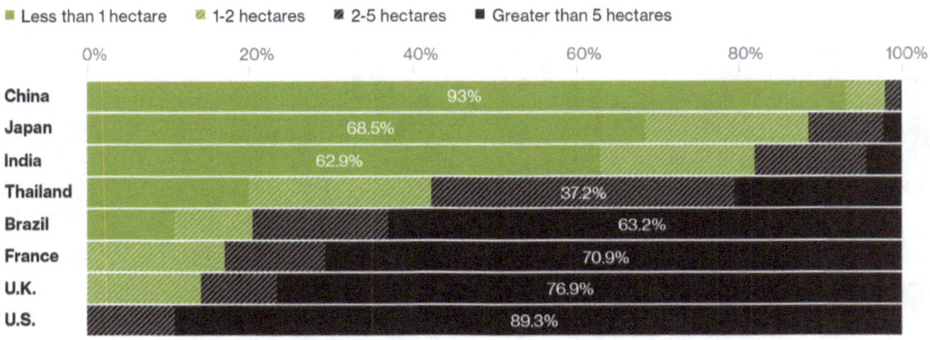

Figure 8: Farmers classification [66].

develop policies and practices that support sustainable and equitable specialty crop production worldwide.

Globally, a similar pattern can be observed. In countries like India, tomatoes are produced year-round, providing employment for millions of farmers. Tomato for paste production, unlike in California, involves labor-intensive operations. This is also the case in countries like Turkey and China. By recognizing these global patterns and the diverse needs of farmers and industries, we can work toward creating sustainable and equitable agricultural practices that benefit communities worldwide.

	Fresh produce	**Paste**
Employment	Florida produces more than 50% for US needs. Labor intense	California is leading producer. Highly mechanized
Farm size		
Farm type	Family farms	Industrialized

Specialty crops represent a significant revenue generator for Northern American commerce. In 2020, Golden State's fruit-tree-farms, dairy farms, and potted plant garden centers made a staggering $49 billion in money earnings, despite a 3% decrease from previous fiscal-year. Agricultural exports from Golden State also experienced a dip of 2.8% to $20.8 billion, reflecting the pandemic's effects and the redirection of supplies from the food service sector to food banks. Nevertheless, approximately 69,600 California farms continue to flourish, propelled by strong family principles, an unrivaled dedication to work, and a definite objective toward sustainability [73].

The agricultural industry in California provides employment opportunities to 1.2 million individuals, which includes indispensable farm laborers that work tirelessly to gather, handle, and convey California's agricultural produce to consumers across the globe. By supporting sustainable and equitable agricultural practices and investing in the well-being of our farmers and workers, we can ensure the continued success and prosperity of our communities [73].

The AIFS (AI Institute for Next Generation Food Systems) is wholly dedicated to accelerating the adoption of advanced AI techniques for the efficient production, processing, and delivery of healthy and safe food.

Critical industry needs

Crop growers face a range of risks, including unexpected weather events, pest and disease losses, regulatory uncertainty, price volatility, and labor access issues. These risks are particularly acute for specialty crops, which are often sold in thinner markets with fewer buyers and sellers. This makes it more difficult for producers to establish accurate prices and forecast cash flows. It also makes it challenging to establish fencing options such as contract markets. By addressing these unique challenges and investing in risk management strategies that address the specific needs of specialty crop producers, we can help ensure the long-term viability and success of this vital sector of our economy.

Specialty crop cultivators encounter several obstacles, such as elevated expenses related to searching for fresh purchasers in case a single agreement falls apart, along with the hazards linked to specialized production and labor procedures. Modifications to programs like the H-2A guest worker visa, which numerous growers depend on, can cause businesses to become uncertain about their capability to obtain required dedicated hardworking passionate agricultural labor. Furthermore, regulations at the state level concerning wage and overtime can add to the financial burden of producers. By proactively addressing these challenges and supporting policies that promote stable labor markets and fair compensation for workers, we can help ensure the continued success of specialty crop production and the well-being of our farming communities [74].

The production of specialty crops is essential in tackling the difficulties posed by climate change and environmental issues, while simultaneously guaranteeing economic sustainability. Environmental changes pose a significant threat. For example, the rapid melting of Himalayan glaciers is causing massive environmental disasters, resulting in the migration of millions of people and impacting the freshwater supply for billions more. It is anticipated that this area will confront severe weather situations and crop failure, which could cause mass migrations and potentially affect ocean currents globally. By investing in sustainable agricultural practices and supporting policies that address the root causes of environmental and climate change, we can help ensure the continued success of specialty crop production and the well-being of our planet and its inhabitants [75].

Vegetables are an essential component of a healthy human diet and offer excellent returns for farmers due to their higher market prices. However, like other crops, vegetables are significantly impacted by climate change. These changes can lead to crop failures, yield shortages, diminished value, and increased bug and infection problems, making vegetable cultivation unprofitable [76]. Many physiological processes and enzymatic activities crucial to vegetable production are temperature-dependent and will be significantly affected by climate change. Delayed monsoons will also impact overall production cycles. By acting in advance to tackle the fundamental reasons behind climate change and by investing in sustainable agricultural techniques, we can make a difference. We can help ensure the continued success of vegetable cultivation and the well-being of our communities.

Climate change also has a substantial impact on fruits, with severe weather situations leading to significant reductions in crop yields. A recent visit to a local farm in Boston, Massachusetts (MA), revealed that strawberries and blueberries [76] were among the crops adversely affected by climate change and extreme weather. In May 2023, a late spring freeze caused by subfreezing temperatures severely damaged thousands of acres of crops, with many farmers experiencing over 25% crop losses. This is not uncommon for New England farmers, who have long dealt with fickle weather patterns. However, the effects of climate change have made these events more frequent and severe, posing a significant threat to the sustainability of fruit cultivation. By investing in sustainable agricultural practices and supporting policies that address the root causes of climate change, we can help ensure the continued success of fruit cultivation and the well-being of our farming communities.

The effect of climate change on fruit crops has been devastating, with many small, local growers struggling to make ends meet. The loss of crops such as peaches and apples due to February and May freeze has had a particularly harsh impact, with some farmers losing up to 80% of their crops. For example, a local grower in Boston, MA, lost 75–80% of their 10,000 blueberry bushes in the May 2024 freeze, which struck just as the green berries began to sprout. By investing in sustainable agricultural practices and supporting policies that promote the resilience of our farming communities [76].

Adaptation strategies such as heaters and sprinkler systems have been employed by some farmers to protect their crops from frost damage. However, these techniques are not entirely reliable due to heavy investments, fixed costs, and economic constraints. Most farmers can only afford to cover a limited area of their farm, typically around 5%, as an adaptation strategy. For example, a 40-acre farm equipped with sprinklers can only cover approximately 1.5 acres, which highlights the significant limitations of these techniques [76].

To ensure continued success of our farming communities and protect our food supply, it is crucial to invest in sustainable agricultural practices and support policies that address the root causes of climate change. By adopting innovative technologies and sustainable practices, we can achieve success.

Dairy industry is an example of an off-farm cash generation industry that requires significant investment from farmers to adopt technological advancements such as sensors and cow necklaces. The lack of such technological advancements can limit productivity and reduce overall food security. Therefore, investing in innovative technologies such as Cow Necklace is crucial for enhancing productivity and ensuring the enduring sustainability of the dairy industry.

In summary, the limitations of adaptation strategies like heaters and sprinkler systems emphasize the need for balanced agricultural practices and strategies that address root causes of climate change. Moreover, investing in innovative technologies is crucial for enhancing productivity and ensuring food security in both on-farm and off-farm cash generation industries.

Maine is a significant international center for the production of wild blueberries and the sole state in the USA where they are commercially gathered (Figure 9). In 2000, Maine achieved a record high production of 110 million pounds of fruit. Nevertheless, beginning in 2021, the state has encountered progressively greater variations in its harvest. In 2022, Maine experienced a cold, rainy May that hindered pollination and a dry summer that affected the final stages of harvest, resulting in a 30% decrease in blueberry production. Although all crops are affected by weather conditions, wild blueberry farmers encounter distinctive obstacles due to the crop's biennial cycle. During the first year, the vines of the wild blueberries grow, and the berries are produced in the second year. By investing in sustainable agricultural practices and supporting policies, we can help alleviate extreme weather impacts on our agrobusiness communities and ensure the continued success of wild blueberry cultivation in Maine [77]. Data is from NAS.

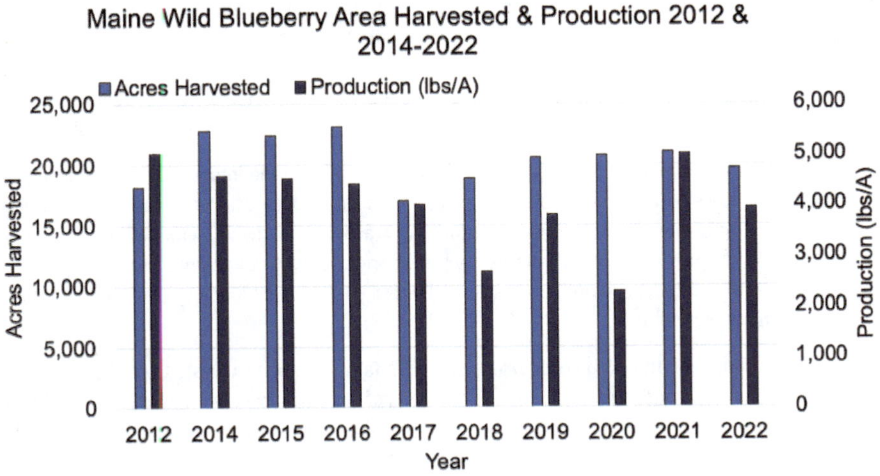

Figure 9: Maine wild blueberry.

Although all crops are affected by weather conditions, wild blueberry farmers encounter distinctive obstacles due to the crop's biennial cycle. During the first year, the vines of the wild blueberries grow, and the berries are produced in the second year [77].

Industry needs are very simple: to have a comprehensive strategy to reduce crop losses, predict unfavorable crop cultivation conditions, and provide adaptation strategies.

Rising temperatures are having a significant impact on vegetable cultivation, resulting in drought and salinity. While increased CO_2 levels may boost crop yields through fertilization, they can also decrease yields. The impact of climate change extends to the prevalence of pests and diseases, the behavior of insects, and their movements between different geographical locations [76, 77, 78].

By studying the subjects presented in this book, we can gain invaluable knowledge that will help us address future environmental challenges more effectively. Additionally, we can use this information to create more accurate climate models that account for changing weather patterns. Furthermore, we will also explore the impact of pests and diseases on specialty crops. Our primary goal is to develop models for pricing, climate, and causation that utilize past production and yield data to improve efficiency, productivity, and profitability in the long run. This includes crafting policies and marketing strategies for specialty crops. By leveraging the potential of ML and AI, we can make remarkable strides in improving the specialty crop industry's sustainability and profitability [76].

The farming of wild blueberries is encountering mounting obstacles as a result of extreme weather and the impact of climate change. The growing frequency of extreme weather events and the decreasing numbers of essential pollinators like honeybees are jeopardizing the sustainability of this crop [78]. The susceptibility of wild blueberries to weather variability makes it an especially precarious endeavor for farmers. Consequently, growers are increasingly relying on weather forecasts and other tools to manage these risks.

Effective adaptation strategies are essential to minimize the impact of these challenges. The development of innovative technologies such data science infused agricultural practices, investment in sustainable farming practices, and the implementation of climate-friendly policies can help mitigate. By prioritizing protection of pollinators plus promoting biodiversity, stakeholders can enhance the resilience of wild blueberry crops to dangerous weather conditions.

In summary, the farming of wild blueberries faces mounting threats from the impact of weather changes and climate. The vulnerability of this crop to weather variability necessitates the adoption of effective adaptation strategies by farmers. By embracing innovative technologies, sustainable farming practices, and climate-friendly policies, stakeholders can enhance the resilience of wild blueberry crops and ensure their continued success.

Production and marketing value chain

The integration of AI/ML has been crucial in advancing green agriculture across every level of the value chain. The primary aim of these technologies is to enable all players in the value chain to enhance food security by increasing productivity. By utilizing the power of AI and ML, stakeholders can optimize crop yield, manage resources more effectively, and minimize waste. This leads to a more efficient and sustainable agricultural system that can meet the rising demand for food while mitigating the effects of climate change. Therefore, incorporating AI and ML throughout the value chain is a promising strategy for creating a more durable and sustainable food system (Table 1).

Table 1: Growers DnA use cases.

Phase	Potential use cases	ML and AI techniques
Growers	Improve productivity and yield	Supervised econometric and data science models
	Fertilizer costs	Commodities forecasting models Markov transition models
	Sustainable water and inputs	Sensors and flow management
	Spot prices	Profit maximization Microtransaction commodity price forecasting models
	Revenue optimization	Markov transition models
	Post-harvest and produce longevity	Transportation heuristics Cluster models

Optimizing fertilizer usage through ML models can bring two significant benefits to communities: prosperity and wellness. This can help small farmers and drive demand economics. Additionally, using fewer fertilizers leads to greener produce, which is more organic and nutrient rich. By embracing these technologies, we can enhance agricultural productivity, profitability, and sustainability, benefiting both farmers and consumers alike.

Field-processed crops: growers and processors

Field processing is a common practice for fresh produce that is intended for markets and supermarkets. This is done by subsistence farmers, small-to-medium commercial farms, and large farms. The growers typically have a business relationship with processors for processed produce, as shown in Figure 10:

Figure 10: Growers and processors.

In nations such as Turkey and the USA, firms in the paste industry have adopted a proactive approach toward securing high-quality raw materials for their production processes. To this end, these firms sign contractual agreements with farms well in advance of the production season, thereby ensuring both the quality and quantity of their raw materials. These contracts also act as a safeguard for growers, guaranteeing their sales at predetermined prices. Furthermore, these firms provide farmers with a host of value-added services such as drip irrigation, extension services, and field demonstrations, which have been shown to significantly enhance productivity [79].

The cultivation of tomatoes is predominantly carried out on small farms that typically span 3–4 hectares, although larger farms may extend up to 50 hectares for processing tomatoes. To ensure a steady and reliable supply of high-quality produce, contractual agreements are signed between processors and growers at the beginning of the season, making up more than half of overall production. Processors supply either kernels or sprouts, the majority of which are high-soluble solids hybrids, and extend technical assistance, fertilizers, financial advances, and pesticides as required. In most cases, the young plants are initially nurtured in specialized plant nurseries [80]. These practices reflect the concerted efforts being made to promote sustainable and efficient agricultural practices that can enhance productivity and ensure a stable supply of high-quality produce for the processing industry.

Figure 11: Growers–cooperatives–processors.

Cooperatives are often used to coordinate between growers and processors for setting contracts [81], terms, agreements, and prices. This provides significant influence on many small growers, as shown in Figure 11.

Growers need to focus on reducing costs and becoming more efficient while maintaining high-quality standards for their produce. Processors also need to recognize the efforts made by growers in improving efficiency and quality. Both parties have invested heavily in expanding the industry, and it is crucial to work together to find new ways to restore profitability without relying solely on contract price adjustments. With the easy options exhausted, there is a need to explore new contract structures for the mutual benefit of both growers and processors [82].

Growers strive to meet quality standards in their contracts while minimizing costs to make farming a profitable venture. The following table lists growers who use advanced data science to derive the best growing practices through data analysis.

Growers ML use cases

Use case	ML technique	Data	Value
Fertilizer usage	Historical yield patterns, weather patterns, forecasting techniques, energy	Historical yield data, weather data, World Bank data, energy	Optimize fertilizer usage to reduce overall input costs
Weather and climate models	Yield to climate patterns, regressive models, causation models	Climate change data, reservoir water data	Maximum yield with the changing Climate
Cost optimization – humans	Human resource optimization	Employment data	Minimize labor cost
Cost optimization – transportation	Heuristics, transportation	Truck rates and availability	Optimize cost of the supply and delivery

Processors focus on developing contract prices with growers and ensuring profitability by meeting market demand and maximizing profits after accounting for grower contract prices. The following table lists processors and their specific data science use cases.

Processor ML use cases

Use case	ML technique	Data	Value
Fertilizer procurement	Macroeconomics, demand and supply, energy cost	Historical energy	Best time to purchase fertilizers to reduce the cost footprint
Price forecasting	Development of demand forecasting, imports and exports, projected energy costs	World Bank data	Profit maximization through demand and macroeconomic data

Market value chain

The market value chain for specialty crops varies between vegetables, fruits, and tree nuts, as illustrated in Figures 12 and 13. For tree nuts, processors typically have contracts with medium-to-large growers, while small growers are often part of cooperatives to have more influence in the process. Processors also have contracts with hullers or shellers, and growers may have similar relationships or vertically integrate as part of their deliverables. Processors have contractual obligations with downstream processes to deliver tree nuts to manufacturers to reach the market. The business steps and contractual obligations differ between each party, as shown in Figure 12.

The process of bringing fruits and vegetables to market is a time-sensitive undertaking, especially when compared to tree nuts. This is attributed to the fact that the goods are perishable, they are only available in specific regions and seasons, and there are limited storage facilities [83]. The speed at which these products reach the market is often dictated by commercial factors, and the value chain typically involves growers, processors, handlers, allied industries, and manufacturers, which is not markedly different from the intermediate steps involved in the case of tree nuts. While competitive and market forces remain dynamic across major agricultural countries and markets, they may vary significantly in specialty crops, particularly in developing economies [84]. Nevertheless, the Porter's five forces model remains a useful tool to derive business strategies and develop ML models that can help small farmers gain equitable market access and information, thereby leveling the playing field and addressing some of the challenges faced by smallholder farmers.

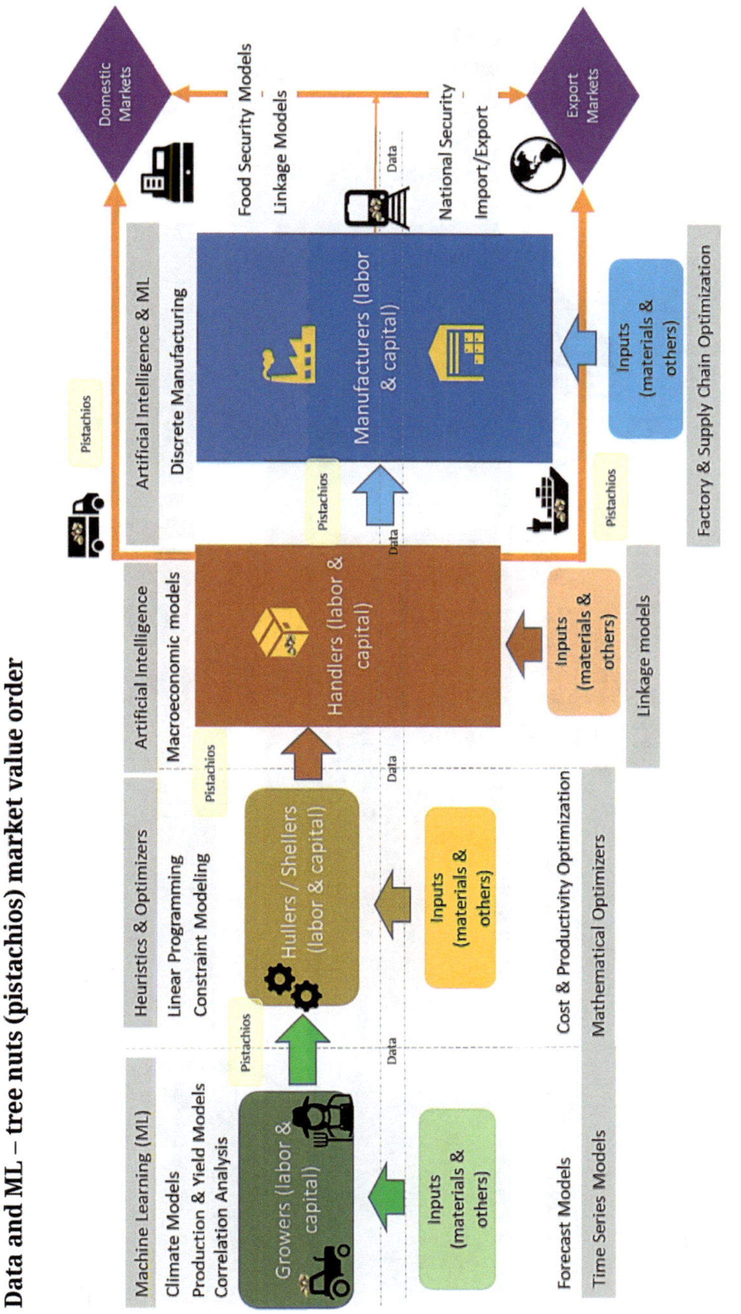

Figure 12: Tree nuts : data and ML value chain model.

Data and ML – tree nuts (tomatoes) market value order

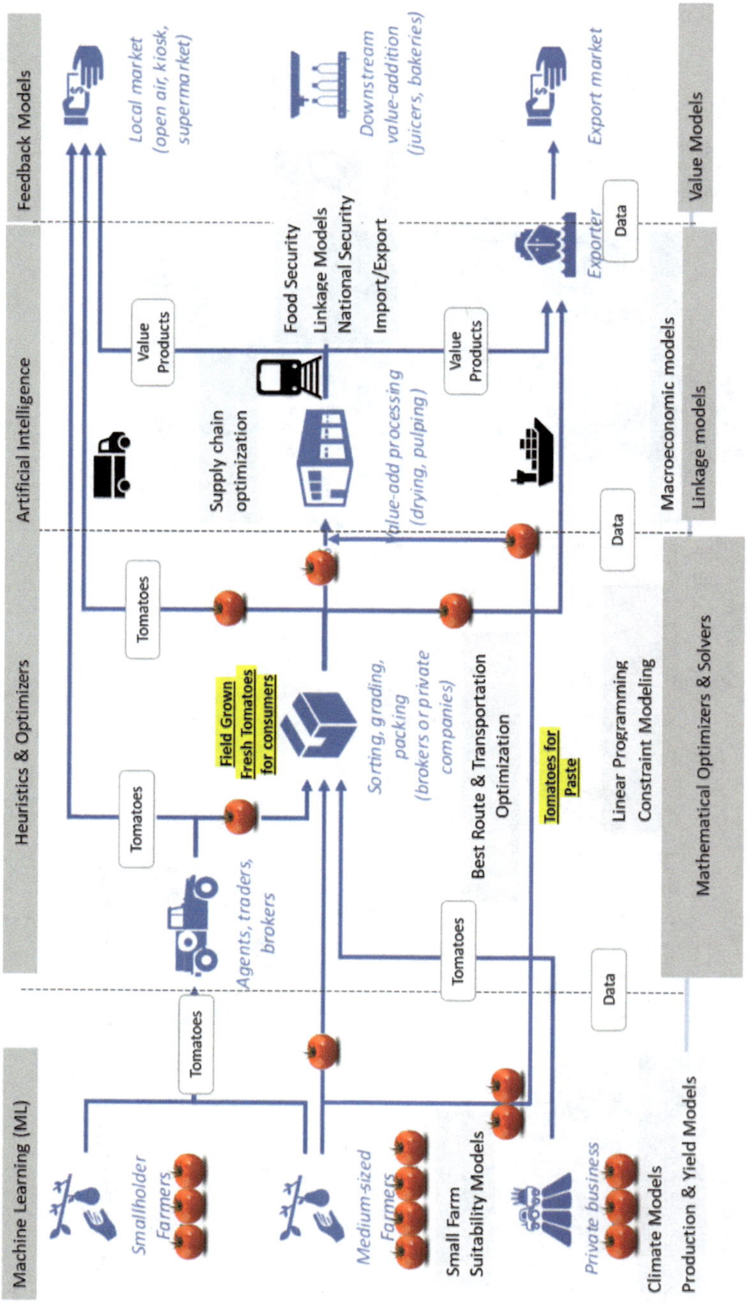

Figure 13: Data and ML value chain model.

Smallholder farmers confront numerous obstacles that hinder their competitiveness in the market. These obstacles comprise small farm size, which limits their participation in price ($) discovery, unpredictable weather patterns, insufficient exchange/trading expertise and timely market intelligence, inadequate information access, inability to take on multiple roles, presence of entrenched traders [85], difficulty in entering the market, and lack of alternative institutional support systems. These factors ultimately lead to lower revenues for farmers and their organizations. To address these difficulties, it is crucial to shift the focus of the vegetable value chain toward meeting demand, enhance the marketing information system, and reinforce the infrastructure for managing produce after harvest (postproduction facilities) [83]. This would enable farmers to have access to efficient data systems and compete with established traders on a more equal footing. The pricing section of the value chain can cover contractual obligations and risks related to yield numbers and quality, ultimately ensuring that farmers receive fair compensation for their efforts.

The integration of data and analytics is pivotal in achieving a more demand-driven vegetable value chain that eliminates the issue of overabundance faced by farmers. Through the utilization of data science and advanced analytics, growers, processors, and traders can make informed decisions regarding supply and demand, market trends, and pricing strategies. By leveraging this information, stakeholders can optimize the value chain, ensuring that farmers receive equitable prices for their produce while meeting the demands of consumers.

Data-driven insights can aid in predicting consumer preferences, thereby reducing food waste and enhancing the efficiency of the value chain. Advanced analytics can also facilitate just-in-time intelligence of market dynamics, providing avenues to foresee bottlenecks and facilitate closed loop active to correct it swiftly. By improving the accuracy of demand forecasting and supply chain management, stakeholders can create a more sustainable and efficient vegetable value chain.

In conclusion, the integration of data and analytics[1] is fundamental in creating a demand-driven vegetable value chain that benefits all stakeholders. By leveraging data science and advanced analytics, growers, processors, and traders can optimize their operations, reduce food waste, and ensure fair prices for farmers. The adoption of innovative technologies and sustainable practices can help create a more resilient and efficient vegetable value chain that meets the demands of consumers while promoting the prosperity of farmers.

Author
Chandrasekar Vuppalapati

1 Hanumayamma Innovations and Technologies, Inc., is an advanced analytics and animal husbandry sensor manufacture company that trailblaze in providing data-driven solutions to farmers, processors, and traders in the agriculture industry. The company offers two distinct services: agriculture analytics and specialty crop analytics.

Specialty crops pricing forecast framework

Specialty crops are the lifeblood of the farming industry in major agricultural nations such as India, which ranks second globally in farm outputs. More than half of the Indian labor force is employed in the agriculture sector, which accounts for around 17–18% of GDP. Key commercial crops in India include tomatoes, onions, and potatoes [85]. At a global level, the market for specialty crops is estimated to be worth a staggering $1.6 trillion in 2022 and reach close to $2 trillion USD by 2026.

Accurately predicting commodity prices is crucial for the entire marketing value chain, from growers to food processors. It enables growers to maximize profits by signing market-driven contracts, optimize input purchase decisions, manage risk, and accurately forecast demand based on lifestyle and food taste changes. For food processors, wholesalers, and retailers, accurate price forecast models provide a competitive differentiator by offering more precise price projections that are more specific than general inflation rates or past patterns. It allows them to monitor prices, make key purchases at the right time, and evaluate supplier price quotes. For governments and public service companies, accurate specialty crop price forecast models enable citizen food security and address governmental food budgets for enhanced food security (Figure 14).

Framework assumptions

The precision of forecasts for specialty crop sales depends on crucial long-term factors such as macroeconomic situations, weather conditions, food preferences of consumers, trade regulations, and supply-chain and transportation systems. Nevertheless, any modifications to these factors can substantially impact the projections, and actual circumstances will inevitably alter the outcomes [71]. The perishable nature of specialty crops imposes a constraint on the market arrivals vs. prices aspects. The correlation

---

Agriculture analytics represents a comprehensive platform that harnesses the power of data science and advanced analytics to enable stakeholders to take actions, supply chain optimization, and market trends. By integrating data from diverse sources, including sensors, weather, and satellite imagery, agriculture analytics can deliver real-time much needed insights into critical parameters such as crop yields and soil moisture levels. This information empowers farmers to optimize their crop management practices, reduce waste, and enhance their bottom line.

Specialty crop analytics, on the other hand, represents a specialized service that focuses on providing insights into the production and trade of cash rich crops such as tree nuts, fruits and seedless fruits, and organic and nonorganic vegetables. By leveraging data from various sources, including market data, consumer trends, and weather forecasts, specialty crop analytics can furnish stakeholders with real-time insights into market demand, pricing trends, and supply chain optimization. Such insights enable farmers and traders to make informed actions/decisions about crop selection, pricing, and logistics, ensuring that they remain ahead of the competition and maximize their profitability.

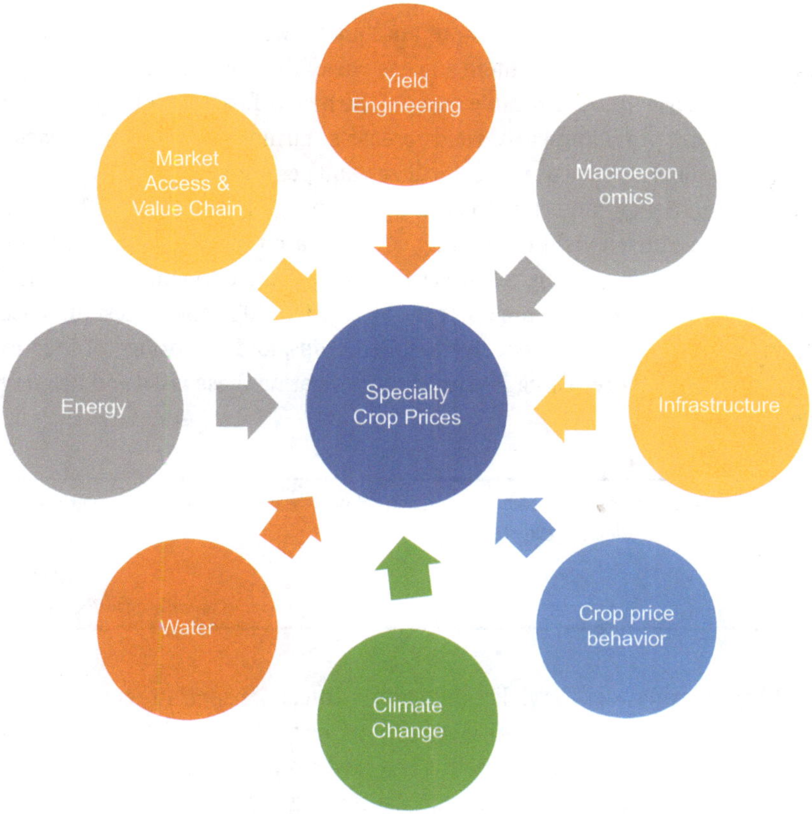

Figure 14: Pricing framework.

between market arrivals and prices can be direct, as seen in bananas, or inverse, as observed in tomatoes. Nevertheless, certain variables such as cold storage amenities, improved export prospects, agro-processing value-addition, modern poly house technologies, digital communications, infrastructure, and climatic conditions can weaken this negative correlation and even transform it into a positive one. Various years and months have been analyzed to account for seasonal variations in vegetable production, determining the extent of the relationship between market arrivals and the prices of selected crops. This study can guide farmers to adapt their crop patterns and sell during periods of optimal pricing [87, 88].

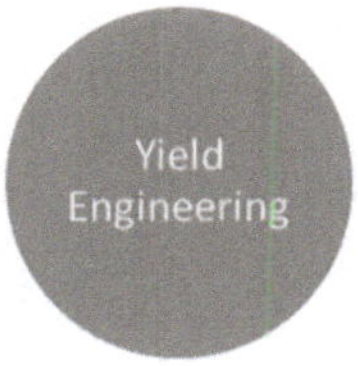

Yield forecasting

Accurate yield forecasting is essential for effective agricultural management, logistics planning, and order fulfillment. It empowers farmers to make informed decisions regarding crop insurance subscriptions and adopt precision management practices, mechanization, and automation that can enhance output and quality while minimizing resource usage and waste [64, 89]. Lack of this intelligence is one of the reasons climate changes is becoming more intense and unbearable as small farmer is forefront of agricultural production systems. By providing early yield forecasts, farmers can automate variable-rate application of inputs such as water, fertilizer, and pesticides, leading to reduced expenses and environmental impact, increased productivity, and improved efficiency. A lack of holistic data-infused yield forecasting can increase risk and costs across the value chain, ultimately leading to higher prices for end customers (Figures 14 and 15). For example, the cost of groceries in the USA rose by 13.5% in 2022, the largest increase in 43 years, due to factors such as heat stress, failed crops, and a shortage of food in the market. Accurate yield forecasting is critical for mitigating these risks and keeping prices stable [90].

> Even the slightest enhancement in agricultural processes can significantly contribute to mitigating the effects of climate change.
>
> Author
> Chandrasekar Vuppalapati

Creating an AI-based framework for yield prediction is crucial for specialty crops, which encompass a wide range of environmental conditions, crop characteristics, and management techniques. Accurate yield forecasting can save money across the farm-to-fork value chain and ensure economic growth and food security. By combining soil quality and composition with weather forecasts, growers can minimize losses during unfavorable weather conditions and maximize crop yield rates during favorable conditions [91]. Proper yield forecasting improves value delivery across the value chain, resulting in lower prices and higher savings for end consumers. In the end, the development of an AI-based framework for predicting crop yields has the power to revolutionize global food systems [92].

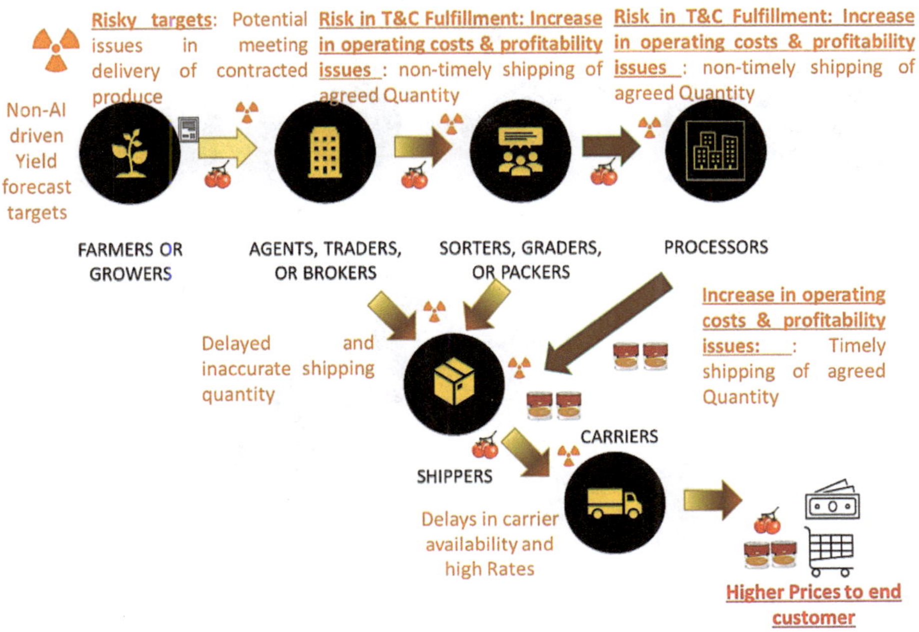

Figure 15: Lack of yield forecasting capability.

Accurate yield forecasts infused with data enable growers and farmers to maximize prices. Proper yield forecasting ensures the fulfillment of terms and conditions among various parties involved in moving produce from growers to the upward value chain through agents, traders, or brokers. This enables timely shipping and delivery of produce to meet market timing and seasonal expectations, while also realizing cost benefits for shippers through planning and operational efficiencies. An end-to-end insight chain creates cost and value synergies across the entire produce-to-home delivery value chain, as illustrated in Figure 16.

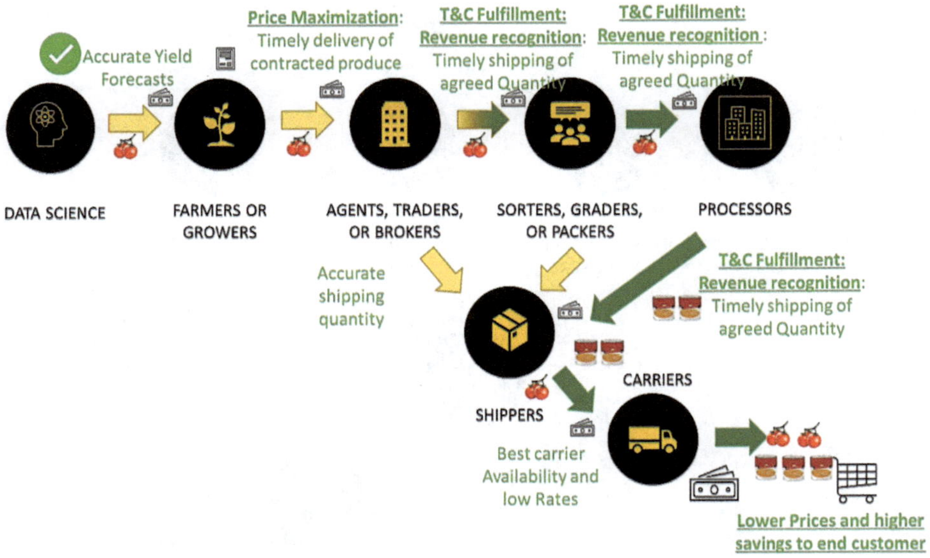

Figure 16: Benefits of yield forecasting.

Following major influencing variables are studied to learn yield signals: historical data (production, area harvested, yield), soil conditions, phenological, agricultural calendar, seasons, climate, weather patterns, farming practices, geospatial, weather events, fertilizers.

Carriers place a premium on proactive shippers and brokers who collaborate with them to plan ahead. To achieve this, these intermediaries depend on growers and farmers to furnish them with precise crop yield forecasts. In turn, farmers and growers rely on data science to generate accurate predictions. Ultimately, data science plays a pivotal role in elevating agricultural productivity, reducing prices, and promoting sustainability [92].

Challenges of pests and diseases in agricultural crop production: Understanding the impact of monocropping and chemical use

Managing pests and diseases in agriculture is a common problem that affects farmers worldwide. However, it is particularly challenging in monoculture systems, where pests and diseases can spread more rapidly and inflict greater harm. As a preventive measure, farmers resort to using pesticides and other chemicals to ensure visually appealing crops, regardless of whether they are regular or specialty crops. The escalating utilization of such chemicals is evident in the producer price index PCU32533253 (Figure 17; eq. (1)).

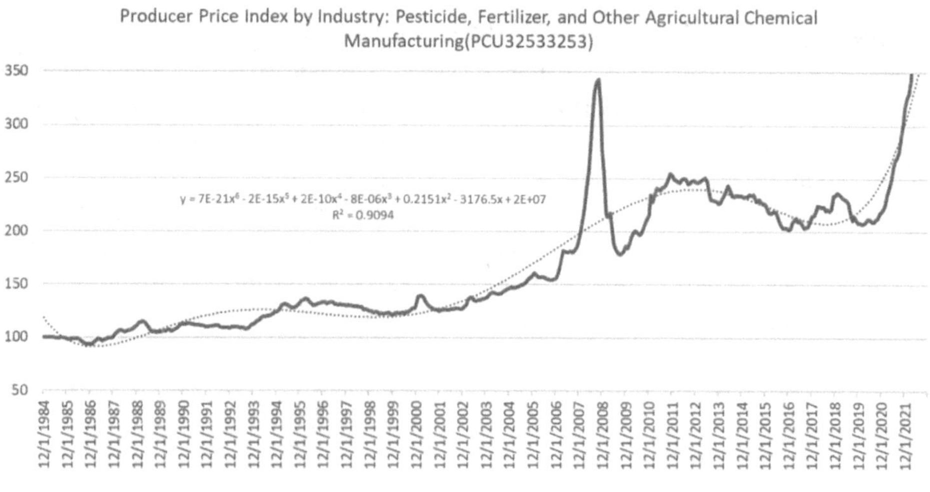

Figure 17: PPI – pesticides.

$$y = 7E{-}21x^6 - 2E{-}15x^5 + 2E{-}10x^4 - 8E{-}06x^3 + 0.2151x^2 - 3176.5x + 2E{+}07 \quad (1)$$

Trendline option	Equation	R^2
Exponential	$y = 7.2338e^{8E-05x}$	0.7814
Linear	$y = 0.0138x - 353.86$	0.7634
Logarithmic	$y = 514.06\ln(x) - 5248.3$	0.7498
Polynomial	$y = 7E{-}21x^6 - 2E{-}15x^5 + 2E{-}10x^4 - 8E{-}06x^3 + 0.2151x^2 - 3176.5x + 2E{+}07$	0.9094
Power	$y = 2E{-}12x^{3.0513}$	0.7796

For instance, consider bananas.

Macroeconomics

Despite agricultural commodity prices being influenced by local governmental policies, macroeconomics plays an important role in forecasting price movements of specialty crops. From farm inputs to market reach, macroeconomic variables have a direct influence on the price of specialty crops. The essential aspect is to identify relevant macroeconomic variables to generate the model. For instance, consider tomato production and the price of tomatoes.

In many countries, tomatoes are produced on open land. In some places, for instance, Turkey, the USA, and others, greenhouses are used to cultivate tomatoes for processing. In this backdrop, when a price forecast model was developed, greenhouse tomatoes production prices, in addition to yield and climate variables, were influenced by energy prices, electricity, and halo bulbs [93, 94, 95]. The Bell curve model (Figure 18) provides a systematic way to understand and analyze the influence of macroeconomic variables on specialty crops [96].

The objective of macroeconomic variables is to consider the prevailing global economic and market conditions that pose ongoing challenges to the agriculture sector in the USA and across the world. These variables include persistent inflation, extreme weather phenomena, interruptions in the supply chain, and exorbitant input costs [71].

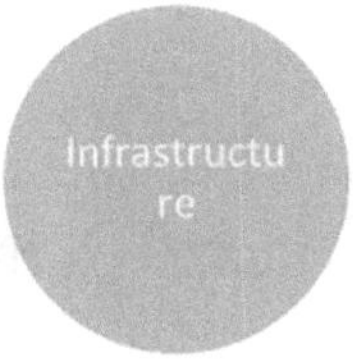

Infrastructure

Farmers have long been intrigued by the challenge of transporting their crops in the most efficient, safe, nutritious, and cost-effective manner [99, 100]. To achieve the farm-to-fork journey, farmers must consider all available modes of transportation, including road, rail, barge, ocean-going ships, pipelines, airplanes, and others. Understanding the various viewpoints and fundamentals of transportation patterns is critical in recommending the most efficient method for farmers. The transportation of food is a multifaceted process, and all means of transportation are vital to the food supply chain. Nevertheless, certain modes of transportation are more critical than others [101, 102]. If you wish to explore this topic further, I recommend referring to my other books.

Machine learning mode: Maine and New Hampshire strawberries pricing model

Effective fresh produce supply chain management is dependent upon accurate price predictions. Inaccurate predictions can lead to overpriced agricultural commodities for suppliers and retailers, as well as price crashes that negatively impact farmers (Figure 19). However, developing price prediction models for fresh produce is a complex process due to the unique characteristics of the produce and its inherent price instability. Additionally, available datasets often contain missing or incorrect data, making the development of reliable models even more challenging. Therefore, assessing data quality prior to model development is essential, and finding a reliable method to address missing values is crucial for achieving more precise and valid predictions [103].

AI-powered forecasting models, including univariate and multivariate models, have been created to analyze strawberry prices. These models have the potential to reduce waste and generate economic advantages for vendors. However, factors such

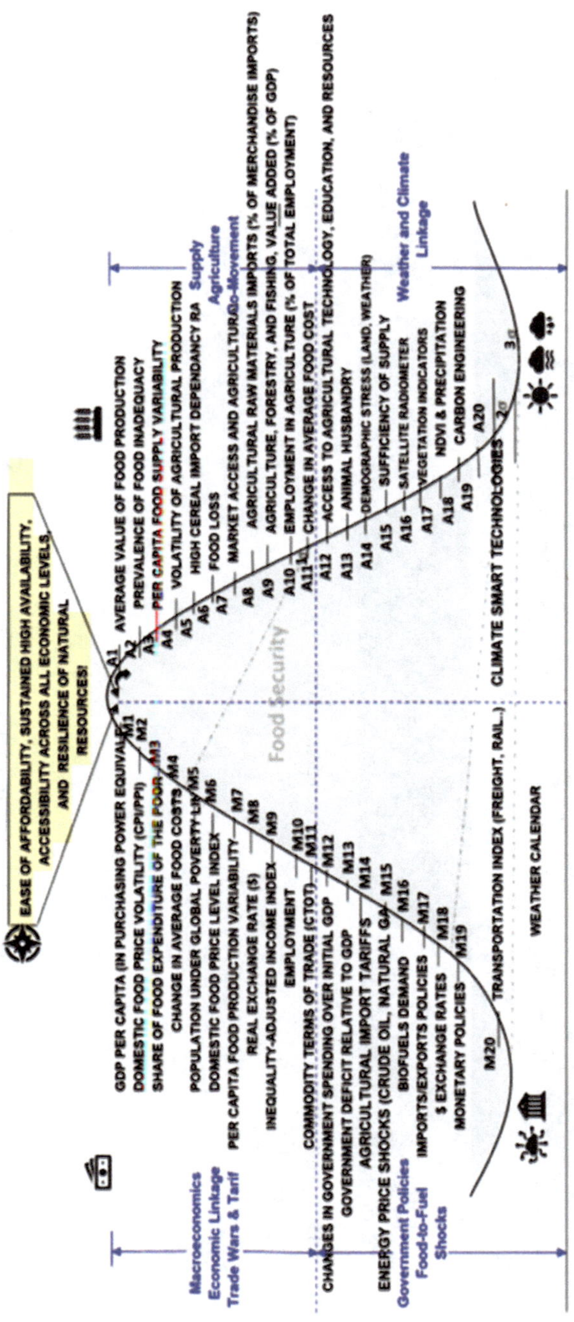

Figure 18: Bell curve modeling.

Figure 19: Specialty crops price forecast framework and component view.

as income, labor, and trade obstacles, along with uncertainties resulting from climate change, can still pose difficulties when making procurement decisions [104, 105].

Suggested varieties

For fruitful strawberry cultivation in New England, it is vital to choose varieties that are resilient to red stele and Verticillium root rots, produce robust plants, and have a reliable record of high-quality fruit and good yields. The following list comprises some reliable varieties suitable for Northern New England [105].

During late fall, typically around mid-November in New England, it is advisable to apply mulch over the strawberry plants to shield them from harsh winter temperatures and potential root damage due to quick freezing and thawing of the soil. Straw is a popular mulch choice, but pine needles or wood shavings can also be utilized, provided they cover the plants without forming a mat. Hay should be avoided as it contains weed seeds that can grow among strawberries in the spring. It is recommended to have a mulch layer that is 6–8 inches deep over the plants.

Around mid-April, the mulch covering the plants should be removed and placed in the spaces between rows, creating a neat walkway while also keeping the fruit dry and clean (Figure 20). If a frost is expected after the mulch has been removed, it can be raked back over the plants overnight to safeguard the flower buds.

Strawberries are vulnerable to fungal diseases such as root rots and gray mold, as well as insects like tarnished plant bugs and strawberry bud weevils. Nevertheless, many issues can be averted with appropriate care and planning. It is recommended to plant varieties that are resistant to red stele and Verticillium root rots. Keeping the planting weed-free can discourage insect pests, while narrow plant rows and mulching between rows can prevent gray mold by improving air circulation (Figure 21).

Figure 20: Strawberry and winter safeguard [105].

Figure 21: Frost protection of strawberry flowers [105].

Although the US strawberry market is mature, household penetration and volume of consumption continue to expand, resulting in a surge in planted crops and imports in the Golden State. This expansion has led to multi-year high acreage in California, enhancing the fruit's availability, and keeping prices stable. Nevertheless, high input expenses remain a significant concern in the short term, and despite being a mature market, the US market shows growth patterns that are unusual for its maturity level.

The journey of fresh strawberries in the USA from 1980 to 2021 is a tale of remarkable growth and increasing consumer demand (Figure 22). From modest beginnings, the industry has expanded significantly, driven by improvements in production, rising imports, and a growing appetite for fresh, healthy food. The consistent increase in per capita consumption highlights strawberries' enduring appeal and their importance in the American diet. This story is not just about numbers; it's about how strawberries have become a beloved fruit, enjoyed by millions across the country.

In the early 1980s, the US strawberry industry was relatively modest. Utilized production hovered around 400 million pounds annually. Imports were minimal, indicating that domestic production was largely sufficient to meet the demand. Per capita use was about 1 pound per person per year, reflecting a limited but steady consumer interest in fresh strawberries.

As the 1990s dawned, both production and per capita consumption began to climb. By the mid-1990s, utilized production had surpassed 1,000 million pounds. This growth was driven by advancements in agricultural practices, better varieties of strawberries, and an increasing consumer appetite for fresh produce. Imports also started to rise slightly, suggesting that domestic production, while increasing, did not entirely keep pace with growing demand. Per capita use edged up to around 3 pounds per person.

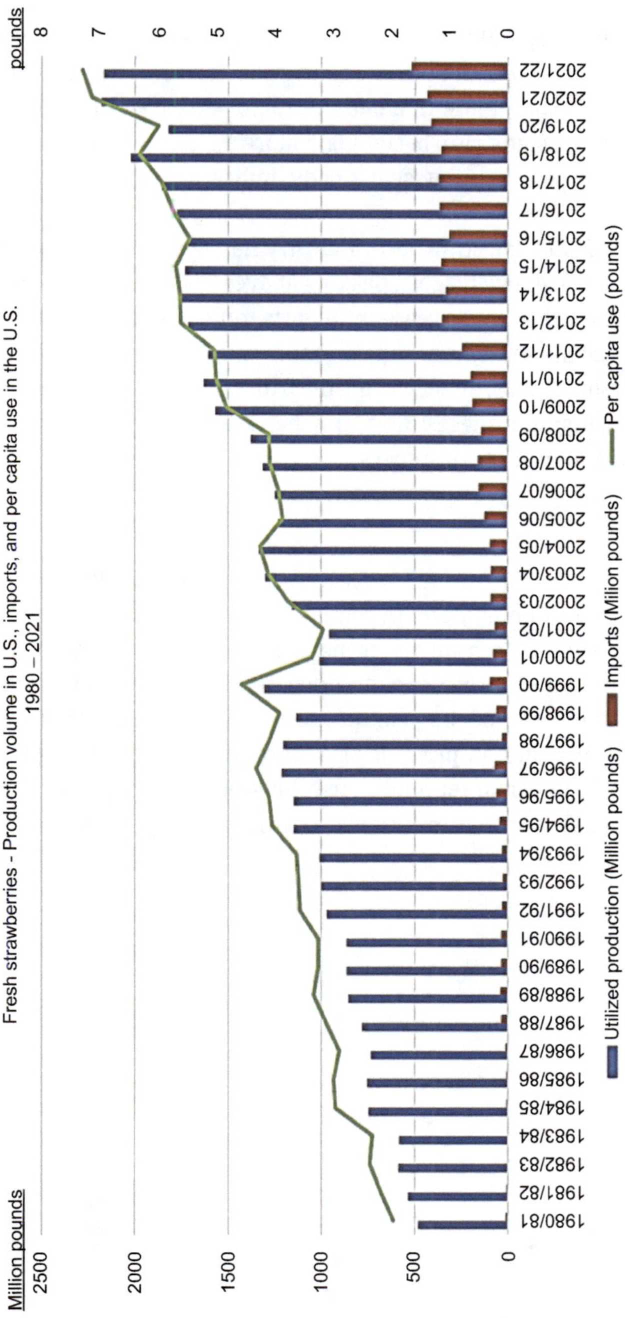

Figure 22: Fresh strawberries – production volume in the USA, imports, and per capita use.

Toward the late 1990s and early 2000s, the strawberry market experienced some fluctuations. Production saw some drops and peaks, reflective of variable growing conditions and market dynamics. Despite these fluctuations, the overall trend remained upward. Imports continued their steady rise, becoming a more significant component of the supply chain. Per capita consumption held steady, indicating consistent consumer demand.

In the last decade (2010s–2021), the strawberry industry has seen unprecedented growth. Utilized production reached new heights, peaking at over 2,000 million pounds by 2021. This period also saw a dramatic increase in imports, reflecting both growing demand and the globalization of the strawberry supply chain. Per capita use hit a record high of over 7 pounds per person in 2021, underscoring the fruit's popularity. The recent spikes in production and consumption suggest that strawberries have cemented their place as a favorite fruit among American consumers.

Seasonality

The price of strawberries (Figure 23) exhibits a clear seasonal pattern. Prices are highest during the winter months (January and December), likely due to lower supply and higher demand during the holiday season. As spring arrives, prices drop and stabilize during the summer months when strawberry production peaks. In the fall, prices begin to rise again, reflecting the end of the peak production season and preparing for the winter holidays. The variability in prices is also more pronounced during the winter months, indicating fluctuating market conditions. This seasonal trend highlights the impact of supply and demand dynamics on strawberry prices throughout the year.

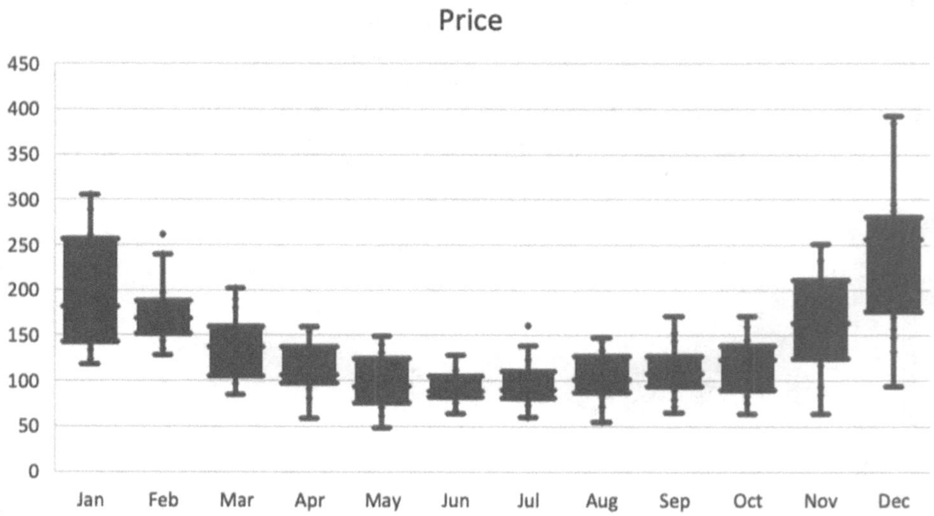

Figure 23: Fresh strawberries prices.

Final Release Strawberries_pricingModel Notebook

Sources

The following table has the list of data sources.

Data source	Name
USDA	Retail prices of fresh and processed vegetables for tomatoes under trade and prices by category.
FRED	Average price: APU0000711415 US diesel sales price (GASDESM) CPI: CPIAUCSL Producer prices: maintenance and repair services for Ag., machinery (PCU8113108113105)
World Bank	Pink Sheet data
NOAA	Maine and New Hampshire weather data

Pricing model framework: variable list

Price forecasting is Following data sources are used as part of the model:

Independent feature time series name	Frequency	Description	Source
Maine weather	Monthly	MaxTemperature(C)', 'MeanTemperature(C)', 'MinTemperature(C)', total_precipitation (kg m^{-2} s^{-1})' measures the mass of precipitation falling on a square meter of land every second	NOAA GSOM
Gas price (GASREGCOVM)	Monthly	Per gallon	Gas Price
CPI	Monthly	CPIAUCSL	CPIAUCSL
Fertilizer	Monthly	PhosphateRock($/mt)', 'Dap($/mt)', 'Tsp($/mt)', 'Urea($/mt)', 'PotassiumChloride($/mt)',	World Bank Commodity Markets
GDP	Quarterly	gross domestic product (GDP)	GDP
Uncertainty index	Monthly	Current price adjusted (GEPUCURRENT)	
S&P 500 dividend by month	Monthly	S&P 500 monthly dividends	Standard and Poor 500 Dividend by Month
Industrial production index (INDPRO)	Monthly	INDPRO	INDPRO
Rail car loadings	Monthly	Rail freight carloads	Rail Freight Carloads (RAILFRTCARLOADSD11)

Step 1: Load data

The code imports various Python libraries that are commonly used in data analysis and ML. These libraries include pandas, numpy, functools, datetime, plotly.graph_objects, seaborn, statsmodels.api, statsmodels.tsa.arima_process, scipy, scipy.stats, matplotlib.pyplot, plotly.express, sklearn.metrics, sklearn.impute, Prophet, and eli5.

```
import pandas as pd
import numpy as np
import functools as ft
from datetime import date
```

```
import plotly.graph_objects as go
import seaborn as sns; sns.set()
import statsmodels.api as sm
from statsmodels.tsa.arima_process import ArmaProcess
from scipy import stats
from scipy.stats import pearsonr
import matplotlib.pyplot as plt
import plotly.express as px
from sklearn.preprocessing importMinMaxScaler
from sklearn.model_selection import train_test_split
from sklearn.linear_model import LinearRegression
from sklearn.metrics import r2_score
from sklearn import metrics
from sklearn.impute import SimpleImputer
from sklearn.metrics import mean_absolute_error
from prophet import Prophet
import eli5
```

And load data (FAOSTAT 2023).

```
df_AreaHarvest = pd.read_csv("StrawberriesHarvest.csv")
df_AreaHarvest
```

Data Table:

	Domain Code	Domain	Area Code (M49)	Area	Element Code	Element	Item Code (CPC)	Item	Year Code	Year	Unit	Value	Flag	Flag Description
0	QCL	Crops and livestock products	840	United States of America	5312	Area harvested	1354	Strawberries	1961	1961	ha	35770	A	Official figure
1	QCL	Crops and livestock products	840	United States of America	5312	Area harvested	1354	Strawberries	1962	1962	ha	35580	A	Official figure
2	QCL	Crops and livestock products	840	United States of America	5312	Area harvested	1354	Strawberries	1963	1963	ha	32400	A	Official figure
3	QCL	Crops and livestock products	840	United States of America	5312	Area harvested	1354	Strawberries	1964	1964	ha	30330	A	Official figure
4	QCL	Crops and livestock products	840	United States of America	5312	Area harvested	1354	Strawberries	1965	1965	ha	32050	A	Official figure
...	...	...	...	...	...	...	...	...	...	...	...	...	...	...
178	QCL	Crops and livestock products	840	United States of America	5510	Production	1354	Strawberries	2017	2017	t	1234130	A	Official figure

Code below processes the data in the 'df_AreaHarvest' dataframe by pivoting it to rearrange the data for better analysis. The 'pivot' function is used to pivot the data so that the 'Year' column becomes the index, the 'Element' column becomes the columns, and the 'Value' column becomes the values. This creates a new dataframe called 'df_AreaHarvest1'. Finally, the 'tail' function is used twice to display the last five rows of the 'df_AreaHarvest1' dataframe. This is done to verify that the data has been processed correctly and to inspect the data to see if there are any anomalies or issues.

```
df_AreaHarvest1 = df_AreaHarvest.pivot(index="Year",columns="Element",values="Value")
df_AreaHarvest1['Date']=pd.to_datetime(df_AreaHarvest1['Year'],format='%y')
df_AreaHarvest1.drop("Year", axis = 1,inplace = True)
df_AreaHarvest1.tail()
df_AreaHarvest1 tail()
```

Output: Perform data manipulation and convert year into date format.

Element	Area harvested	Production	Yield	Date
56	21530	1234130	573214	2017-01-01
57	19720	1183870	600340	2018-01-01
58	17600	1035100	588125	2019-01-01
59	18818	1209730	642858	2020-01-01
60	19992	1211090	605787	2021-01-01

To get harvest data on a monthly basis, please add 365 days to the dataframe and split the rows by week start. The code below is used to manipulate and merge data from the 'df_AreaHarvest1' dataframe. The first line of code initializes a new variable called 'enddt' and sets it to the last date in the 'Date' column of the 'df_AreaHarvest1' dataframe, plus 365 days and 334 days. This creates a new date that is one year and nine months after the last date in the 'Date' column. The 'pd.date_range' function creates a date range between the first date in the 'Date' column of the 'df_AreaHarvest1' dataframe and the 'enddt' date that was created earlier. This is done using a monthly frequency ('freq="MS"') to create a list of dates that span the entire time period between the start and end dates.

```
from datetime import datetime, timedelta
enddt = df_AreaHarvest1["Date"].iloc[-1] + timedelta(days = 365+334)
```

```
df_AreaHarvest1.rename(columns = { "Area harvested": "Area harvested(ha)", "Production":
"Production(tonnes)","Yield":"Yield(100 hg/ha)"},inplace = True)
```

```
tempdt = pd.date_range(start = df_AreaHarvest1["Date"].iloc[0], end = enddt,freq = "MS")
```

```
Tempdf["Date"] = tempdt
```

```
df_AreaHarvest2 = Tempdf.merge(df_AreaHarvest1,on = "Date", how = "left")
df_AreaHarvest2.head(13)
```

Output:

	Date	Area harvested(ha)	Production(tonnes)	Yield(100 hg/ha)
0	1961-01-01	35770.0	230110.0	64330.0
1	1961-02-01	NaN	NaN	NaN
2	1961-03-01	NaN	NaN	NaN
3	1961-04-01	NaN	NaN	NaN
4	1961-05-01	NaN	NaN	NaN
5	1961-06-01	NaN	NaN	NaN
6	1961-07-01	NaN	NaN	NaN
7	1961-08-01	NaN	NaN	NaN
8	1961-09-01	NaN	NaN	NaN
9	1961-10-01	NaN	NaN	NaN
10	1961-11-01	NaN	NaN	NaN
11	1961-12-01	NaN	NaN	NaN

This study focused on the importance of filling in missing data to make accurate predictions using ML models. Various techniques were examined, including both deep learning and non-deep learning approaches. Among the non-deep learning methods analyzed were linear functions and the last observation carried forward (LOCF) method. LOCF is a technique used to handle missing data by using the most recent available observation to fill in the gaps. The researchers found that the LOCF method resulted in the lowest prediction errors for both price and yield. This means that filling in missing data using the LOCF technique helped to make the ML models more accurate in predicting prices and yields [103].

```
df_AreaHarvest3 = df_AreaHarvest2.ffill()
```

	Date	Area harvested(ha)	Production(tonnes)	Yield(100 hg/ha)
0	1961-01-01	35770.0	230110.0	64330.0
1	1961-02-01	35770.0	230110.0	64330.0
2	1961-03-01	35770.0	230110.0	64330.0
3	1961-04-01	35770.0	230110.0	64330.0
4	1961-05-01	35770.0	230110.0	64330.0
...	...	...	...	...
739	2022-08-01	19992.0	1211090.0	605787.0
740	2022-09-01	19992.0	1211090.0	605787.0
741	2022-10-01	19992.0	1211090.0	605787.0
742	2022-11-01	19992.0	1211090.0	605787.0

The rationale for imputing on a monthly basis is to develop a pricing model through the independent features. Plus, by imputing at the monthly level, the same as they appear at yearly, we are not changing the signature on the data as it's applicable to all months in a year.

Step 2: Weather data: NOAA GSOM

Load data from NOAA GSOM

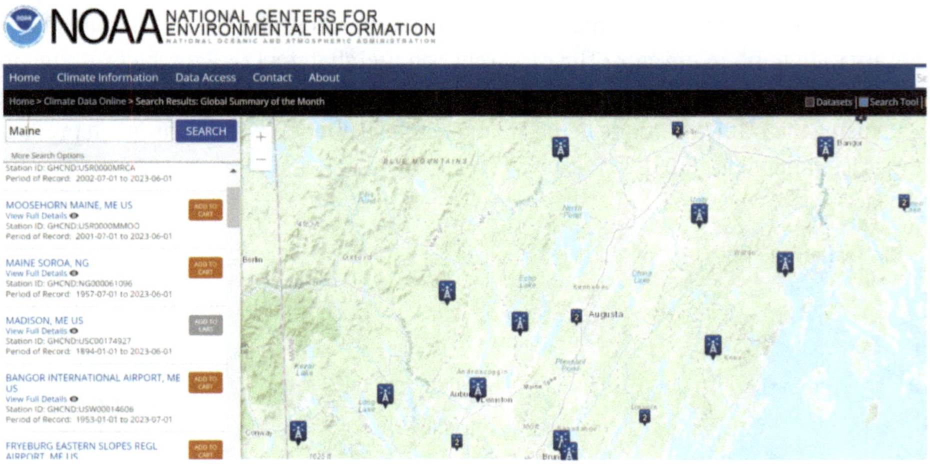

```
weatherdf = pd.read_csv("Maine_NewHampshire_weather_monthly.csv")
weatherdf
```

```
weatherdf.drop('Unnamed: 0', axis=1, inplace = True)
```

```
weatherdf["Date"] = pd.to_datetime(weatherdf["date"])
```

```
weatherdf.drop("date",axis = 1, inplace = True)
```

Output:

	MaxTemperature(C)	MeanTemperature(C)	MinTemperature(C)	total_precipitation(kg m-2 s-1)	Date
0	-7.237036	-12.428717	-17.472281	3.032537e-05	1980-01-01
1	-6.446844	-11.672919	-16.868933	2.978275e-05	1980-02-01
2	3.533838	-3.458319	-9.693121	1.913348e-05	1980-03-01
3	17.994012	10.821130	3.321405	1.565766e-04	1980-04-01
4	26.958643	19.356683	10.692285	9.107852e-05	1980-05-01
...	...	...	...	...	...
515	22.765344	16.305841	9.127924	2.306271e-06	2020-09-01
516	33.471735	26.513574	17.093256	5.615588e-09	2021-06-01
517	35.498438	28.896204	20.415491	3.001805e-05	2021-07-01
518	33.666101	26.935693	18.720850	5.547929e-09	2021-08-01
519	25.790186	18.202112	10.091364	2.350058e-07	2021-09-01

520 rows × 5 columns

The dynamics of strawberry supply and demand are a global phenomenon. In India, for instance, the supply of strawberries from Mahabaleshwar decreased in 2021 due to several factors, causing prices to skyrocket to as much as 250 per kilogram. Weather conditions significantly influence strawberry prices, and the combination of the COVID-19 pandemic and extended rainfall delayed both cultivation and production. The head of the Strawberry Growers Association of Maharashtra noted that late cultivation resulted in the fruit arriving late in the market, while cloudy conditions negatively impacted the quality and size of the strawberries, leading to subpar production levels. However, prices are expected to decline next month with the arrival of other seasonal fruits like grapes, apples, and watermelon in the market.

Step 3: Load fertilizer data from World Bank Pink Sheet data

Load fertilizer data from World Bank.

```
df_fert = pd.read_csv(r"Fertilizers.csv",index_col=0)
df_fert
```

```
df_fert["Date"] = pd.to_datetime(df_fert["Date"])
```

```
df_fert.dtypes
```

Output:

```
Date                          datetime64[ns]
PhosphateRock($/mt)                  float64
Dap($/mt)                            float64
Tsp($/mt)                            float64
Urea($/mt)                           float64
PotassiumChloride($/mt)              float64
dtype: object
```

```
df_fert ['PotassiumChloride($/mt)'].plot()
```

Output:

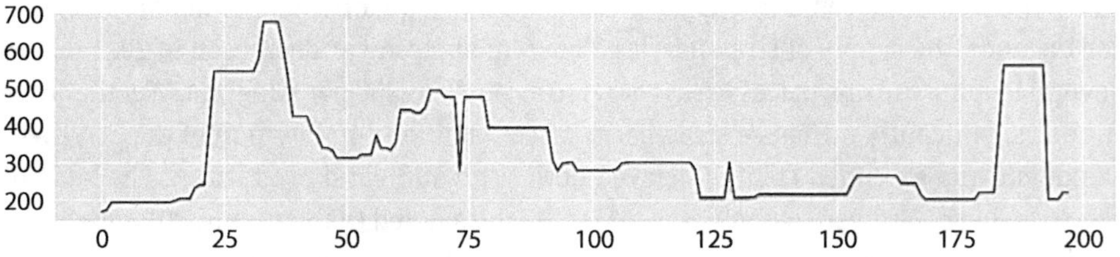


```
df_fert [Urea($/mt)'].plot()
```

Output:

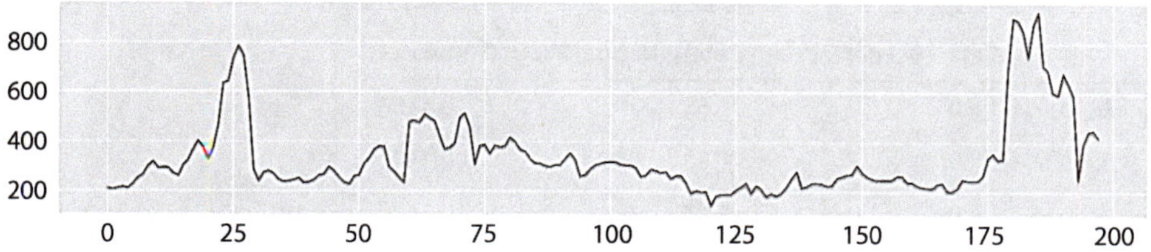


```
df_fert ['PhosphateRock($/mt)'].plot()
```

Output:

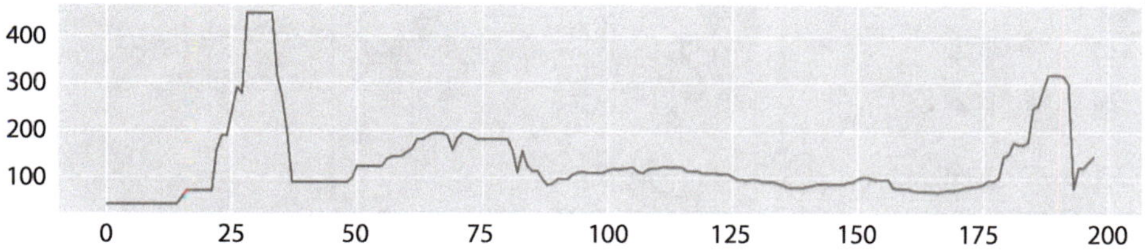

Step 4: Load energy costs

Load energy costs data from World Bank.

```
Energy_df = pd.read_csv(r"Energy.csv",index_col=0)
Energy_df.head(3)
```

```
BrentOil = Energy_df[['Date', 'CrudeOilBrent($/bbl)', 'NaturalGasUs($/mmbtu)']]
BrentOil
```

```
BrentOil.plot()
```

Output:

	Date	CrudeOilBrent($/bbl)	NaturalGasUs($/mmbtu)
0	01-01-1960	1.63	0.1400
1	02-01-1960	1.63	0.1400
2	03-01-1960	1.63	0.1400
3	04-01-1960	1.63	0.1400
4	05-01-1960	1.63	0.1400
...	...	...	...
750	07-01-2022	108.92	7.2561
751	08-01-2022	98.60	8.7854
752	09-01-2022	90.16	7.7629
753	10-01-2022	93.13	5.6195
754	11-01-2022	91.07	5.2769

755 rows × 3 columns

Step 5: Global Economic Policy Uncertainty Index: GEPUCURRENT

To comprehend how pricing is affected by demand, you can utilize a valuable resource called the "Global Economic Policy Uncertainty Index." This index is an amalgamation of economic policy uncertainty metrics from 20 different nations, including the USA, China, and Japan. By examining this index, you can gain a deeper understanding of the level of economic policy uncertainty in diverse regions and its impact on the demand for goods and services.

```
uncertainitydf = pd.read_csv(r"GEPUCURRENT.csv",parse_dates=["DATE"])
uncertainitydf["Date"] = pd.to_datetime(uncertainitydf["DATE"])
```

```
uncertainitydf.drop(["DATE"],axis=1,inplace = True)
```

```
uncertainitydf.dtypes
```

Output:

```
GEPUCURRENT              float64
Date              datetime64[ns]
dtype: object
```

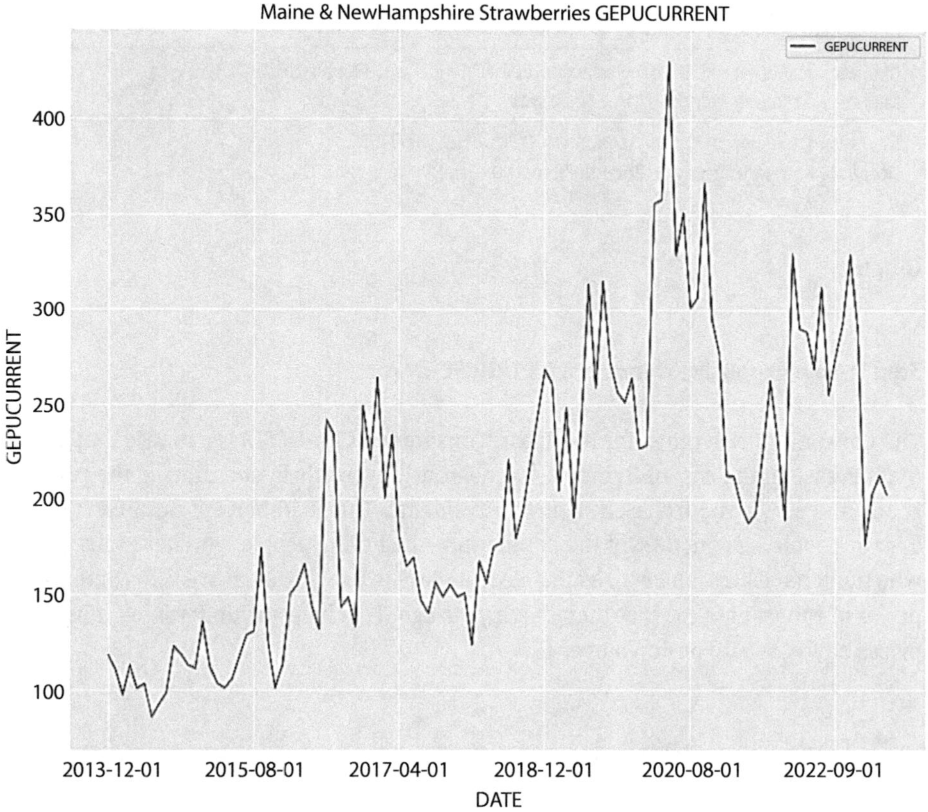

Step 6: Producer Price Index by Industry: Commercial Machinery Repair and Maintenance: Maintenance and Repair Services for Agricultural, Construction, and Mining Machinery (PCU8113108113105)

California's thousands of agricultural workers play a vital role, yet they often work without adequate safety measures and benefits while harvesting strawberries in Ventura County for supermarkets [105]. Although some mechanized processes for harvesting fresh berries have been developed, their widespread commercial use is still a long way off. As a result, nearly all of the 27 billion pounds of American strawberries harvested in 2021 were picked by hand, demanding significant labor. The industry faces notable challenges due to the availability of local labor and the seasonal nature of picking. Most farm production occurs in rural areas where the workforce is neither large nor skilled enough, and the limited seasonal harvest periods mean that even if sufficient workers were available, there might not be another job opportunity once the picking season concludes.

```
MaintenanceRepair_df = pd.read_csv("RepairMaintenancePPI(PCU8113108113105).csv")
MaintenanceRepair_df
```

```
MaintenanceRepair_df["Date"] = pd.to_datetime(MaintenanceRepair_df["DATE"])
MaintenanceRepair_df.drop(["DATE"], axis=1)
```

```
MaintenanceRepair_df.rename(columns = {"PCU8113108113105":
"RepairMaintenanceProducerPriceInd"}, inplace=True)
```

Output:

Step 7: How expensive things are (CPIAUCSL)

The Consumer Price Index for All Urban Consumers (CPIAUCSL) is a metric that gauges the increase in the cost of living over time. It achieves this by monitoring the prices of goods and services purchased by urban residents. This is important because it covers a lot of people – about 88% of the population – including people who have jobs, people who don't have jobs, and retired people. One way to use this measure is to compare the prices of things now to what they cost a year ago. This helps us understand how much prices have gone up or down over time.

```
CPI = pd.read_csv(r"CPIAUCSL.csv")
CPI
```

```
CPI["Date"] = pd.to_datetime(CPI["DATE"])
```

```
CPI.drop("DATE",axis=1, inplace = True)
CPI.plot()
```

Output:

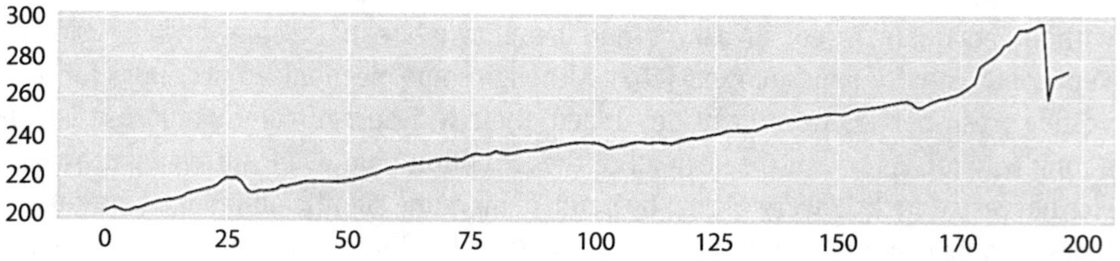

Step 8: US diesel sales price (GASDESW)

Price of diesel – the most basic transportation fuel.

```
df_diesel=pd.read_csv("GASDESW.csv")
df_diesel["Date"] = pd.to_datetime(df_diesel["DATE"])
df_diesel.drop("DATE",axis=1, inplace = True)
df_diesel.plot()
```

Output:

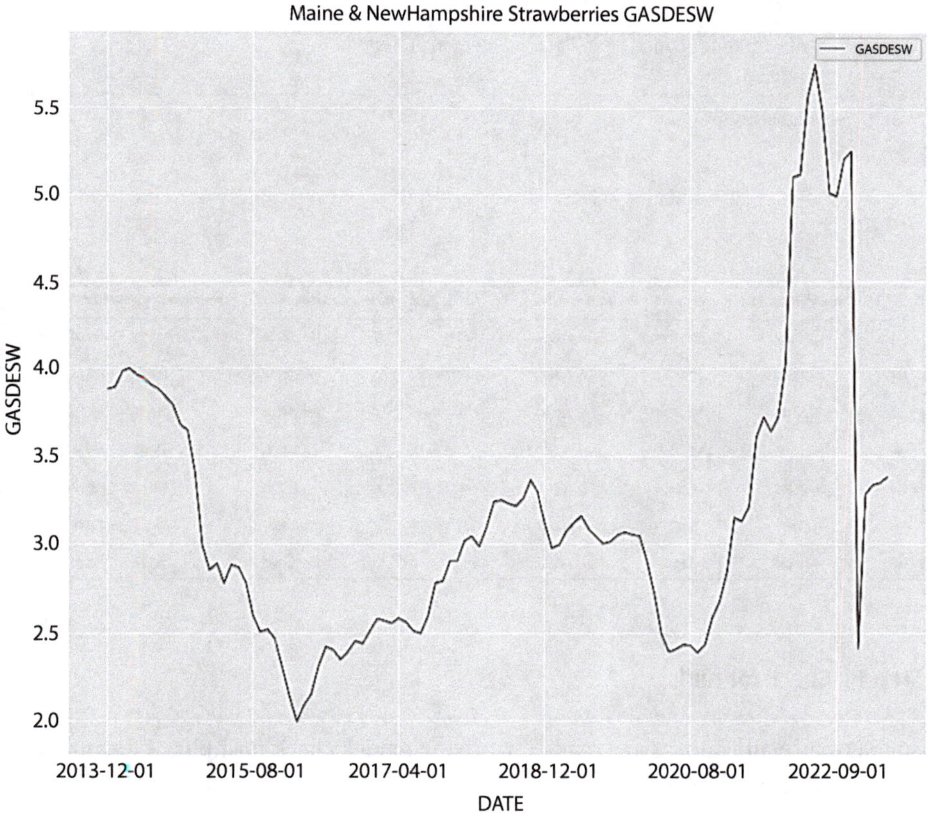

Step 9: Combine all data frames

The code above merges several data frames into a single DataFrame called 'combined_df'. The DataFrame being merged are Weather, Dollar Index, Fertilizer, CPI, Uncertainty,

Area Harvested, Employment, Industrial Production, Producer Price Index of Fertilizer, Diesel Prices, and Strawberries. The 'reduce' function is used to apply a 'merge' function to each pair of DataFrame in the list of data frames. This 'merge' function combines the DataFrame by matching rows based on the 'Date' column.

Once all the DataFrame have been merged, the resulting DataFrame 'combined_df' contains all the columns from each of the original DataFrame. This makes it easier to analyze the data and draw insights from multiple sources. Now, combine all independent feature variable data frames.

```
dfList1 = [ weatherdf,df_dollarIndex1,df_fert,
    CPI,uncertainitydf,df_AreaHarvest3                                    ,df_emp,
df_indIndustry,df_PPfertilizer,df_diesel, strawberries_df]

combined_df = ft.reduce(lambda left, right: pd.merge(left, right,
on="Date"), dfList1)
```

```
ombined_df.tail(12)
```

Output:

	MaxTemperature(C)	MeanTemperature(C)	MinTemperature(C)	total_precipitation(kg m-2 s-1)	Date	dollarIndex_close	PhosphateRock($/mt)	Dap($/mt)	Tsp($/mt)
186	27.356317	20.507440	12.237299	1.838540e-04	2022-05-01	101.750000	255.00	842.50	827.50
187	34.499200	27.449915	18.763940	1.061797e-05	2022-06-01	104.690002	287.50	783.75	730.13
188	35.356165	28.886469	20.380823	7.024366e-06	2022-07-01	105.900002	320.00	784.00	736.00
189	30.810510	24.545801	16.732965	2.634108e-05	2022-08-01	108.699997	320.00	749.38	703.75
190	27.545282	20.124841	12.483636	7.495123e-06	2022-09-01	112.120003	320.00	752.00	708.00
191	16.245416	9.158136	2.550134	6.278431e-05	2022-10-01	111.529999	317.50	725.00	675.00
192	3.986230	-0.414221	-4.043951	9.307604e-05	2022-11-01	105.949997	300.00	665.63	625.00

Step 10: Check for nulls

To make sure all features are ready for pricing model, check for nulls. If any nulls are discovered, impute them.

```
combined_df.isna().sum()
```

Output:

```
MaxTemperature(C)                                    0
MeanTemperature(C)                                   0
MinTemperature(C)                                    0
total_precipitation(kg m-2 s-1)                      0
Date                                                 0
dollarIndex_close                                    0
PhosphateRock($/mt)                                  0
Dap($/mt)                                            0
Tsp($/mt)                                            0
Urea($/mt)                                           0
PotassiumChloride($/mt)                              0
CPIAUCSL                                             0
GEPUCURRENT                                          0
Area harvested(ha)                                   0
Production(tonnes)                                   0
Yield(100 hg/ha)                                     0
employmentInAgriculture(LNS12034560)                 0
ProductionPriceIndexIndustry(PCU811310811310)        0
ProductionPriceIndexIndustry(PCU325311325311)        0
GASDESW                                              0
strawberries_PPI                                     0
dtype: int64
```

Step 11: Perform Prophet model

First, we need to make sure time series column ‘ds’ and the class column ‘y’ are present in the Prophet DataFrame.

```
Prophet_df=combined_df
Prophet_df["Date"] = pd.to_datetime(Prophet_df["Date"])
Prophet_df.rename(columns = {'strawberries_PPI': 'y', "Date":'ds'}, inplace= True)
Prophet_df.columns
```

Output:

```
Index(['MaxTemperature(C)', 'MeanTemperature(C)', 'MinTemperature(C)',
    'total_precipitation(kg m-2 s-1)', 'ds', 'dollarIndex_close',
    'PhosphateRock($/mt) ', 'Dap($/mt) ', 'Tsp($/mt)','Urea($/mt)',
    'PotassiumChloride($/mt)','CPIAUCSL','GEPUCURRENT',
    'Area harvested(ha)','Production(tonnes)','Yield(100 hg/ha)',
    'employmentInAgriculture(LNS12034560)',
```

```
    'ProductionPriceIndexIndustry(PCU811310811310)',
    'ProductionPriceIndexIndustry(PCU325311325311)', 'GASDESW', 'y'],
   dtype='object')
```

Split the DataFrame:

```
n_obs=int(Prophet_df.shape[0]*0.8)
Prophetdf_train,Prophetdf_test=Prophet_df[0:n_obs],Prophet_df[n_obs:]
print(Prophetdf_train.shape,Prophetdf_test.shape)
```

The provided code divides a DataFrame named 'Prophet_df' into two segments for training and testing a Prophet model for time series forecasting.

Output:

```
(158, 21) (40, 21)
```

We have 21 columns.

```
col_list =list( Prophet_df.columns)
col_list
```

Output:

```
['MaxTemperature(C)',
'MeanTeamperature(C)',
'MinTemperature(C)',
'total_precipitation(kg m-2 s-1)',
'ds',
'dollarIndex_close',
'PhospateRock($/mt)',
'Dap($/mt)',
'Tsp($/mt)',
'Urea($/mt)',
'PotassiumChloride($/mt) ',
'CPIAUCSL',
'GEPUCURRENT',
'employmentInAgriculture(LNS12034560)',
'ProductionPriceIndexIndustry(PCU811310811310)',
'ProductionPriceIndexIndustry(PCU325311325311)',
'GASDESW',
'y']
```

Only list feature columns.

```
remove_items = ['ds','y' ]
for i in remove_items:
  col_list.remove(i)
```

```
Prophet_cols = col_list
```

```
multi_model = Prophet(interval_width = 0.95)
```

Output:

```
<prophet.forecaster.Prophet at 0x7fa36aa78390>
```

Step 12: Prepare future DATAFRame: multivariate

This is a critical step. Add all feature variables as history to the time series.

```
future = multi_model.make_future_dataframe(periods = Prophetdf_test.shape[0],freq='Ms',
include_history=True)
future.tail(15)
```

```
for col in Prophet_cols:
   future[col]=Prophet_df[col]
```

```
forecastProphet=multi_model.predict(future)
```

```
forecastProphet[['ds', 'yhat', 'yhat_lower','yhat_upper']].tail()
```

Add columns to the Prophet DataFrame and observe the forecasted Prophet values.

	ds	yhat	yhat_lower	yhat_upper
193	2022-07-01	61.980807	8.081817	124.368821
194	2022-08-01	72.526936	9.943812	133.129646
195	2022-09-01	77.951483	18.773455	138.657477
196	2022-10-01	81.180094	21.987859	142.300221
197	2022-11-01	149.493710	88.690147	210.334879

```
fig1 = multi_model.plot(forecastProphet);
```

Output:

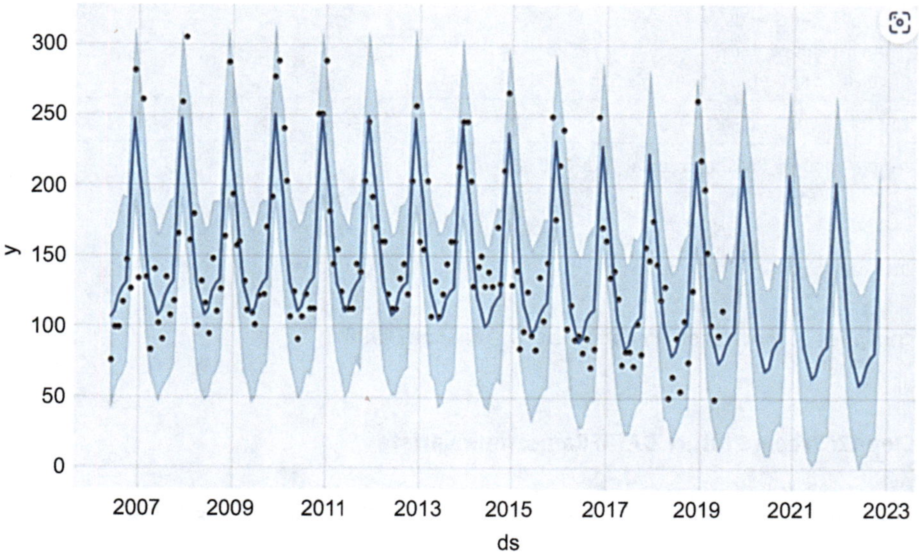

Step 13: Overall performance of prophet model

Combine all data and perform overall performance.

```
combined_prophet_df1 = pd.merge(Prophetdf_test1[['ds', 'y']],forecastProphet1[['ds', 'yhat',
'yhat_lower', 'yhat_upper']],on='ds')
combined_prophet_df1
```

```
from sklearn.metrics import mean_absolute_error,mean_absolute_percentage_error
#Check MAE value
MAE1 = mean_absolute_error(combined_prophet_df1['y'], combined_prophet_df1['yhat'])
print(f'The MAE for the baseline model is {MAE1}')
```

Output:

The MAE for the baseline model is 35.683

```
plt.rcParams.update({'figure.figsize': (15,3), 'figure.dpi': 300})
fig,ax = plt.subplots()

sns.lineplot(data=combined_prophet_df1, x = 'ds',y = 'y', label = 'Original')
sns.lineplot(data=combined_prophet_df1, x = 'ds',y = 'yhat', label = 'Forecast')
plt.grid(linestyle ='-',linewidth = 0.3)

plt.legend(["Original","forecast"])
```

Output:

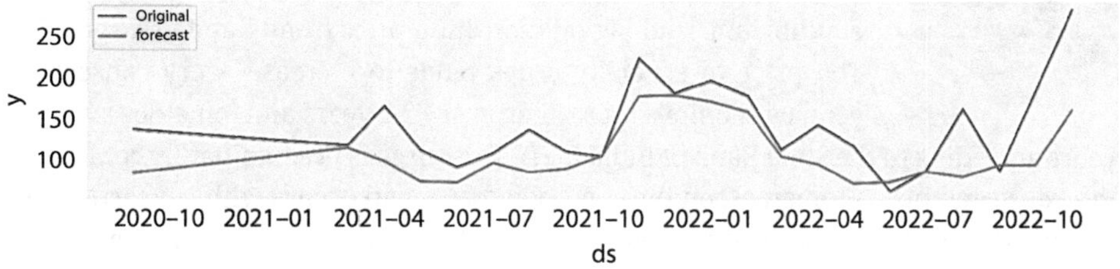

Include the entire dataset to calculate MAE.

```
combined_prophet_fulldf1= pd.merge(Prophet_df1[['ds', 'y']],forecastProphet1[['ds',
'yhat', 'yhat_lower', 'yhat_upper']],on='ds')
combined_prophet_fulldf1
```

```
#Check MAE value
MAE_fulldf1 =mean_absolute_error(Prophet_df1['y'],
combined_prophet_fulldf1['yhat'])
print(f'The MAE for the baseline model is {MAE_fulldf1}')
```

Output:
The MAE for the baseline model is 28.660. The model is off by $28.660.

```
fig, ax = plt.subplots()

sns.lineplot(data = Prophet_df1 , x = 'ds', y = 'y' ,label = 'Original')
sns.lineplot(data= combined_prophet_fulldf1, x = 'ds', y = 'yhat', label = 'Forecast')
plt.grid(linestyle = '-', linewidth = 0.3)

plt.legend(["Original","forecast"])
```

Output:

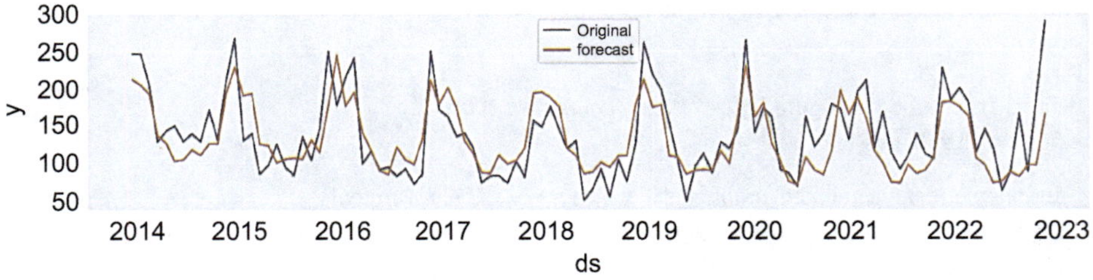

Crop price behavior

Specialty crops exhibit various price behaviors, including long-run equilibrium, lead-lag relationships, price trends, and price gouging. The price of specialty crops tends to increase every consecutive year, with onions increasing every 2.8 years and tomatoes every 2.4 years according to the State Bank of India (SBI). This surge is predominantly confined to the key vegetables – tomatoes, onions, and potatoes – and occurs with concerning frequency, leading to a significant concentration risk. Crises involving potatoes and onions tend to happen every other year. Onion prices might adhere to a cobweb model, which accounts for the erratic fluctuations in prices and quantities. However, potato prices do not appear to follow this model, suggesting the possibility of cartel behavior or deliberate cultivation choices made by vested interests in any given year [95] (Figure 24).

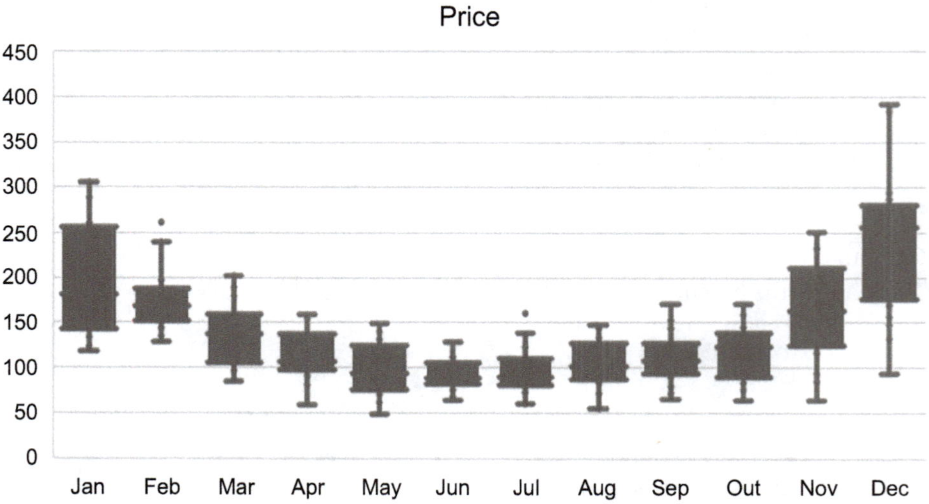

Figure 24: Onion prices.

Throughout the year, onion prices in India exhibit a cyclical pattern with two distinct peaks – one at the beginning and another at the end of the year. The mid-year period is marked by relative stability and lower prices. This pattern underscores the seasonal nature of onion cultivation and market supply, with potential influences from harvesting cycles, storage capabilities, and market demand. The significant price variations toward the year-end may reflect challenges in supply chain management, possible adverse weather conditions, or increased demand during festive seasons.

Cobweb model

The cobweb model is an economic theory that explains periodic fluctuations in certain markets, as observed in SBI's research on vegetable prices. This model describes cyclical supply and demand in a market where production must be chosen before prices are observed. Specialty crops, particularly those with a longer shelf life, may adhere to the cobweb model. This model posits that the supply for the current year is influenced by the prices from the previous year. When an external shock disturbs the market equilibrium, both prices and quantities tend to fluctuate with each annual production cycle.

Market and weather influenced vegetable and fruit price uncertainties

The prices of agricultural commodities greatly influence the decisions of farmers and ranchers. These prices affect the supply of agricultural products, which depends on factors like the acreage of planted and harvested crops or the inventory of livestock [95]. Unstable prices can jeopardize the financial stability and sustainability of small farmers, as these fluctuations introduce unnecessary risks. Several factors contribute to the instability of food prices, including rising energy costs, the demand for biofuels (indirectly), a weakening US dollar (USD), adverse weather conditions, and policy actions by major exporting and importing countries [95, 96].

Farmers bear the risks and costs of production without any assurance that the selling price will offset their expenses. While certain governments provide minimum support prices (MSP) for staple grain crops, numerous specialty crops are not included, rendering small farmers susceptible to the volatility of market prices. By examining market trends and offering predictive models, it becomes feasible to reduce market uncertainties and create a safeguard against price volatility. Identifying variables that help predict market trends is crucial to achieving this goal [107, 109, 110, 111, 112].

Over the observed period (January 2018 to November 2022), the graph (Figure 25; Table 2) illustrates the interplay between various economic factors and their impact on the prices of fruits and vegetables in US cities. The data highlights the effects of global economic uncertainty, the pandemic, rising oil prices, and increasing costs of agricultural inputs on consumer prices. The overall trend suggests a period of relative stability followed by significant volatility and inflationary pressures, culminating in higher consumer prices for fruits and vegetables by the end of 2022. This is especially true for

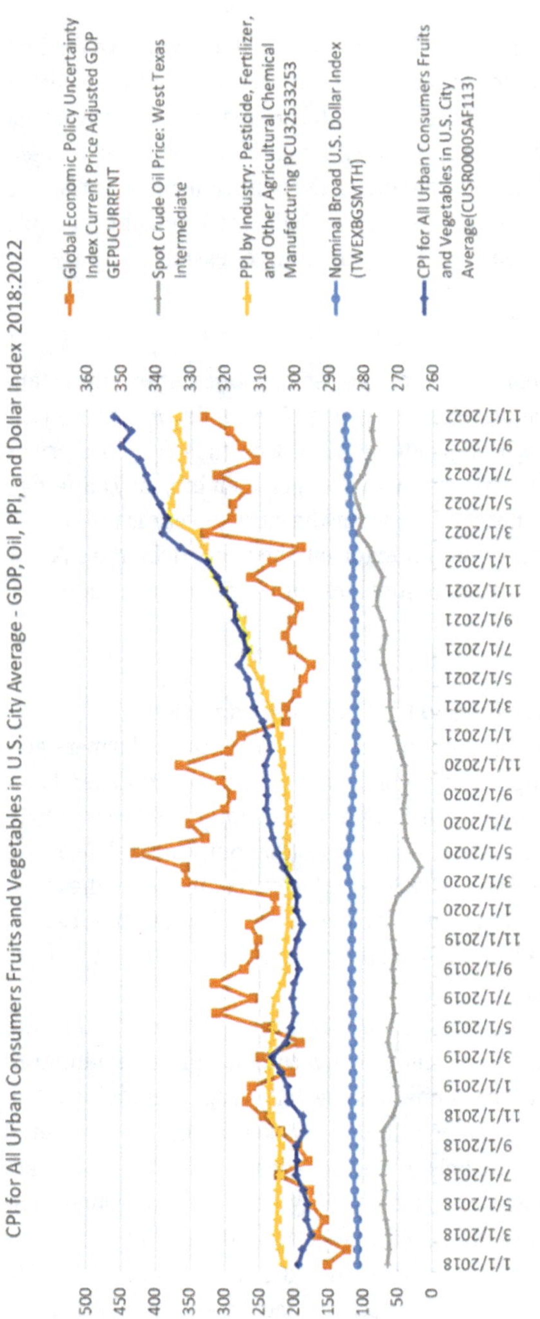

Figure 25: CPI.

economies that rely on agriculture. Adverse weather conditions, such as inconsistent rainfall and heatwaves, have resulted in a decline in the production of key crops like tomatoes and onions, driving higher prices. The cost of food items, which constitute roughly half of the CPI basket, has nearly tripled in the past month. This surge has had the most severe impact on low-income households [107].

Table 2: Food price indices.

	CPI for All Urban Consumers: Fruits and Vegetables in U.S. Average (CUSR000 0SAF113)	**Global Economic Policy Uncertainty Index Current Price Adjusted GDP (GEPUCUR-RENT)**	**Spot Crude Oil Price: West Texas Interme-diate**	**PPI by Industry: Pesticide, Fertilizer, and Other Agricultural Chemical Manufacturing (PCU3253)**	**Nominal Dollar Index (TWEXBGSMTH)**
CPI for All Urban Consumers: Fruits and Vegetables in U.S. Average (CUSR0000SAF113)	1	0.2433			
Global Economic Policy Uncertainty Index Current Price Adjusted GDP (GEPUCURRENT)	0.2433	1			
Spot Crude Oil Price: West Texas Intermediate	0.7198	-0.2799	1		
PPI by Industry: Pesticide, Fertilizer, and Other Agricultural Chemical Manufacturing (PCU3253)	0.9495	0.0937	0.8493	1	
Nominal Dollar Index (TWEXBGSMTH)	0.5845	0.7091	0.1149	0.4771	1

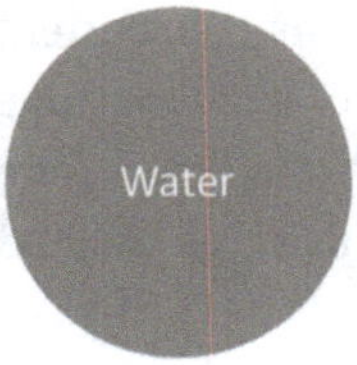

Water

Water is an essential component in agriculture, especially for specialty crops, and without it, nothing can happen [73, 96]. Climate change is anticipated to profoundly influence the water cycle, resulting in uneven effects across the globe [113, 114, 115]. For more information on the impact of water, climate, and agriculture, please refer to my other books.

Evapotranspiration: Watching over water use

Evapotranspiration is the process where water from plants, soil, and other surfaces is transferred into the air as water vapor through evaporation and transpiration. This process requires energy, making it a critical measurement for farmers to estimate the water usage of their fields and crops. Understanding how much water is transferred to the atmosphere enables farmers to more accurately determine crop water needs, facilitating efficient water use and improved irrigation planning. OpenET is a tool that offers satellite-based information on evapotranspiration by utilizing publicly available data from the Landsat program, a collaboration between NASA and the US Geological Survey. The latest satellite in the series, Landsat 9, was successfully launched on September 27, 2021, contributing over 700 daily images of Earth to the mission's archive (Figure 26). OpenET provides data at various scales, from millions of individual fields to custom reports with specified boundaries, time frames, and summarized data.

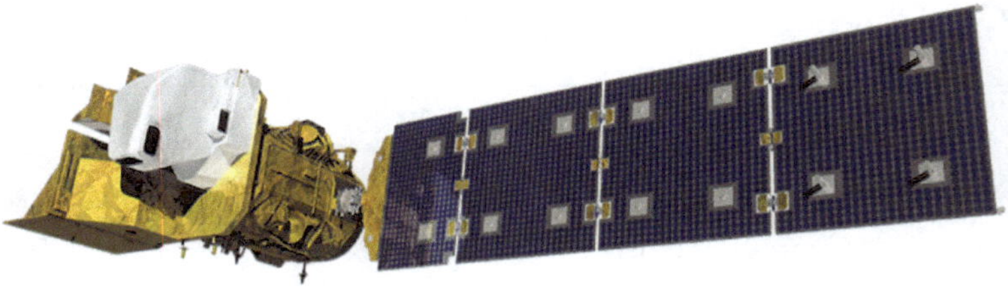

Figure 26: Satellite and OpenET.

View gridded data

The following data collected for Fresno, California.

Selected year	2017
Variable	**ET** or NDVI
Data	Cumulative ensemble evapotranspiration (mm)
Cities	Selected
Units	**mm/in**

The ensemble ET value is determined by averaging all models, excluding any outliers. Outliers are flagged and removed based on the median absolute deviation (MAD) approach, using a threshold of ±2* MAD.

Reference evapotranspiration (ET_0) is an estimate of the evaporation from a hypothetical reference grass surface grown under well-watered conditions. Reference ET can be calculated from data collected by a network of agricultural weather stations or from gridded weather data (Figure 27).

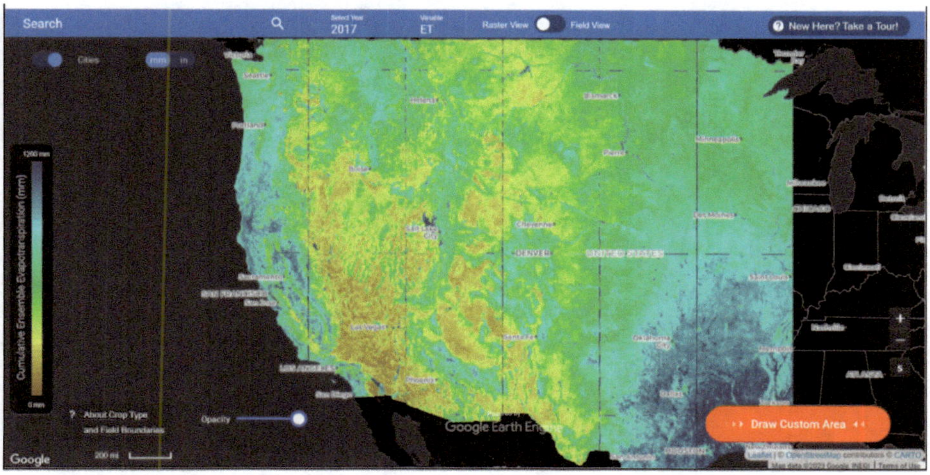

Figure 27: Evapotranspiration.

The Normalized Difference Vegetation Index (NDVI) is a satellite-based metric used to assess the density and health of vegetation. It is calculated by analyzing the visible and near-infrared light reflected by plants. Chlorophyll, the pigment in plant leaves, absorbs visible light for photosynthesis, whereas the cell structures in plants reflect near-infrared wavelengths.

Fresno California evapotranspiration data (Figure 28).

For Tulare County, California, please find evapotranspiration graph for 2017–2023. There is considerable difference between referenced ET_0 and ensemble ET, that is, more water needs to be applied to meet agricultural needs.

Market access and value chain

Specialty crops provide immediate earnings upon sale. Some of these crops, such as tree nuts (Figure 46), command high premiums, like pistachios and tree nuts. Economic exchange in agriculture can be achieved through various coordination mechanisms, including

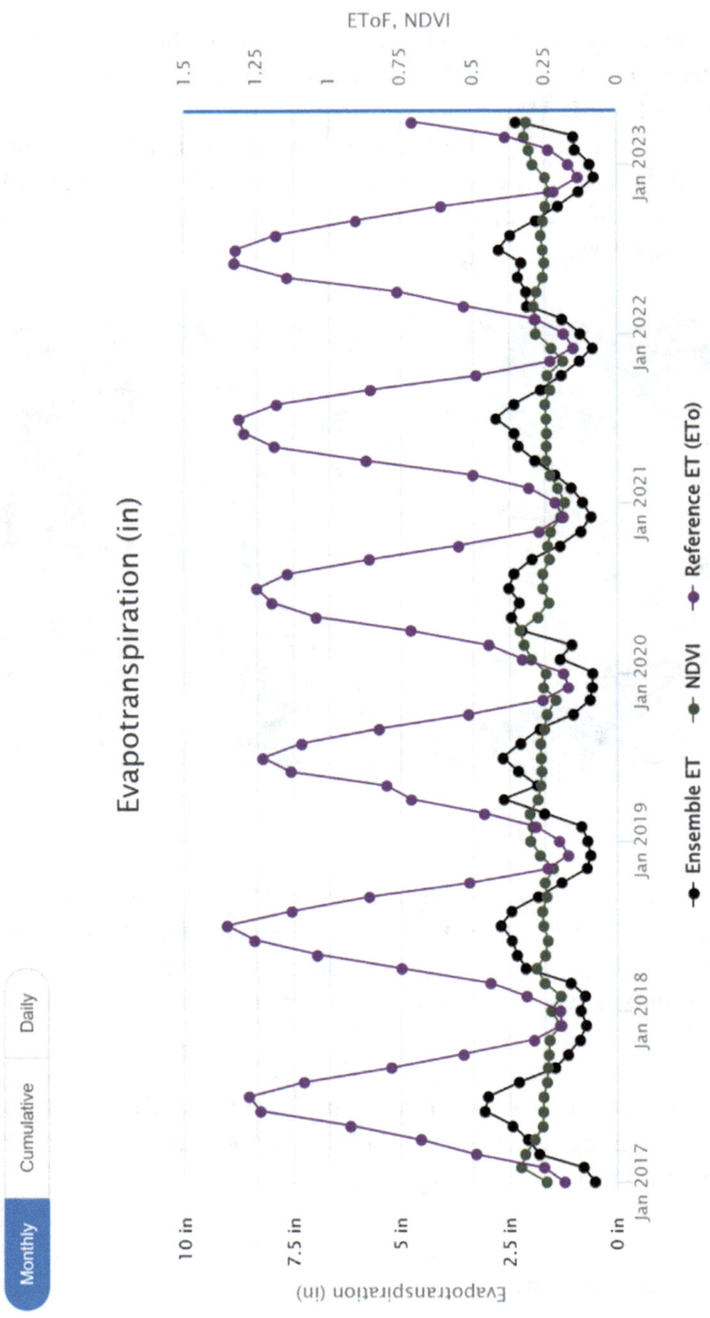

Figure 28: Evapotranspiration Fresno, California.

spot market and bilateral contract arrangements [94]. Farmers often participate in both to safeguard their expected benefits against market uncertainty, with bilateral market coordination typically providing higher benefits than spot market coordination. Bond or contract farming serves as an alternative marketing arrangement that protects farmers from risk while promoting innovation and the adoption of new technologies. While contract farming has many benefits, it often favors large and medium farmers with greater access to capital and technology adoption. However, organizing small and marginal farmers into collectives like Farmer Producer Organizations can overcome these impediments and enable their participation in contract farming [83].

Studies indicate that farmers engaging in both spot markets and bilateral contracts earn twice as much as those solely relying on spot markets, despite no significant yield differences among various farmer groups [119]. In Uganda, each dollar spent on labor generates \$1.1 under single market coordination and approximately \$1.5 under double market coordination. To promote bilateral contracts, it is essential to implement measures that allow farmers to participate in multiple markets while minimizing the risk of contract breaches.

Consider a profit-maximizing monopsonistic processor (Figure 29) that sources specialty crop production from a group of producers through production contracts. In Stage I, the processor offers contracts to producers, who then choose either to accept the contract or grow a commodity crop instead. In Stage II, producers who accept the contract adhere to specific management guidelines for cultivating the specialty crop. In Stage III, farmers harvest their crops, and each farmer's actual yield remains private information, while market and macroeconomic factors play a crucial role in managing market risks. In Stage IV, ex post spot market transactions may take place among producers, influenced by the type of contract offered and the yield outcomes. In Stage V, contracts are settled, and in Stage VI, the processor handles the processing and sells the output to a downstream user. Any surplus specialty crop contracted is sold at its salvage value on the commodity market.

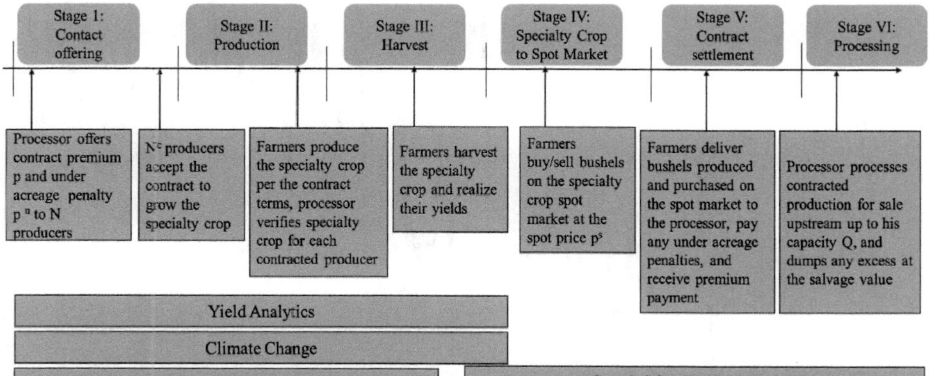

Figure 29: Agricultural contract processing.

Chapter ML experiments

Transportation costs

As shown in the following figure, a total of 2.5 billion pounds of strawberries have been shipped from California Central since January 2000. What impact would it have to include the cost of transportation on the price of strawberries?

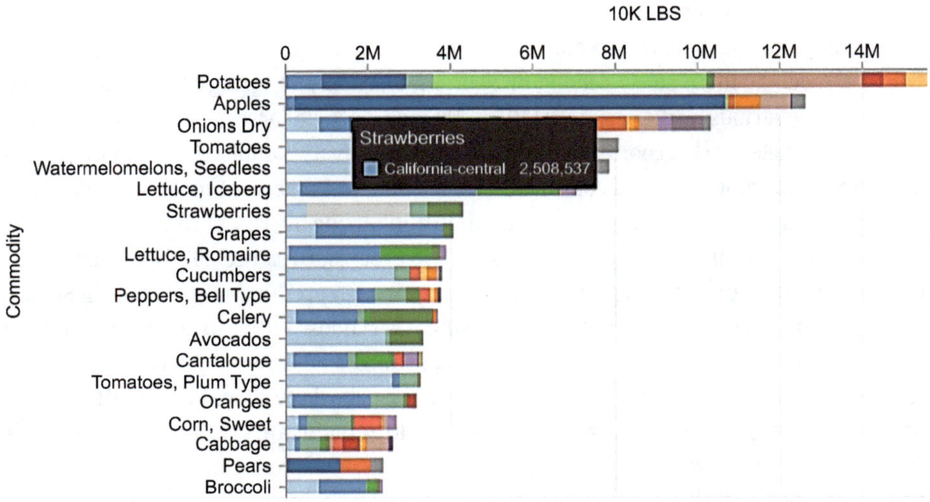

Transportation costs: recent weekly US average refrigerated truck rates.

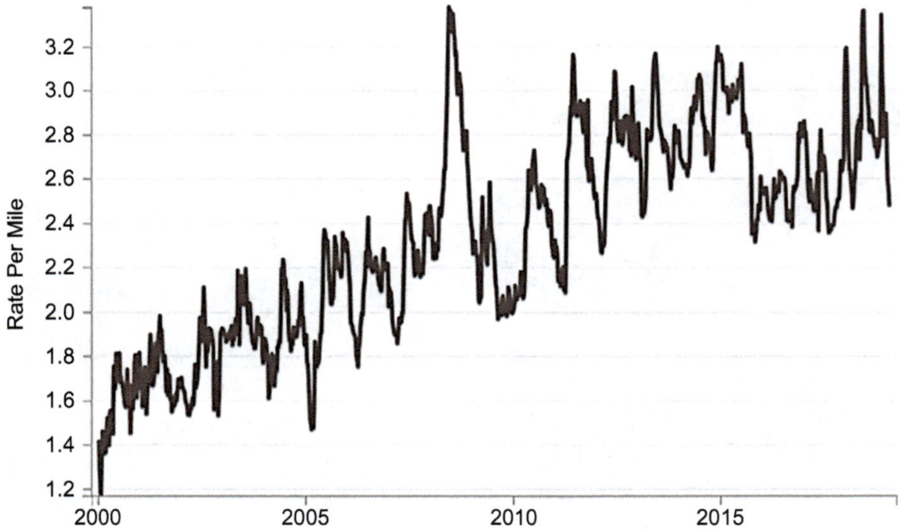

Strawberries' prices

To forecast New Hampshire strawberry prices for the upcoming five years (2025–2029), future data on independent time series variables is essential. The necessary information for these variables can be found in the book available from the Climate Change Knowledge Portal. Farmers' decision-making processes generally determine the area harvested, and assuming historical trends will continue, a future dataset for the area harvested for 2025–2029 can be prepared using a trend equation for the area harvested.

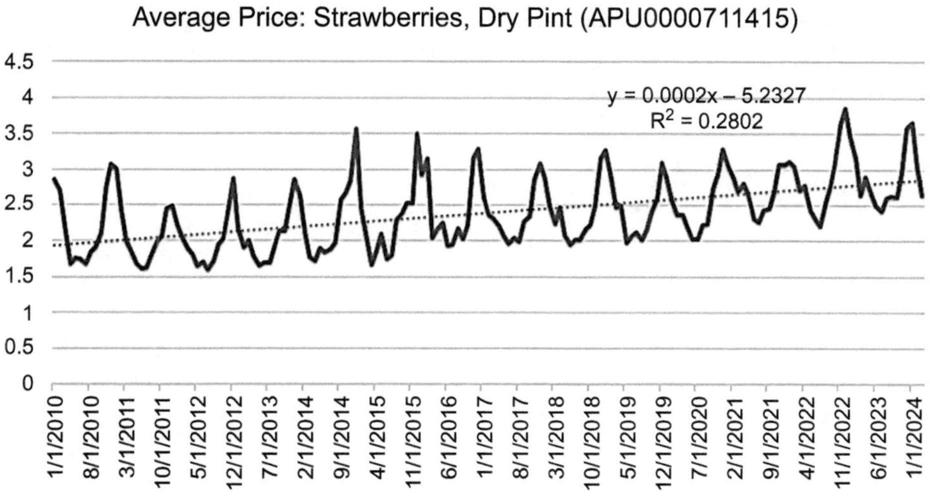

A) Linear

New Hampshire strawberry	Regression line	R^2
Exponential	$y = 7E{+}30e^{-0.006x}$	0.42
Linear	$y = -3091.1x + 9E{+}37$	0.59
Logarithmic	$y = -5E{+}09\ln(x) + 20E{+}90$	0.78
Polynomial order 6	$y = -0.3345x^6 + 9.34x^5 - 1303x^4 + 9E{+}8x^3 - 4E{+}13x^2 + 6E{+}12x - 5E{+}98$	0.993
Power	$y = 7E{+}98x^{-10.95}$	0.9001

$$y = -8906.1x + 8E{+}12$$

B) Exponential

$$y = 7E{+}10e{+}30e^{-0.006x}$$

Where X is the index of 2025 – 01/January {180}, 2025 – 02/February {181},2025 – 03/March {183}, and 2025 – 04/April {184}.

Upon completing this chapter, you would have gained a comprehensive understanding of specialty crops, including their USDA classification and cash receipts revenue modeling. Furthermore, you will have the ability to recognize the economic significance of specialty crops and the employment opportunities they provide. You will also have a thorough understanding of market value chain models and the pricing framework for specialty crops.

Lastly, you will have the ability to utilize ML models to develop a pricing model for specialty crops, such as the Maine and New Hampshire strawberries pricing model. This chapter will equip you with expertise and skills necessary to make educated determinations regarding specialty crops, their pricing, and their value chain.

Chapter 3
Climate change and adaptation strategies

This chapter covers:
- Climate change adaptation strategies
- Shared socioeconomic pathways
- The federal crop insurance program
- RMA crop insurance
- Adaptation strategies
- Sustainability analysis
- ML models
  - Financial sustainability ML models: crop insurance go/no-go decision based on field-grown tomatoes price forecast model

This chapter is important for anyone who wants to understand climate change and shared socioeconomic pathways and how they affect agriculture. It also explains different types of crop insurance programs, like federal crop insurance (FCIP), Risk Management Agency (RMA), and AgRisk Viewer.

The chapter includes an inventory of crop insurance models that helps stakeholders make informed decisions about their coverage options. It covers guarantees related to yield, revenue, and percent-of-damage. This model provides useful insights into the complexities of crop insurance.

Finally, the chapter introduces a financial sustainability machine learning (ML) crop insurance go/no-go decision model for a field-grown tomatoes price forecast model. This model uses advanced ML techniques to predict the price of field-grown tomatoes accurately. This can help stakeholders make informed decisions about crop insurance coverage and ensure the financial sustainability of their agricultural operations.

Climate change

Climate change and variability are causing changes in the seasons and more frequent and severe natural disasters like floods, heat waves, and droughts [121]. These events are having devastating effects on various industries such as insurance, retail, healthcare, citizen services, governance, public services, and infrastructure. Asia's agriculture has been severely impacted by climate shifts, with over $49 billion in damage to crops and livestock since 2010, the highest among all regions [122]. The sector faces recurrent heatwaves, inconsistent rainfall, flooding, and other severe climate events. These events threaten the sustainability of various industries and the livelihoods of billions of people.

Extreme weather events have led to annual yield losses of around 40 million hectares in China since 2000, and a flash flood in Bangladesh in May 2022 caused $6 million in crop losses, impacting 24,000 farmers. Asia's agriculture sector, which supports over 350 million small farmers, is significantly suffering from these climate-related challenges [122].

India, the second-largest tomato producer globally [122], has seen a 300% surge in tomato prices due to climate change-induced crop failures. The staggering cost of tomatoes has led to an increase in theft, creating public security concerns. Tomato growers have experienced significant thefts, with reports of thieves stealing boxes of tomatoes weighing up to 150 kg (330 pounds). Authorities have cautioned all vegetable vendors to exercise vigilance and caution due to the incidents. The sustainability of small farmers is at risk as the burden of high loans and crop failures push many to the brink of poverty [124].

Public safety and small farmer sustainability!

Climate change-induced crop failures in India in 2023 have caused an unprecedented demand for tomatoes, resulting in exorbitant prices. This has been a significant burden on small farmers who are already struggling with high-interest loans. The vicious cycle of produce theft and crop failure has pushed many small farmers below the poverty line, creating a significant imbalance in society [124, 125].

The climate crisis poses a significant threat to the US economy and human welfare, and we have a limited window of opportunity to invest in measures that can help us avoid the worst effects [126]. Climate change can make extreme weather events worse, which can disrupt supply chains and cause damage to infrastructure due to elevated ocean levels and flooding. The impact on businesses and communities is widespread, causing significant costs, lost revenue, and escalating expenses due to the impact of a changing climate. Over the past five years, estimated damages from climate-related weather events have grown to about $120 billion annually, affecting vulnerable inhabitants.

The climate crisis poses a major threat to the federal budget, as economic damage from climate change continues to escalate. This includes increased costs for infrastructure repairs, healthcare, and destabilized insurance programs, alongside global security concerns. Immediate action is essential to mitigate the severe impacts on vulnerable populations and the broader economy [126].

The effect of climate change is causing two of California's largest insurance providers, State Farm General Insurance Co & All State, to no longer sell new residential insurance policies. The elevated wildfire risk and construction costs due to climate change have led to State Farm's decision in May 2023 to stop accepting new applications for property and casualty coverage in California. Mortgage lenders typically require proof of insurance before approving transactions to protect their investment in the property. Without insurance, buyers would be forced to make all-cash purchases, limiting growth in the housing industry [127].

Climate change has led to soaring temperatures in Texas, causing both days and nights to become hotter and setting new record highs. This upward shift in the entire spectrum of Texas heat disproportionately affects work environments and frontline workers [128]. As tens of millions in the USA face extreme weather conditions, much of the western US is enduring the first major heat wave of the year, with temperatures soaring 20–30 °F above the June average. In the Southwest, temperatures persistently exceed 100 degrees.

In Southeast Asia, temperatures generally rise in April and May before monsoon rains bring relief. However, in 2023, they reached unprecedented levels. The impact of climate change has far-reaching consequences on various industries and communities, with urgent action needed to mitigate its effects [127].

In the past year, we have seen record-breaking temperatures on land and in the oceans, along with a relentless series of heat waves, droughts, floods, wildfires, and storms. These extreme events highlight the severe impact of carbon dioxide pollution on our climate system. Urgent action is needed to rapidly reduce fossil fuel use to mitigate further damage.

The graph shows the monthly average concentration of CO_2 in parts per million (ppm) recorded at the Mauna Loa Observatory in Hawaii from 1960 to May 2024. The CO_2 levels have consistently increased over time, starting at around 315 ppm in 1960 and reaching approximately 426.9 ppm in May 2024. The graph also displays a seasonal fluctuation pattern, with CO_2 levels peaking and dipping each year but following an overall upward trend.

Climate change's impact on agricultural production in low-resource regions can diminish land productivity, increase pest attacks, crop returns, and the output of forests and specialty crops. This situation results in lower incomes, decreased climate-resilience, and reduced availability to nutrient-rich foods, ultimately harming the nutritional status and food security of marginalized population. For instance, Michigan State University Extension noted that drought conditions in 2018 and 2022 reduced blueberry yields by up to 40%. This issue is not confined to Michigan, as the Pacific Northwest also faces yield losses due to heat domes and early spring weather impacts [129].

The combination of climate change and the periodic El Niño phenomenon [130], which occurs every 2–7 years, can have a compounded effect, leading to reduced agricultural yields. In India [131], for instance, reduced precipitation during El Niño times has triggered extreme droughts, devastated crops and pressing authorities to restrain grain exports, according to the IMD[1]. Globally, farmers, pastoralists, forest-dependent communities, and fisherfolk are confronted with significant challenges in building resilience to environment adjustment [121]. Coping mechanisms that increase resilience to El Niño and climate change will be crucial for regions affected by this phenomenon [132].

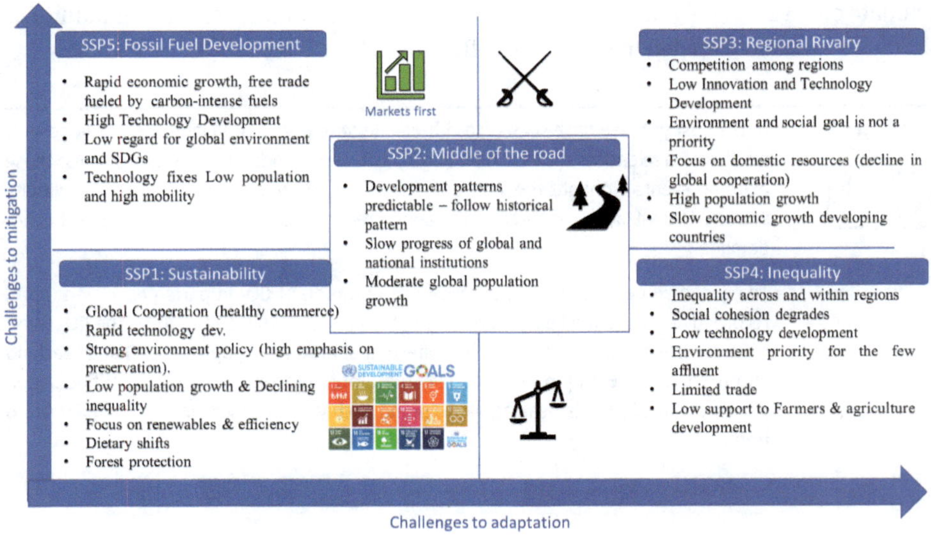

Figure 1: SSPs.

Shared socioeconomic pathways (SSPs; see Figure 1 and Table 1) offer different scenarios for how society may evolve in the coming decades [133, 134, 135, 136].

There are five different scenarios that describe possible futures based on how we deal with sustainability and development. Please refer to other author's books on it.

- SSP1 is about being sustainable, which means taking care of the Earth and using its resources in a way that doesn't harm it [134, 135].
- SSP5 is about focusing on money and using resources like oil and gas to generate more profit [136].
- SSP3 is about countries competing with each other for resources, which means things that we need to live [137, 138].
- SSP4 is about some people having more money and possessions than others.
- Finally, SSP2 is in the middle; it wants to use technology but doesn't want to go too fast.

1 Indian Metrological Department: https://mausam.imd.gov.in/

Projection models

There are different ways that people think the Earth might get hotter in the future [133].

Table 1: Projection models.

Socioeconomic factors impact & projection models
One way, called SSP 1-2.6, imagines that we will try to be more careful with the earth and not hurt it as much. But even if we do that, the earth might still get a little bit hotter, about 1.8 degrees Celsius by the end of the century.
Another way, called SSP 2-4.5, imagines that we will keep doing things the way we have been doing them. We won't try very hard to be careful with the earth. If we do that, the earth might get hotter, about 2.7 degrees Celsius by the end of the century.
Another way, called SSP 3-7.0, imagines that we won't be very good at being careful with the earth. We won't use technology to help us as much, and we won't care as much about the environment. If we do that, the earth might get a lot hotter, about 3.6 degrees Celsius by the end of the century.
The last way, called SSP 5-8.5, imagines that we will keep using things like oil and gas to make money, and we won't care about the environment at all. If we do that, the earth might get really, really hot, about 4.4 degrees Celsius by the end of the century.

Crop indemnity maps – 2022 RMA crops' indemnities

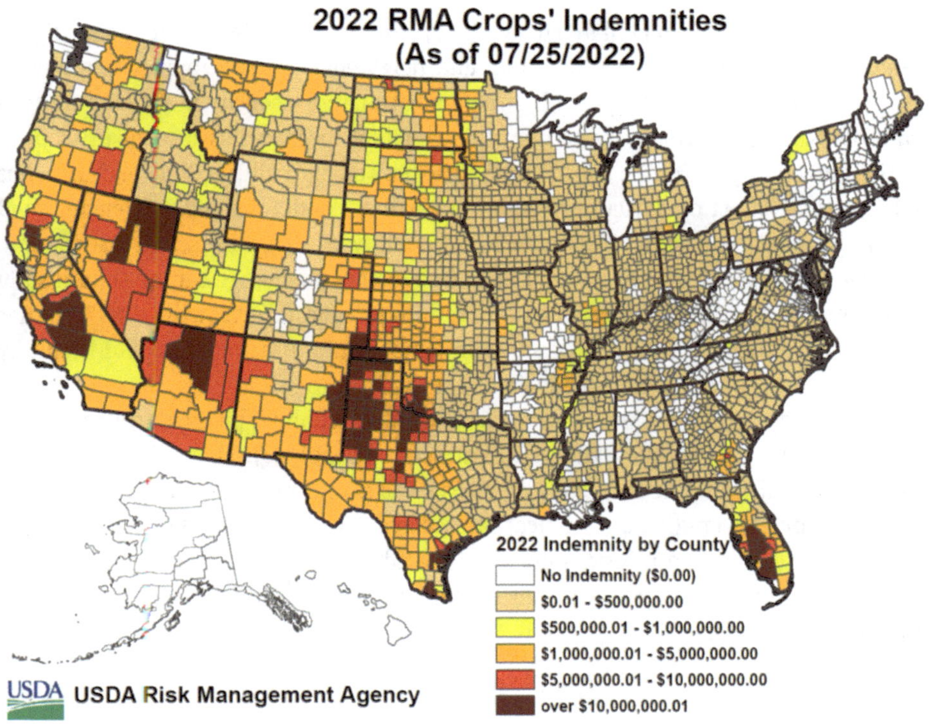

Figure 2: 2022 RMA crops' indemnities.

The risk to both the US economy and the federal budget is evident across various exposure points. However, the process of quantifying the total potential risk for American taxpayers and Federal programs is still in its early stages. A 2016 preliminary report by OMB/CEA [139] estimated that climate change impacts could increase annual federal expenditures by $34–$112 billion by later this century, as depicted in Figure 2. This report also highlights the significant potential for economic and federal revenue losses. It emphasizes that the available evidence indicates that the economic hazards to the National Government could be substantial throughout this century unless we take significant steps to diminish greenhouse gas emissions and adjust our societies to a varying climate [139, 140].

Climate change is causing more erratic weather patterns in the US, with once-rare rainstorms now occurring frequently, heat waves becoming hotter and longer, and hurricanes gaining strength. These significant weather events happen more often and with greater intensity, presenting a complex challenge.

Adaptation strategies

The connection between climate change [141] and farming is interdependent. Higher temperatures, diminished precipitation, and heightened rainfall unevenness have a consequential impact on crop yield, threatening nutrition security in developing agricultural economies. This is particularly detrimental to countries located in tropical Africa and other parts of the world that rely heavily on agriculture. Climate change has a biophysical effect on agriculture, altering weather conditions and influencing food and nutritional security by affecting food availability, quality, access, and distribution. The consequences of decreased crop yield due to climate change can be significantly reduced with appropriate investment to restrain temperature growth to 1.5 °C rather than 2 °C. By 2050, unprecedented shifts in temperature, precipitation, and humidity are projected to increase worldwide food costs by 3–84%.

Monocropping is highly susceptible to climate change, particularly in Africa, with summer warming being the most significant threat [142]. Farmers need to adopt diverse agricultural practices, have no barriers to accessing diverse-markets, institutional and private credit, data science, and receive government support for education and climate adaptation information. Effective adaptation strategies should focus on agricultural sustainability and farmer livelihoods, necessitating training and motivational support [143].

Investing in data science, applying data analytics to specialty crops, and developing localized classifier models tailored to specific regions and market segments are crucial advancements needed to combat yield declines caused by climate change.

The book utilizes several models to examine the impact of climate change on agriculture. By leveraging historical data, it creates yield and pricing models to identify data signals and causative factors. Climate models are then applied to assess agricultural impacts under different climate scenarios. Ultimately, pricing and economic models are employed to recommend the most cost-effective climate strategies [144].

Farmers globally recognize the significant impact of climate change on their agricultural practices, which is crucial for developing future adaptation and mitigation strategies. They have observed changes such as altered rainy seasons, increased extreme weather events, and hotter winters, leading to lower crop productivity and depleted water resources. Additionally, there has been a rise in weeds, pests, and diseases, alongside higher cultivation costs. These factors contribute to shorter crop seasons and overall challenges in farming sustainability [144].

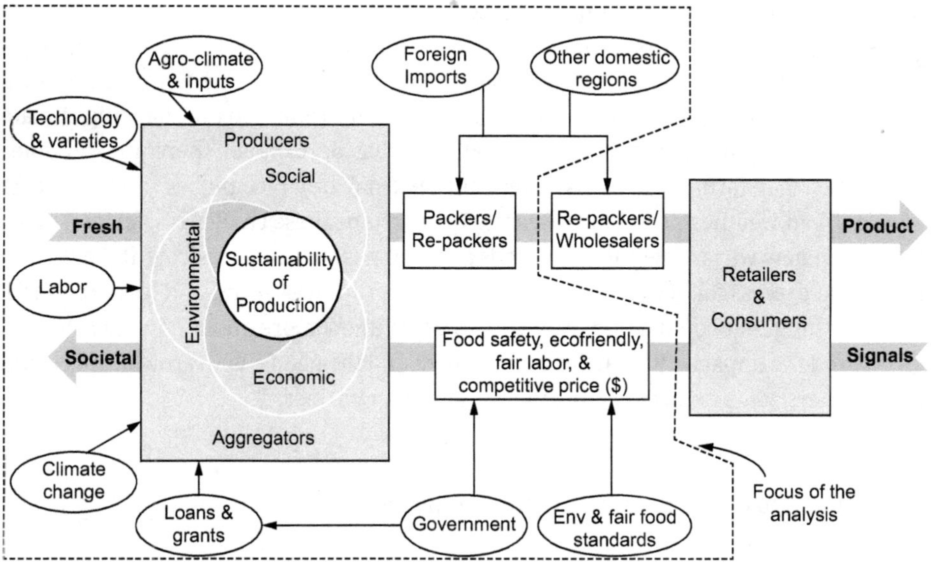

Figure 3: Sustainability analysis [144].

To assess the bearing of extreme weather events on agricultural output, farmers' perceptions were quantified using 18 selected parameters, including areas under harvest, yield, and production, changes in duration, productivity of crops, shape and size of individual crop characteristics, incidence of weeds, pests, diseases, water table, duration of water availability, cost of water supply, labor cost, cost of cultivation, productivity of other crops, soil salinity, forced migration, inflation, and urbanization. Farmers' responses were recorded to determine changes in the parameters over the last 10 years [144].

The sustainability analysis (Figure 3) graph highlights the interconnectedness of factors and stakeholders in achieving sustainable agricultural production. It ensures that consumers receive safe, eco-friendly, and fairly produced food products. Sustainability in agriculture encompasses social, environmental, and economic dimensions, with producers and aggregators playing a central role. Factors like agro-climate inputs, technology, varieties, labor, societal factors, and climate change influence sustainability. Government loans and grants further support these efforts. Post-production, goods are processed by packers/re-packers and wholesalers, sourced from domestic regions and foreign imports. These entities ensure food safety, eco-friendliness, fair labor practices, and competitive pricing by adhering to standards. The entire supply chain, from production to consumption, is analyzed to ensure its sustainability and efficiency. Farmers can adopt various adaptation measures to address changing conditions, such as crop insurance, adjusting sowing times and crop sequences, diversifying crops, and implementing integrated farming systems. They can also practice mixed cropping, select water-efficient varieties, switch crops, construct new bore wells, and use water-saving technologies. Water conservation, rainwater harvesting, and integrated pest and disease management are additional strategies.

Specialty crop farmers in the USA are facing a lot of challenges. These challenges include climate change, competition from other countries, and the rising cost of producing crops. To keep their farms going, farmers need to adapt to the changing climate and the evolving preferences for how food is produced. However, there are still other challenges that farmers face, like competition from other countries, a shortage of workers, bad weather, pests, and diseases. To overcome these challenges, farmers need to develop new ways of selling their crops and find new products to grow. It would also help if the process for getting certified to sell their crops was easier and less expensive. Another thing that could help farmers is if people knew more about how their food is grown and the impact it has on the environment and the people who grow it. This could help farmers compete better with others and stay in business.

The cost and coverage of crop insurance in the USA

The RMA as part of the USDA facilitates farmers and ranchers financially in case something bad happens to their crops, like bad weather or low prices [145]. The program is called "federal crop insurance," and it works like this: First, farmers or producers buy insurance to cover their crops (Figure 4). The insurance can be based on how much their crop produces or how much money they make from selling it. Next, private insurance companies help manage the insurance policies. They work with the farmers to make sure everything is covered, and they pay out money if the crops are lost. Finally, FCIC (operated by RMA) helps oversee programs and make sure everything is fair. The government helps pay for some of the insurance premiums, which makes it easier for farmers to participate in the program. The amount of help the government gives can change depending on different factors, like how much coverage the farmers want and how much they pay in premiums. In essence, Figure 4 illustrates the flow of premiums and indemnities within the crop insurance system, highlighting the roles of farmers, private insurance companies, and the FCIC in maintaining agricultural financial stability.

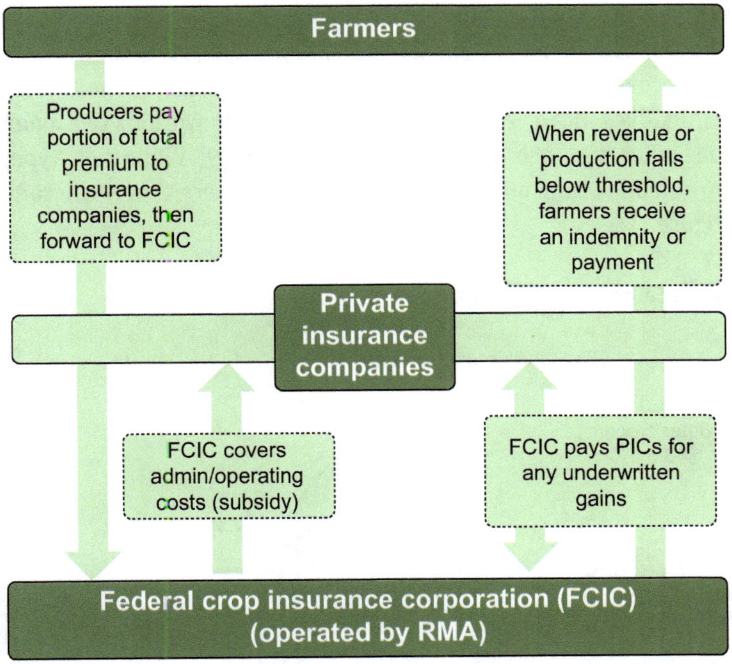

Figure 4: Flow of premiums and indemnities [145, 146].

For the crop year 2022, the FCIP covers over 480 million acres with a total liability exceeding $193 billion. The program offers written agreements, manually underwritten policies that provide improved coverage or terms not available in the county. This process, covering over $1.2 billion annually, identifies changing farming practices and growing crops in new areas, ensuring the program's adaptability and effectiveness [147].

The US government has spent a lot of money, around $120 billion in the last 10 years, to help farmers manage risk in agriculture. This includes things like crop insurance [148]. The most commonly insured crops are maize, soybeans, and wheat because they make up a big portion of the money farmers make and account for a lot of the land that is insured. These crops contributed over half of the money made by US agriculture in 2021. By law, crop insurance premiums have to be "actuarially fair," which means they should match the expected losses on insured land. However, the government pays for almost two-thirds of the premiums, which cost over $6.15 billion in 2020 [149].

Federal crop insurance: supporting traditional and specialty crops

The FCIP is an encompassing insurance program that helps farmers protect themselves against bad weather or low prices. The government pays for part of the cost of the insurance, which has cost over $66 billion between 2010 and 2020.

The program mostly covers traditional long crops, which are assisted by the government's earnings aid initiatives. However, the government has been working to expand the program to include other types of crops, like specialty crops [149]. While these types of crops still make up a small portion of the policies bought by farmers, they are becoming more popular (Figure 5).

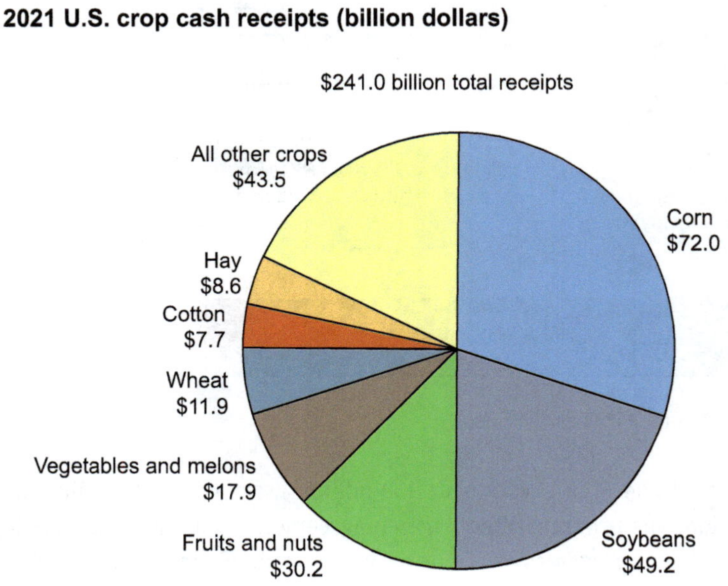

Figure 5: Crop cash receipts.

The cost of inaction is significantly more severe than the cost of taking appropriate measures. Furthermore, the financial burden of climate impacts in a scenario with no adaptation is much more pronounced than when taking green and resilient climate adaptation steps. These insights are derived from recent research conducted by climate scientists.

The FCIP covers around 38 specialty crop categories, with insured liabilities growing from nearly $1 billion in 1989 to almost $18.5 billion in 2017. In 2017, the program insured approximately 9 million acres of specialty crops, 800,000 bee colonies, 100,000 tons of raisins, and 600,000 fruit and coffee trees, with the Whole Farm Revenue Protection (WFRP) policy addressing gaps for uninsured crops. The FCIP for specialty crops and WFRP accounted for about 17% of the total portfolio by liability in the 2017 crop year, with an average premium subsidy rate of about 70% for WFRP.

	FCIC Insured Acres	Percent Eligible Acres Insured	Liability ($)
Total	**8,134,316**	**76%**	**14,770,562,149**

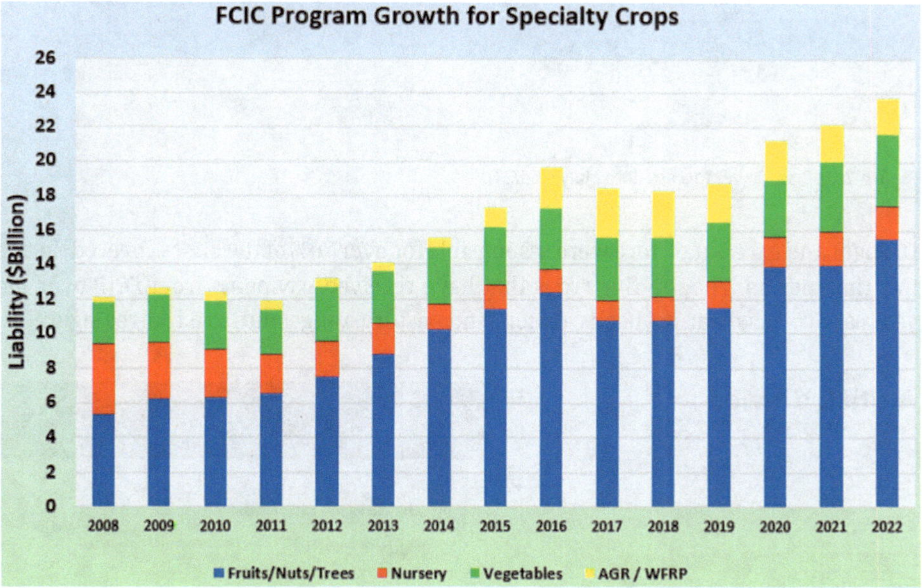

Figure 6: FCIC program growth.

The *costs of premiums for FCIP can help us understand how much it costs for farmers to adapt to climate extremities.* The FCIP is a program that helps farmers manage risk and get paid if they experience losses due to things like drought, bad weather, or price changes [150]. The program has been around since the 1930s and is an important way the government supports agriculture in the USA. It offers financial protection to farmers against things that are influenced by climate change, like extreme weather events, disease, and price fluctuations (Figure 6).

The FCIP covers many different types of risks that farmers face, including things like adverse weather conditions, earthquakes, fires, insects, and plant diseases. Since

2000, the program has covered an average of 284 million acres annually and has supported 133 different types of agricultural commodities [151].

Climate extremities caused major FCIP losses from 2001 to 2016.

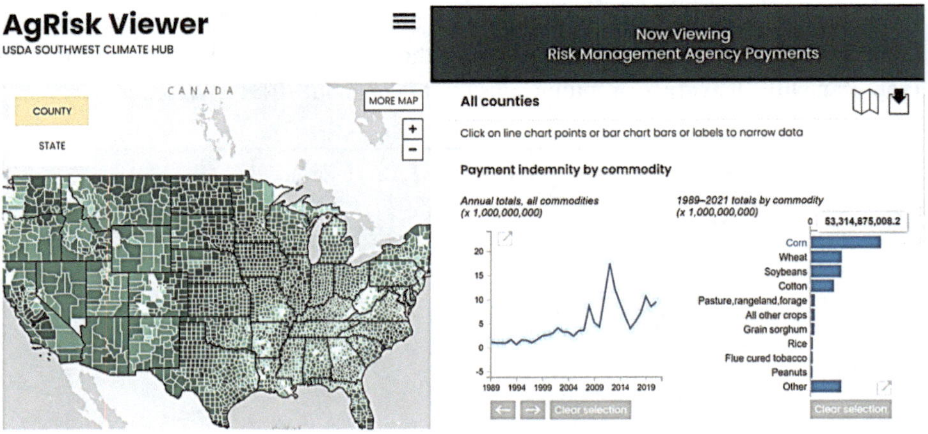

Figure 7: AgRisk Viewer (access date : July 5, 2023).

Drought and excess moisture were responsible for over 70% of the losses covered during this time period. The top five crops that have received payments from FCIP over the years are corn, wheat, soybeans, cotton, and pasture, rangeland, and forage (Figure 7).

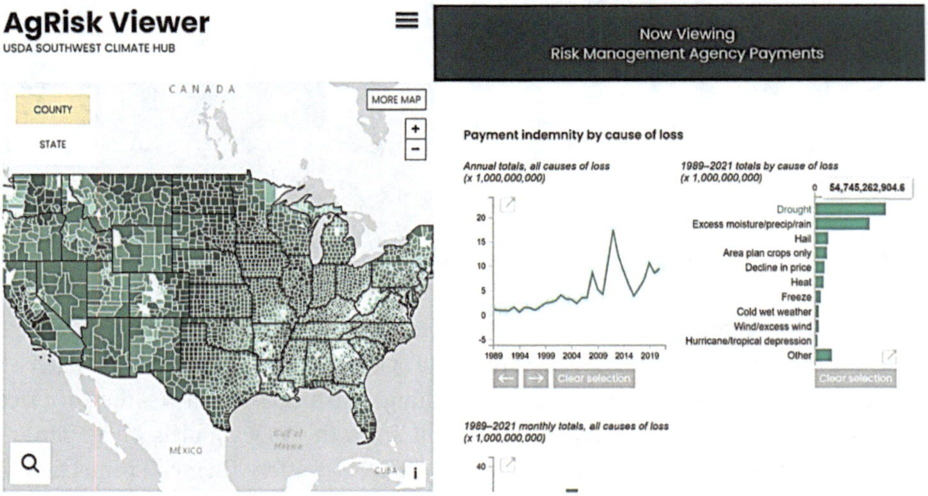

Figure 8: RMA.

Drought ($54.745 billion), excessive moisture/precipitation/rain ($42.293 billion), and hail ($10.725 billion) events caused most of payments from 1989 to 2021 (Figure 8). These three causes of losses accounted for more than 78% of payments nationally (Figure 9) [145].

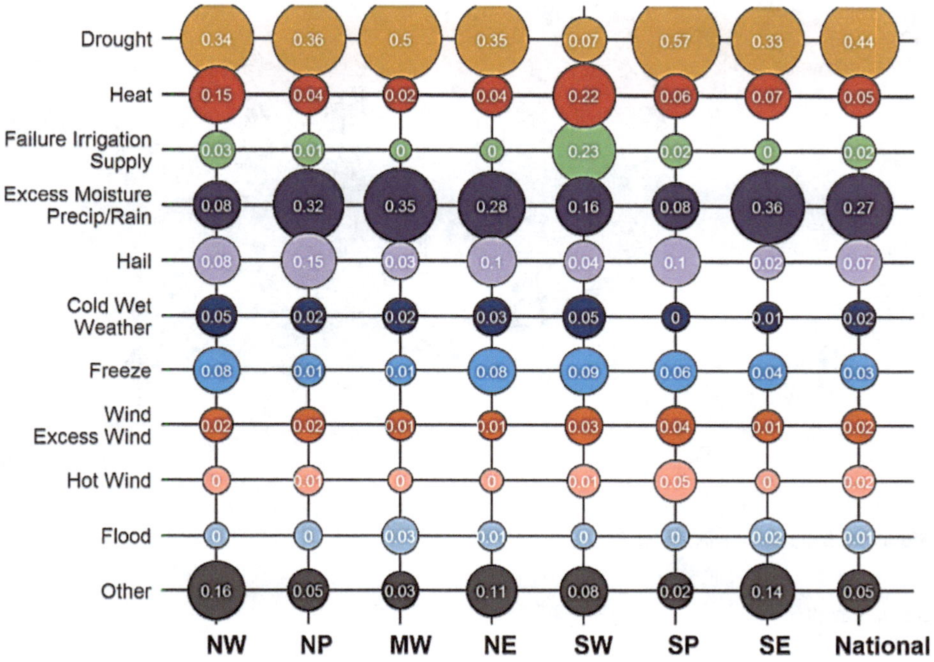

Figure 9: Indemnities : 2001–2016 [145].

In Figure 9, larger bubbles indicate a greater contribution of a reported payment out of all payments made, while bubbles at zero represent contributions of less than 1%. The US regions are categorized as northwestern (NW), northern-plains (NP), middle west (MW), northeastern (NE), southwestern (SW), southern-plains (SP), and south-eastern (SE). To see which states are included in each region, you can refer to supplementary Figure 9 (Figure 10).

Crop insurance performance is often judged by loss ratios. A loss ratio is simply calculated as indemnity payments divided by total premium (eq. (1)). A loss ratio of 1.0 means that indemnity payments equaled total premiums. A loss ratio greater than 1.0 means indemnity payments exceed premiums and a loss ratio less than 1.0 means total premiums exceed indemnity payments [152].

$$\text{Loss Ratio} = \frac{\text{indemnity payment}}{\text{total premium}} \tag{1}$$

The law states that the premium (the amount of money paid for insurance) should be enough to pay for expected losses and have some extra money saved up just in case. This is called a "reasonable reserve" [152, 153].

Figure 10: Spatial unit analysis [151].

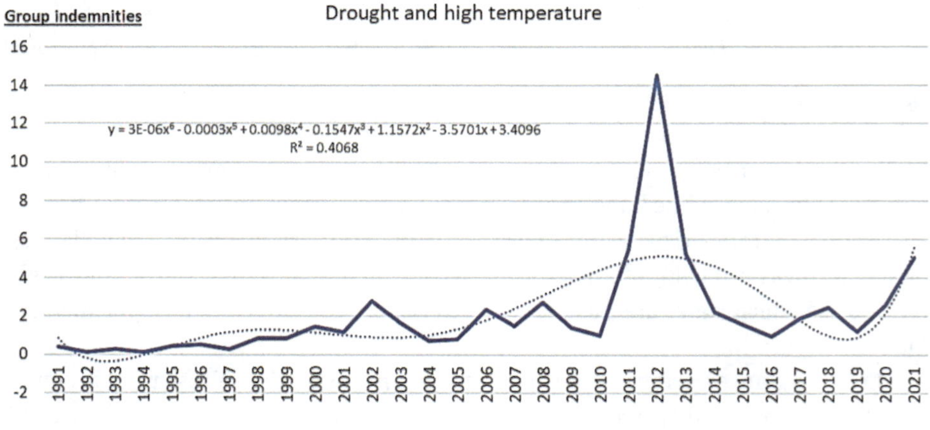

Figure 11: Drought and high temperature.

There are many factors that can affect how much money the FCIP pays out for losses. Some of these factors include changes in the number of farmers who want to buy insurance, the frequency of often extreme weather events occur, and the value of different crops. Since 2000, the amount of money paid out by FCIP has been increasing by an average of 15.8% per year. Even though the amount can vary yearly due to weather conditions, drought and high temperatures have consistently been among the main reasons why losses are covered by the program. In fact, 42.1% of all indemnity payments made since 2000 were for losses caused by drought or high temperatures (Figure 11). Excess moisture, like too much rain or humidity, is also a common cause of large indemnity payments. Since 2000, 27.5% of all indemnity payments made were for losses caused by excess moisture (Figure 12).

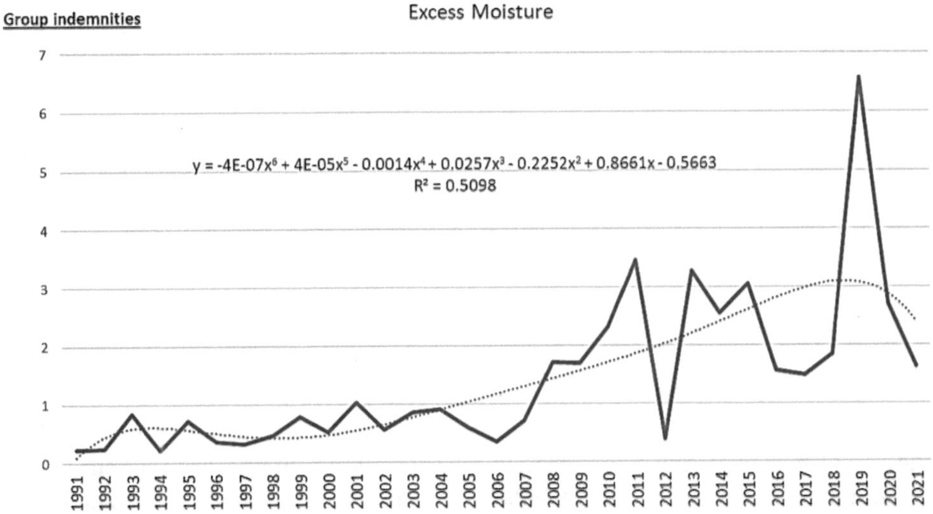

Figure 12: Excess moisture.

The amount of crop losses covered by the FCIP[2] has fluctuated over time, with the highest losses happening in 2012, 2008, and 2002 due to widespread drought. Wine grapes in the Pacific region have been hit particularly hard by factors like frost, freezes, and hot or wet weather. You can find data on crop losses on websites like USDA Crop Insurance at a Glance and AgRiskViewer (Figure 12) [154]. Overall, the FCIP program has been performing better in recent years, with an average of 80% of total premiums being paid out in indemnities since 1997. This means that the program is better able to cover losses without losing money [145, 151].

However, the cost of running the FCIP program has been going up, especially due to the subsidies provided to farmers to help them pay for insurance. In 2020, these subsidies totaled $3.11 billion, making up the largest portion of the program's cost. The cost (Figure 13) of the program due to subsidies has been increasing in a polynomial trend with order 6, which is a mathematical way of saying that it has been going up a lot (R^2 = 0.9628) (eq. (2)).

2 FCIP Indemnities by cause: https://www.ers.usda.gov/media/htyauvqe/fcip_indemnities_by_cause_of_loss.xlsx

$$Y_{\text{fcip program cost – premium subsidies}} = 3E{-}08x^6 - 0.0004x^5 + 1.8743x^4 - 4995.6x^3 + 7E{+}06x^2 - 6E{+}09x + 2E{+}12 \quad (2)$$

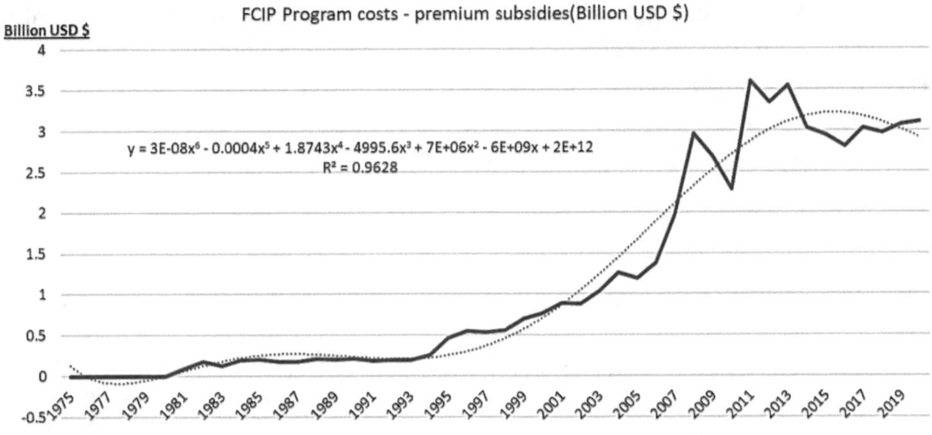

Figure 13: FCIP program costs.

In addition, FCIP works with commercial assurance providers, called "approved insurance providers" (AIPs), to provide insurance to farmers. These companies get paid by the government to provide this service. In 2020, the cost of running the program, including administrative costs, was $1.68 billion. An additional $1.36 billion was paid to the AIPs as a profit for participating in the program. You can find more information on these costs in Figure 14, which is part of the FCIP program data provided by the USDA (Figure 14). This public–private partnership structure, which is defined by the standard reinsurance agreement, can lead to additional costs for the program [155, 156].

$$Y_{\text{fcip program cost}} = 7E{-}07x^6 - 0.0001x^5 + 0.0066x^4 - 0.1221x^3 + 0.9954x^2 - 2.7704x + 3.9108 \quad (3)$$

Over the past decade (2011–2020), the FCIP has averaged annual payouts of $6.06 billion, exceeding the previous decade's average of $3.76 billion. This rise is partly due to climate change, which is expected to heighten program costs by increasing the variability in crop yields and values [148]. When there are more adverse weather events, like droughts, the FCIP has to pay out more in insurance claims than it receives in premiums. Premiums are adjusted based on recent payout histories, so if there are more losses due to climate change, premiums will increase as well.

As climate change causes more variability in crop yields and prices, the Federal Government's financial risk from the FCIP could also increase. There may be more frequent losses, which would raise the cost of payouts and require higher premiums and subsidies. You can see more information on this in Figure 15 and eq. (3), which are part of the FCIP program data [148].

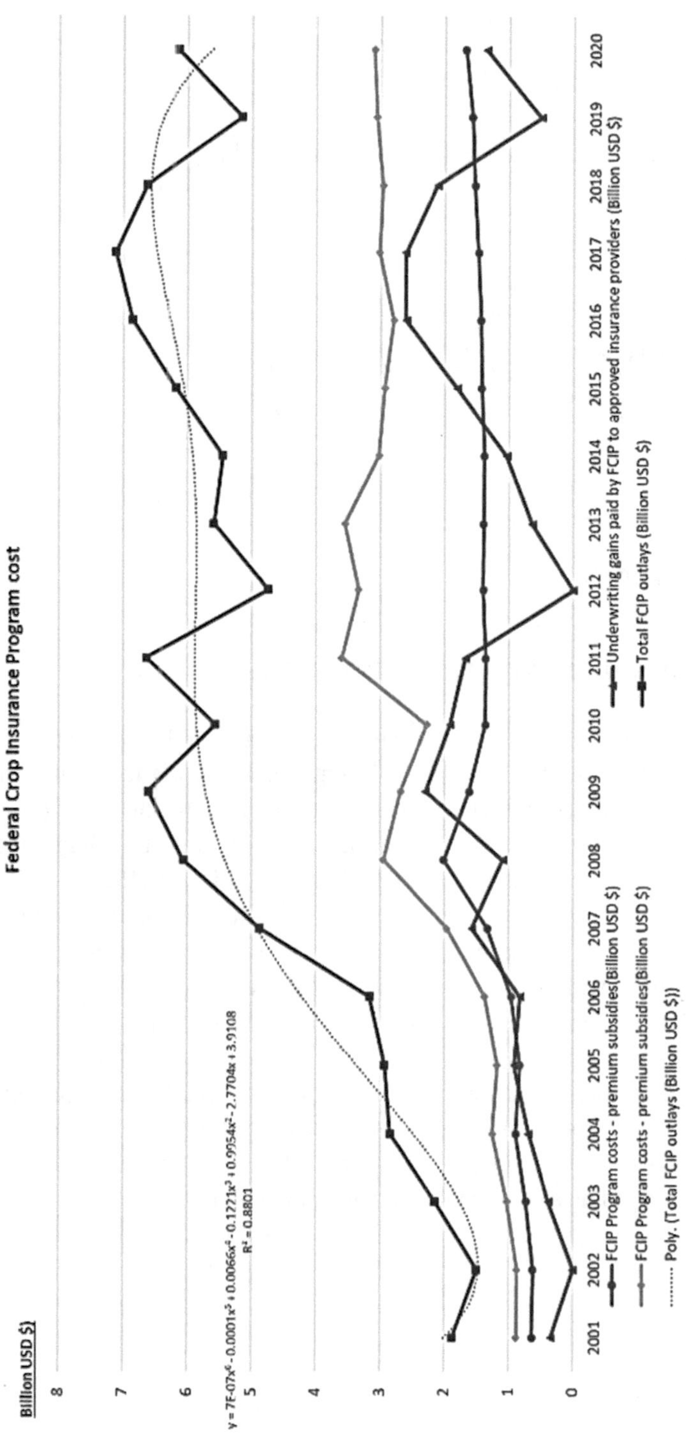

Figure 14: FCIP costs.

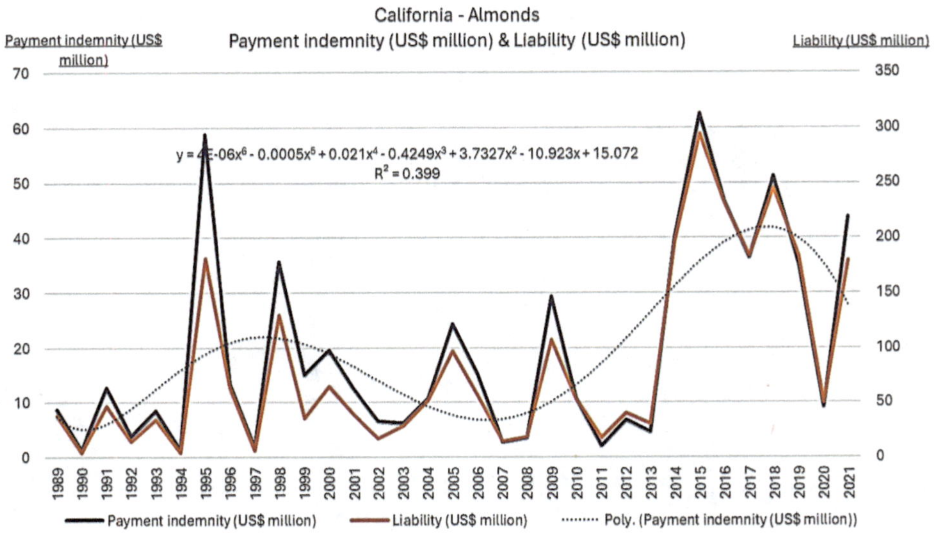

Figure 15: California almonds payment.

ML model use case: almonds payment indemnity

In California, crop insurance is available for nearly all crops, animal husbandry, milk production, chicken farming, and beekeeping, with almonds being the most insured commodity, followed by pistachios and paddy. Fresno tops the nation with the highest insurance liability. Excess moisture, precipitation, and rain are the most dominant causes of loss, followed by cold wet weather, heat, hail, frost, and freeze [156]. In 2018, frost and high winds damaged parts of the almond crop in California's Central Valley, affecting the pollination season. Almonds are becoming increasingly important [157] to California and consumers, with the crop rebounding to a record 2.14 billion pounds of shelled nuts in 2017, more than triple the amount of walnuts and four times that of pistachios [145, 151].

While rain and cold temperatures were welcome amid drought, the 2018 precipitation knocked blossoms off trees and negatively affected the short-lived pollination season (Table 2). Bees are necessary for pollination, but the colder temperatures discourage them from flying, posing a concern for the industry [158, 159].

Table 2: Totals by cause of loss.

Year	Totals by cause of loss [145, 151]	Monthly totals
2019	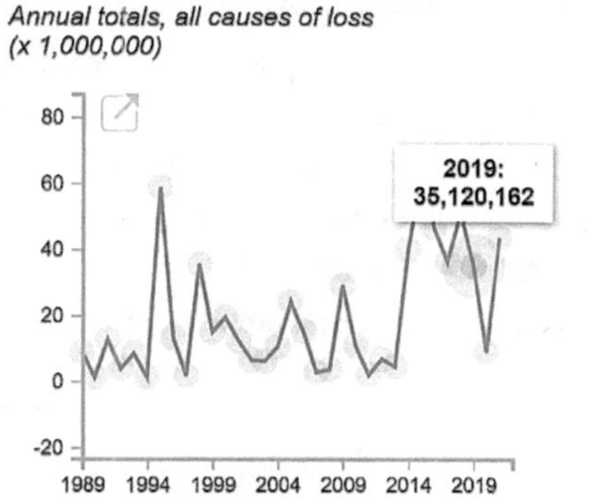	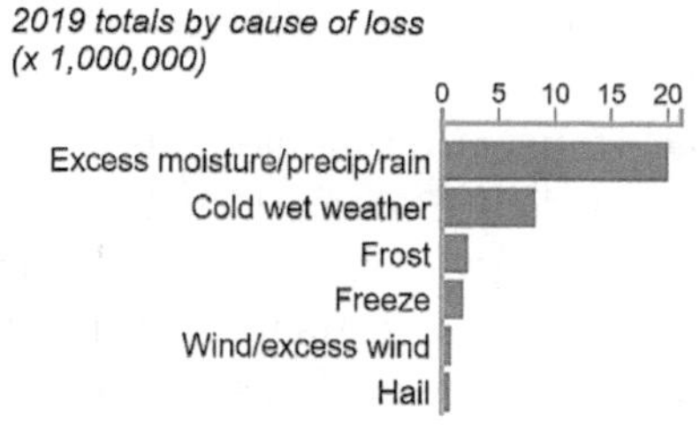
2019 Total Payment indemnity $35,120,162 or $35.120 million USD		
2018	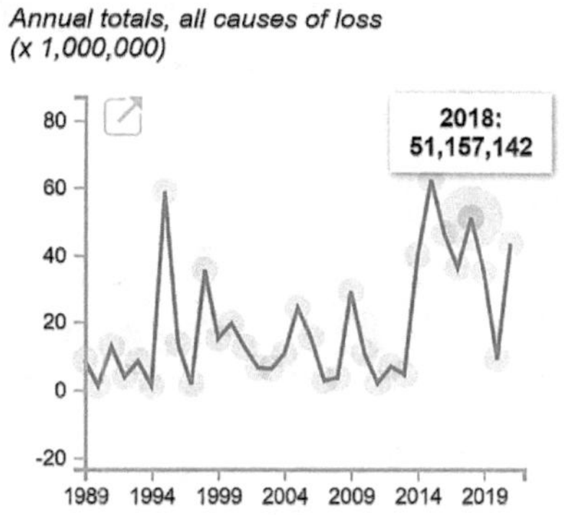	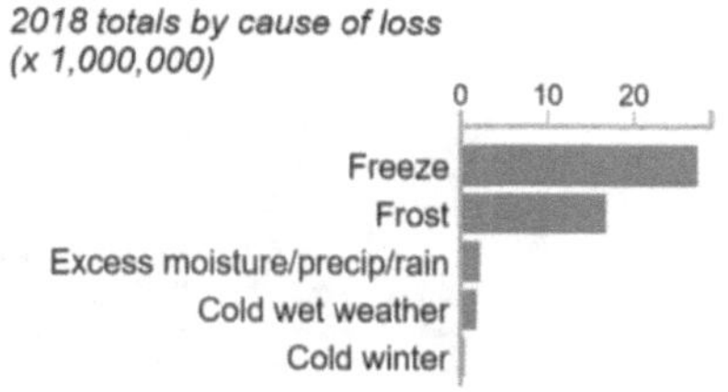
2018 Total Payment indemnity $51,157,142 or $51.157 million USD		
2015	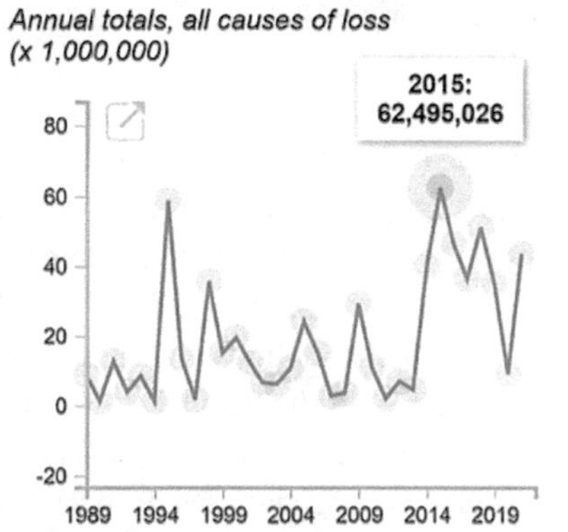	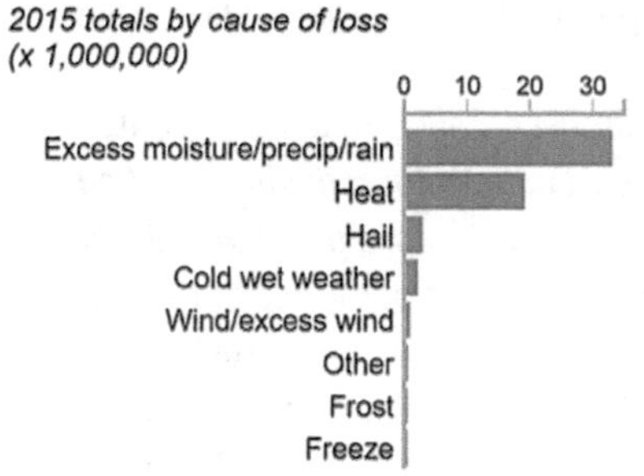
2015 Total Payment indemnity $62,495,026 or $67.495 million USD		

Figure 16 shows how much more money the federal government may have to spend on crop insurance premium subsidies if climate change continues at its current rate. According to the USDA Economic Research Service, without any efforts to reduce greenhouse gas emissions, annual premium subsidy costs for crops like corn, soybeans, and wheat could increase by 40% by 2080 [139] compared to a scenario where historical weather patterns continue. This is an average estimate across different climate models used by the USDA. However, if some greenhouse gas reductions are put in place, the average projected cost increase for the crop insurance program across these models is about 23%. It's important to note that these estimates assume that the government will continue to pay the same portion of total premiums and that coverage rates will remain constant.

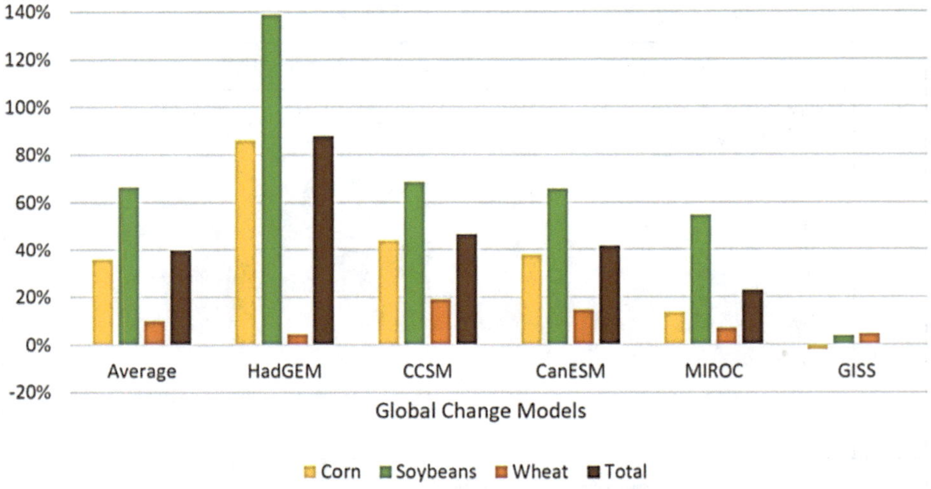

Figure 16: Projected change in total annual premium subsidies in 2080 [139].

The cost of inaction is significantly more severe *than the cost of taking appropriate measures. Furthermore, the financial burden of climate impacts in a scenario with no adaptation is much more pronounced than when taking green and resilient climate adaptation steps.* These insights are derived from recent research conducted by climate scientists.

Researchers examined the potential impacts of climate change on the FCIP using global change models such as the Hadley Centre Global Environment Model (HadGEM) [160] and the Goddard Institute for Space Studies model (GISS). They compared various climate scenarios based on greenhouse gas emissions levels to a hypothetical future resembling the climate of the past several decades. In a scenario with moderate emissions reductions and farmer adaptation, FCIP costs would increase by approximately 3.5% on average. However, if emission trends continue without adaptation, the costs would rise by an average of 22% (Figure 17). These estimates vary across different climate models, with some being more optimistic and others more pessimistic.

The study underscores that higher costs are linked to scenarios where there is no adaptation to climate change [160, 161].

It is therefore unsurprising that climate action and political ideologies prioritizing climate measures have gained prominence, as seen in the recent European elections of 2024, where governments in Europe and other regions have adopted these principles as sovereign policies.

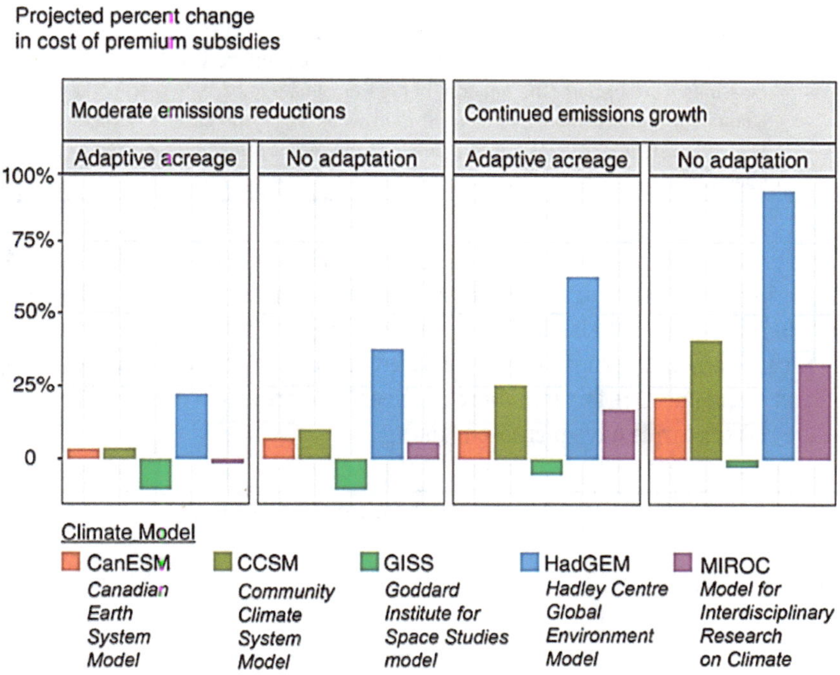

Figure 17: Projected changes to the cost of the FCIP by climate model and emission scenario [160].

Recent wildfires[3] in California from 2017 to 2021 have underscored the significance of crop insurance [162]. While premium rates have risen in some affected counties and fallen in others, annual increases are capped at 20% to prevent dramatic price swings [156].

This book employs statistical models to forecast crop yields by leveraging historical weather data and simulations derived from climate models. They then used these predictions to build scenarios projecting how yields and yield variability might change due to climate change by the year 2100. An economic model was used to translate these

3 History of California Wildfires: https://wfca.com/articles/history-of-california-wildfires/

changes in yield into changes in crop production and prices under two different scenarios. The study considers two scenarios: one where farmers can adapt to yield changes by altering crop choices, planting quantities, and management techniques, and another where they cannot. It then compares these scenarios under different climate conditions based on greenhouse gas emission levels to a hypothetical future resembling the climate of recent decades. Overall, this research helps us understand how climate change might impact crop yields, production, and prices in the future [148, 156].

The cost of inaction is significantly more severe than the cost of taking appropriate measures. Furthermore, the financial burden of climate impacts in a scenario with no adaptation is much more pronounced than when taking green and resilient climate adaptation steps. These insights are derived from recent research conducted by climate scientists.

Crop insurance is designed to help farmers recover from losses due to physical damage caused by an insurable cause of loss, such as a natural disaster. However, it does not cover crop marketing related losses. There are four different types of FCIP plans that are used to insure specialty crops, which are based on yield, revenue, dollar amounts, and whole farm revenue. The fact that there has been an increased payout of FCIP indicates that the risks to farms have increased [150].

Agriculture's importance for US food and national security is paramount today [150].

"Parametric" and weather-based index insurance

Climate crop insurance helps small farmers mitigate risks by transferring them to better-equipped entities, unlike traditional insurance, which is often time-consuming and costly. Parametric insurance, favored by governments, uses predefined parameters for quicker, more transparent payouts during adverse weather events. While it stabilizes farmers' income, challenges like design flaws and insufficient payouts must be addressed to ensure a robust market [122].

Weather-based index insurance is a highly effective tool for ensuring stable incomes for farmers.

Barriers for effective adaptation

Constraints such as lack of coordination among government departments, inadequate staff, and resources can hinder farmers from adapting to climate change. Other barriers include social, cognitive, psychological, and demographic factors. Investment in crop diversification, water use technologies, soil management, and strengthening allied sectors such as livestock rearing [144], and aquaculture can help farmers handle the effects of climate change. Early warning systems and data science models can also improve adaptation measures. To meet the essential needs of an estimated 9 billion people by 2050, global food production must increase by 70%, achievable through the integration of data science, technological innovations, advanced genomics, and climate-resilient crops, alongside improved human labor productivity. Essentially, the future relies on the synergy of people, processes, and technologies working together globally (Table 2: indemnities maps). However, adaptation is costly and varies by country, crop, and impact on agriculture, and lack of action can severely impact global food security and future generations.

Inventory of crop insurance model and ML feature engineering

The inventory of the crop insurance model includes the following feature variables:

1. Yield Guarantee: This is a group of crop insurance products that guarantee a percentage of historical yield to farmers and pay indemnities if the actual yield falls short, with three models: Individual, Mixed, and Area [163].

	Yield guarantees		
	Individual	**Mixed**	**Area**
Defining attributes	Current individual yield	Comparison yield	Comparison area yield
 Machine learning variables	Historical Production Historical acreage Historical yield		
Assurance	Individual	Comparison	Comparison
 Machine learning variables	Historical average yield Timely planting for the full guarantee		
Examples	Actual production history (APH)	Obsolete	Corn group risk plan (GRP)

(continued)

	Yield guarantees		
	Individual	**Mixed**	**Area**
Liability[†]	Indemnity	Max. indemnity	Indemnity per acre
w	Rating	Territorial	Crop

† To calculate the guarantee for each insurance period, we multiply the guaranteed amount per acre by the number of acres that are insured. We then multiply the guarantee by a percentage of the FCIC maximum price (this is called the "indemnity").

Acreage refers to land that is covered by the crop insurance policy. There are very few restrictions on what land can be insured, so most of the land used for commercial crop production can be insured. However, the most important limitation is that the guarantee is only valid if the crops are planted on time (as defined in the policy). If the crops are not planted on time, the guarantee will be reduced for the affected acreage.

Artificial intelligence improves America's food system!

	Yield guarantees		
Model	**Individual**	**Mixed**	**Area**
Hazards[±]	Comprehensive	Open-ended	Open-ended
Mandatory acreage [Δ]	County-wide	Same	Same
Units	Subdivided	County	Units by county
Benchmarked[¶]	Requirement	Same	Same
 Machine learning variables	County average yield based on 10 years historical data	Same	Same
Marginalizations	Exclusions	Exclusions	None

[±] The insurance policy for crops covers events that can limit the amount of crops a farmer can produce. These events can last for a long time, from the beginning of planting to the end of the harvest season.
[Δ] The insurance policy requires that all the cropland that the insured person owns or shares with others in the county must be covered. This rule is the same for both the acreage- and individual-based yield guarantee models.
[¶] The same revenue and percent-of-damage guarantee.

Indemnity payments

When analyzing data on indemnity payments, it's important to note that these payments often underrepresent crop losses because some losses are too minor to trigger payments and some crops remain uninsured. Despite potential selection bias, the distribution patterns of indemnity payments for various causes and months are likely similar for both insured and uninsured producers, though data limitations allow only one cause of loss to be reported and regional variations exist [154].

Additionally, adapting to climate change could cost India up to $360 billion annually by 2030, resulting in a cumulative adaptation gap of over $1 trillion. The bearing of climate change has already been felt in many areas, and cost of adaptation varies by crop. Delayed implementation of adaptation strategies increases costs, and investing in costly solutions requires high yields and higher crop prices. The cost of preventing coastal flooding in San Francisco Bay by midcentury is estimated to be $110 billion, but other climate models predict more than 6 feet of ocean level increase by the conclusion of the era [165, 166, 167]. The cost of adaptation is exponentially higher if increased temperatures (Figure 18) are not prevented, with melting glaciers impacting billions of people and causing food shortages and other disasters [168, 169, 170].

Scenario	SSP Model	potential scenarios for the glaciers of the HKH [50]
SSP 1-2.6	SSP 1	If there is a 1.5-2 degree Celsius increase in the Earth's average temperature above pre-industrial levels, the glaciers will lose 30% to 50% of their ice volume by 2100.
SSP 2-4.5	SSP2	If the global temperature rises by 3 degrees Celsius, the glaciers could lose 75% of their ice
SSP 3-7.0	SSP3	By the end of the century, average temperatures have risen by 3.6 °C.
SSP 5-8.5	SSP5	With a 4-degree rise, the researchers say there will be a loss of up to 80% of the ice in the HKH.

In layman's language, it means we have no doubt whatsoever that at 2 °C of global warming, we will lose 50% of the glacial ice mass in the region. The report notes that the Himalayan glaciers lost ice at a rate 65% faster between 2010 and 2019 than over the previous decade (2001–2010). And this is unprecedented. The impacts of the rapid glacial melt in the Himalayas will be felt around the world.

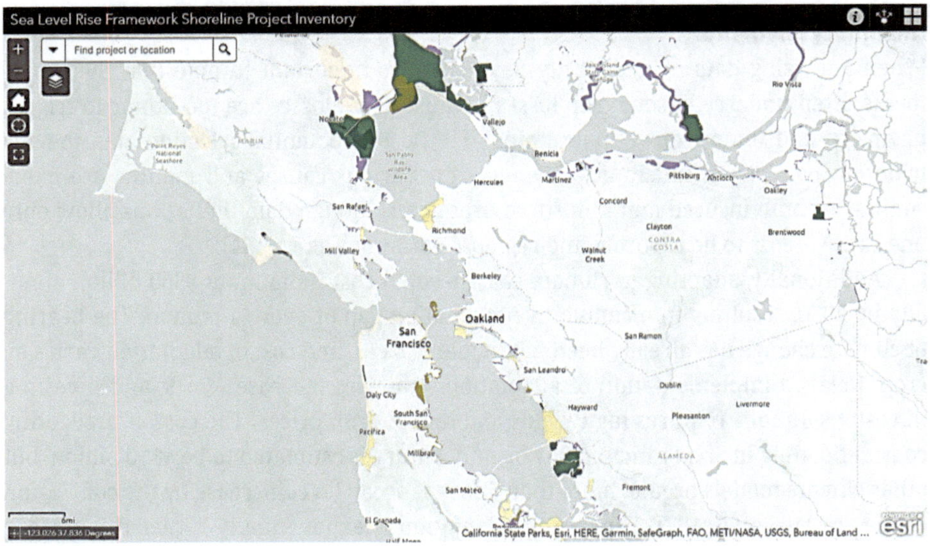

Figure 18: Sea level rise.

Role of data science in increasing adoption of crop insurance

Governments in developing countries have increasingly supported commercial agricultural insurance programs, with China notably expanding its market to become the second largest globally by 2008 through substantial support and premium subsidies. India and Mexico have developed extensive weather-based crop insurance schemes, while other countries have explored or initiated pilot programs for agricultural insurance [171]. Here is the classification of risks posed by agricultural producers [171] and data science techniques to model and provide proactive insights (Table 3).

Table 3: AgRisk and data science techniques.

Type of risks	Idiosyncratic ⟷		Systemic	Model	
Natural disaster	Hail	Flood, pest infestation	Drought	Prognostics, what-if	
Diseases and pests			Contagious animal disease	Prognostics, what-if	Sensors[10] and Internet connected devices
Price			Commodity, input, exchange rates	Forecast	Regression and time series forecasting

4 Hanumayamma Innovations and Technologies, Inc. Cow Necklace: https://internet-of-things.cioreview.com/vendor/2020/hanumayamma_innovations_and_technologies

Table 3 (continued)

Type of risks	Idiosyncratic	⟷	Systemic	Model	
Financial			Interest rates	Prognostics, what-if	Decision models
Operational		Availability of inputs	Evolution of production techniques (for example, data science technique for yield improvement)	Forecast and heuristics	Regression, time series forecasting, and heuristics
Environmental		Pollution, deforestation		Prognostics, what-if	CO_2
Policy			Public subsidies, agricultural policy	What-if	Risk modeling and what-if analysis
Health	Illness, injury, disability	Epidemic diseases		Prognostics, what-if	
Property	Fire, theft		Earthquake, floods	What-if	

Agriculture insurance can de-risk lending to the farm sector, reduce budget volatility, increase fiscal space during shock years, and stimulate growth of the agriculture sector. It can also reduce fiscal leakages and corruption. Current adaptation strategies include crop insurance, changes in planting time, crop diversification, and others [172]. Despite its benefits, farmers in developing countries are not adopting crop insurance due to economic, social, demographic, educational, and structural factors [173]. Trust in the insurance market is critical, and timely payouts and local agents can increase adoption. Agricultural insurance is the antidote to many economic illnesses [174].

Adapting to climate change involves two steps: perceiving climate change and responding by adjustment [141]. Crop insurance schemes with new product designs and innovations, and funding, address low coverage and penetration, with data science playing an important role in enabling proactive recommendations and risk mitigation. Farmers need proactive recommendations, training, and motivational support to address uncertainties related to market, macroeconomic, climatic, and commerce factors to mitigate risks as much as possible. ML techniques can help address the gap in data science and support farmers' adaptability to climate change [143, 173] (see in the above figure, farmers get a prediction interval for a chosen metric for a given horizon).

The demand for fruits and vegetables has increased rapidly, and value chains must be financially sustainable for stakeholders without putting undue pressure on the environment. Sustainability focuses on positive agriculture that uses regenerative practices and sustainably sourced ingredients, evaluating value chains for both financial and environmental sustainability. Positive value chains incorporate net-zero emissions, net water positivity, sustainable employment, and inclusive practices. Sustainability is crucial for the future (Figure 19).

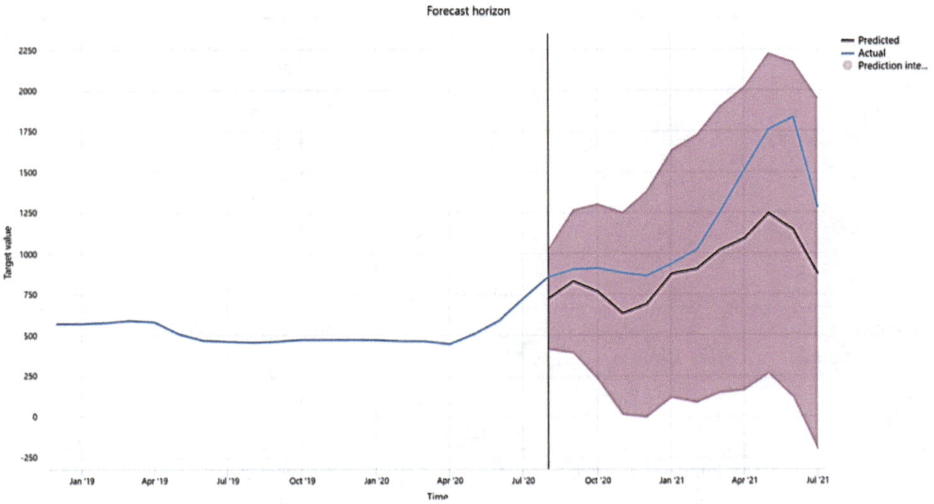

Figure 19: Forecast.

Although horticultural crop production has greatly increased, farmers are not benefiting from the high levels of production due to market inefficiencies and a lack of well-integrated value chains. Despite the record levels of production, farmers are not making more money because of low prices offered compared to the cost of growing their crops. Farmers growing tomatoes, onions, and potatoes often have to sell their crops at a loss or discard them due to fluctuating wholesale and retail prices combined with production costs. This cycle of price volatility perpetuates their financial instability [175].

Farmers growing tomatoes, onions, and potatoes often have to sell their crops at a loss or discard them due to fluctuating wholesale and retail prices combined with production costs. This cycle of price volatility perpetuates their financial instability.

Specialty crops often experience boom-and-bust cycles, a trend increasingly common as the agricultural sector shifts toward high-value perennial tree and vine crops [175]. These cycles are driven by long lead times, delayed adjustments for breeding stocks and investment decisions, and time lags for land development and nonbearing periods. In California, such cycles have led to new plantings exceeding market demand, causing commodity prices to fall and attracting significant outside investment due to the lucrative returns of tree and vine crops.

Financial sustainability ML models: crop insurance go/no-go decision based on field-grown tomatoes price forecast model

The purpose of the go/no-go crop insurance is to apply ML techniques to assess the prices of field-grown tomatoes would be at the end of the harvest cycle and ensure financial sustainability prevails. If not, opt for crop insurance choices.

Data sources:

Data source	Name
USDA	Retail prices of fresh and processed vegetables for tomatoes under trade and prices by category.
FRED	Tomatoes average price (APU0000712311).
IBRD-IDA	Emissions indicator and Pink Sheet data of monthly prices of commodities.

Retail prices can be downloaded from USDA ERS or from FRED. An interesting fact is that the share price spread from farm to consumer is higher to farms for tomatoes. This could be an additional factor for farms to seed tomatoes (Figure 20).

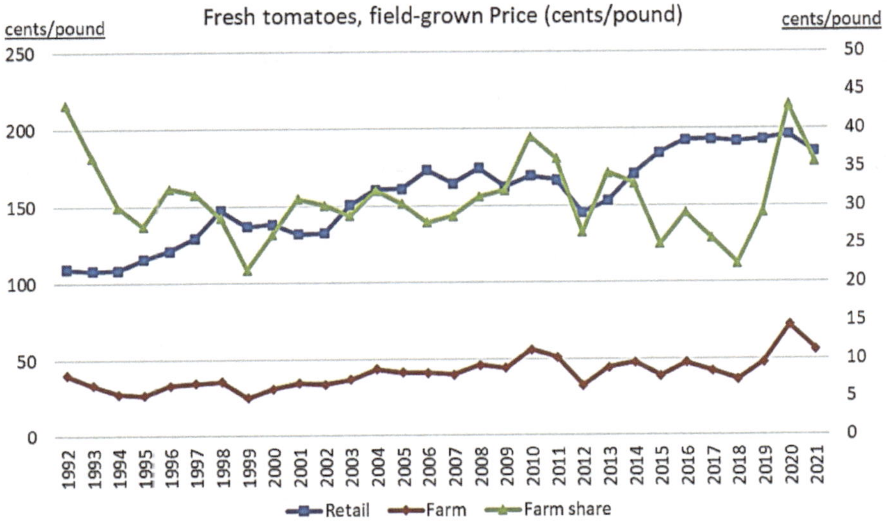

Figure 20: Fresh tomatoes retail and farm share.

$$Y_{\text{Tomatoes fresh procured farm share}} = 4\text{E-}06x^6 - 0.0003x^5 + 0.0106x^4 - 0.1867x^3 + 1.9067x^2 - 10.472x + 50.977$$

Except for the polynomial regressor of order 6 ($R^2 = 0.5009$) all other trend options have resulted less than 5% accuracy.

Tomatoes, field grown farm share		R^2
Exponential	$y = 30.852e^{-7E-04x}$	$R^2 = 0.0006$
Linear	$y = -0.0144x + 31.158$	$R^2 = 0.0006$
Logarithmic	$y = -1.274\ln(x) + 34.105$	$R^2 = 0.044$
Polynomial order 6	$y = 4\text{E-}06x^6 - 0.0003x^5 + 0.0106x^4 - 0.1867x^3 + 1.9067x^2 - 10.472x + 50.977$	$R^2 = 0.5009$
Power	$y = 33.612x^{-0.039}$	$R^2 = 0.048$

Step 1: Load important feature engineering parameters

There are various factors that influence tomatoes retail prices. On inputs side, chemicals (DAP, TSP, urea, and others) play an important role. Next, energy prices have a huge impact on prices. To forecast the retail prices of fresh grown tomatoes, we collected historical data on retail tomato prices.

Understanding the chemicals PPI

In particular, the PPI for chemicals and allied products, which includes industrial chemicals, has fluctuated over time. In March of 2022, it reached a record high of 352.97500, while in June of 1939 it hit a record low of 16.70000. Trading economics is a website that provides current and historical data, as well as related indicators, for this PPI. The most recent update is from July of 2023 and includes information from the US Federal Reserve.

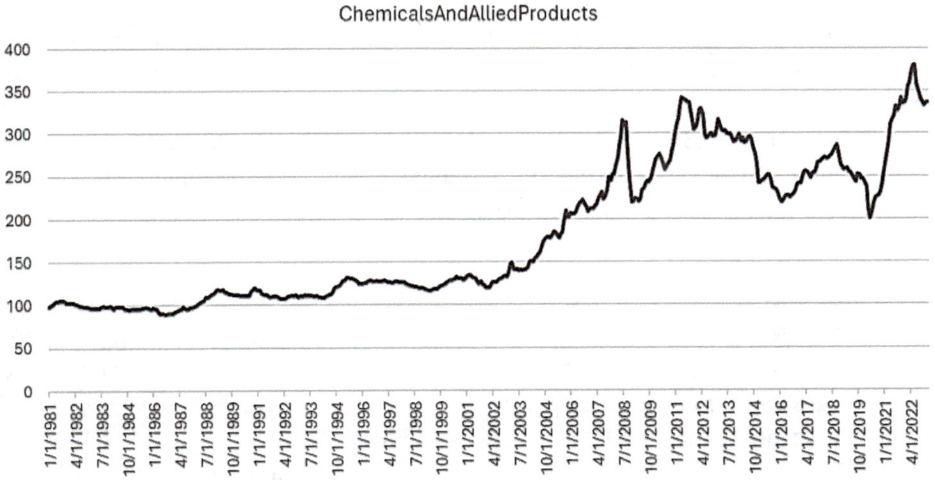

Load phosphate rock, DAP, and TSP prices

Tomatoes require complete fertilizer with low nitrogen content and high levels of potash and phosphoric acid for optimal growth and yield. The appropriate fertilizer depends on the soil's characteristics, mechanical condition, and composition, and economic considerations and potential seasonal factors should also be considered. Phosphorus is essential for healthy fruit setting in tomatoes, and common chemicals like phosphate rock, diammonium phosphate (DAP), and TSP are used, with TSP treatment involving a film coat to remove tomato mosaic virus from seeds, and Thiram being a widely used fungicide for vegetable crop seeds [176].

Phosphate rock is a crucial mineral in global agriculture, used primarily for fertilizer production. Its availability and price greatly impact worldwide agricultural production costs. Phosphate rock is a sedimentary rock containing minerals with phosphate ions.

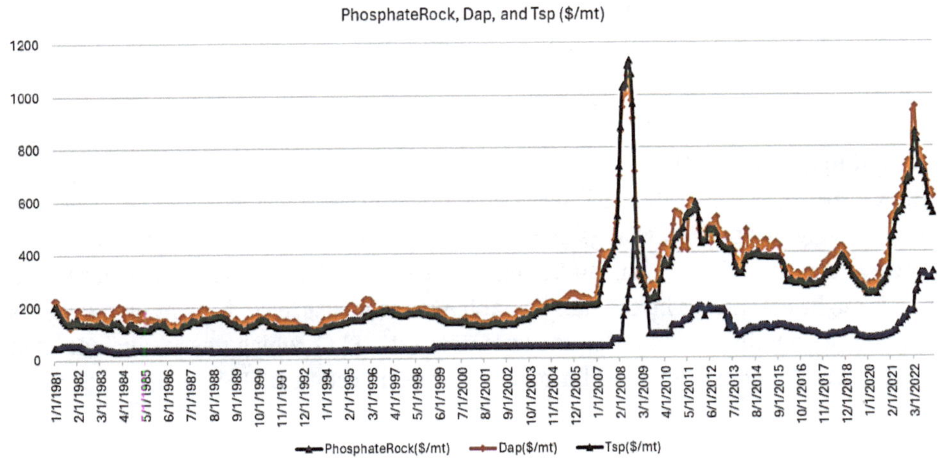

DAP prices rose to 772 USD per metric ton in 2022 due to several factors, but prices are projected to decrease in 2023 and 2024, with estimates of 580 USD and 570 USD per metric ton, respectively. The decline in pricing is attributed to a deal between Russia and India in April 2023 that caused a significant drop in DAP prices. There are concerns about excess supply due to strong DAP production and declining input costs for raw materials, which is also affecting TSP pricing.

Load urea prices

Urea is a mineral fertilizer in the form of white granules, containing the highest concentration of nitrogen of all existing fertilizers. It is safe for plants and fruits and widely used in agriculture to make seedlings strong and hardy. Urea price swings are in line with other fertilizers such as DAP and TSP. Two noticeable trends include a 37.02% jump in May 2008 during the Great Recession and a +46% spike in October 2021, reaching $695 per metric ton due to a sharp slump in production caused by eminent natural gas costs.

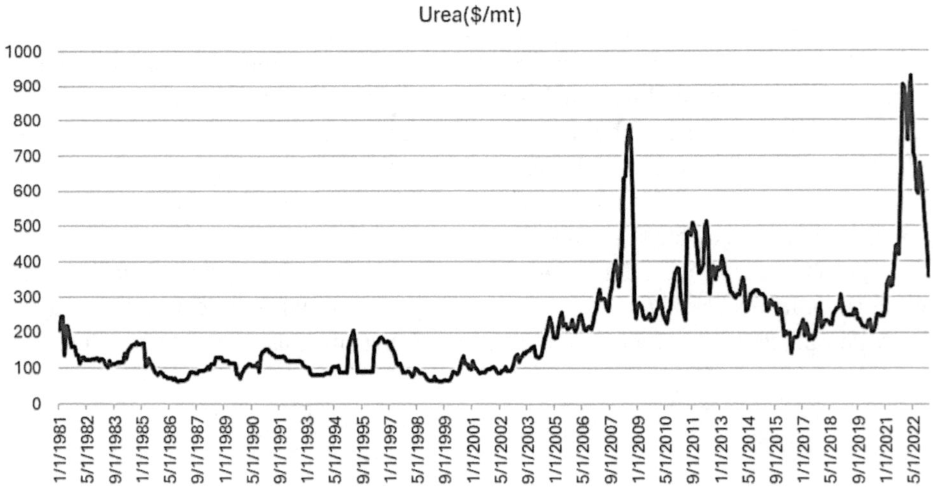

Analyzing the CPIAUCSL

The CPIAUCSL is a tool that measures how much prices for goods and services that people living in cities pay change over time. It includes things like food and gas prices. However, because the index includes things like food and gas, which can be very volatile, it might not always be the most reliable way to measure changes in prices. That's why there's another index called the core CPI (CPILFESL), which doesn't include food and gas prices and is often used for more accurate detection [177].

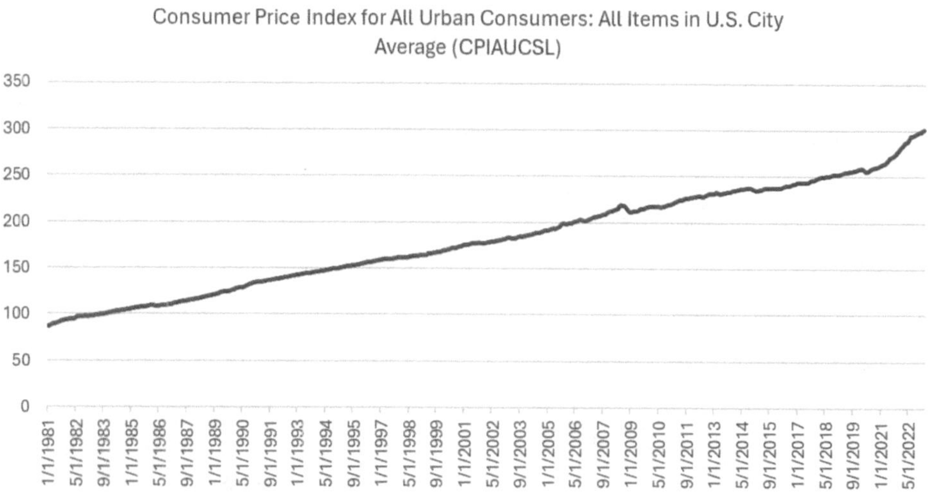

Load consumer GDP: Normalized for US (USALORSGPNOSTSAM)

In the same way, economists in other countries focus on final sales, which is gross domestic product (GDP). Following provides GDP for the USA.

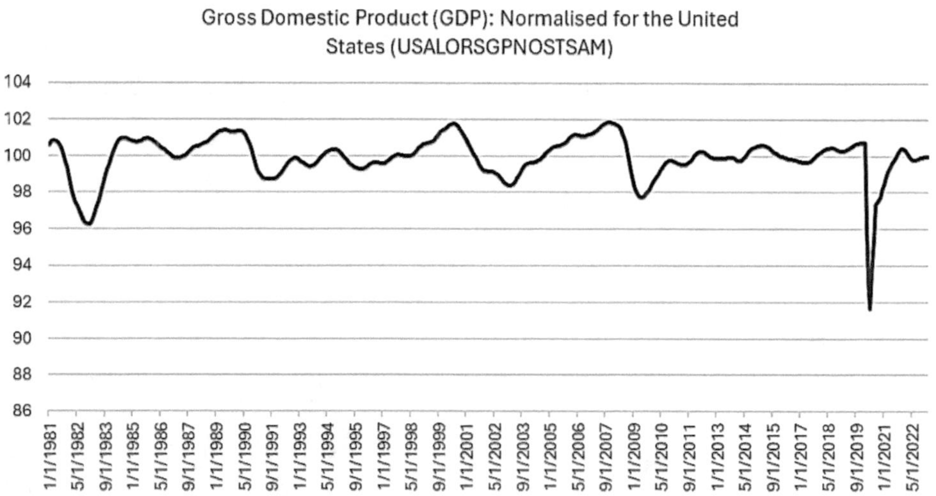

Load industrial production

Assesses output of important companies in US, covering manufacturing, mining, and electric and gas utilities: It, along with construction, accounts for most of the variation in national output over the business cycle.

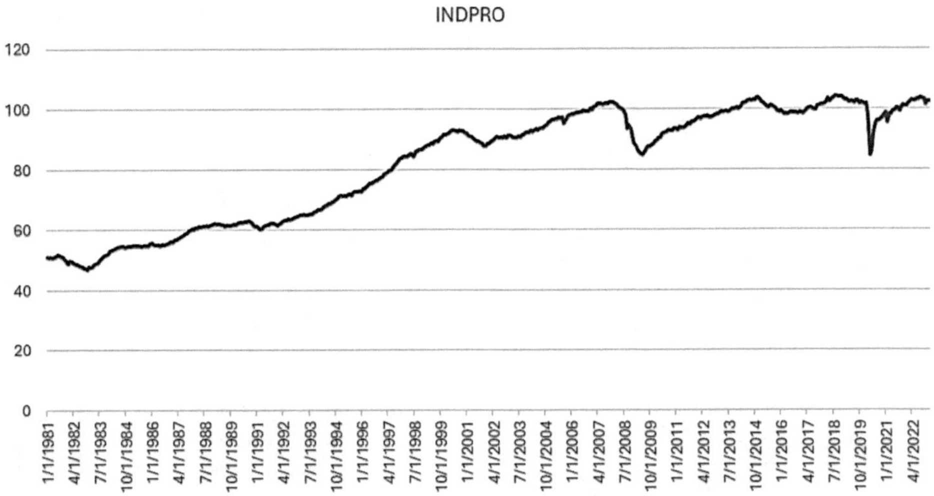

Natural gas

A gaseous mixture of hydrocarbon compounds, the primary one being methane: The data is collected from World Bank Pink Sheet and the same can be accessed from FRED. There is a direct connection between prices of natural gas and prices of tomatoes. Recently, in 2023, the price of tomato products has doubled due to the rise in natural gas prices. Industry tomato prices in food service channels have more than doubled to account for the increased energy costs, particularly gas, which has increased by 620% [178].

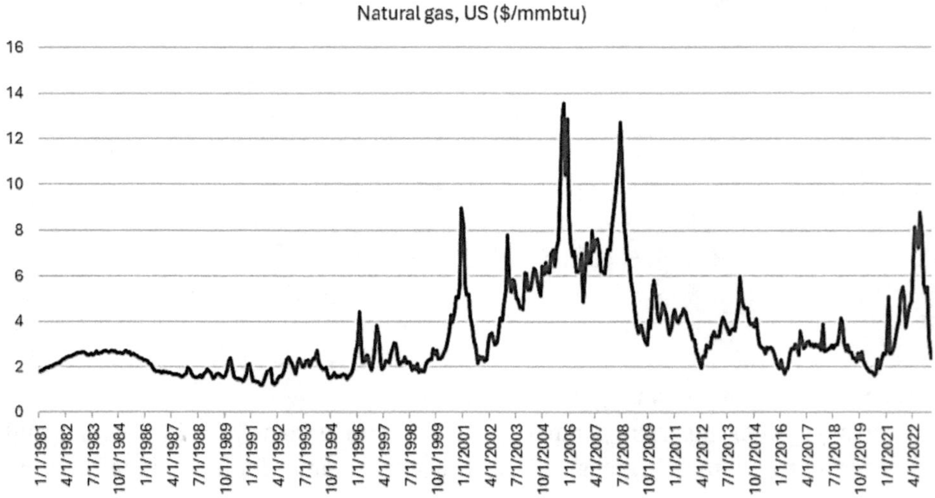

The largest annual increase in natural gas prices since 1935 occurred in 2000, with crude oil, gasoline, and household fuel prices also increasing sharply in 1999 and 2000 [179].

In 2005, natural gas prices spiked due to supply disruptions caused by hurricanes and high demand from colder weather [180]. In July 2023, US natural gas futures rose over 3% due to expectations of higher cooling demand driven by hot weather and limited LNG exports. Declining US natural gas production and high net withdrawals from storage caused the price to increase in Q1 2022, with significant day-to-day price changes [181].

Load PPI for machinery and equipment (WPU111)

President Truman approved Public Law 78 in 1951 to ensure better living and working conditions for all farm workers.[5] However, in 1964, the US government declined to extend the provision that allowed foreign nationals to assist with crop production and harvesting [182]. As a result, tomato harvesting machines became crucial, eliminating about 3.5 million man-hours of labor annually by 1966. However, mechanizing tomato production involves more than just the harvester, and successful mechanization requires designing crops to be harvested by machines (Figure 21).

Figure 21: Tomato harvester [183].

Tomato planting operations are done simultaneously, including forming planting beds, applying fertilizer, precision-planting seeds, and applying weed control chemicals. The producer price index is the best way to capture agricultural machinery and equipment costs [182, 183].

5 Public Law 78: https://historyengine.richmond.edu/episodes/view/6780

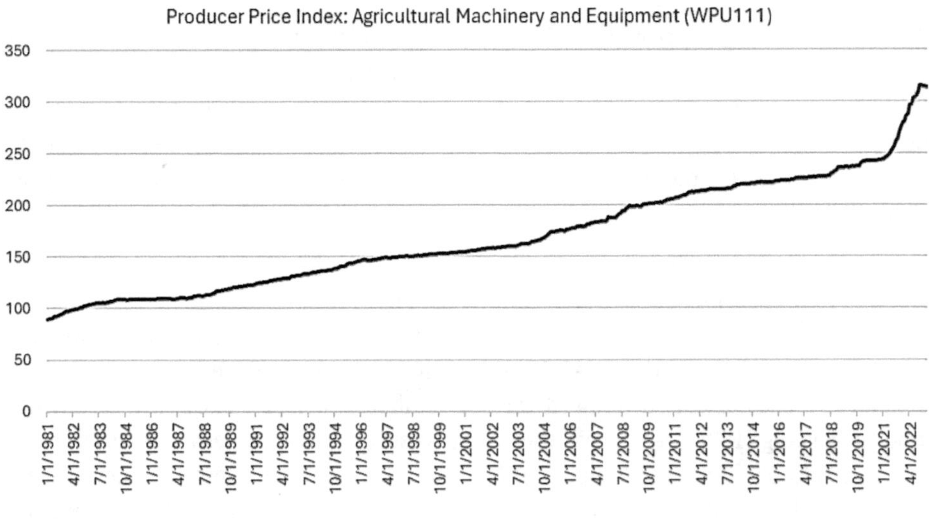

Load refrigerated truck rates by distance

Weekly US average refrigerated truck rates.

Recent Weekly US Average Refrigerated Truck Rates

This chart shows US average refrigerated truck rates, by default including the past two years. Filterable by region, origin, destination, distance, and com...

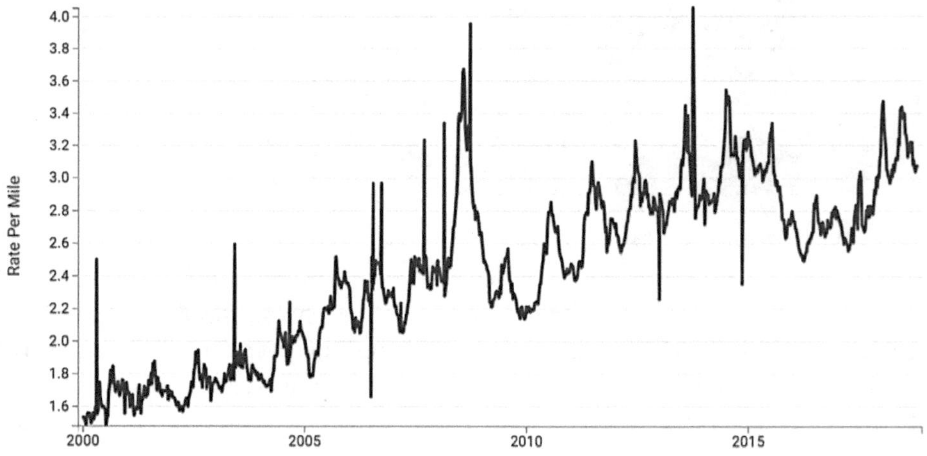

Step 2: Load tomatoes prices and feature variables DATAFRAme

Load combined tomato prices and feature variables.

```
df = pd.read_csv(r"FinalCropInsuranceModelsTomatoesFieldGrownCombinedFrame.csv")
df
```

Output:

	Date	U.S. Recession	Methylbromide_ban	sp_500_pe_ratio	ChemicalsAndAlliedProducts	PhosphateRock($/mt)	Dap($/mt)	Tsp($/mt)	Urea($/mt)
0	1/1/1981	0	0	9.02	97.700	44.0	227.50	202.50	207.00
1	2/1/1981	0	0	8.76	99.900	44.0	226.00	204.50	242.50
2	3/1/1981	0	0	9.14	100.500	44.0	207.50	187.50	242.50
3	4/1/1981	0	0	9.13	102.800	47.5	193.00	177.50	135.00
4	5/1/1981	0	0	8.86	104.500	51.0	195.50	161.00	215.00
...	...	...	...	...	...	...	...	...	...
501	10/1/2022	0	0	20.44	341.677	317.5	725.00	675.00	636.25
502	11/1/2022	0	0	22.07	337.539	300.0	665.63	625.00	588.75
503	12/1/2022	0	0	22.65	332.219	300.0	625.00	584.38	519.38
504	1/1/2023	0	0	22.93	335.513	300.0	631.00	569.38	443.75
505	2/1/2023	0	0	23.62	336.535	322.5	612.50	547.50	357.50

506 rows × 19 columns

Check data frame columns:

```
df.columns
```

Output:

```
Index(['Date', 'U.S. Recession', 'Methylbromide_ban', 'sp_500_pe_ratio',
       'ChemicalsAndAlliedProducts', 'PhosphateRock($/mt)', 'Dap($/mt)',
       'Tsp($/mt)', 'Urea($/mt)', 'PotassiumChloride($/mt)', 'CPIAUCSL',
       'USALORSGPNOSTSAM', 'employmentInAgriculture(LNS12034560)', 'INDPRO',
       'NitrogenousFertilizerManufacturingProductionPriceIndexIndustry(PCU325311325311)',
       'Natural gas, US ($/mmbtu)',
       'PPI_MachineryandEquipment: Agricultural Machinery and Equipment (WPU111)',
       'Commercial Refrigeration', 'y'],
      dtype='object')
```

Step 3: Prepare prophet data frame for tomatoes prices

Prepare Prophet data frame.

```
Prophetdf = df[[ 'U.S. Recession', 'Methylbromide_ban', 'sp_500_pe_ratio',
    'ChemicalsAndAlliedProducts', 'PhosphateRock($/mt)', 'Dap($/mt)',
    'Tsp($/mt)', 'Urea($/mt)', 'PotassiumChloride($/mt)', 'CPIAUCSL',
    'USALORSGPNOSTSAM', 'employmentInAgriculture(LNS12034560)', 'INDPRO',
    'NitrogenousFertilizerManufacturingProductionPriceIndexIndustry(PCU325311325311)',
    'Natural gas, US ($/mmbtu)',
    'PPI_MachineryandEquipment: Agricultural Machinery and Equipment (WPU111)',
    'Commercial Refrigeration', 'y', 'ds']]#.rename({'APU0000712311' :'y'},axis = 'columns')
```

Step 4: Prepare train and test data

Prepare Prophet train and test data.

```
n_obs = int(Prophetdf.shape[0] * 0.9 )
Prophetdf_train, Prophetdf_test =
Prophetdf[0:numberofobservations],Prophetdf[numberofobservations:]
print(Prophetdf_train dataset shape,Prophetdf_test dataset shape)
```

Result:
(455, 19) (51, 19)

Step 5: Check time series data for nulls

Check data nulls before modeling time series.

```
Prophetdf.isna().any()
```

Output:

```
U.S. Recession                    False
Methylbromide_ban                 False
sp_500_pe_ratio                   False
ChemicalsAndAlliedProducts        False
PhosphateRock($/mt)               False
Dap($/mt)                         False
Tsp($/mt)                         False
Urea($/mt)                        False
PotassiumChloride($/mt)           False
```

```
CPIAUCSL                                                          False
USALORSGPNOSTSAM                                                  False
employmentInAgriculture(LNS12034560)                              False
INDPRO                                                            False
NitrogenousFertilizerManufacturingProductionPriceIndexIndustry(PCU325311325311)  False
Natural gas, US ($/mmbtu)                                         False
PPI_MachineryandEquipment: Agricultural Machinery and Equipment (WPU111)  False
Commercial Refrigeration                                          False
y                                                                 False
ds                                                                False
dtype: bool
```

Step 6: Prepare the time series model

First, get the time series columns and set up the model.

```
Prophet_cols = ['U.S. Recession', 'Methylbromide_ban', 'sp_500_pe_ratio',
      'ChemicalsAndAlliedProducts', 'PhosphateRock($/mt)', 'Dap($/mt)',
      'Tsp($/mt)', 'Urea($/mt)', 'PotassiumChloride($/mt)', 'CPIAUCSL',
      'USALORSGPNOSTSAM', 'employmentInAgriculture(LNS12034560)', 'INDPRO',
      'NitrogenousFertilizerManufacturingProductionPriceIndexIndustry(PCU325311325311)',
      'Natural gas, US ($/mmbtu)',
      'PPI_MachineryandEquipment: Agricultural Machinery and Equipment (WPU111)',
      'Commercial Refrigeration'
      ]
multi_model = Prophet(interval_width = 0.95)
# adding all columns in add regressor
for col in Prophet_cols:
  multi_model.add_regressor(col)
multi_model.fit(Prophetdf_train)
```

Prophet is a tool that helps predict. To use it, you first need to set up a Prophet object and configure it with the type of model you want to use. Then, you fit the model to your data. Prophet ML has many options to customize your model, such as how to handle growth and seasonality, but it can also figure out these things automatically if you prefer. When fitting the model, you need to make sure your dataset is in a specific format, with one column containing the date-times and another column containing the observations you want to predict [184, 185].

Output: <prophet.forecaster.Prophet at 0x7fae29ddc320>

Step 7: Predict freshly grown tomato prices

This line of code creates a new DataFrame called "future" using the make_future_dataframe() function from the multi_model object. This function takes in three arguments: periods, freq, and include_history. The "periods" argument specifies the number of time periods to forecast into the future, which is set to Prophetdf_test. "freq" argument specifies the frequency of the time series, which is set to 'MS' for monthly data. The "include_history" argument is set to True, which means that the original historical data will be included in the future data frame along with the forecasted values. Overall, this line of code sets up the data frame for the multi_model to make predictions for the future time periods [64] [65].

```
future = multi_model.make future dataframe (periods = Prophetdf test
shape[0],freq='MS', include_history=True)
future.tail(15)
```

Output:

	ds
491	2021-12-01
492	2022-01-01
493	2022-02-01
494	2022-03-01
495	2022-04-01
496	2022-05-01
497	2022-06-01
498	2022-07-01
499	2022-08-01
500	2022-09-01
501	2022-10-01
502	2022-11-01
503	2022-12-01
504	2023-01-01
505	2023-02-01

```
for col in Prophet_cols:
  future[col] = Prophetdf[col]
forecastProphet = multi_model.predict(future)
forecastProphet[['ds', 'yhat', 'yhat_lower', 'yhat_upper']].tail()
```

The predict() function generates a DataFrame with important information about the predicted values and the uncertainty surrounding them.

```
forecastProphet[['ds', 'yhat', 'yhat_lower', 'yhat_upper']].tail()
```

Output:

	ds	yhat	yhat_lower	yhat_upper
501	2022-10-01	1.944083	1.600592	2.322102
502	2022-11-01	2.053463	1.667256	2.424090
503	2022-12-01	2.225157	1.861327	2.612933
504	2023-01-01	2.272105	1.905263	2.644052
505	2023-02-01	2.261524	1.929723	2.596311

Step 8: Tomatoes prices estimate

Prophet has a feature that allows you to visualize the predicted values in comparison to the original data. This helps to give a clear visual representation of how well the model is predicting future values and how much uncertainty there is in the predictions. In summary, the plot() function is a useful tool for understanding how accurate the model is and how much confidence you can have in its predictions [64, 65].

```
fig1 = multi_model.plot(forecastProphet);
```

Output:

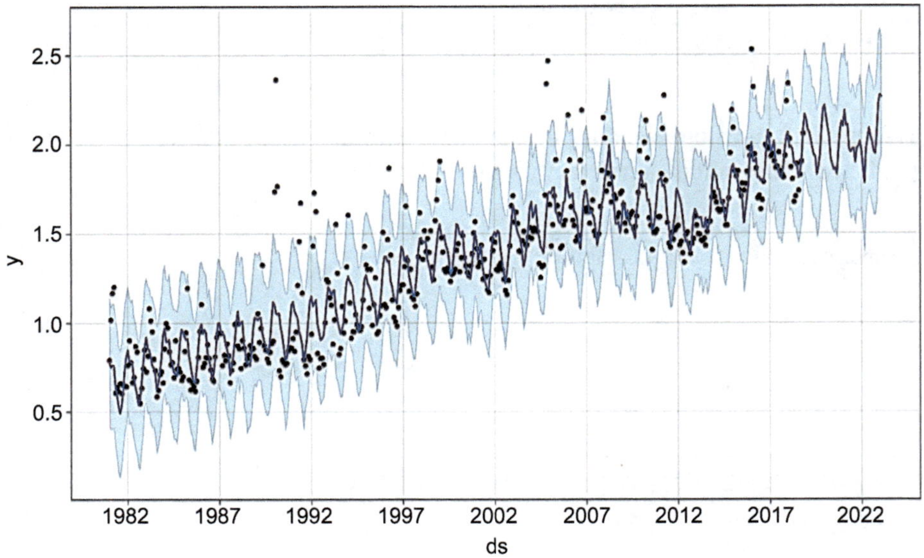


```
Prophetdf.plot(x = 'ds', y = 'y')
```

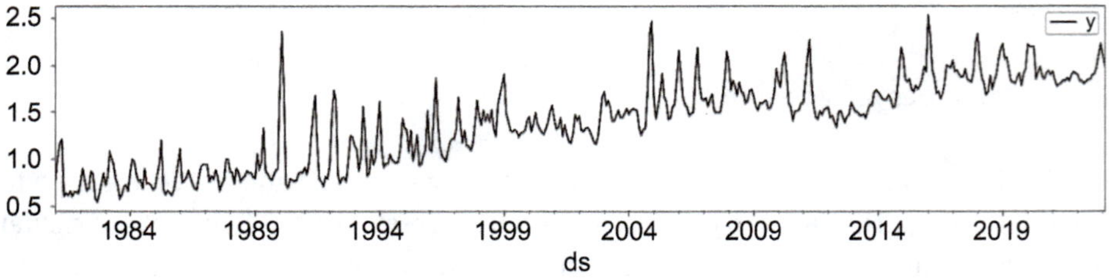

Step 9: Visualize forecast components

Visualize Prophet components:

```
multi_model.plot_components(forecastProphet);
```

Output:

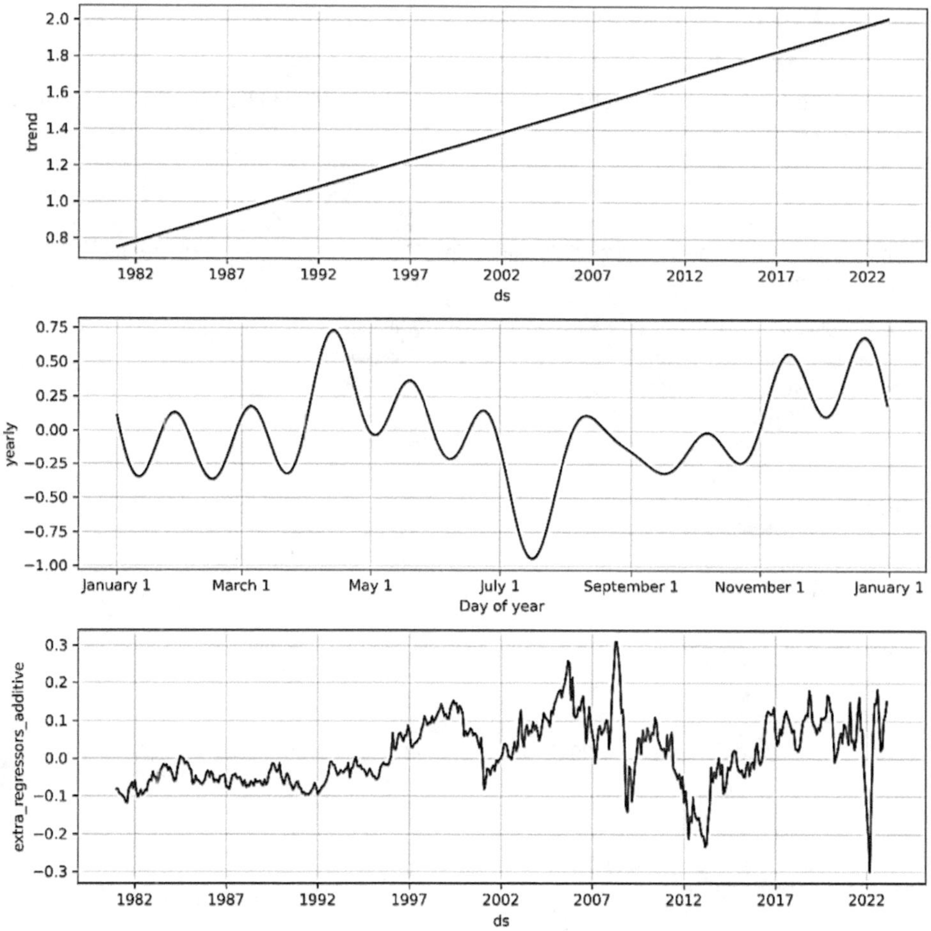

Step 10: Calculate performance metrics (MAE) and visualize the forecasted prices

To calculate model performance metrics, combine the test data frame and the forecast Prophet data frame to compute mean absolute error metrics.

```
#Check MAE value
MAE = mean_absolute_error(combined_df['y'],combined_df['yhat'])
print(f'The MAE for the baseline model is {MAE}')
```

```
combined_df = pd.merge(Prophetdf_test[['ds', 'y']],forecastProphet[['ds', 'yhat', 'yhat_lower', 'yhat_
upper']][-15:], on='ds')
combined_df
```

Output: The MAE for the baseline model is 0.1190819845093926. That is, the model is predicting 11 cents off!

```
import seaborn as sns
plt.rcParams.update({'figure.figsize': (15,3), 'figure.dpi': 300})
fig,ax = plt.subplots()

sns.lineplot(data = combined_df, x = 'ds', y = 'y' ,label = 'Original')
sns.lineplot(data = combined_df, x= 'ds', y = 'yhat',label = 'Forecast')
plt.grid(linestyle = '-', linewidth = 0.3)
plt.legend(["Original", "forecast"])
```

Output:

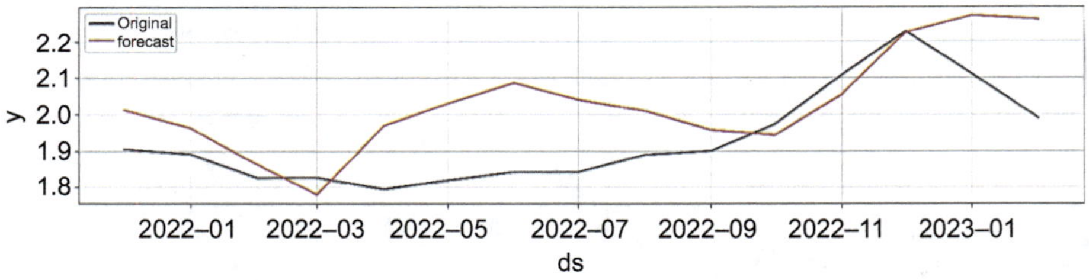

Step 11: AutoML model

Running the same model on automated ML, a driverless architecture. It provides model validation. The key features that have higher influence on time series prediction include:

– Industrial production
– CPI
– Chemical and allied inventories
– TSP

Metrics:

– normalized_root_mean_squared_error

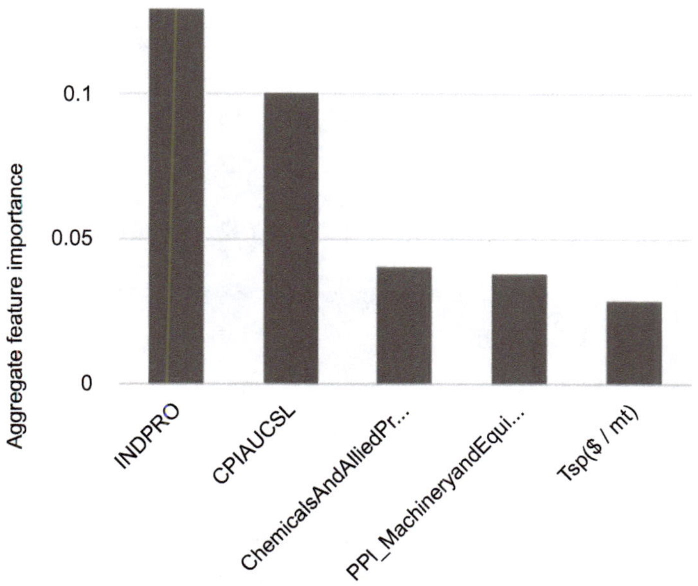
Aggregate feature importance
0.1
0.05
0
INDPRO
CPIAUCSL
ChemicalsAndAlliedPr...
PPI_MachineryandEqui...
Tsp($ / mt)

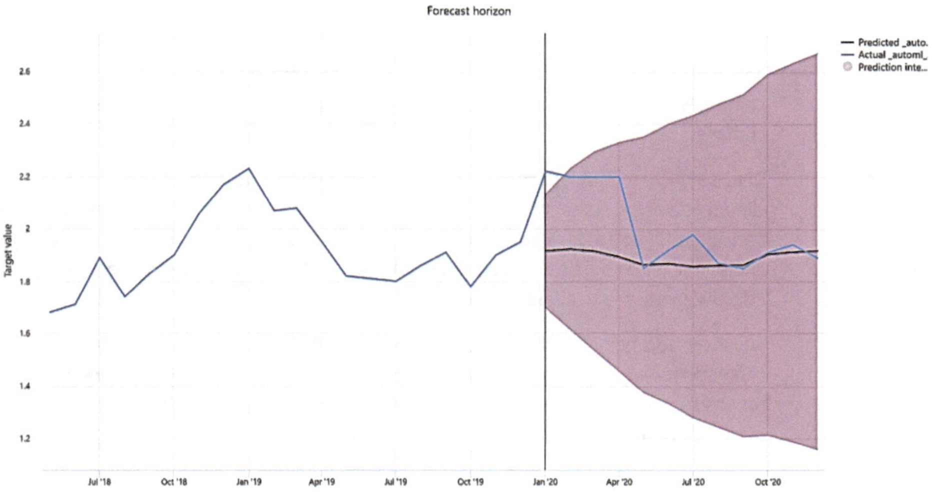
Forecast horizon
Predicted _auto.
Actual _automl_
Prediction inte...
Target value
2.6
2.4
2.2
2
1.8
1.6
1.4
1.2
Jul '18
Oct '18
Jan '19
Apr '19
Jul '19
Oct '19
Jan '20
Apr '20
Jul '20
Oct '20

Step 11: KPI: crop insurance decision

mean_absolute_error	mean_absolute_perce...	median_absolute_error	normalized_mean_abs...	normalized_median_a...
0.06262329	3.177992	0.03706933	0.03162792	0.01872189

normalized_root_mea...	normalized_root_mea...
0.04329795	0.03518166

To provide crop insurance decisions as to go or no-go, we need to calculate the forecast price trend. A positive upward trend indicates that prices of tomatoes will increase in the forecasted horizon, while a downward trend implies that the prices will fall. Based on it, we can inform our decisions.

Data-driven insights for addressing the challenges of agriculture in a changing climate.

Data is vital for mitigating the impact of climate change on crop yields due to unpredictable climate patterns. Data analysis provides insights into how climate change affects agricultural production, including weather phenomena like monsoon swings. Gathering and analyzing data helps understand challenges in the agricultural sector and establish effective strategies to address them.

Advanced technologies like ML and predictive analytics are necessary to analyze data comprehensively. Investing in data-driven solutions and advanced technologies is crucial for ensuring the long-term sustainability and success of agricultural systems in the face of climate change.

Author
Chandrasekar Vuppalapati

Chapter ML experiments

Financial sustainability what-if models

ML experiment: The financial sustainability ML model developed for evaluating options for field-grown tomatoes, the crop insurance go/no-go decision was based on

the historical trend of feature variables. Remodify the model to incorporate what-if scenarios based on the following market and agricultural conditions:
- Scenario: 150% increase in 'Natural gas, US ($/mmbtu)' prices
- Scenario: 200% increase in 'Commercial Refrigeration' rates
- Scenario: hyper inflationary trends 0 increase in 209% 'CPIAUCSL'
- Economic events such as 'U.S. Recession'

Yield guarantees model

Re-run the financial sustainability ML model for field-grown tomatoes, with prices for input costs: DAP ($/mt), TSP ($/mt), and urea ($/mt) trending at an exponential level, assuming all other feature variables exhibit historical trends.

Does exponential growth in input costs result in yield loss for farmers, assuming that farmers scaled down usage of inputs due to acreage reduction?

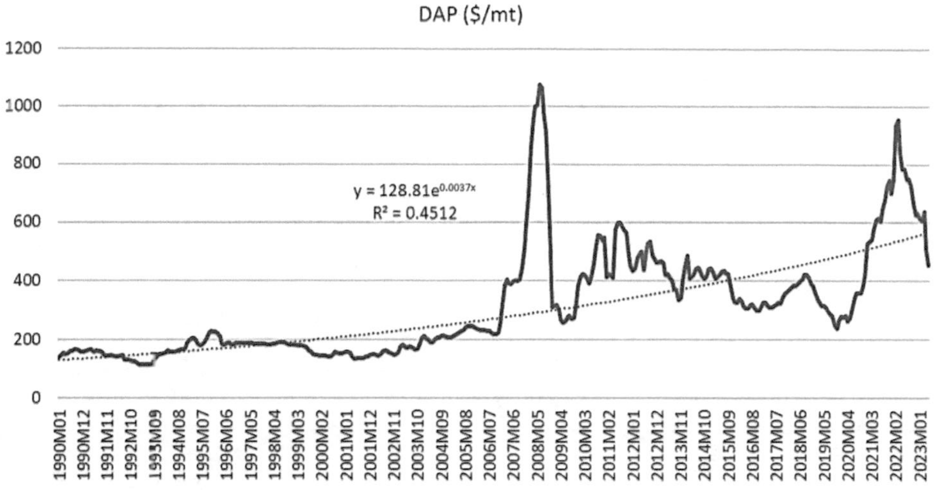

DAP ($/mt)	$y = 128.81e^{0.0037x}$ $R^2 = 0.4512$

TSP ($/mt)	$y = 111.52e^{0.0038x}$ $R^2 = 0.3937$

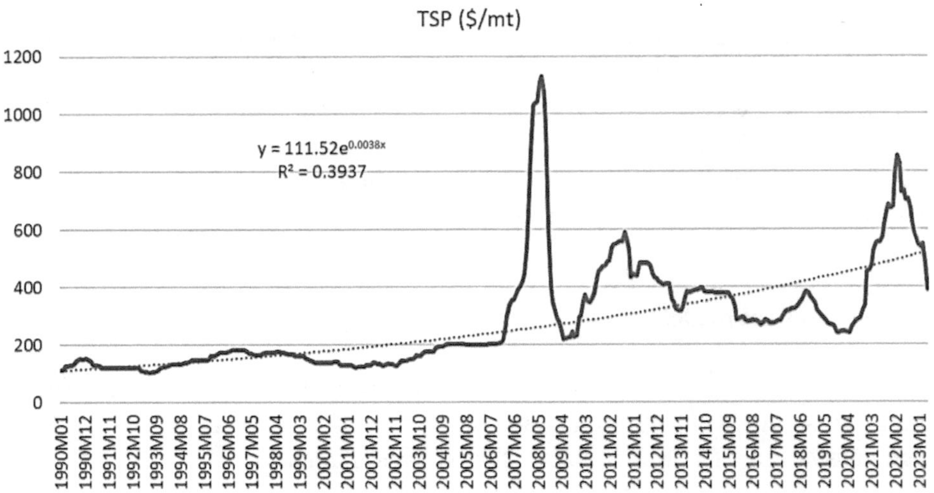

Urea ($/mt)	$y = 86.102e^{0.004x}$ $R^2 = 0.4249$

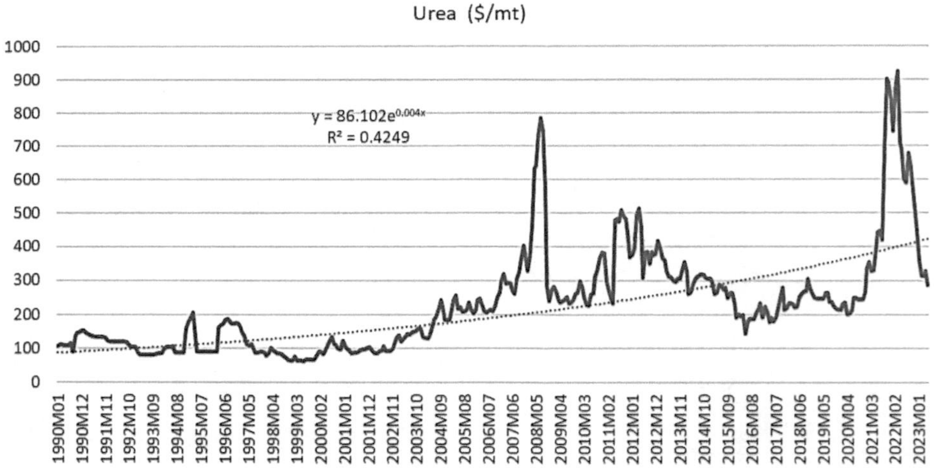

Revenue guarantees model

Re-run

The financial sustainability ML model for field-grown tomatoes considers the sudden increase in the S&P P/E ratio, where higher values imply a higher stock price over its earning potential. The P/E ratio is a metric that shows if a stock is undervalued or overvalued, with a lower PE being safer for the marketplace. The average P/E ratio is typically 20–25, but different industries may have different average P/E ratios. Does an exponential drop in S&P PR index result in revenue loss for the farmers?

P/E ratio	$y = 98.786x - 605305$ $R^2 = 0.1969$

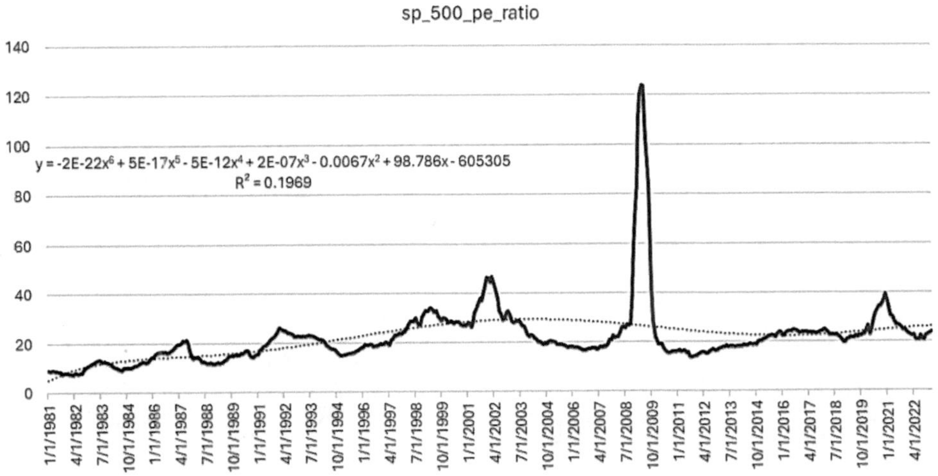

By completing this chapter, you will learn about climate change and SSPs and how they impact agricultural production. You will also gain knowledge about different crop insurance programs, such as FCIP, RMA, and AgRisk Viewer. These programs offer yield, revenue, and (%) percent-of-damage guarantees to farmers.

Moreover, you will apply advanced ML to the financial sustainability ML crop insurance go/no-go decision model. This model provides accurate price forecasts for field-grown tomatoes and ensures the financial stability of agricultural stakeholders. This chapter equips you with valuable skills and knowledge to thrive in the agricultural industry.

Section II: **Specialty crops: pistachios**

Chapter 4
Specialty crops pistachio: production and yield

This chapter covers:
- Focuses on pistachios
- Explores yield patterns in key producing countries, including the USA, Turkey, and Iran
- Delves into the nutritional benefits and food security aspects of pistachios, while also identifying the factors that influence their yield
- Introduces framework for analyzing yield across different countries
- Investigates the influence of weather events on pistachio yield projection models in California's Central Valley, USA
- Introduces a polynomial regression model that can predict the future harvest area of pistachios in California, USA

This chapter delves into the world of pistachios, a type of specialty crop. It provides an in-depth analysis of yield patterns in major producing countries like the USA, Turkey, and Iran. The chapter explores the nutrition and food security traits of pistachios and investigates the factors that impact their yield. Furthermore, the chapter presents a framework that can be used to analyze yield across different countries and examines how weather events can affect pistachio yield projection models in Central Valley, California, USA. The chapter also introduces a polynomial regression model that can predict the future harvest area of pistachios in California, USA. Overall, this chapter provides valuable insights into the yield patterns, nutrition, and food security aspects of pistachios. It also offers a framework and predictive model that can be used to analyze and forecast pistachio yield.

Pistachios, often mistakenly referred to as nuts, are actually the mildly sweet seeds of the pistachio tree. This tree is dioecious, meaning that male and female flowers grow on separate trees, both of which are necessary for nut production. The female flowers lack petals and nectar, relying on the wind for pollen dispersal. Pistachio trees shed their leaves in the fall and remain dormant throughout the winter. Classified as phreatophytes, these trees have extensive root systems that allow them to endure long periods of drought [186, 187]. Predominantly a desert plant, pistachios are mainly cultivated in the arid regions of inland California [188, 189].

Pistachios have enjoyed popularity as a food source for millennia, with records of their consumption tracing back to 7,000 B.C. The pistachio tree originally hails from Western Asia and was introduced to the USA in the mid-nineteenth century [190]. Commercial production of pistachios in the USA began in earnest during the 1970s.

Today, pistachios have emerged as a significant crop in California, benefiting from robust export markets, high prices, and lower water needs compared to other crops such as almonds. This is especially advantageous in the water-constrained Central Valley.

Remarkably, the past two years have witnessed record-breaking pistachio production in California, and experts anticipate that the acreage dedicated to pistachios will continue to expand rapidly in the coming years [191].

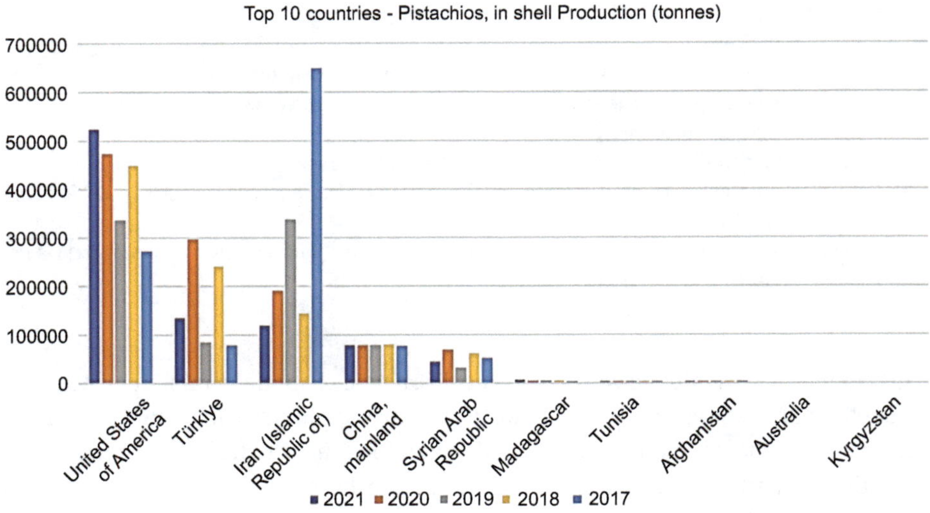

Figure 1: Top 10 countries – pistachios.

By the early twentieth century, California's pistachio industry was already thriving, with several popular nut varieties developed through crossbreeding. Over the last three decades, the yield of pistachios in California has surged dramatically. Today, more than half a million acres in the San Joaquin, Fresno, and Sacramento valleys are devoted to pistachio cultivation.

California currently stands as the world's leading producer of pistachios, contributing approximately 80% of the global supply. Pistachios represent California's top agricultural export and are the most valuable tree nut crop in terms of both revenue (US $) and acreage. Furthermore, they are the foremost specialty crop export for the USA. This underscores the remarkable expansion and significance of the pistachio industry in California, making it a pivotal player in both the state's economy and the global food market.

Pistachios are a well-loved nut cultivated in over 20 countries across the world, including the USA, Turkey, Iran, China, Syria, Madagascar, Tunisia, Afghanistan, Australia, and Kyrgyzstan (Figure 1). The global pistachio industry is worth billions of dollars and continues to grow in value as the nut becomes more popular as food [192].

The USA holds the title of the world's largest pistachio producer, with an anticipated output of 523,900 metric tons for the 2021/22 season. This surge in production is attributed to an "on-year" in the *alternate-bearing cycle and the expansion of bearing acreage.* Comparatively, in the 2020/21 marketing year, the USA produced 474,000 tons, marking an increase of 49,900 tons for the current season [193].

The global pistachio industry, a multi-billion dollar sector, continues to expand as pistachios gain increasing popularity worldwide.

Despite being an exogenous variable, the *alternate-bearing crop cycle* is an essential machine learning (ML) variable that has significantly improved the accuracy of yield, climate, and pricing models for pistachios. This variable has proven to be a valuable tool in predicting pistachio production levels and has performed a fundamental role in enhancing overall precision and reliability of pistachio yield forecasting models.

Furthermore, the alternate-bearing crop cycle has enabled stakeholders in the pistachio industry to make more learned findings about pricing and resource allocation, leading to increased profitability and sustainability of agricultural operations.

In summary, the alternate-bearing crop cycle may be an exogenous variable, but it has proven to be an indispensable asset in the development of ML models for pistachios. Its inclusion has enhanced the accuracy and reliability of yield, climate, and pricing models and has played a decisive role in driving growth and success of pistachio industry.

Author
Chandrasekar Vuppalapati

Turkey is second-largest producer of pistachios globally, and it is projected to produce 135,000 metric tons in 2021/22, a decrease of nearly 65% from 296,376 metric tons in 2020/21. This drop in production is due to low yields resulting from the alteration of the crop.[1]

Pistachios demand
Worldwide, pistachios industry has enjoyed explosive growth rates due to perceived health benefits offered such as potential lower chances aimed at cardiovascular disease plus lower of blood sugar, blood pressure, and cholesterol [5].

However, there was a considerable increase in production in 2020/21, with output nearly tripling that of 2019/20 at 85,000 metric tons. This was due to good conditions in southeastern Turkey, where most of the country's pistachio orchards are located, and a boost from the on-year.

The majority of Turkey's pistachio harvest is enjoyed within the country, leaving only a small portion available for international export. Domestic consumption in Turkey is projected to reach 211,000 tons [193].

Iran ranks as the third-largest pistachio producer in the world, with an estimated output of 119,355 tons in the 2021/22 season, a decline from 190,000 tons in 2020/21. Back in 2017, Iran's pistachio production reached 648,934 tons, but unfavorable weather conditions [194] led to a significant drop in 2018. Despite strong exports to China, the trade volume is anticipated to decrease as the available supply shrinks. On the domestic front, pistachio consumption in Iran is expected to remain steady at 30,000 tons for the 2020/21 season [193].

1 World pistachio production falls 2021/22: https://pistachosluna.com/en/world-pistachio-production-falls-2021-22/

Global pistachio industry has experienced explosive growth due to the perceived health benefits of the nut, including a potential lower risk of cardiovascular disease and reduced blood sugar, blood pressure, and cholesterol levels. Pistachios are an excellent source of protein, low in saturated fat, and completely free of cholesterol.

The surge in pistachio consumption in China has significantly contributed to market growth. In the 2020/21 season, China accounted for 35.5% of the world's total pistachio imports, amounting to an estimated 150,000 tons. This figure marks a 45% increase from the 2019/20 season, largely driven by higher shipments from both Iran and the USA.

Amid the COVID-19 pandemic, America's food banks have received donations of pistachios, other tree nuts, and surplus seafood. Notably, the highest funding allocation for these donations, amounting to $40 million [195], has been dedicated to pistachios, which are predominantly cultivated in the deserts of inland California. This investment is nearly double the amount allocated for any other food item [196].

The area of land where pistachios are grown has increased significantly over the years. In 1961, the worldwide area harvested was only 35,393 hectares, but in 2021 it increased to 817,025 hectares. There was a sharp increase to 1,046,964 hectares in 2019 due to the introduction of new plants [197].

The expansion rate of the harvested area can be accurately described using a linear trend or a regression equation (as shown in eq. (1)). This means that the growth rate follows a consistent pattern that can be predicted using mathematical models. The R^2 values for these trends are relatively high, indicating a strong correlation between the growth rate and time.

The production of pistachios has increased significantly over the years. In 1961, the worldwide production was only 20,714 tons, but in 2021 it increased to 915,717 tons according to FAOSTAT 2022. The growth rate of pistachio production can be reliably explained with a polynomial regression equation (as shown in eq. (2)). This means that the growth rate follows a more complex pattern that can be predicted using mathematical models. Furthermore, the yield of pistachios has also increased significantly from 5,853 hg/ha in 1961 to 11,208 hg/ha in 2021. The trend of yield growth can be characterized by a polynomial order 6 yield eqs. ((2) and (3)). This means that the yield growth follows a more complex and nonlinear pattern that can be predicted using mathematical models.

$$Y_{\text{Area Harvested}} = -0.0004x^6 + 4.59x^5 - 22917x^4 + 6\text{E}{+}07x^3 - 9E + 10x^2 + 7E + 13x - 2E + 16 \quad (1)$$

$$Y_{\text{Production}} = -0.002x^6 + 0.3663x^5 - 24.573x^4 + 766.45x^3 - 10846x^2 + 64886x - 78328 \quad (2)$$

$$Y_{\text{Yield}} = -2E{-}05x^6 + 0.0038x^5 - 0.2369x^4 + 7.1942x^3 - 112.98x^2 + 995.9x + 4344.9 \quad (3)$$

Note that, except for the power regression trend fit, the area harvested regression types (linear, exponential, logarithmic, and polynomial) have higher accuracy (Figure 2).

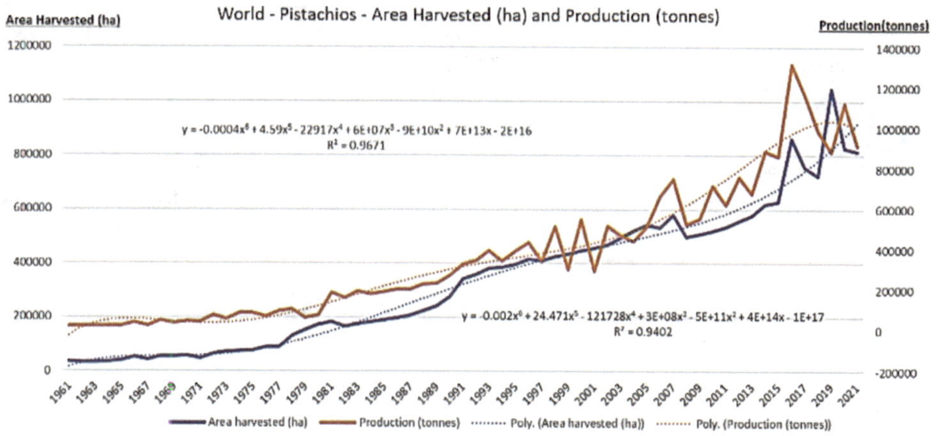

Figure 2: World pistachios area harvested.

Area	Equation	R^2 value
Exponential	$y = 1E{-}43e^{0.0558x}$	$R^2 = 0.9053$
Linear	$y = 13825x - 3E{+}07$	$R^2 = 0.9284$
Power	$y = 0x^{111.27}$	$R^2 = 0$

Area harvested is a function of bearing acreage and the time to maturity of nonbearing acreage.

$$\text{Area harvested} = (1 - d^{ba}) * \text{BA} + \int_{t=1}^{t=N} \text{nBA maturity function (nBA Trend)}$$

where

- BA is bearing acreage.
- d^{ba} is a damping constant, and it's a time function of how long acreage is under production. Longer years (> 30 years) would have a higher number of trees that have reached the peak of yield and the cost function would need to be carved. For now, assume a constant (0.0001).
- *nBA* maturity function is the subject of nonbearing acreage trend. It varies from orchard to orchard; a management decision to expand production through increased area harvested and potential increase in yield.
- F(nBA Trend): It's a regression equation that expresses the nonbearing acreage maturity trend.
- T is time to maturity of nonbearing acreage maturity [198].

The area of land where pistachios grow has increased significantly over time, and as a result, more trees are reaching maturity and producing nuts. This is known as "bearing acreage." As nonbearing acreages continue to mature, there is an expectation of substantial growth in pistachio production. This means that as more trees reach maturity and start producing nuts, there will be a significant increase in the amount of pistachios produced.

The distinctive characteristic of pistachios, which naturally split open before being harvested, poses a considerable challenge for farmers. Therefore, it is essential to ensure that these fragile nuts do not touch the ground, as they are susceptible to contamination by soil bacteria.

To preserve the quality and safety of the pistachio crop, farmers must rigorously supervise the harvesting process. Careful collection and handling are vital to minimizing contamination risks. This process requires exceptional precision and attention to detail, as even slight variations in technique can have a significant impact on the crop's quality and safety.

Production: Except for logarithmic (56.48%), all other regression types provide higher accuracy (> 86%).

	Equation	R^2
Exponential	$y = 27218e^{0.0665x}$	$R^2 = 0.8923$
Linear	$y = 17450x - 167948$	$R^2 = 0.8609$
Logarithmic	$y = 278237\ln(x) - 506136$	$R^2 = 0.5648$
Polynomial order 6	$y = -0.002x^6 + 0.3663x^5 - 24.573x^4 + 766.45x^3 - 10846x^2 + 64886x - 78328$	$R^2 = 0.9402$
Power	$y = 3867.8x^{1.2698}$	$R^2 = 0.8932$

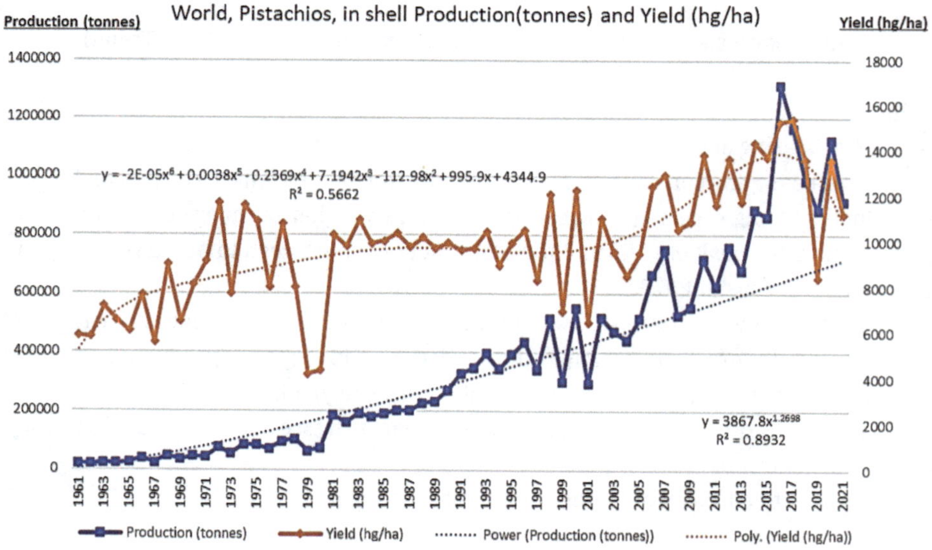

Figure 3: World pistachios production.

Pistachios production is unique as they exhibit clearly alternate-bearing repetition, following an "on"/"off" cycle. As a result, year over year would vary [198] as shown in Figure 3. As a result, the R^2 value that explains yield would be very low.

Yield curve: The yield of pistachios has experienced more fluctuations compared to production. From 1961 to the mid-1970s, the yield shows an increasing trend. From the late 1970s to the early 2000s, the yield fluctuates significantly, with notable drops and recoveries. Post-2000, while there are still fluctuations, the overall trend appears to be upward [199].

Pistachios demand
Pistachios split before they are harvested. Thus, they must not fall on ground, because they run the risk of contamination from soil microorganisms.

The worldwide pistachios yield could be observed using eq. (4). Except for the polynomial order (56.62%), all other regression trend types exhibit lower R^2 values. Figure 3 effectively illustrates the growing trend in pistachio production and the more variable but overall upward trend in yield over the past six decades. The trendlines and their equations provide a mathematical representation of these trends.

$$Y\,\text{yield} = -2E{-}05x^6 + 0.0038x^5 - 0.2369x^4 + 7.1942x^3 - 112.98x^2 + 995.9x + 4344.9 \qquad (4)$$

$$\text{Yield Function (chill, bloom, harvest)} = \sum_{\text{Climate}} \sum_{\text{Age}} \sum_{\text{Farm Inputs}} \text{F (Climate, Age, Farm Inputs)}$$

The bloom period is impacted by many factors, such as wind, rain, cold, and heat. At the end of this period, we can evaluate yields based on the conditions experienced during the bloom season [199]. Likewise, the harvest season depends on several of the same factors: accumulated heat units, the amount of irrigation water available to the trees, and the overall growing season will determine the size, onset, duration, and quality of the harvest [199]. Yield curves are representative of nature, phenology, climate, botany, human labor, and soil engineering (Figure 4).

Other yield curves:

Yield trendline options	Equation	R^2 Value
Exponential	$y = 6831.2e^{0.0106x}$	$R^2 = 0.4734$
Linear	$y = 100.73x + 6746.4$	$R^2 = 0.4729$
Logarithmic	$y = 1868.5\ln(x) + 3965.3$	$R^2 = 0.4198$
Polynomial order 6	$y = -2E{-}05x^6 + 0.0038x^5 - 0.2369x^4 + 7.1942x^3 - 112.98x^2 + 995.9x + 4344.9$	$\mathbf{R^2 = 0.5662}$
Power	$y = 4965.9x^{0.2053}$	$R^2 = 0.4456$

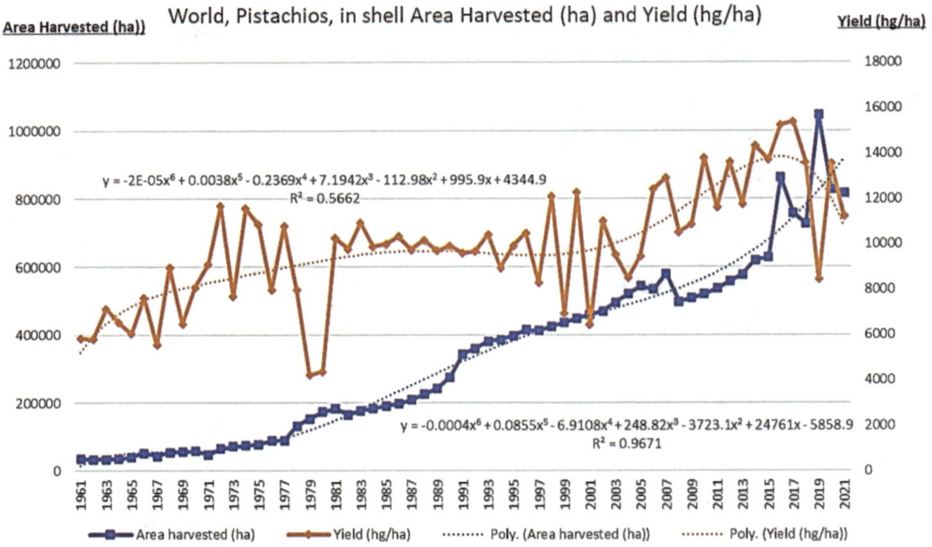

Figure 4: Area harvest and yield.

The age of plants makes a considerable difference in the yield analytics. The other factors that impact yield include climate change, weather, fertilizers, water, and human labor availability.

In 2020, the USA emerged as the world's leading producer of pistachios, with California standing out as a major production hub. Among the popular pistachio varieties cultivated in California are carmel, nonpareil, types, and mission (Figure 4).

Yield is influenced by wind, rain, cold, heat, frost, timing of fertilizer, water quality, bearing, nonbearing, and age of the trees.

The USA accounts for over 90% of the global pistachio production, with California leading the way. California is not only the top producer of pistachios, contributing approximately 40% to the world's supply, but also dominates almond production, supplying more than 80% of the world's almonds [186].

Pistachio production follows an alternate-bearing pattern, which can pose marketing challenges. This pattern leads to large harvests being succeeded by smaller ones, creating an "on" and "off" year cycle. Unfortunately, no solutions to this phenomenon are currently known, and it must be factored into production models. As a result of this pattern, grower prices can fluctuate significantly based on changes in supply. Prices tend to rise in off years when the crop is short and decline in on year when the crop is larger [198].

In a race against warming

The effects of climate change on California pistachio growers' livelihoods have become strikingly clear. Recent reports highlight that they have endured a billion-dollar loss due to an unexpectedly warm winter.

This underscores the very real threat that climate change poses to industry, and the urgent need for proactive measures to address this issue. The loss of such a significant amount of revenue is not only detrimental to the growers themselves but also has broader implications for the local economy and the global pistachio market [198].

> The most bountiful yields in pistachio production are typically achieved in orchards that are irrigated and located in regions with long, hot summers and minimal rainfall.

Pistachios are highly valued for their hea lth benefits, particularly due to their growing focus on healthy eating. In the past, nuts and pistachios were considered unhealthy due to their high fat content. However, research has demonstrated that pistachios contain good fats, such as monounsaturated fat that have a positive effect on the body. These good fats decrease the danger of heart disease and improve cholesterol health [194].

Although saturated fats found in animal products and processed foods have been associated with higher cholesterol levels and cardiovascular disease, pistachios present numerous health benefits. They can aid in reducing cholesterol and blood sugar levels, while also delivering antioxidants that support heart health and weight management.

This highlights the unique advantages of incorporating pistachios into one's diet and underscores the importance of making informed choices when it comes to nutrition. By choosing nutrient-rich foods like pistachios, individuals can support their overall health and well-being, while also enjoying delicious and satisfying meals [190].

Pistachios are an excellent source of energy, iron, calcium, vitamins, and polyunsaturated fatty acids. They contribute to maintaining balanced cholesterol levels and lowering the risk of cardiovascular disease. Additionally, they are well-regarded for their weight-loss advantages, with studies indicating that including nuts in a weight-loss regimen can result in more significant weight reduction.

Pistachios are high in fiber and protein, making them a satisfying snack. They also offer a satisfying crunch and chewing experience when consumed. These benefits have contributed to the increasing popularity of pistachios and other tree nuts [190].

Pistachios and blood pressure [190]

Combining a low glycemic index food, like almonds, with a higher glycemic index food, such as fresh fruit or crackers, can help moderate the increase in blood sugar levels after a snack [190].

Pistachios are renowned for their unique growth patterns, which include a long juvenile period where few nuts are produced before the tree reaches five years of age. Full bearing is typically achieved between 10 and 12 years of age, making careful management of the young trees essential. The tree's upright growth habit, characterized by a strong apical dominance and a lack of lateral vegetative buds in older trees, further underscores the importance of proper training and pruning techniques. These practices are critical for promoting healthy growth and rejuvenation.

In recent years, the USA has seen a significant increase in pistachio production. However, this growth has decelerated somewhat due to economic conditions. Despite this slowdown, the overall trend remains upward. US pistachios are exported to numerous countries, including Germany, Turkey, China, Japan, and Spain. From 2016 to 2021, production has grown at a compound annual growth rate ranging from 0.53% to 15.11% per year. Notably, some countries have experienced more substantial increases in production than others. For instance, Turkey and Iran have achieved double-digit growth rates of 15 % and 13%, respectively, while Pakistan and Jordan's growth has been more modest, at 0.53% and 0.93%, respectively. This information is shown in Figure 5.

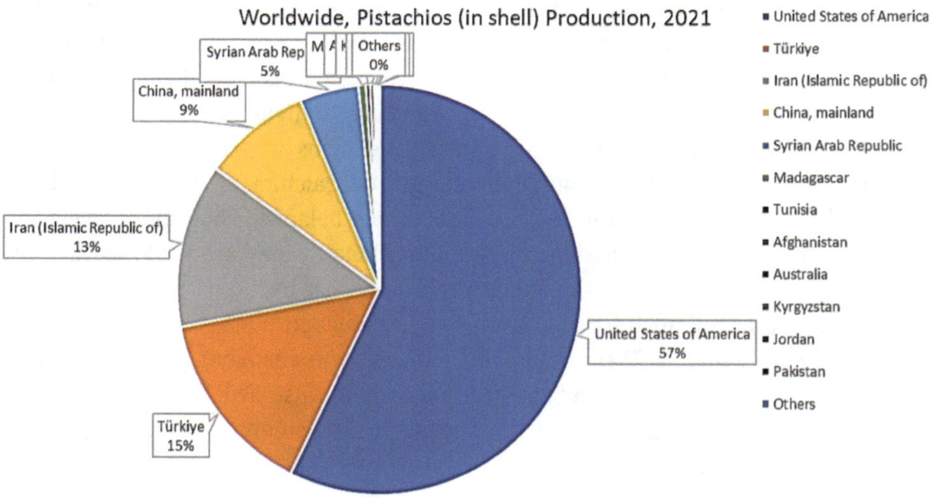

Figure 5: Worldwide pistachios production, 2023.

Top cultivating sources of pistachios

The USA holds the position of the world's leading pistachio producer. In 2021, the value of pistachio production in the USA reached $2.910 billion. Pistachios play a crucial role in the American tree nut industry, accounting for approximately 30% of the total tree nut production value, which amounted to $9.742 billion in 2021.

On/off season – ML feature variable

Pistachio production follows an alternate-bearing pattern, which can complicate marketing and distribution efforts. This pattern is marked by abundant harvests in one year, followed by smaller yields the next, creating a cyclical "on" and "off" year effect. Unfortunately, no remedies for this phenomenon currently exist, necessitating its inclusion in production models. Growers and producers must meticulously manage their crops to achieve optimal yields and maintain consistent quality, even during years of reduced production [198].

The United States

Figure 6 depicts the trend in the production of pistachios (in shell) in the USA from 1977 to 2021, measured in tons. The USA has emerged as the largest supplier of pistachios worldwide, with the value of production in 2021 totaling $2.910 billion (Figure 6). Pistachios contribute significantly to the tree nut industry in the USA, making up around 30% of the absolute worth of production, which was $9.742 billion in 2021. Over the past two decades, the production of pistachios in the USA has grown significantly. In 2000/2001, the USA produced approximately 114 million pounds of pistachios, but by 2021/22, production had grown to over 580 million pounds. Overall, there has been an upward trend in pistachio production in the USA over the years, with some fluctuations, particularly a notable dip around 2015.

As per USDA-NAS (Figure 6), the 2021 crop is estimated to be 580 million pounds, which is a 10% increase from the previous year's record of 526 million pounds [192]. In 2014, the pistachio industry faced a substantial decline in production caused by hot and dry weather conditions in the western region. This led to the damage of half the harvest and reduced earnings for 2015 by nearly $1.5 billion. The impact of weather on pistachio production is reflected in both the price and quantity of pistachios produced. California, Arizona, and New Mexico are three pistachio-producing states.

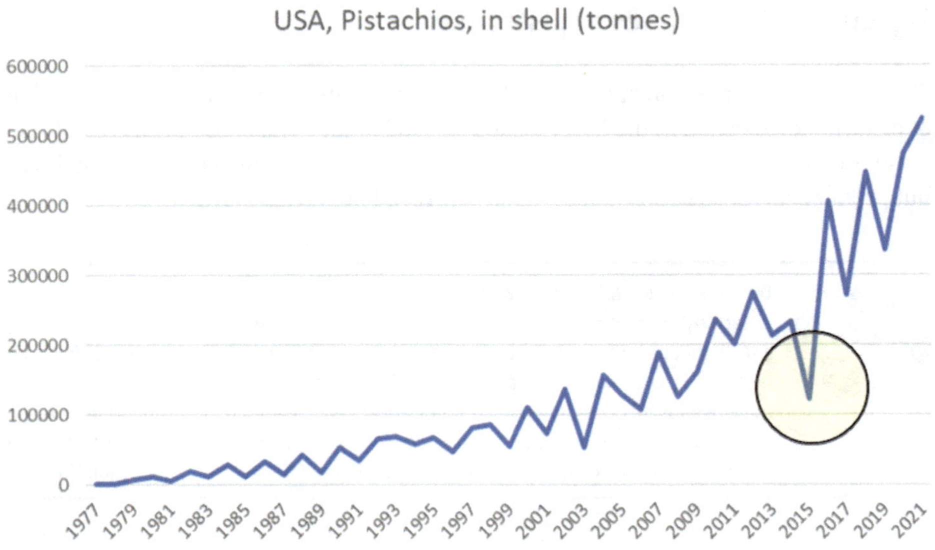

Figure 6: USA pistachios production.

California

California contributes 99% of pistachios production in the USA [200]. Pistachios are the California's sixth largest agricultural commodities by revenue, generating $2.91 billion in 2022. In terms of export ranking,[2] they are #2, with export earnings of $2.010 billion in 2019 and 16% export value growth from 2018 to 2019. Put it simply, pistachios are a cash crop for the state of California (Figure 7).

California's San Joaquin Valley encompasses 312,000 acres dedicated to pistachio farming, with 96% of the production originating from the prominent counties of Fresno, Kern, Kings, Madera, and Tulare. The winter of 2014/15 [201], the warmest ever recorded in the southern San Joaquin Valley, issued a stark warning to the pistachio industry. To guarantee a successful harvest, the number of heating degree days – measured when the daily average temperature drops below 65 °F (18.3 °C) – needs to be adequately high during December and January [202]. The production drop (Figure 8) from 514 million pounds in 2014 to 329 million pounds in 2015 resulted in higher grower prices, as demand outstripped supply. The grower demand in California can be observed in Figure 8.

2 2019 Export data: https://aic.ucdavis.edu/wp-content/uploads/2021/07/2019_CDFA_TablesFinal.xlsx

Figure 7: California pistachios grown areas.

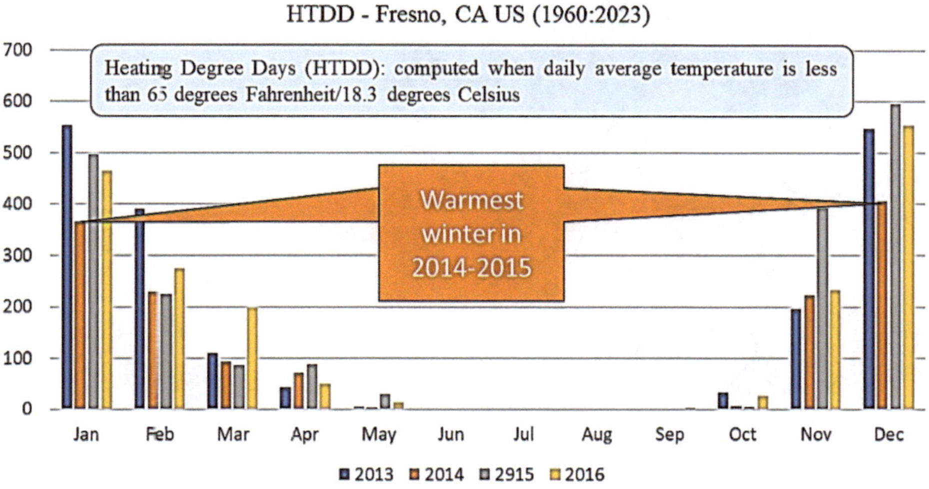

Figure 8: HTDD, CA.

Historically, orchards situated 125 miles north of Los Angeles thrived under the benefits of cool, rainy winters and thick fog. However, in the past century, average temperatures across the state have risen by more than 2 °F. Notably, the valley's winter lows have increased at a rate four times faster than its summer highs. Additionally, the renowned Tule fog, a dense ground fog that typically blankets the San Joaquin and

Sacramento Valleys in California's Central Valley, has diminished by 46% [202].

Tule fog [203], a common winter phenomenon in California's Sacramento and San Joaquin valleys, often leads to significant freeway accidents due to its dense, zero-visibility conditions (Figure 9). Despite the dangers, this fog is highly valued by farmers growing almonds, apricots, cherries, peaches, and pistachios. It aids the trees in meeting their dormancy needs, which is crucial for the development of flowers and fruit. The rest period facilitated by the fog is essential for ensuring high yields during the growing season.

San Joaquin Valley and Sacramento Valley areas of California's Central Valley have enjoyed cool, rainy winters, and dense fog, satisfying the dormancy requirement necessary to produce flowers and fruit. The trees need this rest period to produce high yields during the growing season.

Figure 9: Tule fog.

The agriculture sector in the Central Valley, which accounts for 95% of the US' fruit and nut output, highly depends on winter chills to ensure the healthy development of buds, sprouts, flowers, flora, and fruit. Fruit trees need extended durations with temperatures below approximately 44 °F (6.66 °C) during the persistent Tule fog to attain optimal yields. Consequently, Tule fog is a crucial predictor of fruit production in the valley [203].

- In the winter of 2014/15, the southern San Joaquin Valley saw only half the necessary chill hours for pistachio cultivation and experienced no Tule fog at all. This resulted in the industry's lowest yield in over two decades. Similarly, cherry production suffered a significant decline, with output dropping by 63%. Grower prices rose due to low production but fell sharply in 2015/16 due to bumper crops [204].
- The 2021 pistachio season began favorably with dry weather in February, providing ideal conditions for blooming and pollination. However, the spring's deficiency of precipitation and record-high temperatures in June sparked concerns about water availability. This prompted some farmers to strip their trees of nuts before the harvest. Despite low disease and pest pressure, the average nut set per tree dropped by 18% compared to the previous year, with the Nonpareil variety seeing a 20% decrease in its average nut set (Figure 10).

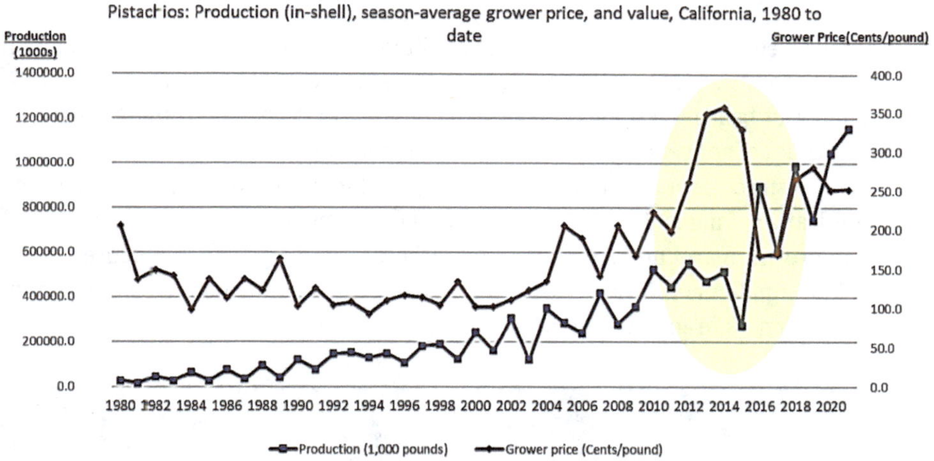

Figure 10: Pistachios production, CA.

Pistachio production in California showed a general upward trend from 1980 to 2020, with notable fluctuations and significant increases from 2010 onward. The grower price for pistachios fluctuated over the years, with a significant rise around 2010–2014, a sharp drop in 2016, and a recovery by 2020. Figure 10 highlights the relationship between production volume and grower price, showing how both metrics have evolved over the past four decades.

Agriculture, in many ways, resembles gambling in Las Vegas. We've always had uncertainty. But now there is even more uncertainty.

Rob Yraceburu,
President of Wonderful Orchards

The weather data for Fresno, California, is collected from the Global Summaries dataset, known as GSOM for monthly [205].

Türkiye

Spring rain is crucial for Turkey's pistachios orchards.

In Turkey, pistachios are primarily grown without irrigation, making spring rain (March through May) crucial for the health and productivity of the orchards. Improved rainfall, especially during winter and spring, will immensely benefit the production [206]. A fact that can be observed through historical correlation of precipitation (2004:2023) and production data (Figure 11). It can be seen the exponential growth ($y = 6189.9e^{0.0539x}$ $R^2 = 0.7215$).

As reported by the Turkish Statistical Institute (TSI), Turkey had about 54 million bearing trees and 22 million nonbearing trees at the start of the marketing year 2021/22. The number of bearing trees grew by 4.7% compared to the previous marketing year, while the count of nonbearing trees rose by approximately 8.2%. This increase in bearing trees has bolstered production, especially compared to earlier off-years, emphasizing the significance of meticulous management and future planning [206]. Although pistachios are grown in around 56 provinces in Turkey, only five provinces (Figure 11) are the leading suppliers of Turkish pistachios. These provinces include Gaziantep, Sanliurfa, Adiyaman, Kahramanmaras, and Siirt [207].

Figure 11: Pistachios leading producing areas.

According to the 2017 data from the TSI, Gaziantep boasts a pistachio cultivation area of 136,347 hectares, accounting for 41.47% of the total. Following Gaziantep are Şanliurfa with 25,809 hectares (7.85%), Adıyaman with 18,807 hectares (5.72%), and Siirt. Collectively, these regions contribute 93.18% of the total pistachio production. Şanliurfa leads in production with 28,507 tons, representing 36.55% of the total, while Gaziantep produces 14,762 tons, making up 18.92% [208]. The following figure shows the precipitation pattern for Gaziantep – weather station: Oguzeli, TU (GHCND:TUM00017260) (Figure 12).

Figure 12: NOAA GSOM.

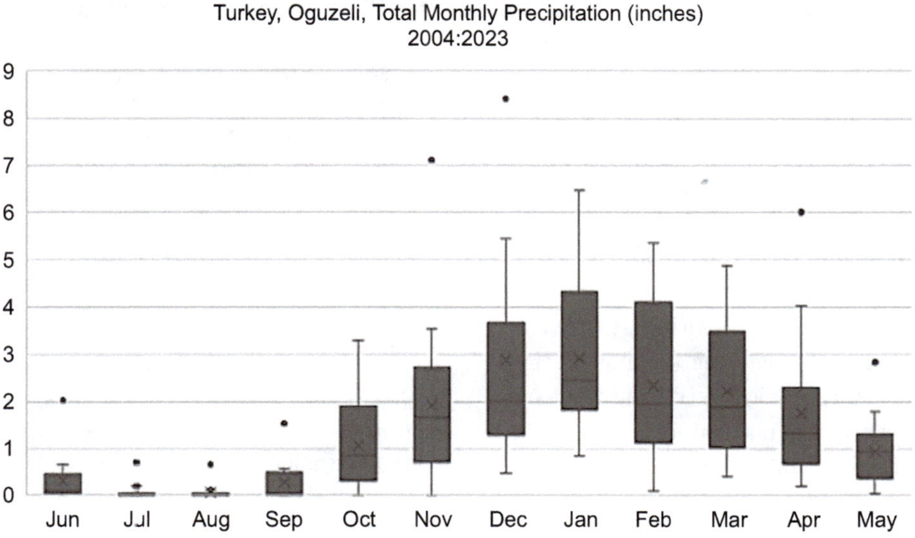

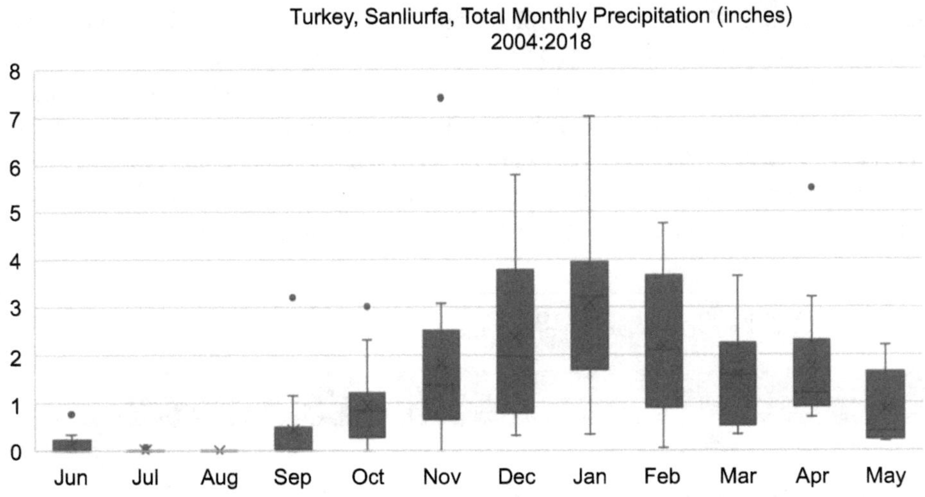

Turkey is home to two main types of pistachios, which are different from the varieties found in Iran and California. The most prevalent pistachio variety in Turkey is the Gaziantep (Antep) type, which is known for being thinner and smaller compared to the standard Iranian pistachio. The second type is the Siirt variety, which makes up approximately 15% of total production. This variety is known for its high-yielding properties and is less susceptible to production fluctuations than the Gaziantep variety.

Siirt pistachios have a size and shape that falls in between the Gaziantep and Iranian varieties. In Turkey, the quality of pistachios is determined based on their size. First-quality pistachios are those with fewer than 90 nuts per 100 g, while second-quality pistachios have between 90 and 100 nuts per 100 g. Third-quality pistachios have between 100 and 120 nuts per 100 g, and fourth-quality pistachios have more than 120 nuts per 100 g [206]. With the rising number of new saplings being planted in the Sanliurfa and Siirt regions, the production of premium-quality pistachios is anticipated to grow in outlook. At present, the average pistachio yield in Turkey is approximately 4 kg per tree (kg/tree) during on-years and 2 kg/tree during off-years. Notably, the marketing year 2020/21 was an exceptional on-year, with yields surpassing 4½ kg/tree (Figure 13).

Pistachio cultivation demands specific temperature conditions, with optimal growth occurring at around 45 °C (113 °F) in the summer and 20 °C (68 °F) in the winter. However, pistachio trees are susceptible to late spring frost, and temperatures close to or below freezing can inflict significant damage on the crop. Conversely, the summer heat is vital for the advance and enhancement of pistachio kernels, making it a critical factor for a successful harvest. By cultivating pistachio trees in favorable temperature conditions and shielding them from late spring frost, growers can maximize their yields and ensure the production of high-quality crops.

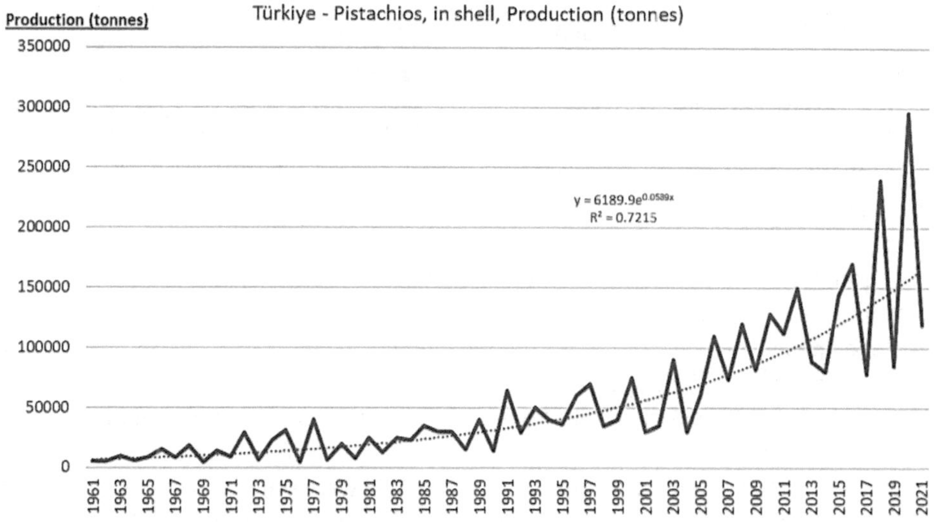

Figure 13: Pistachios production in Türkiye.

Iran

Pistachio farming boasts a long and storied history in Iran, with evidence of cultivation stretching back thousands of years. In comparison, the USA began growing pistachios in the 1930s after importing Persian seeds [192]. Iran, situated in a semi-arid region, has around 50 million hectares of land suitable for agriculture. Unfortunately, a significant portion of this land remains uncultivated due to insufficient irrigation water. Despite this, some horticultural crops are still produced in rainfed conditions, with 400,000 hectares of rainfed orchards in Iran, accounting for 16.5% of total orchards [205]. The province of Kerman is the primary area for pistachio production in Iran, where the crop has been widely cultivated and is regarded as one of the country's most important horticultural products. This information highlights the unique challenges and opportunities associated with pistachio farming in Iran, as well as the country's rich history and tradition in the industry. By understanding the specific conditions and factors that impact pistachio cultivation in different regions, growers and producers can make informed decisions and optimize their yields and profitability over time [208].

The Rafsanjan region (Figure 14) in Kerman province, Iran, has the largest number of different pistachio varieties with recognizable characteristics in cultivation and use compared to other [209] areas in Iran or any other country. According to FAOSTAT 2022, Iran's harvested area for pistachios spans 125,544 hectares. Together, the USA and Iran have consistently controlled between 70% and 80% of the global pistachio production over the past decade, dominating the international pistachio trade. Over the last 40 years, Iranian farmers have faced challenges due to sanctions, tariffs, market accesses, and limitations on accessing global financial services. However, the implementation of the Joint Comprehensive Plan of Action in 2016, following an agreement with the USA and its allies, lifted these sanctions, thereby facilitating trade for Iranian pistachio growers [209].

> Pistachios are renowned for their exceptional resilience to water stress, making them a vital agricultural commodity in Iran's rainfed areas.

Iran, once a prominent exporter of pistachios, has experienced a decline in production in recent years due to several limiting factors identified by experts [206]. These include inadequate farming and operation practices, insufficient rainfall in water capture regions, and inadequate temperatures (low) in March and April that can harm the flowers. Furthermore, certain areas suffer from severe pest infestations and diseases, which further hinder production.

The Iran data captured for Kerman and Zahedan were collected using NOAA GSOM for weather stations: Kerman, IR (IR0000408) and Zahedan, IR (IR000408560) (Figure 15).

Figure 14: Rafsanjan region.

Figure 15: GSOM region selection.

Seasonal phenology and climatic requirements

Pistachio trees thrive in specific climatic and environmental conditions, requiring *very cold winters and long, hot summers*. Optimal temperatures for pistachio growth are around 45 °C (104 °F) in summer and 20 °C (68 °F) in winter. While late spring frosts can be detrimental to pistachio trees, the summer heat is crucial for their growth and kernel development. Today, Iran produces pistachios at lower altitudes and has a successful production cycle (Figure 16 for the value chain).

Pistachio trees rely on wind for pollination rather than bees. Male and female flowers grow on separate trees, so a female tree will not produce nuts unless a male tree is nearby. For optimal pollination, it is advisable to plant a male tree upwind of every 10–15 female trees. The variety of commercial pistachio cultivars is limited, with most growers choosing Kerman for the female trees and Peters for the male trees. The 'Famoso' cultivar (Figure 17) is a newly developed male pistachio variety intended to replace 'Peters' in California's 'Kerman' orchards [210].

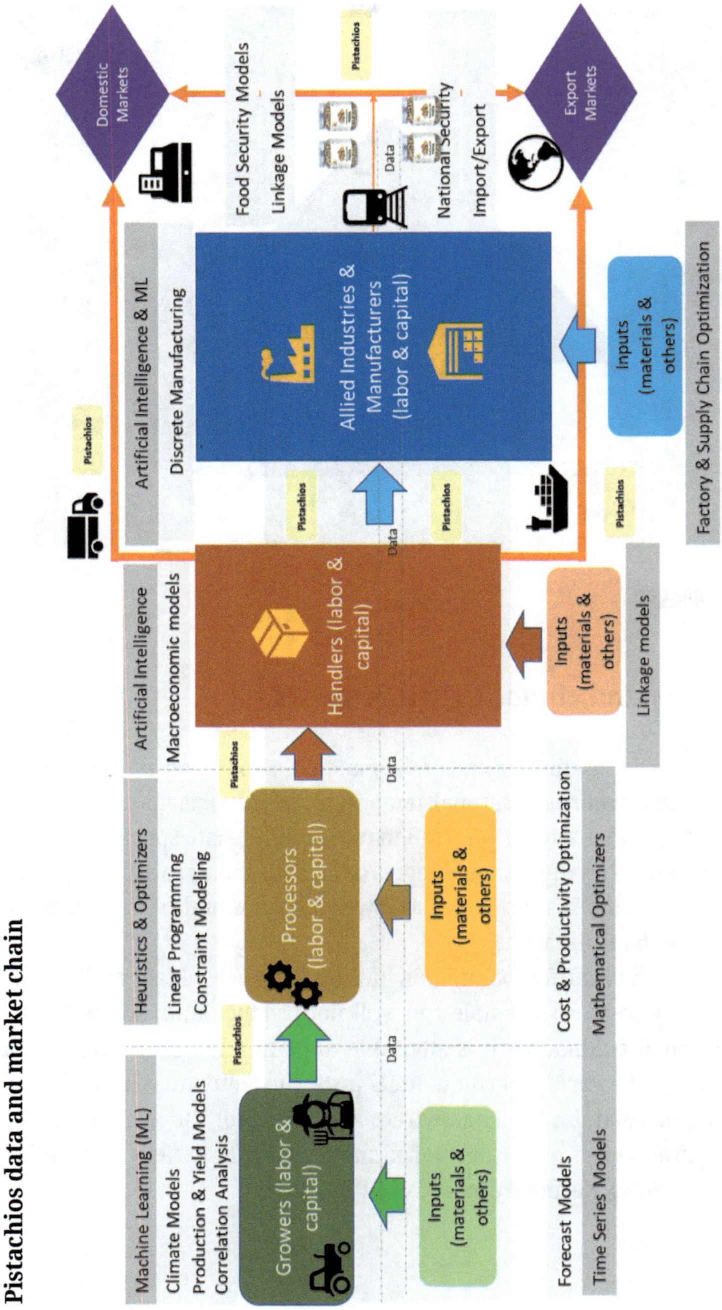

Figure 16: Pistachios.

Figure 17: 'Famoso' [210].

The 'Famoso' pistachio tree is a new type of male tree made to work better with the female 'Kerman' pistachio trees in California. 'Kerman' trees need a male tree to help produce nuts, but the old male tree, 'Peters', didn't always bloom at the right time. 'Famoso' blooms at the right time more often, even when winters are not very cold. This makes it a great match for 'Kerman' trees, helping them grow lots of nuts [210].

When you first pick pistachios, you get about 5 pounds of nuts, but after 10th harvest, you can get 50 pounds or more. Some pistachios do not open, and a few have nothing inside. Pistachio trees produce lots of nuts one year and fewer nuts the next year. Watering and trimming the trees can help, but they cannot stop this from happening completely.

The United States of America

The timing of the pistachio harvest is determined by nature. In the American West, this occurs between late August and early October when the pistachios are ripe and their shells have split [211]. For American pistachio growers, the culmination of the year's efforts is a well-coordinated collaboration between member growers and processors to harvest and deliver the crop swiftly and efficiently. This meticulous process guarantees top-quality pistachios every year (Figure 18).

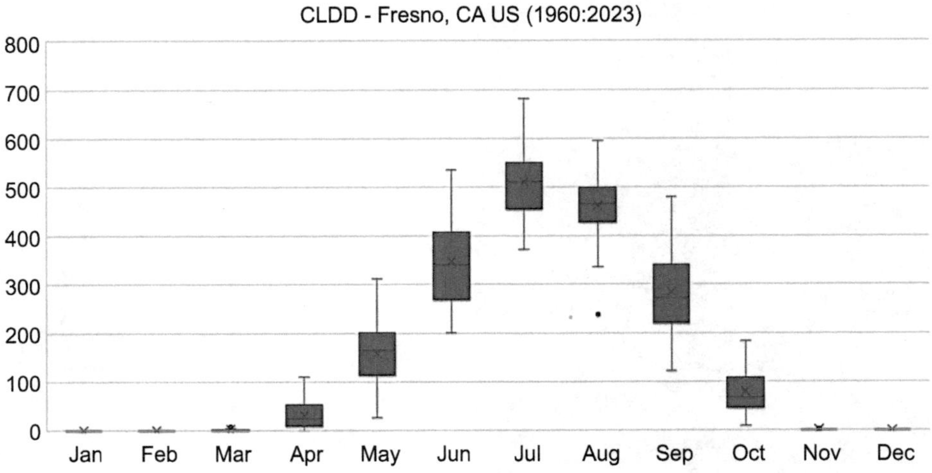

Figure 18: CLDD Gresno.

Pistachios require a significant amount of chilling[3]: approximately 850 h below 45 °F (7.2 °C) from November 1 to March 30. Additionally, they need warm, dry conditions from July to early September for proper kernel development. Although pistachio trees can withstand brief periods of winter cold down to 27 °F (–2.8 °C), early fall and spring frosts can damage their leaves and flowers. Heavy rainfall during pollination can also negatively impact fruit set and lead to wet-weather diseases like Botrytis and Alternaria blights [212].

Please find Fresno cooling degree days (CLDD) – 1969:2023 (Figure 18). The idea of climate degree days (CLDD) involves a calculation made whenever the average daily temperature exceeds 65 °F (18.3 °C). This calculation is performed for each day of the month, and the resulting values are then added up to produce a monthly total. In essence, CLDD is a measure of the amount of heating or cooling needed to maintain a certain temperature in a given area over a period of time. By tracking CLDD, researchers and scientists can gain insights into temperature trends and patterns, as well as make informed decisions about energy usage and efficiency. As can be expected, CLDD would have higher value during the summertime (May through October). The warmest months in Fresno, CA, with the highest CLDD values, are June, July, and August, while the cooler months with negligible CLDD values are January, February, November, and December.

3 The pistachio tree: https://www.heartofthedesert.com/pistachio-tree-info-from-heart-of-the-desert/

The concept of cooling degree days (CDSD) refers to a calculation used to track how much cooling is needed in a certain area. In this case, we are specifically looking at the CDSD in Fresno, which is a running total of how many cooling degree days have been recorded so far this season.

To determine the CDSD, we sum the cooling degree days for each month, considering the difference between the average temperature and a specified base temperature (typically around 65 °F). The following graph (Figure 19) illustrates the CDSD data for Fresno, CA, from 1960 to 2023. The graph demonstrates a steady accumulation of degree days throughout the year, peaking in the later months (October, November, and December) with the highest cumulative values. The early months (January to March) show negligible cumulative degree days, indicating lower temperatures. It is important to remember that the season begins in January for the Northern Hemisphere and in July for the Southern Hemisphere. Additionally, November and December are months that generally require higher cooling requirements due to colder temperatures. November and December mostly meet the high chilling requirement (Figure 19).

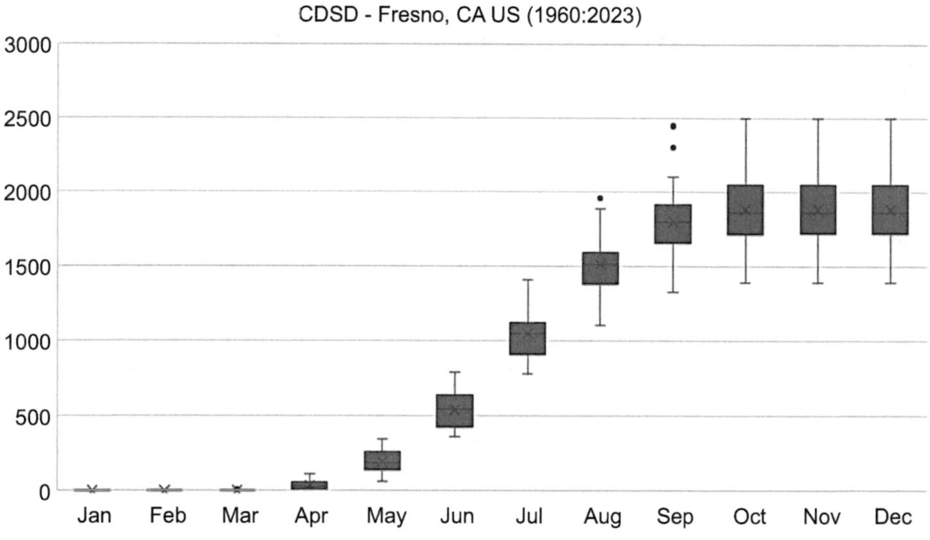

Figure 19: CDSD for Fresno, CA.

To achieve maximum production and yield, it is essential to consider various factors such as weather patterns, climatology, and agricultural calendars. By carefully considering these factors and taking proactive steps to mitigate risks and maximize opportunities, growers and producers can achieve success and thrive in a highly competitive industry.

Pistachio trees attract few pests, making them an excellent option for organic gardeners [212].

Figure 20: Pistachios harvest [199].

California

Wind-pollination takes place in April, with male trees providing pollen and female trees producing the nuts. During June and July, the pistachio kernel matures, causing the shell to naturally split before hardening (Figure 20). The outer hull remains intact, acting as a protective layer for the nut. As the nut ripens, the hull detaches from the shell and can be easily removed by pinching. When fully ripened, the hull often turns a rosy color. Timely harvesting is crucial to maximize the number of naturally split nuts, with growers closely monitoring their fields to determine the optimal start date. Harvesting generally begins in late August to early September and continues for about six weeks (Figure 21) [213].

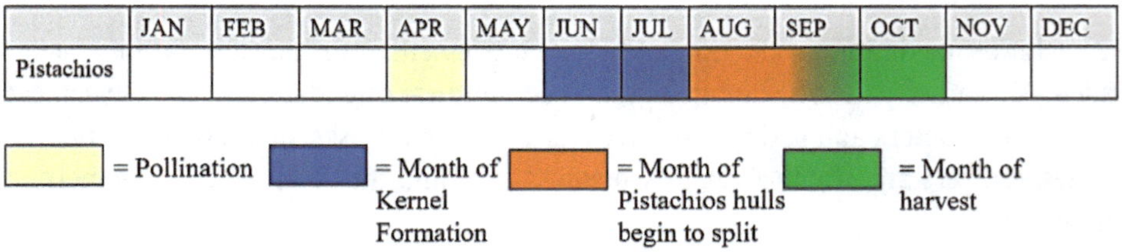

Figure 21: Pistachios agriculture calendar.

Phenological state	Months	Notes
Tree buds, *Blooming†*	*April*	Pollination
Kernel forming	*June and July*	Mature with shell hardening and kernel forming
Pistachios hulls begin to split	*August to early September*	Harvest commences.
Pistachios	*Late August through October*	Harvest

† Pistachios represent the top cash crop in the state, and an unexpected temperature drop during the early spring months in the Central Valley could be disastrous for the industry. This vulnerability arises because pistachios are particularly sensitive to temperature fluctuations, especially in the initial stages of their growth and development. If temperatures fall too low, it can damage the flowers and buds, which can result in a reduced yield and lower quality nuts. This can have a significant impact on the industry as a whole, as pistachios are an essential crop for many farmers and producers in the region.

Pistachios are highly temperature sensitive, and yield can vary greatly even within the same county depending on weather conditions. In 2015, the San Joaquin Valley's blazing hot temperatures resulted in a disaster for millions of pistachio trees, with 90% of the nuts being hollow or "blanks." Drought, heat, and abnormal West Coast weather [214] are the culprits behind the blanks, as with many ongoing agricultural crises. Pistachios need a substantial amount of cold during the winter, a requirement that farmers term as "chilling hours." More information on adaptation strategies can be covered [215, 216].

In the below graph, heating degree days (HTDD) for Fresno are depicted, spanning from 1960 to 2023. The concept of HTDD refers to a calculation used to track how much heating is needed in a certain area. This calculation is performed when the daily average temperature is below 65 °F/18.3 °C. HTDD can also be used as a proxy for chilling hours, which is a measure of the number of hours at a certain temperature range that a plant needs to complete its life cycle. The graph (Figure 22) indicates that the coldest months, requiring the most heating, are January and December, while the warmest months, requiring little to no heating, are June through September [217, 218, 219].

To study the yield acreage of pistachios in California, different trend lines were analyzed to determine the best fit. A polynomial order 6 trend line was found to be the most accurate, as it had a higher R^2 value compared to other trend lines. By using the trend line with a high R^2 value, we can better understand the yield trends of pistachios in California and make informed decisions about management practices to optimize yields and ensure the long-term success of the industry (Figure 23).

$$Y_{\text{pistachios yield}} = 1E\text{-}04x^6 - 0.0107x^5 + 0.4436x^4 - 8.9976x^3 + 84.118x^2 + 782.48x + 6805.5$$

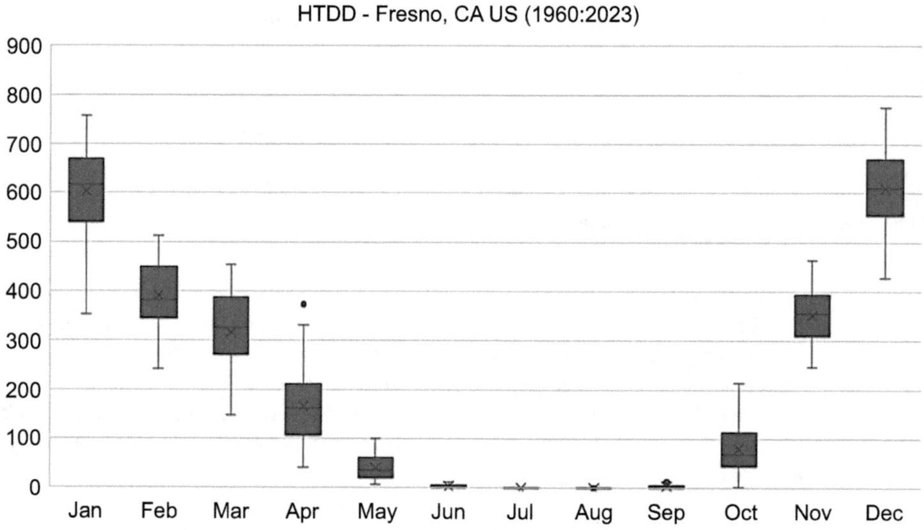

Figure 22: HTDD, Fresno, CA.

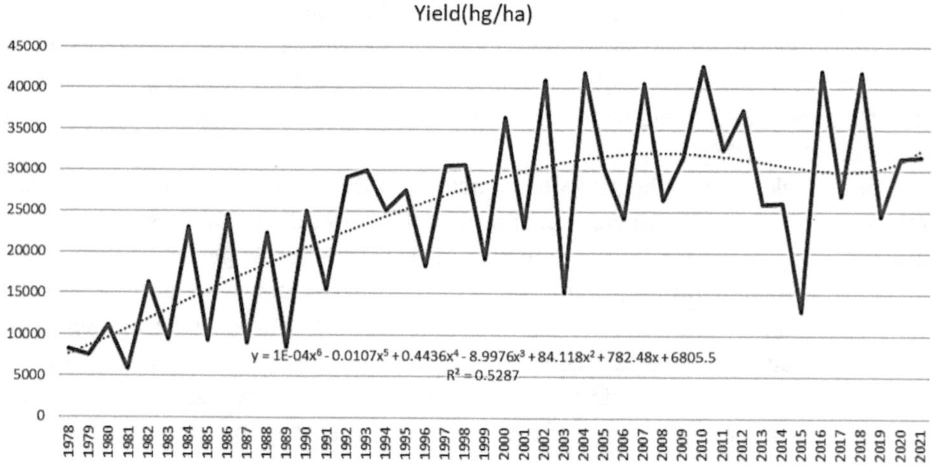

Figure 23: Annual California pistachios yield.

	Equation	R^2 value
Exponential	$y = 11718e^{0.0281x}$	$R^2 = 0.3614$
Linear	$y = 547.52x + 12522$	$R^2 = 0.4312$
Logarithmic	$y = 8470.2\ln(x) + 717.07$	$R^2 = 0.4847$

(continued)

	Equation	R^2 value
Polynomial order 6	$y = 1E{-}04x^6 - 0.0107x^5 + 0.4436x^4 - 8.9976x^3 + 84.118x^2 + 782.48x + 6805.5$	$R^2 = 0.5287$
Power	$y = 6024.5x^{0.4555}$	$R^2 = 0.4853$

Turkey

Turkey is a country that is well-known for being an excellent environment for growing pistachios. The weather and climate in Turkey provide ideal conditions for cultivating and harvesting these delicious nuts. In Turkey, the pistachio harvest season usually spans from the *end of August to the beginning of October, commencing when pistachio trees reach about 5–7 years of age.*

The different phenological stages of the pistachio tree in Turkey begin with tree buds and blooming in April, marking the start of pollination. During June and July, the kernel starts to form (Figure 24) and the shell hardens, which is crucial for the development of the pistachio nut. From August to early September, the pistachio hulls begin to split, which is an indicator that it is time to start the harvest. The actual harvest season usually commences from the end of August to the beginning of October when the pistachios are ready to be picked.

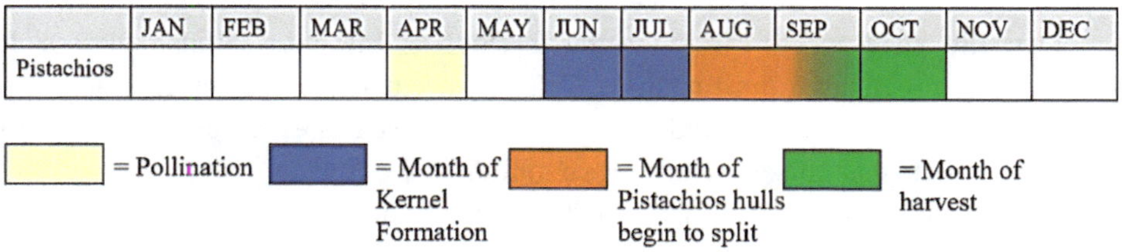

Figure 24: Turkey calendar.

In both Turkey and the USA, producers expect lower yields due to the ongoing “off-year”; however, extreme heat and drought in spring and summer have an additional negative impact on the crops. The Turkish pistachio trees are in a so-called off-year in 2021, so lower production is expected for the 2021/22 season. Moreover, the severe drought in the southeast region during the spring and summer results in crop yields being even lower than anticipated. Problem is that Turkish pistachio plantations manage almost without artificial irrigation and usually get their moisture from the spring rains, which were almost nonexistent this year. In many cases, this led to the death of the branches [220].

Nature!

The beauty and power of nature is awe-inspiring. From pollinating trees to producing life-giving oxygen through photosynthesis, and even sequestering carbon to create a healthy environment, nature tirelessly works to provide for us every day of the year.

As humans, it is our responsibility to understand and appreciate the incredible processes that enable nature to sustain life on our planet. We must recognize the essential role that nature plays in our lives and strive to live in harmony with her, rather than working against her.

Genuine intelligence and wisdom are not found in dominating or controlling nature but in appreciating and respecting her power, collaborating with her to foster a sustainable and prosperous future for everyone. By cherishing the marvels of nature and striving to safeguard and preserve her, we can secure a healthier, more vibrant world for future generations.

In summary, nature is an extraordinary force that offers us numerous benefits and opportunities. As intelligent and responsible beings, it is crucial that we acknowledge the significance of living in harmony with nature and value the essential role she plays in our lives. Only through respecting and safeguarding nature can we secure a sustainable and prosperous future for ourselves and the generations to come. Let us treasure and protect this magnificent gift that nature has bestowed upon us.

Author
Chandrasekar Vuppalapati

Pistachios yield analysis

Yield curves have several benefits in data analysis. They provide a visual representation of the data and can be used to identify correlations between variables.

Crucially, yield curves can guide the selection of the most suitable regression or trend for predicting future datasets. This is particularly beneficial in macro-micro-econo-metric linkage, demand analysis, and short-sell sales calculations that are vital for small- to medium-sized farming communities worldwide.

In this chapter, harvest returns are examined to comprehend historical tendencies and offer predictive movements based on environmental patterns. By analyzing yield curves, researchers can make informed decisions about future farming practices and optimize yields to ensure sustainable and profitable farming for small- to mid-level farmers.

The United States of America (USA)

During the California drought from 2012 to 2016, the prices of pistachios increased. This led farmers and investors to plant new plantations in zones that do not have consistent rainwater supplies, which can be a problem for sustainable farming practices [200]. Looking at the data from 1980 to 2022, there has been a significant increase in the amount of land being harvested for pistachios in recent years. The national average for harvested area during the period of 2010–2022 was 135,321.5 hectares, which is higher than the average of 59,311.49 hectares for the period of 1980–2022.

The data distribution for the harvested area is positively skewed, meaning that there are more hectares of land being harvested at the higher end of the distribution. The minimum harvested area is 10,930 hectares, the mean is 59,311.49 hectares (shown with a dashed line), the median is 31,565 hectares (shown with a dash-dot line), and the mode is 10,930 hectares (shown with a dotted line). The maximum harvested area is 543,900 hectares (Figure 25).

Overall, this data shows that there has been a substantial boost in the amount of land being harvested for pistachios in recent years, particularly during the California drought. However, this increase in harvesting also raises concerns about the sustainability of farming practices, especially in areas with unreliable water supplies.

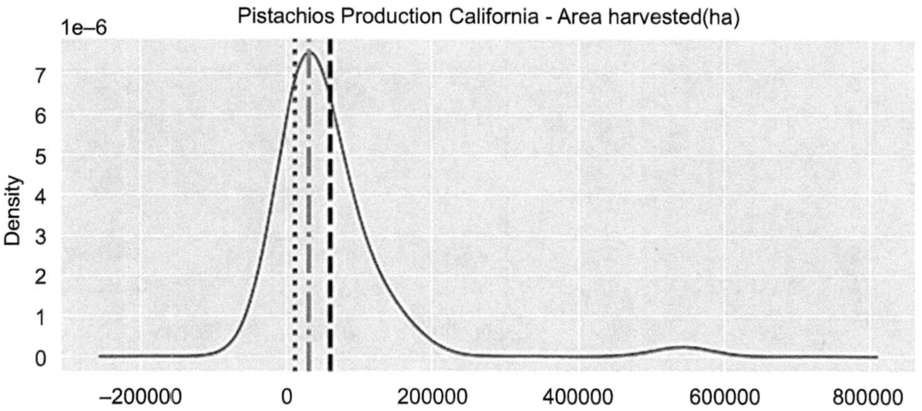

Figure 25: California – pistachios area harvested.

The left-tail of the data distribution, which is positively skewed, is due to a significant increase in the area of land being harvested for pistachios. This has been driven by growth in investment in new pistachio plantings, particularly in California [188], resulting in nearly $1.9 billion.

What's even more impressive is the amount of money invested by growers in new acreage during that period. It amounted to more than $153 million per month and $10,000 plus per acre. What it highlights is the significant economic impact that pistachio farming can have on a region, but it also raises concerns about sustainability and the long-term viability of farming practices, particularly if new plantings are being made in zones with undependable aquatic provisions.

Looking at the data, the national average of pistachio production between 2010 and 2022 was 321,855 tons. This is higher than the average of 145,354 tons for the period between 1980 and 2022. In the recent decade (2010–2022), there has been a

121.42% increase in production. The data distribution for pistachio production is positively skewed, which means that there are more tons of pistachios being produced at the higher end of the distribution. The minimum production is 6,622 tons, the mean is 145,354.68 tons (shown with a dashed line), the median is 85,280 tons (shown with a dash-dot line), and the mode is 6,622 tons (shown with a dotted line). The maximum production is 523,900 tons (Figure 26).

This data shows that there has been substantial growth in the production of pistachios in recent years, particularly in the last decade. However, as with the increase in harvested land, this also raises concerns about the sustainability of farming practices and the long-term viability of pistachio farming, particularly if production continues to increase in areas with unreliable water supplies.

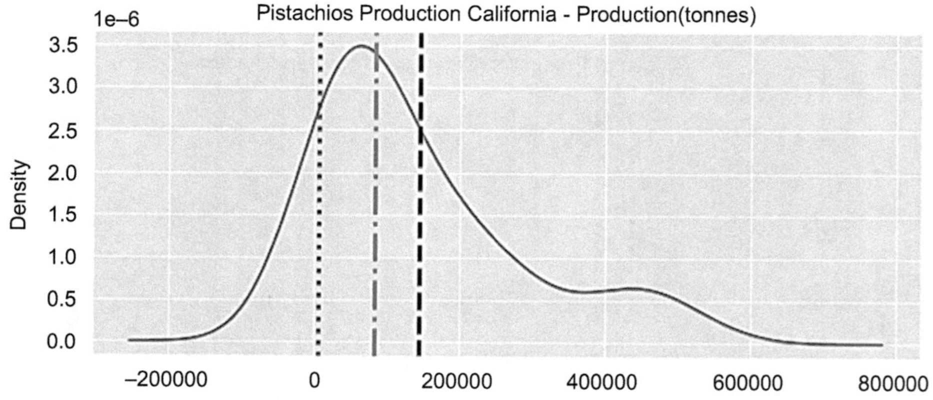

Figure 26: California pistachios production.

Looking at the data, the average national yield of pistachios between 2010 and 2022 was 31,301.92 hg/ha. This is higher than the national average of 25,766.91 hg/ha for the period between 1980 and 2022. In the recent decade (2010–2022), there has been a 21.48% increase in yield (Figure 27).

The data distribution for the yield of pistachios is also positively skewed, which means that there are more yields of pistachios at the higher end of the distribution. The minimum yield is 5,824 hg/ha, the mean is 25,766.91 hg/ha (shown with a dashed line), the median is 26,068 hg/ha (shown with a dash-dot line), and the mode is 5,824 hg/ha (shown with a dotted line). The maximum yield is 42,707 hg/ha. This data indicates a notable rise in pistachio yields in recent years, especially over the past decade. However, as with the increase in harvested land and production, this also raises concerns about the sustainability of farming practices and the long-term viability of pistachio farming, particularly if yields continue to increase in areas with unreliable water supplies.

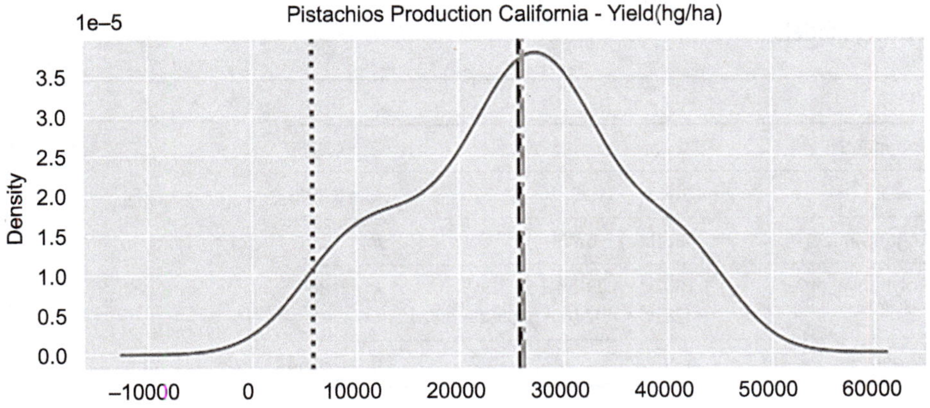

Figure 27: Pistachios California yield.

When looking at the trendline for the area harvested (ha), the best way to fit the data is with a polynomial of order 6. This means that the data can be modeled using a mathematical function with a degree of 6. The R^2 value for this model is 86.88%, signifying that it fits the data well. Alternative trendlines, such as linear, exponential, or power, would not provide as dependable trend predictions as the polynomial regression model. This means that a polynomial order 6 model is the best way to predict the trend for the area harvested (ha) data (Figure 28).

$$Y_{\text{pistachios area harvested}} = 0.0107x^6 - 1.2915x^5 + 59.319x^4 - 1282x^3 + 13124x^2 - 54668x + 73824$$

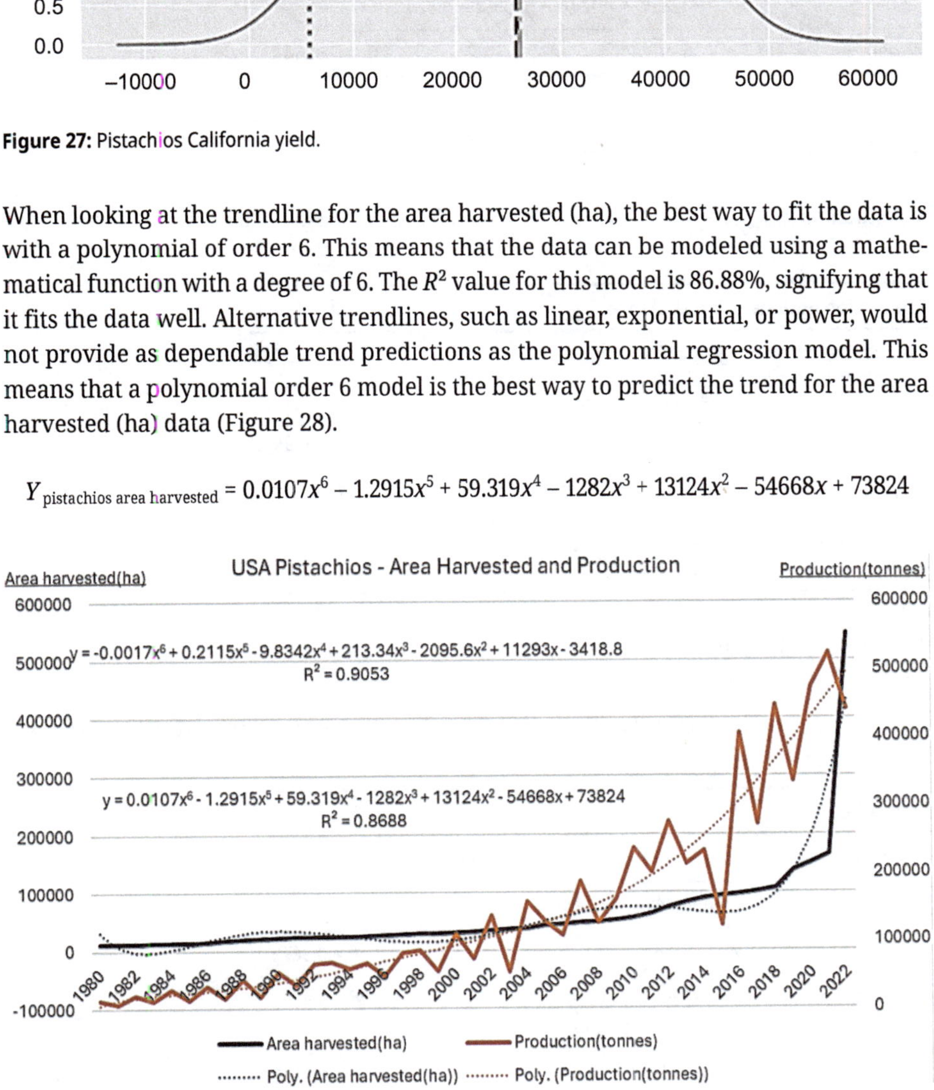

Figure 28: USA pistachios – area harvested and production.

Fitting models:

		R^2
Exponential	$y = 8814.6e^{0.0662x}$	$R^2 = 0.5765$
Linear	$y = 4249.6x - 34179$	$R^2 = 0.3916$
Logarithmic	$y = 44861\ln(x) - 67480$	$R^2 = 0.2137$
Polynomial order 6	$y = 0.0107x^6 - 1.2915x^5 + 59.319x^4 - 1282x^3 + 13124x^2 - 54668x + 73824$	$R^2 = 0.8688$
Power	$y = 3678.3x^{0.8249}$	$R^2 = 0.3654$

Pistachios production(tons) trendline details:

$$Y\text{pistachios}_{\text{Production}} = -0.0017x^6 + 0.2115x^5 - 9.8342x^4 + 213.34x^3 - 2095.6x^2 + 11293x - 3418.8$$

Production options	**Line balance**	**R^2 value**
Exponential	$y = 12826e^{0.0862x}$	$R^2 = 0.9033$
Linear	$y = 9862.9x - 71628$	$R^2 = 0.7661$
Logarithmic	$y = 112166\ln(x) - 171665$	$R^2 = 0.4852$
Polynomial order 6	$y = -0.0017x^6 + 0.2115x^5 - 9.8342x^4 + 213.34x^3 - 2095.6x^2 + 11293x - 3418.8$	$R^2 = 0.9053$
Power	$y = 3078.3x^{1.1762}$	$R^2 = 0.7941$

Pistachios yield (hg/ha):

$$Y_{\text{pistachios yield}} = -2E{-}05x^6 + 0.2181x^5 - 1101.3x^4 + 3E + 06x^3 - 4E + 09x^2 + 4E + 12x - 1E + 15$$

Pistachios		R^2
Exponential	$y = 2E{-}17e^{0.0242x}$	$R^2 = 0.3124$
Linear	$y = 490.94x - 956594$	$R^2 = 0.366$
Logarithmic	$y = 983718\ln$	$R^2 = 0.367$
Polynomial order 6	$y = -2E - 05x^6 + 0.2181x^5 - 1101.3x^4 + 3E + 06x^3 - 4E + 09x^2 + 4E + 12x - 1E + 15$	$R^2 = 0.4664$
Power	$y = 1E - 156x^{48.559}$	$R^2 = 0.3135$

Hot winter and lack of chill hours have decimated pistachios yield in 2015. Second, a lot of growers were caught off guard this past fall of 2014–2015 because many of the trees that looked normal had plenty of shells, but they were blank.

Forecasting the annual pistachio crop size accurately is exceptionally challenging, unlike most other tree crops[4]. This difficulty arises from various factors, including nut sizing, nut total, and genuine nut development or formation, combined with the alternate-bearing nature of pistachios. As a result, pistachio growers can only estimate the total yield until the nuts are harvested and processed [213]. The yield of pistachios is influenced by weather, climate, bearing cycles, human labor, and other factors.

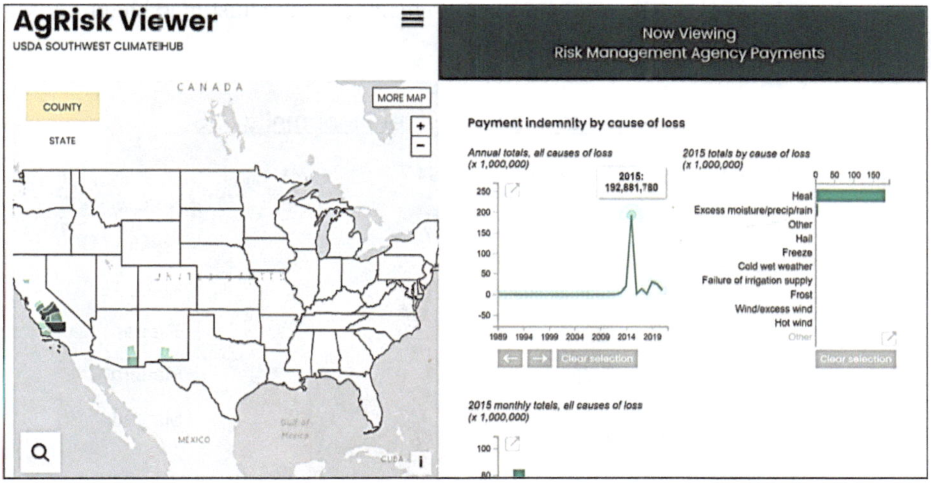

Figure 29: AgRisk viewer.

Other significant historical factors that shaped the yield curves include (Figure 29):

- In March 1991, Fresno experienced over 7 inches of rainfall. This came after an exceptionally dry winter, and the storms that soaked California that year were widely referred to as the "March Miracle" [221]. Similarly, during the El Niño year of 1969, Fresno received 8.56 inches of rain in January, marking the beginning of its wettest year on record[5] (Figure 27).
- In 2015, there was a significant decrease in yield (−47.47%), which *resulted in insurance RMA payments amounting to $192.881 million. This drop was attributed to the unseasonably warm winter, with minimum and maximum temperatures from November through February being higher than usual.* However, the winter of 2015

4 Growing and harvesting: https://keenanfarms.com/about-our-pistachios/growing-harvesting

5 24-hour storm puts month's rain totals well above average: https://www.fresnobee.com/news/local/article56323570.html

experienced a substantial increase in chill hours – temperatures below 45 °F that allow trees to enter dormancy. During the 2014–15 winter, Fresno recorded 589 chill hours, whereas in the 2015 winter, growers anticipated between 800 and 900 chill hours. In the Wetlands district (Figure 30), only 567 chill hours were recorded, but by mid-February 2016, the region had accumulated 897 chill hours. The reduced chill hours during the 2014–2015 winter contributed to the lower yield [222].

- Additionally, many growers were surprised in the fall of 2014–2015 because numerous trees appeared normal and had plenty of shells, but the shells were empty. This issue arose because the female pistachio trees, which produce the nuts, were not adequately pollinated. The male trees, responsible for pollinating the females through a wind-aided process, did not mature at the same rate as the female trees. With a ratio of one male tree to every 20 female trees, the mistimed bloom caused significant problems in some orchards.

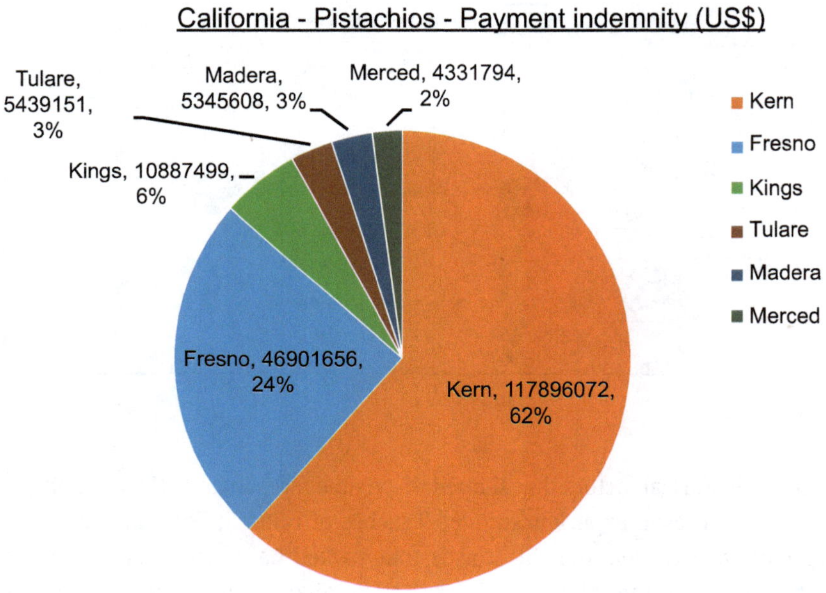

Figure 30: California pistachios payments.

Yield and elevation

As noted above, in 2015 farms in San Joaquin Valley have experienced considerable yield losses. One measure of it is risk management agency (RMS) payments [223]. See Figure 31. I would like to underscore that within San Joaquin Valley all farms are affected. As it can be seen clearly, Kern County received the highest payment (62%) in

2015 for pistachios; next, Fresno with 24%. Merced and Madera have received less than 5% of the payment. *In the higher-elevation* areas of the expansive agricultural valley and in the southern regions, pistachios have not received sufficient chilling hours for at least two consecutive winters, specifically in 2014 and 2015. Consequently, yields in these areas have significantly declined [214]. However, not all growing regions are exhibiting high ratios of blank nuts. *In the lower-lying areas of the San Joaquin Valley*, where cold air tends to accumulate during winter, the crop is performing relatively well. One grower [214] with approximately 1,200 acres of pistachios in Merced and Madera counties is experiencing a successful year. This demonstrates that within the county, elevation levels do indeed affect yield outcomes.

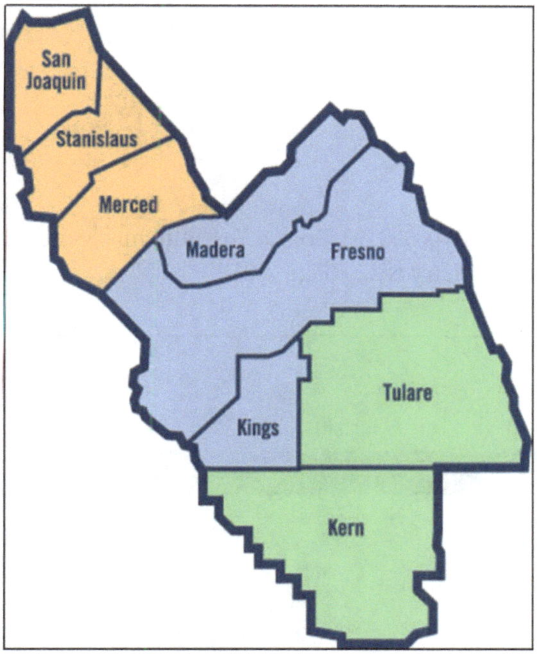

Figure 31: San Joaquin Valley map.[6]

Let's look at HTDD – January, November, and December show higher influence (Figure 32).

6 San Joaquin Valley: https://ww2.valleyair.org/about

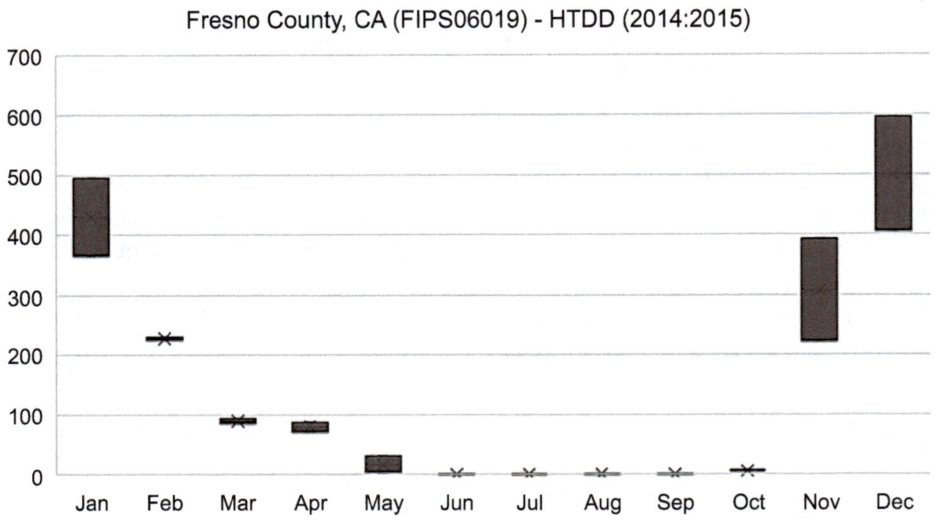

Figure 32: Fresno, HTDD.

Let's look at HTDD for Fresno – station: USW00093193, Fresno Yosemite International, CA, US. In January, HTDD are 400–500. February is 220 (Figure 33).

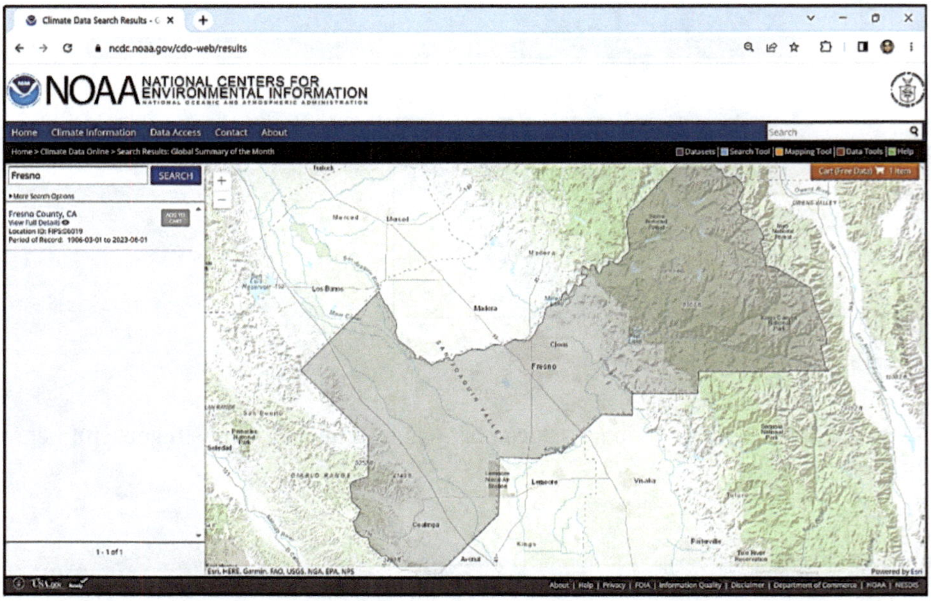

Figure 33: USW00093193 station map.

Let's look at Merced (Figure 34).

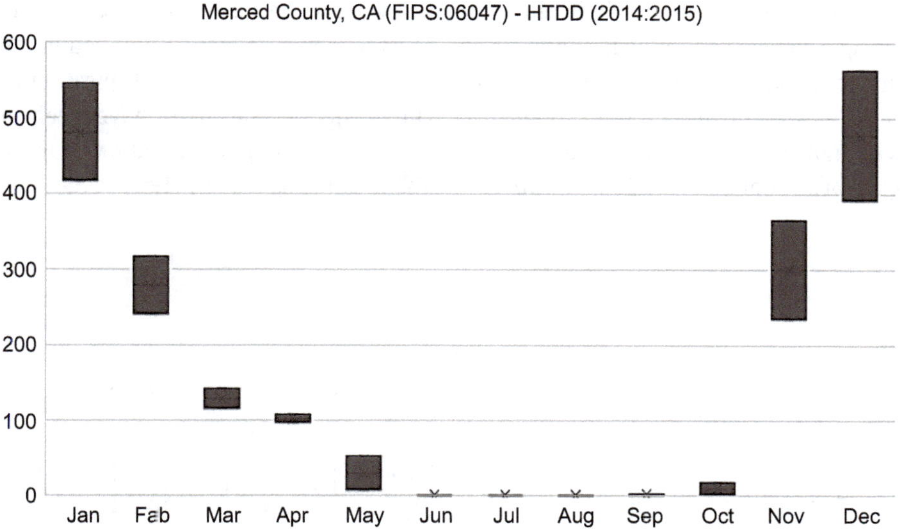

Figure 34: HTDD Merced.

As can be seen, January and February HTDDs are 410–550 and 230–310, respectively, for Merced, which are higher compared to Fresno (Figure 35).

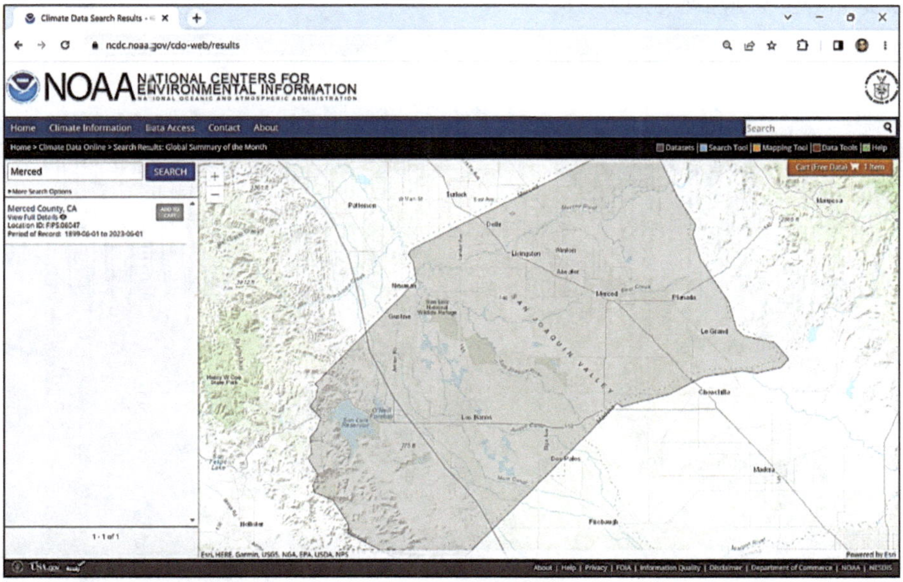

Figure 35: Merced weather stations.

A grower with approximately 1,200 acres of pistachios in Merced and Madera counties is experiencing a successful year [214]. Cold temperatures ranging from 32 to 45 °F are essential for setting buds that will blossom into flowers in the spring and subsequently develop into fruits and nuts in the summer. The issue, however, is the reduction in the number of hours these tree crops are exposed to such temperatures [224]. Typically, pistachio trees require over 700 chill hours each winter, but in Fresno, many have received fewer than 500 hours of this necessary dormancy. Please find other climatic variables: Fresno precipitation (1980:2023) – with an overall mean of 0.92 inches (Figure 36).

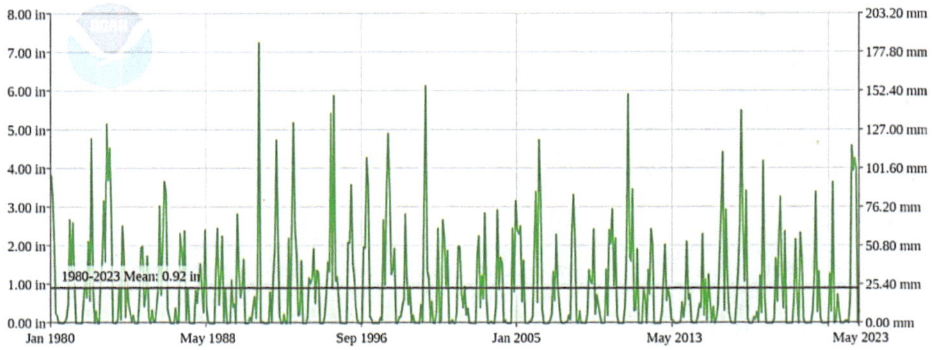

Figure 36: NOAA mean precipitation.

The following picture shows maximum temperatures, Fresno, 1980:2023 – with mean temperatures of 76.9 °F (Figure 37).

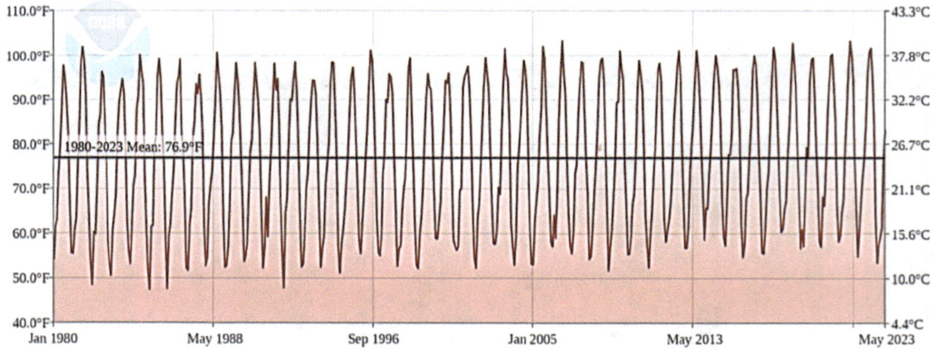

Figure 37: Average temperature.

Elevating yield analytics: how analyzing elevation can improve pistachio crop predictions!

Elevation plays a crucial role in the evaluation and modeling of yield analytics for pistachios. The altitude at which pistachio orchards are situated can greatly affect the growth and development of the trees, impacting variables such as temperature, soil quality, and water availability.

By carefully analyzing the relationship between elevation and pistachio yield, researchers and growers can develop more accurate and reliable models for predicting crop output. This can assist in the development of more effective management strategies, allowing growers to optimize their operations and maximize their yields.

Moreover, the importance of elevation in pistachio yield analytics underscores the need for precision agriculture techniques, which enable growers to collect and analyze highly detailed data on a range of variables, including elevation. By leveraging the latest technologies and techniques, growers can gain critical insights into the complex interplay of factors that impact pistachio growth and development, ultimately leading to more productive and profitable operations.

In conclusion, elevation plays a crucial role in assessing and modeling yield analytics for pistachios. By carefully analyzing the impact of elevation on pistachio growth and development, researchers and growers can develop more accurate and reliable models for predicting crop output. This highlights the importance of precision agriculture techniques, which enable growers to gather and analyze data on a range of variables, ultimately leading to more productive and sustainable agricultural operations.

The variations in pistachio yield, production quantity, and harvested area are being scrutinized to identify potential relationships among these factors. Correlation analysis is being employed to detect patterns within the data. The findings reveal a statistically significant positive correlation between yield and production quantities, indicating that an increase in yield corresponds with a rise in production. Similarly, there is a statistically significant positive correlation between yield and the harvested area, suggesting that higher yields are associated with an expanded area of land harvested for pistachios. Additionally, the analysis confirms a statistically significant positive correlation between yield and the harvested area. This means that when there is an increase in yield, there is also an increase in the production of pistachios (Figure 38).

	Area harvested (ha)	Yield (hg/ha)	Production (tons)
Area harvested (ha)	1		
Yield (hg/ha)	0.2509188	1	
Production (tons)	0.6983245	0.605402	1

In summary, the table indicates that there are positive correlations between all pairs of variables, with the strongest relationship being between the area harvested and production, followed by the yield and production. The weakest relationship is between the area harvested and yield, but it is still positive.

- Area harvested (ha) and yield (hg/ha):
  - Correlation coefficient: 0.2509188
  - Interpretation: There is a weak positive correlation between the area harvested and the yield. This suggests that as the area harvested increases, the yield also tends to increase, but the relationship is not very strong.
- Area harvested (ha) and production (tons):
  - Correlation coefficient: 0.6983245
  - Interpretation: There is a strong positive correlation between the area harvested and the production quantity. This indicates that as the area harvested increases, the production quantity also increases significantly.
- Yield (hg/ha) and production (tons):
  - Correlation coefficient: 0.605402
  - Interpretation: There is a moderate positive correlation between yield and production. This means that as the yield per hectare increases, the total production quantity also increases considerably.

Figure 38: Pistachios.

Pistachios production, California, USA

Future dataset imputation model: USA/California pistachios polynomial regression

Interpolation is a technique employed to predict and estimate values that are absent in a given dataset. This can be useful when you have some known values, but there are gaps in the data that you need to fill in. Interpolation works by using the values that are known to estimate the values that are missing. In the realm of data analysis, interpolation is frequently employed to address gaps in a dataset by estimating missing values. This practice is crucial as incomplete data can hinder accurate analysis. By leveraging the values of adjacent data points, interpolation provides an estimate for the missing entries.

Sometimes, simply taking an average of the available data points is not the best way to fill in missing values. In these cases, interpolation can be a more accurate method. Interpolation is also useful for preparing datasets for future analysis, as it can help to fill in gaps in the data. Another technique that can be used in future dataset preparation is trend-based forecasting. This involves looking at the trends in the data to make predictions about future values. By combining interpolation with trend-based forecasting, you can create more accurate and reliable datasets for analysis.

Step 1: Setup the environment

Load library.

```
from sklearn import datasets
from sklearn.model_selection import train_test_split
from sklearn.datasets import load_boston
from sklearn.linear_model import LinearRegression
from sklearn.preprocssing import PolynomialFeatures
```

```
import numpy as np
import pandas as pd
import functools
from datetime import date
import plotly.graph_objects as go
import seaborn as sns; sns.set()
import statsmodels.api as sm
from statsmodels.tsa.arima_process import ArmaProcess
from scipy import stats
from scipy.stats import pearsonr
import matplotlib.pyplot as plt
import plotly.express as px
```

```
from sklearn.preprocessing import MinMaxScaler
from sklearn.model_selection import train_test_split
from sklearn.linear_model import LinearRegression
from sklearn.metrics import r2_score
from sklearn import metrics
from sklearn.impute import SimpleImputer
import eli5
```

Step 2: Load California pistachios data (1977:2023)

Download Pistachios data from FAOSTAT, 2023.

```
Productiondf = pd.read_csv("FAOSTAT_data_en_California_Pistachios_7-24-2023.csv")
Productiondf
```

Result:

	Domain Code	Domain	Area Code (M49)	Area	Element Code	Element	Item Code (CPC)	Item	Year Code	Year	Unit	Value	Flag
0	QCL	Crops and livestock products	840	United States of America	5312	Area harvested	1375	Pistachios, in shell	1977	1977	ha	690.00	A
1	QCL	Crops and livestock products	840	United States of America	5312	Area harvested	1375	Pistachios, in shell	1978	1978	ha	1420.00	A
2	QCL	Crops and livestock products	840	United States of America	5312	Area harvested	1375	Pistachios, in shell	1979	1979	ha	10280.00	A
3	QCL	Crops and livestock products	840	United States of America	5312	Area harvested	1375	Pistachios, in shell	1980	1980	ha	10930.00	A
4	QCL	Crops and livestock products	840	United States of America	5312	Area harvested	1375	Pistachios, in shell	1981	1981	ha	11370.00	A

Step 3: Partition the data

When working with a dataset, it can be useful to divide the data. Column 1 and column 2 refer to two different sets of data within the dataset. By separating these data into X and y, we can analyze them separately and use them for different purposes. X is typically used as the input data for a model or analysis, while y is used as the output or target variable. By separating the data in this way, we can more easily analyze and manipulate it to achieve our desired results.

```
Production_df=pd.pivot(Productiondf, columns = "Element", index = "year", values = "Value").reset_
index()
Production_df.rename(columns={'Area harvested': 'Areaharvested'},inplace = True)
```

```
X_areaharvest = Production_df.iloc[:,0:1].values
y_areaharvest = Production_df.iloc[:,1].values
```

Step 3 : Signature of the dataset

Apply Pistachios polynomial regression – $R^2 = 99.28\%$. The polynomial function:

$$y = 0.0002x^6 - 0.0253x^5 + 1.1622x^4 - 22.599x^3 + 136.71x^2 + 1599.1x + 588.74$$

Let's model:

```
# Fitting Linear Regression to the dataset
from sklearn.linear_model import LinearRegression
lin = LinearRegression()

lin.fit(X_areaharvest,y_areaharvest)
```

```
#Visualising the Linear Regression results
plt.scatter(X_areaharvest, y_areaharvest,color = 'blue')

plt.plot(X_areaharvest, lin.predict(X_areaharvest), color = 'red')
plt.title('Linear Regression')
plt.xlabel('Year')
plt.ylabel('Area Harvested')

plt.show()
```

Output:

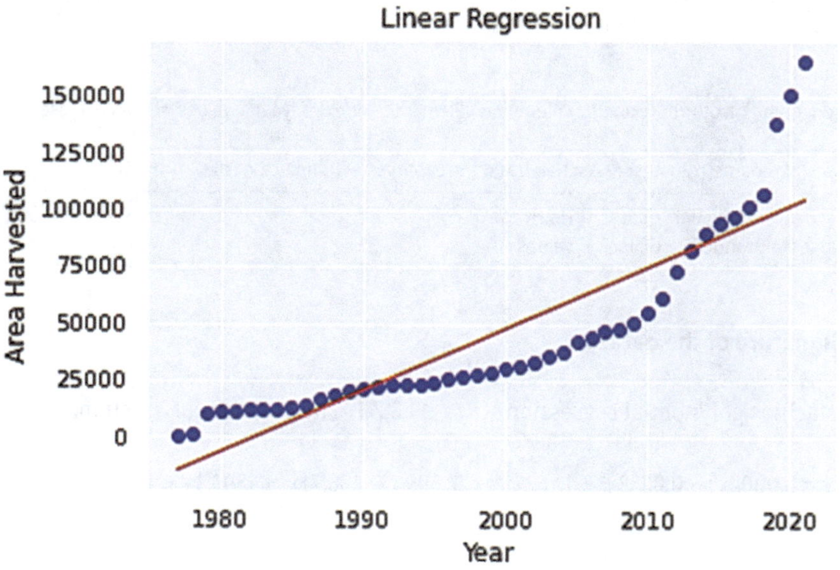

Step 4: Evaluate the model

When forecasting the future area to be harvested, assessing the reliability of these predictions is crucial. One method to gauge this reliability is through a statistical measure known as the root mean square error (RMSE). The RMSE is determined by comparing the predicted values with the actual values from previous harvests, quantifying the average deviation of the predictions from the actual data. A lower RMSE signifies more precise and dependable predictions.

By calculating the RMSE, we can get a better sense of how reliable the area harvest forecast is. This can help us make more informed decisions about how much to plant, how much labor and resources to allocate, and how to plan for the future.

```
from sklearn.metrics import mean_squared_error,r2_score

mse = mean_squared_error(y_areaharvest, lin.predict(X_areaharest))
print("MSE:", mse)

rmse = np.sqrt(mse)
print("RMSE:", rmse)

r2 = r2_score(y_areaharvest, lin.predict(X_areaharvest))
print("R2:", r2)
```

Output:

```
MSE: 335906387.4918955
RMSE: 18327.749111440156
R2: 0.7852339225387015
```

Step 5: Increased accuracy with polynomial regression

Let's apply polynomial regression.

```
#Fitting Polynomial Regression to the dataset
from sklearn.preprocessing import PolynomialFeatures

polyareaharvest = PolynomialFeatures(degree = 6)
X_polyareaharvest = polyareaharvest.fit_transform(X_areaharvest)

polyareaharvest.fit(X_polyareaharvest,y_areaharvest)
lin2 = LinearRegression()
lin2.fit(X_polyareaharvest, y_areaharvest)
```

```
#Visualising the Polynomial Regression results
plt.scatter(X_areaharvest, y_areaharvest, color = 'blue')

plt.plot(X_areaharvest, lin2.predict(polyareaharvest.fit_transform(X_areaharvest)), color = 'red')
plt.title('Polynomial Regression')
plt.xlabel('Year')
plt.ylabel('Area Harvested')

plt.show()
```

When working with data in ML, sometimes we want to create additional features that can help us make more accurate predictions. One way to do this is by using polynomial features. Polynomial features involve taking the original features of the data and creating new features by raising them to different powers. For example, if we have a two-dimensional input sample that looks like [a, b], we can create degree 2 polynomial features by taking the original features, adding their squares, and adding their product. So, our new features would be [1, a, b, a2, ab, b2].

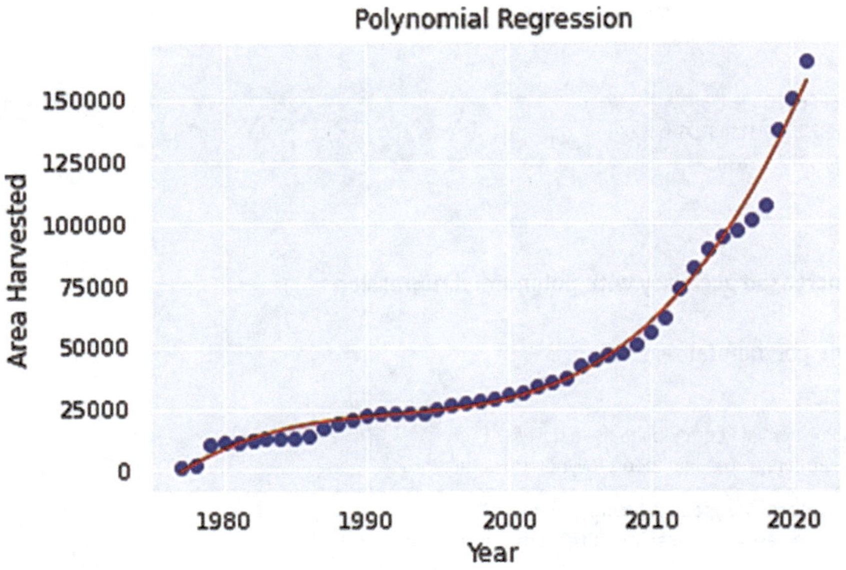

Step 6: Evaluate polynomial regression model metrics

Let's compute coefficients of regression:

```
from sklearn.metrics import mean_squared_error, r2_score

mse = mean_squared_error(y_areaharvest, lin2.predict(polyareaharvest.fit_transform(X_areaharvest)))
print("MSE:", mse)

rmse = np.sqrt(mse)
print("RMSE:", rmse)

r2 = r2_score(y_areaharvest, lin2.predict(polyareaharvest.fit_transform(X_areaharvest)))
print("R2:", r2)
```

```
r2_score(y_areaharvest,lin2.predict(polyareaharvest.fit_transform(X_areaharvest)))
```

Output:

```
MSE: 15639446.508574368
RMSE: 3954.6740078765492
R2: 0.9900007183388456
```

```
0.9900007183388456
```

As it can be seen, a higher accuracies due to 99.00% R^2 values.

Step 7: Area harvest forecast till century end: 2020:2100

We want to make a forecast of how much area will be harvested from now until the end of the century (from 2020 to 2100). To do this, we will use a technique called "polynomial regression" with a transformation called "rensdormaton."

```
year = [i+1961 for i in range(130)]
print(year)
```

```
predictions_value=[]
prediction_year=[]
for x in year:
    pred2array = np.array([[x]])
    prediction_year.append([x][0])
    predictions_value.append(lin2.predict(polyareaharvest.fit_transform(pred2array))[0])
    print(x,lin2.predict(polyareaharvest.fit_transform(pred2array))[0])
```

Output:

```
1978 2424.114483356476
1979 5504.010454893112
1980 8218.513967037201
1981 10594.872673988342
1982 12660.461490631104
1983 14442.782853841782
1984 15969.467006444931
1985 17268.272206783295
1986 18367.085040330887
1987 19293.920647859573
1988 20076.923003673553
1989 20744.365167617798
...........
2082 3936966.418823719
2083 4072372.2502601147
2084 4210976.316963434
2085 4352820.531178951
2086 4497946.960546255
2087 4646397.828390598
2088 4798215.5140452385
2089 4953442.553045511
2090 5112121.637508869
```

Polynomial regression enables the prediction of the harvest area for the year 2090. However, it is essential to recognize that not all trendlines offer accurate long-term predictions. In the case of pistachios, the trendline has a higher R^2 value, which suggests that it may be more reliable for making long-term predictions.

Step 8: Impute future of pistachios production in California till 2100

Prepare pistachios production till 2100.

```
newployAreaHarvestedDF = pd.DataFrame({'Year':prediction_year,'Areaharvested':predictions_value})
```

```
newployAreaHarvestedDF = newployAreaHarvestedDF.iloc[60:130]
```

```
historicalproduction = Production_df.copy()
```

```
historicalproduction.drop(columns=['Production','yield'], inplace = True)
```

```
import pandas as pd
frames = [historicalproduction,newployAreaHarvestedDF]
pistachiosProductionUSA2100=pd.concat(frames)
```

```
pistachiosProductionUSA2100.head(10)
```

Output:

Element	Year	Areaharvested
0	1977	690.0
1	1978	1420.0
2	1979	10280.0
3	1980	10930.0
4	1981	11370.0
5	1982	12100.0
6	1983	12590.0
7	1984	12460.0
8	1985	13070.0
9	1986	13840.0

Let's plot.

```
# Visualising the Polynomial Regression results
plt.scatter(X_areaharvest,y_areaharvest, color = 'blue')

plt.plot(pistachiosProductionUSA2100['Year'], pistachiosProductionUSA2100['Areaharvested'], color = 'red')
plt.title('Polynomial Regression')
plt.xlabel('Year')
plt.ylabel('Area Harvested')

plt.show()
```

Display:

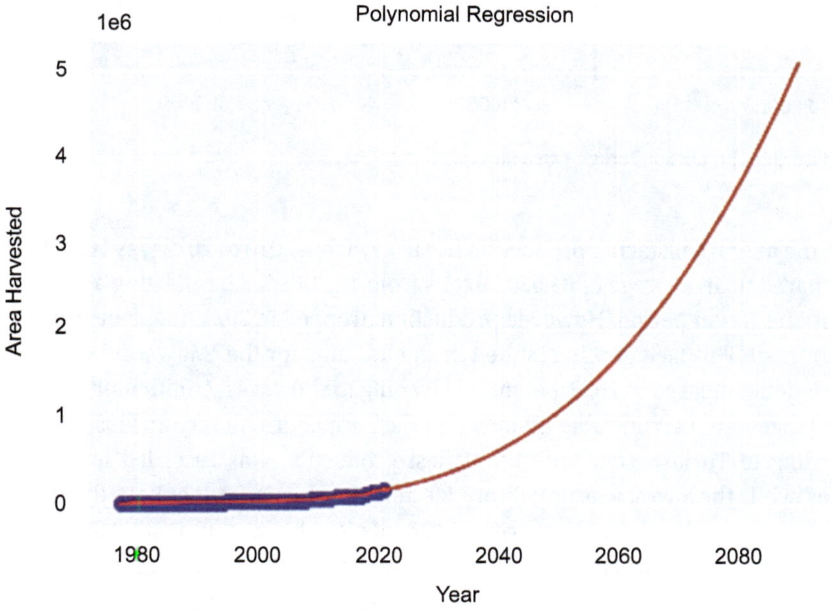

Turkey

The average area of land being harvested in Turkey has increased in recent years. Specifically, between 2010 and 2022, the average area harvested was 190,236.15 hectares. The average area harvested between 1961 and 2022 was 61,026.56 hectares. This means that the amount of land being harvested in Turkey has also increased over time. The minimum value is the smallest area of land being harvested (13,893 hectares), and the maximum value is the largest area of land being harvested (543,900 hectares). The mean value (61,026.56 hectares) is the average of all the areas being harvested, and the median value (30,771.50 hectares) is the middle value when all the areas are put in order. The mode value (24,857 hectares) is the most commonly occurring value [225]. The data is positively skewed, meaning that there are more data points with higher values than lower values (Figure 39).

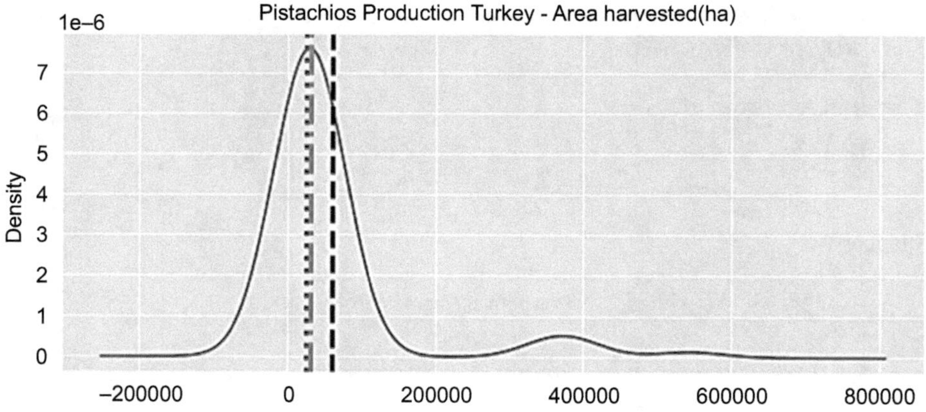

Figure 39: Pistachios production Turkey – area harvested.

Similarly, the average pistachio production in Turkey from 2010 to 2022 was 164,025.46 tons, compared to an average of 61,030.56 tons from 1961 to 2022, reflecting a 168.75% increase in the recent period. However, production dropped in 2021 due to insufficient summer rainfall. This lack of rain resulted in smaller nuts for the "Mawardi" and "Red Type" varieties compared to 2020, potentially leading to shortages. Additionally, Turkey faced challenges from an unstable financial market, impacting all sectors [225].

According to Turkish statistics, the highest production was recorded in 1991 at 64,000 tons, while the lowest was in 1980 at 7,500 tons. Production values have fluctuated over the years due to the alternate-bearing nature of pistachio nut cultivars. Adverse climatic conditions such as late spring frosts, hail storms, and dry, hot winds from southern deserts have also contributed to yield reductions, notably in 1980 and 1988 [226].

While most pistachio cultivars, including those from Iran and the USA, exhibit alternate bearing, this phenomenon is more pronounced in Turkish, Syrian, Greek, Italian, and Tunisian cultivars. The Iranian cultivars and Turkish Siirt cultivar show a "relative" alternate-bearing habit, with high yields in "on years" and about half in "off years." Consequently, Turkey has been establishing new pistachio plantations with the Siirt cultivar over the past decade [227].

Pistachios (tons) production data distribution: The least value of production is 4,300 tons, and the maximum value is 441,000 tons. The mean value of production is 61,030.56 tons, which is the average of all the production values. The median value of production is 35,000 tons, which is the middle value when all the production values are put in order. The mode value of production is 30,000 tons, which is the most commonly occurring value. The data is positively skewed, meaning that there are more data points with higher values than lower values (Figure 40).

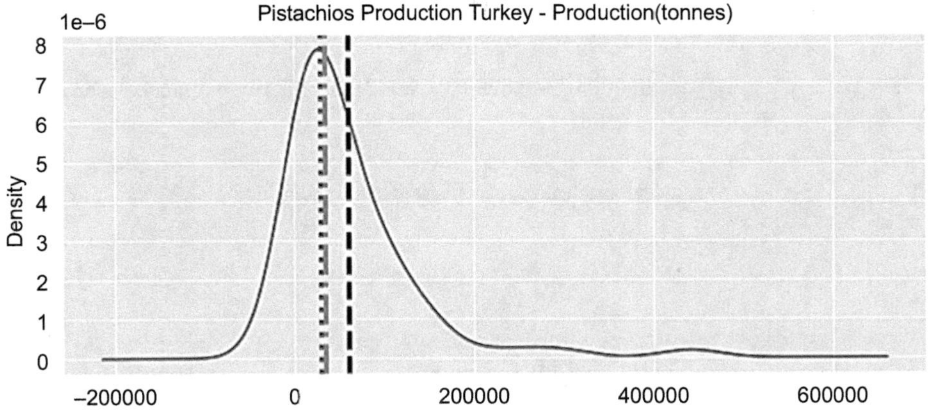

Figure 40: Pistachios production Turkey – production.

The average yield of Turkey (measured in hectograms per hectare) between 2010 and 2022 was 17,646.92 hg/ha, while the national average for the years 1961–2022 was 12,611.24 hg/ha. This represents an increase of 39.93% in the recent decade, from 2010 to 2022. The yield of pistachios (also measured in hg/ha) has a data distribution as follows: the minimum yield is 2,321.00 hg/ha, and the maximum is 30,852.00 hg/ha. The mean yield is 12,611.24 hg/ha (represented by the dashed line), while the median yield is 10,590.00 hg/ha (represented by the dash-dot line). The most commonly occurring value (mode) is 10,058.00 hg/ha (represented by the dotted line). The distribution of data is positively skewed, meaning that there are more data points with higher values than lower values (Figure 41).

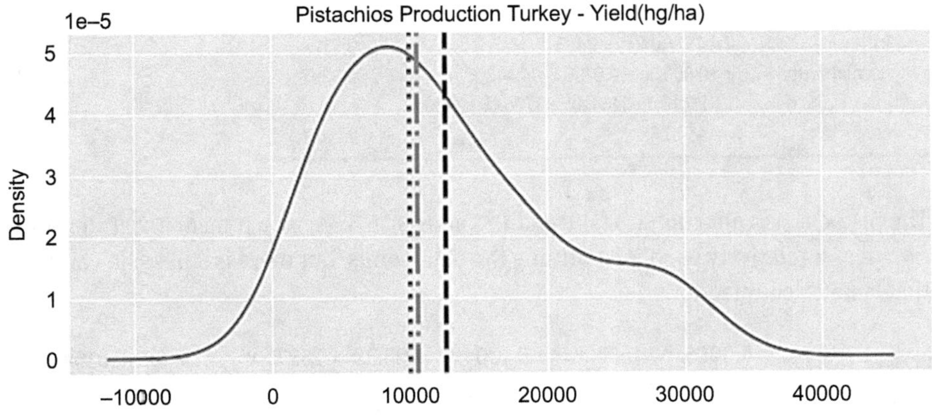

Figure 41: Pistachios production Turkey – yield.

The trendline for the area of land in Turkey where pistachios are being harvested has R^2 value of 92.97%, which suggests that the equation (Figure 42) does a good job of fitting the data points and accurately represents the trend in the area of land being used to harvest pistachios in Turkey over time (Figure 36). Lower R^2 values for other trends!

$$Y_{\text{Turkey Area Harvest Pistachios}} = 0.0005x^6 - 0.0786x^5 + 4.4421x^4 - 117.16x^3 + 1464.4x^2 - 7206.1x + 23861$$

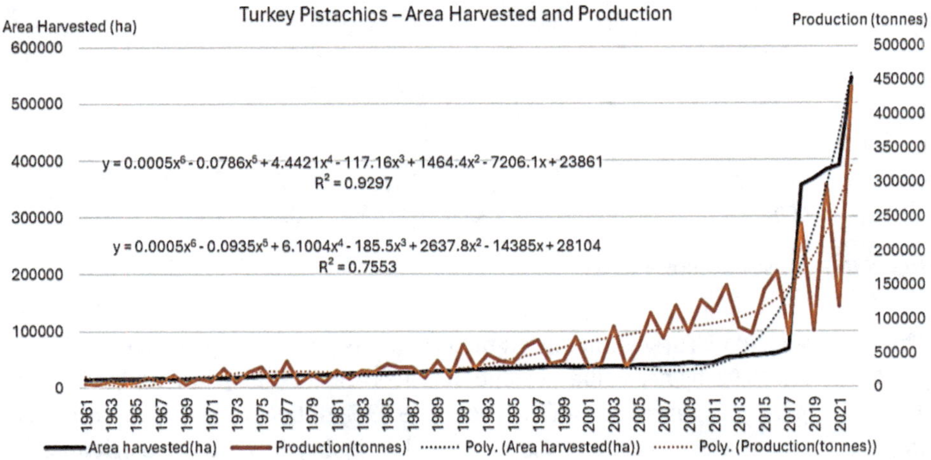

Figure 42: Turkey pistachios area and production.

Other trends:

Turkey pistachios	Regressor line	R^2 fitting value
Exponential	$y = 10076e^{0.0393x}$	$R^2 = 0.5072$
Linear	$y = 3319.7x - 43544$	$R^2 = 0.3191$
Logarithmic	$y = 45778\ln(x) - 84331$	$R^2 = 0.1519$
Polynomial order 6	$y = 0.0005x^6 - 0.0786x^5 + 4.4421x^4 - 117.16x^3 + 1464.4x^2 - 7206.1x + 23861$	$R^2 = 0.9297$
Power	$y = 4566.6x^{0.6386}$	$R^2 = 0.2627$

The pistachios production (tons) trend R^2 value is 75.53%, which means that the equation does a relatively good job of fitting the data points, but there is still some variation that is not accounted for.

$$Y_{\text{Production}} = 0.0005x^6 - 0.0935x^5 + 6.1004x^4 - 185.5x^3 + 2637.8x^2 - 14385x + 28104$$

Production trend line options	Equation	R^2 value
Exponential	$y = 6007.7e^{0.0553x}$	$R^2 = 0.6876$
Linear	$y = 2990x - 33156$	$R^2 = 0.5143$
Logarithmic	$y = 45356\ln(x) - 82985$	$R^2 = 0.2963$
Polynomial order 6	$y = 0.0005x^6 - 0.0935x^5 + 6.1004x^4 - 185.5x^3 + 2637.8x^2 - 14385x + 28104$	$R^2 = 0.7553$
Power	$y = 1450.7x^{0.9961}$	$R^2 = 0.5137$

The trendline for the yield of pistachios in Turkey (measured in hectograms per hectare) can be better fitted with a complex polynomial equation of the 6th order, and the R^2 value is around 39.53%. This means that the equation does not do a great job of fitting the data points, and there is a lot of variation that is not accounted for. Despite the area of land being used to harvest pistachios increasing year over year, the yield (or amount of pistachios produced per hectare) is going down (Figure 43).

$$Y_{\text{Turkey Pistachios Yield}} = 7E{-}05x^6 - 0.0136x^5 + 0.9252x^4 - 28.258x^3 + 376.79x^2 - 1521.6x + 6458.9$$

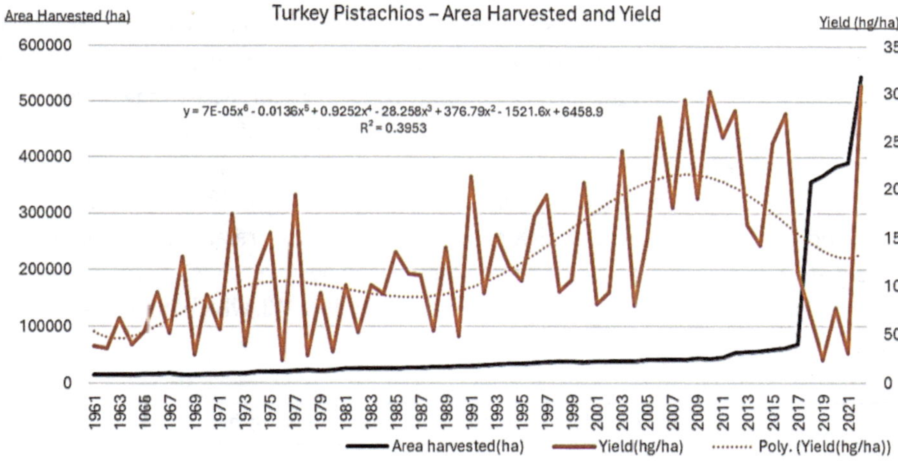

Figure 43: Turkey pistachios – area harvested and yield.

Additional crop trends:

Turkey pistachios yield	Regressor	R^2 fitting value
Exponential	$y = 5711e^{0.0181x}$	$R^2 = 0.2411$
Linear	$y = 228.11x + 5425.7$	$R^2 = 0.2645$
Logarithmic	$y = 4347.4\ln(x) - 1192.8$	$R^2 = 0.2406$
Polynomial order 6	$y = 7E\text{-}05x^6 - 0.0136x^5 + 0.9252x^4 - 28.258x^3 + 376.79x^2 - 1521.6x + 6458.9$	$R^2 = 0.3953$
Power	$y = 2992.7x^{0.383}$	$R^2 = 0.2652$

> Alternate bearing of pistachios is the reason the swing of yield.

Turkish pistachio production has experienced variations over the years, reaching its peak at 64,000 tons in 1991 and hitting its lowest point at 7,500 tons in 1980. Unfavorable weather conditions, *including late spring frosts, hailstorms, and dry, hot winds from southern deserts*, have contributed to reduced yields in specific years, notably 1980 and 1988 [227]. Extreme heat and drought in spring and summer also negatively impact crops. The Turkish pistachio trees are currently in an "off-year" in 2021, resulting in lower production for the 2021/22 season. The extreme drought in the southeast of the country in spring and summer is expected to further reduce crops [220]. High daytime temperatures can be damaging to agriculture, and pistachios require cool night temperatures for optimal growth.

Heat waves can exacerbate droughts and wildfires, creating detrimental effects on the agriculture sector. In 2021, the drought in the western USA forced cattle ranchers in North Dakota to sell their livestock due to a shortage of winter feed. Meanwhile, wildfires in California have ravaged agricultural lands and driven up insurance costs for farms and wineries.

The analysis results indicate a positive correlation between yield and area harvested, production and yield, as well as production and area harvested. This suggests that an increase in one of these factors generally leads to an increase in the others.

The following table provides the correlation analysis of pistachios in Turkey. By analyzing how these three factors are related to each other, we can compare Turkey's data with other countries. The table shows the correlation coefficient for area harvested and production is 0.802, which shows a confirmed correlation. The coefficient for yield and production is 0.547, which also indicates a positive correlation, but it is not as strong. The coefficient for yield and area harvested is 0.048, which indicates a weak positive correlation.

	Area harvested (ha)	Production (tons)	Yield (hg/ha)
Area harvested (ha)	1		
Production (tons)	0.802394743	1	
Yield (hg/ha)	0.048176956	0.546862347	1

Iran

Harvested area for pistachios in Iran: The average area harvested between 2010 and 2022 was 323,621.76 hectares, while the average for the years 1961–2020 was 180,313.51 hectares. This represents a considerable increase in the recent decade (79.47%). The distribution of data for the harvested area is positively skewed, which means that there are more data points with higher values than lower values. The minimum harvested area is 15,000 hectares, and the maximum is 552,870 hectares. The mean harvested area is 180,313.52 hectares (represented by the dashed line), while the median harvested area is 144,586 hectares (represented by the dash-dot line). The most commonly occurring value (mode) is 15,000 hectares (represented by the dotted line). The statistical range is 537,870 hectares. The variance is 18,477,377,085.20. The standard deviation is 135,931.52, which is another measure of how spread out the data is (Figure 44).

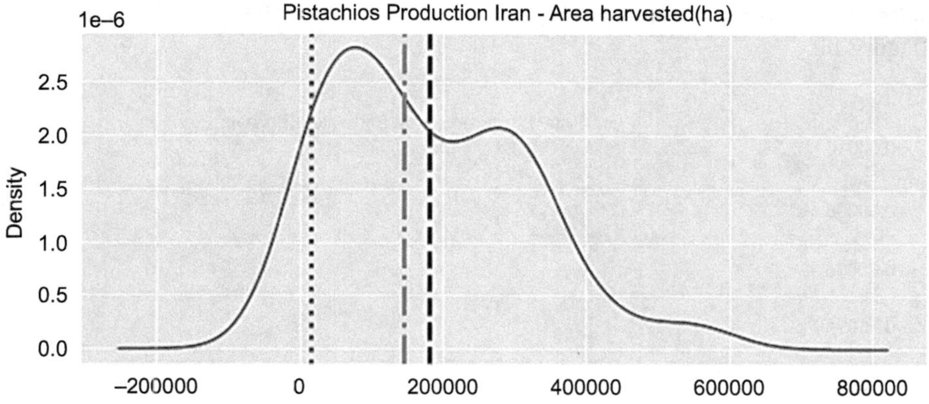

Figure 44: Pistachios production Iran – area harvested.

Similarly, minimum production is 4,000 tons, and the maximum is 648,934 tons. The mean production is 159,921.85 tons (represented by the dashed line), while the median production is 130,765.40 tons (represented by the dash-dot line). The most commonly occurring value (mode) is 7,000 tons (represented by the dotted line). The distribution of data is also positively skewed (Figure 45).

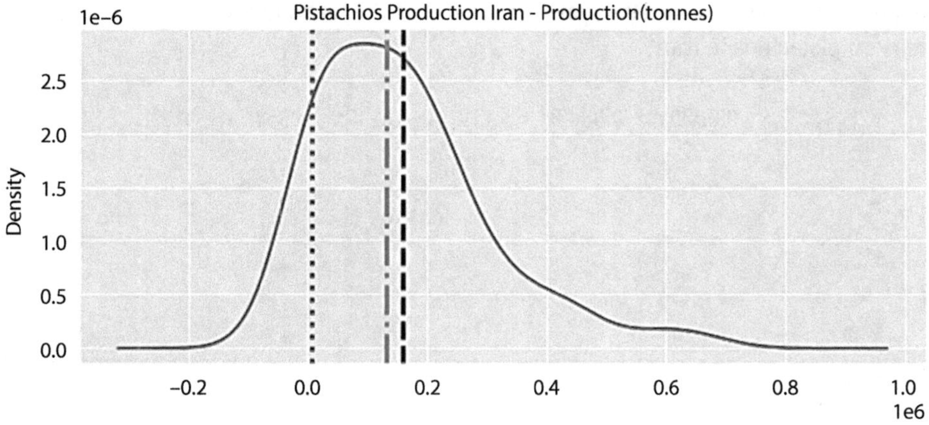

Figure 45: Pistachios production Iran – production.

The average national yield of pistachios in Iran for the period 2010–2022 was 11,553.30 hectograms per hectare (hg/ha), while the national average for the years 1961–2022 was 8,395.75 hg/ha. This represents a growth of 37.60%. The distribution of data for the yield of pistachios is also positively skewed, which means that there are more data points with higher values than lower values. The minimum yield is 938 hg/ha, and the maximum is 30,852 hg/ha. The mean yield is 8,395.76 hg/ha (represented by the dashed line), while the median yield is 8,212.50 hg/ha (represented by the dash-dot line). The most commonly occurring value (mode) is 938 hg/ha (represented by the dotted line) (Figure 46).

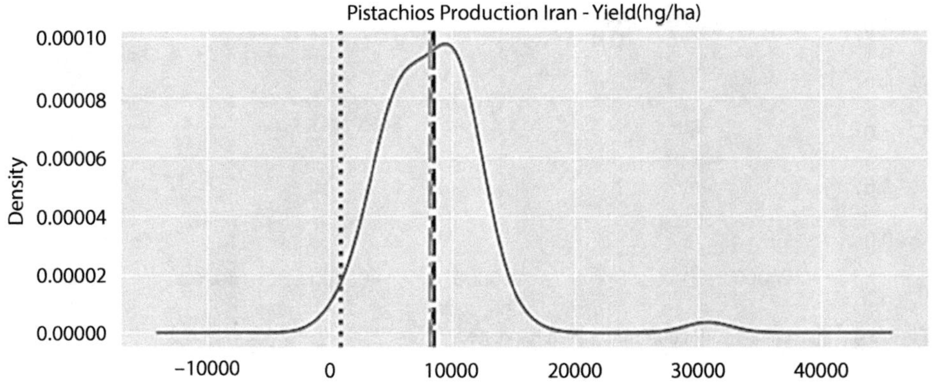

Figure 46: Pistachios production Iran – yield.

The trendline R^2 value of 93.4% is the most reliable one. Other trend fittings result in lower R^2 values, which means that the equation does not fit the data as well. Figure 47 likely shows the different trendlines and their corresponding R^2 values, which helps to determine the most accurate one for predicting the trend in the area of land used to harvest pistachios in Iran.

$$Y_{\text{area harvested}} = 0.0005x^6 - 0.0843x^5 + 5.4318x^4 - 161.17x^3 + 2363.2x^2 - 11818x + 31709$$

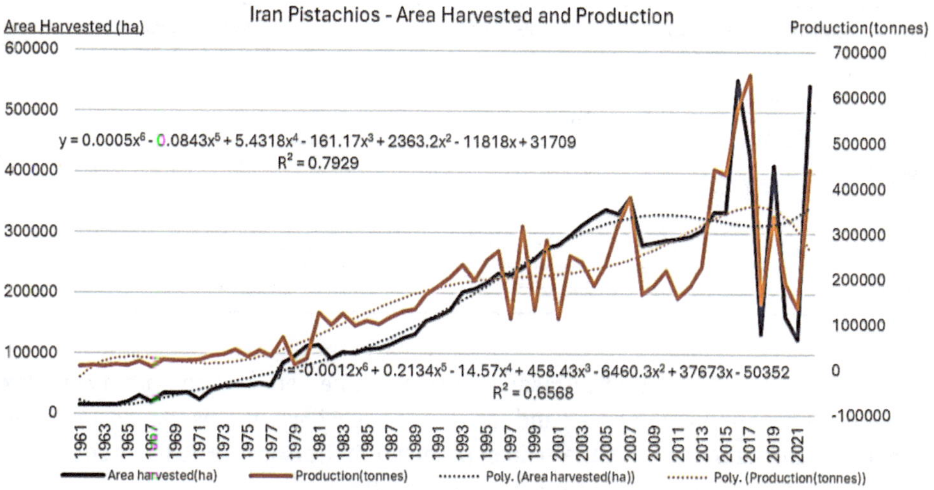

Figure 47: Iran area harvested and production.

Iran pistachios area of land	Regressor	R^2 fitting value
Exponential	$y = 23751e^{0.0517x}$	$R^2 = 0.6069$
Linear	$y = 6539.9x - 25694$	$R^2 = 0.7535$
Logarithmic	$y = 115491\ln(x) - 186400$	$R^2 = 0.5883$
Polynomial order 6	$y = 0.0005x^6 - 0.0843x^5 + 5.4318x^4 - 161.17x^3 + 2363.2x^2 - 11818x + 31709$	$R^2 = 0.7929$
Power	$y = 4205x^{1.0578}$	$R^2 = 0.7534$

The trendline for the production of pistachios in Iran can be better fitted with either a polynomial equation of 6th order or a power equation. The R^2 value for the polynomial equation is 0.6568, while the R^2 value for the power equation is 0.6253.

$$Y_{\text{Iran Pistachios production}} = -0.0012x^6 + 0.2134x^5 - 14.57x^4 + 458.43x^3 - 6460.3x^2 + 37673x - 50352$$

Pistachios production in Iran	Trend regressor	R^2 fitting value
Exponential	$y = 11449e^{0.0647x}$	$R^2 = 0.5022$
Linear	$y = 6303.3x - 38633$	$R^2 = 0.6263$
Logarithmic	$y = 109967\ln(x) - 189251$	$R^2 = 0.4773$
Polynomial order 6	$y = -0.0012x^6 + 0.2134x^5 - 14.57x^4 + 458.43x^3 - 6460.3x^2 + 37673x - 50352$	$R^2 = 0.6568$
Power	$y = 1250.1x^{1.339}$	$R^2 = 0.6253$

The trendline for the yield of pistachios in Iran can be better fitted with a complex polynomial equation of 6th order, and the R^2 value of 53.56% that is the most reliable one for predicting the trend in the yield of pistachios in Iran. Figure 39 likely shows the trendline and the corresponding R^2 value (Figure 48).

$$Y_{\text{Iran Pistachios Yield}} = 5E{-}06x^6 - 0.0005x^5 + 0.0257x^4 - 1.2173x^3 + 34.201x^2 - 144.74x + 4299.2$$

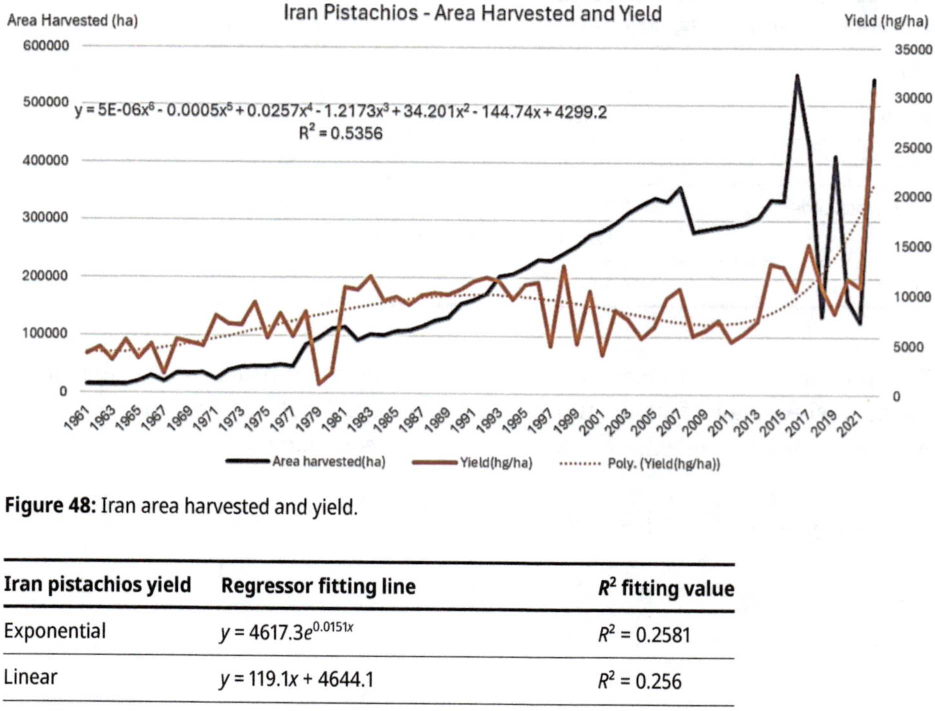

Figure 48: Iran area harvested and yield.

Iran pistachios yield	Regressor fitting line	R^2 fitting value
Exponential	$y = 4617.3e^{0.0151x}$	$R^2 = 0.2581$
Linear	$y = 119.1x + 4644.1$	$R^2 = 0.256$
Logarithmic	$y = 2291.9\ln(x) + 1118.2$	$R^2 = 0.2374$
Polynomial order 6	$y = 5E{-}06x^6 - 0.0005x^5 + 0.0257x^4 - 1.2173x^3 + 34.201x^2 - 144.74x + 4299.2$	$R^2 = 0.5356$
Power	$y = 2800.7x^{0.3068}$	$R^2 = 0.2545$

The table presents the correlation coefficients between three variables related to Iran pistachios: area harvested (ha), yield (hg/ha), and production (tons).

- Area harvested (ha)
  - The correlation coefficient between area harvested and yield is 0.5015, which suggests a moderate positive correlation. This means that as the area harvested increases, the yield tends to increase as well, though not perfectly.
  - The correlation coefficient between area harvested and production is 0.8959, indicating a strong positive correlation. This implies that an increase in the area harvested is strongly associated with an increase in production.
- Yield (hg/ha)
  - The correlation coefficient between yield and production is 0.6480, suggesting a moderate-to-strong positive correlation. This means that higher yields are generally associated with higher production levels.

In summary, the table indicates that there are positive correlations among the area harvested, yield, and production for Iranian pistachios. The strongest correlation is between area harvested and production, while the weakest, though still positive, is between area harvested and yield.

Iran pistachios	Area harvested (ha)	Yield (hg/ha)	Production (tons)
Area harvested (ha)	1		
Yield (hg/ha)	0.501539298	1	
Production (tons)	0.895952682	0.546862347	1

USA pistachios

Climate change on Fresno, San Joaquin Valley, California pistachio yield: an ML approach

To assess the effects of climate change, CO_2 levels, and environmental factors, ML techniques such as linear regression, logistic regression, and random forest are employed. For market analysis, pricing, and spot price recommendations, time series techniques are implemented. Additionally, forecasting time series techniques using Prophet models are applied.

Fresno, California, pistachios model:

Final release California pistachios yield and climate change model notebook software code

Final release California pistachios yield and climate change model GSOM notebook software code

Fresno pistachios production and climate data

Figure 18 likely shows the different data sources used for the ML model. These features include:

- Age of tree or bearing acreage: pistachio trees that are between 5 and 9 years old are more likely to have a higher yield.
- Bearing acreage: Pistachio trees that are over 20 years old and are still bearing fruit are more likely to have a higher yield.
- Frost events: Frost events in February can impact the yield of pistachios, so this information can be useful in predicting the yield.
- Fertilizer consumption: The amount of fertilizer used can impact the yield of pistachios, so this information can be helpful in predicting the yield.
- Honeybee pollination: This can also impact the yield of pistachios, so this information can be useful in predicting the yield.

Overall, these additional data features can be used to help improve the accuracy of the ML model in predicting the yield of pistachios. By including these features, the model can better account for the different factors that impact the yield of pistachios.

Data source	Name
Food and Agriculture Statistics	USA pistachios production

(continued)

Data source	Name
NOAA	Time series dataset includes information about minimum, maximum, and average temperatures, as well as precipitation, for Fresno and San Joaquin county.
UN[7]	Data related to CO_2 emissions. The measurement is in kT, which likely stands for kilotons, and the data is labeled "EN.ATM.CO2E."

Fresno climate and environmental readings drift

Weather station in Fresno, FRIANT Government Camp, is identified with the code GHCND:USC00043261 (Figure 49) and there is a clear shift in the data from 1940 to 1980 and from 1981 to 2023. This means that there was a noticeable change in the weather patterns during these time periods. The shift has already occurred, regardless of any future climate change predictions for 2050. In simpler terms, the data shows that there has already been a change in the weather patterns in Fresno and this change occurred before any future predictions.

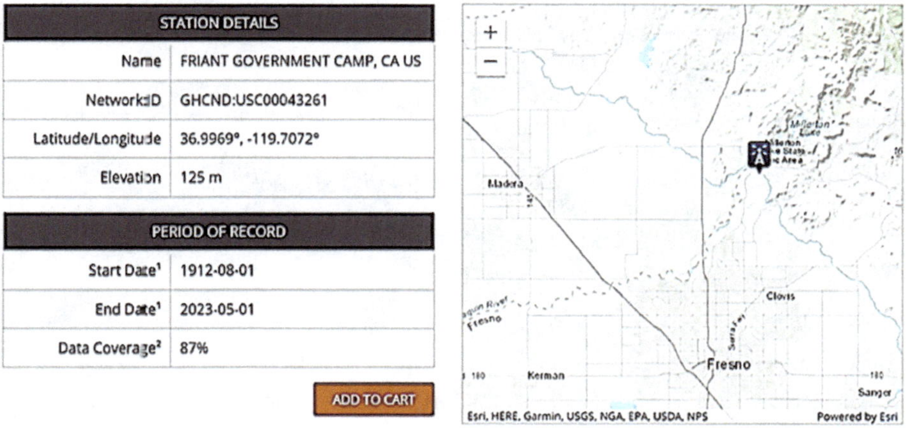

Figure 49: GHCND:USC00043261.

7 IBRD.IDA: https://www.un-ilibrary.org/content/books/9789210574983s011-c006

Minimum temperature: As minimum temperature distribution clearly shows that the mean temperatures have *risen (1.62 °F)* from 1940:1980 and 1981:2022. The data drift is moving toward right of the distribution, clearly indicating the temperature is increasing (Figure 50).

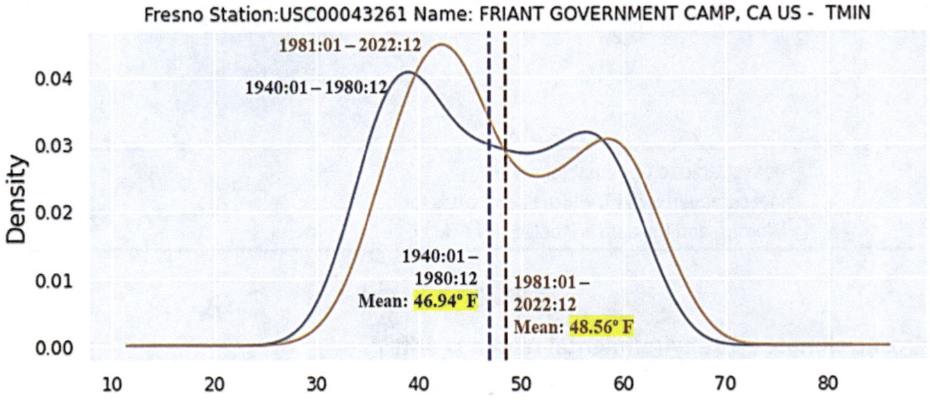

Figure 50: GHCND:USC00043261 temperature drift.

Average temperature: As average temperature distribution clearly shows that the mean temperature of TAVG has *risen (1.03 °F)* from 1940:1980 and 1981:2022. The data drift is moving toward right of the distribution, clearly indicating the temperature is increasing (Figure 51).

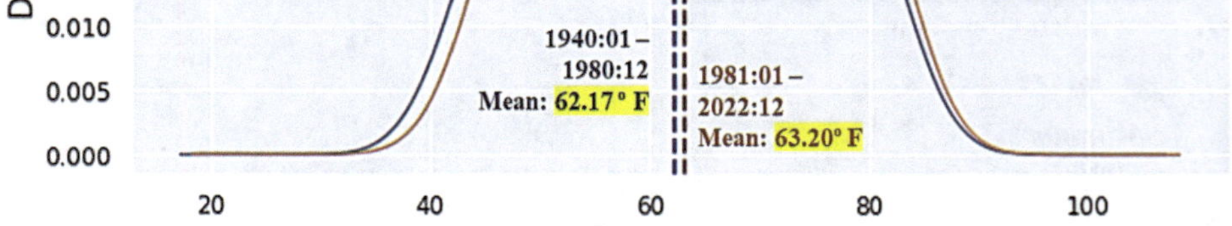

Figure 51: GHCND:USC00043261 average temperature drift.

Maximum temperature: Maximum temperature distribution clearly shows that the mean temperature of TMAX has *risen (0.54 °F)* from 1940:1980 and 1981:2022. The data drift is moving toward right of the distribution, clearly indicating the temperature is increasing (Figure 52).

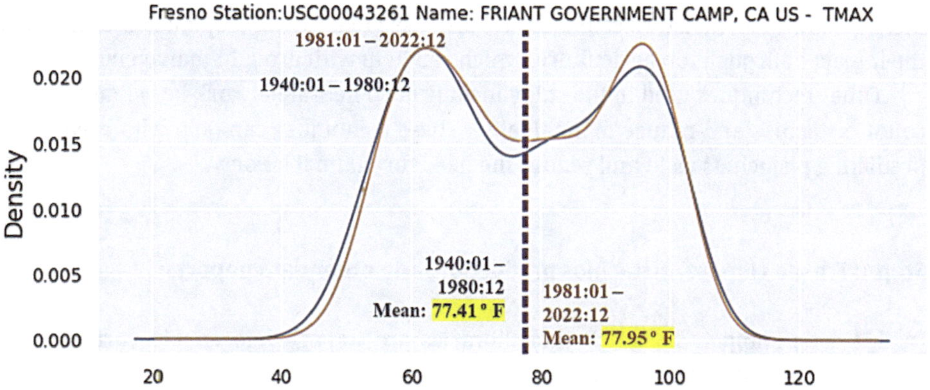

Figure 52: GHCND:USC00043261 maximum temperature drift.

Precipitation: Distribution clearly shows that the mean precipitation has *risen (0.04 inches)* from 1940:1980 and 1981:2022. This is significant as California has seen drought[8] in the last five years (2012–2016), The data drift is moving toward right of the distribution, clearly indicating the temperature is increasing (Figure 53).

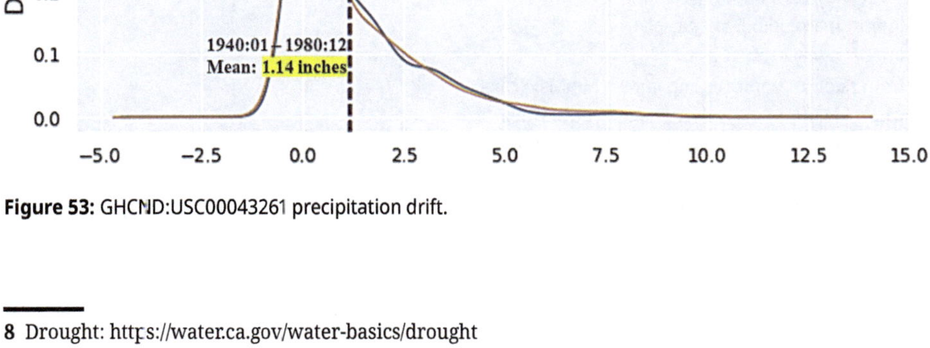

Figure 53: GHCND:USC00043261 precipitation drift.

8 Drought: https://water.ca.gov/water-basics/drought

ML algorithms

This section discusses a new approach to predicting pistachios yield using AI/ML. While similar studies have been done for predicting pistachio yield, this study is the first to use these methods for predicting pistachios yield. The study focuses on counties where there are a significant number of acres planted for pistachios, which makes the analysis more reliable. Soil moisture estimates are also used to improve crop models and assess the impact of drought on agriculture, which can help with drought management.

Other techniques used in the study include deep neural network-based methods to count pistachios and reduce manual labor. These techniques can help with accurately predicting pistachios yield and reduce the need for manual labor.

Step 1: Fresno climate, pistachios production, and other data imports

In this code snippet, several Python libraries are imported to enable various data analysis and visualization tasks. These libraries include NumPy, Plotly, Statsmodels, and Matplotlib for creating plots and charts. Other libraries imported include Eli5 for debugging and SimpleImputer for imputing missing data. The code also imports various functions from these libraries, such as the ArmaProcess function from Statsmodels for time series analysis, MinMaxScaler for data normalization, and Linear Regression for linear regression modeling.

```
import numpy as np
import pandas as pd
import functools
from datetime import date
import plotly.graph_objects as go
import seaborn as sns; sns.set()
import statsmodels.api as sm
from statsmodels.tsa.arima_process import ArmaProcess
from scipy import stats
from scipy.stats import pearsonr
import matplotlib.pyplot as plt
import plotly.express as px
from sklearn.preprocessing import MinMaxScaler
from sklearn.model_selection import train_test_split
from sklearn.linear_model import LinearRegression
from sklearn.metrics import r2_score
from sklearn import metrics
from sklearn.impute import SimpleImputer
import eli5
```

Step 2: Pistachios FAO 1991:2021 data

In this code snippet, a CSV file containing data on US pistachio production is imported using the Pandas library. The file is read using the read_csv function, with the file path specified using the r prefix to indicate a raw string. The resulting DataFrame is assigned to the variable dfPistachiosProdUSA. The unique values in the "Unit" column of this DataFrame are then displayed using the unique function. Finally, the DataFrame is pivoted using the pivot function, with "Year" specified as the index, "Element" specified as the columns, and "Value" specified as the values. This creates a new DataFrame where the rows correspond to years and the columns correspond to different elements of pistachio production, such as harvested area, yield, and production quantity.

```
dfPistachiosProdUSA = pd.read_csv(r"Pistachos_USA.csv")
dfPistachiosProdUSA
dfPistachiosProdUSA["Unit"].unique()
dfPistachiosProdUSA = dfPistachiosProdUSA.pivot(index = "Year", columns = "Element", values= "Value")
dfPistachiosProdUSA.reset_index(inplace = True)
dfPistachiosProdUSA.tail(10)
```

Output:

Element	Year	Area harvested(ha)	Production(tonnes)	Yield(hg/ha)
36	2013	82151.0	213188.00	25951.0
37	2014	89436.0	233146.00	26068.0
38	2015	94292.0	122470.00	12988.0
39	2016	96720.0	406646.00	42044.0
40	2017	101170.0	272290.00	26914.0
41	2018	106840.0	447700.00	41904.0
42	2019	137593.0	336112.04	24428.0
43	2020	150545.0	474000.00	31486.0
44	2021	165518.0	523900.00	31652.0
45	2022	543900.0	441000.00	30852.0

Step 3: Alternate cropping flag

Pistachios worldwide follow an alternate-year cropping model. The following code enables the flag.

```
dfPistachiosProdUSA["Flag"] = [0 if x%2 == 0 else 1 for x in range(len(dfPistachios-
ProdUSA))]
dfPistachiosProdUSA
```

Output:

Element	Year	Area harvested(ha)	Production(tonnes)	Yield(hg/ha)	Flag
36	2013	82151.0	213188.00	25951.0	0
37	2014	89436.0	233146.00	26068.0	1
38	2015	94292.0	122470.00	12988.0	0
39	2016	96720.0	406646.00	42044.0	1
40	2017	101170.0	272290.00	26914.0	0
41	2018	106840.0	447700.00	41904.0	1
42	2019	137593.0	336112.04	24428.0	0
43	2020	150545.0	474000.00	31486.0	1
44	2021	165518.0	523900.00	31652.0	0
45	2022	543900.0	441000.00	30852.0	1

Step 4: Visualize pistachios production data (California, USA)

This code defines a function called "show_timeseriesplot" that creates a time series plot of Fresno pistachios production using the Matplotlib library in Python. The function takes four arguments: the title of the plot, the date variable, the data variable, and the name of the column being plotted.

Within the function, the YearLocator and MonthLocator functions are used to specify how often the *x*-axis should display year and month labels. The DateFormatter function is used to format the *x*-axis labels as year values. The function then creates a Matplotlib figure with the specified title and *y*-axis label. The tick_params function is used to set the font size.

```
#Import Library
import pylab
import numpy as np
import datetime
from matplotlib.dates import YearLocator, MonthLocator, DateFormatter

def show_timeseriesplot(title, var_date, var_data, colname):
    from matplotlib import pyplot as plt

    years = YearLocator() # every year
    months = MonthLocator() # every month
    yearsFmt = DateFormatter('%Y')

    fig = plt.figure(figsize=(12,6))
    ax = plt.gca()

    #Plot density
    #var_data.plot(figsize=(12,6), kind='line')

    #Add titles and labels
    plt.title(title + '-'+ colname, fontsize= 12)
    plt.ylabel (colname, fontsize= 12)
    plt.tick_params(axis = 'both', which = 'major', labelsize = 12)
    plt.tick_params(axis = 'both', which = 'minor', labelsize = 12)
    plt.plot(var_date, var_data)
    # Show the figure
    plt.show()
```

```
numerical_features = ['Area harvested(ha)', 'Production(tonnes)','Yield(hg/ha)']
for col in numerical_features:
    show_timeseriesplot('Pistachios Production California',
dfPistachiosProdUSA['Year'], dfPistachiosProdUSA[col],col)
```

Plot display: Display Fresno pistachios production from 1980 to 2020.

Production shows that the amount of a certain product being made is increasing every year. This can be observed in a graph or chart that displays the production data over time.

However, when looking at the yield data, a different trend pattern is observed. The yield is decreasing over time. This means that even though more of the product is being produced overall, the amount produced per unit of area is decreasing.

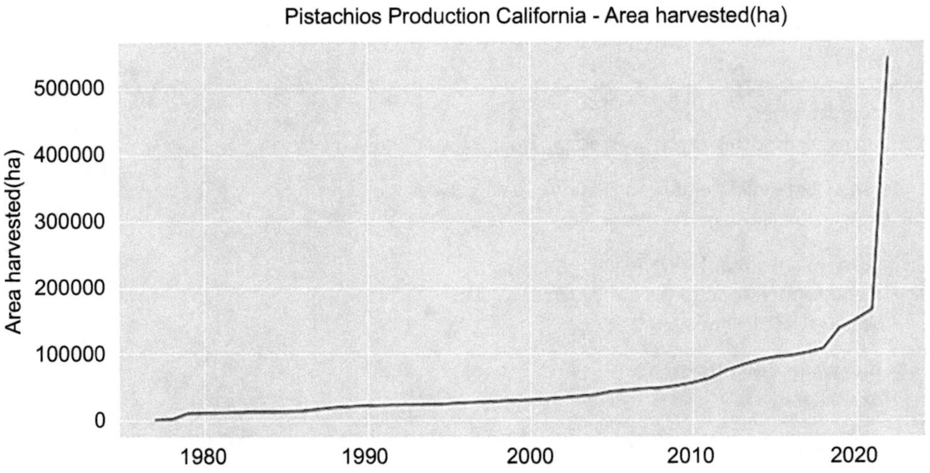
Pistachios Production California - Area harvested(ha)
Area harvested(ha)
500000
400000
300000
200000
100000
0
1980
1990
2000
2010
2020

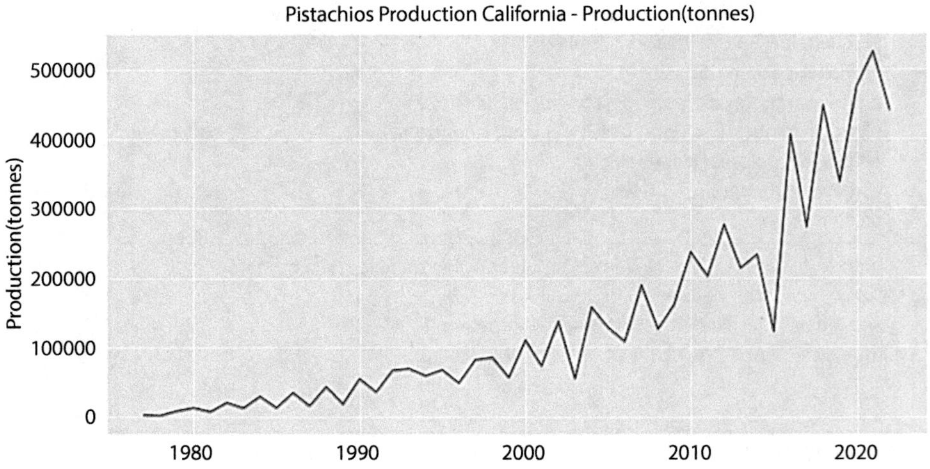
Pistachios Production California - Production(tonnes)
Production(tonnes)
500000
400000
300000
200000
100000
0
1980
1990
2000
2010
2020

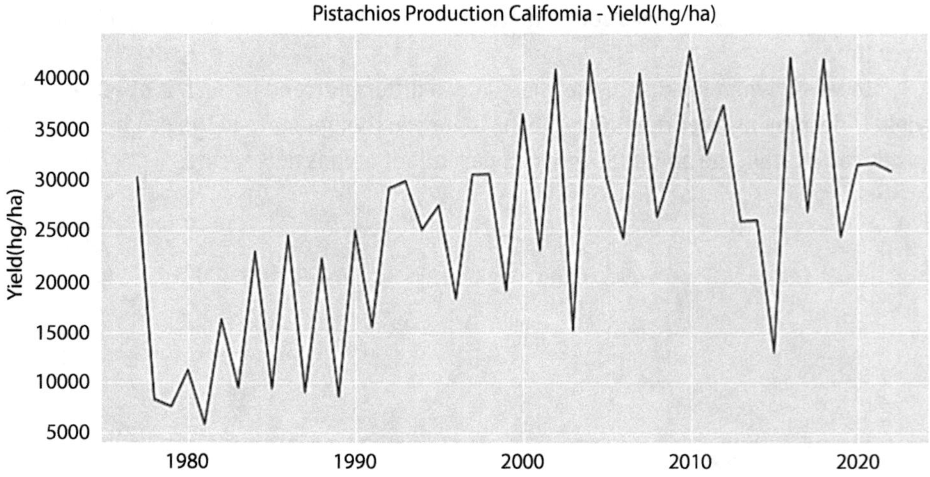
Pistachios Production Califomia - Yield(hg/ha)
Yield(hg/ha)
40000
35000
30000
25000
20000
15000
10000
5000
1980
1990
2000
2010
2020

Step 4: Plot US CO_2 1990:2020

This code imports and manipulates data on CO_2 emissions in the USA and creates a line plot to visualize the trend in these emissions over time.

```
co2df = pd.read_excel("co2Emissions_USA.xlsx",sheet_name = "Data")
co2df
```

```
co2_df = co2df.T.reset_index()
co2_df.columns = co2_df.iloc[0]
```

```
co2_df1["year"] = co2_df1["Series Name"].apply(lambda x : x.split("[")[0])
```

```
co2_df2["year"] = co2_df2["Year"].astype(int)
co2_df2["CO2 emissions (kt)"] = co2_df2["CO2 emissions(kt)"].astype(float)
```

```
fig = px.line(co2_df2,x="Year", y="CO2 emissions(kt)",title='UnitedStates Co2 Emissions')
fig.show()
```

Output:

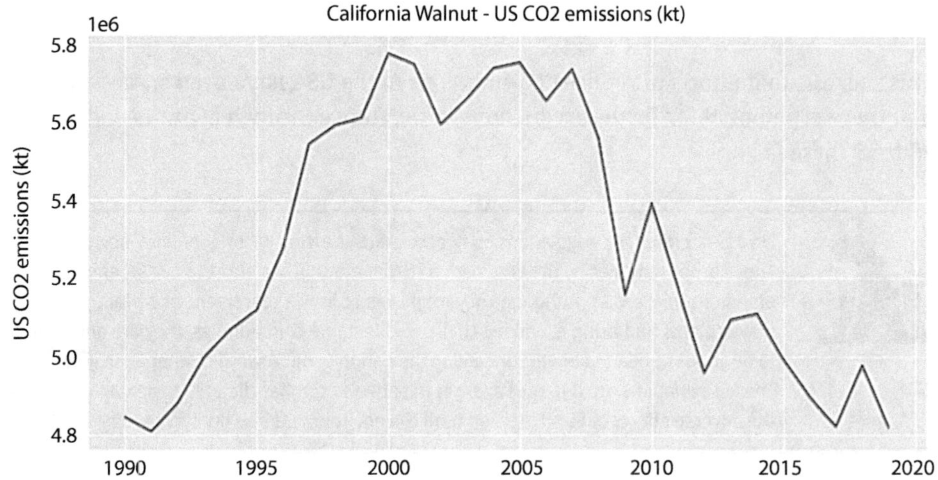

The data on CO_2 emissions in the USA reveals a downward trend over time. This trend can be clearly seen in a graph or chart illustrating the emissions data across several years. For instance, in 2020, the USA released 5,981 million metric tons (equivalent to 13.2 trillion pounds) of carbon dioxide. This represents a 7% reduction since 1990 and a 20% reduction since 2005. Thus, it is evident that CO_2 emissions in the USA have been consistently declining over the years.

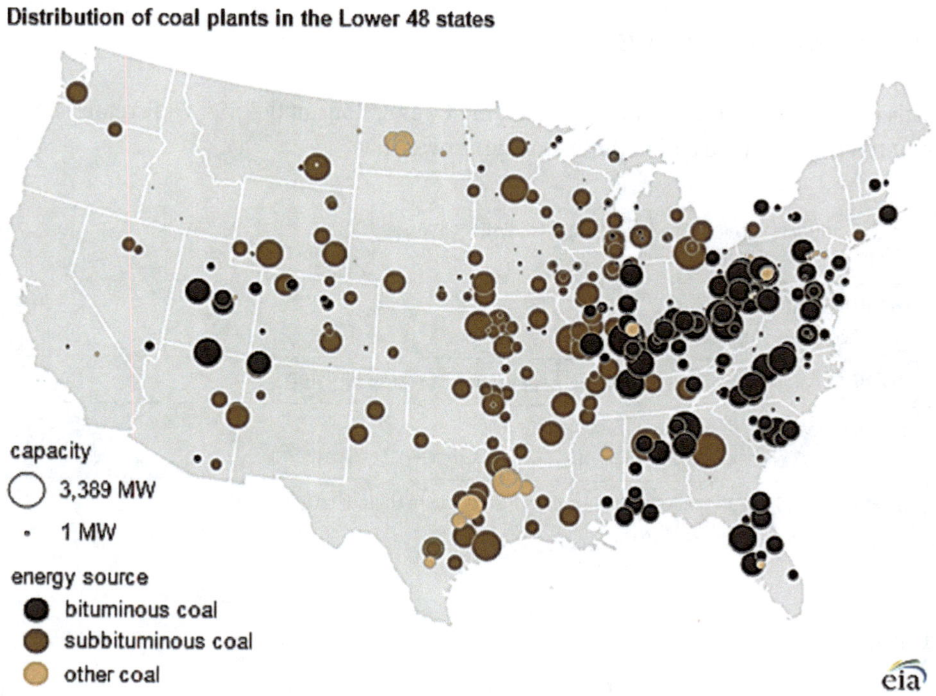

This suggests that efforts to reduce CO_2 emissions in the USA have been successful, and that there is potential for further reductions in the future through continued efforts to address these factors.

New EPA emissions regulations may accelerate the closure of coal-fired power plants. These proposed rules by the EPA mark a crucial move in the effort to cut greenhouse gas emissions in the USA. Although they might result in the retirement of certain coal-fired power plants and bring economic challenges to some communities, they are anticipated to offer public health benefits and aid in the nation's shift toward cleaner energy sources. These regulations are a part of a larger initiative to combat climate change and mitigate the adverse effects of fossil fuels on both the environment and human health.

Step 5: Visualize California historical and projected drought conditions (SPEI)

This code provides a way to visualize and analyze historical and projected drought conditions in California. The data and visualizations produced can enhance our understanding of the effects of drought on various natural and managed systems. They can also serve as valuable tools for informing decisions related to water resources and other sectors impacted by drought conditions.

```
speidf_1986_2005=pd.read_csv("spei12_timeseries_annual_cmip5_historical_ref_ensemble_1986-2005_
p90USA.csv")
```

```
spei_1986_2005_df = spiedf_1986_2005[["Year","California"]]
```

```
speidf_2006_2100 = pd.read_csv("spei12_timeseries_annual_cmip5_rcp26_ensemble_2006-2100_p90_
USA.csv")
spei_2006_2100_df_rcp26 = spiedf_2006_2100[["Year","California"]]
spei_2006_2100_df_rcp26
```

```
speidf_1986_2100.rename(columns={'California' :'SPEI_droughtIndex'},inplace=True)
```

```
show_timeseriesplot('California Walnut',speidf_1986_2100['Year'],
speidf_1986_2100 ['SPEI_droughtIndex'],'California SPEI_droughtIndex')
```

SPEI is a tool that uses climate data to determine how dry or wet a particular area is compared to normal conditions. The data is shown in a table with different categories based on the SPEI value, ranging from extremely wet to extreme drought.

The table also shows the minimum/maximum SPEI values, the highest wet year (2010) and the normal range (1990). Understanding these values can help us to better understand the severity of drought conditions in different areas and make informed decisions about how to manage natural resources in response.

Categorization	**Classifiation**
Extremely wet	SPEI ≥ 2
Severely wet	1.5 ≤ SPEI < 2
Moderately wet	1 ≤ SPEI < 1.5
Mildly wet	0.5 < SPEI < 1
Normal	−0.5 ≤ SPEI ≤ 0.5
Mild drought	−1 < SPEI < −0.5
Moderate drought	−1.5 < SPEI ≤ −1
Severe drought	−2 < SPEI ≤ −1.5
Extreme drought	SPEI ≤ −2

Output:
Based on analysis of climate data using the Standardized Precipitation-Evapotranspiration Index (SPEI), it has been determined that even under low emissions scenarios, California may experience drier conditions. This finding is based on projections of SPEI data from 2006 to 2100 using the RCP2.6 emissions scenario. SPEI is a multi-scalar drought index that is widely used to evaluate drought conditions in different natural and managed systems. Its application to climate data for California has revealed that even with reductions in greenhouse gas emissions, future drought conditions in the state may worsen.

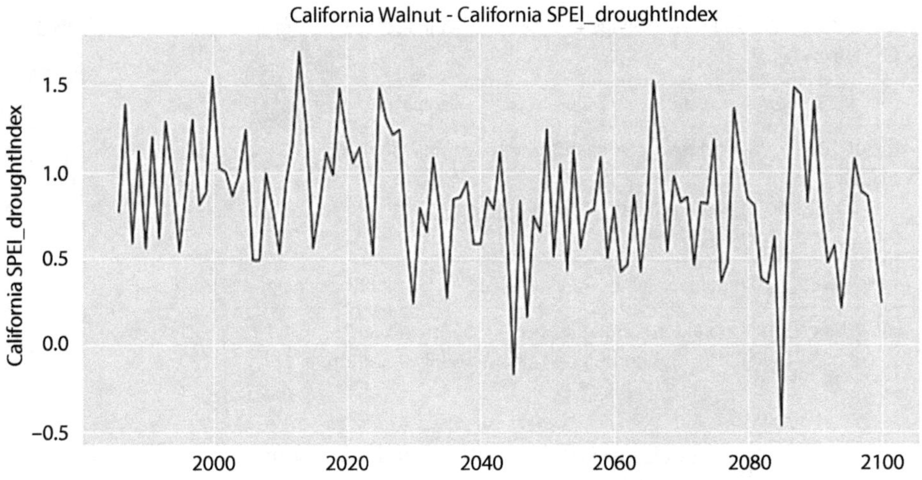

Step 6: California: Fresno county weather data 1991:2020

This code loads temperature data and renames the columns. Specifically, it calculates the average or mean temperature for a given time period, monthly, and stores that data in a DataFrame. Then, it renames the columns in the DataFrame to better reflect the data that is stored in each column.

```
weather_df = pd.read_csv(r"Fresno_county_Weather.csv", index_col="date")
weather_df
```

```
weather_df.drop('Unnamed: 0', axis=1, inplace = True)
```

```
weather_df.reset_index(inplace=True)
```

```
weather_df
```

This output indicates that the data being analyzed spans a period of 43 years, from 1980 to 2023. Specifically, the data is monthly data, which means there are 12 data points for each year. This results in a total of 520 rows of data.

	date	MaxTemperature(C)	MeanTemperature(C)	MinTemperature(C)	total_precipitation(kg m-2 s-1)
0	1980-01-01	2.334131	-2.273688	-6.125128	0.000015
1	1980-02-01	4.689233	-1.033362	-5.164252	0.000022
2	1980-03-01	10.396387	4.479791	0.005518	0.000036
3	1980-04-01	16.833643	10.494165	5.215051	0.000300
4	1980-05-01	25.352472	18.083429	11.640741	0.000616
...	...	...	...	...	...
515	2022-12-01	3.427637	-0.947424	-4.218237	0.000005
516	2023-01-01	3.690240	-0.982703	-4.436926	0.000038
517	2023-02-01	6.852960	1.561304	-1.974799	0.000013
518	2023-03-01	15.910211	8.614282	3.050012	0.000002
519	2023-04-01	19.494806	13.175745	8.039575	0.000112

520 rows × 5 columns

The code provides a way to analyze temperature data and identify patterns in maximum monthly temperatures over time. This information could be useful for understanding climate trends and making decisions related to weather-sensitive activities, such as agriculture or outdoor recreation.

```
weather_df["Date"] = pd.to_datetime(weather_df["date"])

weather_df.drop("date",axis = 1, inplace = True)

weather_df["Month"] = weather_df["Date"].apply(lambda x:x.strftime(‚%b'))

weather_df["Year"] = weather_df["Date"].dt.year

max_df = weather_df[["Date", "Month","Year", ‚MaxTemperature(C)']]

max_df1 = max_df.pivot(columns= "Month", index="Year", values= "MaxTemperature(C)").reset_index()
max_df1

max_df2 = max_df1[:-1]

max_df2.rename(columns = { "Jan": "Jan_max", "Feb": "Feb_max", "Mar": "Mar_max", "Apr": "Apr_
max", "May":"May_max", "Jun": "Jun_max","Jul":"Jul_max","Aug": "Aug_max",
"Sep": "Sep_max", "Oct": "Oct_max","Nov": "Nov_max", "Dec": "Dec_max"}, inplace=True) max_df3 =
max_df2.apply(lambda x: round(x,2))

max_df3.head()
```

Box plot view: This code provides a way to visually represent the maximum monthly temperature data for each month of the year using a box plot. Box plots can be useful for identifying trends and patterns in the data, such as seasonal variations in temperature.

```
import pandas as pd
import matplotlib.pyplot as plt
from matplotlib.cbook import boxplot_stats import numpy as np

df=max_df3[['Jan_max','Feb_max','Mar_max','Apr_max','May_max','Jun_max', 'Jul_max',
'Aug_max','Sep_max', 'Oct_max', 'Nov_max', ,Dec_max'
   ]]
# plot the dataframe as needed
ax = df.plot.box(figsize=(15, 8), showmeans=True, grid=True)
```

Observations: Fresno experiences significant seasonal variations, with a hot, arid summer from early June to mid-September, where temperatures often exceed 90 °F (32.22 °C), peaking in July. In contrast, the winter season, lasting from late November to late February, is characterized by cold temperatures, averaging daily highs below 60 °F (15.56 °C), and frequent precipitation, with 10–11 rainy days per month. Overall, Fresno's climate features distinct hot, dry summers and cold, wet winters.

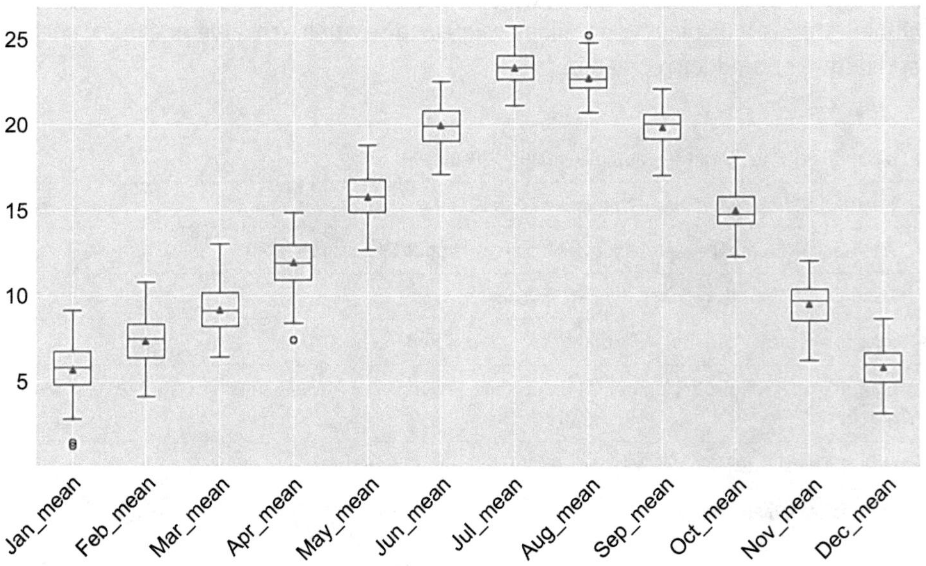

Similarly, load minimum temperature, mean temperature, and precipitation.

```
df_prcp = pd.read_csv("pr_timeseries_monthly_cru_1901-2021_USA_3218.csv")
df_prcp
```

```
df_prcp.rename(columns = { "Jan": "Jan_prcp", "Feb": "Feb_prcp", "Mar": "Mar_prcp", "Apr": "Apr_prcp",
"May":"May_prcp", "Jun": "Jun_prcp", "Jul":"Jul_prcp", "Aug": "Aug_prcp","Sep": "Sep_prcp", "Oct":
"Oct_prcp","Nov": "Nov_prcp", "Dec": "Dec_prcp"}, inplace=True)
```

```
import pandas as pd
import matplotlib.pyplot as plt
from matplotlib.cbook import boxplot_stats
import numpy as np
df = df_prcp[['Jan_prcp', 'Feb_prcp', 'Mar_prcp', 'Apr_prcp', 'May_prcp',
    'Jun_prcp', 'Jul_prcp', 'Aug_prcp', 'Sep_prcp', 'Oct_prcp', 'Nov_prcp',
    'Dec_prcp']]

# plot the dataframe as needed
ax = df.plot.box(figsize=(15, 8), showmeans=True, grid=True)
```

Load average temperature: This code provides a way to analyze temperature data and identify patterns in mean monthly temperatures over time. This information could be useful for understanding climate trends and making decisions related to weather-sensitive activities, such as agriculture or outdoor recreation.

```
mean_df=weather_df[["Date", "Month","Year", 'MeanTemperature(C)']]
```

```
mean_df1 = mean_df.pivot(columns= "Month", index = "Year", values=
"MeanTemperature(C)").reset_index()
mean_dfl.head()
```

```
mean_df2= mean_dfl[:-1]
```

```
mean_df2.rename(columns = { "Jan": "Jan_mean", "Feb": "Feb_mean", "Mar": "Mar_mean", "Apr":
"Apr_mean", "May":"May_mean", "Jun": "Jun_mean", "Jul":"Jul_mean", "Aug": "Aug_mean", "Sep":
"Sep_mean", "Oct": "Oct_mean","Nov": "Nov_mean", "Dec": "Dec_mean"}, inplace = True)
```

```
mean_df3 = mean_df2.apply(lambda x: round(x,2))
```

```
mean_df3
```

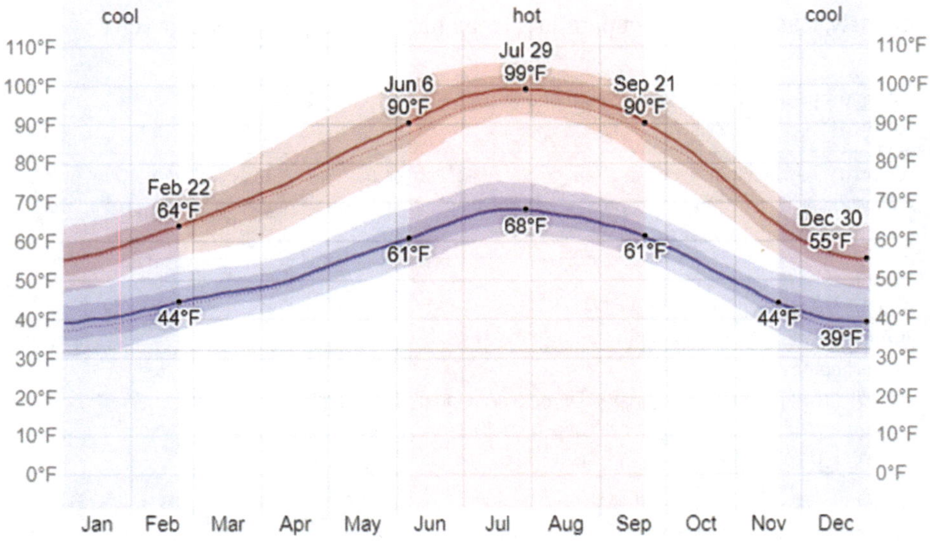

Extract average temperature data: This process involves first setting the date as the index. Next, collect the year and month date time components. Pivot the data frame and rename the columns.

Box plot view:

```
import pandas as pd
import matplotlib.pyplot as plt
from matplotlib.cbook import boxplot_stats
import numpy as np

df=mean_df3[['Jan_mean', 'Feb_mean','Mar_mean', 'Apr_mean','May_mean','Jun_mean', 'Jul_mean',
'Aug_mean',
        'Sep_mean', 'Oct_mean','Nov_mean', 'Dec_mean']]
# plot the dataframe as needed
ax = df.plot.box(figsize=(15, 8), showmeans=True, grid=True)
```

Observations: Fresno experiences a cool season from late November to late February, with average daily high temperatures below 64 °F (17.78 °C) and December is the coldest month. This period contrasts with the hot, arid summer season, which lasts from early June to mid-September.

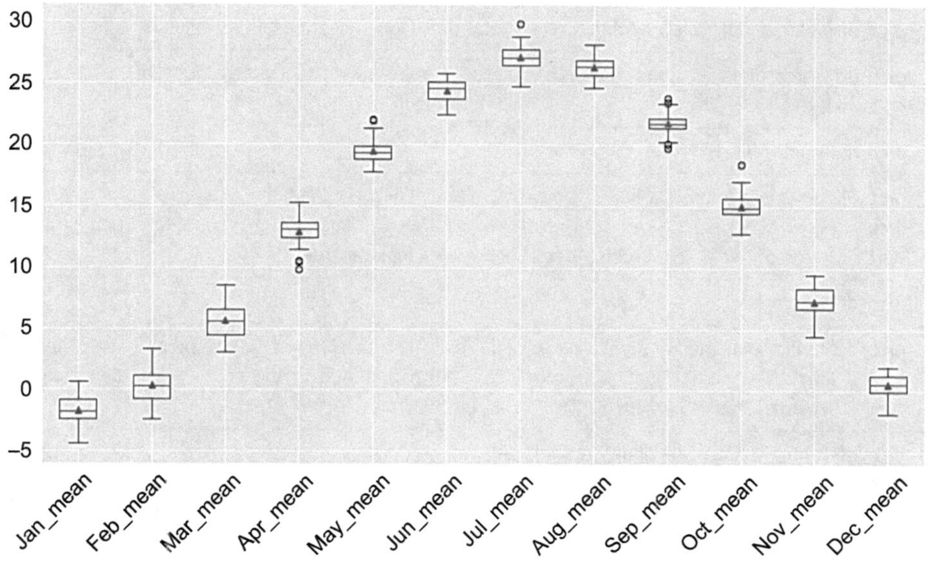

The climatic data for Fresno suggests that the region experiences significant seasonal variations in temperature and precipitation, with a cool winter season and a hot summer season. Understanding these seasonal variations is important for making decisions related to activities such as agriculture or outdoor recreation in the region.

Analyze Fresno precipitation dataset:
The following code provides a way to analyze precipitation data and identify patterns in total monthly precipitation over time in Fresno. This information could be useful for understanding climate trends and making decisions related to weather-sensitive activities, such as agriculture or water management.

First, the code selects the total precipitation data from the original DataFrame and creates a new DataFrame with columns for each month of the year. This is done using the Pandas pivot function, which rearranges the data so that the total precipitation for each month is shown in a separate column.

Next, the column names in the new DataFrame are changed to reflect the month and type of precipitation being recorded. The total precipitation values are also rounded to six decimal places.

```
prcp_df=weather_df[["Date", "Month","Year", 'total_precipitation(kg m-2 s-1)']]
```

```
prcp_df1 =prcp_df.pivot(columns="Month", index="Year", values= 'total_precipitation(kg m-2 s- 1)').
reset_index()
```

```
prcp_df2 = prcp_dfl[:-1]
```

```
prcp_df2.rename(columns= { "Jan": "Jan_prcp", "Feb": "Feb_prcp", "Mar": "Mar_prcp", "Apr": "Apr_
prcp", "May":"May_prcp", "Jun": "Jun_prcp", "Jul":"Jul_prcp", "Aug": "Aug_prcp","Sep": "Sep_prcp",
"Oct": "Oct_prcp","Nov": "Nov_prcp", "Dec": "Dec_prcp"}, inplace=True)
```

```
prcp_df2 = prcp_df1[:-1]
```

```
prcp_df2.rename(columns= { "Jan": "Jan_prcp", "Feb": "Feb_prcp", "Mar": "Mar_prcp", "Apr": "Apr_
prcp", "May":"May_prcp", "Jun": "Jun_prcp", "Jul":"Jul_prcp", "Aug": "Aug_prcp","Sep": "Sep_prcp",
"Oct": "Oct_prcp","Nov": "Nov_prcp", "Dec": "Dec_prcp"}, inplace=True)
```

```
prcp_df3 = prcp_df2.apply(lambda x: round(x,6))
prcp_df3
```

Box plot view: This code provides a way to visually represent the total monthly precipitation data for each month of the year using a box plot. This information could be useful for understanding climate trends and making decisions related to weather-sensitive activities, such as agriculture or water management.

This code creates a box plot of the total monthly precipitation data for each month of the year in Fresno. First, the Pandas library is imported as pd, and the Matplotlib library is imported as plt. The boxplot_stats function from the Matplotlib cbook module is also imported, as well as the NumPy library, which is used for array operations. Next, the code selects the total monthly precipitation data from the DataFrame created in the previous code block and creates a new DataFrame with columns for each month of the year.

Finally, the code creates a box plot of the total monthly precipitation data using the plot.box function from Matplotlib. The figsize parameter sets the size of the plot, and showmeans=True displays the mean total precipitation for each month in the plot. The grid=True parameter displays a grid in the plot.

```
import pandas as pd
import matplotlib.pyplot as plt
from matplotlib.cbook import boxplot_stats
import numpy as np

df = prcp_df3 [['Jan_prcp', 'Feb_prcp','Mar_prcp','Apr_prcp','May_prcp','Jun_prcp', 'Jul_prcp',
'Aug_prcp','Sep_prcp', 'Oct_prcp', 'Nov_prcp', 'Dec_prcp'
    ]]

# plot the dataframe as needed
ax = df.plot.box(figsize=(15, 8), showmeans=True, grid=True)
```

In Fresno, the number of wet days varies throughout the year, with a wet season from November 5th to April 8th and a dry season from April 8th to November 5th. February is the wettest month, averaging 6.8 wet days, and rain is the most common form of precipitation, peaking on February 20th. Understanding these variations is crucial for planning and managing agricultural and other activities in the region.

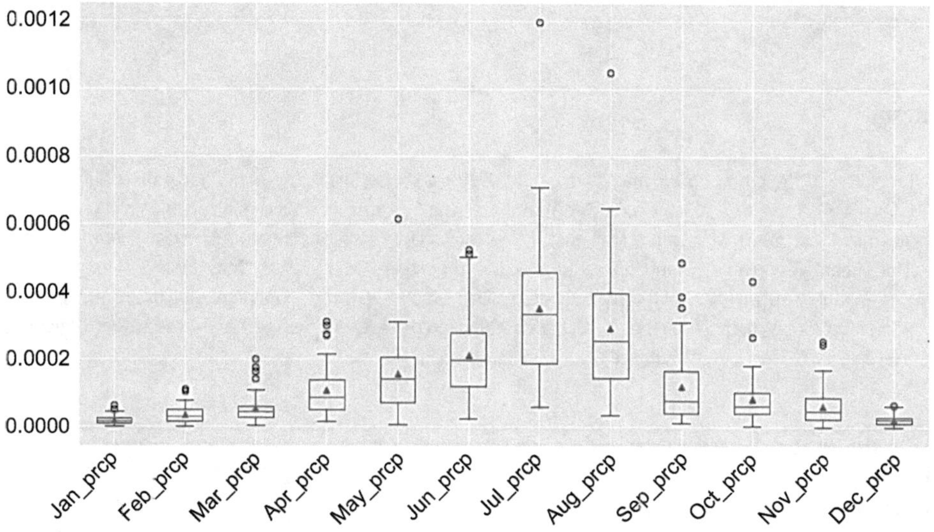

Step 7: Prepare Fresno climatology and pistachios combined dataset

This code block combines several DataFrames using the Pandas merge function and the reduce function from the functools library. First, a list of DataFrames is created, including max_df3, min_df3, mean_df3, prcp_df3, and dfPistachiosProdUSA. These DataFrames contain maximum, minimum, and mean temperature data, precipitation data, and pistachio production data for different years in Fresno. Next, the reduce function is used to merge these DataFrames into a single DataFrame based on the "Year" column. The merge function combines the data from the DataFrames by matching the data for each year. Finally, the shape function is used to display the dimensions of the combined DataFrame, and the tail function is used to display the last few rows of the DataFrame.

This code block provides a way to combine multiple DataFrames into a single DataFrame for further analysis.

```
dfList1 = [max_df3, min_df3, mean_df3, prcp_df3,
dfPistachiosProdUSA]
combined_df = ft.reduce(lambda left, right: pd.merge(left, right,
on="Year"), dfList1)
```

```
combined_df.shape
```

```
combined_df.tail()
```

```
combined_df
```

Result:

```
Index(['Year', 'Apr_max', 'Aug_max', 'Dec_max', 'Feb_max', 'Jan_max', 'Jul_max', 'Jun_max', 'Mar_max',
'May_max', 'Nov_max', 'Oct_max', 'Sep_max', 'Apr_min', 'Aug_min', 'Dec_min', 'Feb_min', 'Jan_min',
'Jul_min', 'Jun_min', 'Mar_min', 'May_min', 'Nov_min', 'Oct_min', 'Sep_min', 'Apr_mean', 'Aug_mean',
'Dec_mean', 'Feb_mean', 'Jan_mean', 'Jul_mean', 'Jun_mean', 'Mar_mean', 'May_mean', "Nov_mean',
'Oct_mean', 'Sep_mean', 'Apr_prcp', 'Aug_prcp', 'Dec_prcp', 'Feb_prcp', 'Jan_prcp', 'Jul_prcp', 'Jun_prcp',
'Mar_prcp', 'May_prcp', 'Nov_prcp', 'Oct_prcp', 'Sep_prcp', 'Area harvested(ha)', 'Production(tonnes)',
'Yield(hg/ha)', 'Flag'], dtype='object')
```

	Year	Apr_max	Aug_max	Dec_max	Feb_max	Jan_max	Jul_max	Jun_max	Mar_max	May_max	...	Jun_prcp	Mar_prcp
38	2018	21.13	32.83	4.40	5.37	2.14	32.98	31.39	14.12	26.27	...	0.000356	0.000198
39	2019	19.63	31.58	6.82	5.71	4.11	34.24	32.05	14.34	28.34	...	0.000276	0.000044
40	2020	18.70	30.83	4.14	8.10	4.71	30.30	30.85	14.88	26.10	...	0.000513	0.000022
41	2021	18.32	30.42	6.69	9.42	3.38	31.63	30.47	13.95	24.94	...	0.000206	0.000045
42	2022	20.95	30.75	3.43	5.15	3.19	31.07	31.06	13.13	27.06	...	0.000217	0.000078

5 rows × 53 columns

Step 8: Fresno pistachios correlation matrix

This code block provides a way to analyze the correlation between different Fresno pistochios and weather variables in a merged DataFrame and visualize the results using a heatmap. The corr() function is used to calculate the correlation matrix for several variables in the DataFrame.

```
mergedframe1 = mergedframe.ffill()
```

```
mergedframel[['Production_Tonnes','Area harvested','Yield','CO2 emissions
(kt)','SPEI_droughtIndex']].corr()
```

```
# Visualizing a Pandas Correlation Matrix Using Seaborn
import pandas as pd
import seaborn as sns
import matplotlib.pyplot as plt

matrix = mergedframe1[['Production_Tonnes','Area harvested', 'Yield','CO2 emissions
(kt)','SPEI_droughtIndex']].corr().round(2)
sns.heatmap(matrix, annot=True)
plt.show()
```

Display:

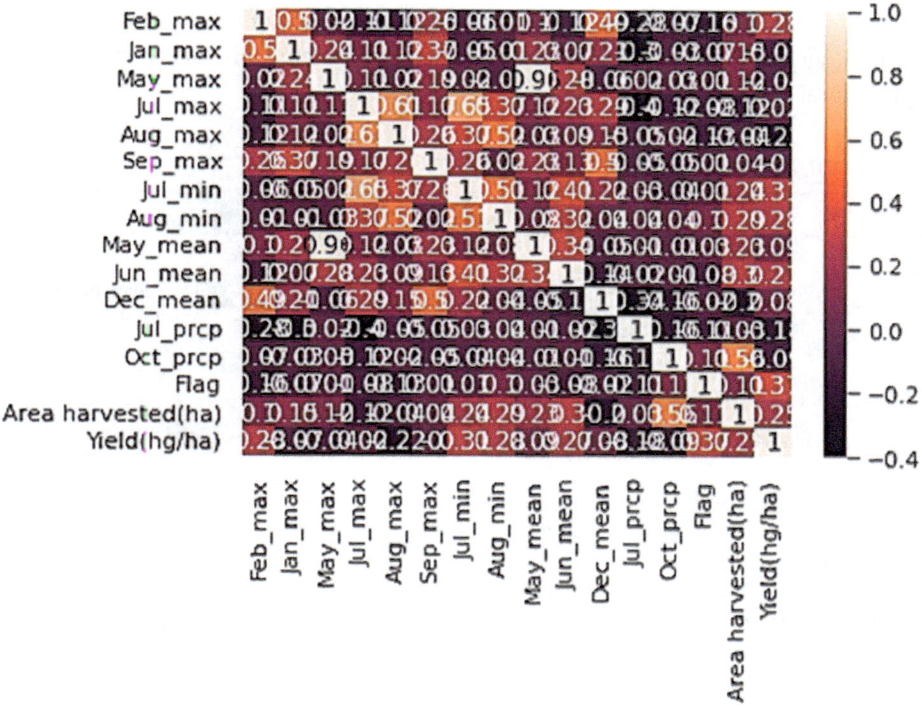

In Fresno, California, pistachio yields positively correlate with both the harvested area and overall production. Additionally, there is a positive correlation between pistachio yields and other alternate-bearing crops. These correlations suggest that increases in harvested area and production, as well as the cultivation of alternate-bearing crops, may enhance pistachio yields.

Step 9: ML model: gradient boosting regressor

In the pursuit of optimizing pistachio yield, an ML model was developed based on the agricultural calendar. This model aimed to predict pistachio yield by analyzing independent time series attributes. The results of this study revealed that these variables significantly influenced yield, highlighting their importance in the development of accurate yield forecasting models.

It is worth noting that other factors that may impact pistachio yield, such as tree age and fertilizer consumption, were not included in the model.

In conclusion, the development of ML models has revolutionized domain of agricultural forecasting, enabling researchers and growers to predict crop yields with unprecedented accuracy. However, it is essential to consider all factors that impact crop production, such as honeybee pollination, to ensure the sustainability and profitability of agricultural operations.

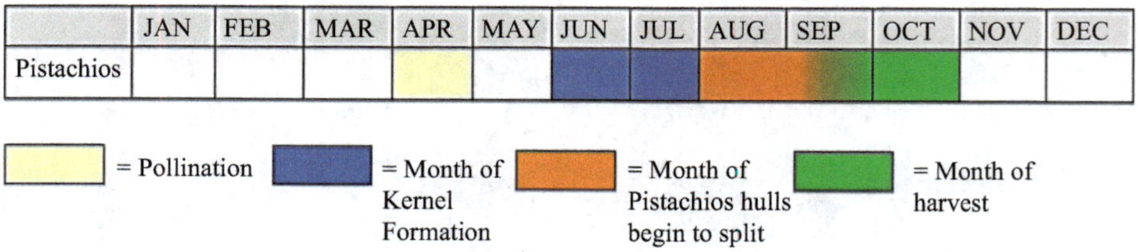


```
gbr = GradientBoostingRegressor(random_state=0)
X=combined_df[[
        'Feb_max', 'Jan_max', 'May_max', 'Jul_max', 'Aug_max', 'Sep_max',
  'Jul_min', 'Aug_min', 'May_mean', 'Jun_mean', 'Dec_mean', 'Jul_prcp',
  'Oct_prcp',
    'Flag',
  'Area harvested(ha)'
                    ]]
y= combined_df['Yield(hg/ha)']
X_train,X_test, y_train, y_test = train_test_split(X,y, test_size = 0.2,random_state=0 ) y= combined_
df['Yield(hg/ha)']
X_train,X_test, y_train, y_test = train_test_split(X,y, test_size = 0.2,random_state=0)

gbr.fit(X_train,y_train)
gbr.score(X_test,y_test)

y_pred = gbr.predict(X_test)
y_pred
r2_score(y_test,y_pred)
```

Gradient boosting for regression: Gradient boosting is a powerful method for predicting numerical values. Gradient boosting builds a model by adding new components to it in a step-by-step manner.

In this code block, a GradientBoostingRegressor model is used to predict pistachio yield based on several environmental variables. The model is trained using a subset of the combined DataFrame, which includes variables such as maximum and minimum temperature, precipitation, and area harvested, among others.

Overall, the above code provides a way to train and evaluate a gradient boosting regressor model for predicting pistachio yield based on environmental variables. This can be useful for farmers and other stakeholders in the agricultural industry.

Result:

$$R^2 \text{ value} = 0.7582 \text{ or } 75.82\%$$

Step 10: Gradient boost explainability

The code block uses the Eli5 library to explain and visualize the feature weights of an ML model that predicts pistachio yield based on environmental variables. The explain_ weights function is used to generate an explanation of the feature weights of the GradientBoostingRegressor model, with feature names specified by the list of columns in the X DataFrame. This function provides insights into which features are most important in predicting yield and how they contribute to the model's overall performance.

```
eli5.explain_weights(gbr, feature_names = list(X.columns))
```

```
eli5.show_weights(gbr, feature_names =list(X.columns), target_names = "California Pistachios
Yield Predict")
```

Explainability variable list:

Weight	Feature
0.4748 ± 0.3493	Area harvested(ha)
0.1233 ± 0.2373	Jan_max
0.1046 ± 0.3858	Feb_max
0.0898 ± 0.1436	Flag
0.0462 ± 0.3222	Dec_mean
0.0342 ± 0.1701	Jul_min
0.0322 ± 0.2144	Jul_max
0.0283 ± 0.2838	Jul_prcp
0.0155 ± 0.2063	Oct_prcp
0.0139 ± 0.2687	Aug_min
0.0120 ± 0.0647	May_max
0.0118 ± 0.1406	Jun_mean
0.0093 ± 0.3170	Sep_max
0.0029 ± 0.2449	Aug_max
0.0014 ± 0.2717	May_mean

In this ML model, the area harvested variable has the highest importance in predicting pistachio yield. This means that the area of land on which the pistachio trees are grown has the biggest impact on the yield. Additionally, Fresno maximum temperatures in January and February have a positive impact on the yield. This means that when the temperatures are higher during these months, it leads to a better yield of pistachios. Another factor that has a positive influence on the model is the alternative bearing flag. This flag indicates whether the tree is in a year of high yield or low yield. When the flag is set to high yield, it leads to a better overall yield of pistachios.

Step 12: Maximizing Fresno pistachio yield: insights from random forest regressor

The code creates an ML model created using the random forest regressor algorithm to predict pistachio yield based on environmental variables.

```
from sklearn.ensemble import RandomForestRegressor
X=combined_df[[ 'Feb_max', 'Jan_max', 'May_max', 'Jul_max', 'Aug_max', 'Sep_max',
   'Jul_min', 'Aug_min', 'May_mean', 'Jun_mean', 'Dec_mean', 'Jul_prcp',
   'Oct_prcp',
      'Flag',
'Area harvested(ha)'
          ]]
y= combined_df['Yield(hg/ha)']
X_train,X_test, y_train, y_test = train_test_split(X,y, test_size = 0.2,random_state=0 )
regr = RandomForestRegressor(max_depth=3, random_state=0)
regr.fit(X_train, y_train)
regr.score(X_test,y_test)
```

Model performance:
0.17556 or 17.556%

Other climatology insights derived from ML models:
- In this ML model, we discovered that temperature variables from November through January significantly influence pistachio yield. Specifically, the variables Dec_Mean and Jan_Max emerged as particularly crucial. This is due to the fact that pistachio trees require a dormant period during the winter to ready themselves for the upcoming growing season, shedding their leaves and undergoing a chilling period in California's cool, wet winters. The Dec_Mean and Jan_Max variables serve as key indicators of temperature during this dormancy, positively affecting pistachio yield.

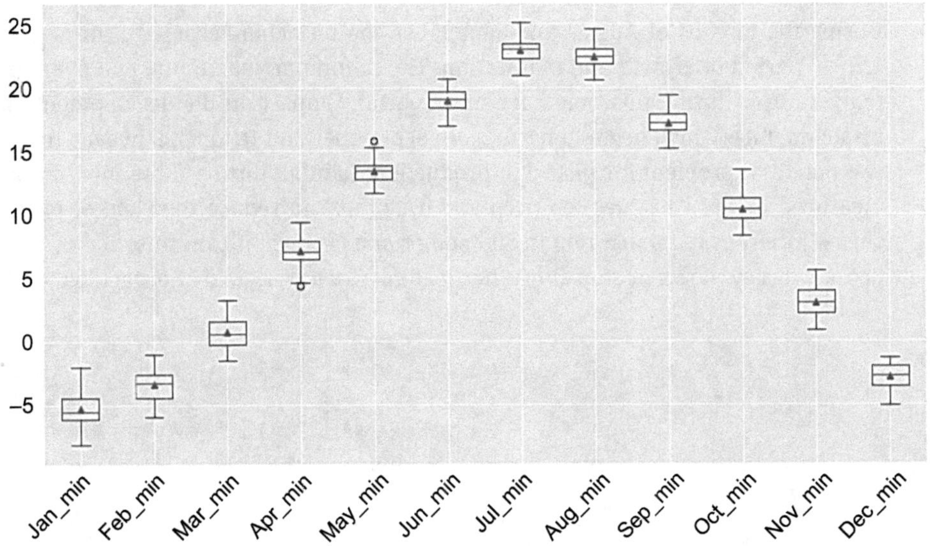

– Between mid-June and mid-July, a captivating transformation occurs in pistachio orchards. The buds on the trees unfurl into stunning yellow and nimble pinkish (light pink) flowers. This period is crucial as it marks the time of pollination, leading to the development of pistachio nuts. To ensure that the pistachio trees are properly pollinated, beekeepers bring hives into the orchards during this time. Bees are very important pollinators for pistachios, and they help to ensure that the trees produce a good crop of nuts.

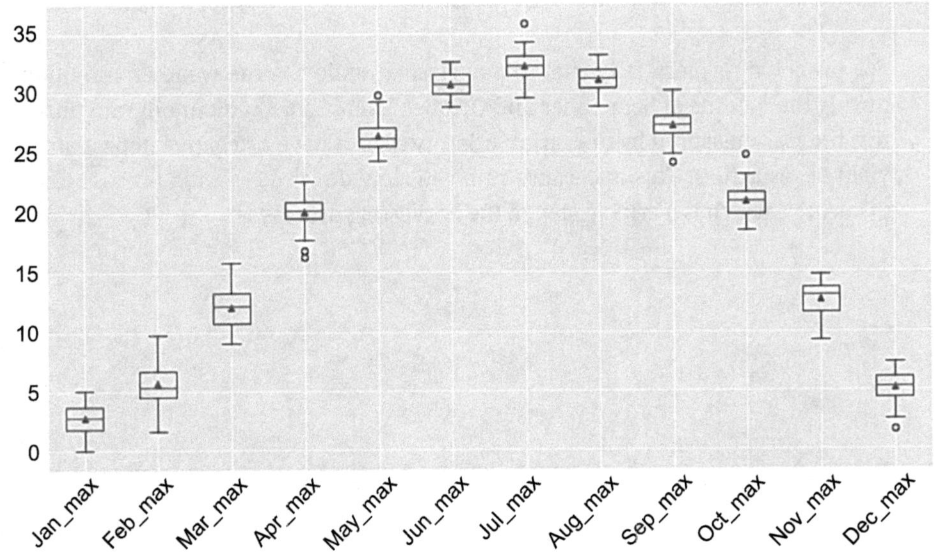

- During the months of August and September, the pistachio kernels go through a critical period of growth and maturation. The minimum, maximum, and average temperatures during this time have an important impact on the development of pistachio nuts (which begin to harden). In September and October, however, there is a potential problem for pistachio production. Rainfall during these months, as measured by the variables sep_prcp and oct_prcp, can reduce the yield of pistachios. If there is too much rain in September and October, it can cause the drying process to slow down or stop altogether, leading to a lower yield of pistachios.

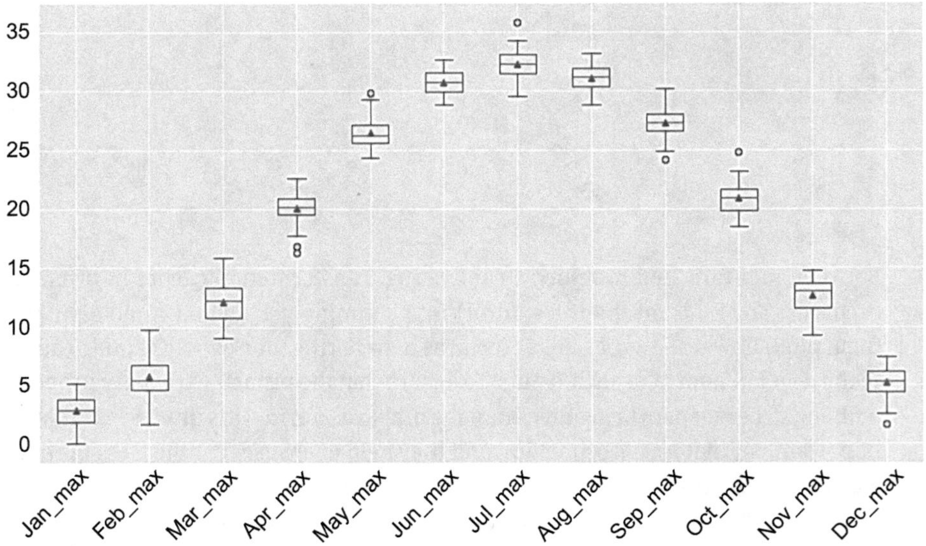

- For pistachio farmers, it is vital to pay close attention to the weather conditions during the months of September and October. Even a small amount of rain during this time, as measured by the variable Sep_prcp, can have a negative impact on the yield of pistachios. This is because rain can slow down the drying process of the pistachios, which is a critical step in the harvesting process.

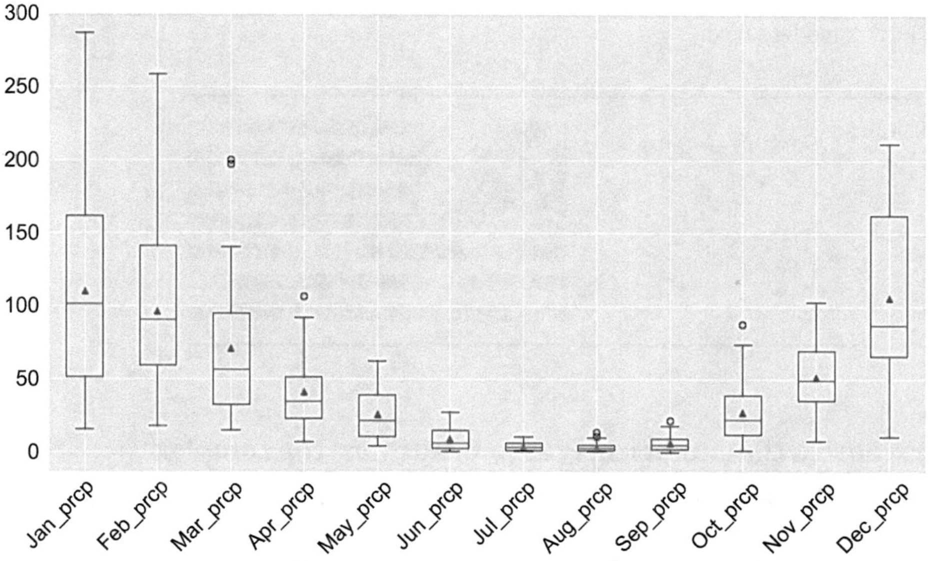

Overall, this information gives insight into the complex and carefully managed process of harvesting pistachios. By understanding the impact of weather conditions on pistachio production, farmers can make more informed decisions about when to harvest their crops and how to optimize the drying process for the best possible yield.

Step 13: Saving and loading Fresno pistachios yield ML mode

The line of code “import pickle” may seem like a small detail in the world of computer programming, but it is vital in persisting the model for later use. In this particular case, the code is being used to save a model that predicts the yield of pistachios in the USA. The line of code “pickle.dump(gbr, open(“Pistachios_usa.pkl”,”wb”))” is what actually saves the model to a file called “Pistachios_usa.pkl”. This file can then be loaded into other programs or used to make predictions about pistachio yields in the future. By using the pickle library in Python, developers are able to save and load complex ML models with ease. This makes it possible to reuse models across different projects and to share them with others in the data science community.

```
import pickle
pickle.dump(gbr, open("Pistachios_usa.pkl","wb"))
```

Output: model saved.

USA pistachios

Extensive climatological Fresno pistachios: the complex relationship between climate and yield

The ML model is utilized to examine the impact of essential ecological and climatical variables, such as temperature, precipitation, wind speed, CDSD, HTDD, and HDSD, on pistachio yields. Its goal is to understand these influences better and predict future yields using various climate models. While climate projections are available for basic variables like temperature and precipitation, they are not available for computed variables like CDSD and HDSD. Despite this limitation, the model is instrumental in studying the complex relationships between climate and pistachio yield, aiming to foster more sustainable and productive farming practices.

Let's build models for USA pistachios:

Final Release California Pistachios Yield And Climate Change Model GSOM Notebook

Key variables and data elements:
The ML model we are discussing uses data from various sources to predict the yield of pistachios. These sources include the Climate Change Portal, FAO Statistics Data, Fresno County Weather data, World Meteorological Organization Data, and NOAA STAR. The data being used includes information on minimum and maximum temperatures, precipitation, and CO_2 emissions. The model also uses Earth Observation data from FAO and Global Vegetation Health Products from NOAA STAR.

Data source	Name
Food and Agriculture Statistics	Fresno Pistachios Time Series Yield, Production, and Area Harvest.
National Oceanic and Atmospheric Administration	NOAA's Climate at a Glance County Time Series provides data on minimum, maximum, and average temperatures, as well as precipitation, for Fresno county. This information helps us understand the weather patterns in this region.
UN[9]	Data related to CO_2 emissions. The measurement is in kT, which likely stands for kilotons, and the data is labelled "EN.ATM.CO2E."

Steps 1 through 4 of this model are identical to the previous model, "Climate Change on California Pistachio Yield: A Machine Learning Approach." As a result, we can reuse the same code from the previous model.

Step 5: Fresno Yosemite International, Station 1980:2023 weather data

This code loads temperature data and renames the columns. Specifically, it calculates the average or mean temperature for a given time period, monthly, and stores that data in a DataFrame. Then, it renames the columns in the DataFrame to better reflect the data that is stored in each column.

9 IBRD.IDA: https://www.un-ilibrary.org/content/books/9789210574983s011-c006

```
weather_df = pd.read_csv(r"USW00093193_Fresno_county_Weather_GSOM.csv", index_col=
"date")
weather_df
```

```
weather_df.drop('Unnamed: 0', axis=1, inplace = True)
```

```
weather_df.reset_index(inplace=True)
```

```
weather_df
```

This output indicates that the data being analyzed spans a period of 43 years, from 1980 to 2023. Specifically, the data is monthly data, which means there are 12 data points for each year. This results in a total of 520 rows of data.

/leanTemperature(F)	MaxTemperature(F)	MinTemperature(F)	total_precipitation(kg m-2 s-1)	FatestWindSpeed	DirectionOfWind	AverageWindSpeed	CDSD	CLDD
49.1	54.2	44.0	3.83	21.9	100	NaN	0	0
53.4	61.7	45.2	3.30	28.0	90	NaN	0	0
53.3	63.0	43.7	2.05	25.9	300	NaN	0	0
61.5	73.4	49.6	0.25	30.0	310	NaN	36	36
66.8	79.4	54.3	0.18	25.1	310	NaN	151	115
...	...	...	...	...	...	...	...	...
50.3	57.7	42.9	3.95	35.1	130	5.6	0	0
49.2	59.5	39.0	4.26	38.9	280	5.8	0	0
53.3	61.5	45.0	4.00	35.1	170	7.4	0	0
64.0	76.4	51.6	0.00	33.1	310	7.4	88	88
71.3	83.4	59.3	0.35	21.0	310	8.5	302	213

The code provides a way to analyze temperature data and identify patterns in maximum monthly temperatures over time. This information could be useful for understanding climate trends and making decisions related to weather-sensitive activities, such as agriculture or outdoor recreation.

The Yosemite Fresno Weather Station CLDD (cooling degree day) is a measure of the amount of cooling required to maintain a certain level of comfort indoors during the summer months. The CLDD value is used as an indicator of the energy demand for air conditioning during the summer months. In the context of the previous code, the CLDD value is extracted from the weather data for the Yosemite Fresno Weather Station and organized by month and year to analyze the cooling degree days over time.

```
weather_df["Date"] = pd.to_datetime(weather_df["date"])
```

```
weather_df.drop("date",axis = 1, inplace=True)
```

```
weather_df["Month"] = weather_df["Date"].apply(lambda x : x.strftime(‚%b‘))
```

```
weather_df["Year"] = weather_df["Date"].dt.year
```

```
CLDD_df = weather_df[["Date", "Month","Year", ‚CLDD‘]]
```

```
CLDD_df1 = CLDD_df.pivot(columns= "Month", index = "Year", values=
"CLDD").reset_index()
CLDD_df1
```

```
CLDD_df2=CLDD_df1[:-1]
```

```
CLDD_df2.rename(columns = { "Jan": "Jan_cldd", "Feb": "Feb_cldd",
        "Mar": "Mar_cldd", "Apr": "Apr_cldd",
        "May":"May_cldd", "Jun": "Jun_cldd",
        'Jul':"Jul_cldd","Aug": "Aug_cldd",
        "Sep": "Sep_cldd", "Oct": "Oct_cldd",
        "Nov": "Nov_cldd", "Dec": "Dec_cldd"}, inplace=True)
```

```
CLDD_df3 = CLDD_df2.apply(lambda x: round(x,2))
CLDD_df3.head()
```

In this code, we import the “pandas” and “matplotlib.pyplot” libraries using the “import” statement. We also import the “boxplot_stats” function from the “matplotlib.cbook” module and the “numpy” library using the “import” statement. Next, we create a new dataset called “df” by selecting the columns from “CLDD_df3” that correspond to the CLDD values for each month of the year. We use the double square brackets notation to select multiple columns.

Box plot view:

```
import pandas as pd
import matplotlib.pyplot as plt
from matplotlib.cbook import boxplot_stats import numpy as np
df = CLDD_df3[['Jan_cldd', 'Feb_cldd','Mar_cldd','Apr_cldd','May_cldd','Jun_cldd',
'Jul_cldd', 'Aug_cldd','Sep_cldd', 'Oct_cldd','Nov_cldd', 'Dec_cldd'
  ]]
# plot the dataframe as needed
ax = df.plot.box(figsize=(15, 8), showmeans=True, grid=True)
```

Display CLDD box plot: The Yosemite International Weather Station has high values of CLDD during May to August. The units used to report CLDD values may vary, with Fahrenheit being used in the PDF output and either Fahrenheit or Celsius being used in the CSV output, depending on user specification.

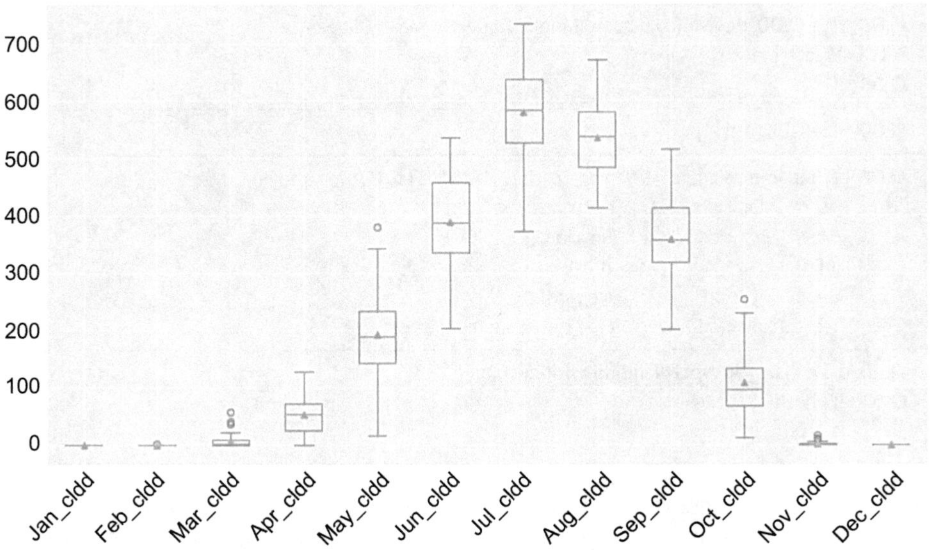

CLDD is a computed parameter that reflects values based on environmental factors such as temperature. To better understand this, one can observe temperature curves and note the similarities in the data.

Similarly, load HTDD, average wind speed, and other parameters. Heating degree days (HDD) is a calculated parameter that reflects values based on environmental factors such as temperature. The units used to report HDD values may vary, with Fahrenheit being used in the PDF output and either Fahrenheit or Celsius being used in the CSV output, depending on user preference. This information can be useful for understanding the energy demand for heating during the colder months, which can have implications for energy consumption and utility costs.

```
htdd_df=weather_df[["Date", "Month","Year", ,HTDD‘]]
```

```
htdd_df1 = htdd_df.pivot(columns="Month", index = "Year", values=
"HTDD").reset_index()
htdd_dfl
```

```
htdd_df2 = htdd_dfl[:-1]
```

```
htdd_df2.rename(columns= { "Jan": "Jan_htdd", "Feb": "Feb_htdd",
    "Mar": "Mar_htdd", "Apr": "Apr_htdd",
    "May":"May_htdd", "Jun": "Jun_htdd",
    "Jul":"Jul_htdd","Aug": "Aug_htdd",
    "Sep": "Sep_htdd", "Oct": "Oct_htdd",
    "Nov": "Nov_htdd", "Dec": "Dec_htdd"}, inplace = True)
```

```
htdd_df3 = htdd_df2.apply(lambda x: round(x,2))
htdd_df3.head()
```

Display HTDD:

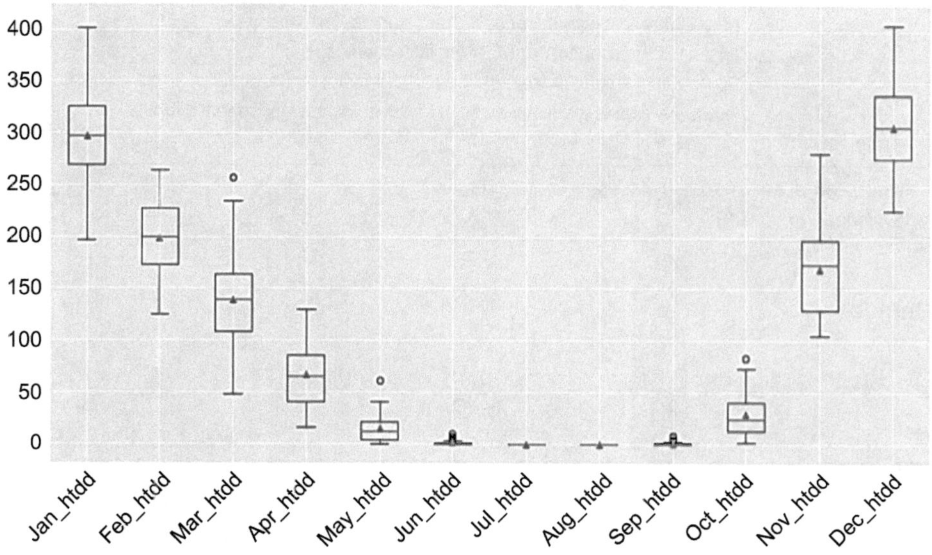

Load fast wind speed: This code pertains to wind speed data collected at the Yosemite Fresno Weather Station. Specifically, it selects the columns for date, month, year, and fastest wind speed from a larger dataset called "weather_df". The resulting dataset is then pivoted to display the fastest wind speeds for each month of the year. Next, the resulting dataset is modified by removing the last row and renaming the columns to reflect the corresponding month of the year and the fastest wind speed for that month. The final dataset is rounded to two decimal places and the first few rows are displayed using the "head()" function. Overall, this code is used to manipulate and analyze wind speed data for the Yosemite Fresno weather Station, which could provide insight into weather patterns and conditions in the area.

```
fastwindspeed_df=weather_df[["Date", "Month","Year", 'FatestWindSpeed']]
```

```
fwndspeed_df1 = fastwindspeed_df.pivot(columns= "Month", index = "Year", values=
"FatestWindSpeed").reset_index()
fwndspeed_dfl
```

```
fwndspeed_df2 = fwndspeed_dfl[:-1]
```

```
fwndspeed_df2.rename(columns = { "Jan": "Jan_fastestwindspeed", "Feb":
"Feb_fastestwindspeed",
                    "Mar": "Mar_fastestwindspeed", "Apr": "Apr_fastestwindspeed",
                    "May":"May_fastestwindspeed", "Jun": "Jun_fastestwindspeed", "Jul":
                    "Jul_fastestwindspeed","Aug": "Aug_fastestwindspeed",
                    "Sep": "Sep_fastestwindspeed", "Oct": "Oct_fastestwindspeed",
                    "Nov": "Nov_fastestwindspeed", "Dec": "Dec_fastestwindspeed"}, inplace
=True)
```

```
fwndspeed_df3 = fwndspeed_df2.apply(lambda x: round(x,2))
fwndspeed_df3.head()
```

Output:

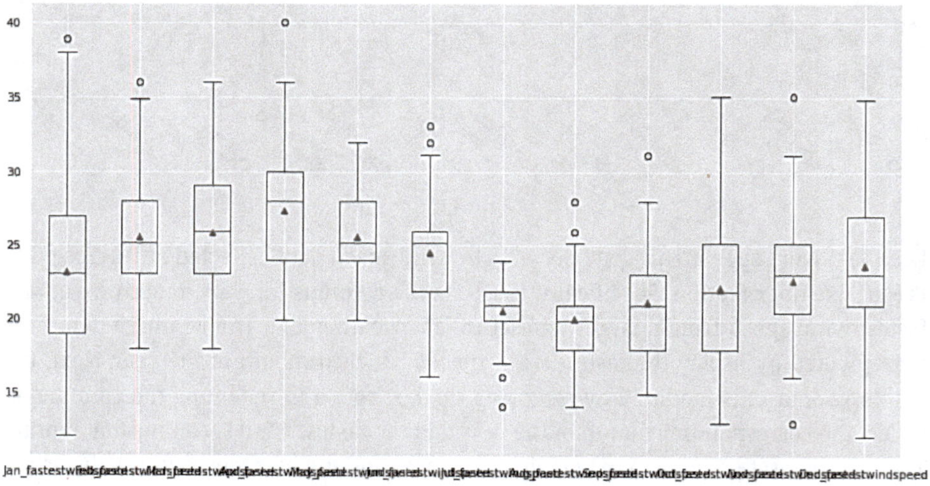

The wind speed during the month of April is very important for pollination. This is because wind plays a crucial role in carrying pollen from one plant to another, which is necessary for fertilization and the production of seeds. To better understand the wind patterns during this critical time, a box plot is shown above that displays wind speed data for the months of February through April. This box plot can help identify any trends or patterns in wind speed during this important period, which can be useful for predicting and managing pollination and crop yields.

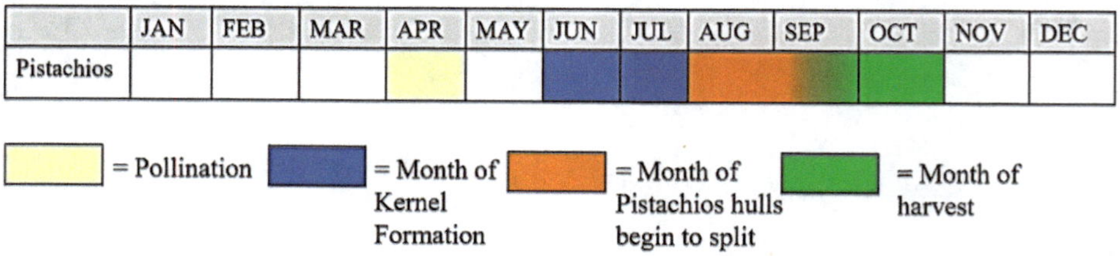

Precipitation:

```
prcp_df=weather_df[["Date", "Month","Year", 'total_precipitation(kg m-2 s-1)']]
```

```
prcp_df1 = prcp_df.pivot(columns= "Month", index = "Year", values= 'total_precipitation(kg m-2 s- 1)').
reset_index()
```

```
prcp_df2 = prcp_df1[:-1]
```

```
prcp_df2.rename(columns = { "Jan": "Jan_prcp", "Feb": "Feb_prcp", "Mar": "Mar_prcp", "Apr": "Apr_
prcp", "May":"May_prcp", "Jun": "Jun_prcp", "Jul":"Jul_prcp", "Aug": "Aug_prcp","Sep": "Sep_prcp",
"Oct": "Oct_prcp","Nov": "Nov_prcp", "Dec": "Dec_prcp"}, inplace=True) prcp_df2 =
```

```
prcp_df1[:-1]
```

```
prcp_df2.rename(columns = { "Jan": "Jan_prcp", "Feb": "Feb_prcp", "Mar": "Mar_prcp", "Apr": "Apr_
prcp", "May":"May_prcp", "Jun": "Jun_prcp", "Jul":"Jul_prcp", "Aug": "Aug_prcp","Sep": "Sep_prcp",
"Oct": "Oct_prcp","Nov": "Nov_prcp", "Dec": "Dec_prcp"}, inplace=True) prcp_df3 =
```

```
prcp_df3=prcp_df2.apply(lambda x: round(x,6))
prcp_df3
```

Box plot view:

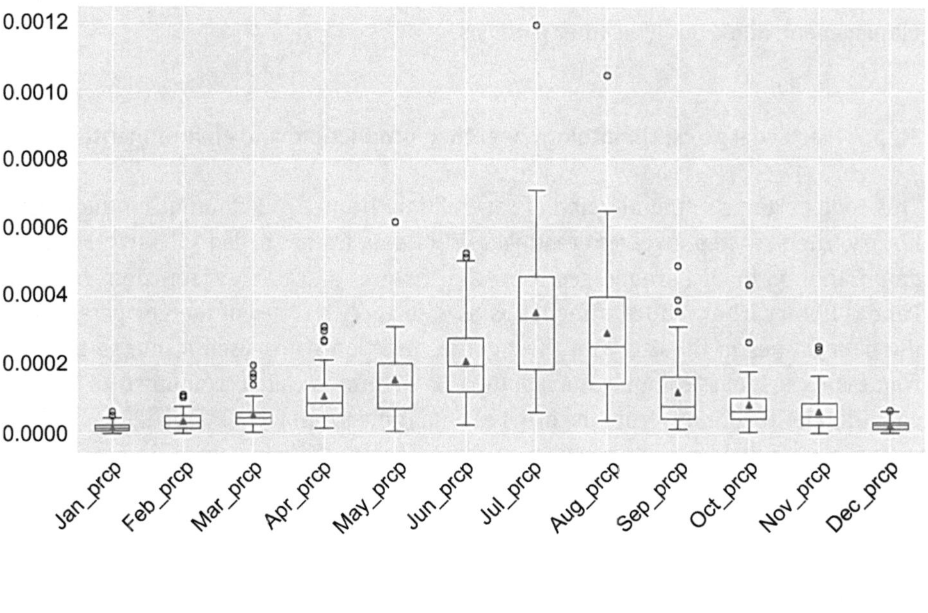

```
import pandas as pd
import matplotlib.pyplot as plt
from matplotlib.cbook import boxplot_stats
import numpy as np

df=prcp_df3[['Jan_prcp',
'Feb_prcp','Mar_prcp','Apr_prcp','May_prcp','Jun_prcp', 'Jul_prcp',
'Aug_prcp','Sep_prcp', 'Oct_prcp', 'Nov_prcp', 'Dec_prcp'
    ]]

# plot the dataframe as needed
ax = df.plot.box(figsize=(15, 8), showmeans=True, grid=True)
```

Fresno, California, experience wet days, which are days with at least 0.04 inches of precipitation or liquid equivalent. The likelihood of a wet day changes throughout the year, with a period of wetter weather lasting 5.1 months from November 5 to April 8, during which there is a greater than 13% chance of a wet day. The wettest month in Fresno is February, with an average of 6.8 wet days. On the other hand, there is a drier season lasting 6.9 months from April 8 to November 5, with August having the fewest wet days (0.1 days on average). Rain is the most common type of precipitation, with a peak probability of 27% on February 20. Among the wet days, rain alone is the most frequent form of precipitation. This information can be helpful in understanding the precipitation patterns and seasons in Fresno, which can have implications for agriculture, water management, and overall weather patterns.

Step 7: Merge datasets: climatology, weather, production, and environmental

This code pertains to the merging of several data frames in Python using the Pandas library. The first step involves creating a list of data frames called "dfList1". Next, the data frames in the list are merged using the "reduce" and "merge" functions from the Pandas library. The "reduce" function is used to apply a series of merge operations to the data frames in the list, with the "merge" function being used to merge the data frames on the "Year" column. The resulting DataFrame is called "combined_df", which contains all the columns from the original data frames that were merged.

```
dfList1 = [ max_df3, min_df3, mean_df3, prcp_df3,
htdd_df3,dfPistachiosProdUSA]
combined_df = ft.reduce(lambda left, right: pd.merge(left, right, on="Year"),
dfList1)
```

```
combined_df.shape
```

```
combined_df.tail()
```

```
combined_df
```

Output:

```
Index(['Year', 'Apr_max', 'Aug_max', 'Dec_max', 'Feb_max', 'Jan_max',
   'Jul_max', 'Jun_max', 'Mar_max', 'May_max', 'Nov_max', 'Oct_max',
   'Sep_max', 'Apr_min', 'Aug_min', 'Dec_min', 'Feb_min', 'Jan_min',
   'Jul_min', 'Jun_min', 'Mar_min', 'May_min', 'Nov_min', 'Oct_min',
   'Sep_min', 'Apr_mean', 'Aug_mean', 'Dec_mean', 'Feb_mean', 'Jan_mean',
   'Jul_mean', 'Jun_mean', 'Mar_mean', 'May_mean', 'Nov_mean',
'Oct_mean',
   'Sep_mean', Apr_prcp', 'Aug_prcp', 'Dec_prcp', 'Feb_prcp', 'Jan_prcp',
   'Jul_prcp', 'Jun_prcp', 'Mar_prcp', 'May_prcp', 'Nov_prcp', 'Oct_prcp',
   'Sep_prcp', 'Apr_htdd', 'Aug_htdd', 'Dec_htdd', 'Feb_htdd', 'Jan_htdd',
   'Jul_htdd', 'Jun_htdd', 'Mar_htdd', 'May_htdd', 'Nov_htdd', 'Oct_htdd',
   'Sep_htdd', 'Area harvested(ha)', 'Production(tonnes)', 'Yield(hg/ha)',
   'Flag'],
   dtype='object')
```

	Year	Apr_max	Aug_max	Dec_max	Feb_max	Jan_max	Jul_max	Jun_max	Mar_max	May_max	...	Jun_prcp	Mar_prcp
38	2018	21.13	32.83	4.40	5.37	2.14	32.98	31.39	14.12	26.27	...	0.000356	0.000198
39	2019	19.63	31.58	6.82	5.71	4.11	34.24	32.05	14.34	28.34	...	0.000276	0.000044
40	2020	18.70	30.83	4.14	8.10	4.71	30.30	30.85	14.88	26.10	...	0.000513	0.000022
41	2021	18.32	30.42	6.69	9.42	3.38	31.63	30.47	13.95	24.94	...	0.000206	0.000045
42	2022	20.95	30.75	3.43	5.15	3.19	31.07	31.06	13.13	27.06	...	0.000217	0.000078

5 rows × 53 columns

Step 8: Climatic and wind pollination pistachios yield ML regressor

An ML was created to forecast pistachio yield based on the agricultural calendar. The model found that temperature, alternate flag, and precipitation were significant factors that influenced yield. However, the model did not consider other factors like tree age and fertilizer consumption, which could also have an impact on yield.

```
#AgRisk Manager
X = combined_df[[
      'Mar_max', 'Apr_max', 'Aug_max',
     'Jun_mean', 'Jul_mean', 'Oct_mean', 'Apr_mean',
  'Oct_min', 'Aug_min',
        'Aug_prcp', 'Jan_prcp', 'Feb_prcp',
     'Flag', 'Nov_htdd', 'Feb_htdd',
  'Area Harvested(ha)'
          ]]
```

```
y= combined_df['Yield(hg/ha)']
X_train,X_test,y_train, y_test = train_test_split(X,y,test_size = 0.2,random_state=0)

regressor = LinearRegression()
regressor.fit( X_train,y_train)

y_pred = regressor.predict(X_test)
y_pred

r2_score(y_test,y_pred)
```

Model performance:
R^2 value = 0.61269 or 61.269%

Get the metrics:
The coefficient of determination is 61.269%.

Step 10: Formulate Fresno pistachios regression equation

This code is useful in creating a readable and interpretable equation that can help to understand yield patterns.

```
mx=""
for ifeature in range(len(X.columns)):
    if regressor.coef_[ifeature]<0:
        #format & beautify the equation
        mx+= "-" +"{:.2f}".format(abs(regressor.coef_[ifeature]))+ " * " + X.columns[ifeature]
    else:
        if ifeature ==0:
            mx += "{:.2f}".format(regressor.coef_[ifeature]) + " * " + X.columns[ifeature]
        else:
            mx += " + " +"{:.2f}".format(regressor.coef_[ifeature]) + " * " + X.columns[ifeature]

print(mx)
```

Equation:

```
871.20 * Mar_max – 2247.24 * Apr_max + 10.56 * Aug_max – 1061.79 * Jun_mean + 35.33 * Jul_mean – 4713.74 * Oct_mean + 2603.71 * Apr_mean + 4723.85 * Oct_min – 797.29 * Aug_min – 181383.46 * Aug_prcp + 604.50 * Jan_prcp + 125.33 * Feb_prcp + 7428.86 * Flag – 110.19 * Nov_htdd + 58.35 * Feb_htdd + 0.06 * Area harvested(ha)
```

```
# y=mx+c
if(regressor.intercept_<0):
    print("The formula for the "+ y.name +" linear regression line (y=mx+c) is = "+"-
{:.2f}".format(abs(regressor.intercept_)) + "+"+ mx)
else:
    print("The formula for the"+ y.name +" linear regression line (y=mx+c) is = "+
"{:.2f]".format(regressor.intercept_) + "+"+ mx)
```

Output:

```
Fresno Pistachios Yield(hg/ha) = 162325.18 + 871.20 * Mar_max - 2247.24 * Apr_max + 10.56 * Aug_
max - 1061.79 * Jun_mean + 35.33 * Jul_mean - 4713.74 * Oct_mean + 2603.71 * Apr_mean + 4723.85 *
Oct_min - 797.29 * Aug_min - 181383.46 * Aug_prcp + 604.50 * Jan_prcp + 125.33 * Feb_prcp + 7428.86
* Flag - 110.19 * Nov_htdd + 58.35 * Feb_htdd + 0.06 * Area harvested(ha)
```

Step 10: ML model: gradient boost explainability

This code uses the ELI5 library to explain and display the feature importance weights of a gradient boosting regressor model. The "explain_weights" function first takes in the trained regressor model, the list of feature names, and the number of top features to display. It then calculates the weights of each feature and returns an explanation of the model's prediction. The explanation is based on the magnitude and direction of the feature weights.

```
eli5.explain_weights(regressor, feature_names = list(X.columns), top=100)
```

```
eli5.show_weights(gbr, feature_names = list(X.columns), target_names = "California
Pistachios Yield Predict")
```

Explainability:
The first feature means that the "Alternative production flag" is the most important feature in the model. The amount of rainfall in the months of January and February, second important influencer, has a positive effect on the yield of pistachios. In other words, more rainfall during these months can lead to higher yields. The third feature means that August precipitation has a negative impact on pistachio yield. This is because rain during August can cause the pistachios to drop prematurely, resulting in a lower yield.

y top features

Weight?	Feature
+162325.185	<BIAS>
+7428.858	Flag
+4723.850	Oct_min
+2603.706	Apr_mean
+871.200	Mar_max
+604.500	Jan_prcp
+125.327	Feb_prcp
+58.351	Feb_htdd
+35.332	Jul_mean
+10.564	Aug_max
+0.057	Area harvested(ha)
-110.187	Nov_htdd
-797.291	Aug_min
-1061.792	Jun_mean
-2247.242	Apr_max
-4713.739	Oct_mean
-181383.457	Aug_prcp

Step 12: Gradient boosting regressor

Develop gradient boosting regressor to model the yield.

```
gbr = GradientBoostingRegressor(random_state=0)

# Fit train data t 'MaxTemperature(C)',
X =combined_df[[    'Mar_max','Apr_max',     'Jul_max',
'Sep_max',
    'Mar_mean', 'Jun_mean',    'Jul_mean',    'Oct_mean',
'Aug_min',
  'Nov_min',   'Oct_min',
          'Aug_prcp',    'Jan_prcp',
      'Flag', 'Oct_htdd','Nov_htdd','Dec_htdd', 'Feb_htdd',
   'Area harvested(ha)'
            ]]

y= combined_df['Yield(hg/ha)']
X_train,X_test, y_train , y_test = train_test_split(X ,y,
test_size = 0.2,random_state=0 )

gbr.fit(X_train,y_train)
gbr.score(X_test,y_test)
```

Output: 0.6503 or 65.03%

Weight	Feature
0.4949 ± 0.3708	Area harvested(ha)
0.0981 ± 0.2072	Oct_mean
0.0887 ± 0.2311	Oct_min
0.0815 ± 0.1947	Mar_max
0.0667 ± 0.1546	Flag
0.0407 ± 0.2156	Jan_prcp
0.0375 ± 0.3670	Oct_htdd
0.0261 ± 0.2609	Aug_min
0.0222 ± 0.1984	Jun_mean
0.0111 ± 0.2492	Nov_min
0.0070 ± 0.2302	Mar_mean
0.0065 ± 0.0645	Feb_htdd
0.0051 ± 0.2500	Nov_htdd
0.0049 ± 0.1801	Jul_max
0.0027 ± 0.1152	Apr_max
0.0026 ± 0.0993	Jul_mean
0.0019 ± 0.3339	Dec_htdd
0.0018 ± 0.1884	Sep_max
0.0000 ± 0.0316	Aug_prcp

The statement highlights the significance of specific temperature variables, such as nov_htdd and nov_min, during the months of November through January for pistachio trees. During this period, pistachio trees must enter a state of quiescence, shedding their leaves and experiencing California's cool and wet winter conditions. Consequently, these temperature variables play a crucial role in ensuring that the trees successfully undergo this essential dormancy phase.

Chapter ML experiments

Water and yield sustainability

For the ML model developed as part of Pistachios Production Model in California, USA, consider adding water resources data from the USGS and see how the water influences the ML model?

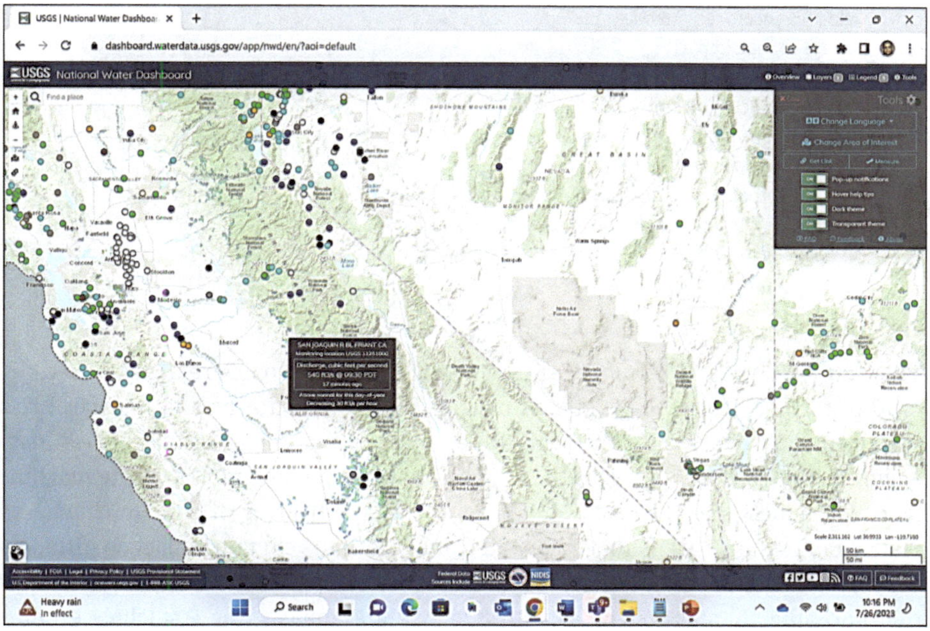

Upon completing this chapter, you will acquire the ability to conduct advanced analysis and interpretation of specialty crop pistachio yield patterns worldwide. This will involve a deep dive into the statistical and mathematical harvest trends of major producing countries such as the USA, Turkey, and Iran, providing with a comprehensive understanding of the factors that impact pistachio yield.

Furthermore, you will develop the skills to leverage polynomial regression ML models to forecast and prepare future datasets for climate modeling. This will enable you to generate accurate estimates about forthcoming pistachio yields constructed on a varied selection of variables, counting temperature, precipitation, and other climatic factors.

In addition to these capabilities, you will be equipped to obtain ML and thunderstorm events classifiers related to pistachio yield. This will involve harnessing the power of ML procedures to evaluate massive volumes of data related to pistachio production and identify trends and patterns that can inform more effective management strategies.

Chapter 5
Specialty crops pistachio: climate change adaptation strategies

This chapter covers:
- Pistachios: historical risk management (RMA) payments
- Yield influencers
- Climate change impact
- In-depth analysis of climate impact on pistachio yield and framework for analyzing yield across various producing countries
- Pistachio yield and climate impact assessment
- Climate projections model for the years 2021–2100
- Pistachios production model specific to California, USA
- Valuable insights into production of pistachios in California
- Possible effects of climate change on future pistachio yield
- Policy recommendations

The chapter delves into resources that cover a range of topics related to specialty crop pistachios. It provides detailed insights into yield patterns and historical risk management payments for pistachios as well as an analysis of historical risk management issues. The chapter also presents a range of demonstrated climate machine learning models that offer valuable insights into the bearing of climate change on pistachio produce. This includes a detailed analysis of the climate impact on pistachio yield and a framework for analyzing yield across various producing countries. Furthermore, the chapter concludes with two essential models, the Pistachios Production Model specific to California, USA, and a Climate Projections Model for the years 2021–2100. These models offer valuable insights into the production of pistachios in California and the prospective influence of climate swings on pistachio yield in the coming years.

Pistachios are actually seeds, not nuts, that come from the pistachio tree. These trees have separate male and female flowers, so both types of trees are needed in order to produce the seeds. Interestingly, the female flowers of the tree do not have petals or nectarines, so they rely on the wind to pollinate them instead of attracting bees. In the winter, the pistachio tree is dormant and loses its leaves, but it has a strong root system that allows it to survive long periods of drought. This root system is called a phreatophyte [228, 229].

Pistachios have been adored for eras by civilizations from around the globe! The United States has consistently been the largest producer of pistachios over the years (Figure 1). Türkiye and Iran have shown significant fluctuations in production [230], with Türkiye experiencing a notable increase in 2021. China, mainland, and the Syrian Arab Republic have maintained stable production levels over the years. Other countries

© 2026 the author(s) | https://doi.org/10.1515/9783111438894-005

like Madagascar, Tunisia, Afghanistan, Australia, and Kyrgyzstan have relatively low and stable production levels [231].

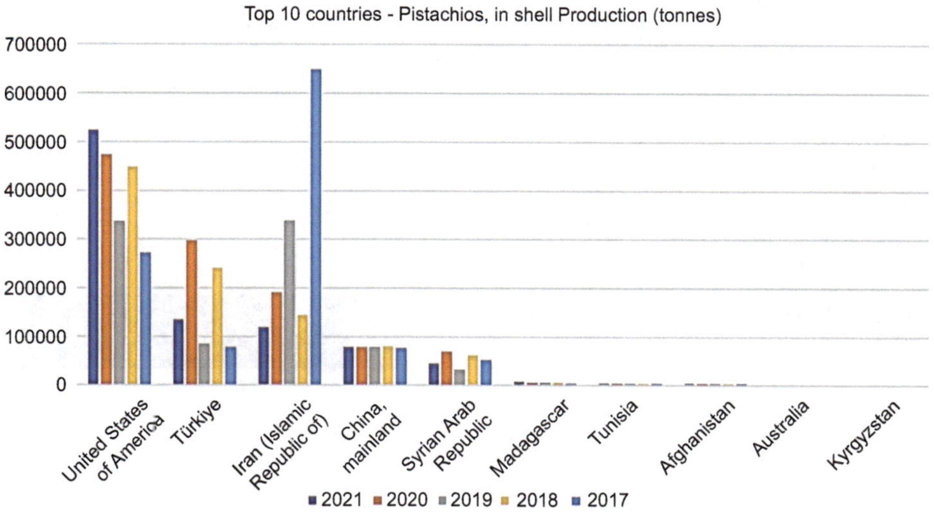

Figure 1: Top pistachios producing countries.

Farmers worldwide recognize the magnitude of knowing the influence of weather alter on cultivation in order to develop applicable adjustment and easing strategies. These farmers have observed a variety of changes including an overdue onset and hasty end to monsoon cycle, higher occurrences of dehydrated spells, heatwaves, foggy days, floods, droughts, and storms, as well as a decrease in monsoon, winter, off-season, and pre-monsoon rains. They have also seen an increase in summer temperatures and a shorter winter season. These shifts have led to a reduction in crop productivity, depletion of water tables, shorter water availability in ponds, and an increase in weeds, pests, diseases, and cultivation costs. Additionally, crop seasons have been shortened [232]. For climate change adaptation, see Figure 2.

Unprecedented challenges demand holistic true leaders: climate Resilience Program Manager

A Climate Resilience Program Manager is responsible for developing and implementing strategies to help communities, organizations, and governments become more resilient to climate change. This involves identifying vulnerabilities and risks associated with climate change and developing plans to mitigate them. The program manager works closely with stakeholders to ensure that the plans are exclusive needs of the specific group or organization. They may also work with policymakers to advocate for policy changes that support climate resilience.

The program manager must have an in-depth knowhow of scientific theories behind climate change plus its impacts on different sectors. They must also have excellent communication skills to effectively communicate complex scientific information to stakeholders and policymakers. Additionally, they must be able to work collaboratively with various power centers of society, and industry leaders, to ensure that resilience plans are effective and sustainable. Overall, the Climate Resilience Program Manager instrumental for helping communities and organizations prepare for the future of climate initiatives.

USDA Agriculture Risk Viewer.

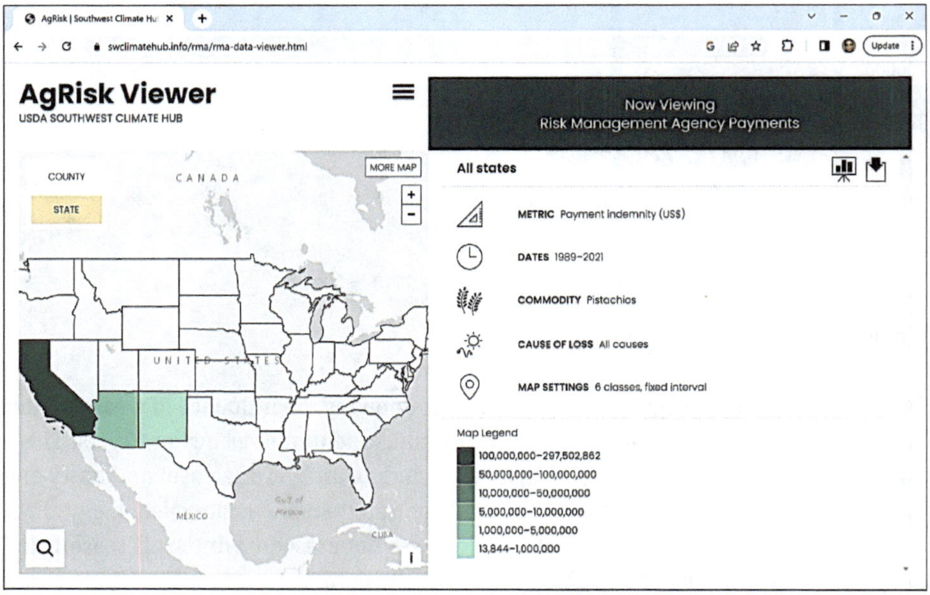

Figure 2: Pistachios AgRisk Viewer.

Historical risk management (RMA) payments

The FCIP administer by USDA, which provides financial protection for agricultural producers against losses caused by adverse and extreme weather events and market movements, all of which are influenced by climate change. The FCIP covers eligible perils that have substantial material impact on the financial sustainability of farmers. Common causes of losses include excess precipitation, drought, hail, heat, declining prices, cold and wet weather, freeze, wind, and flood. Data is obtained from AgRisk Viewer [233, 234].

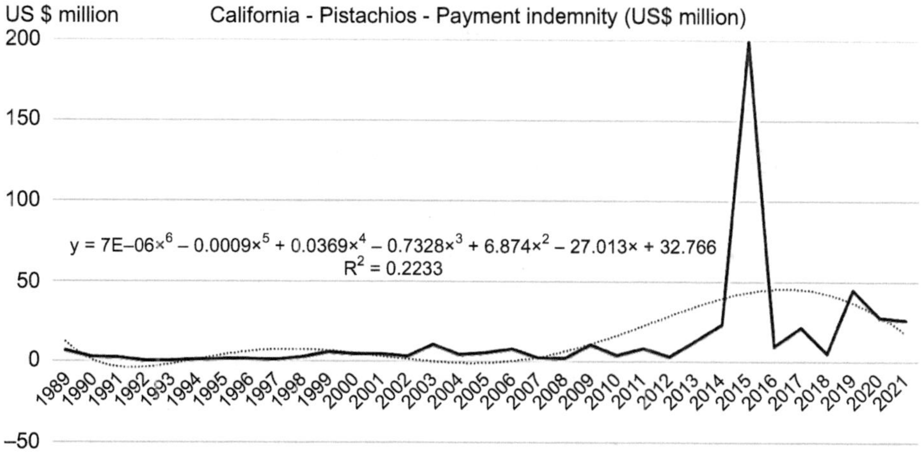

Figure 3: Pistachios payments.

$$Y_{\text{Indemnity payment California}} = 7\text{E-}06x^6 - 0.0009x^5 + 0.0369x^4 - 0.7328x^3 + 6.874x^2 - 27.013x + 32.766 \quad (1)$$

Figure 3 consists of payment indemnity (US $ million) for pistachios crops in California from 1989 to 2021. The overall trend in payment indemnity for pistachios in California shows a gradual increase over the years, with a significant peak in 2015. As can be seen, indemnity payments in 2015 were $199.13 million. Post-2015, indemnity payments remain higher than the initial years but do not reach the extreme levels seen in 2015. The polynomial trend line suggests a complex relationship with multiple factors potentially influencing the indemnity payments over time (Figure 3 and eq. (1)). In 2015, unusually warm winter and spring temperatures led to over $240 million in indemnity payments to various fruit and nut growers in California [235], significantly impacting the state's substantial agricultural sector. Notably, Fresno County holds the highest insurance liability in the nation, and in 2020, grape wildfire losses surpassed the indemnity payments made to pistachio growers in 2015 by nearly $42 million [236].

Indemnity payment: pistachios, California

	Equation	R^2 value	
Exponential	$y = 0.991e^{0.0977x}$	$R^2 = 0.1411$	(2)
Linear	$y = 1.3263x - 8.442$	$R^2 = 0.1371$	(3)
Logarthimic	$y = 11.518\ln(x) - 15.581$	$R^2 = 0.0815$	(4)
Polynomial order 6	$y = 7\text{E-}06x^6 - 0.0009x^5 + 0.0369x^4 - 0.7328x^3 + 6.874x^2 - 27.013x + 32.766$	$R^2 = 0.2233$	(5)
Power	$y = 0.5565x^{0.8684}$	$R^2 = 0.1324$	(6)

County view of pistachios production in California (Figure 4):

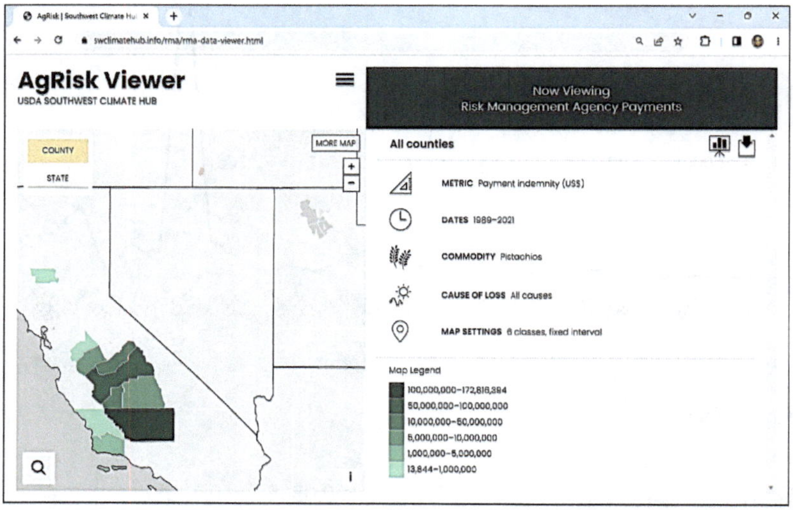

Figure 4: AgRisk Viewer.

In California, crop insurance covers almost all agricultural products through specific policies or Whole Farm Revenue Insurance, with pistachios being the most insured commodity, and Fresno County leading the nation in insurance liability [237].

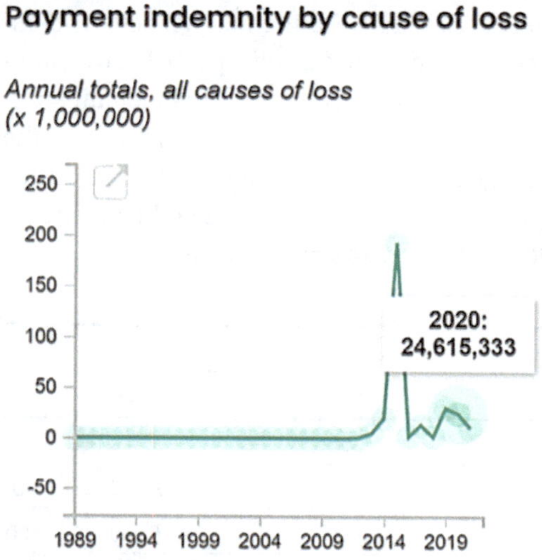

Source: AgRisk Viewer.

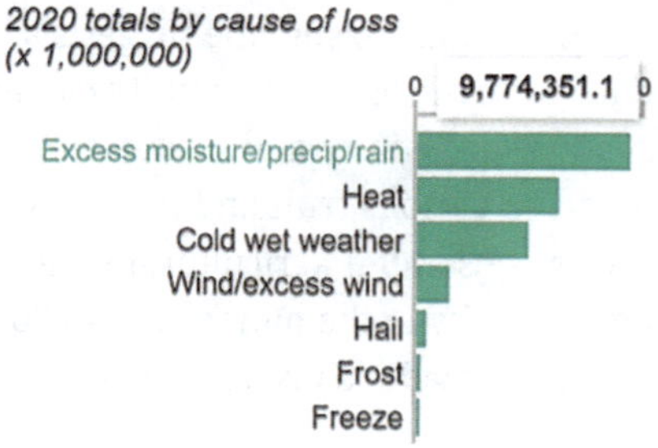

In 2020, California pistachios farms received $24.615 million indemnity. The major losses include excessive moisture/precipitation/rain ($9.774 million), heat ($6.579 million), Cold wet weather ($5.211 million), wind/excess wind ($1.656 million), and hail ($596K) losses. In 2020, the American pistachio industry suffered a devastating season with nearly half the crop lost due to warm temperatures and water shortages, causing profits to drop by approximately $1.4 billion compared to 2014. [238].

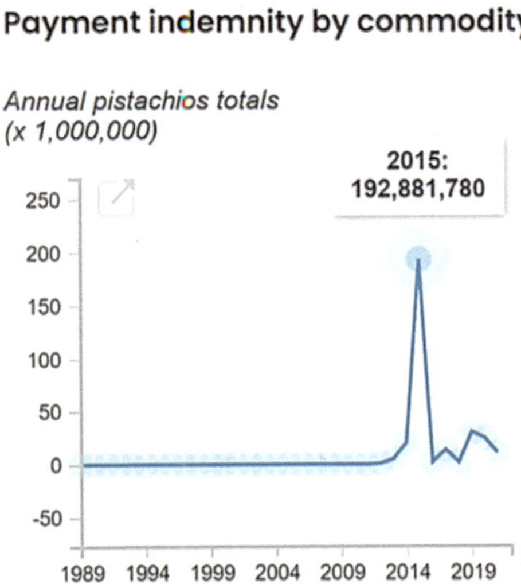

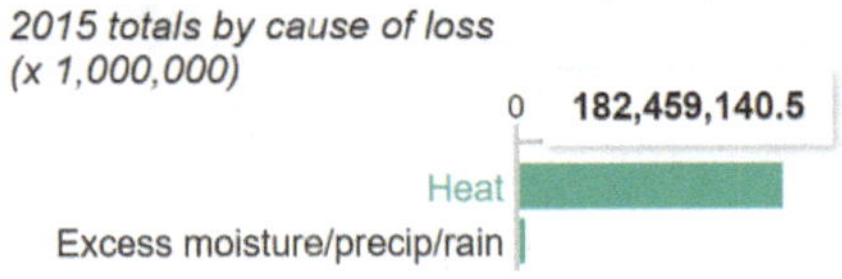

In 2015, California pistachios farms received $192.881 million indemnity. The major losses include heat losses that are attributed to $182.459 million and excess moisture caused another $6 million [238].

In 2015, the San Joaquin Valley heatwave in California proved disastrous for millions of pistachio trees. About 90% of the harvested nuts were hollow compared to the typical 10% blanking rate. The American Pistachio Growers estimated a drop of $120 million from 2014. The drought, heat, and abnormal West Coast weather were responsible for the high blanking rate. Pistachios require sufficient winter chilling hours, which are essential for proper blooming and pollination between female and male trees. In 2015, an unusually warm winter in interior California, with minimal fog and rain, caused male trees to release pollen too late, missing the female trees' bloom period due to unmet chilling requirements. Hollow pistachios are identified during postharvest processing by placing them in a water bath, where empty shells float and full nuts sink [239].

Hollow pistachios are identified during postharvest processing by placing them in a water bath, where empty shells float and full nuts sink.

Adverse conditions can result in hollow pistachio nuts, as the trees produce shells even after a winter of insufficient chilling hours. This can mislead farmers into thinking they have a good crop, but the blanks are revealed after harvest when they float in the water bath during processing. Erratic blooming also leads to timing issues with harvesting, as the longer bloom period during warmer winters results in a spread-out fruiting season. Processors incur higher costs by having to operate two to three times longer to handle a smaller-than-usual crop (Figure 5).

Figure 5: Pistachios blanks [239].

Erratic blooming and timing issues for processors [239]

In the San Joaquin Valley, pistachio harvest typically occurs within a 21-day window, accounting for 90% of the annual crop yield. However, in 2015, this pattern was disrupted due to unusual weather conditions, including excessive heat and warm winters, which resulted in a significant delay in the harvest season.

As a result, the harvest commenced in mid-August, two weeks later than usual, and is expected to extend into October. This deviation from the typical harvest window highlights the effect of climatic factors on agricultural harvesting and underscores need for effective climate adaptation strategies to ensure the sustainability and profitability of agriculture in the region.

Despite the challenges posed by this abnormal harvest season, growers in the San Joaquin Valley remain committed to producing high-quality pistachios and implementing innovative management techniques to optimize yield and adapt to changing climatic conditions. By embracing the latest technologies and techniques, growers can continue to thrive despite a changing climate and positive factor-in sustained sustainability of cultivation in the region.

In 2015, California pistachios farms paid $192.881 million indemnity. The major losses include heat losses that're attributed to $182.459 million and excess moisture caused another $6 million. In 2015, the American pistachio industry faced a disastrous season with nearly half the crop lost due to warm temperatures and water shortages, causing profits to drop by about $1.4 billion compared to 2014 [238].

To help pistachio farmers adapt to warmer winters, experts suggest understanding tree responses to unmet chilling requirements, which can lead to better predictions and chemical treatments to increase yields. Long-term solutions include breeding new pistachio varieties that need fewer chilling hours to bloom together. Additionally, selecting female cultivars with specific male pollinizers that bloom in sync is recommended for regions with high fall and winter heat accumulation, with a list provided for those expecting warmer and drier winters in the San Joaquin Valley [239, 240].

Female	Early male	Primary male	Adjunct male
Gumdrop	Zarand (50%)	Tejon (50%)	
Golden Hills	Tejon (25%)	Randy (75%)	
Lost Hills	Tejon (25%)	Randy (75%)	
Kalehghouchi	Tejon (25%	Randy (75%)	
Kerman	Randy (25%	Famoso (50%)	Peters (25%)

If you consider the unusual weather conditions of 2014 and 2015 to be rare anomalies, you can use the recommended primary male pollinizers, with the exception of Kerman, for which Peters remains suitable [241]. However, given the extreme climates and the possibility that these conditions may become the new normal, the opposite approach may be more appropriate.

Yield influencers

As climate adjustment brings ascending temperatures and extreme climate patterns, food production systems are increasingly threatened with low yields. This raises concerns about which foods consumers may have to cut back on or abandon entirely. While plants use carbon dioxide (CO_2) to fuel photosynthesis, the benefits of adding more CO_2 may be outweighed by other factors such as water availability, temperature swings, and plant stress. Yield data from corn and wheat production already shows negative impacts from climate change, as do fruit and nut trees which require a certain number of cold, wintry days for optimum production. Reduced yields can lead to more frequent price spikes in many foods. Yield curves also differ between Iran and the USA [242, 243]. The resulting harvest influences make the difference:

Weather adjustment

Climate adjustment is threatening California, planet's prominent pistachio producer, since numerous orchards are facing water shortages and practicing "deficit irrigation." Fresno, Kern, Kings, Madera, and Tulare counties in California, which have large acreage pistachio plantings, are at risk due to projected increases in winter temperatures that may not satisfy the high chill requirements of pistachios. Transitioning to lower-chill varieties like Mateur pistachio may provide some adaptation, and advocating for the development of new low-chill varieties can help growers prepare for future warming. Pest pressures, which are moderately vulnerable to pistachios, are also likely to increase under warming conditions. Managing uniform maturity timing could help mitigate any summer pest pressure [244].

Water and climate change [230]

Access to water is vital for farming activities yet impacts of global climatic trends and changes have made it increasingly challenging for farmers to sustain their crops. As a result, many farmers are forced to make difficult decisions at the time of harvest season, sacrificing crops and investments they have made in their orchards.

This loss is particularly devastating for those who have invested significant time and resources into growing trees, only to see their efforts go to waste due to water shortages. The influence of climate change on water availability underscores need for effective water management strategies and policies that prioritize sustainable and equitable access to this critical resource.

Freeze during fall

When young pistachio trees are between 1 and 8 years old, they are most likely to be damaged by freezing temperatures that occur in the fall, between late October and the end of December. This is not a new problem, as there were instances of trees being damaged by cold temperatures in the 1980s [241].

Young pistachio trees can experience two main types of damage from fall freezes, with the first being "mild" damage where leaves freeze and remain on the branches, delaying normal leaf drop. This type of damage is usually identified by pruning crews [245, 246].

The second type of damage, called "severe" damage, is not obvious until the spring when the trees start to grow new leaves. In severely affected trees that are at least 3 years old, the new growth usually only appears from the lower part of the tree, and it occurs later than in unaffected trees. In the winter of 2011–2012, there was severe frost damage in some pistachio orchards in Kern and Fresno counties, and some blocks lost up to 20% of their trees. Severe frost damage typically occurs after trees have started but not yet completed their dormancy, usually between late November and late December.

Understanding radiation frosts

Radiation frosts are a type of frost that occurs when the sky is clear, the wind is calm, and the humidity is low. Unlike other types of frosts, which occur when cold air moves into an area, radiation frosts happen when heat is radiated from the existing air mass to the sky, causing the temperature to drop.

During radiation frosts, the leaves of trees lose heat to the cold night sky, and this can cause the temperature to drop low enough to cause frost damage to crops. Advection frosts, on the other hand, are associated with cold air masses moving into an area and are usually accompanied by high winds.

For farmers, understanding the different types of frosts is important because it helps them prepare for potential crop damage. By monitoring weather conditions and taking appropriate measures, such as using frost protection mechanisms, farmers can reduce the impact of frosts on their crops and ensure the long-term sustainability of their operations.

Managing heat stress in young plants: strategies for shade and protection

Intense summer heat can seriously harm or even kill young plants. To protect them, one option is to plant arhar plants nearby for shade, keeping a distance of at least 1 m. Another effective method is to whitewash or wrap the tree trunks to reflect sunlight and prevent bark damage, which is crucial for the tree's nutrient and water transport, ensuring its survival. By implementing these measures, farmers can promote the survival and well-being of their young plants, even during hot summers. This is essential for maintaining a sustainable and productive agricultural system.

The pistachio industry is facing significant challenges, and the profitability of growing pistachios is not as it once was. As a result, some industry experts predict that the world may start to see a decline in pistachio production.

Factors such as changing climate patterns, water scarcity, and increasing production costs have contributed to a decline in profitability for growers. Moreover, competition from other crops and regions has further impacted on the economic viability of pistachio production.

Chilling hours

Cold winters are crucial for nut and fruit trees, especially pistachios (Figure 6). Pistachios require approximately 850 h, or 5 weeks, at temperatures below 45° to end dormancy and facilitate pollen distribution [247, 248]. As the San Joaquin Valley experiences warming and diminishing cooling fogs, growers are noticing a misalignment in their orchards: many male trees are no longer producing pollen when the female trees need it.

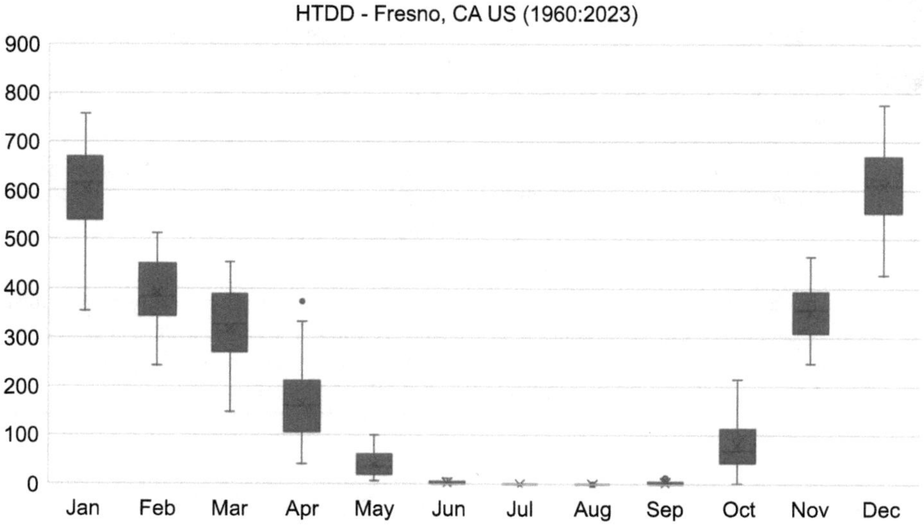

Figure 6: HTDD Fresno, CA.

The field of livestock health monitoring is rapidly evolving in agriculture. This practice includes tracking key indicators such as vital signs, activity levels, and food consumption. Utilizing cutting-edge technologies like the Cow Necklace, a Class 10 Wearable veterinary sensor developed by Hanumayamma Innovations and Technologies, Inc., farmers can gather comprehensive data on a cow's vital signs. This data helps optimize milk production and enhance the overall health of the cows.

Using monitoring sensors also helps in detecting food-borne diseases, preventing their spread, and identifying the source of infection. This is important for maintaining the health of livestock and ensuring the safety of food products. Companies that use AI and machine learning to promote optimal livestock health are making a significant contribution to sustainability efforts. Some of these companies have even received recognition for their achievements, including the Fast Company's Best Designs[1] of 2023 award, among other esteemed honorees in the field.

1 Fast Company is a leading business media brand that emphasizes innovation in technology, leadership, transformative ideas, creativity, and design. Founded in November 1995 by former Harvard Business Review editors Alan Webber and Bill Taylor, the magazine was created to document how evolving businesses are reshaping the world. It aims to inspire progressive business leaders to think broadly, lead with purpose, and embrace change while showcasing new business practices and the pioneers driving the future of business. https://www.fastcompany.com/about-us

Insect behavior and global warming

The impact of global warming on insect behavior is a complex issue that poses significant challenges to agriculture. As temperatures continue to rise in California's Central Valley, insects like the navel orange worm may expand their range and reproduce at faster rates, potentially causing substantial damage to crops. Climate change is expected to accelerate the growth rate of these pests, which could have devastating consequences for small tree nut farmers, who may face significant losses due to increased pest pressure.

In Spain, the bacterium *Xylella fastidiosa* threatens tree nut production and other fruit tree plantations. To combat its spread, Spain has implemented measures such as destroying infected plants, tightening border controls, and restricting plant material movement from affected areas, in accordance with EU Commission Decision 2015/879. Addressing the impact of global warming on insect behavior and bacterial spread is crucial for protecting crop production and the economy.

Despite the challenges posed by *Xylella fastidiosa*, growers in Spain are working tirelessly to find innovative solutions to protect their crops and ensure the long-term sustainability of their operations. By adopting best practices in phytosanitary management and leveraging cutting-edge technologies, growers can optimize yields and minimize the risk of damage caused by this and other pests and diseases, safeguarding the future of tree nut production in Spain and beyond [247].

USA pistachios

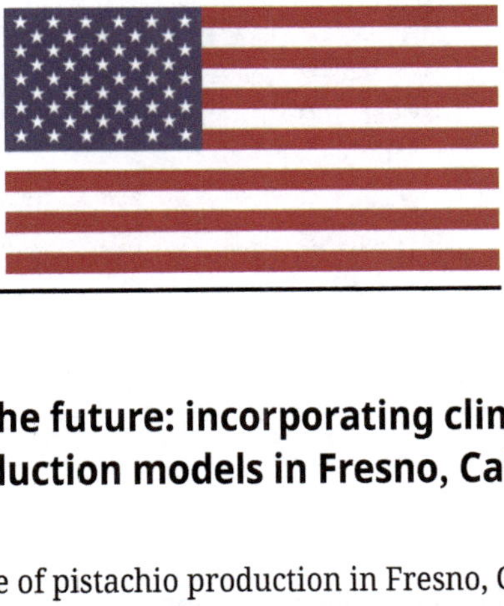

Preparing for the future: incorporating climate projections into pistachios production models in Fresno, California (2021–2100)

To secure the future of pistachio production in Fresno, California, it is essential to integrate climate projections into the existing production model. This requires downloading various SSP projections from the World Bank's Climate Knowledge Portal and analyzing the data to predict the impact of climate change on pistachio yields. By understanding changes in temperature, precipitation, and other climate factors, farmers and policymakers can adapt their practices to mitigate these effects. This proactive approach ensures sustainable agriculture and helps maintain a stable food supply for future generations.

Let's continue from Step 11 of the previous chapter model – climate change on California Pistachio Yield: A machine learning approach,

Step 11: Load climate data

The script loads data from the "ClimateKnowledgeSSPData.csv" file into the variable "SSP_df" using the "pd.read_csv" function for further analysis.

```
SSP_df=pd.read_csv("ClimateKnowledgeSSPData.csv")
SSP_df
```

	Unnamed: 0	Jan_mean	Feb_mean	Mar_mean	Apr_mean	May_mean	Jun_mean	Jul_mean	Aug_mean	Sep_mean	...	Mar_prcp
0	0	8.78	9.82	11.08	13.46	17.48	21.92	25.48	26.05	23.26	...	138.83
1	1	8.78	9.72	11.15	13.77	17.91	21.91	25.72	26.26	23.60	...	136.16
2	2	8.86	9.94	11.37	13.50	17.66	22.22	25.70	26.30	23.76	...	137.79
3	3	8.95	9.93	11.53	13.57	17.33	22.17	25.59	26.13	23.60	...	134.35
4	4	8.80	9.68	11.17	13.80	17.56	21.94	25.97	26.55	23.89	...	132.05
5	5	9.44	10.42	11.91	14.52	18.24	22.72	26.76	27.32	24.59	...	133.79
6	6	9.84	10.88	12.40	14.95	18.82	23.25	27.36	27.84	25.24	...	143.95
7	7	10.21	11.35	12.92	15.28	19.22	23.45	27.69	28.33	25.83	...	139.50
8	8	8.97	9.83	11.28	13.89	17.71	22.18	26.17	26.56	23.68	...	133.67
9	9	9.95	10.76	12.25	14.87	18.79	23.09	27.22	27.47	25.06	...	131.40
10	10	11.17	12.05	13.54	16.04	20.17	24.63	28.70	29.17	26.65	...	137.28
11	11	12.41	13.16	14.85	17.50	21.35	26.04	30.19	30.97	29.03	...	140.62

2 rows × 51 columns

Load different SSPs and corresponding temperature and precipitation values.

Step 12: Load pickle model

Use the model that was created in the previous chapter.

```
pickledmodel = pickle.load(open("Pistachios_usa.pkl","rb"))
```

Output: model is loaded.

Step 13: Climate projections: SSP119, 2020–2039

Load Python code that filters the data stored in the "SSP_df" variable based on certain conditions and selects specific columns for analysis. The resulting data is stored in a variable called "result." To view the values stored in the "result" variable, simply type "result.values" in the Python shell or notebook and press enter. This will display the values in the selected columns of the filtered data in an array format. Load the SSP 119 data and call model prediction.

```
#result = SSP_df[(SSP_df["Period"]=="2020-2039") & (SSP_df["SSP"]=="ssp119")][['Feb_max',
'Jan_max', 'May_max', 'Jul_max', 'Aug_max', 'Sep_max', 'Jul_min', 'Aug_min', 'May_mean', 'Jun_mean', 'Dec_
mean',Jul_prcp', 'Oct_prcp',]]

result.values
```

Output

```
array([[15.11, 14.08, 24.86, 33.66, 33.87, 30.96, 17.03, 18. , 17.48, 21.92, 9.14,
9.26, 40.8 ]])tmin     624tmean     624
Name: Variable, dtype: int64
SSP1-1.9    832
SSP2-4.5    832
SSP5-8.5    832
Name: Scenario, dtype: int64
2020-2039    624
2040-2059    624
2060-2079    624
2080-2099    624
Name:year, dtype: int64
```

```
sampleData = np.append(result,[1,543900.0])
sampleData
```

Output:

```
rray([1.511e+01, 1.408e+01, 2.486e+01, 3.366e+01, 3.387e+01, 3.096e+01,
      1.703e+01, 1.800e+01, 1.748e+01, 2.192e+01, 9.140e+00, 9.260e+00,
      4.080e+01, 1.000e+00, 5.439e+05])
```

Call the model

```
yield_2020_2039 = pickledmodel.predict([sampleData])
# percentage change
result_2020_2039 = ((yield_2020_2039 – PreviousYield)/PreviousYield) * 100
if result_2020_2039 < 0:
  print(f"{result_2020_2039} Decrease in Yield for the years 2020_2039 for SSP119")
else:
  print(f"{result_2020_2039}% increase in Yield for the years 2020_2039 for SSP119")
```

Output:

```
[8.55521846]% increase in Yield for the years 2020_2039 for SSP119
```

Step 14: Climate projections: SSP119, 2080–2099

Load SSP119, 2080–2099 data and call model prediction.

```
result_80_99 = SSP_df[(SSP_df[“Period”]==”2080-2099”) & (SSP_df[“SSP”]==
“ssp119”)][[‘Feb_max’, ‘Jan_max’, ‘May_max’, ‘Jul_max’, ‘Aug_max’, ‘Sep_max’, ‘Jul_min’,
‘Aug_min’, ‘May_mean’, ‘Jun_mean’, ‘Dec_mean’, ‘Jul_prcp’, ‘Oct_prcp’,]]
result_80_99.values
```

Output:

```
array([[15.18, 14.01, 24.04, 33.8, 34, 31.08, 17.21, 17.96, 17.33,
    22.17, 9.34, 9.47, 51.69]])
```

```
sampleTestData_80_99 = np.append(result_80_99,[1,543900.0])
sampleTestData_80_99
```

Output:

```
array([1.518e+01, 1.401e+01, 2.404e+01, 3.380e+01, 3.400e+01, 3.108e+01,
    1.721e+01, 1.796e+01, 1.733e+01, 2.217e+01, 9.340e+00, 9.470e+00,
    5.169e+01, 1.000e+00, 5.439e+05])
```

Call the model

```
yield_2080_2099 = pickledmodel.predict([sampleTestData_80_99])
# percentage change
percentageChange_2080_2099 = ( (yield_2080_2099 – PreviousYield)/ PreviousYield) * 100
if percentageChange_2080_2099 < 0:
  print(f"{percentageChange_2080_2099}% Decrease in Yield for the years 2080_2099 for SSP119")
else:
  print(f"{percentageChange_2080_2099}% increase in Yield for the years 2080_2099 for SSP119")
```

Output:

```
[8.55521846]% increase in Yield for the years 2080_2099 for SSP119
```

Continue with all other projections.

Step 25: Future ready insights

Based on climate projections, it is expected that the yield of pistachios in California will increase. The increase in yield is more pronounced for the SSP118 and SSP245 scenarios, while the increase is less significant for the SSP585 scenario.

It is important to note that these models assume a constant area of pistachios harvested each year. This means that the increase in yield is solely due to the changes in climate factors such as temperature and precipitation.

These findings (Figure 7) are significant for farmers and policymakers as they can use this information to plan for the future and adapt their practices accordingly. By understanding how climate change will impact pistachios production, they can take steps to ensure the sustainability of agriculture and maintain a stable food supply.

Climate adaptation strategies

In 2013, scientists sounded the alarm on the worsening global hunger crisis, citing declining crop yields, increased pest and disease pressure, rising water demand, and the disappearance of highly vulnerable crops. Urgent action was needed to adapt to these challenges and ensure that the expected population of 10 billion by 2050 could be fed. A complete overhaul of the food system was identified as necessary in a report published in the prestigious journal Science.

In California's San Joaquin Valley, the warming climate is severely impacting pistachio trees that need cold winters to break dormancy and pollinate. The reduction

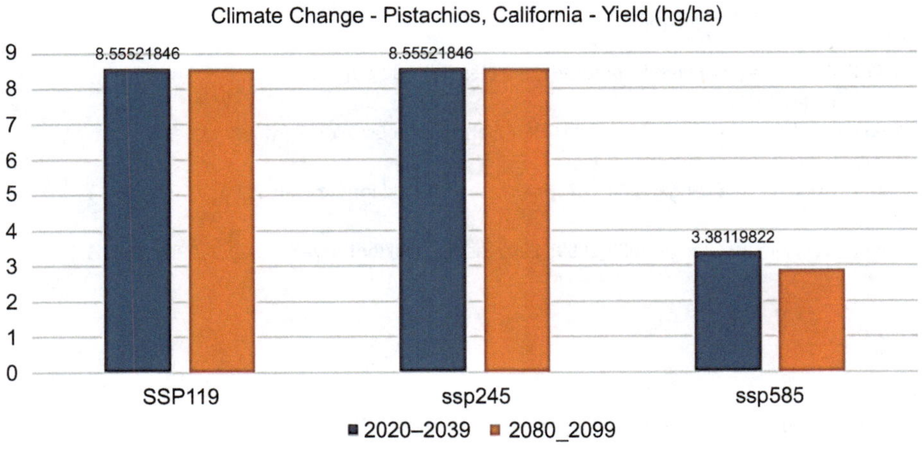

Figure 7: Future of pistachios in California.

in cooling fogs has caused male trees to produce pollen out of sync with female trees, resulting in significant losses. Consequently, California's pistachio growers are facing billion-dollar financial setbacks.

To survive in a warmer world, scientists are developing new trees that can adapt to changing conditions, while growers are experimenting with planting trees that require fewer chilly days and other innovative adaptations [248, 249].

Global agricultural adaptations to climate change: innovations and crop shifts: Pistachio farmers are leading the adaptation to changing climate patterns affecting global agriculture. Worldwide, farmers are adopting innovative strategies and switching crops to better suit the new conditions, such as Costa Rican coffee farmers turning to oranges and Kenyan herders replacing cattle with camels. Additionally, farmers in various regions are making similar adjustments, including Midwestern US farmers planting corn earlier, Chinese farmers in drought-prone areas growing apples instead of wheat and corn, Indian farmers switching from rice to millet, and Bangladeshi farmers converting rice fields to shrimp farms due to seawater intrusion [251].

Adapting society and the economy to climate change is a gradual and complex process that requires research, courage, patience, and financial resources. California's specialized crop growers have the resources to experiment with climate-resilient varieties, but farmers in poorer countries struggle and need support. Fresno County in California's San Joaquin Valley is a key agricultural hub, producing more than 25 states combined, with California contributing over a third of the nation's vegetables and two-thirds of its fruits and nuts. The failure of California growers to adapt could lead to nationwide food shortages and significant economic consequences. Vulnerable crops like cherries, pistachios, walnuts, and wine grapes need cold winters or cannot tolerate extreme heat, while some crops like melons and broccoli may thrive in warmer conditions, though staples like wheat and corn remain essential, and climate change threatens many tree-derived pleasures like chocolate, wine, and coffee.

Adaptation strategies are tools, but their effectiveness varies depending on several factors. These factors include the location, historical climate patterns, local market conditions, and economic models used. Adaptation strategies are not a universal solution, as different regions/communities may require different approaches to effectively adapt to the changing climate. For example, a strategy that works well in one location may not be effective in another due to differences in climate patterns or economic conditions. Therefore, it is important to consider multiple adaptation strategies and assess their effectiveness in a given context. This approach helps policymakers and communities make informed decisions to effectively prepare for climate change and ensure long-term sustainability [247, 250].

Adapting to climate change in agriculture: strategies for.

As climate change impacts the environment, farmers need to adapt by switching to crop varieties better suited to the new conditions. This proactive approach helps prevent market disruptions and ensures a stable food supply. Ignoring climate change could lead to serious problems for the agriculture industry, making it crucial for farmers to adopt new technologies and practices for long-term sustainability.

Author
Chandrasekar Vuppalapati

Pesticides and climate change

The implications of climate change for insect pests are significant, with warmer temperatures providing a hospitable environment for these organisms to thrive. Monocropping practices, which create a continuous food source, are expected to exacerbate this issue, as warmer conditions extend the duration of the available food supply. Additionally, milder winters are projected to reduce insect mortality rates, further contributing to population growth. As temperatures rise, we may also see the expansion of pest ranges into northern regions, where previously unsuitable environmental conditions may now be suitable for their survival and reproduction.

Mitigating the effects of frost on crops: best practices for optimal soil moisture levels

To protect crops from the damaging effects of frost, it is important to maintain optimal soil moisture levels in the upper foot of soil. This region should be moist, without any dry surface crusts that can hinder daytime heat absorption and nighttime release. If there is not enough rainfall, it is recommended to irrigate the field before frost events occur. To retain warmth, the soil should be bare, firm, and moist, with groundcover mowed to no more than two inches for better soil-heat management. If the ground cover is taller than two inches, such as with cover crops or weeds, it can block solar radiation and increase frost damage.

The presence of IN bacteria, which live on grasses and weeds, can also worsen the effects of frost. However, if the orchard has full tree canopy coverage, ground cover is less critical since the foliage shades the soil from sunlight. By taking these measures, farmers can help protect their crops from the damaging effects of frost and ensure a successful harvest.

Using AI/ML for farming yield modeling is essential for ensuring food security in the future. Failure to do so could lead to a significant increase in hunger, which would negatively impact the growth of future populations.

AI/ML can help us equip and predict changes in weather patterns, soil quality, and other factors that affect crop yields. By utilizing these technologies, we can develop more effective strategies for managing and improving agricultural production.

Without these tools, our time to response to changes in the environment results in reduced crop yields and potential food shortages. This highlights the importance of investing in and utilizing machine learning and artificial intelligence for agricultural yield modeling as a means of ensuring food security for future generations.

Author
Chandrasekar Vuppalapati

Integrating data science and weather into agricultural and governmental policies

Recent weather patterns provide strong evidence that extreme climate models are becoming more accurate. In May 2023, Vietnam experienced its highest-ever recorded temperature, while Thailand reported a record-equaling temperature and a town in Myanmar recorded the highest temperature in a decade. It is clear that accurately patterning severe climate events and forecasting their effect should be a crucial part of governmental policies, as such events will become increasingly common in the future.

However, many governmental policies [251] respond to extreme weather events reactively due to a lack of integration between data science and food security policies. By merging data science, ML, AI, climate, and farming, we can better understand and mitigate the impacts of changing dynamics of weather.

Economic benefits and higher citizen satisfaction that can be derived from data modeling of extreme weather events are substantial for local, state, and international governments. Forecasting future weather events with agricultural calendars can reduce insurance policy costs and help control inflation. However, as demonstrated by the historic heat wave and drought that occurred during summer 2022 across the USA, Europe, and China, extreme weather events can have devastating impacts on economies worldwide and exacerbate existing inflation issues.

Farmers in major food-producing countries are facing crop failures due to heat waves, leading to increased energy costs and food price inflation, which particularly impacts those with limited incomes. For millions in India living in poverty or near the poverty line, rising food prices are reducing their ability to afford other essentials, highlighting the importance of incorporating extreme weather models into food security policies to mitigate the effects of climate change.

Adaptation strategies: under extreme heat

In May 2023, Vietnam broke records with a scorching temperature of 44.1 °C (111.38 °F), prompting weather experts and authorities to advise the population to remain indoors during the hottest parts of the day. The extreme heat in the central city of Danang compelled workers to commence their daily routines earlier than ever before, with many finishing before 10 am to avoid the blistering temperatures [249, 250].

A farmer

Pistachios additional experiments

Q1. The below data table shows yearly pistachios production in the United States from 1961 to 2020. The production trendline has been created using the area harvested and polynomial regression order 6, which provides a reliable trend with R^2 0.9807.

a) Using the trendline equation, we can estimate future values for the years 2021, 2022, and 2023. To do this, we should input the respective years into the equation and solve for the predicted production value.

$$Y_{\text{USA pistachios area harvested}} = 4\text{E-}05x^6 - 0.0086x^5 + 0.6736x^4 - 24.876x^3 + 416.35x^2 - 1910.1x$$

Year	Area harvested(ha)	Year	Area harvested(ha)	Year	Area harvested(ha)
1961	57590	1981	70860	2001	82556
1962	57790	1982	72030	2002	84984
1963	57020	1983	71220	2003	86198
1964	57950	1984	72030	2004	86603
1965	56860	1985	72440	2005	87007
1966	58920	1986	72840	2006	87007
1967	59250	1987	71220	2007	88222
1968	59570	1988	71630	2008	93078
1969	60860	1989	72440	2009	97125
1970	62000	1990	73250	2010	103195
1971	63290	1991	73250	2011	107242
1972	66000	1992	72030	2012	109269
1973	66040	1993	74870	2013	113311
1974	67900	1994	76480	2014	117359
1975	68920	1995	78100	2015	121406
1976	70540	1996	77700	2016	127480
1977	73170	1997	79130	2017	135570
1978	73410	1998	79130	2018	141640
1979	72520	1999	79130	2019	147710
1980	72800	2000	78100	2020	153781

b) Alternatively, we can use Python interpolation to estimate future values. Interpolation is a method of estimating unknown values between known data points. Python has a built-in function called "interp1d" that can be used to perform linear or polynomial interpolation. We would input the known data points (years and corresponding production values) into the function and specify the degree of the polynomial regression. The function would then provide estimated values for the years 2021, 2022, and 2023 based on the trend in the data.

Q2. This report describes a severe frost/freeze event in California's San Joaquin Valley from January 11–24, 2007, which heavily impacted the citrus industry. The incursion of cold Arctic air and a lingering cold-core low prevented the temperature inversions that growers typically use to mitigate freeze damage, resulting in extensive crop losses totaling $586.60 million. The provided figure shows temperature changes during the event, highlighting areas where frost damage likely occurred.

Based on the figure, potential indications of frost damage could be when the temperature difference line falls below zero, indicating that the temperature is below freezing. This occurred on several occasions during the event, including on the mornings of January 12, 13, 14, and 15, which could have caused significant frost damage to crops.

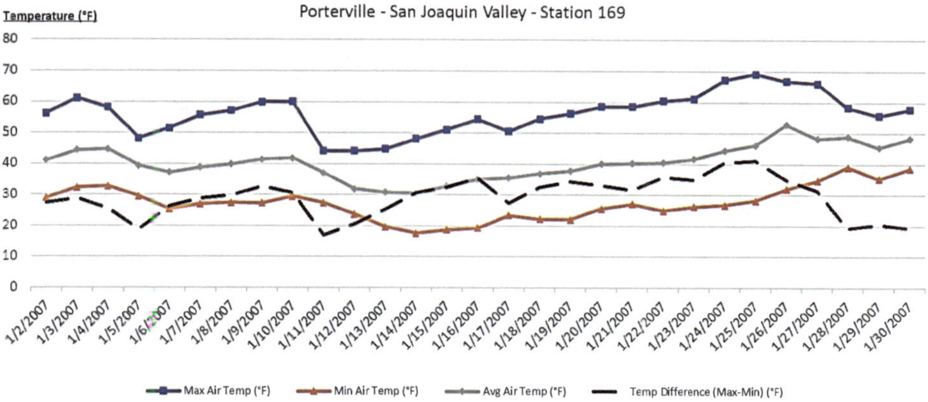

Q3. This is a study that aims to develop a weather model for four types of weather events (flash floods, floods, hail, and heavy rain) that occurred in California between January 1, 1990, and August 1, 2020, specifically in the San Joaquin.

To develop this model, the study will be applying NOAA Storms event DB, which contains information on weather events such as their type, location, and date. The goal is to identify patterns in the data that can help predict when these weather events are most likely to occur in the selected counties.

The study will also consider the production of pistachios in the USA 1961–2020, as this source can help identify any potential correlations between weather events and pistachio production in the selected counties. By examining these correlations, the study can determine if certain weather events are more probable to levy a significant influence on pistachio output in these counties. This information can be useful for developing strategies to mitigate negative effects of climate on pistachios in the future.

Year	Area harvested. (ha)	Yield (hg/ha)	Year	Area harvested. (ha)	Yield (hg/ha)	Year	Area harvested. (ha)	Yield (hg/ha)
1961	57590	10633	1981	70860	28806	2001	82556	33515
1962	57790	12543	1982	72030	29471	2002	84984	30103
1963	57020	13221	1983	71220	25348	2003	86198	34309
1964	57950	14120	1984	72030	26822	2004	86603	34044
1965	56860	12811	1985	72440	27430	2005	87007	37014
1966	58920	14781	1986	72840	22419	2006	87007	36493
1967	59250	11698	1987	71220	31452	2007	88222	33728
1968	59570	14559	1988	71630	26469	2008	93078	42494
1969	60860	15726	1989	72440	28672	2009	97125	40818
1970	62000	16359	1990	73250	28109	2010	103195	44307
1971	63290	19551	1991	73250	32082	2011	107242	38997
1972	66000	16054	1992	72030	25567	2012	109269	45484
1973	66040	24040	1993	74870	31508	2013	113311	39390
1974	67900	20909	1994	76480	27518	2014	117359	44138
1975	68920	26233	1995	78100	27183	2015	121406	45282
1976	70540	23625	1996	77700	24286	2016	127480	49031
1977	73170	23867	1997	79130	30936	2017	135570	42158
1978	73410	19772	1998	79130	26024	2018	141640	43489
1979	72520	26019	1999	79130	32444	2019	147710	40228
1980	72800	24549	2000	78100	27762	2020	153781	46014

This chapter explores the key aspects of pistachio farming including yield patterns, the impact of climate change, and risk management indemnity payments based on historical yield or revenue issues. It provides guidance on developing a machine learning Pistachios Production Model in California and implementing a Climate Projections Model from 2021 to 2100. By the end, readers will gain a comprehensive understanding of pistachio production, factors affecting yield and revenue, and strategies for risk management and future planning in the context of climate change.

Chapter 6
Specialty crops pistachio: pricing models

This chapter covers:
- Pistachio pricing
- Economic importance and opportunities
  - USA
  - Turkey
  - Iran
- Pistachios prices and crop insurance
- Pistachios pricing behavior
- Machine learning models
  - Pistachios pricing models
  - Optimized pricing model with limited high influence parameters
  - Forecasting: what-if modeling
- Yield improvement strategies

The yield patterns of pistachios are examined in leading producer nations such as the USA, Turkey, and Iran. This chapter also delves into pricing models and introduces an impact parameter to assist in pricing decisions. It thoroughly investigates the pricing behavior of pistachios and presents a framework for analyzing yields across various producing countries, culminating in a proactive pricing model that offers price recommendations to farmers. By the chapter's conclusion, readers will gain a comprehensive understanding of pistachio production and pricing, empowering them to make informed decisions and maximize their profits.

Pistachios, often mistakenly referred to as nuts, are actually the mildly sweet seeds of the pistachio tree. This tree is dioecious, meaning that male and female flowers grow on separate trees, both of which are necessary for nut production. The female flowers lack petals and nectar, relying on the wind for pollen dispersal. Pistachio trees shed their leaves in the fall and remain dormant throughout the winter. Classified as phreatophytes, these trees have extensive root systems that allow them to endure long periods of drought [252, 253]. Predominantly a desert plant, pistachios are mainly cultivated in the arid regions of inland California [254, 255].

Pistachios have enjoyed popularity as a food source for millennia, with records of their consumption tracing back to 7,000 B.C. The pistachio tree originally hails from western Asia and was introduced to the United States in the mid-nineteenth century [256]. Commercial production of pistachios in the United States began in earnest during the 1970s.

Today, pistachios have emerged as a significant crop in California, benefiting from robust export markets, high prices, and lower water needs compared to other crops such as almonds. This is especially advantageous in the water-constrained Central Valley. Remarkably, the past 2 years have witnessed record-breaking pistachio produc-

 | https://doi.org/10.1515/9783111438894-006

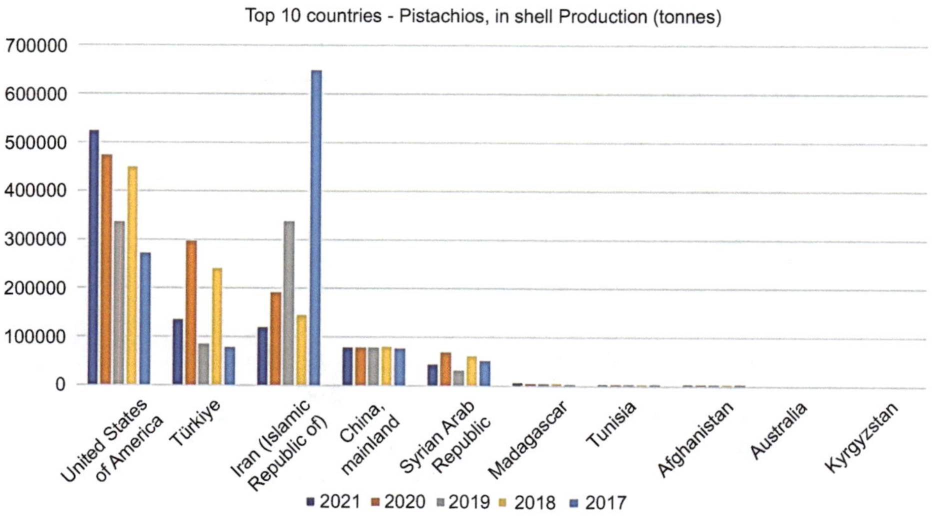

Figure 1: Top 10 countries: pistachios.

tion in California, and experts anticipate that the acreage dedicated to pistachios will continue to expand rapidly in the coming years [257].

By the early 20th century, California's pistachio industry was already thriving, with several popular nut varieties developed through crossbreeding. Over the last three decades, the yield of pistachios in California has surged dramatically. Today, more than half a million acres in the San Joaquin, Fresno, and Sacramento valleys are devoted to pistachio cultivation.

California currently stands as the world's leading producer of pistachios, contributing approximately 80% of the global supply. Pistachios represent California's topmost agricultural export and are the most valuable tree nut crop in terms of both revenue (USD $) and acreage. Furthermore, they are the foremost specialty crop export for the United States. This underscores the remarkable expansion and significance of the pistachio industry in California, making it a pivotal player in both the state's economy and the global food market.

Pistachios are a well-loved nut cultivated in over 20 countries across the world including the USA, Turkey, Iran, China, Syria, Madagascar, Tunisia, Afghanistan, Australia, and Kyrgyzstan (Figure 1). The global pistachio industry is worth billions of dollars and continues to grow in value as the nut becomes more popular as food [258].

The United States holds the title of the world's largest pistachio producer, with an anticipated output of 523,900 metric tons for the 2021/2022 season. This surge in production is attributed to an *"on-year"* in the *alternate-bearing cycle and the expansion of bearing acreage*. Comparatively, in the 2020/21 marketing year, the USA produced 474,000 tons, marking an increase of 49,900 tons for the current season [257].

Global pistachios industry is a multi-billion-dollar industry that is growing as popularity of pistachios grows!

Turkey is the second largest producer of pistachios globally, and it is projected to produce 135,000 metric tons in 2021/22, a decrease of nearly 65% from 296,376 metric tons in 2020/21. This drop in production is due to low yields resulting from the alteration of the crop.

Pistachios demand
Worldwide, pistachios industry has enjoyed explosive growth rates due to perceived health benefits offered such as potential lower chances aimed at cardiovascular disease plus lower of blood sugar, blood pressure, and cholesterol [5].

However, there was a considerable increase in production in 2020/21, with output nearly tripling that of 2019/20 at 85,000 metric tons. This was due to good conditions in southeastern Turkey, where most of the country's pistachio orchards are located, and a boost from the on-year.

The majority of Turkey's pistachio harvest is enjoyed within the country, leaving only a small portion available for international export. Domestic consumption in Turkey is projected to reach 211,000 tons [259].

Iran ranks as the third largest pistachio producer in the world, with an estimated output of 119,355 tons in the 2021/22 season, a decline from 190,000 tons in 2020/21. Back in 2017, Iran's pistachio production reached 648,934 tons, but unfavorable weather conditions [260] led to a significant drop in 2018. Despite strong exports to China, the trade volume is anticipated to decrease as the available supply shrinks. On the domestic front, pistachio consumption in Iran is expected to remain steady at 30,000 tons for the 2020/21 season [259].

Global pistachio industry has experienced explosive growth due to the perceived health benefits of the nut, including a potential lower risk of cardiovascular disease and reduced blood sugar, blood pressure, and cholesterol levels. Pistachios are an excellent source of protein, low in drenched fat, and completely free of cholesterol.

The surge in pistachio consumption in China has significantly contributed to market growth. In the 2020/21 season, China accounted for 35.5% of the world's total pistachio imports, amounting to an estimated 150,000 tons. This figure marks a 45% increase from the 2019/20 season, largely driven by higher shipments from both Iran and the United States.

Amid the COVID-19 pandemic, America's food banks have received donations of pistachios, other tree nuts, and surplus seafood. Notably, the highest funding allocation for these donations, amounting to $40 million [261], has been dedicated to pistachios, which are predominantly cultivated in the deserts of inland California. This investment is nearly double the amount allocated for any other food item [262].

The area of land where pistachios are grown has increased significantly over the years. In 1961, the worldwide area harvested was only 35,393 hectares, but in 2021 it increased to 817,025 ha. There was a sharp increase of 1,046,964 ha in 2019 due to the introduction of new plants [263].

The expansion rate of the harvested area can be accurately described using a linear trend or a regression equation (as shown in eq. (1)). This means that the growth rate follows a consistent pattern that can be predicted using mathematical models. The R^2 values for these trends are relatively high, indicating a strong correlation between the growth rate and time.

The production of pistachios has increased significantly over the years. In 1961, the worldwide production was only 20,714 ton, but in 2021 it increased to 915,717 ton according to FAOSTAT 2022. The growth rate of pistachio production can be reliably explained with a polynomial regression equation (as shown in eq. (2)). This means that the growth rate follows a more complex pattern that can be predicted using mathematical models. Furthermore, the yield of pistachios has also increased significantly from 5,853 hg/ha in 1961 to 11,208 hg/ha in 2021. The trend of yield growth can be characterized by a polynomial order 6 yield equation (eqs. (2) and (3)). This means that the yield growth follows a more complex and nonlinear pattern that can be predicted using mathematical models.

$$Y_{\text{Area Harvested}} = -0.0004x^6 + 4.59x^5 - 22917x^4 + 6\text{E}{+}07x^3 - 9\text{E}{+}10x^2 + 7\text{E}{+}13x - 2\text{E}{+}16 \quad (1)$$

$$Y_{\text{Production}} = -0.002x^6 + 0.3663x^5 - 24.573x^4 + 766.45x^3 - 10846x^2 + 64886x - 78328 \quad (2)$$

$$Y_{\text{Yield}} = -2\text{E}{-}05x^6 + 0.0038x^5 - 0.2369x^4 + 7.1942x^3 - 112.98x^2 + 995.9x + 4344.9 \quad (3)$$

Please note that except power regression trend fit, the area harvested regression types (linear, exponential, logarithmic, and polynomial) have higher accuracy (Figure 2).

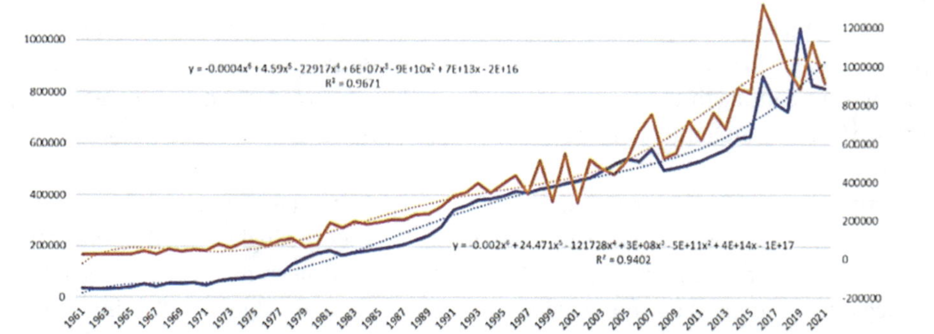

Figure 2: World pistachios area harvested.

Area	Equation	R^2 value
Exponential	$y = 1E{-}43e^{0.0558x}$	$R^2 = 0.9053$
Linear	$y = 13825x - 3E + 07$	$R^2 = 0.9284$
Power	$y = 0x^{111.27}$	$R^2 = 0$

Area harvested is function of bearing acreage and time maturity of nonbearing acreage.

Production: Except logarithmic (56.48%), all other regression types provide a higher accuracy (>86%).

	Equation	R^2
Exponential	$y = 27218e^{0.0665x}$	$R^2 = 0.8923$
Linear	$y = 17450x - 167948$	$R^2 = 0.8609$
Logarthimic	$y = 278237\ln(x) - 506136$	$R^2 = 0.5648$
Polynomial order 6	$y = -0.002x^6 + 0.3663x^5 - 24.573x^4 + 766.45x^3 - 10846x^2 + 64886x - 78328$	$R^2 = 0.9402$
Power	$y = 3867.8x^{1.2698}$	$R^2 = 0.8932$

Pistachios production is unique as they exhibit clearly alternate bearing repetition, follows "on"/"off" cycle. Pistachio production shows a. As a result, year over year would vary [264] as in Figure 3. As a result, the R^2 value that explains yield would be very low.

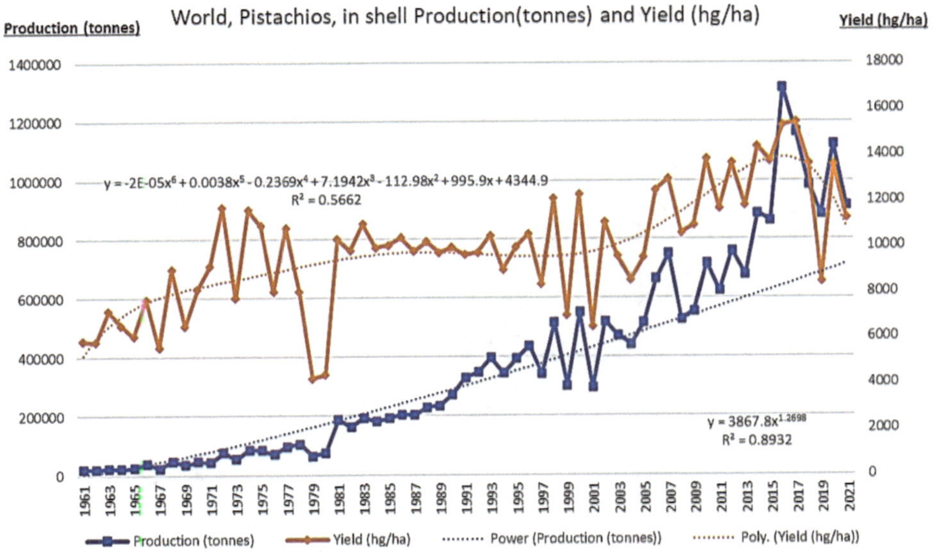

Figure 3: World pistachios production.

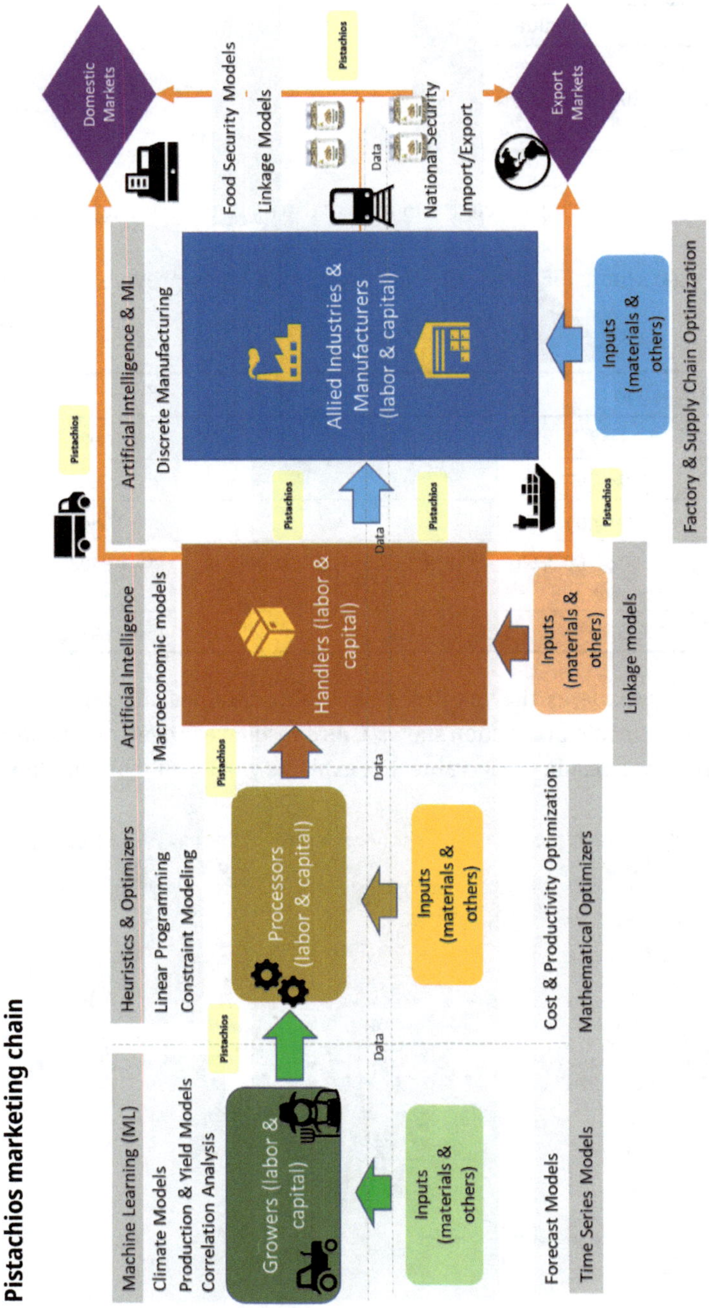

Figure 4: Flow of pistachios.

Economic importance and opportunities

Managing a pistachio orchard entails making numerous economic decisions throughout the long productive life of the trees. Initially, one must decide on the orchard's design, including its location, type of irrigation system, and floor management plan. Subsequent decisions involve regular evaluations of production practices such as pest and disease control, pruning, fertilization programs, and irrigation scheduling [263]. The market value chain, illustrated in Figure 4, plays a crucial role in this process. Given shifting demographics and the availability of human resources, ensuring economic sustainability is a top priority for agricultural farms, particularly pistachio orchards, as exemplified by the practices in Turkey.

The agricultural sector plays a pivotal role in the development and socioeconomic structure of many countries including Turkey. In 1996–1997, 41.1% of Turkey's population resided in rural areas, with agriculture contributing 16.8% to the national income and 11.7% to exports. Additionally, 45.9% of the active workforce was employed in agriculture [264]. By 2023, only 23.4% of the population lived in rural areas, reflecting significant shifts in agricultural employment. The dynamics have evolved due to economic sustainability and the influence of off-farm incomes.

In the United States, the pistachio industry has emerged as a major economic force. According to a report by the American Pistachio Growers, a trade association representing the US industry, pistachio farming in California, Arizona, and New Mexico generated approximately $5.3 billion in economic activity throughout the region. The majority of this economic impact occurs in California, where most of the production is concentrated. From 2016 to 2020, California saw significant growth in pistachio production, with bearing acreage increasing by 56%, equivalent to 132,000 acres, and nonbearing acres (newly planted trees up to 7 years old) expanding by 41,500 acres. This expansion, along with advancements in varieties and agronomic practices, propelled US pistachio production to surpass the 1-billion-pound mark for the first time with the 2021 season's crop [265, 266].

The primary import markets for pistachios include Hong Kong, China, Canada, Germany, Belgium, the Netherlands, and Russia. Not all of these countries import pistachios directly from the producers, as re-shipping can occur due to strategic business goals, quality control issues, and regulatory considerations. Hong Kong holds a crucial role in the global pistachio trade as the largest re-importer, serving as a gateway to China and facilitating re-exports from China to other destinations. Similarly, Germany, Belgium, Luxembourg, and the United Arab Emirates also engage in re-exporting, holding significant positions in the pistachio market.

USA

California pistachio growers and their approximately six processors contribute an impressive $5.2 billion to the state's economy. This figure is expected to grow as the acreage of bearing plants increases. With this growth, job numbers and tax revenues for the state are anticipated to rise as business activities expand. Within this economic impact, growers alone generated nearly $3 billion through the cultivation, management, and harvesting of pistachios. The remaining economic output was derived from processing and packaging activities. Approximately $2.5 billion in salaries were paid across 47,000 jobs in California [266]. Additionally, nearly $191.9 million in indirect business taxes were generated last year solely from the pistachio growing and processing activities in California. These taxes are produced by businesses that benefit from the resulting economic activity and increased employment (see Table 1 for details) [266].

Table 1: Pistachios production in the United States.

	California 	**Arizona** 	**New Mexico** 
Acreage	132,000 acres plus additional 41,500 acres expansion	9,500 acres (6,000 bearing acres)	
Economic boost to state economy	$5.2 billion	$92 million	$4.5 million
Economic output through growing, management and harvesting	$3 billion	$49 million	$2.7 million
Processing and packaging	$2.2 billion	$43 million	$2.8 million
Salaries paid (approximately)	$2.5 billion	$39.6 million	$150,000
Jobs created	47,000	915	
Net investment – average per acre to produce a crop	$3.45 billion	$3,182	
Processors investment	$1.13 per pound of harvested nut		
Indirect business taxes	$191.9 million	$3 million	

The Sacramento and San Joaquin Valleys in California are renowned for their prolific pistachio production. It's also noteworthy that California is home to approximately 47,000 farmers dedicated to cultivating this valuable crop [266].

Employment

The pistachio industry significantly boosts California's economy. In 2020, growers and processors spent over $2.8 billion, resulting in an economic output exceeding $5.2 billion. This spending generated more than 47,200 full-time equivalent jobs and nearly $2.5 billion in labor income [266]. Additionally, the industry contributed close to $191.9 million in indirect business taxes [267]. Overall, the pistachio sector plays a crucial role in job creation, income generation, and tax revenue for the state [268].

In general, most producers of fruits and nuts in California have fewer than 100 acres, but these smaller producers account for less than half of the total acreage, with the exception of avocados. California pistachios in 2017 shows that for pistachios, 75.97% of farms are less than 100 acres in size, but they contribute to 52.21% of the total acreage. This means that even though most pistachio farms are small, they still occupy a relatively large amount of land. On the other hand, 24.02% of pistachio farms are greater than 100 acres in size, but they only contribute to 47.71% of the total acreage. This suggests that larger pistachio farms are less common, but they occupy a larger proportion of the land [269].

California pistachios in 2017

	Farms	Acres	Farms	Acres
			Percent share > 100 acres	
Pistachios	1,515	334,949		
>100 acres	479	305,668	32	91

Cash receipts and export markets

California's pistachio industry generated $2.12 billion in cash receipts in 2020 as per USDA. This represented an increase from the previous year, when cash receipts for pistachios in California were $1.67 billion. The increase in cash receipts for pistachios reflects the continued growth and demand for pistachios, both domestically and internationally. Table 2 shows the amount of agricultural products that California contributed to the total agricultural exports of the United States in 2019 and 2020. The products included are tree nuts (like almonds, walnuts, and pistachios). In both years, California produced all of the tree nuts that were exported by the United States. The table shows the total value of these exports and the percentage of that value that came from California. While the total value of all tree nut exports decreased slightly from 2019 to 2020, the amount of California's contribution to that value stayed the same. Overall, California is a major contributor to the United States' agricultural exports in the tree nut category.

Table 2: California portion of national cultivated trades by group and product, 2019 and 2020.

Commodity	2019		2020	
	Total U.S. Export Value ($1 Million)	California Share of U.S. Exports (In Percent)	Total U.S. Export Value ($1 Million)	California Share of U.S. Exports (In Percent)
Tree Nuts	8161	100	7573	100
Almonds	4901	100	4659	100
Walnuts	1250	100	1246	100
Pistachios	2010	100	1668	100

The cost of pistachios in the United States has fluctuated over the years, shaped by elements like supply and demand, weather patterns, and international trade regulations. USDA data reveals that, despite some variations, the price of pistachios has generally trended upward over the past several decades.

In the early 1980s, the average price of pistachios was around $2.50 per pound. By the mid-2000s, the price had risen to around $3.50 per pound, and by 2019, it had reached around $4.50 per pound. However, there have been some years when the price has dropped due to oversupplied or other factors such as the impact of tariffs on global trade.

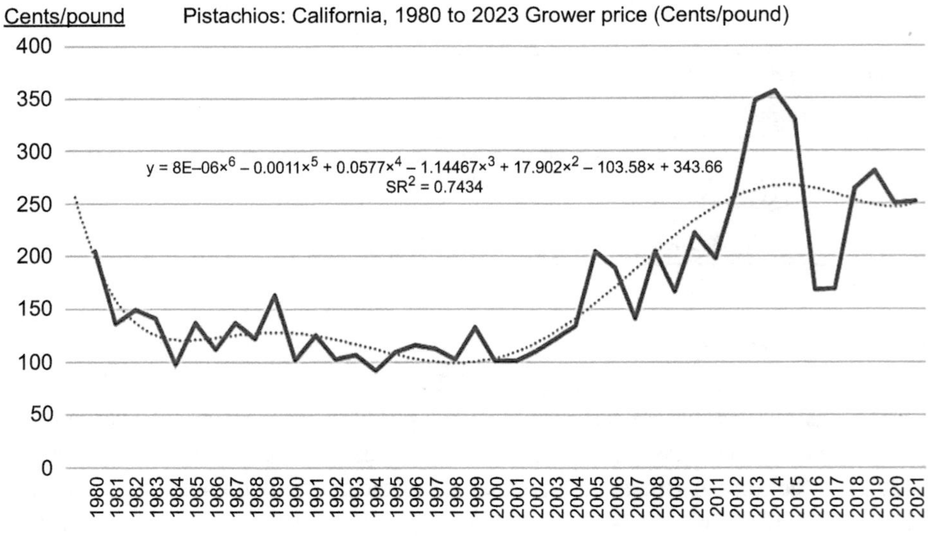

Figure 5: Average grower price.

In recent years, substantial investment in new pistachio plantings has significantly influenced California's economy. Between 2016 and 2020, growers introduced over 173,000 acres of pistachios (Figure 5), generating an economic impact of nearly $1.9

billion. This investment averaged over $5.1 million per day, resulting in the creation of over 16.8K jobs, nearly $0.887 billion in extra labor proceeds [270].

There are several reasons for this surge in pistachio plantings. One is the healthy profits that growers have been making in recent years. Another is the labor landscape, as growers are planting more mechanized crops to reduce their reliance on labor. Additionally, pistachios require less water than many other crops, making them well-suited for low-water situations. They can also tolerate poorer soils, which is important for growers in areas with salty groundwater [270].

Machine learning variable: Commercial machinery repair and maintenance

Pistachio cultivators are striving to minimize their reliance on manual labor by introducing more mechanized crops. The shift toward automation has heightened the demand for services related to commercial machinery repair and maintenance. As a result, leveraging the machinery dataset will be crucial for accurately forecasting pistachio prices[1].

Turkey

Pistachio production in Turkey is marked by significant year-to-year variability, with substantial differences observed across various regions and orchards. Production is cyclical, with some years having significantly larger harvests than others. This means that yields and gross production revenues can differ dramatically from year to year. For example, in MY 2020/21, the gross production value of pistachios in Turkey was $1.763 billion USD, which is three times that of the expected value in the off-year of MY 2021/22, which is only $602.161 million USD. This is due to lower expected yields in the off-year [271]. Despite the fluctuations in production, the pistachio industry in Turkey has a significant impact on farming communities and provides indirect employment. Although anticipated lower revenues during off-years can affect the industry, pistachio production remains a crucial livelihood for many individuals in Turkey.

	 **Turkey**
Acreage	962,354 acres (FAOSTAT 2021)
Economic boost to state economy	USD $1.763 billion (on-year, FAOSTAT 2020) and USD $602.16 million (off-year, FAOSTAT 2021)
Jobs created	Greater 300,000 [272]

1 PCU8113108113105 – https://fred.stlouisfed.org/series/PCU8113108113105

In 2015, at *least 300,000 people were employed* in pistachio farming, and it plays an important economic force, provides huge employment opportunities, strengthens the economy, and prevents possible social security problems [272].

Pistachios are considered a cash crop by many farmers in Turkey because they provide higher returns compared to other crops (Figure 6). The gross production value of in-shell pistachios in Turkey has generally increased from 1991 to 2021 despite some fluctuations. The value rose from $200 million in the early 1990s to peaks of around $1,000 million in 2017 and approximately $1,800 million in 2019, before dropping to about $600 million in 2021. Overall, the trend indicates a significant long-term increase with notable year-to-year variability.

According to the Turkish Statistical Institute, there are approximately 76 million trees (bearing plus nonbearing) in Turkey as of the beginning of MY 2021/22 [271]. *Farmers in Turkey are increasingly planting younger pistachio trees, which are more productive, and recognizing the importance of male trees to boost yields. They are also shifting away from crops like lentils, barley, and wheat, believing pistachios offer higher profits even on nonirrigated land. As a result, pistachios have become a major cash crop, significantly enhancing farmers' incomes.*

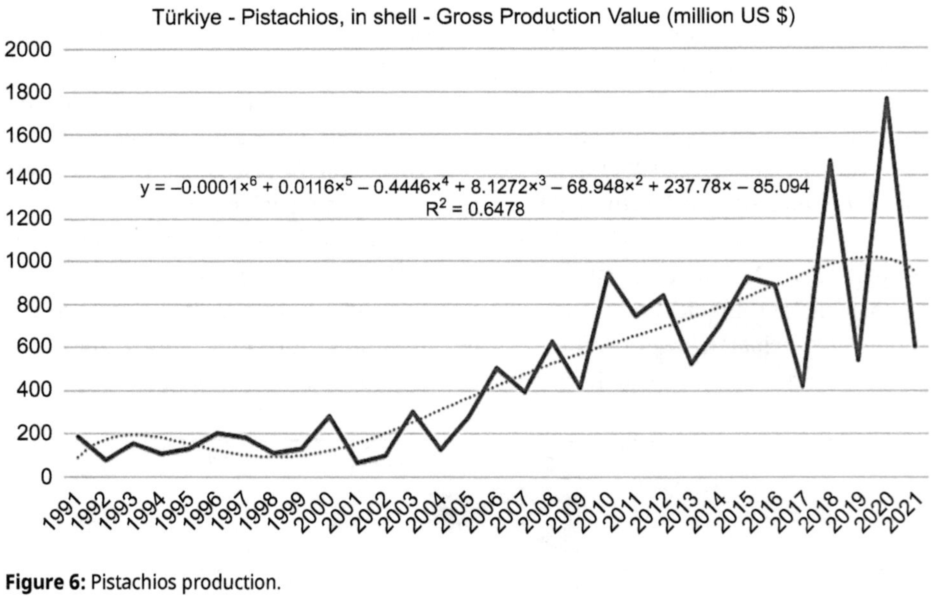

Figure 6: Pistachios production.

$$Y_{\text{gross production value}} = -0.0001x^6 + 0.0116x^5 - 0.4446x^4 + 8.1272x^3 - 68.948x^2 + 237.78x - 85.094$$

Iran

Pistachios thrive in the arid regions of Iran, where rainfall is minimal. Despite Iran possessing approximately 50 million hectares of arable land, a significant portion remains unused due to insufficient water resourc es for irrigation. Nevertheless, pistachios can be grown in these areas because they require less water than other crops and can still be grown economically. In fact, pistachio exports are one of Iran's major sources of income, second only to petroleum. Around 10% of Iran's nonpetroleum export value comes from pistachios. This means that pistachios are an important crop for Iran's economy and provide a significant source of income for the country.

Oil exports in Iran averaged $4,724 billion from 1995 until 2021, reaching an all-time high of $119,148 billion in 2011 and a record low of $10,659.00 million in 1998.

In Iran, pistachios are cultivated in 125,544 hectares of land, with 70% being bearing gardens and 30% nonbearing gardens. In the bearing gardens, the yield is 1.0753 tons per hectare, resulting in a total production of 148,500 metric tons. Iran's pistachio exports generate over $1,500 million in revenue, with the Rafsanjan region alone accounting for a third of this value. This makes Rafsanjan a crucial player in bolstering Iran's economy. In fact, pistachio exports are the second largest export after oil [273]. There are 400,000 ha of rainfed orchards in Iran, which represents 16.5% of the total orchards. The province of Kerman is the main area for pistachio production in Iran and has the largest number of different varieties with recognizable characteristics in cultivation compared to other areas of Iran or any other country [274]. Specifically, the Rafsanjan region in Kerman is known for its high-quality pistachios and is a major contributor to Iran's overall pistachio production and export [275].

Rafsanjan, a central region in Iran, is famous for producing high-quality pistachios and generates nearly $1,000 million yearly, bolstering the local economy. Over 30K people are directly involved in pistachio farming in this area. The region was a major global supplier in the 1980s and 1990s, contributing to over 20% of the world market. Favorable climatic conditions and government subsidies have made Rafsanjan a successful and attractive center for pistachio production [273].

In Iran, pistachios are a vital economic asset, ranking second in export value only to oil.

	 Iran
Acreage	125,544 ha (FAOSTAT 2021)
Economic boost to state economy	USD $1.763 billion (on-year, FAOSTAT 2020) and USD $602.16 million (off-year, FAOSTAT 2021)
Jobs created	Greater 300,000 [272]

Although pistachio production in Rafsanjan provides significant benefits to the state economy, it requires large amounts of water that are not easily available in the region (Figure 7). Pistachios flourish under specific climatic conditions, requiring lingering, hot summers and adequate winter chill, typically found in regions far from surface water sources like rivers or lakes. Consequently, pistachio farmers in Rafsanjan have come to rely heavily on groundwater for their irrigation needs. This dependence on groundwater is essential for the continued success of pistachio cultivation in the region [273].

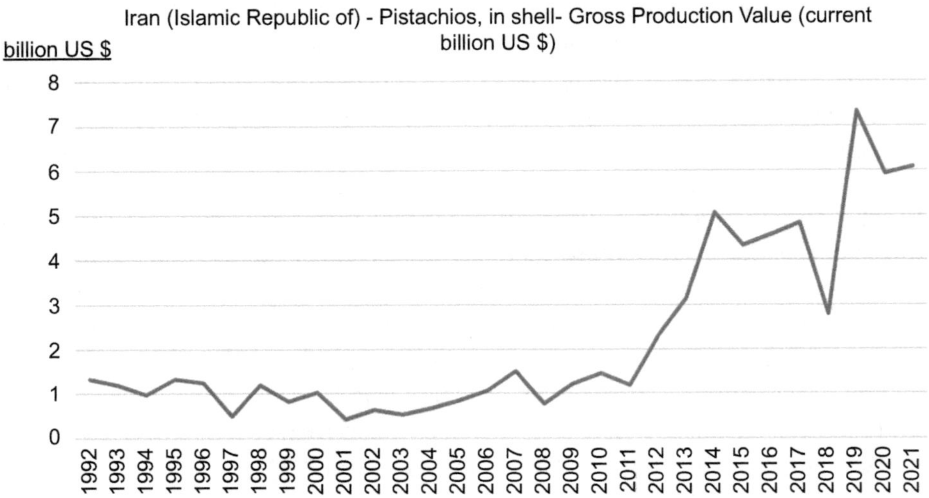

Figure 7: Iran pistachios production.

Pistachios prices

Forecasting pistachios prices in advance is essential for smallholder farmers. The difference is having financial sustainability versus acres of crops will be left unharvested as farmers look to cut their losses despite registering a bumper yield.

Researchers have developed models to simulate and predict pistachio grower prices in the United States. These models take into account various factors, such as import levels and carryover stocks, to forecast price changes. Over the past 13 years, grower prices have seen significant fluctuations due to variations in import levels and domestic production. The number of bearing acres has increased dramatically, indicating that as nonbearing acres mature, production will rise substantially. In 1979, the US pistachio industry produced only 1,000 tons, but by 1990, production had surged to over 58,000 tons. These predictive models are essential for anticipating future grower prices under varying market conditions. They are particularly important as global political conditions continue to change, affecting market dynamics. By simulating US pistachio prices, the models can provide insights into how the market might behave in the future [276]. Alternate bearing acreage plays an important role as demonstrated by price model developed in the chapter.

Please see US pistachios prices[2] received (Figure 8). In 2014, the US prices skyrocketed ($3.57 USD/lb) due to drought in California [275]. In 2016, pistachio prices fell to $1.68 per pound due to the lifting of sanctions against Iran after it reduced its nuclear program [277]. In 2018 and 2019, the prices were in similar range ($2.65 USD/lb and $2.81 USD/lb, respectively).

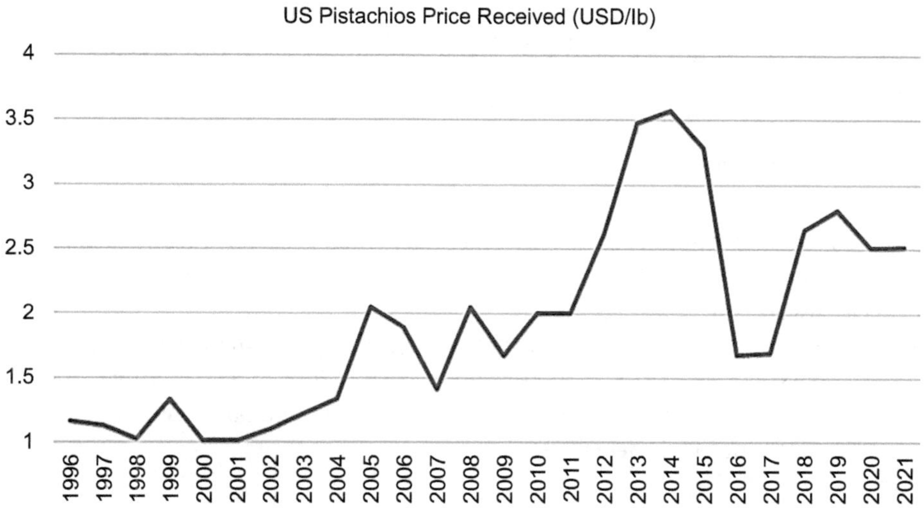

Figure 8: US pistachios price received.

Pistachios, part of the tree nut family, have played a significant role in California's economy [278]. The growth trajectory (Figure 9) of tree nuts underscores their economic importance to the state. Cash receipts for all types rose by 19%, exceeding $2.76 billion, largely due to a recovery in prices.

The advantage of pricing models is many folds [276–279]:

- Yield engineering
  - US pistachio industry has multiplied in acreage and production, bolstered by favorable policies, with a study analyzing these trends and providing short-term production forecasts [276].
- Imports and exports policy
  - A model was created to estimate prices, which was used to predict the potential value ($) at different harvests and trade in. This was done to see how the

2 US Pistachios Prices received – https://ycharts.com/indicators/us_pistachios_price_received

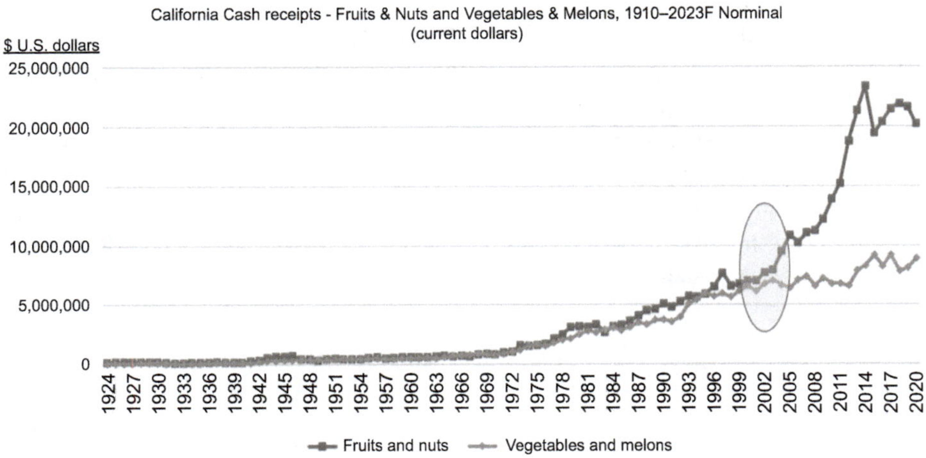

Figure 9: California cash receipts.

increased domestic supply and different levels of imports would impact the industry [276, 279].

- Price oscillations or swings
  - Our simulation model demonstrated that changes in the levels of carryover could help control fluctuations in prices. However, if storage capacity is limited, the price outcome may be determined by these limitations, especially during years with a high yield [276].

US pistachios

Machine learning model: pistachios pricing models, USA

The principle of the model is to develop pistachios forecast pricing model (Figure 10). The pricing model involves various components of fresh produce markets that include macroeconomic variables, infrastructure, crop price behavior, climate change models, energy, and market access & value chain.

The suggested approach is unique and incredibly pioneering. For analyzing pricing models, a traditional approach would apply historical data and link to macroeconomic view. However, in the proposed model, many interwove parameters are considered to model price forecast. Let's build the model for USA pistachios:

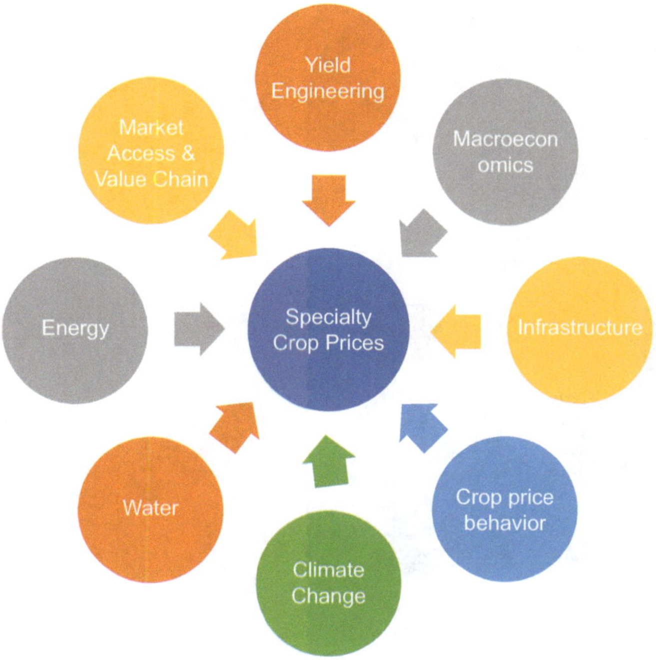

Figure 10: Specialty crops price prediction.

Final release pistachios pricing Prophet model code notebook

Historical pistachios price dataset is available from 2017 onward on FRED – PPI pistachios. Other sources considered was fresh or dried pistachios: US exports by unit value ($ per pound). The data is sparce and missing values. Other source data is the export/import unit values from ERS. The unit value (Figure 11) is calculated by dividing value by volume. For the model developed in the subsequent section, I have used ERS.

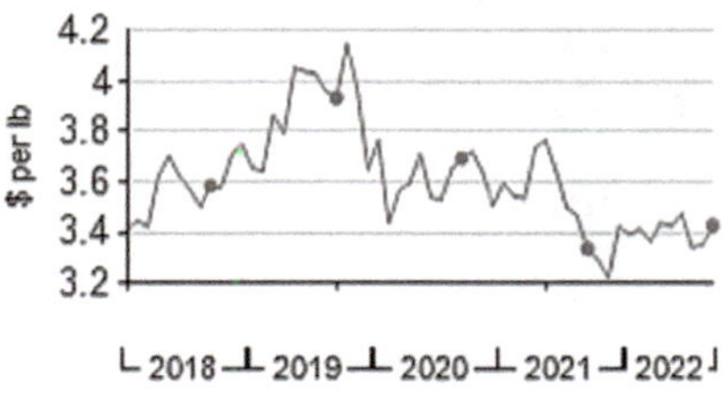

Figure 11: Pistachios export unit value.

Finally, the price forecast developed is based on the proposed framework that links causative factors of many different fields on the price of pistachios (Figure 12).

Figure 12: Specialty crops price components.

Sources of data

The data for the machine learning model comes from various sources such as World Meteorological Organization Data and NOAA STAR. It includes information on minimum and maximum temperatures, precipitation, average temperatures, climate data, and earth observation. The data is collected from different countries and sources, and you can find more information about them in the appendices.

Pistachios pricing framework

Variable list

The price forecasting model leverages the following data sources as key inputs:

Independent feature time series name	Frequency	Description	Source
Fresno weather	Monthly	MaxTemperature(C)', 'MeanTemperature(C)', 'MinTemperature', 'rain'	NOAA GSOM
GASREGCOVM	Monthly	Regular gas prices	Gas price
CPI	Monthly	CPIAUCSL	CPIAUCSL
Fertilizer	Monthly	PhosphateRock($/mt)', 'Dap($/mt)', 'Tsp($/mt)', 'Urea($/mt)', 'PotassiumChloride($/mt)',	World Bank Commodity Markets
GDP	Quarterly	Gross domestic product (GDP)	GDP
GEPUCURRENT	Monthly	GEPUCURRENT	Economic policy uncertainty
S&P 500 dividend by month	Monthly	Major industrial stock dividends	Dividend by month
Industrial production index (INDPRO)	Monthly	Health of industrial production in the United States	INDPRO
Rail car loadings	Monthly	Rail freight carloads	Rail freight carloads (RAILFRTCARLOADSD11)[3]

Step 1: Import libraries

This code imports various software utility python modues: plotly, statsmodels, and sklearn. These modules are used for data manipulation, analysis, and visualization. The code also sets the size of the figure to be plotted using matplotlib.

3 Rail Freight Carloads (RAILFRTCARLOADSD11) – https://fred.stlouisfed.org/series/RAILFRTCARLOADSD11

```
import numpy as np
import pandas as pd
import functools
from datetime import date
import plotly.graph_objects as go
#import seaborn as sns; sns.set()
import statsmodels.api as sm
from statsmodels.tsa.arima_process import ArmaProcess
from scipy import stats
from scipy.stats import pearsonr
import matplotlib.pyplot as plt
import plotly.express as px
from sklearn.preprocessing import MinMaxScaler
from sklearn.model_selection import train_test_split
from sklearn.linear_model importLinearRegression
from sklearn.metrics import r2_score
from sklearn import metrics
from sklearn.impute import SimpleImputer
import matplotlib.pyplot as pltnp
fig = plt.figure()
fig.set_size_inches(8,7)
```

Step 2: Economic analysis of the California pistachios industry using key indicators and market prices

Load California pistachios data

The data has various variables or attributes that can be used for data analysis and modeling. They include weather-related variables such as MaxTemperature(C), MeanTemperature(C), MinTemperature(C), and total_precipitation(kg m^{-2} s^{-1}) as well as economic variables such as ProducerPriceIndex_Pistachios, dollarIndex_close, ChemicalsAndAlliedProducts, PhosphateRock($/mt), Dap($/mt), Tsp($/mt), Urea($/mt), PotassiumChloride($/mt), CPIAUCSL, GEPUCURRENT, employmentInAgriculture(LNS12034560), ProductionPriceIndexIndustry(PCU811310811310), ProductionPriceIndexIndustry(PCU325311325311), and RAILFRTCARLOADSD11. These variables can be used for various statistical analyses and modeling to gain insights into trends, patterns, and relationships in the data.

```
from sklearn.metrics import mean_absolute_error
from prophet import Prophet
```

```
df = pd.read_csv(r"FinalPistachiosCombinedFrame.csv",index_col=0)
df
```

```
df.columns
```

Output:

MaxTemperature(C)	MeanTemperature(C)	MinTemperature(C)	total_precipitation(kg m-2 s-1)	Date	ProducerPriceIndex_Pistachios	dollarIndex_close	DATE	C
4.062555	-0.309088	-3.460669	0.000035	2017-01-01	262.600	99.510002	2017-01-01	
7.469812	1.545831	-2.396613	0.000030	2017-02-01	262.600	101.120003	2017-02-01	
13.163751	6.590570	1.604791	0.000026	2017-03-01	277.200	100.349998	2017-03-01	
22.405664	15.166467	9.009607	0.000124	2017-04-01	262.600	99.050003	2017-04-01	
29.334497	22.008722	15.744470	0.000061	2017-05-01	257.200	96.919998	2017-05-01	
...	...	...	...	...	...	...	...	
31.068170	26.971216	23.387689	0.000336	2022-07-01	257.201	105.900002	2022-07-01	
30.752161	26.576715	23.088403	0.000288	2022-08-01	257.201	108.699997	2022-08-01	
26.847833	21.627832	17.057947	0.000149	2022-09-01	257.201	112.120003	2022-09-01	
18.772760	13.533014	9.138513	0.000436	2022-10-01	257.201	111.529999	2022-10-01	
14.352380	9.456628	5.533319	0.000079	2022-11-01	257.201	105.949997	2022-11-01	

rows × 24 columns

Step 3: Prepare prophet model

Preparing a Prophet model involves using a statistical modeling technique to forecast future trends or patterns based on historical data. This technique is commonly used in the field of data science to predict future values of a given variable such as stock prices, weather patterns, or crop yields. The Prophet model works by analyzing movements and making predictions about future values. It is a popular technique because it is relatively easy to use and can generate accurate predictions with minimal input from the user. Create Prophet model.

```
df["ds"] = pd.to_datetime(df["Date"])
```

```
Prophetdf = df[['MaxTemperature(C)','MeanTemperature(C)','MinTemperature(C)',
    'total_precipitation(kg m-2 s-1)','ds',
    'dollarIndex_close',
    'ChemicalsAndAlliedProducts','PhosphateRock($/mt)','Dap($/mt)',
    'Tsp($/mt)','Urea($/mt)','PotassiumChloride($/mt)',
'CPIAUCSL', 'ProducerPriceIndex_Pistachios',"Flag",
    'GEPUCURRENT','Area harvested(ha)','Production(tonnes)',
    'Yield(hg/ha)','employmentInAgriculture(LNS12034560)',
    'ProductionPriceIndexIndustry(PCU811310811310)',
    'ProductionPriceIndexIndustry(PCU325311325311)','RAILFRTCARLOADSD11',
    'CCUSSP01TRM650N']].rename({'ProducerPriceIndex_Pistachios':'y'},axis = 'columns')
```

```
Prophetdf.shape
```

Output:
(71, 24)

Step 4: Split the time series data model

The above code is used to split the Prophetdf dataset into two separate datasets for training and testing purposes. The first line of code creates a new variable called "n_obs" and assigns it the value of 90% Prophetdf dataset. Multiplying DataFrame size by 0.9 and converting the result to an integer. The second line of code creates two new datasets called "Prophetdf_train" and "Prophetdf_test." The "Prophetdf_train" dataset is created by selecting the first "obs" number of rows from the Prophetdf dataset using the indexing operator. The "Prophetdf_test" dataset is created by selecting the remaining rows from the Prophetdf dataset. Finally, the third line of code prints the shape of the "Prophetdf_train" and "Prophetdf_test" datasets to confirm that they have been split correctly. The shape of a dataset refers to the number of rows and columns it contains, and this information can be used to verify that the dataset has been split into the desired proportions for training and testing.

```
n_obs = int(Prophetdf.shape[0]*0.9)
Prophetdf_train,Prophetdf_test = Prophetdf[0:n_obs],Prophetdf[n_obs:]
print(Prophetdf_train.shape,Prophetdf_test.shape)
```

Output:
(63, 24) (8, 24)

Step 5: Analyze prophet columns

Analyze Prophet columns.

```
Prophetdf.dtypes.tolist()
```

```
Prophetdf.isna().any()
```

Check type of columns and verify any missing data columns.
Output:

```
MaxTemperature(C)                                     False
MeanTemperature(C)                                    False
MinTemperature(C)                                     False
total_precipitation(kg m-2 s-1)                       False
ds                                                    False
dollarIndex_close                                     False
ChemicalsAndAlliedProducts                            False
PhosphateRock($/mt)                                   False
Dap($/mt)                                             False
Tsp($/mt)                                             False
Urea($/mt)                                            False
PotassiumChloride($/mt)                               False
CPIAUCSL                                              False
y                                                     False
Flag                                                  False
GEPUCURRENT                                           False
Area harvested(ha)                                    False
Production(tonnes)                                    False
Yield(hg/ha)                                          False
employmentInAgriculture(LNS12034560)                  False
ProductionPriceIndexIndustry(PCU811310811310)         False
ProductionPriceIndexIndustry(PCU325311325311)         False
RAILFRTCARLOADSD11                                    False
dtype: bool
```

Step 6: Prophet model

Build Prophet model with the following column. The code below is used to create a Prophet model that uses multiple variables to make predictions. The first line of code creates a list called "Prophet_cols" that contains the names of the variables that will be used in the model. These variables include weather-related variables as well as economic variables such as dollarIndex_close, ChemicalsAndAlliedProducts, and ProductionPriceIndexIndustry. The second line of code creates a new Prophet model called "multi_model" and sets the interval width to 0.95. The interval width is used to specify the range of uncertainty around the predicted values. The third line of code creates a loop that iterates over each variable in the "Prophet_cols" list and adds it as a regressor to the "multi_model."

```
Prophet_cols=['MaxTemperature(C)',
        'MeanTemperature(C)', 'MinTemperature(C)',
    'total_precipitation(kg m-2 s-1)',
    'dollarIndex_close',
    'ChemicalsAndAlliedProducts',
     'PhosphateRock($/mt)',
     'Dap($/mt)',
     'Tsp($/mt)',
     'Urea($/mt)',
     'PotassiumChloride($/mt)',
      'CPIAUCSL',
    'GEPUCURRENT',
    'Area harvested(ha)',
    'Production(tonnes)',
    'Yield(hg/ha)',
    'Flag',
      'employmentInAgriculture(LNS12034560)',
      'ProductionPriceIndexIndustry(PCU811310811310)',
      'ProductionPriceIndexIndustry(PCU325311325311)',
      'RAILFRTCARLOADSD11',
        'CCUSSP01TRM650N'
      ]
```

```
multi_model = Prophet(interval_width = 0.95)
```

```
for col in prophet_cols:
  multi_model.add_regressor(col)
```

```
multi_model.fit(Prophetdf_train)
```

Output:

```
<prophet.forecaster.Prophet at 0x7fca3556bb70>
```

Step 7: Create futures data frame

The code above is used to generate a new dataframe called “future” and fills with forecasts. Code creates this dataframe by calling the “make_future_dataframe” method of the “multi_model” object.

```
future = multi_model.make_future_dataframe(periods=Prophetdf_test.shape[0],freq='MS',
include_history=True)
future.tail(15)
```

```
Prophetdf_test['ds']
```

```
for col in Prophet_cols:
   future[col] =Prophetdf[col]
```

```
forecastProphet= multi_model.predict(future)
```

```
forecastProphet[['ds','yhat','yhat_lower','yhat_upper']].tail()
```

Show:

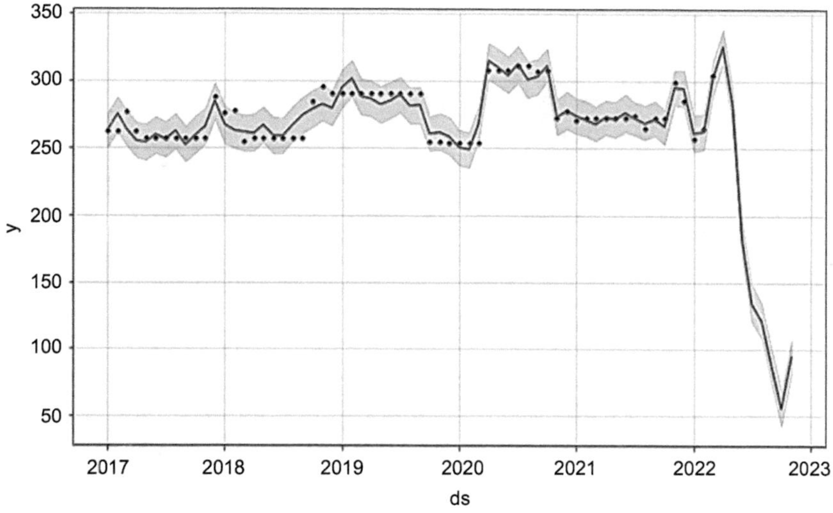


```
rophetdf.plot(x = 'ds',y = 'y')
```

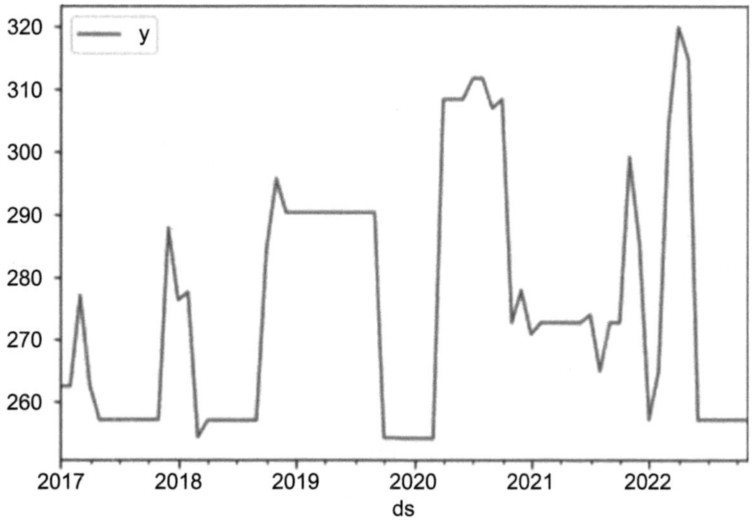

Output:
Print Prophet components.

```
multi_model.
plot_components
(forecastProphet);
```

Output:

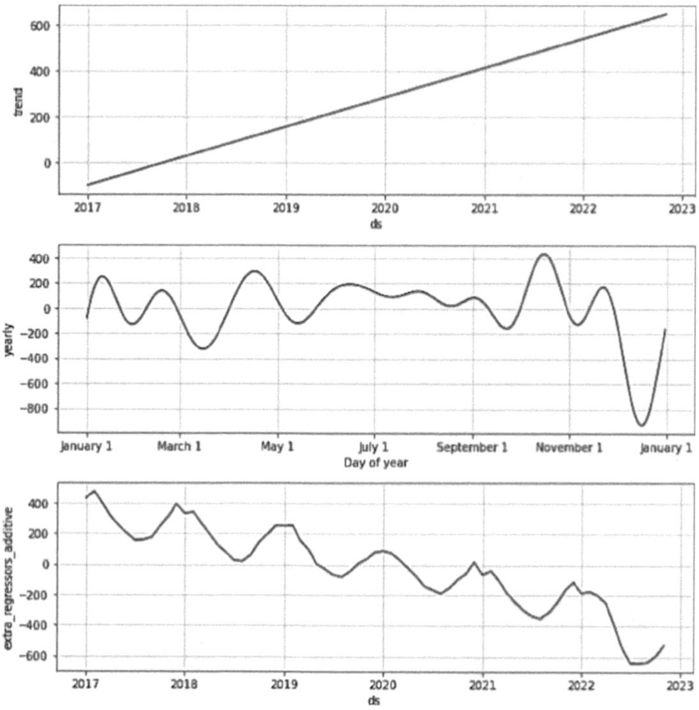

Step 8: Prophet model performance

Combine Prophet test and original data frame to assess model performance.

	ds	y	yhat	yhat_lower	yhat_upper
0	2022-04-01	319.879	325.866510	312.599325	338.693115
1	2022-05-01	314.681	283.248827	269.116179	295.596182
2	2022-06-01	257.201	181.959999	168.310834	195.973889
3	2022-07-01	257.201	134.385069	121.176303	149.025865
4	2022-08-01	257.201	121.534486	108.381475	134.964732
5	2022-09-01	257.201	86.352769	73.150704	99.961910
6	2022-10-01	257.201	55.908185	42.911309	68.965596
7	2022-11-01	257.201	94.643741	80.574966	107.013065

The code provides insights into how accurate its predictions are. By using these metrics, we can identify areas for improvement and work to create more accurate models in the future.

```
rom sklearn.metrics import mean_absolute_error,mean_absolute_percentage_error

 #Check MAE value
MAE = mean_absolute_error(combined_df['y'],combined_df['yhat'])
print(f'The MAE for the baseline model is {MAE}')
```

Output:
The MAE for the baseline model is $128.02. It's very high and future forecasts could be off by MAE.

Step 10: Model output

The code is used to visualize baseline of price model.

```
import seaborn as sns
plt.rcParams.update({'figure.figsize': (15, 3), 'figure.dpi': 300})
fig, ax = plt.subplots()

sns.lineplot(data = combined_df, x = 'ds', y = 'y', label = 'Original')
sns.lineplot(data= combined_df, x = 'ds', y = 'yhat', label = 'Forecast')
plt.grid(linestyle = '-',linewidth = 0.3)

plt.legend(["original","forecast"])
```

Output:
Model shows considerable deviation and forecast errors.

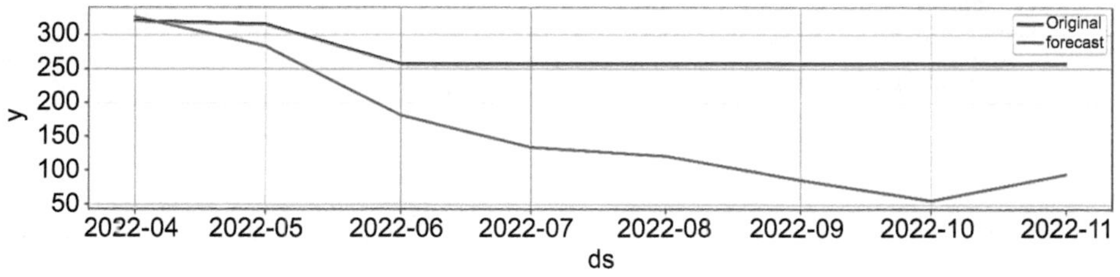

Step 11: Optimized pricing model with limited high influence parameters

The MAE metric used to evaluate model's predictions. In this case, the MAE for a baseline model has been calculated to be $128.0. To improve accuracy, it is recommended to drop the climatology variables and instead use macroeconomic parameters as inputs. By doing so, the model will be trained to make predictions based on more relevant data, which can help to improve the accuracy of its forecasts.

```
Prophet_cols = [
    'dollarIndex_close',
    'ChemicalsAndAlliedProducts',
     'PhosphateRock($/mt)',
       'Dap($/mt)',
     'Tsp($/mt)',
    'Urea($/mt)',
    'PotassiumChloride($/mt)',
     'CPIAUCSL',
    'GEPUCURRENT',
    'employmentInAgriculture(LNS12034560)',
    'ProductionPriceIndexIndustry(PCU811310811310)',
    'ProductionPriceIndexIndustry(PCU325311325311)',
    'RAILFRTCARLOADSD11',
   'CCUSSP01TRM650N']
```

```
multi_model = Prophet(interval_width=0.95)
# adding all columns in add regressor
for col in Prophet_cols:
  multi_model.add_regressor(col)
multi_model.fit(Prophetdf_train)
```

```
future = multi_model.make_future_dataframe(periods = Prophetdf_test.shape[0],freq='MS',
include_history=True)
for col in Prophet_cols:
  future[col] =Prophetdf[col]
forecastProphet = multi_model.predict(future)
forecastProphet[['ds','yhat','yhat_lower','yhat_upper']].tail()
```

```
fig1=multi_model.plot(forecastProphet);
```

Build the Prophet model:

Output:

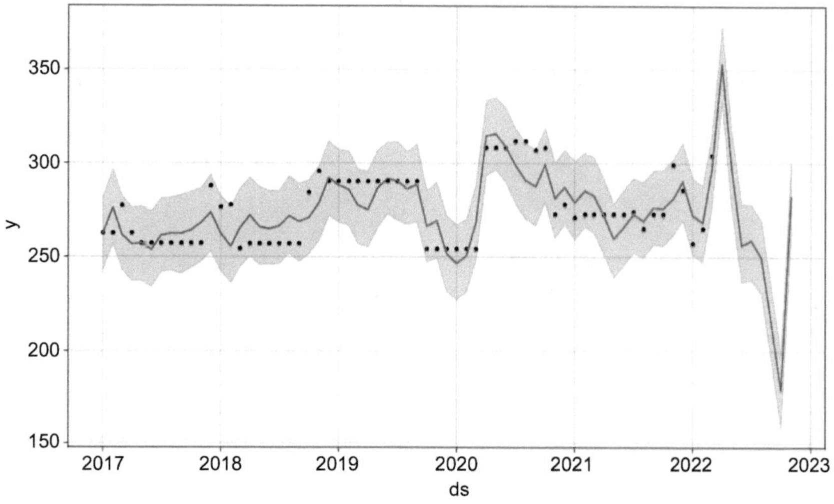

Run model metrics and output is $25.63.

The difference in MAE from $128 to $25 is a significant improvement in the accuracy of the model's predictions. This means that the new model is making much more accurate predictions than the previous model. The improvement in the model can be attributed to the fact that the climatology variables were dropped and replaced with macroeconomic parameters. This change allowed the model to be trained on more relevant data that had a stronger correlation with the target variable. In this case, the target variable is likely related to pistachios, and the macroeconomic parameters are more relevant to predicting the price or demand for pistachios than the climatology variables.

Furthermore, the influence of climate risk on the pistachio market can be mitigated through the use of risk insurance. This means that even if the climate does not cooperate, insurance can provide a safety net that helps to protect pistachio farmers and the market as a whole. By using a combination of accurate predictions and risk management strategies like insurance, it is possible to manage risk.

```
import seaborn as sns
plt.rcParams.update({'figure.figsize': (15, 3),'figure.dpi': 300})
fig, ax = plt.subplots()

sns.lineplot(data = combined_df,x ='ds', y = 'y',label ='Original')
sns.lineplot(data = combined_df,x = 'ds', y = 'yhat', label = 'Forecast')
plt.grid(linestyle = '-', linewidth = 0.3)

plt.legend(["Original","forecast"])
```

Output:

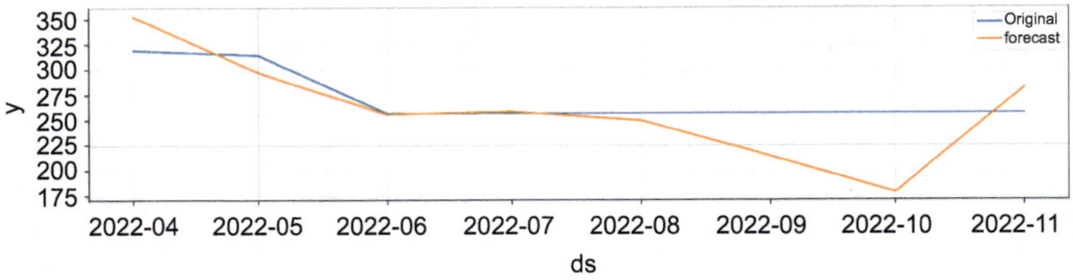

Forecasting: what-if modeling

After developing a forecasting model, the next step is to prepare datasets for future predictions, often requiring imputation to handle missing data points. "What-if" scenario modeling is a widely used imputation method that relies on potential future scenarios informed by industry experts, focusing on anticipated business outcomes rather than detailed domain knowledge. Utilizing these imputation techniques can improve forecast accuracy and support better decision-making, with further exploration of "what-if" modeling to be covered in the subsequent chapters.

Pistachios pricing experiments

Impact of fertilizer prices on California pistachios pricing models

The prices of fertilizers can have a significant impact on the pricing models for California pistachios. Fertilizers are used to provide essential nutrients to the pistachio trees, which help them to grow and produce more pistachios. There are different types of fertilizers that are commonly used in pistachio farming including Phosphate Rock, Dap, Tsp, and urea. Each of these fertilizers has a different cost per metric ton ($/mt),

and changes in these costs can affect the overall cost of growing and producing pistachios. Fluctuations in the prices of fertilizers like phosphate rock and urea can significantly affect the production costs of pistachios, leading to corresponding changes in consumer prices. An increase in phosphate rock prices may drive up production costs and consumer prices, while a decrease in urea prices could lower production costs and consumer prices [29]. Consequently, it is essential to account for these variables when making forecasts or decisions regarding the California pistachio market. As part of the pricing model development, please observe the impact of doubling prices and explain what the impact of fertilizers on the pistachios pricing models is:
- Phosphate rock($/mt)
- Dap($/mt)
- Tsp($/mt)
- Urea($/mt)

Impact of fertilizer prices on California pistachios pricing models

The prices of following variable have a significant impact on the California pistachios pricing. There are several variables that can impact the pricing models for California pistachios. These variables include
- CPIAUCSL – Changes in CPIAUCSL can impact on the overall cost of living, which can affect the demand for pistachios and ultimately their price.
- GEPUCURRENT – This is US gross domestic product (GDP). Changes in GDP can impact on the overall economic conditions, which can affect the demand for pistachios and their price.
- Employment in agriculture (LNS12034560) – Variable measures the number of people employed in the agriculture industry. Changes in employment can impact the supply of pistachios, which can affect their price [280].
- Production Price Index Industry (PCU811310811310) – Variable measures the changes in prices for goods produced in the manufacturing industry. Changes in this index can impact on the cost of producing pistachios, which can affect their price.
- Production Price Index Industry (PCU325311325311) – Variable measures the changes in prices for goods produced in the chemical manufacturing industry. Changes in this index can impact the cost of fertilizers and other chemicals used in pistachio farming, which can affect the cost of producing pistachios and their price.
- RAILFRTCARLOADSD11 – Fluctuations in the number of rail carloads transported can affect the shipping costs and pricing of pistachios in various markets.

Overall, these variables can impact on the pricing models for California pistachios in different ways either by affecting the demand or supply of pistachios or by impacting the cost of producing or transporting them. Develop what-if model on the variables mentioned above for pistachios pricing.

This chapter provides readers the ability to analyze specialty crop pistachios' yield patterns in chief yielding states such as the USA, Turkey, and Iran. Through statistical and mathematical analysis, readers will gain a comprehensive understanding of yield curves for pistachios. Additionally, the chapter covers pistachio pricing models and how to develop a pragmatic pricing model that factors in macroeconomic, climate, and input cost data. Models for predicting and climate modeling are also presented in the chapter, enabling readers to make educated decisions established on data-driven insights. Finally, readers will learn how to develop a machine learning model that factors in macroeconomic data, further enhancing their ability to make effective decisions related to pistachio production and pricing. Overall, this chapter equips readers with the tools and knowledge needed to excel in the pistachio industry.

Section III: **Tomatoes**

Chapter 7
Specialty crops tomatoes: production and yield models

This chapter covers:
- Special types of tomatoes and their yield patterns in different countries
- Nutritional value of tomatoes and their importance for food security
- Factors influencing tomato growth and how to compare production between countries
- The important role of tomatoes in the global economy and job market is highlighted
- Examine the historical yield patterns and RMA payments due to extreme weather
- Weather and other events affecting tomato production in Florida, USA
- Mathematical models used to predict future tomato production in California
  - Tomatoes production model in Plant City, Florida, USA
  - Water use (WU) model: Withlacoochee River and tomatoes production model in Plant City, Florida, USA
- Production and yield patterns of tomatoes in major producing countries are discussed
- Comprehensive understanding of tomato production and projection models for better decision-making and increased profits

In this chapter, we are going to talk about special types of tomatoes and how much they produce in different countries like the United States, Turkey, and India. We'll also look at how nutritious tomatoes are and how important they are for food security. We'll explore what factors affect, how much tomatoes grow, and how we can compare tomato production between different countries. Finally, we'll talk about how weather and other events can affect, and how many tomatoes are produced in Florida, USA. We'll use mathematical models to predict how many tomatoes will be produced in California. By the end of the chapter, you'll have an understanding of decision framework that helps commercialization of tomatoes.

Potatoes and tomatoes are the most commonly consumed vegetables in the USA.

Tomatoes are the world's largest horticultural crop [281] and the second most important vegetable after potatoes [282]. Globally, around 189.134 million tons of fresh tomatoes are produced from 5.1 million hectares. Native to South America, tomatoes spread worldwide following the Spanish colonization of the Americas. Initially deemed poisonous by early American colonists, tomatoes gained popularity by the mid-1800s and are now a staple in the American diet, consumed raw, in dishes and sauces, and in drinks. Products like ketchup, spaghetti sauce, tomato soup, and salsa are common in American kitchens, making tomatoes the second most consumed vegetable in the USA after potatoes. In 2019, the per capita availability of tomatoes was 31.4 pounds, while fresh market and processed tomato consumption were 18.8/18.22 pounds and 59.54/67.42 pounds per capita for 2021/2020, respectively. A reduction in processing tomatoes in California is attributed to drought [283] conditions. The per capita consumption of processed tomatoes far exceeds that of fresh-market tomatoes (Figure 1), with over half of open-field tomato production in the USA serving the foodservice sector. The tomato processing industry in the USA, which primarily produces tomato pastes, sauces, and canned products, operates separately from the fresh-market industry.

Figure 1: Tomatoes.

Tomatoes are not only delicious but also packed with nutritional benefits, including rich sources of vitamin C, vitamin A, and antioxidants. They have garnered attention for their high lycopene content, a powerful antioxidant known for its cancer-protective properties. Additionally, tomatoes are loaded with other essential nutrients such as vitamin B, potassium, iron, and calcium, with a medium ripe tomato providing up to 40% of the Recommended Daily Allowance of Vitamin C and 20% of Vitamin A. There are two primary types of tomatoes: determinate and indeterminate. Most commercial varieties are determinate, meaning they have a set period for flowering and fruiting. In contrast, heirloom garden varieties and greenhouse tomatoes are typically indeterminate, producing flowers and fruit continuous throughout the plant's life [284, 285].

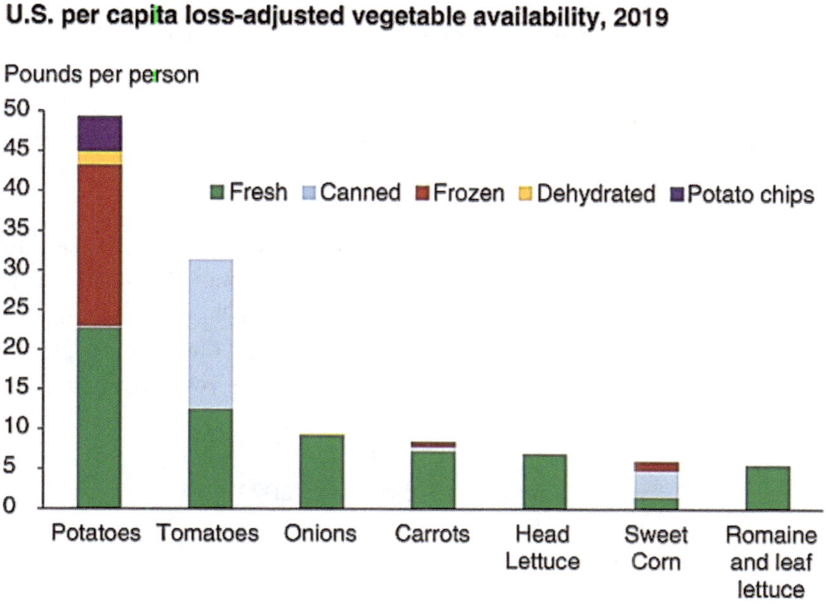

Figure 2: US per capita availability.

Scientifically known as *Solanum lycopersicum*, tomatoes are a globally cherished vegetable native to South and Central America, often debated as either fruits or vegetables. While nutritionists classify them as vegetables (Figure 2) for their nutritional value, botanists consider them fruits due to their development from the plant's ovary and seed content; other popular vegetables include potatoes, onions, chilies, and peppers.

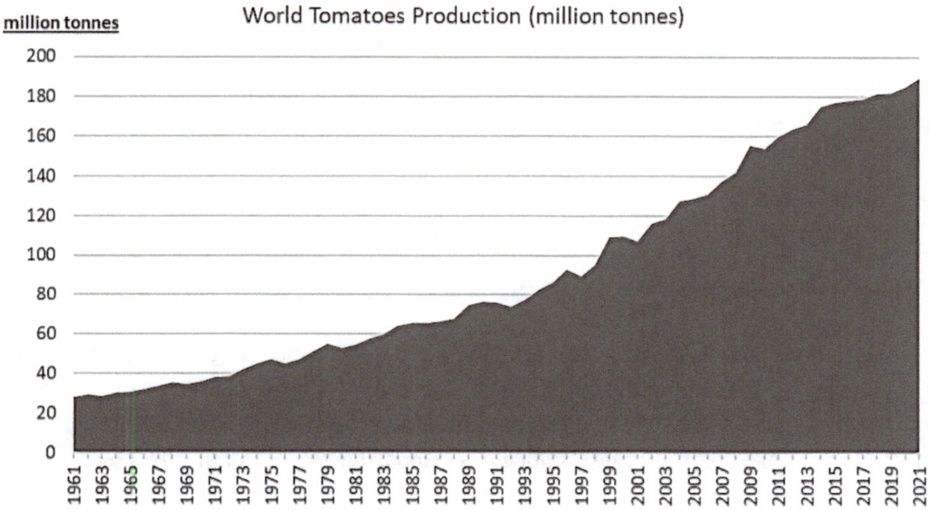

Figure 3: World tomatoes production.

Tomatoes are cultivated worldwide, including in Africa, North America, China, and Asia, and are a key ingredient in many dishes due to their delicious flavor. The Food and Agriculture Organization (FAO) reported that global tomato production exceeded 378 billion pounds (189 million tons) in 2021, covering 12.76 million acres (5.17 million hectares) of farmland, with a consistent increase of over 23% since 2010 [286] (Figures 2 and 3).

China is the leading producer of tomatoes globally, followed by India, Turkey, the USA, Italy, Egypt, Spain, and Mexico, which together account for about 71% of the world's tomato production (Figure 4). In terms of exports, Mexico is the largest exporter, with the Netherlands and Spain also contributing significantly; in 2021, these three countries accounted for 25.89%, 18.61%, and 9.22% of global tomato exports, respectively, totaling $8.694 billion [286].

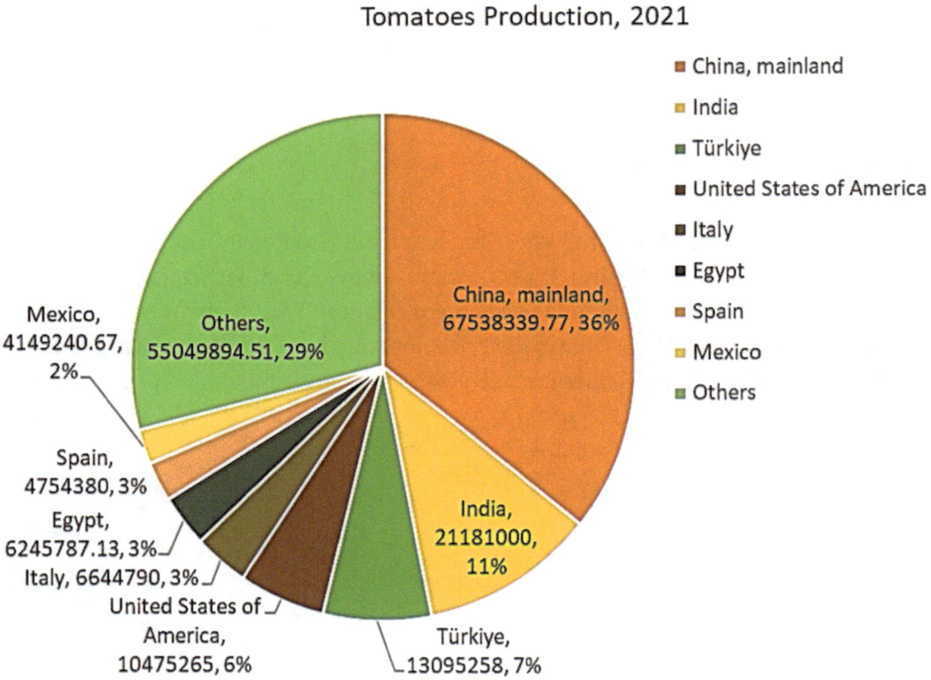

Figure 4: Major tomato producing countries.

In 2021, the United States produced roughly 20.95 billion pounds (10.47 million tons) of tomatoes, with *fresh tomatoes* making up only 8% of this production and valued at *$1.50 billion*, compared to *$1.39 billion* for *processed tomatoes*. Florida and California lead in fresh tomato production, while *California is responsible for 95% of the processed tomato output in the USA* [286].

California is responsible for 95% of the processed tomato output in the United States.

In 2021, China was the world's largest tomato producer (Figure 5), contributing 36% of global production, amounting to approximately 135.07 billion pounds (67.538 million tons) valued at $35.52 billion. Xinjiang led this production due to its optimal geographic conditions, including ample sunshine and significant temperature variations conducive to tomato growth [287].

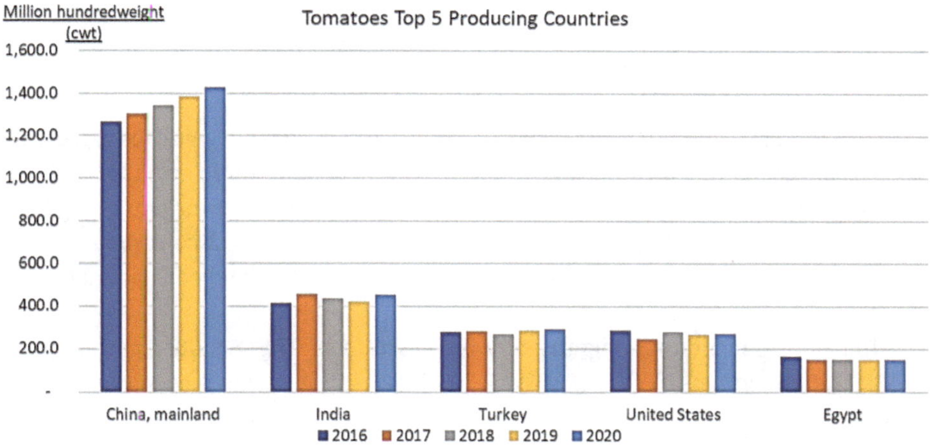

Figure 5: Tomato top 5 producing countries.

In 2021, India was the second-largest tomato producer globally, contributing 11% of the world's supply with around 42.36 billion pounds (21.181 million tons). The leading tomato-producing states were Madhya Pradesh, Andhra Pradesh, and Karnataka, with most of the produce used domestically and only a small fraction exported.

In 2021, Turkey was the third largest tomato producer globally, contributing 7% of the world's supply with around 26.19 billion pounds (13.095 million tons). The country employs contract farming, particularly in the Marmara Region, for *tomato paste production, ensuring quality and sales through preseason agreements, while techniques like drip irrigation have improved productivity* [288].

The global tomato industry has seen significant growth due to the health benefits of tomatoes, including their high vitamin C, potassium, and antioxidant content, particularly lycopene, which is linked to reduced risks of heart disease and certain cancers. Tomatoes are a key component in the food processing industry and are fundamental to cuisines worldwide, making them a staple ingredient that impacts various cultures and everyday life.

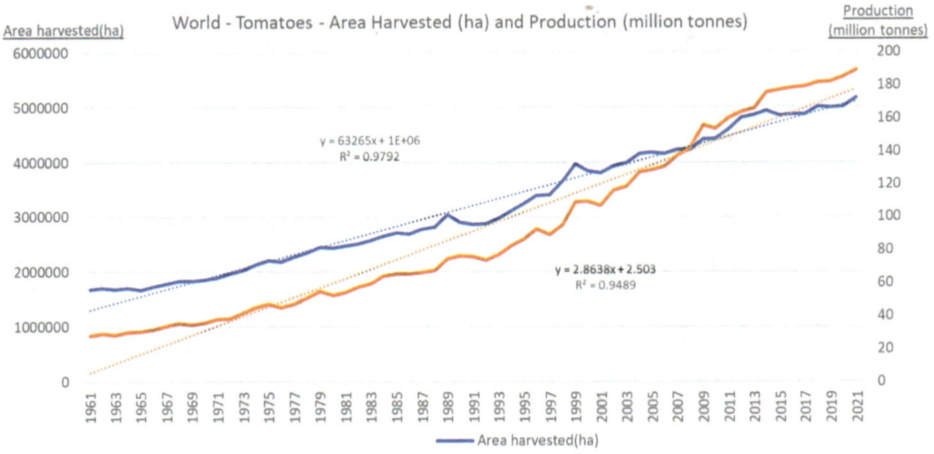

Figure 6: World tomatoes (area harvest and production).

Globally, the area harvested for tomatoes (Figure 6) expanded significantly, growing from 1,680,450 ha in 1961 to 5,167,388 ha in 2021. A notable surge occurred in 1999, with an increase of 3,967,072 ha, as farmers planted more tomatoes for processing than usual[1] [289]. Statistically, the area harvested outgrowth rate could be consistently fitted/described with an exponential ($R^2 = 0.9838$), linear ($R^2 = 0.9792$), and polynomial regression type ($R^2 = 0.9944$; eq. (1)).

Tomato production has significantly increased from 27.617 million tons in 1961 to 189.133 million tons in 2021 (FAOSTAT 2023), driven by raising recognition of their nutritional benefits. In response, governments worldwide have boosted tomato production to ensure food security, with varieties like Alicante, Azoychka, and Aunt Ruby's German Green standing out among the over 10,000 cultivated types [290].

Tomato yields have significantly increased from 164,346 hectograms per hectare (hg/ha) in 1961 to 366,015 hg/ha in 2021, with the production trend effectively modeled by a linear classifier and depicted by a multinomial Order 6 yield model (eqs. (2) and (3)).

$$Y_{\text{Area harvested}} = 63265x + 1\text{E}{+}06 \tag{1}$$

$$Y_{\text{Production}} = 2.8638x + 2.503 \tag{2}$$

$$Y_{\text{Yield}} = -7\text{E}{-}05x^6 + 0.0094x^5 - 0.4727x^4 + 11.286x^3 - 147.66x^2 + 4035.4x + 161006 \tag{3}$$

1 Record tomato harvest may stretch into November- https://www.recordnet.com/story/business/1999/10/16/record-tomato-harvest-may-stretch/50804771007/

The value of eqs. (1) through (3) is to prepare future imputation datasets for predicting the influence of climate change and the price that I cover in the subsequent chapters.

Please note that except power regression trend fit, the area harvested regression types (linear, exponential, logarithmic, and polynomial) have higher accuracy (Figure 7).

Tomatoes Harvested	Equation	R^2
Exponential	$y = 2E + 06e^{0.0206x}$	$R^2 = 0.9838$
Linear	$y = 63265x + 1E + 06$	$R^2 = 0.9792$
Logarthimic	$y = 1E + 06\ln(x) - 182667$	$R^2 = 0.725$
Polynomial order 6	$y = 0.0021x^6 - 0.4167x^5 + 30.821x^4 - 1068.3x^3 + 18163x^2 - 91907x + 2E + 06$	$\mathbf{R^2 = 0.9944}$
Power	$y = 939111x^{0.3679}$	$R^2 = 0.8707$

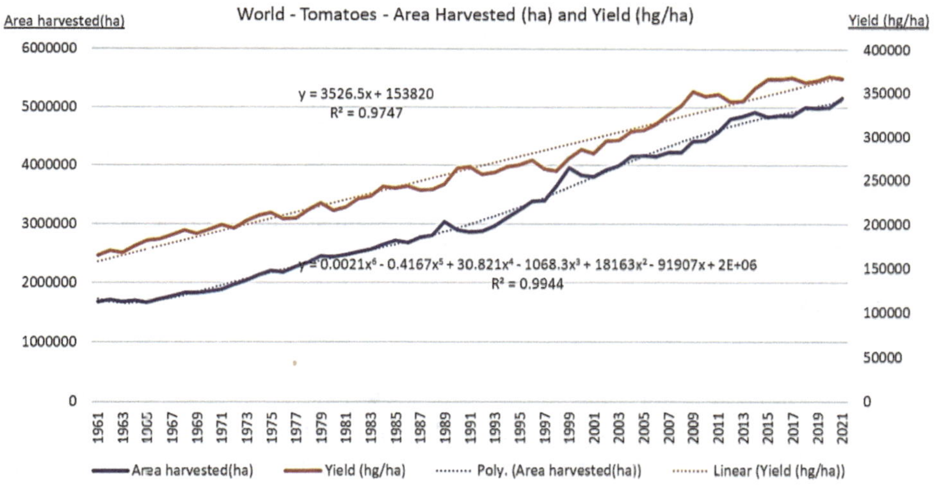

Figure 7: World tomatoes area harvest and yield.

Production: We can use different types of regression models to analyze tomato production data. Except for the logarithmic regression model, all other types of regression models provide a higher accuracy of more than 86%.

Tomatoes production	Equation	R^2 value
Exponential	$y = 26.653e^{0.0341x}$	$R^2 = 0.9863$
Linear	$y = 2.8638x + 2.503$	$R^2 = 0.9489$
Logarthimic	$y = 46.754\ \ln(x) - 56.445$	$R^2 = 0.6526$
Polynomial order 6	$Y = 0.0389x^2 + 0.4496x + 27.852$	$\mathbf{R^2 = 0.9924}$
Power	$y = 11.095x^{0.6123}$	$R^2 = 0.8782$

Area harvested & production: Over the past three decades, the worldwide total acreage of tomatoes has experienced a remarkable increase of 32.31%, 15.52%, and 12.93% between 1990–1999, 2000–2009, and 2010–2019, respectively, with the total harvested output (production) rising by over 43%, 40.4%, and 20.35% in the same periods. The increase in the first two decades exceeded 40%, a significant feat for the agricultural industry. However, the last decade, 2010–2019, saw a drop in the growth rate due to extreme temperatures and the effects of climate change.

Yield curve: Commercial tomatoes farms ensure, during harvest, mechanized machines pick the harvest and tomatoes never touch the ground to avoid contamination [291]. Smallholder farmers, on the other hand, still employ manual steps to pick tomatoes harvest. Hence, one tend to see huge variance in agricultural employment between these two models of farming and operations. The worldwide tomatoes yield could be observed using eq. (4). Except polynomial order ^{6}(99.08%), all other regression trend types exhibit lower R^2 values:

Cosmetics: Of every dozen-plus fruit, only a few had minor cosmetic blemishing on the skin, which usually occurred where the tomatoes contacted the soil [11].

$$Y_{\text{yield}} = -7E{-}05x^6 + 0.0094x^5 - 0.4727x^4 + 11.286x^3 - 147.66x^2 + 4035.4x + 161{,}006 \quad (4)$$

Yield is influenced by wind, rain, cold, heat, frost, fertilizer timing, water quality, bearing, nonbearing, and age of the trees.

The bloom period is influenced by factors such as wind, rain, cold, and heat, which subsequently affect yield assessments. Similarly, the harvest season is dependent on accumulated heat units, irrigation water availability, and the overall growing conditions. These elements collectively determine the size, timing, duration, and quality of the harvest [292]. Yield curves are representative of nature, phenology, climate, botany, human labor, and soil engineering.

Other yield curves:

Tomatoes yield	Equation	R^2 value
Exponential	$y = 167877e^{0.0136x}$	$R^2 = 0.984$
Linear	$y = 3526.5x + 153820$	$R^2 = 0.9747$
Logarthimic	$y = 60762 \ln(x) + 71156$	$R^2 = 0.7467$
Polynomial order 6	$y = -7E{-}05x^6 + 0.0094x^5 - 0.4727x^4 + 11.286x^3 - 147.66x^2 + 4035.4x + 161006$	$\mathbf{R^2 = 0.9908}$
Power	$y = 118140x^{0.2444}$	$R^2 = 0.8425$

The other factors that impact yield include climate change, weather, fertilizers, water, and human labor availability (Figure 8).

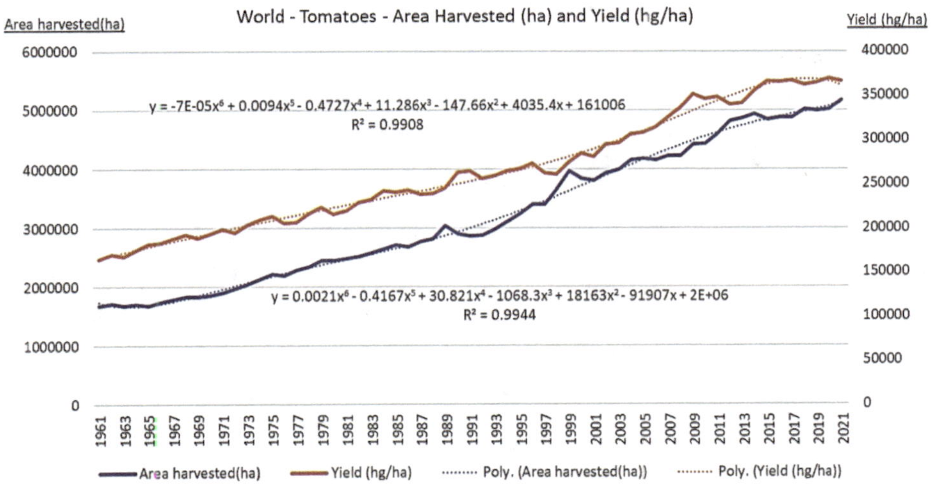

Figure 8: World tomatoes yield.

Area harvested and yield: As stated prior, the worldwide total acreage of tomatoes increased by 36.72%, 15.23%, and 12.61% between 1990–1999, 2000–2009, and 2010–2019, respectively, and the yield increased by over 4.4%, 23.45%, and 5.19% in the same periods. The decade of 2000–2009 was considered a high yield decade for tomatoes production the world.

Top producing countries

Tomatoes are perennial plants grown as annuals in the USA due to their frost sensitivity, preventing continuous outdoor growth. They take about 75 days from transplanting to the first harvest and thrive in daytime temperatures of 70–85 °F and nighttime temperatures of 65–70 °F. These self-pollinating plants rely on wind currents for effective pollination when grown outdoors [284].

In Turkey, tomatoes account for 40% of the total vegetable production, grown primarily in open fields and greenhouses. Vegetables make up 96% of greenhouse cultivation, with tomatoes being produced in half of these greenhouses. The pricing of tomatoes differs notably between open fields and greenhouses due to variations in energy costs, solar radiation, and quality [293].

International exposition[2]

In 1899, Campbell's was invited to participate in the 1900 Paris International Exposition, a grand world fair showcasing the century's achievements and innovations, which included a soup competition!

China

China is the world's largest producer of tomatoes, contributing 36% of global production in 2021 with approximately 135.07 billion pounds (67.538 million tons) valued at $35.52 billion. Major tomato-producing provinces include (Figure 9) Shandong, Xinjiang, Hebei, and Henan, which accounted for about 55% of China's total production in 2006. Xinjiang has emerged as the top producer due to its optimal geographic conditions such as its latitude, abundant sunshine, and significant temperature variations.

Fresh tomatoes are available year-round in China, produced in greenhouses, open fields, or under plastic covers depending on the season. In 2006, open fields accounted for 50% of tomato production, greenhouses for 40%, and plastic-covered areas for 10%. Despite technological advancements, labor concerns have led to Xinjiang's tomato products being labeled "high-risk" under the Uygur Forced Labour Prevention Act, affecting its significant role in the global supply chain [284, 287].

2 Campbell soup -: https://www.campbellsoupcompany.com/newsroom/news/the-new-campbells-condensed-soup/

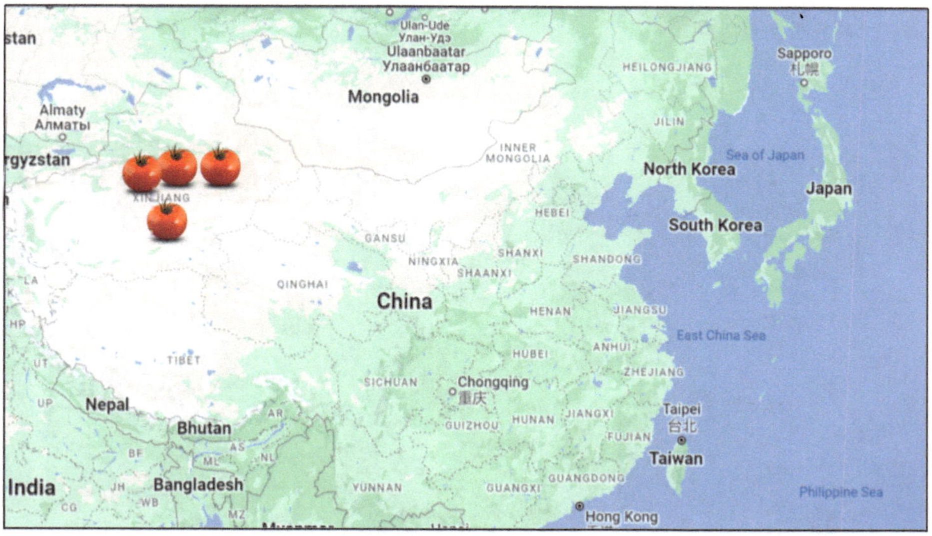

Figure 9: China major tomato-producing provinces.

India

Tomatoes are the most widely cultivated vegetable crop in India, grown for both fresh consumption and processing due to their essential nutrients and popularity in households. However, their perishable nature and susceptibility to weather and supply disruptions limit interstate trade, causing temporary price spikes during shortages. Farmers often face local gluts and significant price volatility due to challenges in safely reaching demand centers, leading to substantial fluctuations in prices [295].

Agriculture plays a crucial role in India's economy, employing over half of the workforce and contributing significantly to the gross value-added. The government has taken steps to promote sustainable farming, improve farmers' incomes, and encourage specialty crop cultivation. As the second largest vegetable producer globally, India excels in producing okra and ranks second in the world for several other vegetables like potatoes, tomatoes, onions, and more [296].

In India, tomatoes are mainly grown during the rainy season (August to October) and the winter season (December to April). Some regions also cultivate tomatoes in the summer (May to July) using protected methods, but this results in lower production volumes and higher prices [296. The primary harvesting period from December to April typically leads to lower prices, while prices rise from July to November [297]. Weather disruptions during the production cycle can cause price spikes, affecting both consumers and producers. Additionally, local production gluts during the main seasons often lead to market oversupply [298] and logistical issues, resulting in price drops and significant losses for farmers [299].

Figure 10: India major tomato-producing states.

The top tomatoes producing states of India include Madhya Pradesh 2.97 million tons (14.63%), Andhra Pradesh 2.21 million tons (10.92%), and Karnataka 2.07 million tons (10.23%) (Figure 10). The three states contributed to 35.78% of total tomatoes production (16.08 million tons) in India 2021. Please find the locations in below India map.

High temperatures exceeding 40 °C in April and May have severely impacted tomato production in key regions of Maharashtra, causing significant flower and leaf drop. Severe drought conditions in these areas have further exacerbated production issues, highlighting the urgent need for efficient water management techniques for tomato farmers. Implementing irrigated cultivation in dry areas or seasons can optimize water use, improve fruit quality, and prevent losses from improper watering.

In July 2023, several McDonald's outlets in India temporarily removed tomatoes from their menus due to crop challenges caused by unusually high temperatures and a delayed southwest monsoon. This seasonal issue is a recurring challenge for the restaurant and food industry during the monsoon season [299].

Türkiye

Tomatoes, originally from South America and introduced to Turkey during World War I, have become a key part of Turkish agriculture, making Turkey the third largest tomato producer globally (Figure 11).

In 2013, Turkey produced 11.8 million tons of tomatoes, with 67.19% *consumed fresh* and 32.81% *processed into tomato paste*. Approximately 25–30% of the total production was used by the food industry, primarily for making paste, canned tomatoes, soup, ketchup, and juice. Around 100 businesses in the agricultural sector rely on tomatoes, which are essential for human nutrition and used in various forms such as frozen, sauces, pickles, and diced products [300].

Tomatoes are typically grown on small farms of 3–4 ha, with larger operations reaching up to 50 ha, and about 50–60% of production is managed through contracts between processors and growers. Processors supply hybrid seeds or young plants, technical assistance, fertilizers, financial advances, and pesticides, with young plants usually starting in nurseries [301].

When not grown under contract, tomatoes are usually sold to brokers who distribute the best quality ones to the table-tomato market and the rest to processors. Traditionally, the harvest was done manually by migrant laborers[3], often Kurdish families, who moved according to demand. Over the past 5 years, labor shortages have led to a rapid increase in the use of mechanical and electrical harvesting machines, now accounting for about half of the harvest [301]. There are an estimated 150–200 machines in use, primarily in the North near Bandirma, with large operators renting

---

3 turkey-ranks-4th-in-tomato-production-across-the-world – https://www.turkishagrinews.com/turkey-ranks-4th-in-tomato-production-across-the-world/

them out to smaller growers, and major production regions including Antalya, Bursa, and Izmir provinces (Figure 11).

Figure 11: Major tomato-producing provinces.

Labor availability!

The availability of labor has always been a problem in agriculture and dairy industries, both in developing and developed economies. It is a significant cost issue, and many agricultural regions have to choose between growing produce or opting for substitutes because most of the agricultural labor has moved to service and manufacturing industries.

To address this issue, the future of agricultural productivity will include machines that incorporate automation at one level of the value chain to alleviate labor nonavailability. This could include tractors or cow necklace[4] devices that function as a farmer's aide to help with tasks that require manual labor. By using these machines, farmers can increase productivity and reduce the cost of labor.

Author
Chandrasekar Vuppalapati

---

4 Introducing the Class 10 Veterinary Diagnostic Equipment, designed to measure the health of cattle and connect veterinarians remotely to provide data-enabled clinical insights. This innovative product is brought to you by Hanumayamma Innovations and Technologies, Inc., a San Francisco-based company specializing in animal husbandry and data science. With this cutting-edge technology, veterinarians can remotely monitor the health of cattle and provide timely, accurate diagnoses, helping to improve overall herd health and productivity.

The United States of America

In 2015, the United States produced 2.7 billion pounds of fresh tomatoes, meeting about 40% of the domestic demand, with the remaining 60% fulfilled by imports from Mexico and Canada. Over the past two decades, US fresh tomato production (Figure 12) has decreased from 3.9 billion pounds in 2000 to 2.7 billion pounds in 2015, largely due to increased competition from Mexico [286].

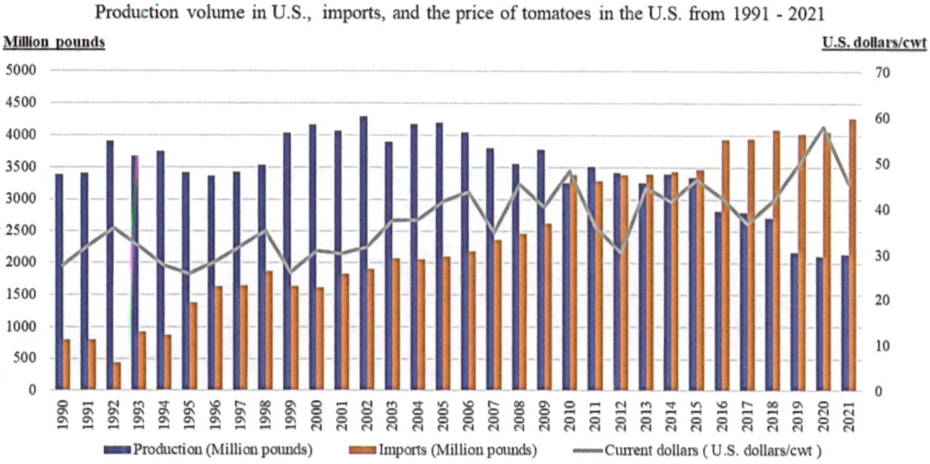

Figure 12: US tomatoes production volume.

California and Florida are the leading producers of fresh tomatoes in the United States, with California growing them year-round except in winter and Florida's production peaking in spring and fall. Other states, including Georgia, North Carolina, Ohio, Tennessee, and Virginia, grow tomatoes in the summer, ensuring a year-round supply (Table 1).

Table 1: Tomatoes for fresh market.

Tomatoes for Fresh Market					
When and	Usual Planting Dates		Usual Harvesting Dates		
Where	Commences	Ends	Commences	Most Active	Ends
Winter					
FL	Nov 1	Dec 1	Dec 1	Dec 15 – Feb 15	Mar 1
Spring					
CA	Jan 15	Mar 1	May 1	May 15 – Jun 30	Jul 31
FL	Dec 1	Mar 15	Apr 1	Apr 1 – May 31	Jul 1
Summer					
CA	Mar 1	Jul 30	Jul 1	Jul 15 – Oct 15	Oct 31
Fall					
CA	Jun 1	Aug 31	Sep 1	Sep 15 – Nov 15	Jan 31
FL	Aug 15	Oct 15	Oct 15	Oct 20 – Dec 20	Dec 31

In 2022, around 200 California farmers produced 95% of the US tomatoes used in canned goods, totaling 10.5 million tons and generating $1.18 billion in revenue, making it the state's eighth largest agricultural commodity [302, 303]. Although 2023 production was initially projected at 12.4 million tons, expectations have decreased due to recent storms (Figure 13).

Tomatoes for Processing					
When and where	Usual Planting dates		Usual Harvesting dates		
	Commences	Ends	Commences	Most Active	End
CA	Jan 1	Mar 31	Jun 1	Jun 25 – Oct 5	Oct 31

Since the tomatoes for processing are grown in open, unlike greenhouses, the climate susceptibility is extremely high for these tomatoes.

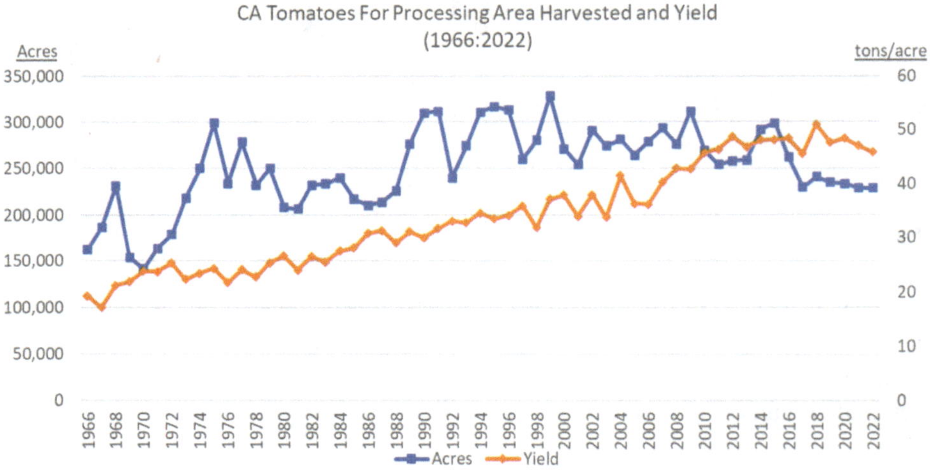

Figure 13: California tomatoes for processing.

The California Tomato Growers Association (CTGA) reported that canning tomato acreage in California was 229,000 acres in both 2021 and 2022, the lowest since 1988. Yields have declined, averaging under 46 tons per acre last year (Figure 14), with total production falling from over 14 million tons in 2015 to under 11 million tons in the past two seasons [304].

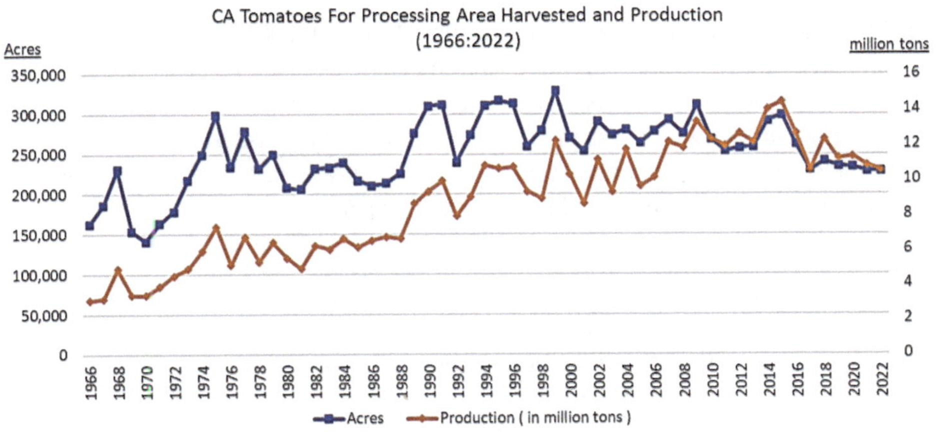

Figure 14: California tomatoes for processing.

In 2023, the price for California canning tomatoes has been set at $138 per ton for conventional crops, a 31% increase from 2022's $105 per ton. The CTGA successfully negotiated this price with the state's canneries including additional premiums of $3–$18 per ton for late-season crops based on delivered tonnage [304] (Figure 15).

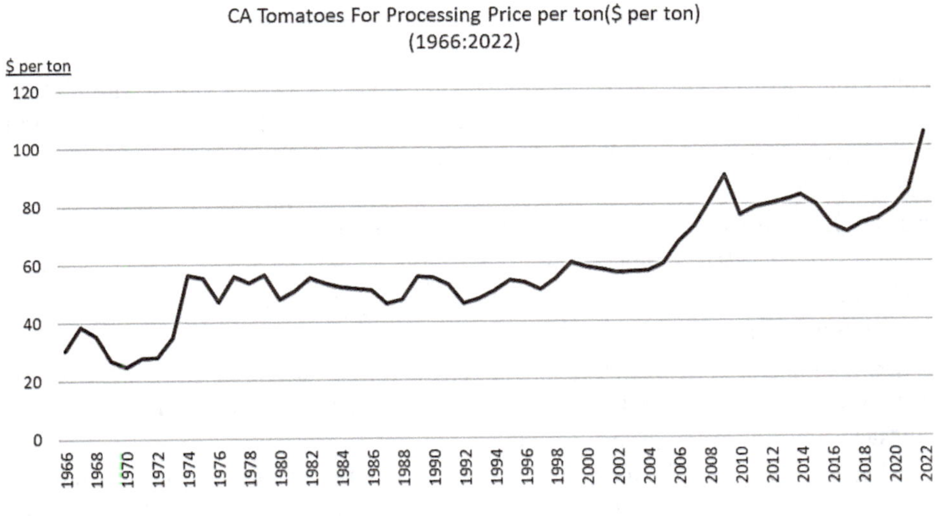

Figure 15: Price per tonne.

The 2004 price increase resulted from the ban on methyl bromide, a fumigant harmful to the ozone layer. The USA, alongside other nations, phased out its production and use, allowing only for critical applications and quarantine preshipment exceptions. A study conducted by the ERS and the University of Florida estimated that this ban could initially lead to annual losses of around $200 million in gross shipping point revenues for both Florida and California, accounting for 20–30% of their revenues from treated commodities, until suitable alternatives are found [305].

The price of processing tomatoes soared in 2009 as a result of strong demand (Figure 15). This price hike was preceded by a nearly 200% rise in export demand in 2008, fueled by a weak US dollar, smaller tomato harvests in Mediterranean regions, and the unpredictable nature of China's production [306].

Price of tomato for processing: machine learning features

- US dollar strength
- Crop size of Mediterranean countries
- China's production
- Fertilizer cost
  - Potash and phosphate
  - Mixed fertilizer
  - Nitrogen
  - Herbicides
- Mixed fertilizer
- Diesel
- Labor
- Equipment
- Repairs

California's prices reflect the rising production costs across North America for all processing vegetables, driven by higher consumer demand for shelf-ready products and increased costs for essentials like fertilizer, fuel, labor, seeds, and equipment [304].

In 2008, export demand surged by nearly 200% due to a weak US dollar, smaller tomato crops in Mediterranean countries, and unpredictable production in China. This summer, staples like ketchup, spaghetti sauce, tomato soup, and salsa may be in short supply and more expensive after record rainfall in California delayed the planting season by 3 weeks, potentially leading to a shortage of tomato-based products [303].

San Joaquin Valley, California's main agricultural region, which is nicknamed "America's salad bowl."

Despite remaining the top state for fresh tomato production, Florida's output has steadily declined since 2000, dropping from 1.56 billion pounds to 950 million pounds by 2015 (Figure 14), alongside a reduction in harvested acreage from 39,400 to 33,000 acres. The average yield also fell from around 40,000 pounds per acre in 2000 to about 28,788 pounds per acre in 2015 (Figure 16), largely due to the ban on the fumigant methyl bromide [306].

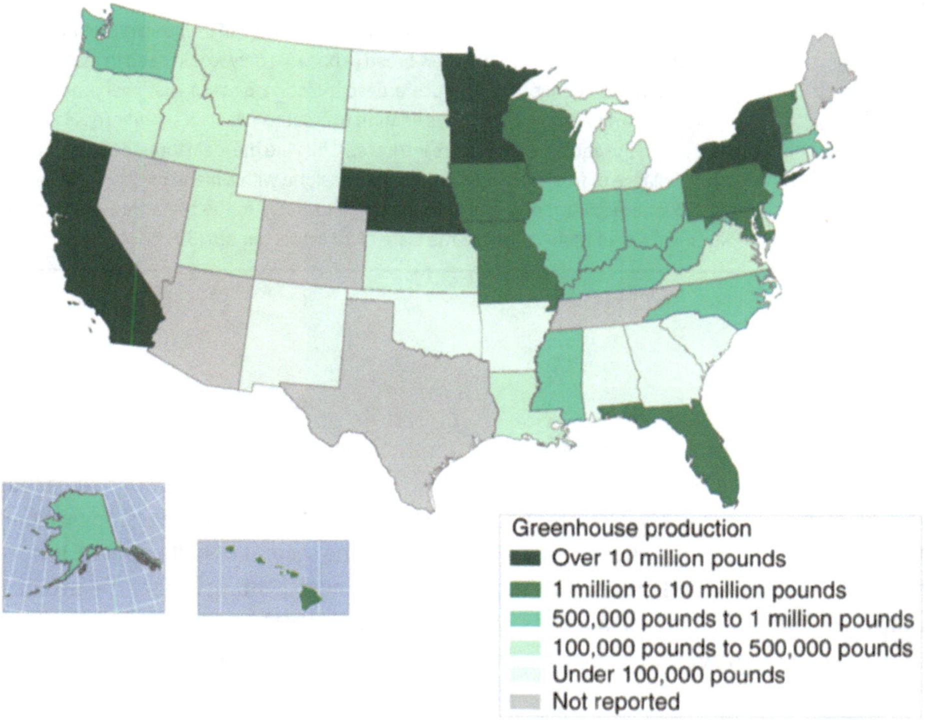

Figure 16: Greenhouse production.

In 2016, Florida and California contributed 76% of US field-grown tomato production, but greenhouse technology has allowed tomato farming to expand to various locations and extend the growing season. Significant greenhouse operations have emerged in states like Nebraska, Minnesota, and New York, offering advantages such as off-season market access and higher yields, despite higher production costs. *Although the United States grows a substantial amount of greenhouse tomatoes domestically, a large portion of consumption is met through imports, with Mexico increasing its share to nearly 84% of greenhouse tomatoes entering the US market since 2004* [307].

California

California is the world's leading producer of processing tomatoes, which are essential for canned goods and commercial kitchens. However, an unprecedented drought is creating a water crisis that threatens this crop and may increase prices for popular products like salsa and spaghetti sauce [283]. In 2021, Fresno County led production with 2.83 million tons, while four other counties – Yolo, Kings, Merced, and Colusa – contributed 71% of the state's total processing tomato tonnage [308, 309].

The tomato flavor is a marvel of complexity, akin to a fine wine in its intricacy. For instance, if a plant breeder aimed to develop a new breed of banana, they would need to incorporate only one signature chemical to produce a decent-tasting banana that everyone would recognize. Similarly, a single chemical is enough to create a flavorful strawberry. However, with tomatoes, the equation is far more intricate. Achieving the ideal tomato taste requires a delicate balance of fructose and citric/malic acid, along with a blend of 19 or 20 different aromatic chemicals. Each of these compounds contributes to the tomato's unique flavor profile, and none of them resemble the taste of an actual tomato [309].

Florida

Florida's 47,500 farms and ranches cover 9.7 million acres and produce a wide variety of safe and reliable food products. The state leads the nation in floriculture sales and the production value of sweet corn, indoor foliage plants, Valencia oranges, sugarcane, fresh market tomatoes, and watermelons, while ranking second in bell peppers, grapefruit, all oranges, strawberries, and non-Valencia oranges [310]. In 2021, the production value for major berries, potatoes, vegetable crops, cantaloupes, and watermelons totaled $1.7 billion, with fresh market tomatoes contributing $324 million despite a 35% drop from the previous year. Florida's tomato industry is struggling due to competition from Mexico, farmland loss to real estate development, and the impact of NAFTA, which has led to a nearly 37% decrease in production since 1991 and a significant increase in cheaper imports (Figure 17).

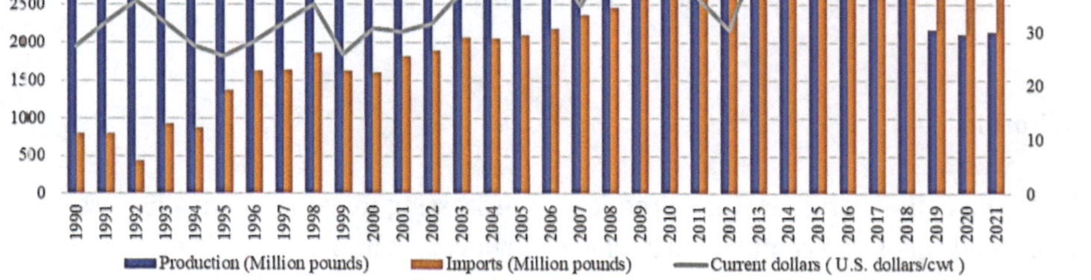

Figure 17: Tomatoes production volume.
(*Source:* USDA-ERS – vegetables and pulses yearbook tables (Table 41 – tomatoes).

The United States mainly imports tomatoes from Mexico and Canada, with Canada's open-field tomatoes available from July to September (Table 2) and greenhouse-grown tomatoes year-round, except January and February. California produces tomatoes from May to November, while Florida's season is from October to June, directly competing with Sinaloa, Mexico's December to April exports and Baja California, Mexico's May to December supplies [310].

Table 2: Tomatoes production.

Country	Places	Open field	Protected condition
USA	California	May to November	Throughout the Year[‡]
	Florida	October to June	
	Other states of the U.S.	July to September	
Mexico	Sinaloa, Mexico	December to April	Throughout the year means all year long, without any breaks or seasonal interruptions.
	Baja California, Mexico	May to December	
Canada		July to September	Throughout the year except extreme cold months that is January and February

Seasonal phenology and climatic requirements

Tomatoes are grown in over 170 countries and thrive in warm temperatures, ideally between 70 °F (21 °C) and 85 °F (29 °C) during the day and 65 °F (18 °C) to 70 °F (21 °C) at night, with extreme temperatures and frost negatively impacting their yield. Rapidly maturing within 90–150 days and being self-pollinating, tomatoes flourish in warm, sunny conditions but are prone to pests, diseases, and fruit rot in high humidity and rainfall (Figure 18).

Tomatoes grow best in well-drained, light loam soil with a pH of 5–7, and require specific fertilizer amounts and adequate watering, with 400–600 mm needed after transplanting. Excessively wet soil can delay planting or reduce yields and increase disease risk, as evidenced by the atmospheric river event in California in winter 2023 [282, 313].

Crop water requirements are determined by the crop factor (K_c) at different growth stages, which is linked to reference evapotranspiration (ETo). Evapotranspiration combines evaporation from soil and surfaces with transpiration from plants. This measurement allows farmers to estimate water usage in their fields, leading to more efficient irrigation planning and is especially crucial in the western USA where irrigation dominates water consumption [314].

Figure 18: Tomatoes production.

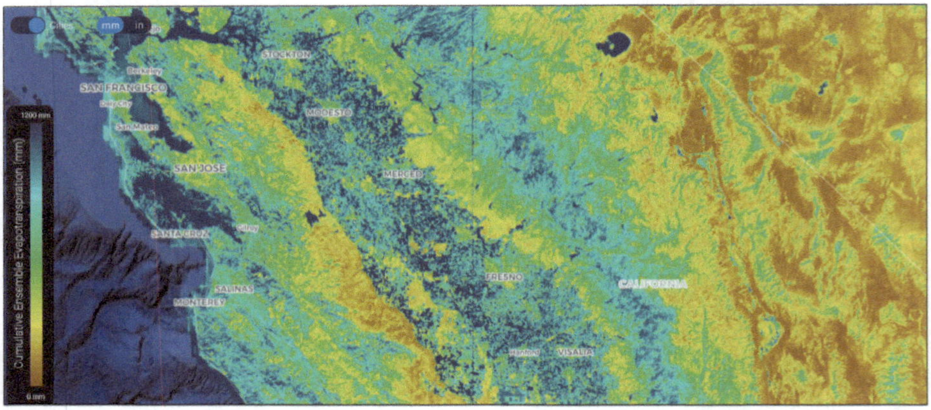

Figure 19: ECOSTRESS Fresno, CA data.[5]

The ECOSTRESS experiment on the International Space Station has an open platform called OpenET, which provides data[6] (Figures 19 and 20).

5 https://explore.etdata.org/custom?#8/36.882/-119.855

6 OpenET – https://explore.etdata.org/custom?#10/36.7736/-119.8705

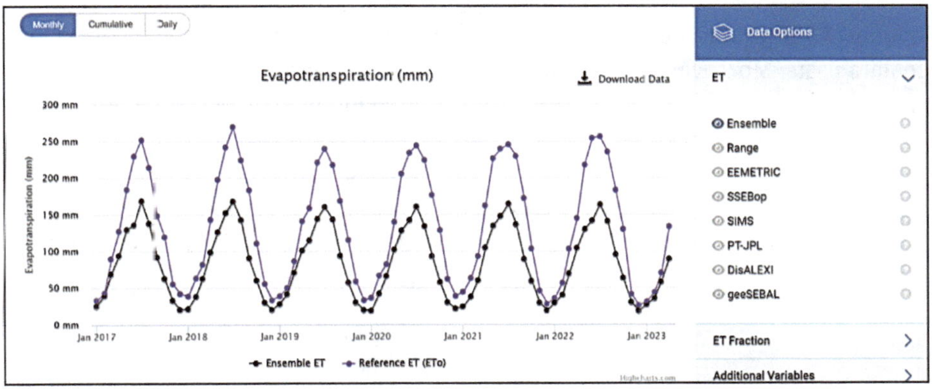

Figure 20: Monthly ECOSTRESS Fresno, CA.

Although the USA grows a substantial amount of greenhouse tomatoes domestically, a large portion of consumption is met through imports, with Mexico increasing its share to nearly 84% of greenhouse tomatoes entering the US market since 2004.

China

Xinjiang is the central hub of China's processed tomato industry, producing over 80% of the country's tomato paste. The region's tomatoes are prized for their vibrant color and high-soluble solid content, attributed to its ideal growing conditions, including abundant sunshine, strong solar radiation, large temperature differences between day and night, and an arid climate [294].

Machine learning features for tomatoes production:
To grow crops effectively, they need plenty of sunshine, typically between 2,500 and 3,500 h per year. It's important that they also receive strong sunshine radiation and experience significant differences between daytime and nighttime temperatures. An arid or dry climate is also ideal for crop growth and development. This means that the weather conditions need to be just right to ensure that crops can grow and thrive.

Author
Chandrasekar Vuppalapati

Tomato processors have recently begun cultivating tomatoes in Inner Mongolia despite its slightly less favorable climate, as a strategy to mitigate risks from adverse weather in Xinjiang Inner Mongolia offers more convenient and cost-effective transportation options, with products easily trucked to Tianjin, the primary export port for China's tomato paste. Moreover, Inner Mongolia's farmers are more responsive to processors' initiatives to expand production compared to those in Xinjiang, which relies solely on railway transport [294].

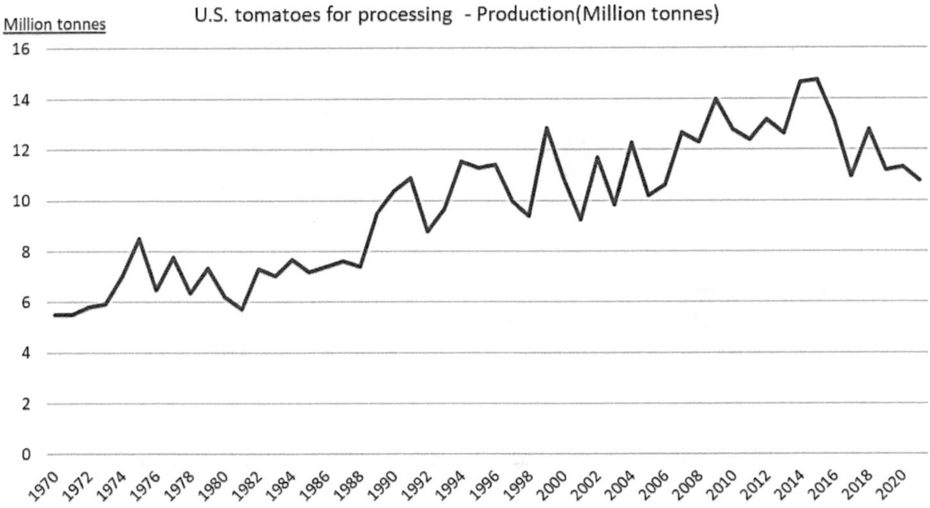

Figure 21: US tomatoes for processing.

US Production, a proxy for the World production, of processing tomato was 11.31 million tons in 2020, which compared 2021, 10.77 million tons, are down, by about 4.75%. China's production of processing tomatoes in the year 2022 was 6.2 million metric tonnes (mT), which is about 16.7% of the worldwide crop. Compared to last year 2021, our production (Figure 21) of processing tomatoes increased by about 29% (the volume last year was 4.8 million tons) [316]:

1. There are several reasons why China's production has increased to this extent. Thirty percent is not a small number. The first reason is the market (Figure 22). The tomato paste market has been going up since last year, providing more incentive to Chinese farmers – they are motivated to plant tomatoes this year.
2. The second reason is that the prices of competing crops have dropped. The major competing crop for tomato is cotton, and the price of cotton in China has dropped by about 30–40%, giving more room to tomatoes.
3. The third reason is that in the past 5–10 years, the use of planting machines and harvesting machines has increased a lot in China. Right now, the Chinese crop is 100% machine-planted and 100% machine-harvested, which is saving a lot on labor. So compared to 5–10 years ago, the labor part of the processing tomato industry has decreased a lot.

4. And the fourth reason is the good cooperation between farmers and processors. They can follow each other, providing advice for each other before the season. So, in the end, processors obtain the required volumes of tomatoes to process, and farmers are getting paid pretty well on time.

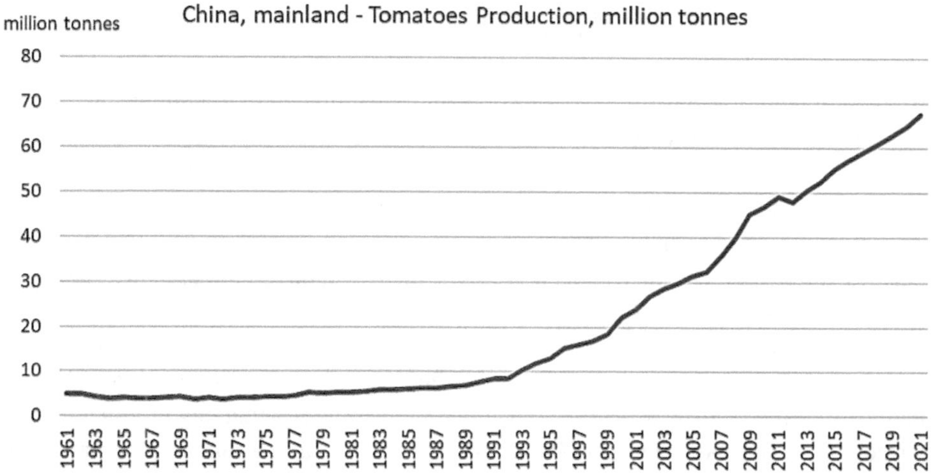

Figure 22: China tomato production.

The reason for increase in production was increase in area harvested (3.4% increase from 2020 to 2021, i.e., from 1,105,513 ha to 1140716 ha – FAOSTAT 2023). The increase in harvest areas was tomato prices fetching higher number as compared to cotton in Xinjiang. Additionally, higher tomato prices helped in increasing more inputs, such as fertilizer and labor. All have positive impact on the yield [294].

India

India grows a wide variety of vegetables across diverse climates, from temperate to humid tropical regions, and from sea level to mountainous areas. These short-duration crops fit well into intensive cropping systems, providing high yields and substantial economic returns for growers. Major tomato-producing states include Andhra Pradesh, Madhya Pradesh, Karnataka, and others, contributing to 90% of the country's tomato production, and India is also a significant exporter of fresh vegetables, including tomatoes, exporting 770,233.19 mT worth Rs. 2,160.72 crores (290.09 USD million) in 2021–2022 [317]:

Table 3: India tomatoes growing season.

India tomatoes growing season		
Region	Transplanting	Harvesting period
Kharif	May–July	July–November
Rabi	October–February	December–June

In India, tomatoes are mainly grown as a Rabi crop (Table 3) in the plains and during the summer and rainy seasons in hilly regions. However, inefficiencies in the logistics network hinder their market value, necessitating improved postharvest management and marketing strategies similar to those used in the dairy industry [295].

Any extreme temperature or weather events during transplanting and harvesting periods would have negative effects. For instance, heatwaves in 2022 have declined tomato and mango crop yields. The scorching heat of the early summer {April–July} in 2022 has severely affected the production of mangoes and tomatoes. According to the Vegetable Growers Association of India, the heatwave has caused the tomato flowers to dry up (given transplanting phenological state), which is impacting production. The Vegetable Growers Association of India also said that due to the change in climatic conditions, pest attack on tomato crop has also gone up. As a result, area that yielded 10 tons of tomatoes earlier is now yielding only 3 tons [312]. Due to extreme weather, the inflated prices can only get normal after July, whereas tomatoes will not cool down until July when the new crop will arrive.

The 4-month monsoon season is crucial for agricultural activities, employment, and food security in India, delivering nearly 70% of the rainfall needed for irrigation and water replenishment, and mitigating extreme heat. With almost half of India's farmland reliant on *the June–September rains, any delay in their arrival can disrupt the planting of essential crops such as rice, cotton, corn, soybean, and sugar cane* [318].

Yield, monsoon, and El Nino connection!
The Indian Meteorological Department has noted that below-average rainfall during most El Nino years leads to severe droughts, significant crop damage, and export restrictions on certain grains [318].

Turkey

Tomato plants are transplanted into fields with microirrigation systems in April, and the harvest in Izmir's southern region begins in mid-July, while in the northern regions, it starts in early August. The season can start as early as late July and end by mid-October, but some growers might not honor their contracts if spot prices are higher than contract prices [301].

Table 4: Turkey tomatoes growing season.

Turkey		
Region	Transplanting	Harvesting period
South near Izmir	April	Mid July–mid October
North	April	August–mid October

The amount of tomatoes harvested in the South has decreased by 20–25%. This is because there has been a drop in the area where tomatoes are grown, and also because of infestations of Tuta absoluta and mildew. In the North, *the temperature has varied widely, and the humidity levels have remained high.* This has led to a decrease in agricultural yields, and many crop protection measures have been needed to address this issue [301].

Accelerated biological clocks in trees: a global phenomenon

In Spain, the weather has been changing, and winters have become more like spring. Past five of six winters were warm. This change in temperature has caused trees, like almond and olive trees, to adjust their hormonal patterns. These trees' natural cycles have been accelerated by 20 days in the past 20 years due to climate change. This same phenomenon is happening to countless other tree species globally. For example, cherry trees in Japan bloomed earlier than they had in the past 1,200 years. Trees are essential for Earth.

Author
Chandrasekar Vuppalapati

Precipitation data is prepared from the Global Historical Climatology Network Monthly dataset (GHCN-M) and the GIEWS. The imputation strategy for preparing precipitation data is from yeidling regression coefficicent between GHCN-M and ECMWF taken from NOAA/FEWSNet.

The United States of America

Tomatoes grow best when the mean daily temperature is between 18 and 25 °C (64.4 and 77 °F), and the night temperatures are between 10 and 20 °C (50 and 68 °F). This means that dry climates are better for growing tomatoes. In California, processing tomatoes are mainly grown in the Central Valley using production centered in several counties including Fresno, Yolo, San Joaquin, Kings, and Colusa. Other counties, such as Merced, Stanislaus, Solano, and Sutter, also produce significant amounts of tomatoes. California, accounting for over 90% of the USA and 35% of the world's tomato production, plants from late January to early June and harvests from late June to October.

California

In California, tomato plants are usually planted in April or May, but high temperatures above 95° in July and August can cause blossoms to wither and halt fruit production [318]. To extend the growing season into late September or beyond, a second crop can be planted in mid- to late June or July, with young plants thriving if regularly watered [319]. Seed germination is influenced by factors like seed condition, water, air, soil conditions, and temperature, with optimal soil temperatures improving success, and a probe-type thermometer recommended for accurate measurement [320].

Table 5: Tomato optimum soil temperature.

	Minimum (°F)	Optimum range (°F)	Maximum (°F)
Tomatoes [41]	50	65-85	105

The time it takes for vegetable seeds to sprout varies with temperature, with optimal soil temperatures ensuring quicker germination, while extreme temperatures can delay or prevent it. For example, tomato seeds germinate in 6–8 days at 65–85 °F but may take over 40 days at 50 °F (Table 5) and are unlikely to germinate at 104 °F [321] (Table 6).

Table 6: Temperature to number of days.

	32°F	41°F	50°F	59°F	68°F	77°F	86°F	95°F	104°F
Tomatoes [41]	0.0	0.0	42.9	13.6	8.2	5.9	5.9	9.2	0.0

Record wet winter could result in planting delays in California. Atmospheric river during winter 2023 has resulted grounds in Petaluma too wet for tomato plantation. As a result, many farmers have to resort to keeping plants in greenhouse before transplanting them to the fields [313].

Rising temperatures are expected to decrease global yields of "processing tomatoes," used in products like ketchup, by 6% by 2050 compared to the 1990–2009 baseline, with Italy being notably affected. Since these tomatoes are typically grown in open fields rather than controlled greenhouse environments, they are particularly vulnerable to climate change [322].

Please find precipitation (inches), minimum temperature, maximum temperature, and average temperature for Fresno, California, one of the major growing regions of pistachios. Average precipitation is 0.92 in – 1980:2023 (Figure 23).

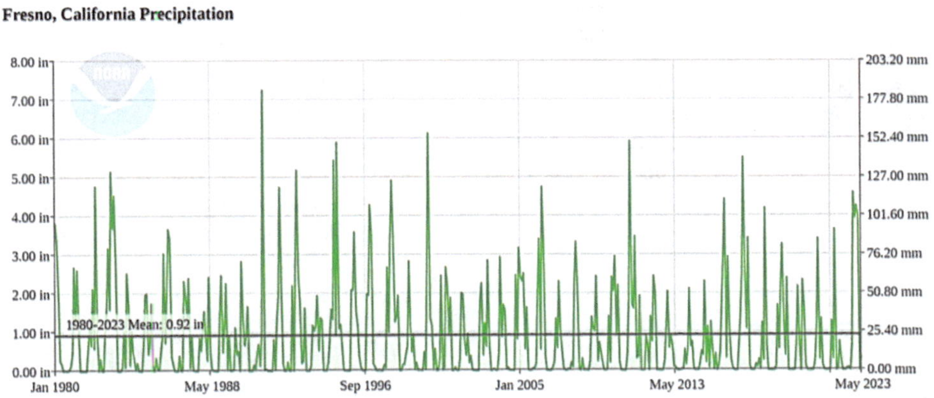

Figure 23: Fresno, Californa precipitation.

To understand how to maximize tomato production and yield, it's important to consider weather patterns, climatology, and agricultural calendars. In most production areas, good weather conditions during the flowering period are essential for successful tomato production. However, in March, there were widespread frosts that impacted several areas of production. Despite these challenges, rainfall has generally been above average, which benefits the vegetative growth of trees. This favorable weather has also led to a low occurrence of fungal diseases. Additionally, some areas have implemented rotation in production, which can help to improve overall yield and production.

Pistachio trees are an excellent option for organic gardeners because they have very few pests. This means that gardeners can grow pistachio trees without the need for harmful pesticides or other chemicals. The trees are naturally resistant to many pests, making them easy to care for and maintain. Organic gardeners can enjoy the benefits of growing pistachios without worrying about harming the environment or their health [323].

Tomato yield curves

Yield curves provide valuable insights, such as data signatures and correlation analysis, and guide the appropriate regression or trend for future data imputation, which is crucial for econometric linkage and pricing analysis. This chapter explores yield curves to uncover historical trends and offer predictive trends alongside climate models, benefiting small to mid-level farming communities worldwide.

Maximizing profitability in agriculture: The role of high-yield plant varieties.

To achieve maximum profitability in agriculture, it's important to prioritize yield profit and cultivate superior plant varieties. Simply expanding planting areas to increase production may not necessarily lead to an overall increase in yield profits. This is because planting more crops does not always result in more profits if the yield per crop is low. Instead, it's important to focus on cultivating high-quality plant varieties that produce a high yield per crop. By doing so, farmers can maximize their profits while also maintaining sustainable agricultural practices.

China

The data (Figure 24) shows increase in tomato land areas in China has increased over the past decade, from 525,504.4 ha from 1961 to 2020 to 1,019,000 ha from 2010 to 2020. This is a significant increase of 14.75%. Tomato cultivation land data is positively skewed, favoring larger areas. The minimum area used for tomato cultivation is 150,000 ha, the maximum is 1,140,716 ha, and the mean is 525,502.41 ha. The median, which is the middle value, is 304,000 ha, and the mode, which is the most common value, is 300,000 ha. The data has a large range of 990,716 ha, a variance of 118,623,163,025.45, and a standard deviation of 344,417.14. Positively skewed distribution means the mean exceeds mode and median [328].

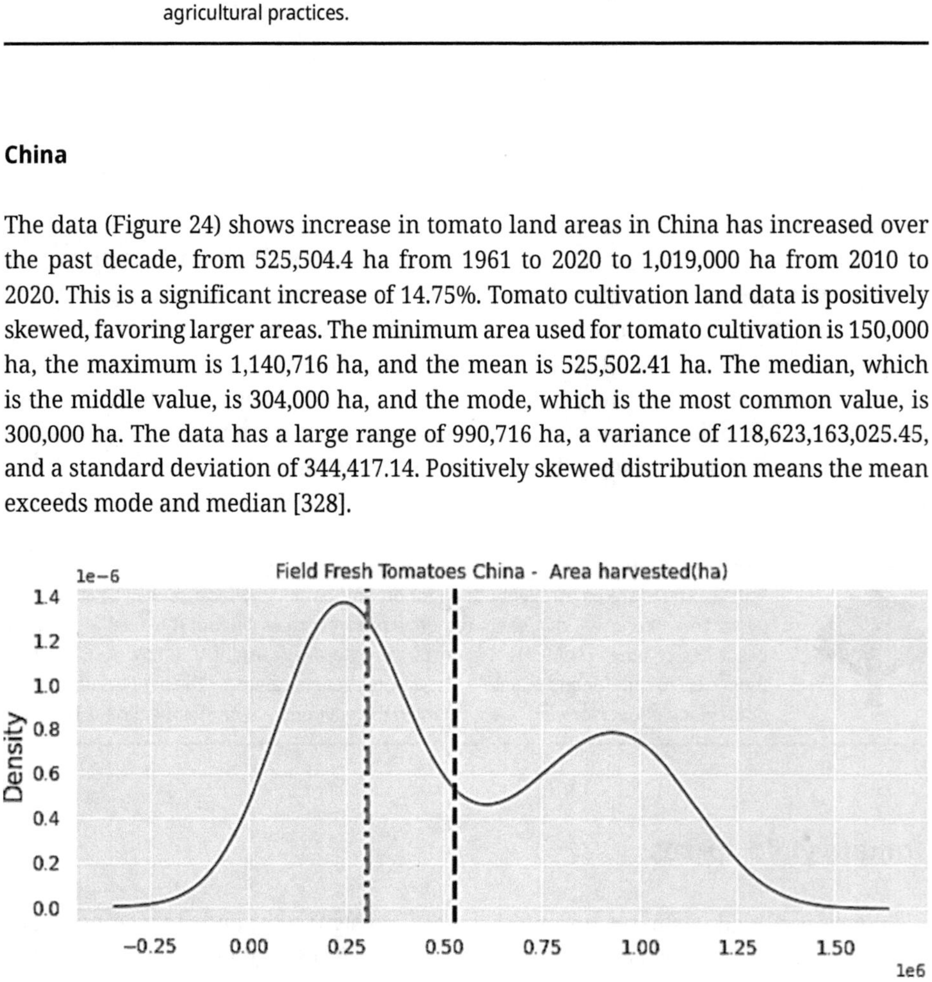

Figure 24: Field fresh tomatoes in China – area harvest.

The data shows that tomato production in China has increased significantly in recent years. From 1961 to 2020, the average tomato production was 19.82 million tons, but from 2010 to 2020, the average was 55.22 million tons, which is a 34.45% increase

(Figure 25). The data on tomato production is positively skewed, meaning that there are more tonnes of tomatoes produced at the higher end of the range. The minimum production is 3,645,000 tons, the maximum is 67,538,339.77 tons, and the mean is 20,610,669.36 tons. The median, which is the middle value, is 8,250,000 tons, and the mode, which is the most common value, is 4,000,000 tons. The data has a large range of 63,893,339.77 tons, a variance of 33,203,475,181,562.57, and a standard deviation of 5,763,827.44. Mean exceeds mode and median in positive skew [328].

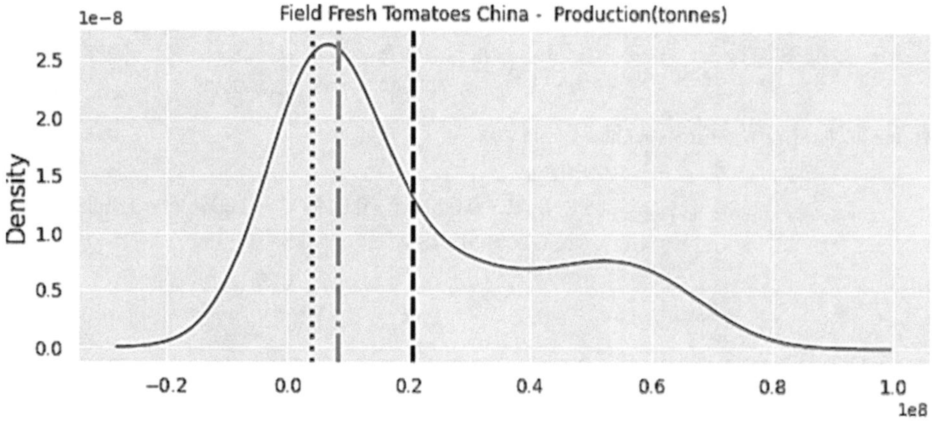

Figure 25: Field fresh tomatoes in China – production.

The data shows that the average yield of tomatoes in China has increased by 17.15% from 2010 to 2020. The average yield during this period was 539,954 hg/ha. The data on tomato yield is positively skewed (Figure 26), meaning that there are more hectares of land with higher tomato yields in the data. The minimum yield is 160,000 hg/ha, the maximum is 592,070 hg/ha, and the mean is 315,138.41 hg/ha. The median, which is the middle value, is 245,455 hg/ha, and the mode, which is the most common value, is 160,000 hg/ha. The data has a range of 432,070 hg/ha, a variance of 46,347,402,926.07, and a standard deviation of 215,192.06. Mean exceeds mode and median in positive skew.

When analyzing the trend of the area used for tomato cultivation in China, an exponential growth model or a polynomial order 6 model provides the best fit. These models have R^2 values of 92.26% and 98.87%, respectively. R^2 shows fit; 1 indicates perfect fit. Therefore, a trendline with an R^2 value closer to 1 is more reliable than one with a lower value. Other trend fittings, such as linear or quadratic, result in lower R^2 values and are therefore not as reliable in predicting the trend of the area used for tomato cultivation in China (Figure 27):

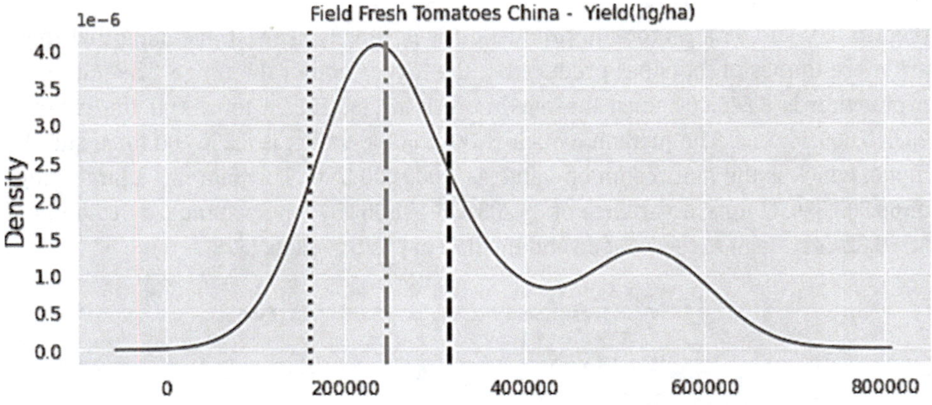

Figure 26: Field fresh tomatoes in China – yield.

$$Y_{\text{China field fresh tomatoes area harvest}} = 2E{-}06x^6 - 0.0003x^5 + 0.0197x^4 - 0.6056x^3 + 9.5039x^2 - 72.564x + 391.78$$

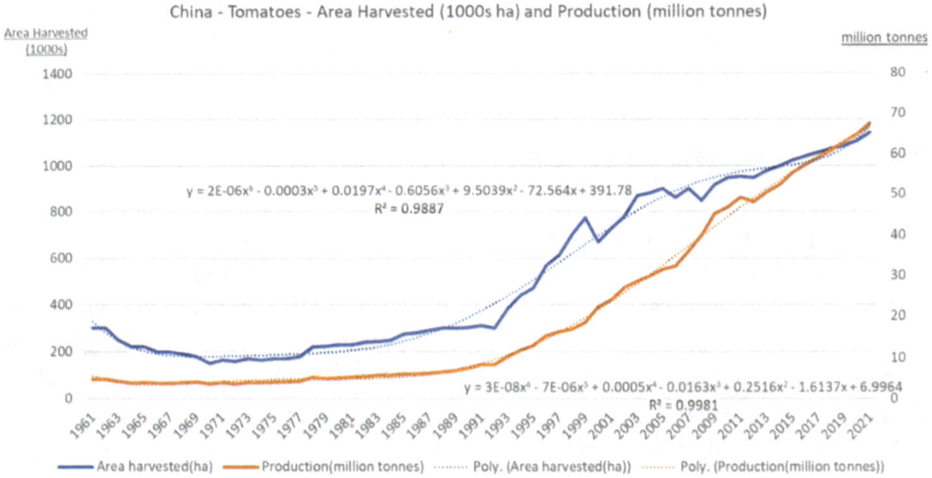

Figure 27: China field fresh tomatoes area harvest and production.

China field tomatoes area harvested	Trend line	R^2 fitting
Exponential	$y = 133.35e^{0.0367x}$	$\mathbf{R^2 = 0.9226}$
Linear	$y = 18.082x - 35.055$	$R^2 = 0.8687$
Logarthimic	$y = 273.5\ln(x) - 338.66$	$R^2 = 0.5128$
Polynomial order 6	$Y = 2E{-}06x^6 - 0.0003x^5 + 0.0197x^4 - 0.6056x^3 + 9.5039x^2 - 72.564x + 391.78$	$\mathbf{R^2 = 0.9887}$
Power	$y = 70.152x^{0.5637}$	$R^2 = 0.758$

To analyze the trend of tomato production in China, an exponential or polynomial order 6 model provides a better fit for the data. These models have R^2 values of 0.9759 and 0.9981, indicating near-perfect trendline fits, with 1 representing a perfect fit. Therefore, a trendline with an R^2 value closer to 1 is more reliable than one with a lower value. The exponential or polynomial order 6 models provide a better fit for the data compared to other trend fittings, such as linear or quadratic models, which have lower R^2 values and are less reliable in predicting the trend of tomato production in China:

$$Y_{\text{production}} = 9\text{E}{-}09x^6 - 1\text{E}{-}05x^5 + 0.0305x^4 - 0.0763x^3 + 0.2226x^2 - 1.3437x + 9.9964$$

China field fresh tomatoes production	Trendline	R^2 fitting values
Exponential	$y = 2.0989e^{0.0567x}$	**$R^2 = 0.9759$**
Linear	$y = 1.0466x - 11.834$	$R^2 = 0.8118$
Logarthimic	$y = 15.428 \ln(x) - 28.136$	$R^2 = 0.4552$
Polynomial order 6	$Y = 9\text{E}{-}09x^6 - 1\text{E}{-}05x^5 + 0.0305x^4 - 0.0763x^3 + 0.2226x^2 - 1.3437x + 9.9964$	**$R^2 = 0.9981$**
Power	$y = 0.712x^{0.8982}$	$R^2 = 0.7869$

In summary, the total area of land used for tomato cultivation in China has increased significantly over the past few decades. From 1990 to 1999, there was a 154.93% increase, from 2000 to 2009, there was a 36.82% increase, and from 2010 to 2019, there was a 14.75% increase. Similarly, the total tomato production in China has also increased by over 146%, 103.9%, and 34.45% in the same periods, except for the last decade where the increase was lower. The increase in tomato production was over 100% in all the previous decades due to various reasons. However, in the last decade, there was a drop in the rate of increase, which could be attributed to the imposition of the Uyghur Forced Labor Prevention Act.

China has experienced significant growth in the cultivation and production of tomatoes. The area of land used for tomato cultivation and the amount of tomatoes produced has increased rapidly over the years. This growth could be described as explosive as it has been very significant and has happened quickly.

Author
Chandrasekar Vuppalapati

The yield of tomatoes in China has been growing rapidly and exponentially over time. A sixth-order polynomial model, with an R^2 value of 98.06%, provides an accurate fit for predicting tomato yields. Therefore, a trendline with an R^2 value closer to 1 is more reliable than one with a lower value. The polynomial order 6 model provides a better fit for the data compared to other trend fittings, such as linear or quadratic models, which have lower R^2 values and are less reliable in predicting the yield of tomatoes in China (Figure 28):

$$y = -6E{-}02x^6 - 1E{-}08x^5 + 0.0092x^4 - 0.021x^3 - 0.0792x^2 + 21.643x + 298.05$$

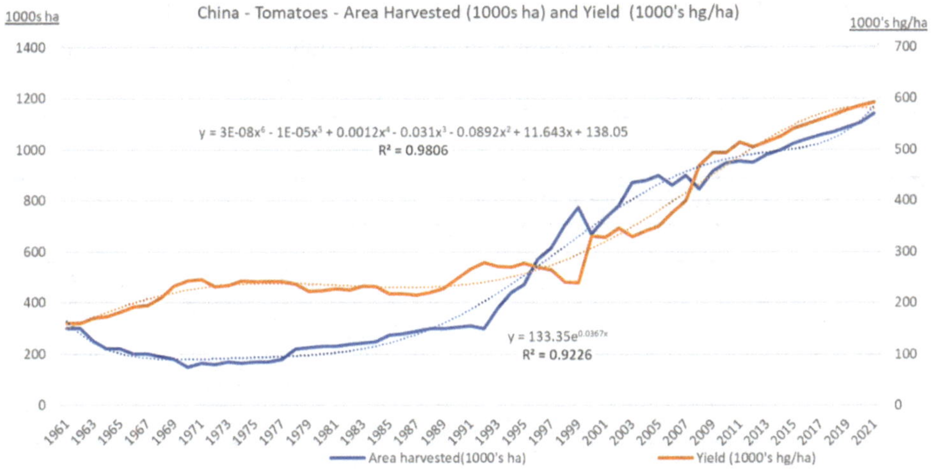

Figure 28: Field fresh tomatoes – area.

Production trendline options	Equation	R^2 value
Exponential	$y = 157.39e^{0.0199x}$	$R^2 = 0.8894$
Linear	$y = 6.6403x + 109.29$	$R^2 = 0.802$
Logarthimic	$y = -104.14\ \ln(x) - 13.895$	$R^2 = 0.509$
Polynomial order 6	$Y = -6E{-}02x^6 - 1E{-}08x^5 + 0.0092x^4 - 0.021x^3 - 0.0792x^2 + 21.643x + 298.05$	$\mathbf{R^2 = 0.9806}$
Power	$y = 101.5x^{0.3345}$	$R^2 = 0.6326$

Chinese domestic consumption has been growing pretty fast. About 10 years ago, 2012, China exported about 900,000 mT of tomato paste, while domestic consumption only amounted to 100,000 mT. But today, China consumes 150,000–180,000 mT. It has almost doubled. There are three reasons for this [316]:

1. First, China's restaurant chains have been well set up – you can find the same restaurants in Beijing, in Shanghai, in Guangzhou, in Urumqi, with the same name restaurants doing dishes that taste the same, which are called "pre-made dishes." All these premade dishes have to keep the same flavor wherever you are. This is done by using stable ingredients, like tomato paste, which is something that cannot be avoided.

2. The second reason is that western dishes are very popular – like pizzas and hamburgers. A lot of McDonald's, KFC, and Pizza Hut have opened in China everywhere. Compared to 10 years ago, I think the number has gone up like 500% or more than that.
3. And the third reason is that many famous local brands of sauces, dipping sauces, and barbecue sauces have been developed and launched to market for 20 years now, accumulating a very good market share. These products use a lot of tomato paste made in China. So speaking of our domestic market, it has grown very rapidly [316].

In summary, the total acreage of tomatoes in China was increased by 154.93%, 36.82%, and 14.75% between 1990 and 1999, 2000 and 2009, 2010 and 2019, respectively, and the yield increased by over −3.243%, 49.02%, and 17.15% in the same periods. The decade of 2000–2009 was considered a high yield decade for tomatoes production in China.

Area harvested and yield: During the decade of 2000–2009, China experienced significant growth in the production of tomatoes. This growth was considered explosive because it happened very quickly and was very significant. One of the main reasons for this growth was the increased demand for tomatoes in both the domestic market and for export opportunities. This decade was also considered a high-yield decade for tomato production in China, meaning that the amount of tomatoes produced per unit of land was very high.

The purpose of the correlation analysis for China's tomatoes was to understand how the different factors of area harvested, yield, and production are related to each other. The analysis was conducted to compare the efficiency of tomato production among major producers. The results showed that all the critical relationships between the three factors were positively correlated. More land for tomatoes increases their production. Additionally, the yield of tomatoes was maintained well during this process, meaning that the amount of tomatoes produced per unit of land remained high. This increase in tomato production is important for food availability and processing within China. Correlation values: production/yield 0.9818, yield/area 0.9082, production/area 0.95704 [323, 324].

Variable	Correlation values
Production/Yield	0.9818
Yield/Area Harvested	0.9082
Production/Area Harvested	0.95704

China is expanding tomato production by promoting greenhouse agriculture to better control growing conditions. The Ministry of Agriculture and Rural Affairs aims to have over 2 million ha of greenhouse facilities by 2025, addressing logistical issues highlighted during the coronavirus pandemic. Currently, only 35% of vegetables are grown in greenhouses, but this is set to increase with new high-tech structures being built near cities for closer consumer access [324].

India

Between the years of 2010 and 2020, the national average of the area of land used for tomato cultivation in India was 808,584 ha. This is a significant increase compared to the average of 364,992 ha for the last six decades (1961–2020), indicating that tomato cultivation is growing in India. The distribution of the data for the area of land used for tomato cultivation is positively skewed, which means that there are more hectares of land with higher values in the data (Figure 29). The minimum area of land used for tomato cultivation is 50,000 ha, while the maximum is 907,000 ha. The mean area of land used for tomato cultivation is 364,992 ha, the median is 308,653 ha, and the mode is 100,000 ha. The statistical range is 857,000 ha, the variance is 75,629,637,465.61, and the standard deviation is 275,008.43.

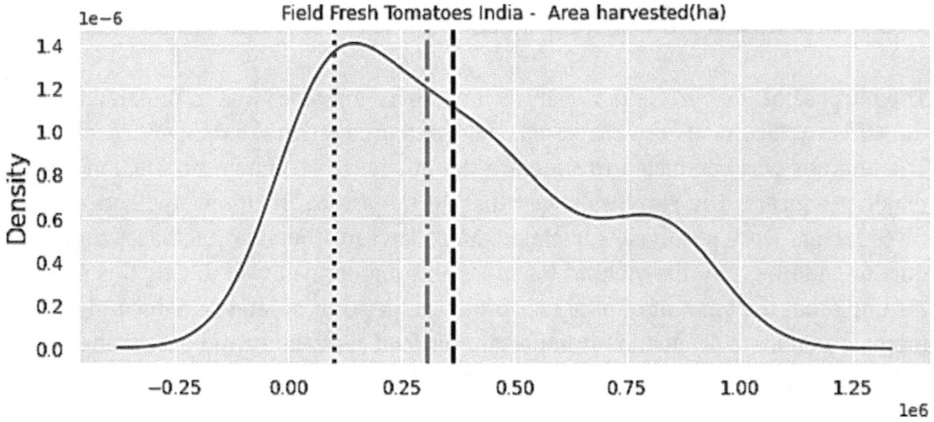

Figure 29: India field fresh tomatoes – area harvest.

Between the years 2010 and 2020, the average production of tomatoes in India was 18.15 million tons. This is a significant increase compared to the average of 6.595 million tons for the period 1961–2020, indicating that tomato production is growing in India. The increase in production over the recent decade was 65.28%. The distribution of the data for tomato production is positively skewed, which means that there are more tonnes of tomatoes with higher values in the data (Figure 30). The minimum production of tomatoes is 464,000 tons, while the maximum is 21,181,000 tons. The mean production of tomatoes is 6,595,176.51 tons, the median is 4,603,446.00 tons, and the mode is 464,000.00 tons. This data indicates that the production of tomatoes in India has been increasing significantly, especially in recent years.

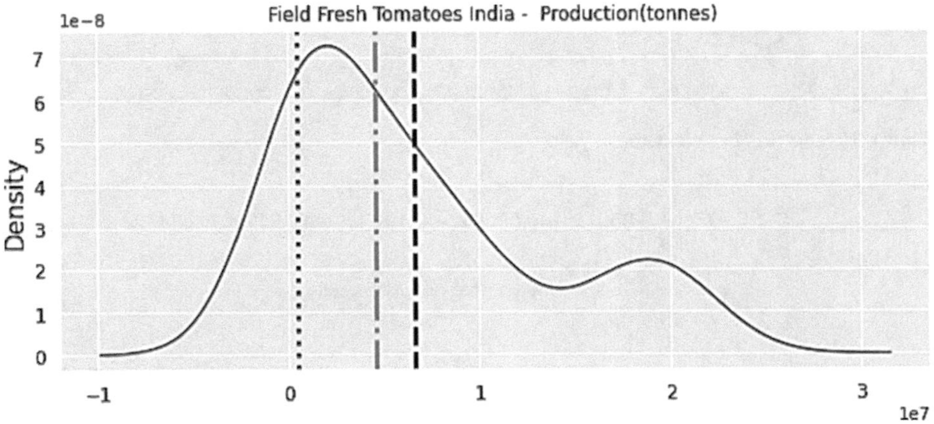

Figure 30: India field fresh tomatoes – production.

The field fresh tomato yield in India for the period of 2010–2020 was 224,792 hg/ha, which is a significant increase compared to the national average of 143,266 hg/ha for the period of 1961–2020. This indicates that the yield of tomatoes per unit of land has increased in India over the years. The growth in yield over the recent decade was 28.18%. The distribution of the data for tomato yield is negatively skewed, which means that there are more hectares of land with lower values in the data. The minimum tomato yield is 81,268 hg/ha, while the maximum is 259,824 hg/ha. The mean tomato yield is 143,266.28 hg/ha, the median is 146,825 hg/ha, and the mode is 91,304 hg/ha. The distribution is negatively skewed: mean < mode and mean < median (Figure 31). This data indicates that the tomato yield per unit of land has been increasing in India, especially in recent years, leading to a higher overall production of tomatoes.

To analyze the trend of the area of land used for tomato cultivation in India, a polynomial order 6 trendline was used. An R^2 value of 97.54% shows the trendline is highly reliable, near perfect fit. Other trend fittings, such as linear or quadratic trendlines, resulted in lower R^2 values, indicating that they are less reliable. Therefore, the polynomial order 6 trendline is the best way to analyze the trend of the area of land used for tomato cultivation in India (Figure 32):

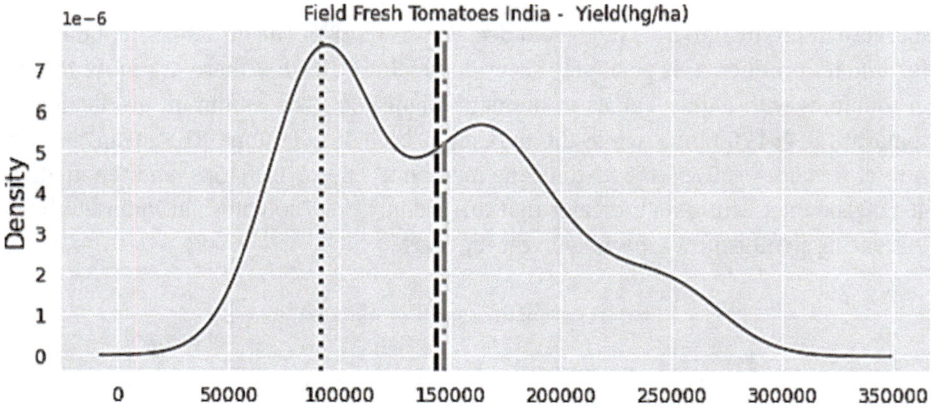

Figure 31: India field fresh tomatoes – yield.

$$Y_{\text{area harvest}} = -8\text{E}{-}07x^6 + 0.0001x^5 - 0.0079x^4 + 0.1995x^3 - 1.7942x^2 + 5.7458x + 49.471$$

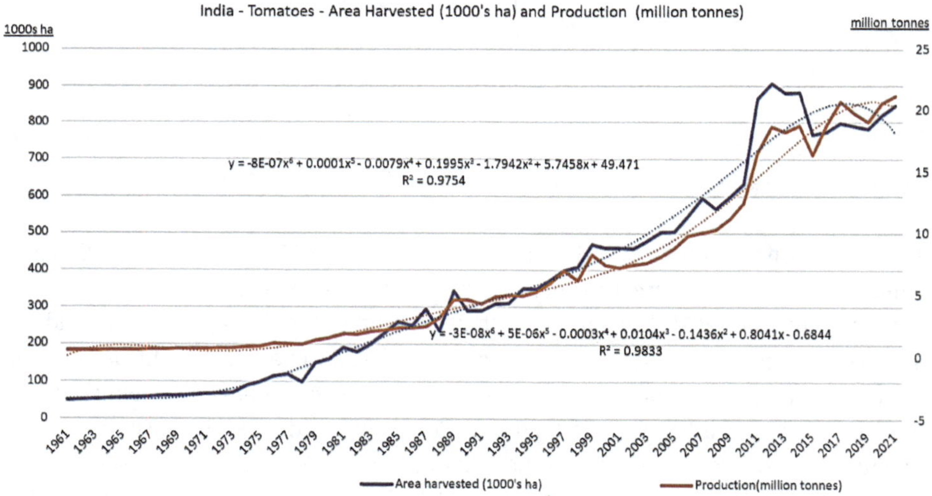

Figure 32: India – fresh field tomatoes – area harvest and production.

India Fresh Field Tomatoes - Area Harvested Trendline options	Equation	R^2 Value
Exponential	y = 49.005e^0.0527x	R^2 = 0.9126
Linear	y = 14.918x - 97.451	R^2 = 0.9273
Logarithmic	y = 243.18ln(x) - 403.38	R^2 = 0.6359
Polynomial Order 6	$y = -8E\text{-}07x^6 + 0.0001x^5 - 0.0079x^4 + 0.1995x^3 - 1.7942x^2 + 5.7458x + 49.471$	R^2 = 0.9754
Power	y = 11.506x^0.976	R^2 = 0.9244

To analyze the trend of tomato production in India, two trendlines were used: an exponential trendline and a polynomial order 6 trendline. Exponential trendline R^2: 0.9491, polynomial order 6: 0.9833; higher values indicate better fit. Both trendlines are reliable, but the polynomial order 6 trendline is slightly more reliable as it has a higher R^2 value. Therefore, the polynomial order 6 trendline is the best way to analyze the trend of tomato production in India:

$$Y_{\text{India field fresh tomoatoes production}} = -18x^6 + 2E{-}16x^5 - 0.1003x^4 + 2.0104x^3 - 1.1436x^2 + 8.041x - 0.6844$$

	Equation	R^2
Exponential	y = 0.3588e^0.0722x	**R^2 = 0.9491**
Linear	y = 0.3464x - 4.1425	R^2 = 0.8481
Logarithmic	y = 5.3012ln(x) - 10.155	R^2 = 0.5126
Polynomial Order 6	$y = -18x^6 + 2E\text{-}16x^5 - 0.1003x^4 + 2.0104x^3 - 1.1436x^2 + 8.041x - 0.6844$	**R^2 = 0.9833**
Power	y = 0.0576x^1.2875	R^2 = 0.8965

Over the last three decades, India has shown significant growth in the production and cultivation of tomatoes. The total acreage of land used for tomato cultivation increased by 61.91%, 30.23%, and 23.10% during the periods of 1990–1999, 2000–2009, and 2010–2019, respectively. In the same periods, the total harvested output or production of tomatoes increased by over 79.68%, 50.05%, and 57.87%. This means that India has exhibited growth of over 50% in the last three decades in terms of both the land used for tomato cultivation and the production of tomatoes. This growth shows that the tomato industry in India is expanding and becoming more important to the country's economy.

Area harvested and production trend: India has exhibited explosive growth in terms of area of harvest and production of tomatoes.

A polynomial order 6 trendline fits yield (hg/ha) data better, with R^2 near 95.96% (Figure 33):

$$y = -4E{-}07x^6 + 7E{-}05x^5 - 0.0053x^4 + 0.1854x^3 - 2.9224x^2 + 17.911x + 65.169$$

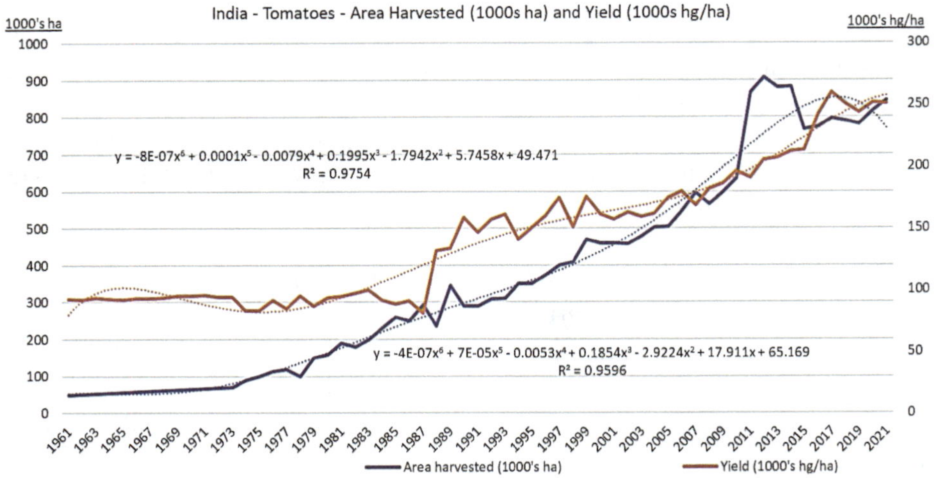

Figure 33: India – fresh field tomatoes – area harvest and yield.

Tomatoes' short growth period and high yields boost their economic importance, expanding cultivation areas [325].

Yield	Equation	R^2 value
Exponential	$y = 73.216e^{0.0195x}$	$R^2 = 0.9196$
Linear	$y = 2.8217x + 55.795$	$R^2 = 0.8655$
Logarthimic	$y = 44.032 \ln(x) + 4.1399$	$R^2 = 0.5439$
Polynomial order 6	$Y = -4E-07x^6 + 7E-05x^5 - 0.0053x^4 + 0.1854x^3 - 2.9224x^2 + 17.911- + 65.169$	$\mathbf{R^2 = 0.9596}$
Power	$y = 50.032x^{0.3115}$	$R^2 = 0.6807$

In summary, the total acreage of tomatoes in India was increased by 61.91%, 30.23%, and 23.10% between 1990 and 1999, 2000 and 2009, and 2010 and 2019, respectively, and the yield increased by over 10.95%, 15.21%, and 24.17% in the same periods. 2010–2019 achieved highest yields due to advanced planting material, drip irrigation, INM/IPM, and pollination systems.

Area harvested and yield: Due to domestic market and export opportunities, India has exhibited an explosive growth during the 2000–2009 decade was considered a high yield decade for tomatoes production in China.

A correlation analysis was performed on the data related to tomato cultivation in India. The analysis aimed to understand the relationship between the area of land used for tomato cultivation, the yield of tomatoes per unit of land, and the total production of tomatoes. Positive correlation: area harvested, production, yield. This means that when the area of land used for tomato cultivation increases, there is a corresponding increase in both the production of tomatoes and the yield per unit of land. Importantly, the yield is maintained well, which means that the increase in production is not at the expense of the quality of the tomatoes produced. This is good news for processors and the availability of tomatoes as food within India. The correlation analysis can also be used to compare the efficiency of tomato production between different regions or countries [323, 324].

	Area harvested	*Production*	*Yield*
Area harvested	1		
Production	0.975775619	1	
Yield	0.93794214	0.960809902	1

In 2019, heavy rains in September and October caused significant damage to the Kharif tomato crop in regions like Madhya Pradesh and Karnataka. This led to lower yields and impacted the tomato paste market [325]. India's minimal presence in the export market is due to high production costs, while China dominates with lower processing costs. As a result, Indian ketchup manufacturers prefer importing Chinese tomato paste, highlighting the need for cost-effective domestic production [326].

Turkey

Turkey field fresh tomatoes is an agricultural area where tomatoes are grown and harvested. The average size of the area where tomatoes were harvested from 2010 to 2021 is 182,344 ha, which means that this much land was used to grow tomatoes during this period. Similarly, the average size of the harvested area from 1961 to 2021 is 142,689 ha. This means that the area where tomatoes were grown and harvested has increased over time. However, there has been a decrease in the harvested area in the recent decade (2010–2020), which is about 2.617%. This indicates that the land used for growing and harvesting tomatoes has diminished over the past decade.

Moving on to the data distribution (Figure 34), we see that the harvested area data is positively skewed. This means that there are more hectares of land where higher numbers of tomatoes were harvested. The minimum harvested area is 57,000 ha, while the maximum harvested area is 213,255 ha. The mean harvested area is 142,684.92 ha, which is the average of all the harvested areas. The median harvested area is 160,915 ha, which is the middle value of all the harvested areas. The mode harvested area is 57,000 ha, which is the most frequently occurring harvested area. Finally, we see that the distribution is positively skewed because the mean (142,684.92 ha) is greater than the mode (57,000 ha). This indicates that there are more harvested areas with higher hectares than lower hectares.

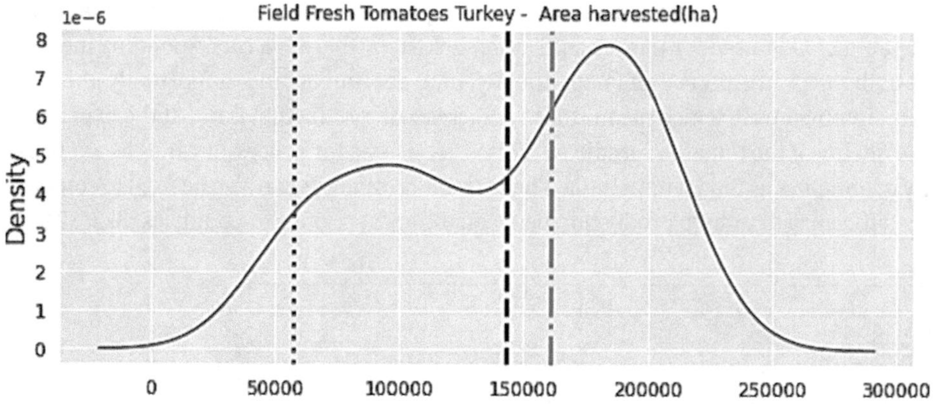

Figure 34: Turkey field fresh tomatoes – area harvest.

Similarly, the Turkey produces tomatoes, and the average production of tomatoes from 2010 to 2021 is 12.021 million tons. Similarly, the average production from 1961 to 2021 is 6.453 million tons. This means that the production of tomatoes has increased over time. In the recent decade (2010–2021), there has been a 31.35% increase in the production of tomatoes. This represents a substantial rise, largely attributed to the abundant harvests in recent years.

Now let's talk about the data distribution (Figure 35) of the production of tomatoes. The distribution is positively skewed, which means that there are more tonnes of tomatoes produced in higher production years. The minimum production of tomatoes is 1,120,000 tons, while the maximum production is 13,204,015 tons. The mean production of tomatoes is 6,453,082.18 tons, which is the average of all the production values. The median production of tomatoes is 6,150,000 tons, which is the middle value of all the production values. The mode production of tomatoes is 3,700,000 tons, which is the most frequently occurring production value. Lastly, we see that the distribution is positively skewed because the mean (6,453,082.18 tons) is greater than both the mode (3,700,000 tons) and the median (6,150,000 tons). This suggests that there are more production values with higher tonnes of tomatoes than lower tonnes of tomatoes.

The Turkey field fresh tomatoes also has a yield of tomatoes, and the average yield from 2010 to 2021 is 671,535 hg/ha. In comparison, the national average yield from 1961 to 2021 is 407,983 hg/ha. This means that the yield of tomatoes has substantially increased over time. In the recent decade (2010–2021), there has been a 41.25% increase in the yield of tomatoes, which is a significant increase. This suggests that the Turkey field fresh tomatoes has been producing more tomatoes per hectare of land.

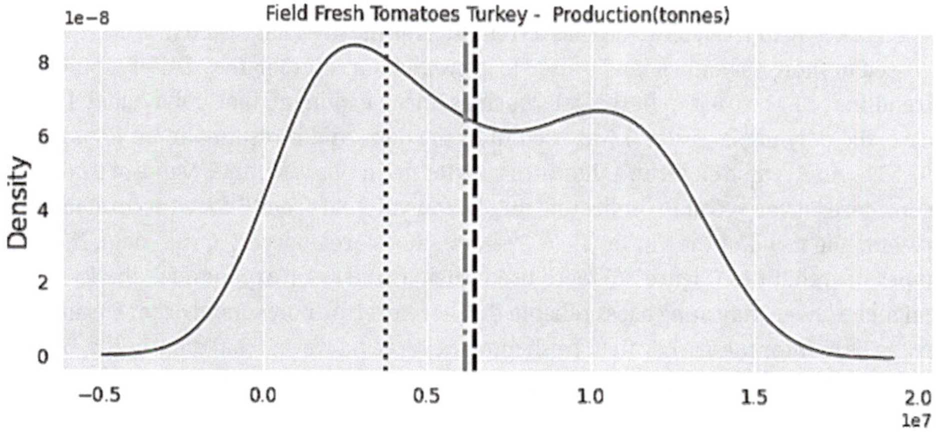

Figure 35: Turkey field fresh tomatoes – production.

Now let's talk about the data distribution (Figure 36) of the yield of tomatoes. The distribution is positively skewed, which means that there are more hectares of land with higher yields. The minimum yield of tomatoes is 196,491 hg/ha, while the maximum yield is 792,672 hg/ha. The mean yield of tomatoes is 407,983.90 hg/ha, which is the average of all the yield values. The median yield of tomatoes is 375,386 hg/ha, which is the middle value of all the yield values. The mode yield of tomatoes is 196,491 hg/ha, which is the most frequently occurring yield value.

Finally, we see that the distribution is positively skewed because the mean (407,983.90 hg/ha) is greater than the mode (196,491 hg/ha). This indicates that there are more yield values with higher hectograms per hectare than lower hectograms per hectare.

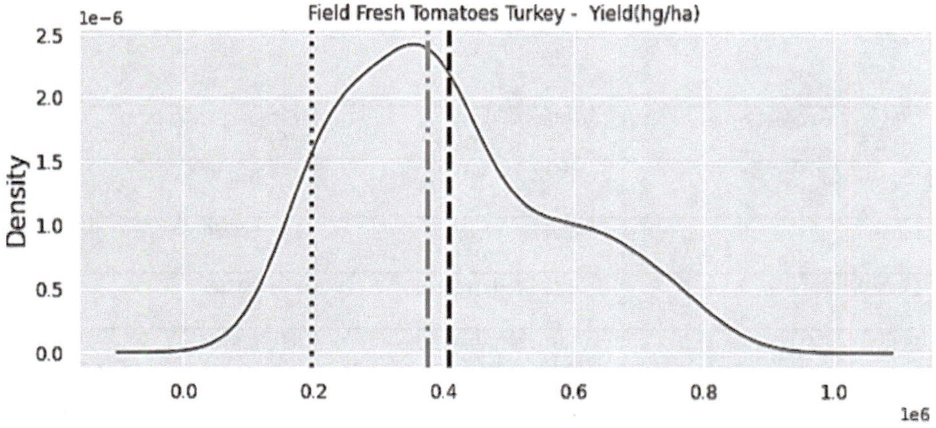

Figure 36: Turkey field fresh tomatoes – yield.

The Turkey field fresh tomatoes has a trendline for the area harvested (ha) data, which is used to show how much land is used to grow and harvest tomatoes. Different types of trendlines can be used to fit the data, such as linear, exponential or polynomial. In this case, the polynomial order 6 was used to fit the data, and it resulted in an R^2 value of 97.65%. An R^2 value closer to 1 indicates a better fit. In this case, an R^2 value of 97.65% is considered a very good fit, indicating that the polynomial order 6 curve accurately represents the trend of the Turkey field fresh tomatoes area harvested (ha) data. If other types of trendlines (Figure 36) were used, such as linear or exponential, the R^2 value might be lower, indicating a less reliable fit. Therefore, the polynomial order 6 trendline is the best fit for the Turkey field fresh tomatoes area harvested (ha) data, as it provides a more accurate representation of the trend over time. (Figure 37):

$$Y_{\text{Area harvest}} = 14\text{E}{-}18x^6 - 0.021x^5 + 6.0789x^4 - 17428x^3 + 07x^2 + 10x + 12$$

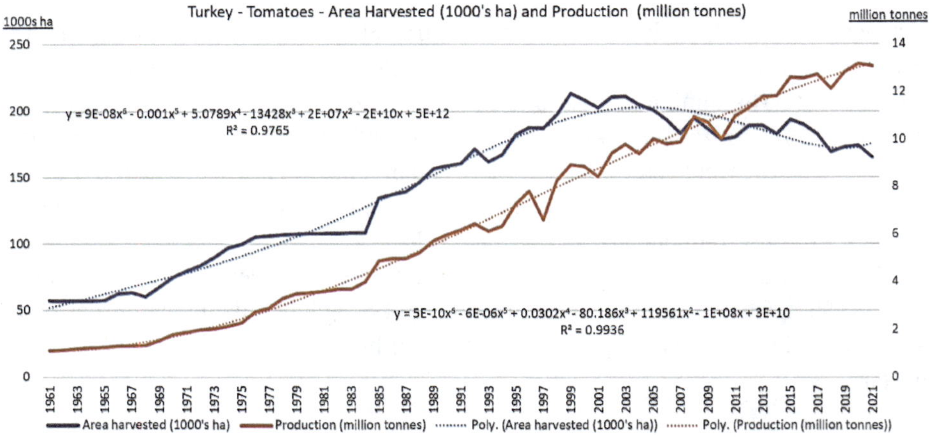

Figure 37: Turkey tomatoes.

Turkey Tomatoes Harvested Area	Trendline	R^2 Fitting Value
Exponential	$y = 2\text{E-}17e^{0.0218x}$	$R^2 = 0.6837$
Linear	$y = 2.6173x - 5068.5$	$R^2 = 0.8086$
Logarthimic	$y = 5218.4\ln(x) - 39498$	$R^2 = 0.8109$
Polynomial Order 6	$y = 14\text{E-}18x^6 - 0.021x^5 + 6.0789x^4 - 17428x^3 + 07x^2 + 10x + 12$	$\mathbf{R^2 = 0.9765}$
Power	$y = 5\text{E-}142x^{43.478}$	$R^2 = 0.687$

The Turkey field fresh tomatoes has a trendline for the production of tomatoes (tonnes), which is used to show how much tomatoes are produced over time. Different types of trendlines can be used to fit the data, such as linear, exponential or polynomial. In this case, all types of trendlines could be used to fit the data, but the polynomial order 6 trendline resulted in the highest accuracy with an R^2 value of 99.36%. Although other types of trendlines could be used to fit the data, the polynomial order 6 trendline is the best fit for the Turkey field fresh tomatoes production (tonnes) data, as it provides the highest accuracy and the most accurate representation of the trend over time.

$$Y_{\text{Production}} = 5\text{E}{-}10x^6 - 6\text{E}{-}06x^5 + 0.0302x^4 - 80.186x^3 + 119561x^2 - 1\text{E}{+}08x + 3\text{E}{+}10$$

Turkey	Trendline	R^2 fitting values
Exponential	$y = 5\text{E}{-}38e^{0.0439x}$	$R^2 = 0.9192$
Linear	$y = 0.2244x - 440.38$	$R^2 = 0.9816$
Logarthimic	$y = 446.66\ \ln(x) - 3386.5$	$R^2 = 0.9809$
Polynomial order 6	$Y = 5\text{E}{-}10x^6 - 6\text{E}{-}06x^5 + 0.0302x^4 - 80.186x^3 + 119561x^2 - 1\text{E}{+}08x + 3\text{E}{+}10$	$R^2 = 0.9936$
Power	$y = 9\text{E}{-}289x^{87.527}$	$R^2 = 0.9214$

The Turkey field fresh tomatoes has a trendline for the yield of tomatoes (hg/ha), which is used to show how much yield is obtained per hectare of land over time. Different types of trendlines can be used to fit the data, such as linear, exponential, logarithmic, or polynomial (Figure 38). In this case, logarithmic and power trend options were not able to fit the data well. However, the exponential and polynomial order 6 trendlines resulted in an R^2 value closer to 97%, which is considered a good fit. Although logarithmic and power trend options were not able to fit the data well, the exponential and polynomial order 6 trendlines provide a good fit for the Turkey field fresh tomatoes yield (hg/ha) data, as they accurately represent the trend over time with an R^2 value closer to 97%:

$$Y_{\text{yield}} = -9\text{E}{-}05x^6 + 0.007x^5 + 0.477x^4 - 55.918x^3 + 1683.3x^2 - 11522x + 225599$$

Turkey tomatoes yield	Trendline	R^2 fitting value
Exponential	$y = 190083e^{0.0221x}$	$R^2 = 0.9748$
Linear	$y = 8869x + 133044$	$R^2 = 0.9279$
Logarthimic	$y = 146469\ \ln(x) - 54808$	$R^2 = 0.653$
Polynomial order 6	$Y = -9\text{E}{-}05x^6 + 0.007x^5 + 0.477x^4 - 55.918x^3 + 1683.3x^2 - 11522x + 225599$	$R^2 = 0.989$
Power	$y = 109591x^{0.3914}$	$R^2 = 0.8047$

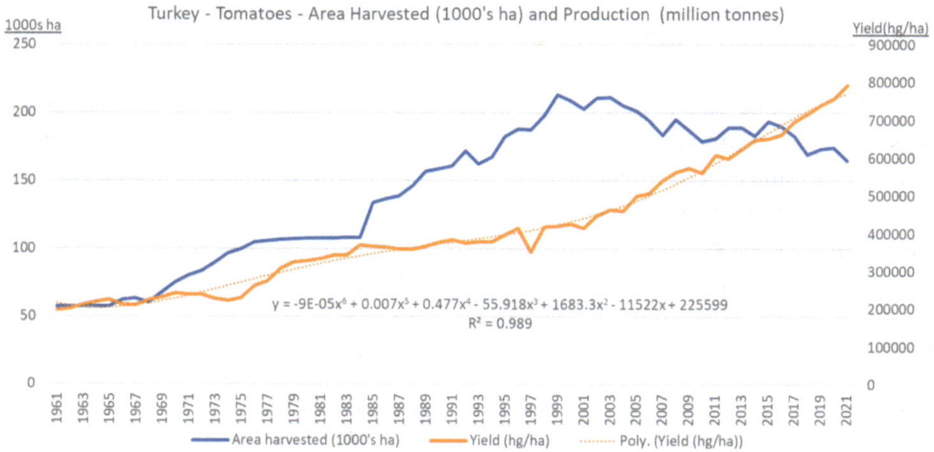

Figure 38: Turkey tomatoes yield.

Correlation analysis was performed for Turkey's tomatoes to understand the relationship between area harvested, yield, and production. The main objective was to compare major producers of tomatoes with respect to production efficiencies.

The analysis reveals a positive correlation between the area harvested, production, and yield of tomatoes. A correlation coefficient of 1 represents a perfect correlation, while 0 indicates none. The study found a strong positive correlation (0.76047) between the area harvested and production, meaning increased harvested area leads to higher production. Similarly, a strong positive correlation (0.979342) between production and yield suggests higher production results in better yields. The correlation between the area harvested and yield (0.74476) also indicates that increasing the harvested area maintains good yield levels. These findings are crucial for supporting processors and ensuring food availability in Turkey, suggesting that expanding the harvested area can boost tomato production while maintaining high yields.

	Area harvested	Production	Yield
Area harvested	1		
Production	0.76047	1	
Yield	0.74476	0.979342	1

The United States of America

Florida tomatoes harvested area has been analyzed for the period of 2010–2021 and compared to the average harvested area for the years 1961–2021, which is 167,954.34 ha. The results show that there has been a considerable decrease in the harvested area in the recent decade, with a decrease of 17.306%. This means that less land is being used to grow and harvest tomatoes in Florida in recent years compared to the average of the past 60 years. The data distribution for the harvested area is positively skewed, which means that there are more data points on the higher end of the range. The minimum harvested area is 109,226 ha, while the maximum is 207,870 ha. The mean harvested area is 167,954.34 ha, which is represented by a dashed line on the distribution graph. The median harvested area is 167,800 ha, represented by a dashed-dot line (Figure 39). The mode harvested area is 109,226 ha, represented by a dotted line. This means that data is skewed towards the higher end of the range, with more data points in the higher harvested area values. Overall, this information shows that there has been a decrease in the harvested area for Florida Tomatoes production in recent years, and the data is positively skewed towards the higher end of the range.

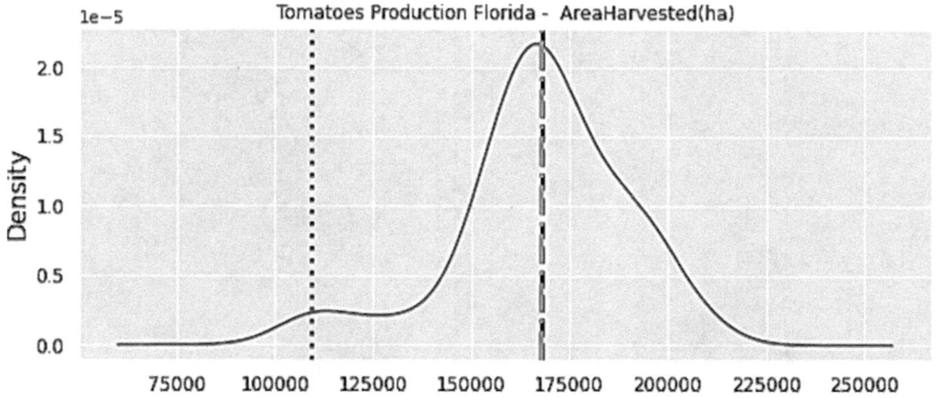

Figure 39: Florida tomatoes area harvest.

The Florida tomatoes production has also been analyzed for the period of 2010–2021 and compared to the average production for the years 1961–2021, which is 9,755,589.869 tons. The results show that there has been an increase in production of 32.612% in the recent decade (2010–2021). This means that more tomatoes are being produced in Florida in recent years compared to the average of the past 60 years.The data distribution for the production of tomatoes is also positively skewed, which means that there are more data points on the higher end of the range. The minimum production is 4,626,881 tons, while the maximum is 15,875,000 tons. The mean production is 9,755,589.87 tons, which is represented by a dashed line on the distribution graph. The median production is 10,232,700 tons, represented by a dashed-dot line (Figure 40). The mode production is 4,626,881 tons, represented by a dotted line. The higher mean compared to the mode signifies a positively skewed distribution, indicating more data points at the higher production values. This suggests an increase in Florida tomato production in recent years, with the data skewing towards higher production levels.

The Florida tomatoes yield (hg/ha) has been analyzed for the period of 2010–2021 and compared to the national average yield for the years 1961–2021, which is 596,926.04 hg/ha. The results show that there has been a substantial increase of 56.74% in the yield of Florida tomatoes in the recent decade (2010–2021). This means that more yield is being obtained per hectare of land in Florida in recent years compared to the national average of the past 60 years. The data distribution for the yield of Florida Tomatoes is positively skewed (Figure 41), which means that there are more data points on the higher end of the range. The minimum yield is 254,496 hg/ha, while the maximum is 990,502 hg/ha. The mean yield is 596,926.05 hg/ha, which is represented by a dashed line on the distribution graph. The median yield is 577,943 hg/ha, represented by a dashed-dot line. The mode yield is 254,496 hg/ha, represented by a dotted line. The higher mean compared to the mode signifies a positively skewed distribution, indicating more data points at the higher production values. This suggests an increase in Florida Tomato yield in recent years, with the data skewing towards higher production levels.

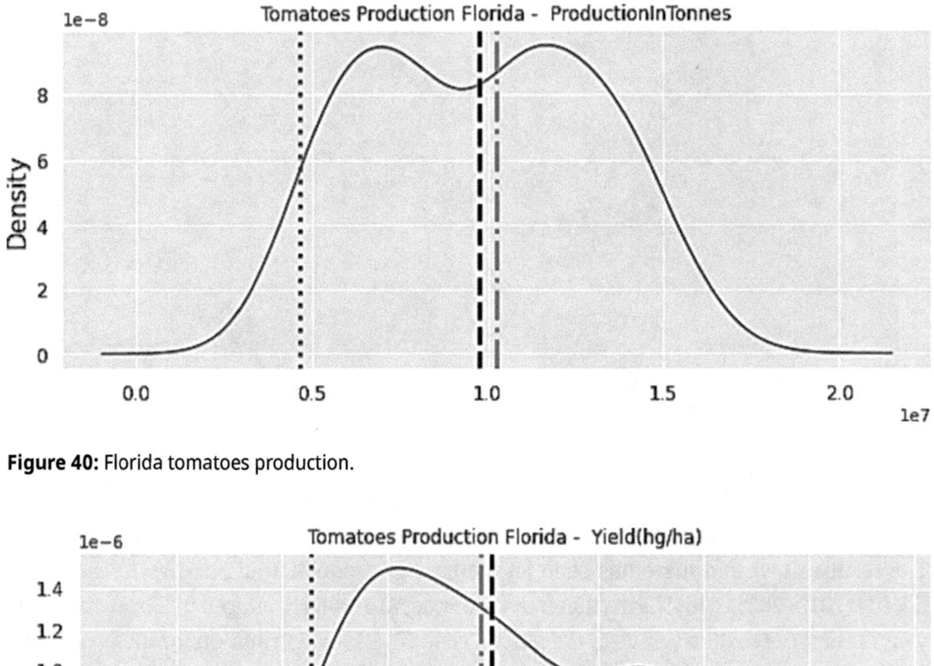

Figure 40: Florida tomatoes production.

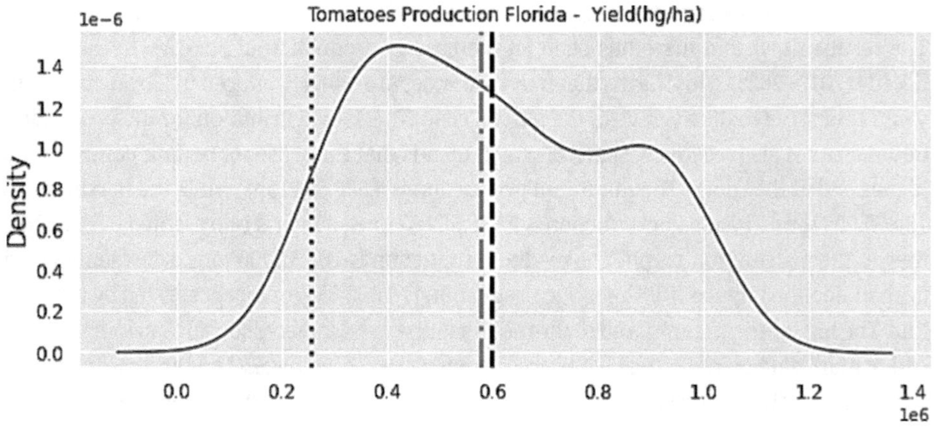

Figure 41: Florida tomatoes yield.

The Florida tomatoes harvest area trendline fits (Figure 42) best with a 6th order polynomial (R^2 = 99.73%):

$$Y_{\text{area harvested}} = -5\text{E}{-}05x^6 + 0.0026x^5 + 0.2027x^4 - 16.852x^3 + 461.02x^2 + 4441.1x + 264778$$

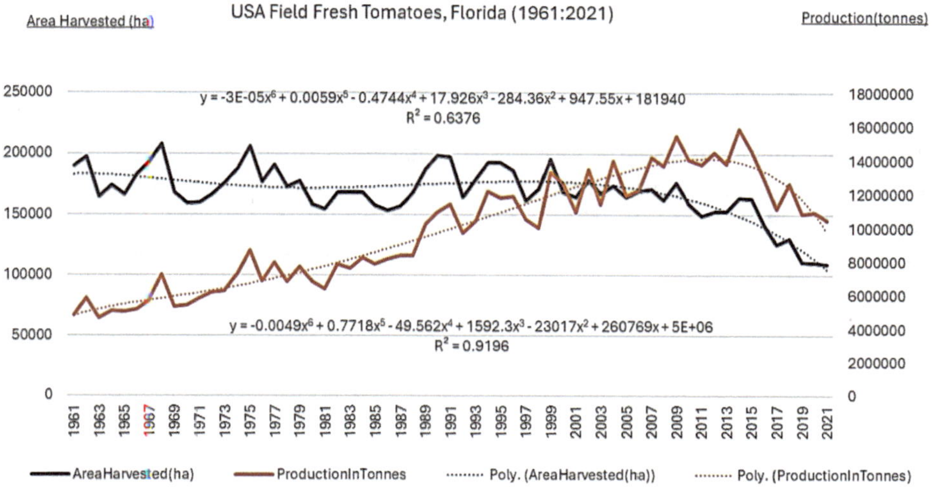

Figure 42: Florida tomatoes.

Florida	Equation	R^2 Value
Exponential	$y = 190931e^{-0.004x}$	$R^2 = 0.3057$
Linear	$y = -677.45x + 188955$	$R^2 = 0.3212$
Logarthimic	$y = -10273\ln(x) + 200412$	$R^2 = 0.1906$
Polynomial Order 6	$y = -3\text{E-}05x^6 + 0.0059x^5 - 0.4744x^4 + 17.926x^3 - 284.36x^2 + 947.55x + 181940$	$R^2 = 0.6376$
Power	$y = 204809x^{-0.066}$	$R^2 = 0.181$

Florida production trendline fits best with sixth-order polynomial (R^2 = 99.73%) over exponential regression:

$$Y_{\text{production}} = -5\text{E}{-}05x^6 + 0.0026x^5 + 0.2027x^4 - 16.852x^3 + 461.02x^2 + 4441.1x + 264778$$

Florida	Equation	R^2 value
Exponential	$y = 5E{+}06e^{0.0181x}$	$R^2 = 0.7392$
Linear	$y = 162038x + 5E{+}06$	$R^2 = 0.8021$
Logarthimic	$y = 3E{+}06 \ln(x) + 376876$	$R^2 = 0.6945$
Polynomial order 6	$Y = -0.0049x^6 + 0.7718x^5 - 49.562x^4 + 1592.3x^3 - 23017x^2 + 260769x + 5E{+}06$	$R^2 = 0.9196$
Power	$y = 3E{+}06x^{0.3453}$	$R^2 = 0.7833$

The Florida tomato industry faces significant challenges from Mexican import competition and farmland loss due to real estate development. Since NAFTA's implementation in 1994, Florida's tomato production has dropped by nearly 37.129%, while imports have increased almost fivefold. This surge in cheaper imports has driven down market prices, reducing profits for local farmers (Figure 43):

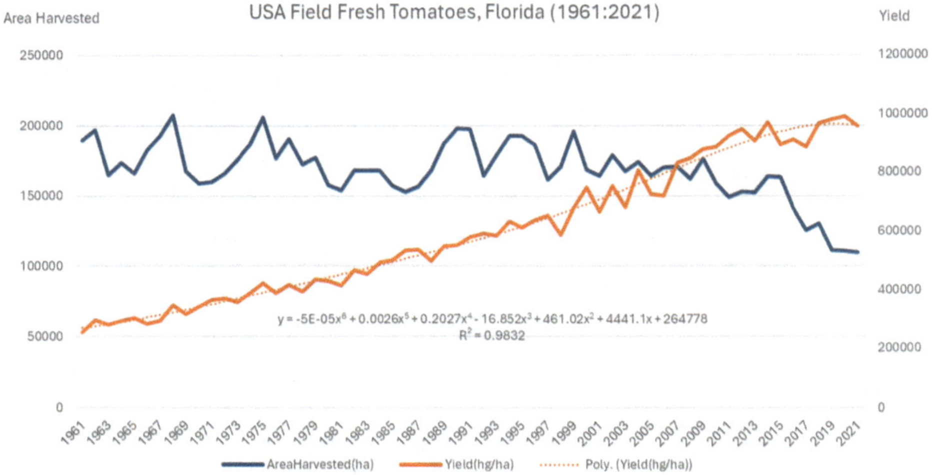

Figure 43: Florida yield.

$$Y_{\text{Yield}} = -5E{-}05x^6 + 0.0026x^5 + 0.2027x^4 - 16.852x^3 + 461.02x^2 + 4441.1x + 264778$$

Florida yield	Equation	R^2 value
Exponential	$y = 275403e^{0.0225x}$	$R^2 = 0.971$
Linear	$y = 12701x + 203201$	$R^2 = 0.9706$
Logarthimic	$y = 217088 \ln(x) - 88998$	$R^2 = 0.7317$
Polynomial order 6	$y = -5E{-}05x^6 + 0.0026x^5 + 0.2027x^4 - 16.852x^3 + 461.02x^2 + 4441.1x + 264778$	$R^2 = 0.9832$
Power	$y = 150921x^{0.4108}$	$R^2 = 0.882$

Over the past decade, the US tomato industrys production capacity has significantly declined by 30%, from 3.8 billion pounds on 136,000 acres in 2005 to 2.6 billion pounds on 97,500 acres in 2015. This decline was especially pronounced in California and Florida, which together produce about 70% of the nation's tomatoes. Increased competition from Mexico has been a major factor, with import volumes in 2015 more than tripling those of Florida's production [327, 328].

	Area harvested (ha)	Production in tonnes	Yield (hg/ha)
Area harvested (ha)	1		
Production in tonnes	−0.188748797	1	
Yield (hg/ha)	−0.565321555	0.90717738	

USA Plant City Florida tomato yield linear regression notebook

USA tomatoes

Florida plant city tomatoes production, USA

The proposed Plant City Florida Tomato Yield model uses machine learning to predict harvest days and yields based on temperature forecasts [329]. Traditional visual assessments of tomato maturity, which determine market prices, are prone to errors and costly in terms of labor and quality control. Transfer learning (TL) offers a more efficient alternative, with experiments showing that the ResNet152V2 model achieved the highest testing accuracy at 99.46% and the lowest training loss among the tested TL models [330]. This chapter introduces innovative methods combining climatology, yield, and environmental factors to develop a machine learning model for tomato cultivation in Florida, a region with ideal warm temperatures similar to the Mediterranean. Since the 1870s, Florida has grown to become the largest producer of fresh tomatoes in the United States, with nearly every southern county contributing to a production that accounts for about 50% of the nation's domestic fresh tomatoes from October through June (Figure 44).

Figure 44: Florida map.

Fresh-market tomatoes are grown in every state, with commercial-scale production in about 20 states, and Florida has overtaken California as the largest producer, likely due to California's ongoing drought. According to the USDA 2012 Census of Agriculture, while total tomato acreage has decreased by 10% since 2007, the number of farms growing tomatoes has increased by 20%, particularly among small-scale farms of five acres or less. In 2020, around 12.6K tons of fresh market tomatoes and 11.3K tons of processing tomatoes were harvested from approximately 272,900 acres, valued at about $1 billion.

Plant city, Florida: weather and climatology details

Plant City has a subtropical climate with long, hot, and humid summers that are mostly cloudy and short, cool winters that are partly cloudy. The temperature typically ranges from 51 °F (10.55 °C) to 91 °F (32.77 °C) throughout the year, rarely falling below 38 °F

(3.33 °C) or rising above 95 °F (35 °C), resulting in a climate with warm summers and mild, relatively dry winters (Figure 45).

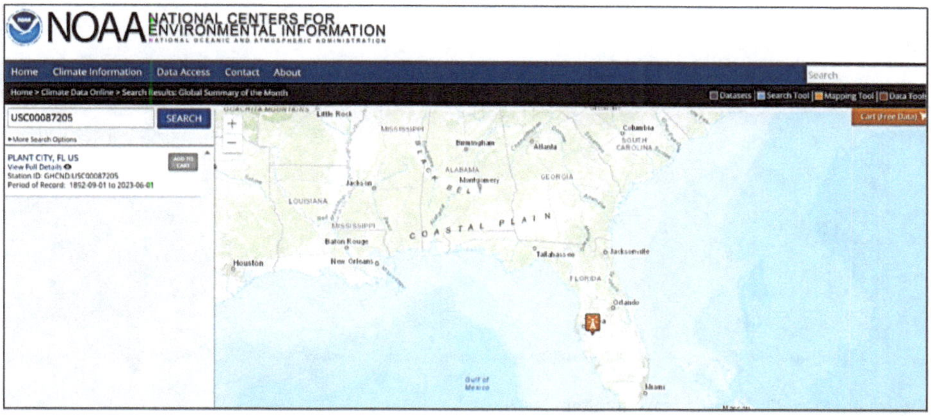

Figure 45: NOAA station selection.

PLANT CITY, FL, USA
View Full Details
Station ID: GHCND:USC00087205
Period of Record: 1892-09-01: 2023-06-01

Average temperature in Plant City

In Plant City, the hot season lasts about 4.7 months, from May 9 to September 30, with average daily high temperatures above 87 °F (30.55 °C). August is the hottest and most humid month, with average highs of 91 °F (32.77 °C) and lows of 74 °F (23.33 °C), characterizing this period with prolonged hot and humid weather. Overall, the graph (Figure 46) indicates that Plant City experiences a pronounced warm season from late spring to early autumn, with the highest temperatures occurring in July and August. The cooler months, from October to March, display a wider range of maximum temperatures but generally remain mild.

In Plant City, the cool season lasts about 2.6 months, from December 6 to February 22, with average daily highs below 76 °F (24.44 °C). January is the coldest month, with average lows of 52 °F (11.11 °C) and highs of 72 °F (22.22 °C), characterized by mild temperatures and reduced humidity. Overall, the graph (Figure 47) indicates that Plant City experiences warmer nights from late spring to early autumn, with the highest minimum temperatures occurring in July and August. The cooler months, from October to March, display lower minimum temperatures but generally remain mild.

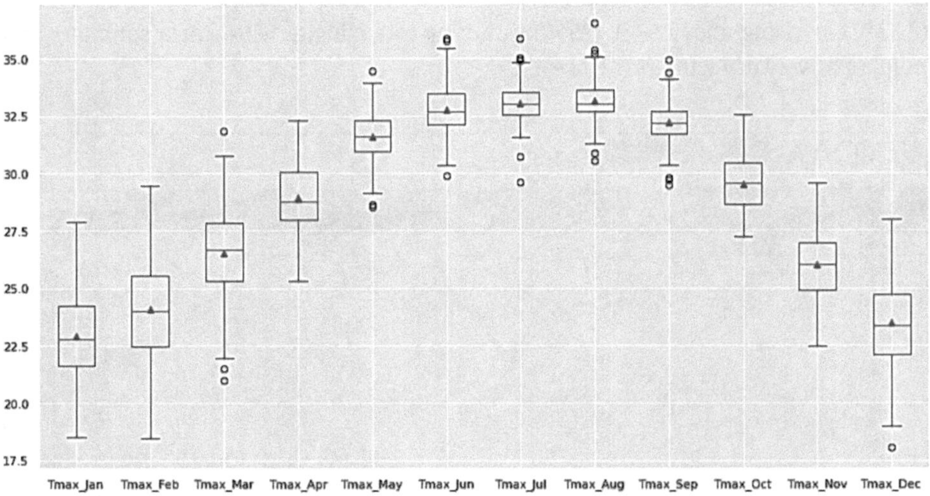

Figure 46: Plant City Florida maximum temperatures.

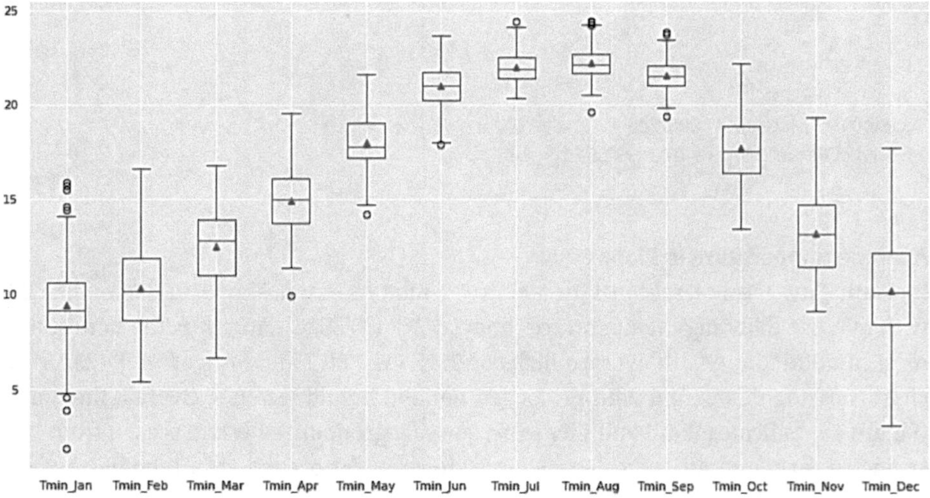

Figure 47: Plant City Florida minimum temperatures.

Growing season: The growing season for tomatoes is defined as the longest continuous period with nonfreezing temperatures, varying globally and applying to the calendar year in the Northern Hemisphere and from July 1 to June 30 in the Southern Hemisphere. In Plant City, freezing temperatures are rare but possible in some winters, with January 10 being the day most likely to fall outside the growing season (64% chance). Based on growing degree days, which measure heat accumulation for plant development, the first spring blooms in Plant City are expected around January 8, assuming temperatures stay within the specified range of 50 °F (10 °C) to 86 °F (30 °C) [329].

Step 1: Import libraries

To process the data, please import following libraries.

```
import numpy as np
import pandas as pd
import functools
from datetime import date
import plotly.graph_objects as go
import seaborn as sns; sns.set()
import statsmodels.api as sm
from statsmodels.tsa.arima_process import ArmaProcess
from scipy import stats
from scipy.stats import pearsonr
import matplotlib.pyplot as plt
import plotly.express as px
from sklearn.preprocessing import MinMaxScalar
from sklearn.model_selection import train_test_split
from sklearn.linear_model import LinearRegression
from sklearn.metrics import r2_score
from sklearn import metrics
from sklearn.impute import SimpleImputer
import eli5
```

Step 2: Access tomato data (1991–2020)

Tomato data from FAOSTAT includes comprehensive statistics on US production, with Florida being a major contributor. Therefore, analyzing this data necessitates considering Florida's impact to accurately understand factors affecting national tomato yields and production dynamics.

```
AreaHarvested_df=
pd.read_csv(r"FloridaTomatoDataV12/productionData/FAOSTAT_USA_Tomato_AreaHarvested.csv")
print(AreaHarvested_df['Element'].unique(),AreaHarvested_df['Unit'].unique())
AreaHarvested_df.rename(column={'Value':'AreaHarvested(ha)'},inplace=True)
AreaHarvested_df=AreaHarvested_df[['Year','AreaHarvested(ha)']]
AreaHarvested_df.set_index('Year',inplace=True)

print(AreaHarvested_df.info())
AreaHarvested_df.head()
```

Output:

	AreaHarvested(ha)
Year	
1961	189422
1962	196808
1963	164454
1964	173454
1965	165800

```
Productiondf=
pd.read_csv(r"FloridaTomatoDataV12/production/FAOSTAT_USA_Tomato_Production.csv")
print(Productiondf['Element'].unique(),Productiondf['Unit'].unique())
Productiondf.rename(columns={'Value':'ProductionInTonnes'},inplace=True)
Productiondf=Productiondf[['Year', 'ProductionInTonnes']]

Productiondf.set.index [['Year',inplace=True)
#Productiondf_m.reset_index(inplace=True)
#Productiondf_m.rename(columns = {'index': 'Date'},inplace=True)
Productiondf.head()

Productiondf.tail()
```

Output:

	ProductionInTonnes
Year	
2017	11138620
2018	12613090
2019	10858982
2020	10939109
2021	10475265

```
Yield_df =
pd.read_csv(r"FloridaTomatoDataV12/productionData/FAOSTAT_USA_Tomato_Yield.csv")
Print(Yield_df['Element'].unique(),Yield_df['Unit'].unique())
Yield_df.rename(columns={'Value':'Yield(hg/ha)'},inplace=True)
Yield_df=Yield_df[['Year','Yield(hg/ha)']]
Yield_df.set_index('Year',inplace=True)

Yield_df.head()
```

Yield:

	Yield(hg/ha)
Year	
1961	254496
1962	296746
1963	281348
1964	293393
1965	302597

Step 3: View tomatoes time series

Chart tomatoes production time series data and trends.

```
#ImportLibrary
import pylab
import numpy as np
import datetime
from matplotlib.dates import YearLocator, MonthLocator, DateFormatter

def show_timeseriesplot(title, var_date,var_data,colname):
    from matplotlib import pyplot as plt

    years = YearLocator() # every year
    months = MonthLocator() # every month
    yearsFmt = DateFormatter('%Y') fig = plt.figure(figsize=(12,6))
    ax = plt.gca()
    #Plot dens ty
    #var_data.plot(figsize=(12,6), kind='line')

    #Add title and lables
    Plt.title(title +'-'+ colname,fontsize=12)
    plt.ylabel(colname,fontsize=12)
    plt.tick_params(axis = 'both',which = 'major', labelsize = 12)
    plt.tick_params(axis = 'both',which = 'minor', labelsize = 12)
    plt.plot(var_date, var_data)

    # Show the figure
    plt.show()
```

```
numerical_features=['Areaharvested','Yield','Production_Tonnes']
for col in numerical_features:
    show_timeseriesplot('AlmondProductionCalifornia',Production_df['Year'],Production_df[col],col)
```

Chart:

Tomatoes data.

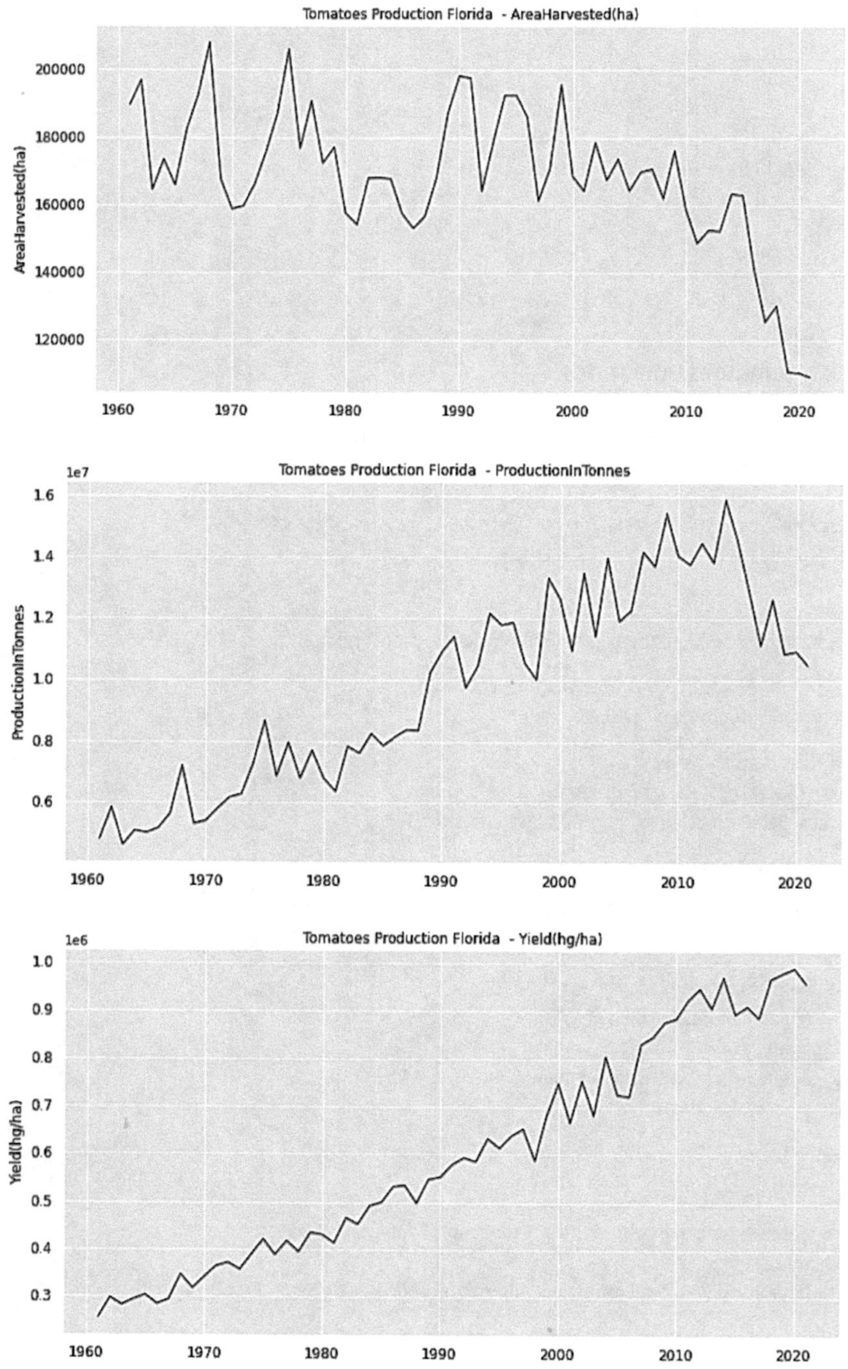

Step 4: US CO_2 1991:2020 emissions data

CO_2 information can be used to track progress toward reducing emissions and to inform policy decisions related to climate change.

```
co2df = pd.read_excel("co2Emissions_USA.xlsx",sheet_name="Data")
co2df
```

```
co2_df=co2df.T.reset_index()
co2_df.columns=co2_df.iloc[0]
```

```
co2_df1["Year"] = co2_df1["SeriesName"].apply(lambda x : x.split("[")[0])
```

```
co2_df2["Year"] = co2_df2["Year"].astype(int)
co2_df2["CO2 emissions (kt)"] = co2_df2["CO2 emissions (kt)"].astype(float)
```

```
fig = px.line(co2_df2,x="Year", y="CO2 emissions (kt)", title='United States CO2 emissions')
fig.show()
```

Output:

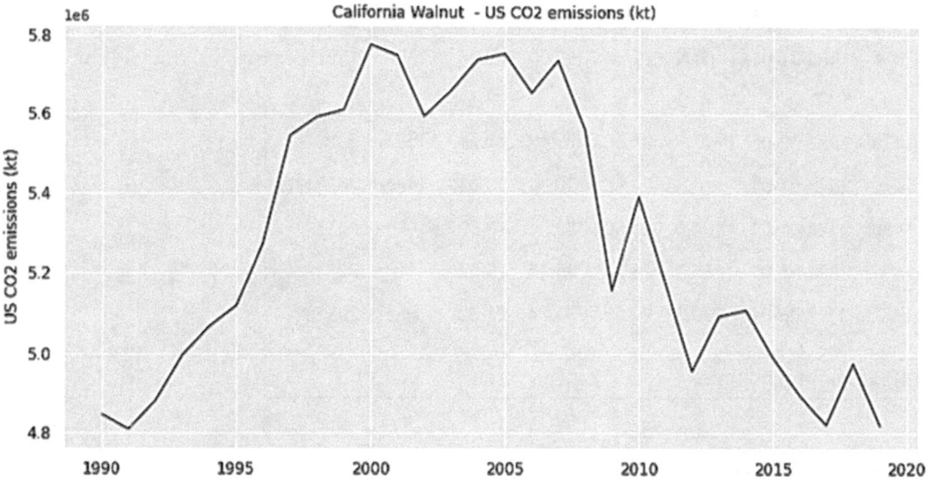

Step 5: Plant city NOAA GSOM data 1991–2020

Plant City, Florida is being loaded into a data frame. A data frame is a common way of organizing and analyzing data in Python. Once the data is loaded, the column names in the data frame are being renamed to reflect the data for each month. This means that the new column names will be based on the average temperature data for each month of the year.

```
weatherdf_Original =
pd.read_csv(r"FloridaTomatoDataV12/FloridaTomato/WeatherData/USC00087205_PlantCityFL.csv")
weatherdf_Original.head()df_mean
```

```
weatherdf = weatherdf_Original.copy()
weatherdf = weatherdf[['DATE','PRCP','TAVG','TMAX','TMIN']]
weatherdf.head()
```

```
weatherdf['DATE'] = pd.to_datetime(weatherdf['DATE'])
```

```
weatherdf['Month'] = weatherdf['DATE'].dt.strftime('%b')
weatherdf['Year'] = weather['DATE'].dt.year
```

Output:

	DATE	PRCP	TAVG	TMAX	TMIN	Month	Year
0	1892-09-01	NaN	26.34	31.49	21.19	Sep	1892
1	1892-10-01	NaN	22.36	28.19	16.52	Oct	1892
2	1892-11-01	NaN	17.71	25.35	10.08	Nov	1892
3	1892-12-01	NaN	16.93	24.11	9.76	Dec	1892
4	1893-01-01	NaN	12.47	19.50	5.44	Jan	1893
...	...	...	...	...	...	...	...
1478	2023-02-01	17.7	21.86	29.48	14.25	Feb	2023
1479	2023-03-01	4.8	22.86	30.34	15.38	Mar	2023
1480	2023-04-01	102.6	25.50	32.31	18.69	Apr	2023
1481	2023-05-01	135.6	26.33	33.14	19.52	May	2023
1482	2023-06-01	260.3	29.02	35.74	22.30	Jun	2023

1483 rows × 7 columns

```
weatherdf.rename(columns = {'PRCP': 'prcp',
                'TMAX':'Tmax',
                'TMIN':'Tmin',
                'TAVG':'TAVG'},inplace=True)
```

```
tempdf = weatherdf.pivot(index = 'Year', columns = ['Month'],values = ['prcp', 'Tavg', 'Tmax','Tmin'])
```

```
tempdf.columns = ['_'.join(col).strip()for col in tempdf.columns.values]
```

```
tempdf.head()
```

PRCP data:

Year	prcp_Apr	prcp_Aug	prcp_Dec	prcp_Feb	prcp_Jan	prcp_Jul	prcp_Jun	prcp_Mar	prcp_May	prcp_Nov	...	Tmin_Dec	Tmin_Feb	Tmin_Jan
1892	NaN	NaN	NaN	NaN	NaN	NaN	NaN	NaN	NaN	NaN	...	9.76	NaN	NaN
1893	60.2	282.0	39.6	78.6	NaN	NaN	251.1	NaN	182.6	65.5	...	9.54	12.61	5.44
1894	8.6	241.6	46.2	50.4	59.7	NaN	NaN	33.8	72.8	NaN	...	NaN	11.46	10.17
1895	128.2	222.2	45.5	NaN	77.0	320.4	89.7	26.6	136.5	54.9	...	8.10	5.40	10.29
1896	42.7	176.1	20.2	92.3	85.6	218.7	417.4	50.3	51.2	23.8	...	9.23	8.78	7.49

5 rows × 48 columns

Box plot view:

```
import pandas as pd
import matplotlib.pyplot as plt
from matplotlib.cbook import boxplot_stats
import numpy as np

df=
tempdf[['Tmax_Jan', 'Tmax_Feb', 'Tmax_Mar', 'Tmax_Apr', 'Tmax_May', 'Tmax_Jun', 'Tmax_Jul', 'T
max_Aug','Tmax_Sep','Tmax_Oct','Tmax_Nov','Tmax_Dec']]
# plot the dataframe as needed
ax = df.plot.box(figsize=(15,8), showmeans=True,grid=True)
```

Box plot:

Plant City, Florida experiences a hot season from May 9 to September 30, with average daily highs above 87 °F (30.55 °C), and August being the hottest month with highs of 91 °F (32.77 °C) and lows of 74 °F (23.33 °C). Understanding the duration and intensity of this hot season is essential for agricultural planning, outdoor activities, public health measures, and preparing for extreme heat events.

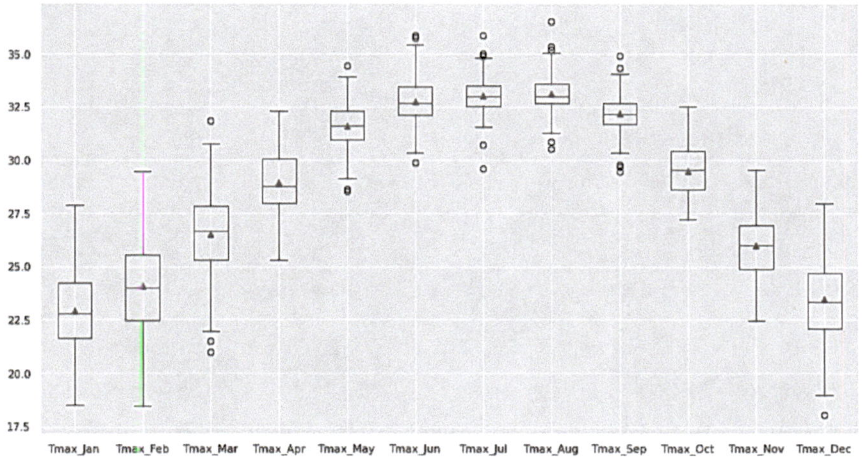

Similarly other climate parameters Boxplot:

```
import pandas as pd
import matplotlib.pyplot as plt
from matplotlib.cbook import boxplot_stats
import numpy as np

df =
tempdf[['Tmax_Jan', 'Tmax_Feb', 'Tmax_Mar', 'Tmax_Apr', 'Tmax_May', 'Tmax_Jun', 'Tmax_Jul','Tmax_Aug','Tmax_Sep','Tmax_Oct','Tmax_Nov','Tmax_Dec']]
#plot the dataframe as needed
ax = df.plot.box(figsize=(15,8), showmeans=True,grid=True)
```

```
df =
tempdf[['prcp_Jan','prcp_Feb','prcp_Mar','prcp_Apr','prcp_May','prcp_Jun','prcp_Jul','prcp_Aug','prcp_Sep','prcp_Oct','prcp_Nov','prcp_Dec']]

# plot the dataframe as needed
ax = df.plot.box(figsize=(15,8), showmeans=True,grid=True)
```

In Plant City, the wetter season lasts from June 1 to September 25, with a daily chance of rain exceeding 44%, and July being the wettest month, averaging 22.1 wet days. The drier season spans from September 25 to June 1, with November being the driest month, averaging just 4.5 wet days, and rain is the predominant form of precipitation throughout the year.

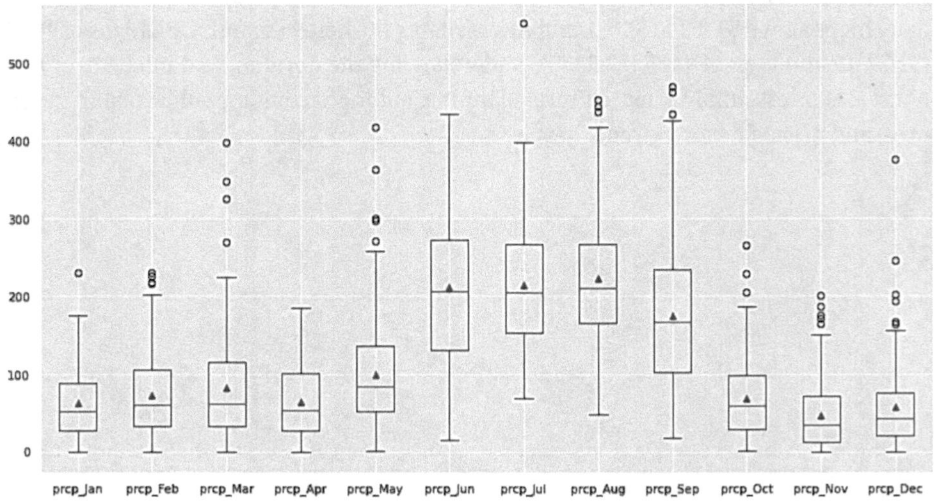

Step 6: Merge Plat City data

Merge completely datasets and verify any nulls. Fill any nulls.

```
finaldf=pd.merge(left=tempdf,right=Yield_df,left_index=True,right_index=True)
finaldf=pd.merge(left=finaldf,right=Productiondf,left_index=True,right_index=True)
finaldf=pd.merge(left=finaldf,right=AreaHarvested_df,left_index=True,right_index=True)
#finaldf=pd.merge(left=finaldf,right=Co2Emissions_df,left_index=True,right_index=True)
finaldf.head()
```

```
finaldfwithnulls = finadldf[finaldf.isna().any(axis=1)]
finaldfwithnulls
```

```
finaldf.fillna(method= 'ffill',inplace=True)
finaldf.fillna(method= 'bfill',inplace=True)
```

```
finaldf
```

Output:

Year	prcp_Apr	prcp_Aug	prcp_Dec	prcp_Feb	prcp_Jan	prcp_Jul	prcp_Jun	prcp_Mar	prcp_May	prcp_Nov	...	Tmin_Jul	Tmin_Jun
1961	65.8	173.7	106.2	59.8	65.2	178.4	38.1	34.9	64.8	11.2	...	22.75	20.03
1962	41.9	266.0	7.1	40.8	40.7	112.3	290.2	89.0	121.0	47.5	...	22.75	21.30
1963	6.9	163.9	56.3	192.1	61.8	198.5	244.8	66.5	90.0	164.2	...	21.93	21.12
1964	26.0	157.8	71.2	135.9	162.3	205.3	155.1	119.5	74.7	8.2	...	21.78	20.72
1965	24.3	234.6	83.0	91.7	41.0	336.6	280.5	53.3	31.5	15.2	...	21.12	20.20
...	...	...	...	...	...	...	...	...	...	...	...	...	...
2017	17.8	191.0	23.8	42.4	33.1	361.5	432.5	10.2	38.7	3.8	...	23.88	22.93
2018	60.6	233.9	201.6	48.5	101.8	295.3	246.7	15.2	362.5	34.8	...	23.68	22.68
2019	56.3	417.2	89.5	56.1	123.0	263.1	308.0	56.4	61.0	27.5	...	24.08	23.70
2020	133.1	241.2	66.0	46.2	16.5	195.2	184.8	0.5	38.4	175.1	...	24.40	23.37
2021	95.3	98.5	19.5	82.9	10.7	289.3	245.2	12.4	22.6	107.4	...	24.08	23.17

61 rows × 51 columns

Step 7: Optimizing tomato yield using machine learning and weather data

ML model has been developed that is designed to predict tomato yield based on weather data. The model considers the agricultural calendar for tomatoes, which means that it considers the timing of different stages in the growing process. The independent variables in the model are related to temperature and precipitation, which are known to have a significant impact on tomato yield. By analyzing patterns in these variables over time, the model can make predictions about how weather conditions will affect tomato yield in the future. The grid below shows when most major crops are typically harvested in Florida.

	Jan	Feb	Mar	Apr	May	Jun	Jul	Aug	Sep	Oct	Nov	Dec
Tomato	✓	✓	✓	✓	✓	✓				✓	✓	✓

```
#Trial 1
X= finaldf[['AreaHarvested(ha)','Tmax_Feb',
    'Tmax_Jan','Tmax_Mar','Tmax_Apr','Tmax_Aug','Tmax_Sep','Tmax_Nov','Tmin_Mar',
'Tmin_Apr','Tmin_Jul','Tmin_Oct','Tmin_Dec','prcp_Jan','prcp_Feb','prcp_Jun','prcp_Aug',
   ]]

Y= finaldf['Yield(hg/ha)']

X_train,X_test,y_train,y_test=train_test_split(X,y,test_size = 0.20,random_state = 0)
print(X_train.shape)
print(X_test.shape)

model = LinearRegression()
model.fit(X_train,y_train)

# predicting the test
Y_pred = model.predict(X_test)
Y_pred

model_features=['AreaHarvested(ha)','Tmax_Feb','Tmax_Jan','Tmax_Mar','Tmax_Apr',
'Tmax_Aug','Tmax_sep','Tmax_Nov','Tmin_Mar','Tmin_Apr',
'Tmin_Jul','Tmin_Oct','Tmin_Dec','prcp_Jan','prcp_Feb','prcp_Jun',' prcp_Aug', ]

mse = mean_squared_error(y_test,y_pred)
print("MSE:",mse)

rmse = np.sqrt(mse)
print("RMSE:",rmse)

r2 = r2_score(y_test,y_pred)
print("R2Linear Regression:",r2)
```

Output:

```
(48, 17)
(13, 17)
MSE: 5784000550.038702
RMSE: 76052.61698349836
R2 Linear Regression: 0.8736847686660374
```

R^2 68.64%, RMSE 3965, plot regression:

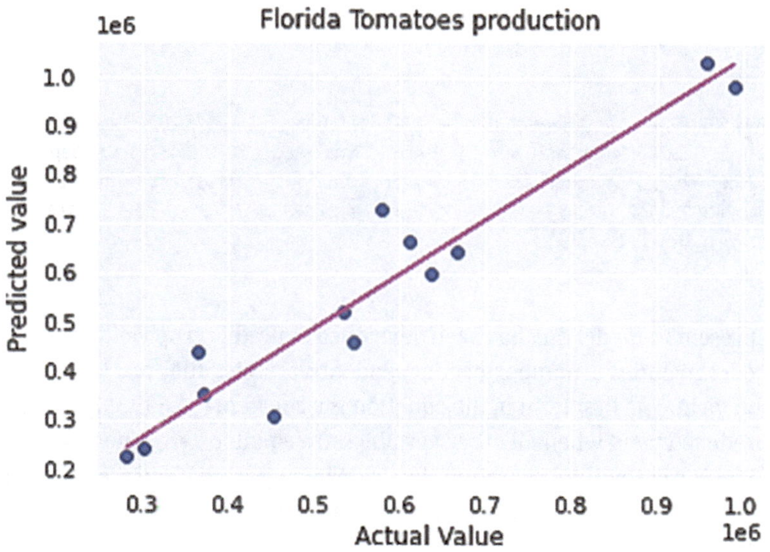

Step 8: Generate regressor line equation

The code below constructs model equation.

```
mx=""
 for ifeature in range(len(X.columns)):
   if model.coef_[ifeature]<0:
     #format & beautify the equation
     mx +="-"+"{:.3f}".format(abs(model.coef_[ifeature]))+"*"+X.columns[ifeature]
   else:
     if ifeature ==0:
       mx +="{:.3f}".format(model.coef_[ifeature])+"*"+X.columns[ifeature]
     else:
       mx +="+"+"{:.3f}".format(model.coef_[ifeature])+"*"+X.columns[ifeature]

print(mx)
```

```
# y=mx+c
if(model.intercept_<0):
   print("The formula for the "+y.name+" linear regression line is ="+"-
{:.3f}".format(abs(model.intercept_))+mx )
else:
   print("The formula for the "+y.name+" linear regression line is ="+"+
{:.3f}".format(model.intercept_)+mx )
```

Output:

```
Yield(hg/ha) = – 1395.592 – 2.879 * AreaHarvested(ha) – 13347.897 * Tmax_Feb – 6578.250 * Tmax_Jan + 28453.973 * Tmax_Mar – 62346.748 * Tmax_Apr – 14461.251 * Tmax_Aug – 20691.646 * Tmax_Sep – 9690.496 * Tmax_Nov – 26712.984 * Tmin_Mar + 62745.250 * Tmin_Apr + 141841.284 * Tmin_Jul + 3168.383 * Tmin_Oct + 19987.142 * Tmin_Dec – 538.175 * prcp_Jan – 1235.847 * prcp_Feb + 320.110 * prcp_Jun – 13.010 * prcp_Aug
```

This equation represents a model that has been developed to predict crop yield in terms of hg/ha. The model includes a number of independent variables that are known to have an impact on yield. The first term in the equation is a constant (−1,395.592), which represents the predicted yield when all other variables are equal to zero. The next two terms (−2.879 * AreaHarvested(ha)) represent the negative impact that the area of land being harvested has on yield. This suggests that as the area of land increases, the yield per unit area decreases.

The remaining terms in the equation represent the impact of various weather variables on yield. For example, higher temperatures in February, March, April, August, September, and November have a negative impact on yield, while lower temperatures in March, April, July, October, and December have a positive impact.

Similarly, higher precipitation in January and February has a negative impact on yield, while higher precipitation in June has a positive impact.

Overall, this equation provides a useful tool for predicting crop yield based on a range of weather and agricultural variables. By considering the impact of different factors on yield, farmers and other stakeholders can make more informed decisions about planting and harvesting crops, ultimately leading to higher yields and better outcomes for the agricultural industry.

Step 9: Explainability

Construct explainability.

This information is about the factors that influence the yield of tomatoes in Florida. First, the maximum temperature in March has an impact on yield. Higher temperatures in March have a negative impact on yield. Second, the minimum temperatures in April, July, October, and December have a positive impact on yield. Lower temperatures in these months are associated with higher yields. Third, precipitation also has an impact on yield. Higher precipitation in June has a positive impact on yield, while higher precipitation in January, February, and August has a negative impact on yield. Finally, the area of land being harvested also has an impact on yield. As the area of land being harvested increases, the yield per unit area decreases. This is likely because it takes more effort to prepare and cultivate a larger area of land. Overall, these factors are important to consider when planting and harvesting tomatoes in Florida. By taking into account the impact of temperature, precipitation, and area of land being harvested, farmers and other stakeholders can make more informed decisions about optimizing their yields and improving the overall productivity of the agricultural industry in Florida.

y top features

Weight?	Feature
+141841.284	Tmin_Jul
+62745.250	Tmin_Apr
+28453.973	Tmax_Mar
+19987.142	Tmin_Dec
+3168.383	Tmin_Oct
+320.110	prcp_Jun
-2.879	AreaHarvested(ha)
-13.010	prcp_Aug
-538.175	prcp_Jan
-1235.847	prcp_Feb
-1395.592	<BIAS>
-6578.250	Tmax_Jan
-9690.496	Tmax_Nov
-13347.897	Tmax_Feb
-14461.251	Tmax_Aug
-20691.646	Tmax_Sep
-26712.984	Tmin_Mar
-62346.748	Tmax_Apr

Step 10: Save binary form of the model (Pickle)

For projecting climate models, let's save the model in binary form.

```
file = open('USA_FLoridaTomatoYield_pklfile', 'wb') # -trail1
```

Output:
Saved model in "'USA_FLoridaTomatoYield_pklfile'" file.

USA tomatoes

Machine learning water use (WU) model: Withlacoochee River and tomatoes production model in Plant City, Florida, USA

The Withlacoochee River, one of only two rivers in Florida that flow northward, originates in the Green Swamp and travels 160 miles to the Gulf of Mexico near Yankeetown. Its name, derived from a Creek Indian term meaning "Little Big Water," likely signifies the river's natural water level fluctuations.

The ML model seeks to improve our understanding of how water and other climatic factors influence tomato production in Florida by analyzing weather data from Plant City to predict yields. This approach helps researchers and farmers optimize growing practices, enhancing both sustainability and profitability in the agricultural industry.

Satellite-based data monitor water levels in global bodies of water by detecting surface elevation variations through radar altimeters from space agency missions. These variations reveal changes in sea levels and continental water fluctuations due to climate changes and human activities, supporting scientific and applied programs such as water resource management, hazard monitoring, and regional security [331].

The study aims to estimate the irrigation water usage for growing fresh tomatoes by analyzing surface water withdrawals, total groundwater withdrawals, and nonrenewable groundwater depletion using the PCR-GLOBWB 2 model across the Continental United States. Findings reveal a significant shift over time, with groundwater now providing 48% of irrigation water compared to 23% historically, indicating its increasing importance [332].

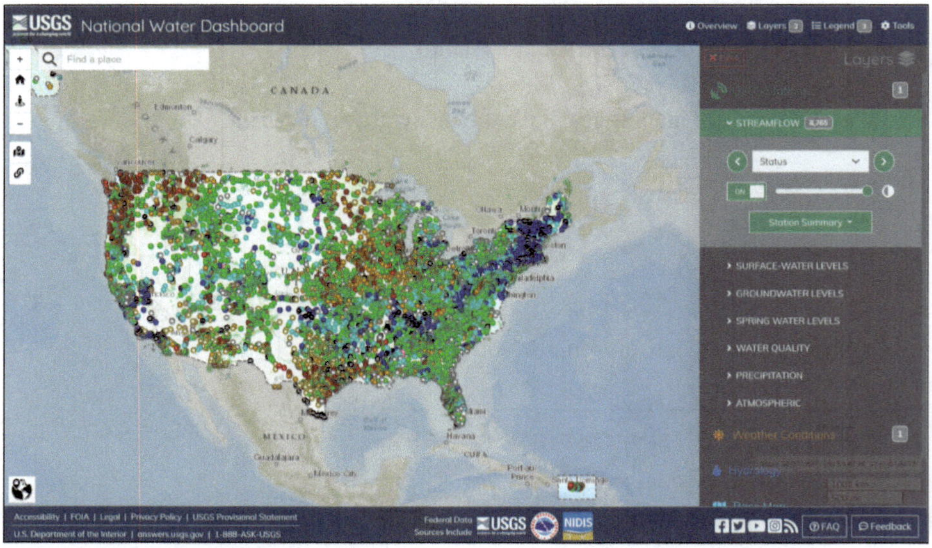

USA Plant City Florida tomato yield linear regression with United States Geological Survey Notebook

Data source	Name
USGS	United States Geological Survey 02312600 WITHLACOOCHEE NEAR FLORAL, FL

Water use source: United States Geological Survey 02312600 WITHLACOOCHEE RIVER NEAR FLORAL CITY, FL (Figure 48)

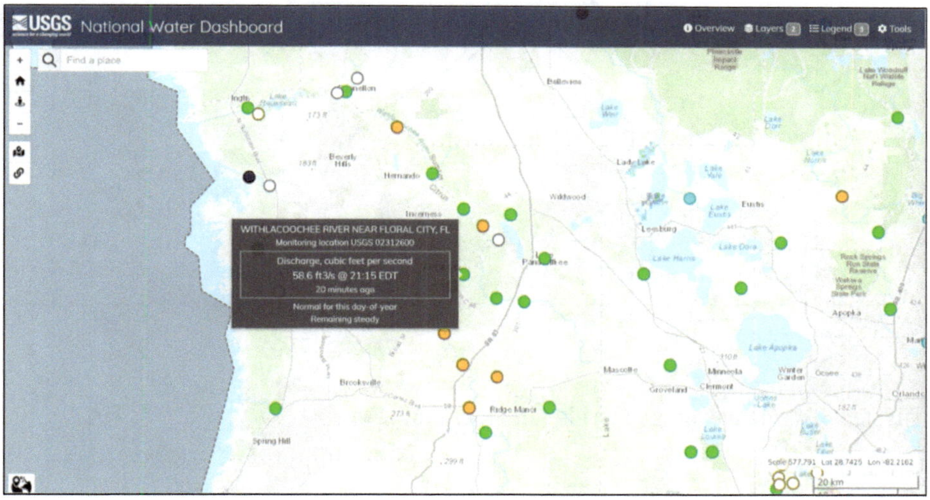

Figure 48: Water dashboard.
Source: 02312600 and data.

03100208 – The model uses gage height as input feature.

The term “gage height” refers to the height of the water surface above a specific reference point, known as the gage datum or zero point. This measurement is often used to monitor water levels in rivers, lakes, and other bodies of water. The term “stage” is a more general term that can refer to the height of the water surface above any arbitrary reference point, not just the gage datum. However, when used in conjunction with a gage reading, it is more appropriate to use the term “gage height” to describe the measurement.

Withlacoochee River Near Floral City, FL – 02312600 data for last year is presented in the following figure [332].

Understanding the relationship between crop coefficients and water use for peppers in Southwest Florida is essential for optimizing yield analytics and enhancing water use efficiency, as a model can accurately determine water needs, establish irrigation schedules, and potentially save 1.7 Mgd while also reducing pollutant loading and providing valuable data for AGMOD [333]:

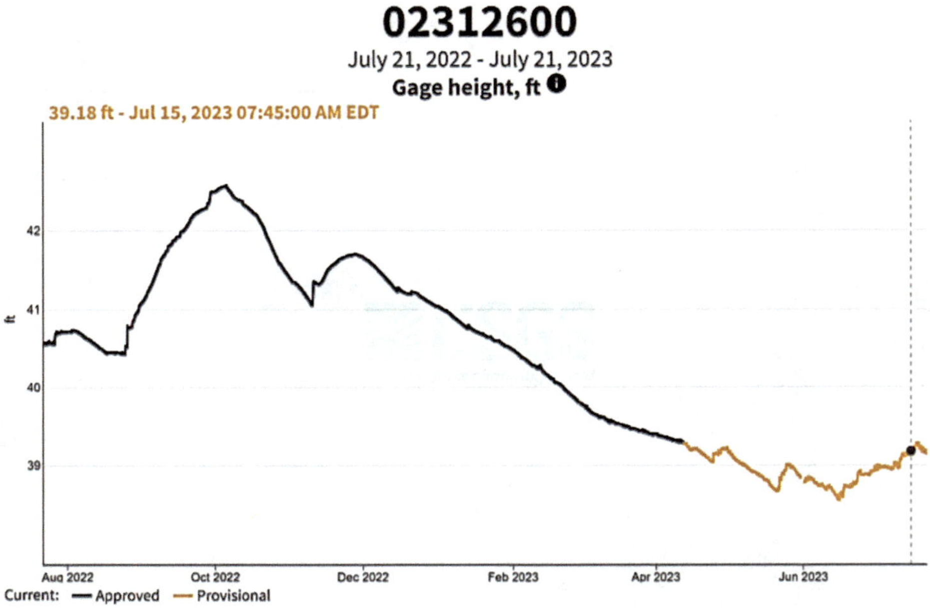

Till step 5, we can leverage Florida tomatoes model.

Step 6: Load water use data for USGC Site Floral City (site number: 2312600)

Withlacoochee River Near Floral City, FL – 02312600 data for last year is presented in the following figure.

```
waterdata_Original = pd.read_csv(r"FloridaTomatoDataV12/FloridaTomato/waterdata/
withlacoocheeRiver_FloralCityFlorida.csv")
waterdata_Original.head()
```

Output:

	AgencyCode	USGCSiteNumber	ParameterCode	TS_id	Year	Month	GageHeightMean(feet)
0	USGS	2312600	65	26227	1983	10	41.505
1	USGS	2312600	65	26227	1983	11	40.986
2	USGS	2312600	65	26227	1983	12	40.849
3	USGS	2312600	65	26227	1984	1	41.569
4	USGS	2312600	65	26227	1984	2	41.368

```
waterdata_Original.info()
```

Output:

```
<class 'pandas.core.frame.DataFrame'>
RangeIndex: 450 entries, 0 to 449
Data columns (total 7 columns):
 #   Column                Non-Null Count  Dtype
---  ------                --------------  -----
 0   AgencyCode            450 non-null    object
 1   USGCSiteNumber        450 non-null    int64
 2   ParameterCode         450 non-null    int64
 3   TS_id                 450 non-null    int64
 4   Year                  450 non-null    int64
 5   Month                 450 non-null    int64
 6   GageHeightMean(feet)  450 non-null    float64
dtypes: float64(1), int64(5), object(1)
memory usage: 24.7+ KB
```

```
waterdata = waterdata_Original[['Year','Month','GageHeightMean(feet)']]
waterdata.head()
```

```
waterdata.rename(columns={'GageHeightMean(feet)':'height'},inplace=True)
waterdata['Month'] = waterdata['Month'].astype(str)
waterdata.head()
```

Output:

	height											
Month	1	10	11	12	2	3	4	5	6	7	8	9
Year												
1983	NaN	41.505	40.986	40.849	NaN	NaN	NaN	NaN	NaN	NaN	NaN	NaN
1984	41.569	40.155	39.264	38.960	41.368	41.366	41.200	40.769	40.474	41.012	41.546	41.152
1985	38.880	41.624	40.528	39.884	38.834	38.733	38.756	38.323	38.285	38.898	41.343	43.123
1986	41.219	41.224	40.789	40.712	41.572	41.304	41.131	40.380	40.178	40.353	40.719	41.796
1987	40.794	40.868	41.069	41.154	40.851	41.290	43.522	41.668	40.653	40.555	40.682	40.955

```
Strip() colimns
```

```
Index(['height_1', 'height_10', 'height_11', 'height_12', 'height_2' 'height_3', 'height_4', 'height_5',
'height_6', 'height_7', 'height_8', 'height_9'],dtype='object')
```

Check for nulls:

```
tempdf.isna().sum()
```

Output:

```
height_1     3
height_10    2
height_11    2
height_12    2
height_2     2
height_3     5
height_4     4
height_5     5
height_6     5
height_7     3
height_8     5
height_9     4
dtype: int64
```

Impute with interpolation technique:

```
tempdf2 = tempdf1.interpolate(method='linear',axis=0)
```

Visualize Box plots per month of water gage heights:

```
import pandas as pd
import matplotlib.pyplot as plt
from matplotlib.cbook import boxplot_stats
import numpy as np

df = tempdf2[['height_1','height_2','height_3','height_4','height_5','height_6','height_7',
     'height_8','height_9','height_10',' height_11','height_12'
         ]]
#plot the dataframe as needed
ax = df.plot.box(figsize=(15,8), showmeans=True,grid=True)
```

Output:

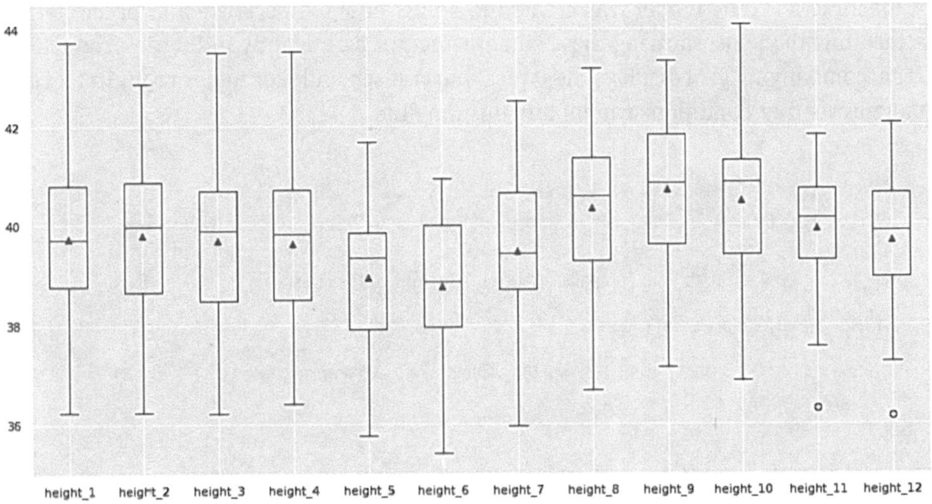

For Withlacoochee River Near Floral City, FL – 02312600 data, as it can be seen, the height of gage varies highly in September.

Step 7: Merge water and other climatology, weather, production, and environmental datasets

Merge all datasets and verify any nulls. Fill any nulls.

```
finaldf_water=pd.merge(left=finaldf,right=tempdf2,left_index=True,right_index=True)
finaldf_water.head()
```

Output:

_May	prcp_Nov	...	height_11	height_12	height_2	height_3	height_4	height_5	height_6
115.7	50.9	...	39.264	38.960	41.368	41.366	41.200	40.769	40.474
17.0	30.2	...	40.528	39.884	38.834	38.733	38.756	38.323	38.285
56.0	10.7	...	40.789	40.712	41.572	41.304	41.131	40.380	40.178
164.5	114.8	...	41.069	41.154	40.851	41.290	43.522	41.668	40.653
62.0	186.6	...	40.532	42.067	41.348	41.816	41.902	40.684	39.914

Step 8: Water use Florida tomatoes model

A machine learning model was created to assess how temperature and precipitation affect tomato yields, showing these climatic factors significantly influence production. An accompanying grid displays the typical harvest schedule for major crops in Florida, though weather conditions can modify this timeline.

```
X = finaldf_water[['AreaHarvested(ha)','Tmax_Feb',
    'Tmax_Jan','Tmax_Mar','Tmax_Apr', 'Tmax_Aug','Tmax_Nov','Tmin_Jan','Tmin_Mar','Tmin_
Apr','Tmin_May','Tmin_Dec',
'prcp_Jan', 'prcp_Feb','prcp_Aug','prcp_Oct','height_1','height_2',]].values

y= finaldf_water['Yield(hg/ha)'].values

X_train,X_test,y_train,y_test = train_test_split(X,y,test_size = 0.20,random_state =0)
print(X_train.shape)
print(X_test.shape)

model = LinearRegression()
model.fit(X_train,y_train)

#predicting the test
y_pred = model.predict(X_test)
y_pred

model_features = ['AreaHarvested(ha)','Tmax_Feb','Tmax_Jan','Tmax_Mar','Tmax_Apr', 'Tmax_
Aug','Tmax_Nov','Tmin_Jan','Tmin_Mar','Tmin_Apr','Tmin_May','Tmin_Dec',
'prcp_Jan','prcp_Feb','prcp_Aug','prcp_Oct','height_1','height_2' ]

mse = mean_squared_error(y_test,y_pred)
print("MSE:", mse)

rmse = np.sqrt(mse)
print("RMSE:",rmse)

r2 = r2_score(y_test,y_pred)
print("R2 Linear Regression:",r2)
```

Output:

```
(30, 18)
(8, 18)
MSE: 3476155374.516577
RMSE: 58958.92955707877
R2 Linear Regression: 0.6709139713295547
```

Step 9: Water use classifier equation

Let's develop model equations that take into gage height changes.

Output:

```
Yield(hg/ha) = – 24812.233 – 4.064 * AreaHarvested(ha) – 16962.522 * Tmax_Feb + 47598.367 * Tmax_Jan – 18421.389 * Tmax_Mar + 1641.164 * Tmax_Apr + 47217.952 * Tmax_Aug – 24031.875 * Tmax_Nov – 30419.832 * Tmin_Jan – 300.197 * Tmin_Mar + 29676.096 * Tmin_Apr + 35327.052 * Tmin_May + 13511.381 * Tmin_Dec + 312.197 * prcp_Jan – 441.100 * prcp_Feb + 286.215 * prcp_Aug – 411.604 * prcp_Oct + 4405.095 * height_1 – 23319.816 * height_2
```

This equation is a mathematical formula used to estimate the yield (in hg/ha) of a particular crop based on several different variables.

The variables used in the formula are:
- AreaHarvested (in hectares)
- Tmax_Feb, Tmax_Jan, Tmax_Mar, Tmax_Apr, Tmax_Aug and Tmax_Nov (maximum temperature in degree Celsius for each respective month)
- Tmin_Jan, Tmin_Mar, Tmin_Apr, Tmin_May and Tmin_Dec (minimum temperature in degrees Celsius for each respective month)
- prcp_Jan, prcp_Feb, prcp_Aug, and prcp_Oct (Precipitation in millimeters for each respective month)
- height_1 and height_2 (height in meters above sea level)

The formula employs regression analysis to link variables with yield. The coefficients (the numbers next to each variable) indicate how much each variable contributes to the overall yield estimate. For example, a higher maximum temperature in January (Tmax_Jan) is associated with a higher yield, while a higher minimum temperature in January (Tmin_Jan) is associated with a lower yield. Similarly, higher precipitation in August (prcp_Aug) is associated with a higher yield, while higher precipitation in October (prcp_Oct) is associated with a lower yield. Overall, this equation estimates crop yield, aiding in informed management decisions.

Step 10: Water use explainability

Output:

Weight?	Feature
+47598.367	Tmax_Jan
+47217.952	Tmax_Aug
+35327.052	Tmin_May
+29676.096	Tmin_Apr
+13511.381	Tmin_Dec
+4405.095	height_1
+1641.164	Tmax_Apr
+312.197	prcp_Jan
+286.215	prcp_Aug
-4.064	AreaHarvested(ha)
-300.197	Tmin_Mar
-411.604	prcp_Oct
-441.100	prcp_Feb
-16962.522	Tmax_Feb
-18421.389	Tmax_Mar
-23319.816	height_2
-24031.875	Tmax_Nov
-24812.233	<BIAS>
-30419.832	Tmin_Jan

- Water levels in January have positive influence on the model.
- Water levels in February have negative impact on the model.

The first statement, “water levels in January have a positive influence on the model,” means that when water levels are higher in January, the model performs better or shows a positive outcome. In other words, higher water levels in January are associated with a positive impact on the model.

The second statement, “water levels in February have a negative impact on the model,” means that when water levels are higher in February, the model performs worse or shows a negative outcome. In other words, higher water levels in February are associated with a negative impact on the model.

These statements suggest that water levels in different months can have different effects on the model being studied. This information can be useful for researchers and other stakeholders who are interested in understanding how water levels impact different systems and processes and can help inform decision-making related to water management and conservation.

Chapter machine learning experiments

ML experiment: water use model Withlacoochee River near Floral city, FL

The figure below showcases the water gage for the Withlacoochee River, a key factor in linking crop coefficients and water use for tomatoes. Given that tomatoes are a primary crop in the region, it is vital to understand the actual amount of water these plants require, which is contingent on various factors such as soil quality, growing season, and climate conditions. By improving water use efficiency and conserving this precious resource, growers and the district can minimize waste and maximize yield. The Florida Tomato model plays a pivotal role in this process, determining optimal irrigation schedules and crop coefficients to help growers make informed decisions. As part of the ML experiment, it is worthwhile to rerun the model for different months and gage heights to assess how the coefficient of the regression model changes over time.

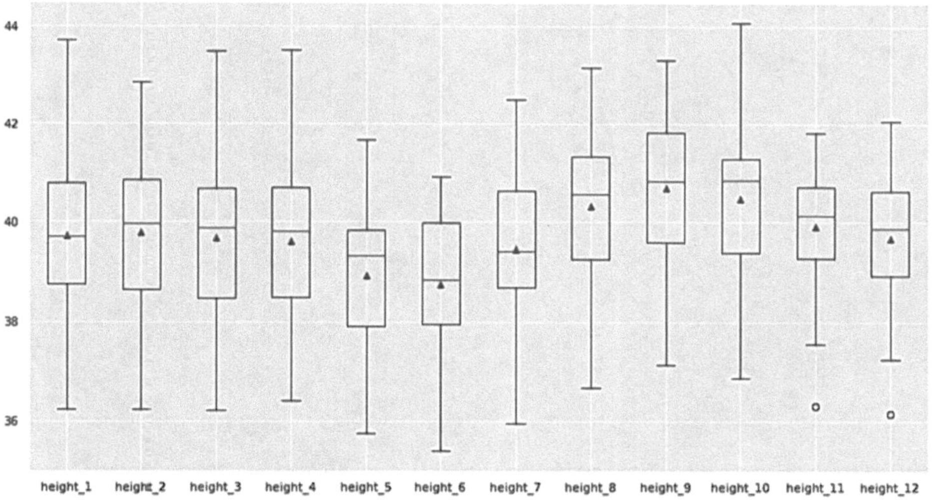

ML experiment: tomatoes' prices and food security

Tomatoes are one of the essential crops. The prices of tomatoes are linked to food security, higher prices, lower food security, and nutrition. How can yield analytics help reduce the price volatility?

This chapter examines yield patterns for specialty crop tomatoes in key producing nations, using statistical and mathematical methods to understand yield curves and production trends. It introduces the development of machine learning models to analyze large datasets and identify relevant patterns. Specifically, the chapter discusses employing polynomial regression models to forecast climate data related to tomato cultivation. It also explores machine learning models that focus on water usage and its impact on tomato yields, helping stakeholders prepare for extreme weather. By the end, readers will have a comprehensive understanding of tomato production, yield influences, and the ability to use machine learning for informed decision-making and future planning.

Chapter 8
Specialty crops tomatoes: climate change adaptation strategies

This chapter covers:
- Tomatoes: historical risk management (RMA) payments
- Yield influencers
- Climate change impact
- The use of methyl bromide in tomato production is explained, including its benefits and drawbacks
- Machine learning models
  - Plant City , Florida , USA, tomatoes production yield model and methyl bromide: Montreal protocol climate sustainability model
  - A projection model is presented that examines the influence of weather events on tomato yield in Plant City, Florida, USA
- Climate adaptation strategies
- Policy recommendations

This chapter is all about tomatoes that are grown for special purposes. It talks about how the weather affects the amount of tomatoes that are produced and how the government helps farmers who experience extreme weather. It also looks at how different countries produce tomatoes and how important tomatoes are to the economy and job market. The chapter provides a lot of information about what affects the amount of tomatoes that are grown and how the use of a chemical called methyl bromide can help or hurt the tomato plants. The chapter ends with a detailed look at how weather events affect the amount of tomatoes grown in a specific area in Florida. After reading this chapter, you will have a good understanding of how tomatoes are produced, what affects their growth, and how to make good decisions to make more money when growing specialty crop tomatoes.

Scientists have thoroughly examined how climate change affects staple crops, but its impact on specialty crops like processing tomatoes is less clear. These tomatoes are crucial as a nutrient source and are widely used in various global food products. In the previous chapter, computer simulations were used to predict how rising temperatures would affect tomato crops in the top-producing countries: the United States (mainly California), India, and China. These countries collectively supply most of the world's processed tomatoes. The simulations, despite varying in specific outcomes, consistently showed that climate change will substantially impact tomato production in the coming decades [334].

Climate change presents significant threats to many crops, with tomatoes being especially vulnerable. These plants thrive at temperatures between 18 °C (64 °F) and 25 °C (77 °F), but deviations cause issues such as poor pollen development and improper fruit formation. When temperatures surpass 35 °C (95 °F) as witnessed recently in San Joaquin valley, tomato yields dramatically decrease. A 2020 study revealed that by the mid-twenty-first century, up to 66% of California's traditional tomato-growing land might become unsuitable and in some cases inhabitant due to rising temperatures. Furthermore, modeling studies suggest that by 2050, large regions in Brazil, sub-Saharan Africa, India, and Indonesia will also lose their optimal climate conditions for tomato cultivation [335].

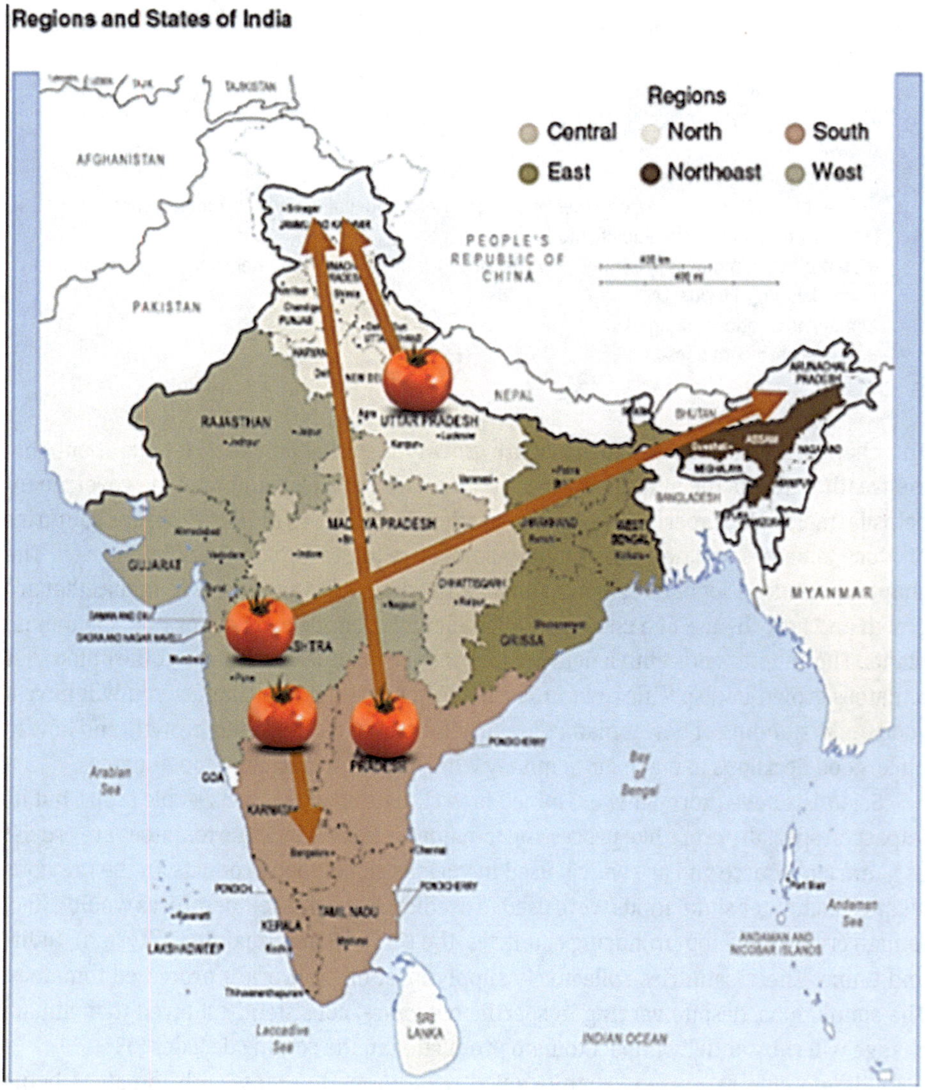

Figure 1: Adaptation strategies for India.

As average temperatures increase, regions that were previously too cold for tomato cultivation may become suitable. In places like California, India, and China, this shift could be beneficial for the cooler northernmost areas. Rising temperatures in these regions may enhance tomato yields, with studies predicting a steady increase in production for the northern Chinese province of Gansu and the neighboring country of Mongolia. In India, rising temperatures in southern regions like Andhra Pradesh and Madhya Pradesh could improve tomato yields in cooler northern areas such as Kashmir (Figure 1), Himachal Pradesh, and Assam. In Himachal Pradesh, tomatoes are becoming an important out-of-season secondary immediate payment crop, benefiting 22,753 smallholder farmers. However, even at peak yields, these northern regions will produce only a fraction of what California and Italy currently achieve and may not fully compensate for future production needs lost in the southern regions. Consequently, we could be facing a future with tomato shortages and increased prices [336].

Kashmir: India's food basket!

Climate change is causing shifts in the regions around the world that are important for growing food. In India, one of the world's most populous countries, Punjab, Uttar Pradesh, and Madhya Pradesh are currently major producers of long and specialty crops. However, these regions will face significant stress on their crop yields due to changing weather patterns and unprecedented weather in the future. Thus, regions like Kashmir may become the future of India's food basket, potentially serving as a source of food for over a billion people.

Author
Chandrasekar Vuppalapati

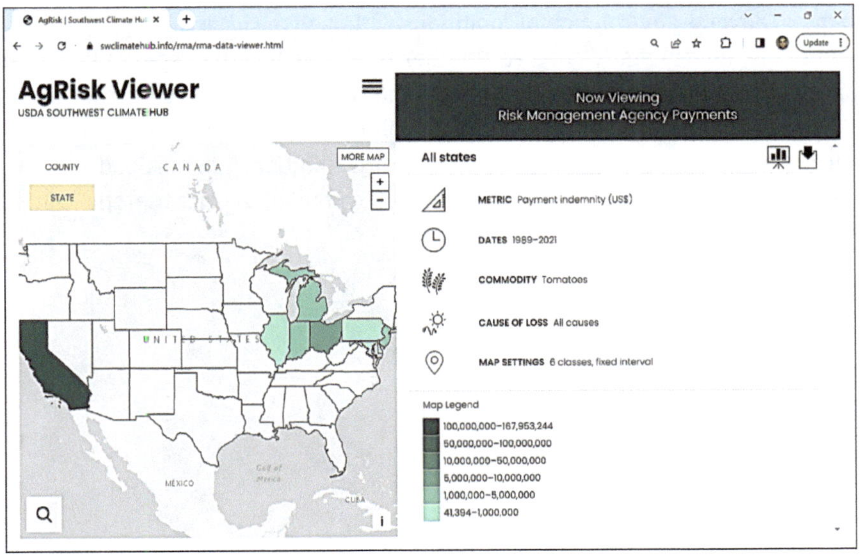

Figure 2: RMA payment for tomato paste.

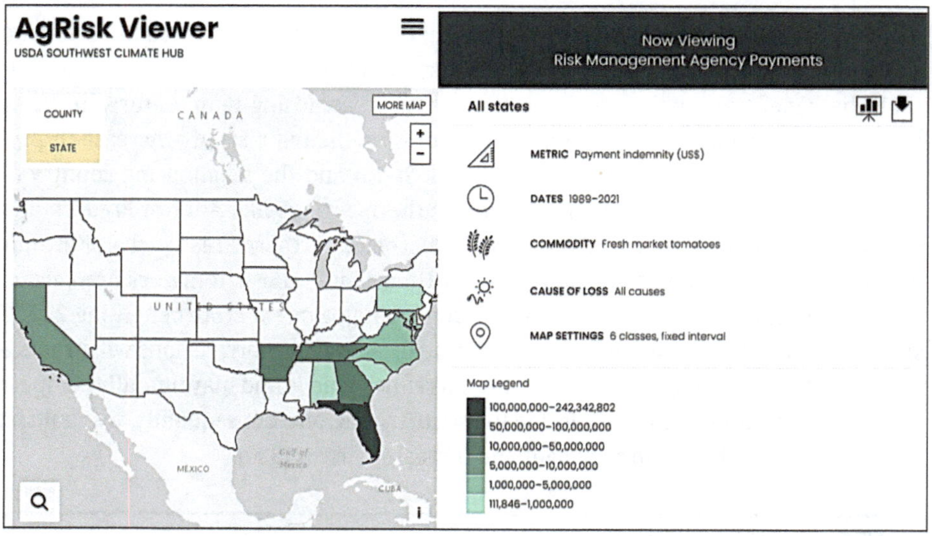

Figure 3: RMA payment for fresh tomato.

Historical RMA payments: fresh market tomatoes

The RMA is slated to monitor Federal Crop Insurance Program (FCIP) and provide financial protection to agricultural producers against losses resulting from adverse events – all of which are directly influenced by climate change (Figures 2 and 3).

The USDA defines eligible perils under the FCIP as including extreme and increasingly frequent adverse environmental conditions. Although the list is expanding in both items and scope, the currently covered weather events include barrage, chill, freeze, gale, famine, and excess rainfall. Additionally, the program covers risks from earthquakes, fires, insect infestations, plant diseases, wildfires, and volcanic eruptions [337]. Common causes of losses include excess moisture, precipitation, famine, flood, extreme heat, downward fluctuations or sudden drop of commodity prices, arctic watery climate, wind or excess wind, and flood (Figure 4).

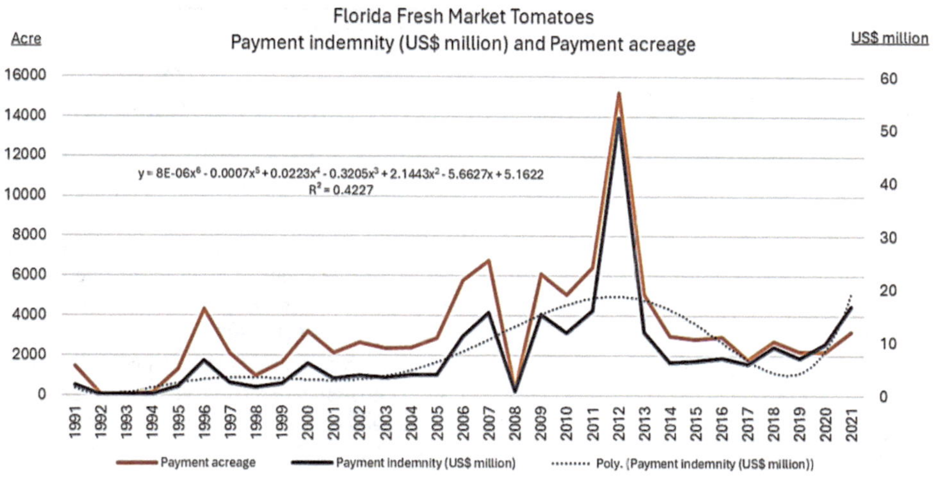

Figure 4: Florida fresh tomatoes.

The above figure consists of payment indemnity (US $ million) for tomatoes crops in California from 1989 to 2021. The data is downloaded from AgRisk Viewer [338].

Indemnity payment: tomatoes, California			
	Equation	**R^2 value**	
Exponential	$y = 0.5623e^{0.119x}$	$R^2 = 0.1012$	(1)
Linear	$y = 0.4721x + 0.2644$	$R^2 = 0.1978$	(2)
Logarthimic	$y = 4.9034\ \ln(x) - 4.5346$	$R^2 = 0.1879$	(3)
Polynomial order 6	$y = 8E{-}06x^6 - 0.0007x^5 + 0.0223x^4 - 0.3205x^3 + 2.1443x^2 - 5.6627x + 5.1622$	$R^2 = 0.4227$	(4)
Power	$y = 0.1261x^{1.3495}$	$R^2 = 0.1836$	(5)

The way that farmers are compensated for growing tomatoes varies depending on how the tomatoes will be used. For tomatoes that will be canned or processed, as well as for tomatoes grown for guaranteed production plans for the fresh market, the indemnity model is based on an individual yield guarantee. This means that the farmers are guaranteed a certain yield of tomatoes, and they will be compensated accordingly if they do not meet that yield. For tomatoes that will be sold in the fresh market, the indemnity model is based on a dollar revenue guarantee. This means that the farmers are guaranteed a certain amount of revenue from their tomato sales, and they will be compensated accordingly if they do not meet that revenue goal [339].

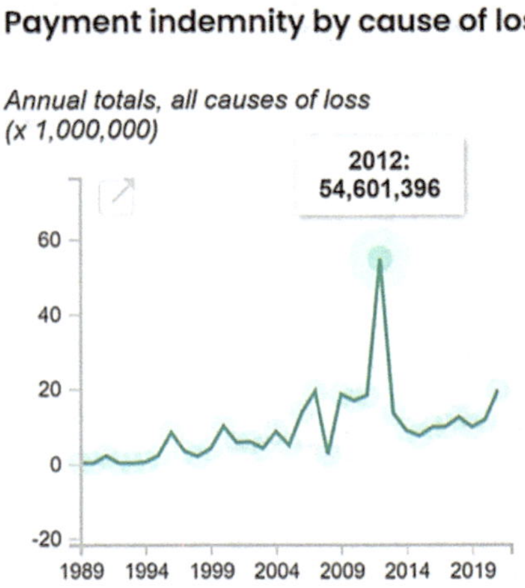

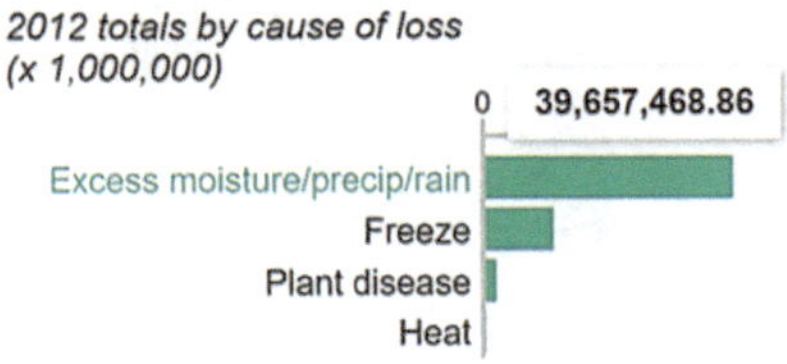

In 2012, Florida fresh tomatoes farms received $54.601 million indemnity payments from FCIP. The major losses include excessive moisture/precipitation/rain ($39.687 million), freeze ($11.346 million), and plant disease ($2.348 million). 2012 was a terrible season for the tomato industry. Excessive moisture/precipitation/rain has contributed to losses of $17.789 [340].

Source: AgRisk Viewer.

Postharvest deterioration damages for field-grown, fresh-market tomatoes often occur during warm and wet harvest conditions, particularly when temperatures exceed 90 °F (32.22 °C) during the day. Prolonged wetness in the fields allows decay pathogens to infect damaged fruit and injuries to petioles and stems. These pathogens spread through the harvested fruit during picking operations, making harvest-related wounds especially susceptible to infection. As a result, growers and packing house managers frequently struggle to save their crops. Although gray mold is not a major issue for Florida tomatoes, most tomato decay pathogens become more active in warm temperatures.

Postharvest decay becomes more common during weather transitions, especially when dramatic temperature shifts due to weather fronts cause prolonged wetness in plant canopies. Indicators like dense fog and persistently wet plants, even without rainfall, can signal these transitions. Heavy dews and extensive guttation further sustain wet conditions, collectively increasing the risk of postharvest decay.

Chilly temperatures during the winter production seasons of 2010 and 2011 resulted in notable postharvest defects, which diminished fruit quality and increased decay. As reported by newspapers, by the close of January 2010, frosts and freezes had decimated 70% of South Florida's tomato crops that were slated for late winter and early spring harvests. The quality of the remaining harvested fruit was poor, and this adverse situation continued until mid-April.

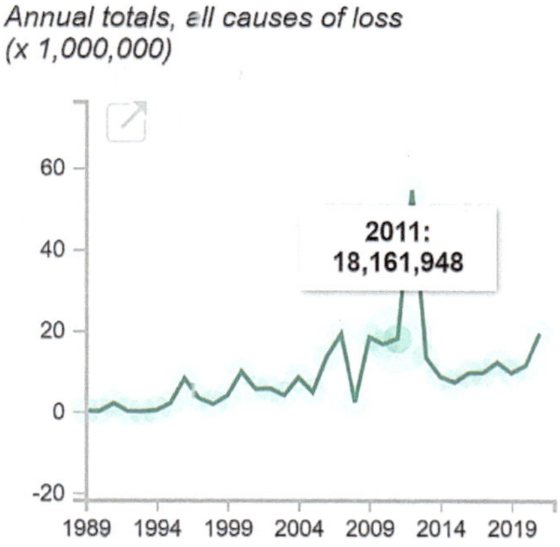

Source: AgRisk Viewer.

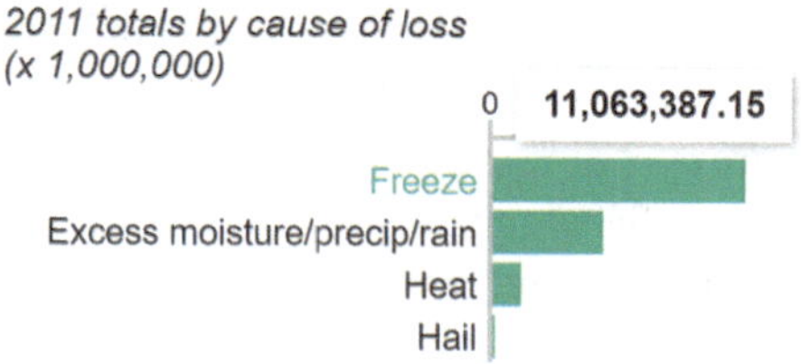

In 2011, Florida fresh tomatoes farms received $18.161 million indemnity payments from FCIP. The major losses include freeze ($11.063 million), excessive moisture/precipitation/rain ($4.938 million), and heat ($1.412 million). 2011 was a terrible season for the tomato industry. Freeze, excessive moisture/precipitation/rain, and heat have contributed to losses of $18.161 million [341].

The tomatoes cultivated in Florida are vastly different from garden varieties, as they are primarily bred for their perfect shape and durability during shipping rather than their flavor. For over 50 years, tomato breeders have prioritized yield, resulting in fruits that can withstand being harvested, packed, and shipped across the country without breaking or cracking. Unfortunately, this focus on yield has come at the expense of taste, as breeders have prioritized shipment over flavor [341, 342]. Despite being the primary source of tomatoes in the USA, Florida may not be the most suitable place to grow them. The majority of the state's tomatoes are cultivated in sandy soil, which is deficient in the essential nutrients and organic matter required for optimal growth. Additionally, the humid climate in Florida attracts large populations of insects, necessitating frequent pesticide applications. In fact, Florida uses over eight times more pesticides and herbicides than California, the second leading tomato grower in the country. While this is partially due to California processing tomatoes for canning rather than fresh consumption, it also reflects consumer demand for aesthetically pleasing tomatoes [341, 342].

Florida stands as the foremost cultivator of fresh tomatoes in the United States; however, since 2000, the quantity of tomatoes grown has been steadily decreasing. In 2015, there was a 40% drop in production compared to 2000. The area where tomatoes are grown has also decreased. Before 2009, Florida had the highest amount of tomatoes produced per acre compared to other states, but now, it has decreased. This decline is primarily due to the banning of a chemical called methyl bromide, which was used to control pests and increase yields [343, 344].

Florida tomato growers face a multitude of unique challenges [345], ranging from unpredictable weather events and poor soil quality to pest and disease pressure, labor shortages, urban development, and strict regulations. The discontinuation of methyl bromide, a widely used soil fumigant, has resulted in higher production costs and lower yields. A study by the Economic Research Service and the University of Florida found that banning methyl bromide could cause an annual loss of approximately $200 million in gross shipping point revenues for both Florida and California. Additionally, the switch to the new industry standard, PicChlor 60, significantly decreased gross revenue and profit for growers during the 2013/2014 season, with higher market prices worsening the losses. These challenges underscore the pressing need for continued innovation and investment in sustainable and cost-effective farming practices for the Florida tomato industry [346].

Methyl bromide (CH_3Br)

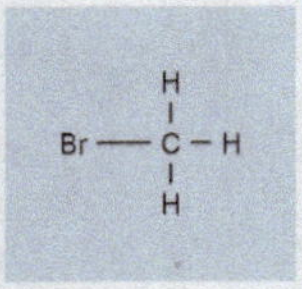

Methyl bromide is a fumigant commonly employed in farming and transport to manage pests like molds, tidies, bugs, roundworms, and gnawers. However, it is a hazardous and toxic chemical that depletes the ozone layer, leading to increased levels of harmful UV radiation. The United States, along with numerous other countries, has gradually eliminated manufacture and application of CH_3Br, except for significant applications and confinement or preconsignment scenarios. Although it is highly effective as sterilize soil before planting, up to 95% of the methyl bromide injected into the soil eventually escapes into the atmosphere. It is also used to handle produce such as wine primary ingredients and sparagus to check pest introduction into the United States. While the phase out of methyl bromide may negatively impact agricultural production and consumers, it is a crucial measure for safeguarding the environment and public health [344].

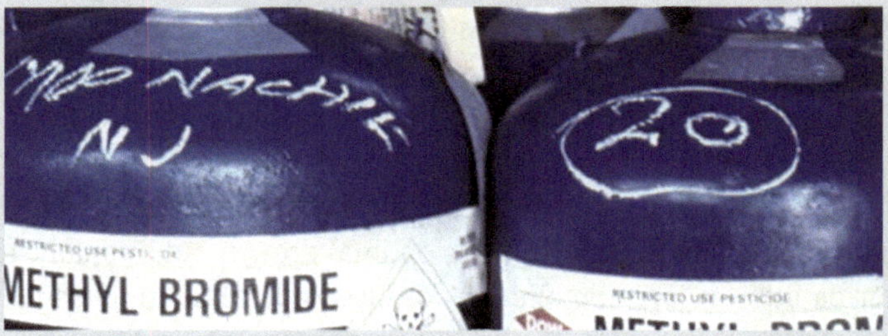

Historical RMA payments: tomatoes for processing

The FCIP is administered by USDA, which provides financial protection to farmers against losses caused by things like drought, excess moisture, freezes, hail, wind, disease, and price fluctuations. These problems are becoming more common due to climate change, which is why it's important for the government to offer support to farmers who are affected by these issues. The FCIP program helps farmers to manage the risks associated with these challenges and helps to ensure that they can continue to produce food for the population.

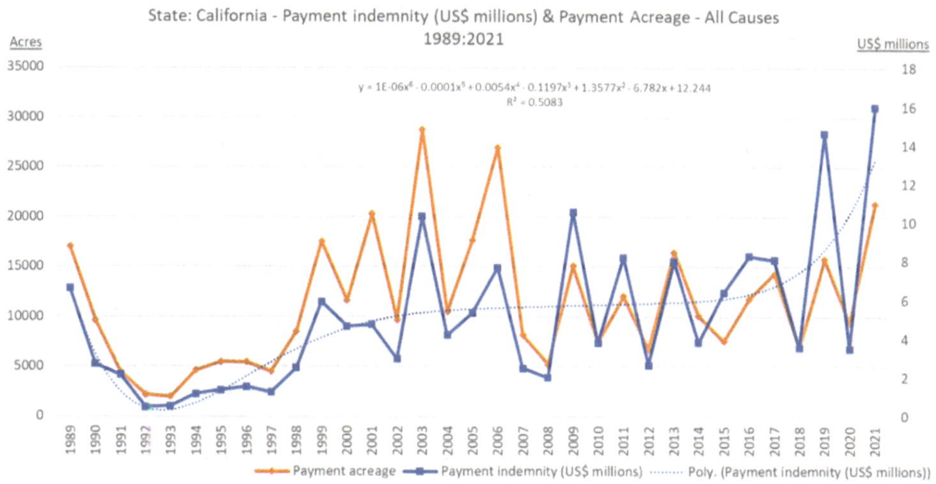

Figure 5: California payment indemnity.

Figure 5 consists of payment indemnity (US $ million) for tomatoes crops in California from 1989 to 2021. The data is downloaded from AgRisk Viewer [338].

Indemnity payment: tomatoes, California

	Equation	R^2 value	
Exponential	$y = 1.4637e^{0.0552x}$	$R^2 = 0.3606$	(6)
Linear	$y = 0.2308x + 1.166$	$R^2 = 0.3378$	(7)
Logarthimic	$y = 2.0179\ \ln(x) - 0.1114$	$R^2 = 0.2035$	(8)
Polynomial order 6	$y = 1E{-}06x^6 - 0.0001x^5 + 0.0054x^4 - 0.1197x^3 + 1.3577x^2 - 6.782x + 12.244$	$R^2 = 0.5083$	(9)
Power	$y = 1.0067x^{0.5095}$	$R^2 = 0.2924$	(10)

A quarter of the world's annual tomato production is sourced from California, yet the state's tomato output is now plummeting at an extraordinary pace. In 2021, tomato yields were about 23% lower than in 2015. This reduced supply has caused a dramatic spike in the prices of popular tomato-based products, including tomato soup, jam, hot pickled tomatoes, marinara sauce, and red salsa, in both the USA and worldwide [347].

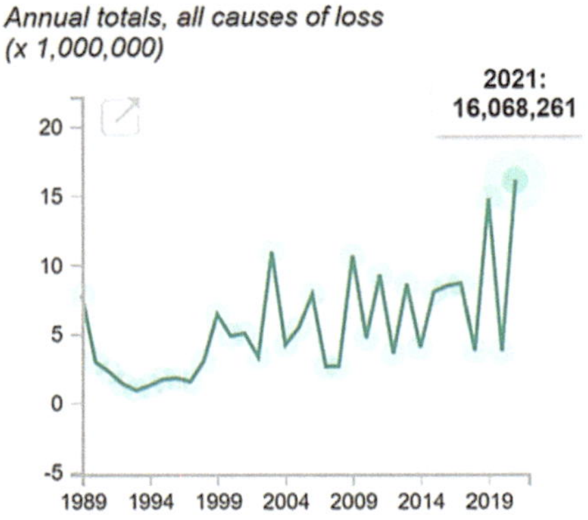

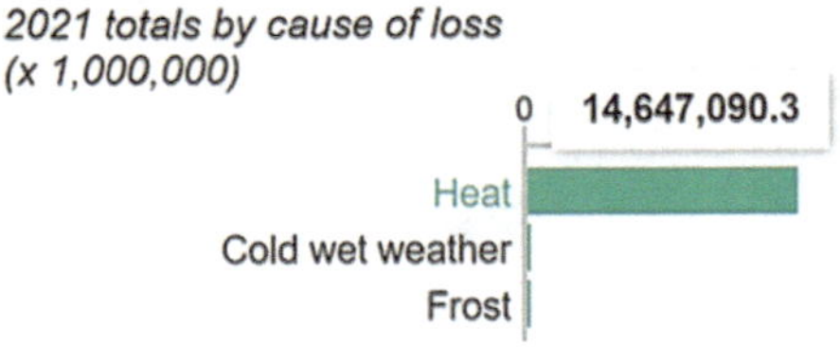

In 2021, California tomatoes for processing farms received $16.068 million indemnity payments from FCIP. The major losses include heat ($14.647 million), cold wet weather ($421K), and frost ($416K). 2021 was a terrible season for the tomato industry. Heat has contributed to losses of $14.647 million [340].

Source: AgRisk Viewer.

The food inflationary trends of tomatoes in the United States have increased by 13–23%, far exceeding the current overall food prices, which the US Department of Agriculture projects will stay between 9% and 11% this year. Essentially, tomato price inflation is significantly higher than overall inflation.

Tomatoes are a cherished staple in the United States, coming in as the second most consumed vegetable after potatoes. In 2021, the North American ketchup market alone reached a remarkable valuation of $1,390 million USD. Even if we momentarily set aside the vital role of tomatoes and ketchup in the food industry, it is hard to imagine many of our meals without this versatile fruit, which is a cornerstone in salsa and a myriad of sauces [347].

Nurturing tomato crops has become incredibly challenging these days. On one hand, drought conditions are causing costs to soar because there isn't enough water for all the fields. On the other hand, escalating fuel and fertilizer prices are driving farm inflation.

Central California is a major agricultural hub in the United States, responsible for growing almost 50% of fruits-nuts-vegetables produced in the country. It's also a significant producer of tomatoes, accounting for 30% of worldwide tomatoes. However, in 2021, tomato yields in Central California were lower than usual due to extremely hot weather conditions. This caused prices for tomatoes to increase by 25%, making them more expensive for consumers to buy [348].

In 2021, there was a significant drop in yield, which can be attributed to the intensity and duration of the hotter spells. According to the president and CEO of the California Tomato Growers Association, these spells are not only hotter but also last longer, significantly impacting the yields that growers can achieve [349]. Additionally, the heat is not the only challenge that growers face. Unusual cold snaps, such as frost in April and unseasonable September rains, have also contributed to reduced tomato crops in 2021, as evidenced by indemnity payments. As a result of water scarcity and extreme weather, farmers are planting fewer acres, and the fields that do produce are yielding lower outputs, which inevitably lead to higher prices [349].

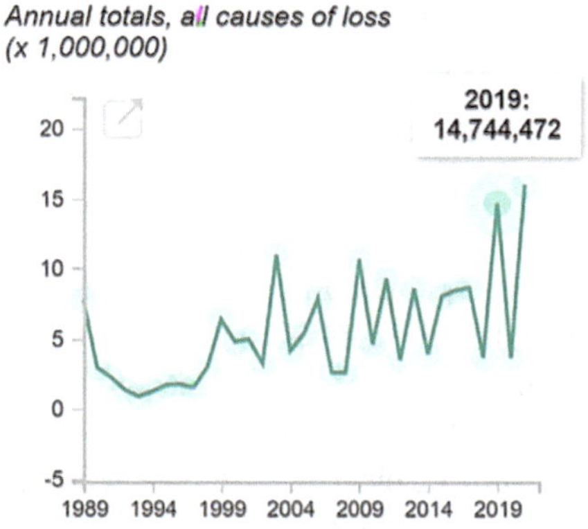

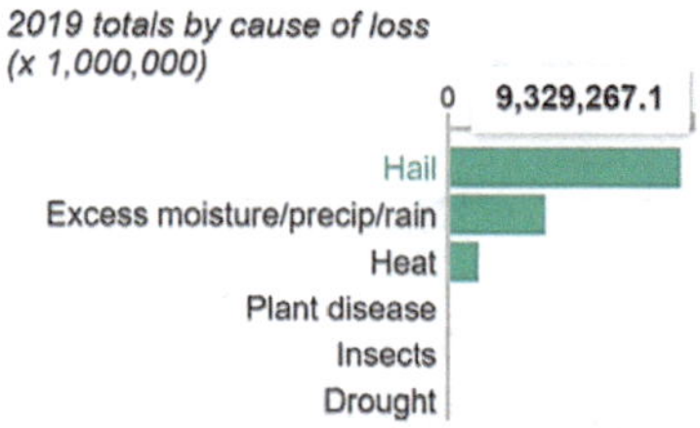

In 2019, California tomatoes for processing farms received $14.744 million indemnity payments from FCIP. The major losses include hail ($9.329 million), excess moisture/precipitation/rain ($3.938 million), and heat ($1.281 million), 2019 [340].

Source: AgRisk Viewer.

The rainy and cool conditions of early spring 2019 stalled planting and hindered crop growth, while hail damage in May in Fresno County reduced expected yields. Additionally, extreme heat in July and August, along with disease pressure, further negatively impacted the crops [350]. 2019 hail impacted year! [351, 352].

In California, severe summer heat in 2016–2017 increased mold and adversely affected crops, while frost damage was reported in Indiana, Michigan, and Ohio around mid-May. Despite these challenges, by June, tomatoes were growing well with no significant disease pressure, and harvesting began on schedule, with Florida experiencing warmer weather and earlier crop maturation due to sufficient moisture.

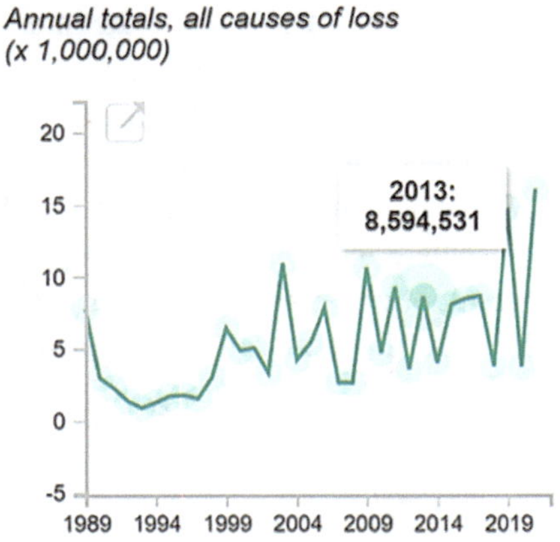

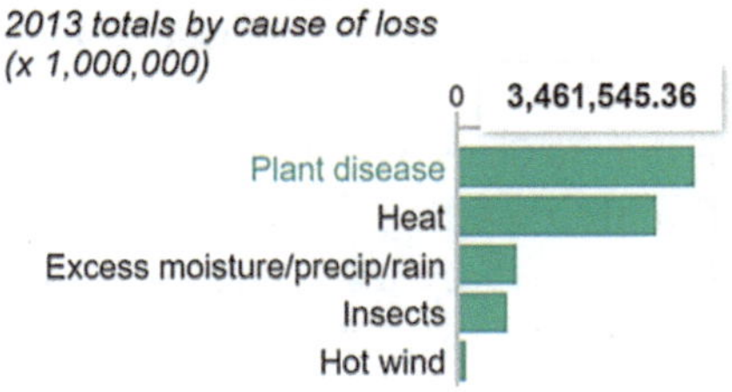

In 2013, California tomatoes for processing farms received $8.594 million indemnity payments from FCIP. The major losses include plant disease ($3.461 million), followed by heat ($2.907 million), excess moisture/precipitation/rain ($879K), and insects ($839K) [340].

Source: AgRisk Viewer.

In 2013, California's tomato growers suffered major losses due to the widespread beet curly top virus, which affected a variety of crops and expanded into new areas including San Joaquin County [352]. The virus, transmitted by the Beet leafhopper, led to over a million tons of tomatoes being lost that year, significantly impacting yields [352]. This prompted California tomato canneries to contract for 13.5 million tons of tomatoes for 2014 in response to the reduced supply [353]. A plant pathologist from the University of California, Davis, highlighted that the virus had reduced the previous year's tomato crop by nearly a million tons [353]. The beet curly top virus, being the most severe threat to tomatoes and uniquely transmitted by the beet leafhopper, has posed a significant challenge for researchers and growers, exacerbated by a recent surge in the leafhopper population [352].

In California, the rapid migration patterns of the beet leafhopper make it difficult to control, as the pest can briefly land on tomato plants, feed, and efficiently transmit disease through phloem feeding. This poses a significant challenge for growers, who may not detect the leafhoppers even though they have briefly visited and spread the disease [353].

Yield influencers

As our planet experiences escalating temperatures and increasingly severe weather patterns, the productivity of numerous food production systems is being jeopardized, resulting in lower yields. This worrisome trend prompts us to ponder which foods may need to be reduced or even abandoned by consumers. One of the primary factors affecting food production is carbon dioxide (CO_2). While plants utilize CO_2 to power photosynthesis, there comes a point where additional amounts of CO_2 become ineffective. Additionally, other considerations such as water availability, fluctuating high and low temperatures, and the impact of stress on plant health may surpass the benefits of a CO_2 boost [354].

California: atmospheric rivers

The indispensability of water in agriculture cannot be overstated, as it is fundamental towards sustainment of crops. However, in March 2023, a series of approximately twelve atmospheric rivers spanning the Pacific Ocean unleashed vast plumes of tropical moisture [355], which fueled storms that inundated the state with trillions of gallons of water. This deluge resulted in farmland being rendered too waterlogged for the planting of tomatoes, causing significant delays in the cultivation process.

The consequences of these disruptions to the tomato supply chain are manifold, including the potential for shortages of preferred tomato-based condiments at retail outlets, and a concomitant increase in prices for ketchup, salsa, and other tomato products. The far-reaching impacts of these phenomena highlight the importance of implementing innovative strategies to ease harmful impacts and enhance agricultural resilience.

Through cutting-edge technologies instrumentation, alongside the adoption of resource-efficient and ecologically sustainable practices, it is possible to ensure the continued availability and affordability of essential food products, including those derived from tomatoes. This requires an unwavering commitment to environmental stewardship, community engagement, and the pursuit of adaptive approaches that can withstand the vagaries of a changing climate.

The latest yield data reveals that the production of corn and wheat, the two essential crops, is already suffering the negative effects of the shifting climate [354, 356]. Furthermore, fruit and nut production is likewise experiencing the impact of climate change. Fruit-bearing trees necessitate "chilling hours," or extended periods in cold, wintery conditions, to achieve optimal production. If they fail to accumulate the required number of cold days, their output, as well as quality, will plummet. These reduced yields result in more frequent price fluctuations across various food items. The yield section unmistakably highlights the contrasting behavior of yield curves in Iran and the USA, which is influenced by various factors.

Climate change

Tomatoes are a beloved staple in American diets, with each person consuming over 18.8 pounds (8.527 kg) of fresh tomatoes and 59.54 pounds (27 kg) of processed tomatoes annually, predominantly in forms like paste, sauce, and ketchup. However, extreme weather conditions, regulatory hurdles, and economic challenges have escalated the costs for growers and processors. These rising production costs are ultimately passed on to consumers, resulting in higher prices for tomato-based products in stores and restaurants.

Vegetables are universally cherished, and tomatoes hold a special place globally. India is the second largest producer of tomatoes, where they are a daily staple alongside onions and feature prominently in popular dishes like Masala and Andhra Tomato Kura. However, a 341% increase in tomato prices as of July 2023 has caused significant unrest and theft. This price surge is attributed to flooding in key tomato-producing states such as Andhra Pradesh, Maharashtra, and Karnataka, which has severely damaged crops and led to widespread theft of the remaining harvests [357, 358].

The economic viability of tomato cultivation has undergone a discernible shift, marked by a notable decrease in profitability. Consequently, the global tomato supply chain is poised to experience a corresponding reduction in availability.

This transformation in the tomato industry is attributable to a confluence of factors, including but not limited to, fluctuations in market demand, changes in production costs, and variable weather patterns. The resulting shift in economic incentives has led to a decline in the cultivation of tomatoes, thereby limiting the availability of this widely consumed fruit.

The implications of this paradigmatic shift are far-reaching and merit careful consideration. As the supply of tomatoes becomes increasingly constrained, consumers may face higher prices, reduced access, and a potential shift in dietary preferences. It is therefore incumbent upon stakeholders in the tomato industry to devise innovative strategies to address this challenge and ensure continued access to this vital food source.

Chandrasekar Vuppalapati

Heinz ketchup tomatoes: all on sustainability!

Our dedication[1] to environmental stewardship is reflected in every facet of our enterprise, from soil management practices to our food production and packaging methodologies. Pursuant to this overarching mission, we have established an audacious aim to source all Heinz ketchup tomatoes through sustainable means by 2025. We intend to realize this goal through the implementation of pioneering soil health strategies and a tenacious pursuit of optimal tomato yields on every acre.

Such an aspirational objective is predicated on our unyielding commitment to safeguarding the planet's natural resources and preserving them for future generations. To this end, we remain steadfast in our resolve to explore innovative methodologies that prioritize the principles of sustainability, biodiversity, and ecological resilience. Through the application of cutting-edge technologies and the cultivation of enduring partnerships with like-minded entities, we are confident in our ability to achieve our sustainability aspirations [359].

---

1 All on sustainability! https://www.heinz.com/who-we-are/

Fall freeze

A fall freeze is an extreme weather event that can damage tomato plants in California, usually occurring from late October to the end of December. Historically, such frozen weather has caused significant harm as seen in the 1980s. The impact on tomato plants can range from minor leaf damage to complete destruction, potentially leading to a significant decline in yield and even plant death (Table 7 for bacterial spot and Table 8 for early blight) [360].

To mitigate the impact of fall freeze on tomato cultivation in California, farmers use various techniques. One such method is to cover the tomato plants with a protective layer to shield them from the cold. Additionally, growers may use irrigation systems to create a thin layer of ice on the plants, which can help maintain a stable temperature around the plants. However, these methods may not always provide complete protection, and the yield may still be affected. In conclusion, fall freeze is a significant challenge for tomato cultivation in California. It can cause damage to the plants and lead to a decline in the yield. Farmers must take appropriate measures to minimize the impact of the fall freeze on their crops.

Table 1: Bacterial spot.

Tomato bacterial spot disease, caused by various species of Xanthomonas bacteria, appears as small, water-soaked spots that darken and may be surrounded by yellow halos, affecting leaves, stems, and fruit. Thriving in warm, wet conditions, the disease spreads through infected seeds, plant debris, and splashing water, leading to defoliation, fruit blemishes, and reduced plant vigor, posing a significant challenge for growers.

Table 2: Early blight.

Tomato early blight disease, caused by the fungus *Alternaria solani*, presents as dark, concentric spots on the lower leaves, progressing upward and leading to defoliation, fruit rot, and reduced plant health. This disease thrives in warm, humid conditions and spreads through infected plant debris, soil, and splashing water, making effective management essential for maintaining crop yield and quality.

Water, evapotranspiration, and irrigation

California produces nearly 95% of the processed tomatoes in the United States and one-third of the global supply. However, recent challenges like drought, extreme heat, and reduced acreage due to competition from other crops have affected production yields and inventory. Despite latest rainfall, drought persists, and California growers face stringent water regulations under SGMA [345, 356, 358, 361].

Water and climate change [336]

The magnitude of water in agriculture cannot be overstated. Amidst the challenges of climate variance and increasing frequency of drought conditions, farmers are frequently compelled to make the difficult decision to forgo entire crops at the close of the harvest season. This, in turn, results in the squandering of significant investments made in the cultivation of crops, including the planting and nurturing of trees that may take years to mature.

The ramifications of such losses are extensive and pervasive, impacting economic, environmental, and social dimensions of agricultural communities. The depletion of finite water resources not only jeopardizes the viability of crop yields but also exacerbates the deleterious outcomes of climate change and further threatens the availability of water for future generations.

In the interest of securing a sustainable future for agriculture, it is imperative that we collectively prioritize the conservation and management of water resources. Innovative approaches that integrate the principles of ecological stewardship, resource efficiency, and community engagement are essential to achieving this objective and ensuring a thriving agricultural sector for all.

Chilling hours

Impact of heat thermal time or heat degree days (HTDD) on tomato production in California is a growing concern for growers. HTDD refers to the accumulation of heat units above a specific temperature threshold, typically 50 °F, through the growing season. This temperature range is key for tomato plant growth plus development (Figure 6).

However, California has been experiencing growth in HTDD, which has led to a reduction in tomato production. This increase in temperature can cause several issues including lower yields, reduced fruit quality, and shorter production cycles.

Moreover, an increase in HTDD can cause water stress in tomato plants, leading to reduced growth and a higher risk of diseases. This can have a terrible sway on the overall health and productivity of the tomato crop.

To mitigate the impact of high HTDD on tomato production, growers are implementing several measures, including the use of shading, misting, and other cooling techniques. Additionally, they are experimenting with new tomato varieties that are more tolerant of high temperatures. Overall, the impact of HTDD on tomato production in California is a significant challenge that requires careful management and innovative solutions to ensure the sustainability of the industry.

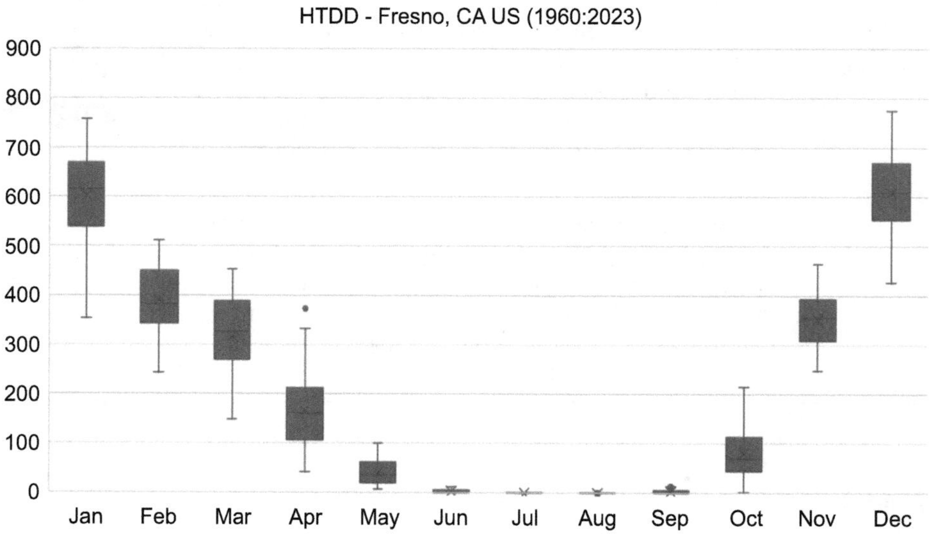

Figure 6: HTDD.

Climate change and viral threats

Tomato production in India has been adversely affected by above-average temperatures during the monsoon months of June and July, along with a delayed onset of the southwest monsoon season. Additionally, the emergence of the tomato mosaic virus from 2020 to 2023 has caused crop damage ranging from partial to total losses [357]. This virus, which manifests as a mottled or mosaic pattern on leaves, reduces the size, quality, and yield of the crop. The tobacco mosaic virus (TMV), a particularly problematic strain, can survive without a host for years and withstand high temperatures, making it difficult to eradicate [362]. It spreads primarily through mechanical means, contaminating workers and their equipment. Symptoms include yellow-green mottling (Figure 7 and table 9) on leaves and smaller, distorted flowers and leaflets, with infected plants producing fewer and smaller fruits, often with internal browning. Another significant threat is the *Pepino mosaic* virus, which is easily transmitted mechanically and contaminates the seed coat, although it has a low seed transmission rate if the seeds are properly cleaned [362].

Figure 7: Viruses turning up in high tunnel tomatoes [362].

Table 3: TMV.

USA tomatoes	

Plant city, Florida, USA, tomatoes production yield model and methyl bromide: montreal protocol climate sustainability model

Methyl bromide, a powerful fumigant used in agriculture and shipping, effectively controls pests but depletes the ozone layer. In response, the United States and other countries are phasing out its production and use, with exceptions for critical and quarantine-related applications. Despite measures to contain it, a significant portion of methyl bromide escapes into the atmosphere, prompting regulatory action under the Montreal Protocol [344]. We will continue from Step 7 from the previous chapter ML model – machine learning model: tomatoes production model in Plant City, Florida, USA, once final data frame constructed.

Step 7: Add methyl bromide feature variable

```
finaldf1 = finaldf.copy()
finaldf1.reset_index(inplace=True)
finaldf1['MethylBromide'] = 0
```

```
finaldf1.head()
```

Output:

Yield(hg/ha)	ProductionInTonnes	AreaHarvested(ha)	MethylBrom:
254496	4820709	189422	
296746	5840198	196808	
281348	4626881	164454	
293393	5089017	173454	
302597	5017059	165800	

Step 8: Set methyl bromide after the Montreal Protocol

Methyl bromide is an effective fumigant for controlling pests in agriculture and shipping, but it depletes the ozone layer, leading to international efforts to phase out its use, except for critical and quarantine-related applications. Despite containment measures, a significant amount of methyl bromide escapes into the atmosphere, prompting regulatory actions under the Montreal Protocol.

```
# adding Methyl bromide usage flag to df,
#flag set to 1 for years 2003-2010

def myfunc(year):
    if year >=2003 and year <=2010:
      return 1
    else:
      return 0
```

```
finaldf1['MethylBromide'] =0

finaldf1['MethylBromide'] = finaldf1.apply(lambda x: myfunc(x,Year),axis=1)

finaldf1.head()
```

```
finaldf1.columns
```

Output:

```
Index(['Year' , 'prcp_Apr' , 'prcp_Aug', 'prcp_Dec', 'prcp_Feb', 'prcp_Jan', 'prcp_Jul',
'prcp_Jun' , 'prcp_Mar' , 'prcp_May', 'prcp_Nov', 'prcp_Oct', 'prcp_Sep', 'Tavg_Apr',
'Tavg_Aug', 'Tavg_Dec' , 'Tavg_Feb' , 'Tavg_Jan', 'Tavg_Jul', 'Tavg_Jun' , 'Tavg_Mar',
'Tavg_May', 'Tavg_Nov' , 'Tavg_Oct', 'Tavg_Sep', 'Tmax_Apr', 'Tmax_Aug' , 'Tmax_Dec' ,
'Tmax_Feb', 'Tmax_Jan' , 'Tmax_Jul', 'Tmax_Jun', 'Tmax_Mar', 'Tmax_May' , 'Tmax_Nov' ,
'Tmax_Oct', 'Tmax_Sep', 'Tmin_Apr', 'Tmin_Aug', 'Tmin_Dec', 'Tmin_Feb', 'Tmin_Jan' ,
'Tmin_Jul', 'Tmin_Jun', 'Tmin_Mar', 'Tmin_May', 'Tmin_Nov', 'Tmin_Oct', 'Tmin_Sep',
'Yield(hg/ha)','ProductionInTonnes','AreaHarvested(ha)','MethylBromide'],
  dtype='object')
```

Step 9: Correlation of methyl bromide to yield

To see the correlations between methyl bromide and yield, perform correlation analysis.

```
finaldf1.corr()
```

Output:
0.342323

Step 10: Linear regressor model

To see the correlations between methyl

```
#Trial 2 – trail1 params + 'MethylBromide'
X = finaldf1[['AreaHarvested(ha)', 'Tmax_Feb',
      'Tmax_Jan', 'Tmax_Mar', 'Tmax_Apr',
         'Tmax_Aug', 'Tmax_Sep', 'Tmax_Nov',
         'Tmin_Mar', 'Tmin_Apr',
      'Tmin_Jul', 'Tmin_Oct', 'Tmin_Dec',
      'prcp_Jan', 'prcp_Feb',
    'prcp_Jun', 'prcp_Aug',
    'MethylBromide'
   ]].values

y= finaldf1['Yield(hg/ha)'].values

X_train,X_test,y_train,y_test = train_test_split(X,y,test_size =
0.20,random_state = 0)
print(X_train.shape)
print(X_test.shape)

model = LinearRegression()
model.fit(X_train,y_train)

# predicting the test
y_pred = model.predict(X_test)
y_pred

model_features = ['AreaHarvested(ha)', 'Tmax_Feb',
      'Tmax_Jan', 'Tmax_Mar', 'Tmax_Apr',
         'Tmax_Aug', 'Tmax_Sep', 'Tmax_Nov',
         'Tmin_Mar', 'Tmin_Apr',
         'Tmin_Jul', 'Tmin_Oct', 'Tmin_Dec',
      'prcp_Jan', 'prcp_Feb',
    'prcp_Jun', 'prcp_Aug',
    'MethylBromide'
   ]

mse = mean_squared_error(y_test,y_pred)
print("MSE:",mse)

rmse = np.sqrt(mse)
print("RMSE:",rmse)

r2 = r2_score(y_test,y_pred)
print("R2 Linear Regression:", r2)
```

Output:

```
(48, 18)
(13, 18)
MSE: 7002152470.0945015
RMSE: 83678.86513388253
R2 Linear Regression: 0.8470818767315389
```

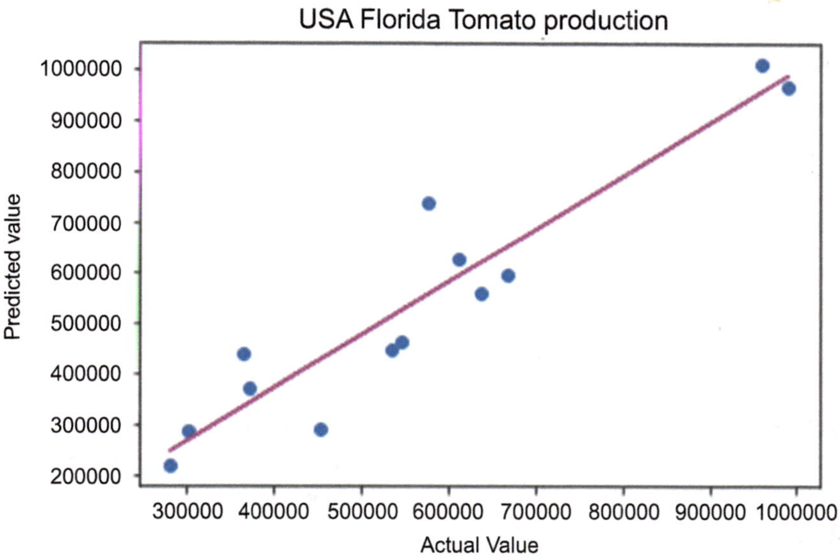

Step 11: Explainability

Perform explainability

```
eli5.show_weights(model,feature_names = model_features)
```

Output:

Weight?	Feature
+152975.281	MethylBromide
+107774.615	Tmin_Jul
+72299.191	Tmin_Apr
+31176.437	Tmax_Mar
+19511.166	Tmin_Dec
+1211.620	Tmin_Oct
+269.553	prcp_Jun
-2.964	AreaHarvested(ha)
-103.206	prcp_Aug
-247.998	prcp_Jan
-1177.515	prcp_Feb
-4686.474	Tmax_Feb
-5156.711	Tmax_Jan
-7348.665	Tmax_Nov
-7772.506	Tmax_Aug
-13864.592	Tmax_Sep
-29587.773	Tmin_Mar
-58341.895	Tmax_Apr
-241046.384	<BIAS>

- Methyl bromide is a chemical that has a significant impact on the yield of tomatoes.
- In Florida, the highest temperatures in March and the lowest temperatures in April, July, October, and December influences tomato yield positively.
- While amount of rain in June influences tomatoes yield positively, on the other hand rain in January, February, and August influences negatively.
- Last, when the area used to cultivate tomatoes in Florida is increased, it can actually have a negative effect on yield because it requires a lot of effort to prepare and maintain a larger area.

USA tomatoes

ML model: plant city, Florida, USA, tomatoes production field model and climate projections model (2021–2100)

To make predictions about future tomato yields in Plant City, Florida, climate projections need to be considered. The previous yield model showed that the area used to grow tomatoes is an important factor in predicting returns. Challenge now is to figure out how to predict the area that will be used to grow tomatoes in the future. This can be done by using interpolation or imputation techniques to estimate the missing data.

To continue with this analysis, we will start from Step 10 of the previous chapter's machine learning model for predicting tomato yields in Plant City, Florida.

Step 11: Download climate projections data

```
Directorypath = r"./allrpcs/"
list_of_files = []
list_of_files = list_files(Directorypath)
list_of_files
```

Load projections.

```
pr_climatology_annual-monthly_cmip5_rcp26_climatology_ensemble_2020-2039_p90_ECU.csv

pr_climatology_annual-monthly_cmip5_rcp26_climatology_ensemble_2040-2059_p90_ECU.csv
pr_climatology_annual-monthly_cmip5_rcp26_climatology_ensemble_2060-2079_p90_ECU.csv
pr_climatology_annual-monthly_cmip5_rcp26_climatology_ensemble_2080-2099_p90_ECU.csv
pr_climatology_annual-monthly_cmip5_rcp45_climatology_ensemble_2020-2039_p90_ECU.csv
pr_climatology_annual-monthly_cmip5_rcp45_climatology_ensemble_2040-2059_p90_ECU.csv
pr_climatology_annual-monthly_cmip5_rcp45_climatology_ensemble_2060-2079_p90_ECU.csv
pr_climatology_annual-monthly_cmip5_rcp45_climatology_ensemble_2080-2099_p90_ECU.csv
```

Step 14: Florida tomatoes climate master data frame

The code combines climate data from multiple files into a single master DataFrame, making it easier to analyze and visualize the data.

```
masterdf = pd.DataFrame()

masterdflength =0
for i in range(0,len(list_of_files)):
   filename = list_of_files[i]
   print(filename)
   tempdf=pd.read_csv(list_of_files[i],header=1)
   #tempdf1 = tempdf.copy()
   if'2020-2039' in filename:
     tempdf1=tempdf.assign(year='2020-2039')
   elif'2040-2059' in filename:
     tempdf1=tempdf.assign(year='2040-2059')
   elif'2060-2079' in filename:
     tempdf1=tempdf.assign(year='2060-2079')
   elif'2080-2099' in filename:
   tempdf1=tempdf.assign(year='2080-2099')

   if'pr_' in filename:
     tempdf1['Variable']= 'precipitation'
   elif'tasmin_' in filename:
     tempdf1['Variable']= 'tmin '
   elif'tasmax_' in filename:
    tempdf1['Variable']= 'tmax'
   elif'tas_' in filename:
    tempdf1['Variable']= 'tmean'

   if'_ssp119_'in filename:
    tempdf1['Scenario'] = 'SSP1-1.9'
   elif'_ssp245_' in filename:
     tempdf1['Scenario'] = 'SSP2-4.5'
   elif'_ssp585_' in filename:
    tempdf1['Scenario'] = 'SSP5-8.5'
   #elif'_ssp85_' in filename:
    #tempdf1['Scenario'] = 'rcp85'

   print(tempdf1.shape[0])
   masterdf = pd.concat([masterdf,tempdf1], ignore_index=True)
   masterdflength = masterdflength + tempdf1.shape[0]

masterdflength
   masterdf.tail()
```

Output:

	Unnamed: 0	Annual	Jan	Feb	Mar	Apr	May	Jun	Jul	Aug	Sep	Oct	Nov	Dec	year	Variable	Scenario
2491	Illinois	19.92	4.12	6.31	10.86	17.67	25.47	32.76	36.72	36.64	31.32	23.59	13.60	6.52	2080-2099	tmean	SSP5-8.5
2492	Idaho	15.50	2.32	4.16	7.05	11.79	18.17	25.83	32.44	32.06	26.44	17.35	8.43	3.37	2080-2099	tmean	SSP5-8.5
2493	Hawaii	27.42	25.95	25.47	25.30	25.61	26.43	27.83	28.89	29.92	30.01	29.69	28.22	26.74	2080-2099	tmean	SSP5-8.5
2494	Georgia	24.11	13.13	15.04	18.35	23.36	29.30	33.16	34.59	33.89	31.55	27.37	20.87	15.32	2080-2099	tmean	SSP5-8.5
2495	Florida	27.29	20.47	21.09	23.08	26.19	29.76	32.22	33.26	33.51	32.52	30.11	26.57	22.66	2080-2099	tmean	SSP5-8.5

Step 15: CMIP5 verification

CMIP5 data is loaded.

```
# verification

print("master df shape:",masterdf.shape)
print(masterdf['Variable'].value_counts())
print(masterdf['Scenario'].value_counts())
print(masterdf['year'].value_counts())
```

Result:

```
master df shape: (2496, 17)
precipitation 624
tmax      624
tmin     624
tmean      624
Name: Variable, dtype: int64
SSP1-1.9   832
SSP2-4.5   832
SSP5-8.5   832
Name: Scenario, dtype: int64
2020-2039   624
2040-2059   624
2060-2079   624
2080-2099   624
Name: year, dtype: int64
```

Visualize climate projections data.

```
masterdf.rename(columns={'Unnamed:0': 'State'},inplace=True)

(masterdf['State'].value_counts())
```

Display:

	State	annual	Jan	Feb	Mar	Apr	May	Jun	Jul	Aug	Sep	Oct	Nov	Dec	year	Variable	Scenario
0	United States	1117.18	94.48	91.32	100.51	104.10	115.54	109.56	107.85	100.08	94.42	90.28	96.00	102.04	2020-2039	precipitation	SSP1-1.9
1	New Jersey	1538.54	132.41	127.82	144.36	137.87	141.03	147.59	155.43	138.93	122.10	130.73	132.98	137.27	2020-2039	precipitation	SSP1-1.9
2	New Hampshire	1672.44	132.49	126.16	134.69	151.32	152.34	167.14	182.42	178.32	130.09	152.69	152.24	144.25	2020-2039	precipitation	SSP1-1.9
3	Nevada	813.61	108.21	113.81	100.00	84.51	77.46	54.99	24.30	24.39	29.53	36.73	73.47	112.23	2020-2039	precipitation	SSP1-1.9
4	Nebraska	884.78	37.86	46.90	72.82	110.50	132.30	126.68	102.42	95.95	80.99	65.26	52.05	37.66	2020-2039	precipitation	SSP1-1.9

```
masterdf['Variable'].value_counts()
```

Output:

```
precipitation  624
tmax      624
tmin      624
tmean     624
Name: Variable, dtype: int64
```

```
masterdf['State'].value_counts()
```

Output:

```
United States        48
New Jersey           48
West Virginia        48
Washington           48
Virginia             48
Colorado             48
California           48
Arkansas             48
Arizona              48
Alaska               48
Vermont              48
Alabama              48
```

The code is a way to verify that all the states. Count should be equal to 64.

```
'Ecuador' , 'Galapagos', 'Esmeraldas' , 'El Oro', 'Cotopaxi', 'Chimborazo',
'Carchi', 'Canar', 'Bolivar', 'Azuay', 'Zona No Delimitada', 'Zamora',
'Chinchipe' , 'Tungurahua', 'Santo Domingo de los Tsachilas', 'Sucumbios',
'Pastaza', 'Orellana', 'Napo', 'Guayas', 'Pichincha' , 'Santa Elena', 'Morona
Santiago', 'Manabi', 'Los Rios', 'Loja', 'Imbabura'
```

	State	Annual	Jan	Feb	Mar	Apr	May	Jun	Jul	Aug	Sep	Oct	Nov	Dec	year	Variable	Scenario
0	Ecuador	3763.98	369.60	378.63	445.44	442.21	354.05	217.78	201.89	221.22	288.16	337.67	386.59	394.52	2020-2039	precipitation	rcp26
1	Galapagos	1157.14	176.45	131.78	164.96	183.27	152.39	47.95	32.40	25.83	23.95	29.07	49.76	161.66	2020-2039	precipitation	rcp26
2	Esmeraldas	4482.58	391.43	384.07	461.76	484.39	530.33	316.01	342.71	332.84	355.48	379.88	457.48	440.71	2020-2039	precipitation	rcp26
3	El Oro	3274.81	437.64	449.46	501.65	439.39	296.26	135.47	138.93	123.78	172.48	254.97	299.29	410.59	2020-2039	precipitation	rcp26
4	Cotopaxi	4482.59	429.56	451.92	527.12	540.79	424.60	271.01	255.20	273.65	370.61	393.71	450.47	464.05	2020-2039	precipitation	rcp26

Step 16: Load florida state climate projections

Load Florida state climate projections data. The code is a way to extract and manipulate data for a specific state and crop from a larger dataset. By filtering the data, it is easier to analyze and visualize trends and patterns specific to a particular state or crop.

```
#separating dsf for California
df_State = masterdf.iloc[np.where(masterdf['State'] =='Florida')]

country = masterdf['State'][0]
state = 'Florida'
crop = 'Tomato'
#df_ES = df_ES.reset_index(inplace=True)
#drop state column to avaoid state_tmax,State_min etc columns

df_State.drop(columns={'State'},inplace=True)
df_State.head()
```

Output:

Ensure that climate projections are available for the years 2020–2100 using RCPS data. This means that the code checks if there are climate projections available for the next 80 years, starting from the year 2020 and going up to the year 2100. The RCPS data is a type of climate scenario that helps researchers make projections about future climate conditions. By ensuring that there are climate projections available for a long period of time, researchers can better understand and predict how climate conditions may change over the coming decades.

```
See the caveats in the documentation: https://pandas.pydata.org/pandas-docs/stable/user_guide/indexing.html#returning-a-view-versus-a-copy
  errors=errors,
```

	Annual	Jan	Feb	Mar	Apr	May	Jun	Jul	Aug	Sep	Oct	Nov	Dec	year	Variable	Scenario
51	1466.47	119.33	100.88	107.16	97.95	106.18	170.86	194.44	200.81	217.57	133.24	95.75	120.58	2020-2039	precipitation	SSP1-1.9
103	1495.81	131.77	103.93	110.70	99.48	107.43	169.40	196.88	196.14	201.36	137.27	103.42	126.64	2040-2059	precipitation	SSP1-1.9
155	1510.09	120.35	102.64	106.28	88.53	114.86	179.87	200.54	202.37	217.50	143.41	97.59	129.38	2060-2079	precipitation	SSP1-1.9
207	1510.47	123.47	113.32	100.05	93.94	105.58	168.19	207.32	184.23	207.01	139.09	99.98	124.16	2080-2099	precipitation	SSP1-1.9
259	1420.79	116.30	108.05	100.06	93.46	122.65	166.84	182.28	196.71	209.19	151.19	105.40	117.81	2020-2039	precipitation	SSP2-4.5

Get annual projections.

```
df_State.drop(columns={'Annual'},inplace=True)
df_State.head()
```

Output:

	Jan	Feb	Mar	Apr	May	Jun	Jul	Aug	Sep	Oct	Nov	Dec	year	Variable	Scenario
51	119.33	100.88	107.16	97.95	106.18	170.86	194.44	200.81	217.57	133.24	95.75	120.58	2020-2039	precipitation	SSP1-1.9
103	131.77	103.93	110.70	99.48	107.43	169.40	196.88	196.14	201.36	137.27	103.42	126.64	2040-2059	precipitation	SSP1-1.9
155	120.35	102.64	106.28	88.53	114.86	179.87	200.54	202.37	217.50	143.41	97.59	129.38	2060-2079	precipitation	SSP1-1.9
207	123.47	113.32	100.05	93.94	105.58	168.19	207.32	184.23	207.01	139.09	99.98	124.16	2080-2099	precipitation	SSP1-1.9
259	116.00	108.05	100.06	93.46	122.65	166.84	182.28	196.71	209.19	151.19	105.40	117.81	2020-2039	precipitation	SSP2-4.5

The code is used to combine data from different DataFrame into a single Dataframe for easier analysis and visualization. By merging the data based on specific columns, the code ensures that only matching data is included in the final DataFrame.

```
# climate predictions data finaldf
finaldf_cl = pd.merge(left = dfState_tmin,right = dfState_tmax,how = 'inner', left_on=['year',
'Scenario'],right_on=['year' , 'Scenario'])
finaldf_cl = pd.merge(left = finaldf_cl,right = dfState_tmean,how = 'inner', left_on=['year',
'Scenario'],right_on=['year' , 'Scenario'])
finaldf_cl = pd.merge(left = finaldf_cl,right = dfState_pr,how = 'inner', left_on=['year', 'Scenario'],right_
on=['year' , 'Scenario'])
finaldf_cl.head()
```

Output:

	Jan_Tmin	Feb_Tmin	Mar_Tmin	Apr_Tmin	May_Tmin	Jun_Tmin	Jul_Tmin	Aug_Tmin	Sep_Tmin	Oct_Tmin	...
0	13.01	13.45	15.14	17.54	20.79	23.69	25.37	25.48	24.32	21.14	...
1	13.55	13.79	15.31	17.76	20.87	23.71	25.45	25.77	24.47	21.48	...
2	13.22	13.58	15.17	17.74	20.92	23.76	25.49	25.74	24.36	21.54	...
3	12.90	13.46	15.02	17.81	20.82	23.76	25.45	25.69	24.04	21.09	...
4	13.50	13.72	15.15	17.72	20.79	23.55	25.11	25.38	24.43	21.51	...

5 rows × 50 columns

```
finaldf_cl.columns
```

Output:

```
Index(['Jan_Tmin', 'Feb_Tmin', 'Mar_Tmin', 'Apr_Tmin', 'May_Tmin', 'Jun_Tmin', 'Jul_Tmin', 'Aug_Tmin',
'Sep_Tmin', 'Oct_Tmin', 'Nov_Tmin', 'Dec_Tmin', 'year', 'Scenario', 'Jan_Tmax', 'Feb_Tmax', 'Mar_Tmax',
'Apr_Tmax', 'May_Tmax', 'Jun_Tmax', 'Jul_Tmax', 'Aug_Tmax', 'Sep_Tmax', 'Oct_Tmax', 'Nov_Tmax', 'Dec_
Tmax', 'Jan_Tmean', 'Feb_Tmean', 'Mar_Tmean', 'Apr_Tmean', 'May_Tmean', 'Jun_Tmean', 'Jul_Tmean',
'Aug_Tmean', 'Sep_Tmean', 'Oct_Tmean', 'Nov_Tmean', 'Dec_Tmean', 'Jan_prcp', 'Feb_prcp', 'Mar_prcp',
'Apr_prcp', 'May_prcp', 'Jun_prcp', 'Jul_prcp', 'Aug_prcp', 'Sep_prcp', 'Oct_prcp', 'Nov_prcp', 'Dec_prcp'],
```

```
finaldf_cl = finaldf_cl[['year', 'Scenario','Jan_Tmin', 'Feb_Tmin', 'Mar_Tmin', 'Apr_Tmin', 'May_Tmin',
'Jun_Tmin', 'Jul_Tmin', 'Aug_Tmin', 'Sep_Tmin', 'Oct_Tmin', 'Nov_Tmin',
'Dec Tmin', 'Jan Tmax', 'Feb Tmax', 'Mar Tmax',
'Apr_Tmax', 'May_Tmax', 'Jun_Tmax', 'Jul_Tmax', 'Aug_Tmax', 'Sep_Tmax',
'Oct_Tmax', 'Nov_Tmax', 'Dec_Tmax', 'Jan_prcp', 'Feb_prcp', 'Mar_prcp',
'Apr_prcp', 'May_prcp', 'Jun_prcp', 'Jul_prcp', 'Aug_prcp', 'Sep_prcp',
'Oct_prcp', 'Nov_prcp', 'Dec_prcp']]
```

Final DF contains all climate projections based data.

Step 17: Load model binary file

The following code loads model pickle file. The following function is designed to extract specific data from a larger DataFrame and convert it into a list for later use. The function considers specific scenarios, year ranges, and agricultural data to create a more focused and targeted dataset.

```
def GetPacketPklInput(SSPInput,yearRange,AreaHarvested_1,df_local):
   tempdf = df_local.iloc[np.where((df_local['Scenario'] ==SSPInput)& (df_local['year'] ==
yearRange))]
   #print(tempdf)
   Xparam =
['Feb_Tmax', Jan_Tmax','Mar_Tmax','Apr_Tmax','Aug_Tmax','Nov_Tmax','Sep_Tmax','Mar_Tmin','Apr_
Tmin','Jul_Tmin','Oct_Tmin','Dec_Tmin','Feb_prcp','Jan_prcp','Jun_prcp','Aug_prcp']
   temp1df =tempdf[Xparam]
   arr=temp1df.iloc[0].tolist()
arr.insert(0,AreaHarvested_1,)
   # arr.append(co2Emissions_1)
   #print(type(arr))
   #print(arr)
    return arr
```

```
# open a file, where you stored the pickled data
file = open('USA_FLoridaTomatoYield_pklfile', 'rb')

# dump information to that file
Data = pickle.load(file)
```

Step 18: Rising temperatures and the consequences of inaction 2080–2099

If we continue our current practices without making changes, the future will experience extreme temperature variations becoming hotter, warmer, and colder. Projected data indicates that temperature and precipitation levels will rise significantly, shifting upward on box plot graphs by at least three degrees or more. This substantial increase could have a profound impact on both the environment and human life.

Precipitation:

```
df = finaldf_cl[['Jan_prcp',

   'Feb_prcp','Mar_prcp', 'Apr_prcp','May_prcp', 'Jun_prcp', 'Jul_prcp',
   'Aug_prcp', 'Sep_prcp', 'Oct_prcp', 'Nov_prcp', 'Dec_prcp']]

#plot the dataframe as needed
ax = df.plot.box(figsize=(15,8),showmeans=True,grid=True)
```

Output:

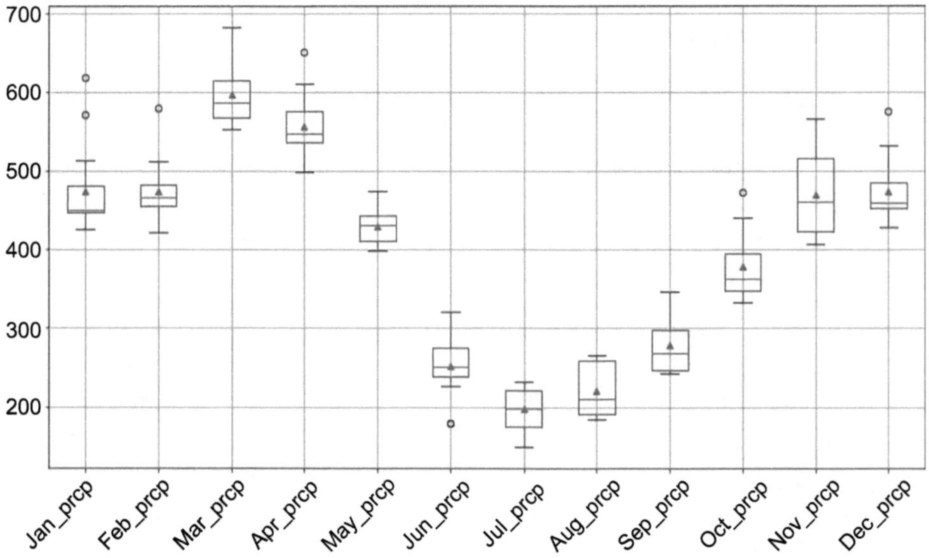

Plant City Florida precipitation March and April precipitation are higher 2020–2040 and 2080–2099 means that based on data projections, the amount of precipitation during the months of March and April in Plant City, Florida is expected to increase during two time periods: from 2020 to 2040 and from 2080 to 2099. This suggests that Plant City may experience more rain or other forms of precipitation during these months in the future. This information is important for farmers, city planners, and other stakeholders who need to plan for potential changes in the local climate and its impact on the environment and human systems.

Minimum temperature

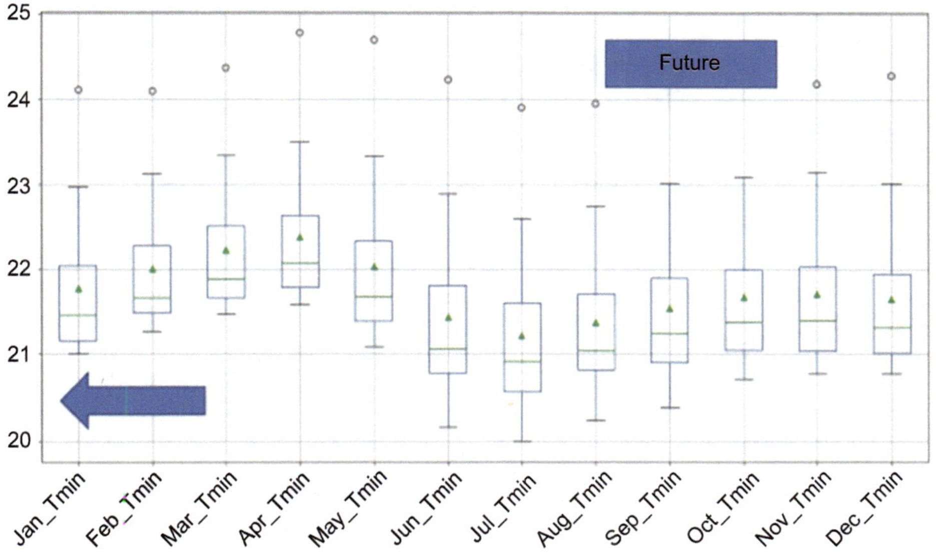

Plant City Florida minimum temperatures are in November, December, and January. 2020–2040 and 2080–2099 means that based on data projections, the lowest temperatures in Plant City, Florida are expected to occur during the months of November, December, and January in two time periods: from 2020 to 2040 and from 2080 to 2099. This suggests that Plant City may experience colder temperatures during these months in the future. This information is important for people living in Plant City, as they may need to prepare for colder weather, such as by wearing warmer clothing or taking steps to protect their homes and other properties from the effects of cold temperatures. Similarly, we can see the temperatures from current and future trends.

Step 19: Florida tomatoes prediction: 'SSP1-1.9'

Import serialized climatic classifier.

```
pkl_input = GetPacketPklInput('SSP1-1.9','2040-2059',Latest_areaHarvested_inHectars,finaldf_cl)
pkl_input
```

```
[109226,
23.5,
23.24,
25.1,
27.89,
33.95,
27.07,
32.63,
15.31,
17.76,
25.45,
21.48,
14.85,
103.93,
131.77,
169.4,
196.14]
```

Get predictions for 'SSP1-1.9'

```
pkl_input = GetPacketPklInput('rcp85', '2040-2059',Latest_areaHarvested_inHectars,2*Latest_
Yieldinhgha,finaldf_cl)
pkl_input
```

SSP result:

```
[195436.2888, 33.75, 34.03, 28.15, 22.25, 22.5, 22.6, 514.2,
488.1,
1.83, 39290.00092]
```

```
pklOutput = data.predict(np.array([pkl_input]))
PredictedTomatoYield = pklOutput[0]
PredictedTomatoYield
percentChange = ((PredictedTomatoYield – Latest_Yield)/Latest_Yield)*100
print(PredictedTomatoYield,Latest_Yield)
percentChange
```

Output:

```
1364362.8732950906 959045
42.26265433791851
```

Step 20: Florida tomatoes prediction: 'SSP5-8.5'

Predict year 2040:2059 predictions:

```
pkl_input = GetPacketPklInput('SSP5-8.5','2040-2059',Latest_areaHarvested_inHectars,finaldf_cl)
pkl_input
```

```
[109226,
24.13,
23.69,
25.99,
28.87,
35.25,
27.92,
34.01,
16.28,
18.93,
26.25,
22.96,
15.82,
112.72,
128.07.
165.56,
180.86]
```

Get predictions for 'SSP5-8.5', 2040-2059

```
pklOutput = data.predict(np.array([pkl_input]))
PredictedTomatoYield = pklOuput[0]
PredictedTomatoYield
percentChange = ((PredictedTomatoYield - Latest_Yield)/Latest_Yield *100
print(PredictedTomatoYield,Latest_Yield)
percentChange
```

Output:

```
50.38120978107157
```

Climate adaptation strategies

Specialty crops, such as the processing tomato, are crucial globally for their nutritional value and role in various cuisines, but there is limited knowledge about the effects of climate change on them. This book offers pioneering global models, making it a unique and valuable resource for understanding these impacts [344].

Recognizing the crucial role of tomatoes in global food security, NIFA and AFRI have awarded $590k to a research scholar at NC State and the Horticultural Science tomato breeding program [343]. The objective of this grant is to cultivate enhanced crop varieties that may possess superior productivity, quality, and environmental tolerance. This will not only preserve grower livelihoods but also provide consumers with nutritious and sustainable food while conserving natural resources. Ultimately, this genetic improvement research for tomatoes aims to promote food security worldwide.

Florida farmers have started adapting to increasing temperatures by using heat-resistant crop varieties and advanced production technologies. However, they face numerous challenges, including rising heat, increased foreign competition, fluctuating prices, higher energy costs, labor shortages, and changing consumer preferences. A study by Florida International University recommends a multifaceted approach involving technology, business innovation, and government policy to tackle these issues. The study predicts continued warming in Florida, especially in summer, which could reduce tomato yields by 7–10% and strawberry yields by 10–17% for non-heat-resistant varieties [363]. Additionally, competition from cheaper Mexican tomato imports has reduced Florida's market share, while shifting consumer preferences toward greenhouse-produced vine-ripe tomatoes pose further challenges due to Florida's humid climate and higher production costs. Labor shortages add another layer of difficulty for the agricultural sector. Despite these obstacles, adopting new business models, technological advancements, consumer education, and policy reforms could help Florida farmers become more resilient, although these strategies require significant capital investment [364].

Feeding the future: analyzing climate shifts on geophysical terrains and temperature zones for safeguard global food security

Through our research, it has become clear that Kashmir holds the key to future food security for over a billion people, representing approximately 60% of the global population. To gain insights into the effects of environmental patterns across different geophysical terrains and temperature zones, we have collaborated with cow necklace, a sensor manufacturing company.[2] These sensors have been deployed globally, enabling us to study climate change impacts in high-altitude areas and various climatic regions.

Hanumayamma innovations and technologies Inc has deployed sensors in several locations to examine changing climate on dairy cattle. These locations include Hyderabad, Telangana; Visakhapatnam, Andhra Pradesh; Patiala, Punjab; Fremont and San Ramon in California, USA; Kerglas in France; and Seoul in South Korea, each with their unique elevation above sea level.

Image and sensor deployment: Jammu and Kashmir's Keran, a border tehsil of Kupwara[3] district, nestled along the banks of the Kishenganga River (Neelum River).

Our findings have been intriguing, showing that body temperature shifts in cattle are more drastic at higher altitudes compared to lower ones. This would have clinical impacts such as heat stress index, lameness, milk fever, and other parameters (below figure). With this information, the company has been able to develop better climate change strategies for dairy and animal husbandry, ensuring the sustainability of the industry in the face of changing environmental conditions.

Temperature: Kashmir, April 25, 2024 – 24 h readings (Sensor Name: HANU_CNECKLACE_0001_0004)

2 Cow necklace manufacturer – Hanumayamma innovations and technologies, Inc., a Delaware registered, Fremont, California HQ Company.

3 Jammu and Kashmir - https://www.hindustantimes.com/lifestyle/travel/jammu-and-kashmirs-keran-village-beckons-travellers-with-open-arms-101690633322348.html

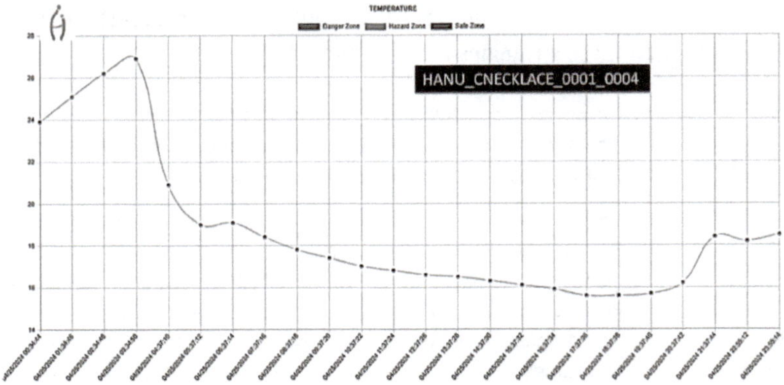

Humidity: Kashmir, April 25, 2024 – 24 h readings (Sensor Name: HANU_CNECKLACE_0001_0004)

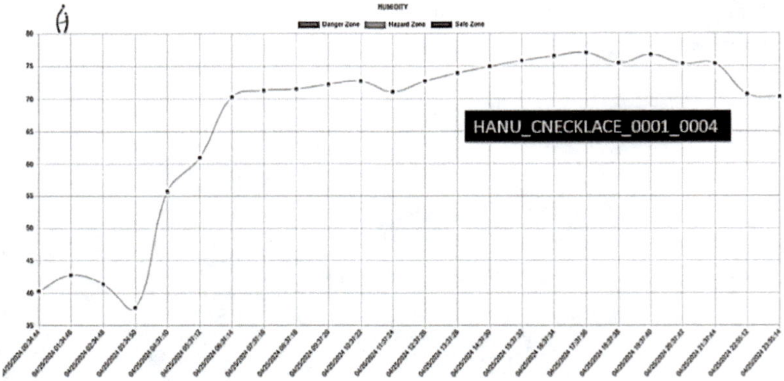

Temperature drop and humidity increase can be observed.

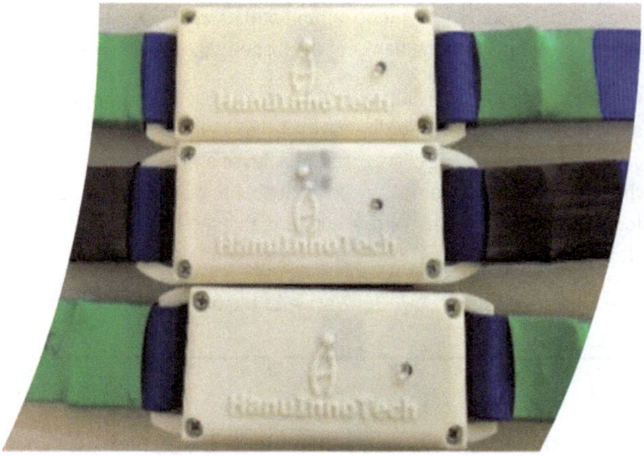

The company has deployed sensors(above figure) in the following locations to study the impact of climate change on the dairy cattle.

Country	Location	Elevation above sea level
India	Hyderabad, Telangana	1,778 ft (542 m)
India	Visakhapatnam, Andhra Pradesh	Elevation 45 m
India	Patiala, Punjab	250 m (820 ft)
USA	Fremont, CA	Elevation above sea level 52 ft (16 m)
USA	San Ramon, CA	337–887 ft
France	Kerglas, 29180 Guengat	7–162 m (23–531 ft)
South Korea	Seoul	38 m (125 ft)

Author
Chandrasekar Vuppalapati

Implementing strong customer acquisition strategies and competitive branding will lead to higher capital and operational costs. Small growers unable to afford these expenses may need to rely on market intermediaries or local sales to remain competitive. It is vital for farmers to invest in these strategies, as the cost of not adapting is much higher in terms of sustainability and livelihood [363].

In 2013, scientists urged farmers to act swiftly to address the food needs of an anticipated 10 billion people by 2050 [361]. They warned that without prompt action, crop yields would decline, pests and diseases would rise, water demand would increase, and vulnerable crops could vanish, worsening global hunger. This call to action underscores the necessity for proactive measures to ensure future food security and mitigate agricultural challenges. The report, published in the journal *Science*, stressed that the entire food system needed to change [364–367].

Adaptation strategies are diverse instruments, and their effectiveness varies. However, world tomato industry has shown remarkable resilience and innovation in addressing these challenges. Identifying and implementing new methodologies is not solely the responsibility of the industry, but rather a collective effort that involves scientists, policymakers, and consumers alike [365–368].

Paradoxical [369]!

Even though there are over 8 billion people in the world, there still aren't enough workers in the agriculture industry. This is a big problem because agriculture is very important for making sure everyone has enough food to eat and for taking care of the planet in the future. To solve this problem, we need to make more people aware of how important agriculture is, and how much value it adds to our lives. By doing this, we can help make sure that there are enough workers in agriculture to support a sustainable future for everyone.

Author
Chandrasekar Vuppalapati

This chapter provides a lot of information about specialty crop tomatoes. It talks about how they're grown and how extreme weather can affect production. The chapter also compares tomato production in different countries like China, India, and the USA and explains how different factors affect how many tomatoes are grown.

The chapter also looks at different things that can affect tomato yield, like weather and chemicals used in production. It explains how these factors can be analyzed to predict how many tomatoes will be grown in a certain area.

After reading this chapter, you'll know a lot about how specialty crop tomatoes are grown and how different factors can affect their production. This knowledge can help you make better decisions and potentially make more money in the tomato industry.

Chapter 9
Specialty crops tomatoes: pricing models

This chapter covers:
- Specialty crop tomatoes\
- Economic importance and opportunities
  - The United States of America
  - Türkiye
  - India
- Tomatoes prices and crop insurance
- Tomatoes pricing behavior
- Machine learning models
  - Tomatoes pricing models
  - Forecasting: what-if modeling
  - Rend-based forecasting
- Yield improvement strategies
- Climate adaptation strategies

This chapter looks at how many tomatoes are grown in different countries, like the USA, Türkiye, and India, and how the prices of these tomatoes are determined. It talks about how pricing models work and provides a tool to help farmers make better pricing decisions. The chapter goes into detail about how the prices of different types of tomatoes, like those grown in fields and those used for processing, are determined. It also provides a framework for analyzing tomato yield in different countries. At the end of the chapter, there's a pricing model that can help farmers determine the best prices for their tomatoes. After reading this chapter, you'll know a lot about how tomato production and pricing work, which can help you make better decisions and potentially make more money in the tomato industry.

Climate change could influence price of your next pizza and tomato sauce.

Tomatoes are the most popular vegetable in the United States, with each American consuming over 31 pounds annually, mostly in processed forms like paste and sauce. However, extreme weather, regulatory challenges, and economic pressures have increased the costs of harvesting and delivering tomatoes. Consequently, consumers can expect higher prices for tomatoes at grocery stores and restaurants, including on their next pizza [370].

Predicting price of tomatoes is very important because they spoil easily and are only available during certain times of the year. Knowing how much tomatoes will cost help farmers make better farming decisions [371]. This is important for everyone involved in the agriculture industry including farmers, consumers, retailers, wholesalers, processors, and the government. Accurate forecasting can also help prevent legal issues that may arise when contract prices are lower than spot prices. Sometimes, farmers disobey contract terms and sell their crops on the open market at higher spot prices for financial reasons. However, this can lead to legal issues with processors and should be avoided. For example, in Turkey, some growers did not comply with contracts during the 2018 season when spot prices were much higher than contract prices. Accurate forecasting can help prevent these types of issues and ensure the economic well-being of farmers [372].

Farmers, especially those in the specialty crops sector, face significant economic uncertainty as the prices they receive for their products are rarely stable or predictable. Recently, increased volatility in agricultural commodity prices has amplified the risks for producers. Precise price estimating has thus become essential, enabling farmers to make informed decisions and better manage price risks [373].

Price estimation is essential for tomatoes due to their perishable and time criticality. Tomatoes are a key agricultural product globally, and accurate price predictions rely on factors such as weather events, commerce, economy, historical data, climate, and soil type. This chapter introduces a new economic-climate-yield model to forecast tomato prices one month in advance with greater accuracy [373]. I will cover machine learning models in the subsequent sections. Moreover, the framework proposed works equally well for both stable behavior vegetables, such as potatoes, and volatile price behavior vegetables such as tomatoes. Due to their volatility, farmers do not always return or profit from the best price for the crop. Additionally, tomatoes have another unique distinction, namely the crop pattern for tomatoes for processing and field-grown crops [374].

Developing effective forecasting models for vegetable prices: considerations for stable and volatile markets

Developing a forecasting model for vegetable prices requires understanding the unique characteristics of this sector. One important consideration is the difference between stable and volatile pricing for vegetables.

Stable prices depend on things like how efficient the supply chain is, how much competition there is, and how many alternatives are available. Volatile prices are caused by unpredictable weather events, transportation issues, or trade disputes.

To create an accurate forecasting model, it's important to consider both stable and volatile pricing scenarios. By analyzing data on supply and demand, weather patterns, and market trends, forecasting models can help predict how vegetable prices will change over time. This information can help growers and other stakeholders make better decisions and maximize their profits while also ensuring a steady supply of healthy vegetables.

Author
Chandrasekar Vuppalapati

For specialty crops' farm to market reach, growers to manufacturers form part of value chain and should be coordinated to have high effectiveness and profit maximization. One can infer from the tomateos for processsing data (Figure 1) that coordinaion between growers and processros in USA.

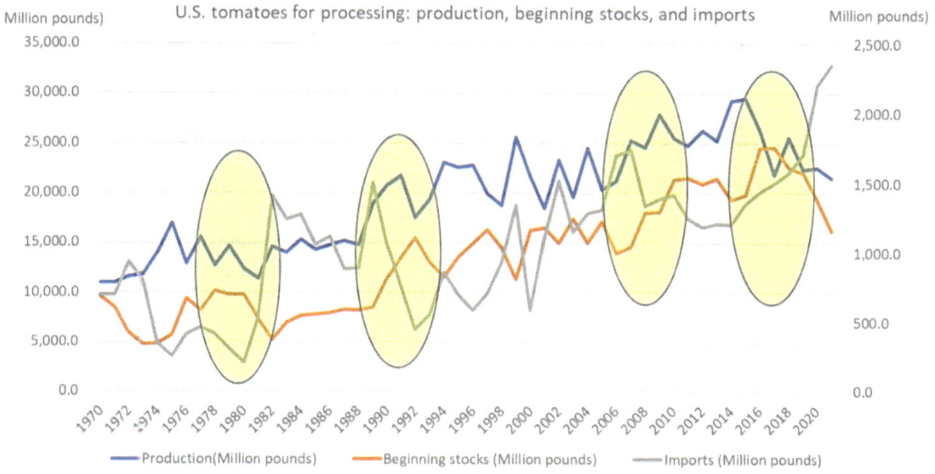

Figure 1: US tomatoes for processing.

In 1982, when the inventory reached a lower level (−28.578%), production increased significantly (27.69%), with imports rising by an impressive 162.90%. Conversely, in 1992, an increase in beginning stock (14.70%) resulted in a decrease in production (−19.273%) and imports (−40.192%). The same trend was observed in 2017 when an increase in beginning stock (23.835%) coincided with a decrease in production (−10.732%). However, in 2021, a drop in beginning stock (−12.212%) led to an increase in production (1.124%) and imports (28.895%). Remarkably, the sum of these three numbers remains stable. The reason for this is that farmers and processors communicate with one another, with processors promising farmers fair prices before they begin planting. Additionally, farmers follow processors' suggestions regarding what to plant, resulting in final numbers that are not disappointing. Both farmers and processors are satisfied with the final outcome. Similarly, in China, the tomato industry has been improving its relationships between farmers and processors since 2015 [375]. China has four main processing areas: southern Xinjiang, northern Xinjiang, Inner Mongolia, and Gansu, with Xinjiang accounting for roughly 80% of production. Both processors and growers coordinate to adjust beginning stock to production levels. Higher beginning stocks imply lower production value, and the opposite is true for lower beginning stocks, pushing production. To achieve this delicate balance, there should be a symbiotic handshake between growers and processors.

Beginning stocks and production sync dance!

Effective communication between farmers and processors is essential to calibrating beginning stocks and production levels, ultimately leading to lower prices and higher profit maximization. By working together, these stakeholders can gain a more accurate understanding of supply and demand dynamics, enabling them to make informed decisions that optimize their yields and profits.

Through open dialogue and the exchange of critical information, farmers and processors can coordinate their activities to ensure that supply meets demand, which is crucial to maintaining stable market prices. This collaboration can involve sharing data on expected crop yields, pricing trends, and other factors that may impact the market.

By working together, farmers and processors can achieve their shared goal of maximizing profits while also ensuring a steady supply of high-quality products to consumers. This collaboration is a critical component of a healthy and sustainable agricultural system, enabling growers and processors to navigate the complexities of the marketplace and meet the evolving needs of consumers.

Author
Chandrasekar Vuppalapati

Data and tomatoes

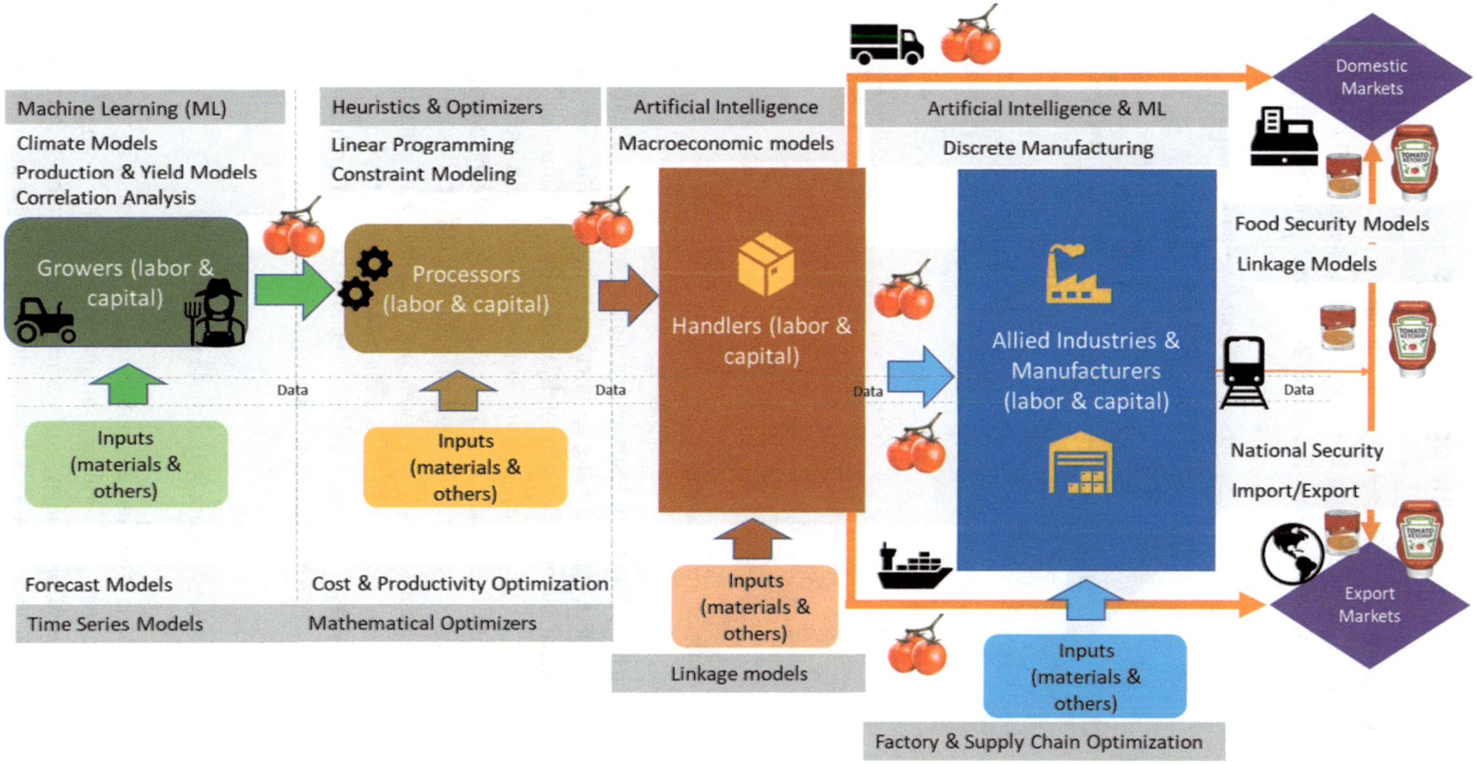

Figure 2: Tomatoes.

Economic importance and opportunities

Many stakeholders in the value chain of major cash crops (Figure 3) are often unaware of the lucrative opportunities in other agricultural markets. The tomato industry, in particular, holds significant potential to quickly improve investment portfolios.

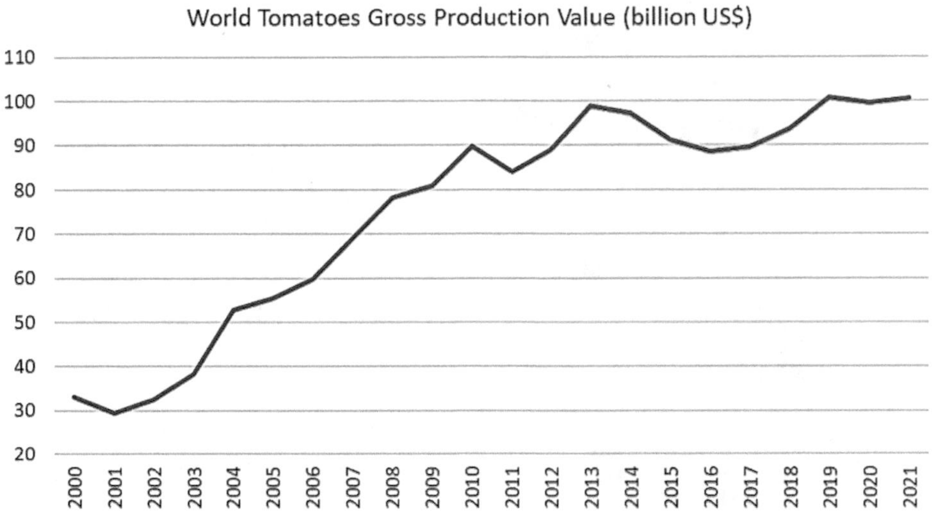

Figure 3: World tomatoes gross production.

Tomatoes are a billion-dollar industry with extensive applications in home cooking, food processing, and snack foods, driving significant market growth. They play a crucial role in the food service sector, including hotels, restaurants, and fast-food outlets, with the fast-food industry's rapid expansion further propelling the market. In the United States, tomatoes contribute $1.505 billion to cash receipts, and globally, their gross production reached $100.52 billion in 2021, growing at a 5.44% CAGR (FAO 2023). Their versatility extends to the production of soups, sauces, purees, juices, and ketchup as well as being used fresh in various dishes. Tomatoes offer essential nutrients for human health, such as maintaining blood pressure and healthy skin, and have anti-inflammatory properties, making them a valuable commodity that ensures high nutritional value and food security.

Government initiatives in boosting tomato production

As global populations grow and the demand for fresh produce increases, governments are intensifying efforts to boost crop production and processing. Utilizing advancements in science and technology, various initiatives have been launched to enhance tomato cultivation and meet agricultural demands. Research institutions funded by governments, such as the California Tomato Research Institute, ARS, and ICAR-IIHR in India, have developed high-yielding, disease-resistant tomato varieties like Pusa Ruby, Pusa Gaurav, and Chhuhara. These initiatives underscore the commitment to sustainable agriculture and food security.

Why has the US ban on Xinjiang's tomato exports had such limited effect? The Chinese tomato industry has demonstrated remarkable resilience, owing to its independence from American imports and its extensive export network, which spans over 80 countries worldwide. This robustness has enabled the industry to weather various economic and geopolitical challenges, including trade disputes and supply chain disruptions.

The Chinese tomato industry's strength lies in its ability to meet domestic demand while also exporting high-quality products to global markets. This has been made possible by the industry's focus on investing in advanced technologies, optimizing production processes, and leveraging its vast agricultural resources.

Surging growth for tomatoes in the food processing industry

The business-to-business market relies heavily on tomatoes, as they are a crucial raw material for producing other processed tomato products. Tomatoes are versatile and used in various forms such as juice, paste, puree, diced, or peeled tomatoes, ketchup, pickles, sauces, and ready-to-eat curries. These processed tomato products have wide applications in the food sector including snacks, culinary dishes, hotels, restaurants, and fast-food chains. The global demand for these products is high, driven by rapid urbanization and a growing preference for ready-made foods in both emerging and developed countries. Food manufacturers and tomato paste processors are focusing on producing ready-to-eat products to meet this increasing demand. The rise in the working population and millennials' preference for convenience foods has significantly boosted the demand for tomatoes in various forms, contributing to market growth in cafes, university dining halls, hotels, inns, catering services, and food processing industries.

Mexico is swiftly becoming a significant force in global tomato exports, having shipped $2.54 billion USD worth of tomatoes in 2021, which is about 24.13% of the world's total exports. The global tomato export market was valued at approximately $10.52 billion USD in the same year. Analysts forecast a promising future for the industry [376], with an expected growth rate of 5.6% CAGR from 2022 to 2027.

Employment

In the USA, the fruit and vegetable industries rely heavily on manual labor for various essential tasks, with labor costs constituting a significant portion of production expenses. The tomato production sector is notably labor-intensive, but farm operators are facing difficulties in finding enough workers, causing farm wages to rise more rapidly than nonfarm wages. These labor shortages and rising costs present substantial challenges for the industry in delivering high-quality produce to consumers [377].

China

From January to July 2022, Italy emerged as the top importer, absorbing nearly 20% of the autonomous region's exports, followed by Russia at 16%, and Ghana and the Philippines each at around 6%, according to China customs data. Large barrels of tomato paste, typically weighing over 5 kg (11 lbs), accounted for more than 96% of tomato trades during this period. These statistics highlight the strong global demand for high-quality tomato products, with China positioning itself as a key player in the industry.

India

Vegetable cultivation is crucial in India for generating income, creating jobs, promoting equity, improving nutrition, and protecting the environment, making it the world's second largest producer after China. In 2020–2021, production reached a record 137.98 million tonnes, with demand expected to double by 2030–2031 [378].

The Indian government has implemented initiatives to boost horticultural production to meet growing demand and ensure food security. Agriculture is the main livelihood for approximately 70% of rural households in India. Therefore, a robust agricultural growth strategy is crucial for the welfare of this large population [379].

Globally, around 1.23 billion people work in agrifood systems, with almost half of the world's population living in households connected to these systems. In India, 539 million rural households depend mainly on agriculture, with 82% of farmers being small and marginal. These statistics highlight the significant role of agriculture in India's economy and the importance of continuous support and investment in the sector.

India's tomato production relies heavily on smallholder farmers, nearly half of the farming community, with landholdings between 1 and 3 acres. The southern and central states of Andhra Pradesh, Telangana, Karnataka, and Maharashtra are key producers. Farmers typically sell their tomatoes to local aggregators or regional traders in mandis. However, the processing industry requires farmers to form clusters for a consistent supply of quality tomatoes. Current production methods focus on reducing crop risks with heavy pesticide use, leading to higher prices for processors.

Various market, nature, and man-made events can lead to economic dampening and pose upside risks to inflation such as El Nino, which could also impact the economic growth of major agricultural economies like India. Geopolitical uncertainties and declining merchandise trade due to a contraction in global trade could also contribute to downside risks to the economy, all of which can significantly influence the price of tomatoes [380].

Tomatoes are highly valuable vegetable crops cultivated for their fleshy fruits. They are essential both commercially and dietarily due to their high yield, short growth cycle, and versatility in preserved products like soups and paste. These qualities make tomatoes economically crucial for India and the global market [381].

Machine learning variable: the significance of rural population percentage in agricultural planning and decision-making

The countryside inhabitants constitute individuals residing in areas designated as rural by country statistical offices and is determined by the variation relating to the total and metropolitan population. The percentage of the countryside population in countries with small farms or independent farmers has a significant influence on the overall rural population percentage. This feature variable holds immense significance in predicting yield and forecasting prices, thereby making it an indispensable factor in agricultural planning and decision-making.

A comprehensive understanding of the rural population percentage is crucial for stakeholders to make informed decisions that support sustainable agriculture, improve the livelihoods of rural communities, and enhance food security. This entails a multifaceted approach that incorporates data on the rural population's demographic, economic, and social factors. This knowledge can be leveraged to advance pointed policies plus programs that address unique needs of rural communities and promote equitable agricultural development.

Moreover, the countryside population's percentage of the overall population is a vital indicator of a nation's overall socioeconomic status and the agricultural policies' effectiveness. By monitoring changes in this variable over time, policymakers and other stakeholders can assess the impact of agricultural interventions and make data-driven decisions to support sustainable and inclusive development.

Author
Chandrasekar Vuppalapati

Turkey

Turkey's agricultural sector is one of the top 10 worldwide, utilizing half of the country's land and employing nearly a quarter of its population. It leads in the production of wheat, sugar beets, milk, poultry, cotton, and tomatoes and excels globally in apricot and hazelnut production. Additionally, Turkey's young and growing population provides ample opportunities for market expansion and the introduction of new products [382].

	 Turkey
Acreage	962,354 acres (FAOSTAT 2021)
Economic boost to state economy	USD $1.763 billion (on-year, FAOSTAT 2020) and USD $602.16 million (off-year, FAOSTAT 2021)
Jobs created	Greater 300,000 [383]

Tomato transportation

Transporting perishable items like Florida tomatoes involves complex processes governed by USDA guidelines and laws such as the Perishable Agricultural Commodities Act and Country of Origin Labeling. California and Florida are the primary tomato producers in the United States, with Florida contributing about half of the nation's tomatoes and California focusing on tomatoes for paste. Efficient logistics management is essential to ensure the safe and timely delivery of these perishable goods to consumers [384].

When transporting goods, senders prioritize several factors such as delivery time, safety during transit, and shipping costs. However, when it comes to transporting fresh produce, such as Florida tomatoes, additional considerations must be considered [384, 385].

For instance, fresh Florida tomatoes require appropriate storage conditions during transport due to their perishable nature. If moved under right conditions and packaging, tomatoes freshness can be prolonged, enabling stores offer to consumers before they spoil. Moreover, transporting fresh produce necessitates careful handling, as fruits and vegetables, including Florida tomatoes, are prone to being squashed, bruised, or even destroyed during transit. Therefore, any mode of transportation must ensure minimal damage to these perishable goods [384, 385]. These factors underscore the importance of proper logistics planning and management to ensure that fresh produce arrives at its destination in optimal condition, meeting the expectations of both senders and receivers.

Farmers have the option to harvest tomatoes either when they are fully ripe and ready for consumption or while they are still green and unripe. During the ripening stage, tomatoes emit ethylene gas, a natural plant hormone that significantly influences physiological processes in plants. Even at very low internal concentrations of 0.1–1.0 parts per million (ppm), ethylene can accelerate the ripening of various fruits such as apples, avocados, bananas, citrus (for degreening), dates, mangoes, some melons, papayas, pears, persimmons, pineapples, and tomatoes. The broad physiological effects of ethylene across many plant species underscore its critical role in agriculture [386, 387].

The production of ethylene is a critical component of climacteric fruit ripening and artificially transforms into red tomatoes, indicating that it is ripe and ready to eat [385]. Ethylene is a gas hormone emitted from specific fruits and vegetables during the ripening process. According to the International Plant Growth Substances Association, all higher plants produce ethylene, but the type of tissue the produce has typically determines the amount of ethylene produced. This is why fruits are commonly seen as ethylene producers compared to vegetables, as they bloom on trees above ground [388]. These details highlight the role of ethylene in the ripening of fruits and vegetables, which is crucial to both farmers and consumers.

After being picked green and hard, unripe tomatoes are typically transported to storage facilities where they are treated with ethylene gas to accelerate aging procedure [389]. Tomatoes produce ethylene gas naturally to start their ripening process, but it can be slow. Companies often use ethylene-filled chambers to hasten the ripening, causing the tomatoes to turn red without developing full flavor naturally.

Some food producers use ethylene gas to hasten the ripening of tomatoes for timely shipment, while others focus on cultivating organic tomatoes without artificial ripening. As a result, Florida tomato producers adopt diverse methods and practices to meet industry standards [385].

One such technique to increase the shelf life of ripe tomatoes is the use of ethylene absorbents, which scavenge away the ethylene hormone responsible for fruit ripening. This method has become increasingly popular in the marketplace, as it can significantly delay the ripening of fruits and vegetables [390]. For instance, ripe tomatoes can be washed, have their surface moisture removed, and then packed in polypropylene packets with 0.002% perforation, or without perforation, to improve their shelf lifespan [391]. These innovative techniques highlight the importance of proper handling and management of fresh produce to ensure its quality and longevity.

While some large commercial tomato operations harvest mature-green tomatoes to ripen them later with ethylene gas, most Georgia growers wait until 10% of their field reaches the "breaker" stage before picking. Quality at harvest is judged by size uniformity and the absence of defects, with ideal tomatoes having a glossy surface, smooth scars, consistent color, and no damage. Although size doesn't typically affect grade quality, it significantly influences commercial buyers' preferences, prompting Georgia growers to focus on harvesting large and extra-large tomatoes [392].

Transporting fresh produce requires careful consideration of the appropriate temperature to maintain the quality of the goods. When shipping Florida tomatoes, it is essential to prevent overheating, as this can accelerate aging progression. On the other hand, if tomatoes are transported at temperatures that are too low, tomatoes can suffer from chilling injury and arrive in a deteriorated state, compromising their quality [384].

To maintain the highest quality, Florida tomatoes should be stored and transported at 12 °C (53.6 °F) with a relative humidity of about 90–95%. If ripening during storage or transit is desired, they should be kept at 20 °C (68 °F) [384]. When transporting Florida tomatoes, the transportation intermediaries must follow stringent guidelines to ensure that the produce arrives in optimal condition, both in terms of appearance and taste, while minimizing the risk of contamination.

The North American Free Trade Agreement (NAFTA), effective from January 1, 1994, has had a notable impact on Florida's tomato production, which decreased by nearly 37.129% from 1991 to 2021. During this period, the volume of tomato imports surged almost fivefold, leading to lower US market prices due to cheaper imports from Mexico and other countries [393]. These changes highlight the profound influence of international trade on the tomato industry and the need for adaptive strategies to manage evolving market dynamics.

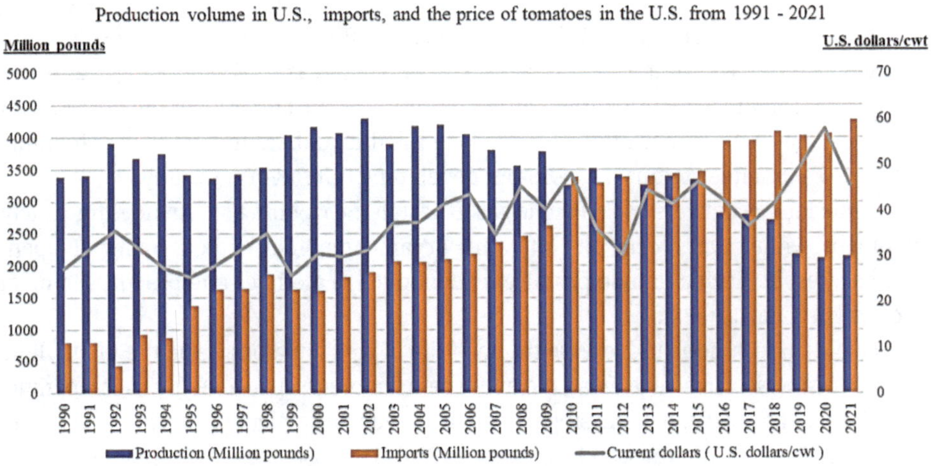

Figure 4: Production value in the USA.

The United States predominantly imports tomatoes from Mexico and Canada, with Canada providing open-field tomatoes from July to September and greenhouse tomatoes year-round, except in January and February. Within the USA, California supplies tomatoes from May to November, while Florida does so from October to June, with Mexico's Sinaloa and Baja California regions filling in during overlapping periods. This import strategy ensures a consistent year-round supply of fresh tomatoes, underscoring the importance of international trade in meeting consumer demand and highlighting the global nature of the food industry [393].

Table 1: The year-round tomato supply chain.

Country	Places	Open field	Protected condition
USA	California	May to November	Entire year ‡
	Florida	October to June	
	Other states of the U.S.	July to September	
Mexico	Sinaloa, Mexico	December to April	Entire Year†
	Baja California, Mexico	May to December	
Canada		July to September	Entire year except extreme cold months - January and February

* nationwide † pan south america

Ethylene is a colorless, sweet-smelling gas that becomes flammable at concentrations between 3.1% and 32% in air, a level much higher than what is used for ripening tomatoes [386]. Different vegetable crops emit varying amounts of ethylene. In contrast, tomatoes breed elevated quantities of ethylene, making them more susceptible to ethylene-induced ripening and aging.

Understanding the role of ethylene in vegetable ripening and senescence is crucial for optimizing postharvest handling and storage. By monitoring ethylene levels and mitigating its effects, growers and processors can stretch the shelf time of their products and reduce decay, thereby maximizing profitability and reducing food waste.

Overall, the natural production of ethylene in vegetable crops highlights the importance of careful handling and storage to ensure optimal quality and shelf life. By leveraging scientific knowledge and advanced technologies, stakeholders can achieve sustainable and profitable agricultural practices that benefit both producers and consumers.

Chandrasekar Vuppalapati

Truck driver shortages have significantly impacted distribution and transportation, with Florida experiencing the highest shortages in early 2022 due to a lack of drivers and rising fuel costs. Companies have responded by investing in technological innovations to improve logistical efficiency and ensure the safety and quality of fresh produce. Nonetheless, the industry continues to face challenges from increasing foreign competition, labor shortages, and rising input costs, necessitating ongoing adaptation and innovation to meet consumer and market demands [394].

Tomato prices

The fresh tomato supply-chain network is unique, driven by consumer demand and encompassing products collected at various ripe thresholds. This results in a go-to market route that sets fresh tomatoes apart from other produce. These delectable fruits are typically marketed through retail or food service channels, with the supply chain divided into different stages that involve various entities [394].

However, due to relatively stagnant consumer demand, the volume of fresh tomato imports and domestic production is expected to shift in favor of importing countries that have observed significant advantages. As a result, North American producers are losing market share to Mexico and Canada, where labor wages are relatively lower and seasonal production overlaps with that of the United States, respectively. This trend has contributed to a reduction in the number of Florida's growers and consolidation within the industry [394].

Forecasting tomato prices (Table 2) in advance is crucial for smallholder farmers as it can make the difference between financial sustainability and leaving acres of crops unharvested, despite registering a bumper yield. In other words, investing in labor and agricultural inputs becomes futile if the price received is not sufficient to break even, resulting in the abandonment of the crop [395].

As tomato prices plummet (Figure 5) in the open market, farmers may choose to desert standing crops, as further expenditure on harvesting, labor, and transportation charges may not be remunerative. However, unlike field tomatoes, where harvesting can result in a loss despite a bumper yield, tomatoes for processing are governed by a price contract between growers and processors. This minimizes the possibility of loss for growers, making it a more secure option [395].

These challenges faced by smallholder farmers highlight the importance of accurate price forecasting and effective risk management strategies, such as price contracts, to ensure the financial sustainability of the industry. By prioritizing these measures, farmers can continue to produce high-quality fresh produce that meets the needs of consumers and markets worldwide.

Table 2: Tomato price behavior.

	Price behavior	
	Tomatoes for Field	**Tomatoes for processing**
Mode of business	Between smallholder farmers and intermediaries	Contract between growers and processors.
Price contracts	Market determined	Well established prior crop season
Price behavior at Harvest	Higher risk to farmers as prices are market determined	Well established contract; Recently, 2022/2023, reference prices negotiated between growers and processors have soared, once again taking the value of processing tomatoes to unprecedented levels‡ [6]

‡ The World Processing Tomato Council reports that for the 2023 season, the global average field-gate value of a metric ton of tomatoes is approximately US $136, representing a 40% increase from 2022's record level and a 60% rise compared to the average price from 2020 to 2022 [375].

Supply and demand are crucial in determining the price levels of goods and services in an economy. In India, factors such as weather changes, production rates, labor shortages, and transportation costs significantly influence the inflation of onion, tomato, and potato prices. Tomato prices have exhibited a generally increasing trend with notable fluctuations post-2006, supported by statistical data indicating a steady linear rise [381].

Various factors can impact the market price of tomatoes, including changes in farming land use, weather patterns, and tomato (table 41 – tomatoes) imports from Mexico. The average price for fresh-market tomatoes in the United States increased (Table 1)

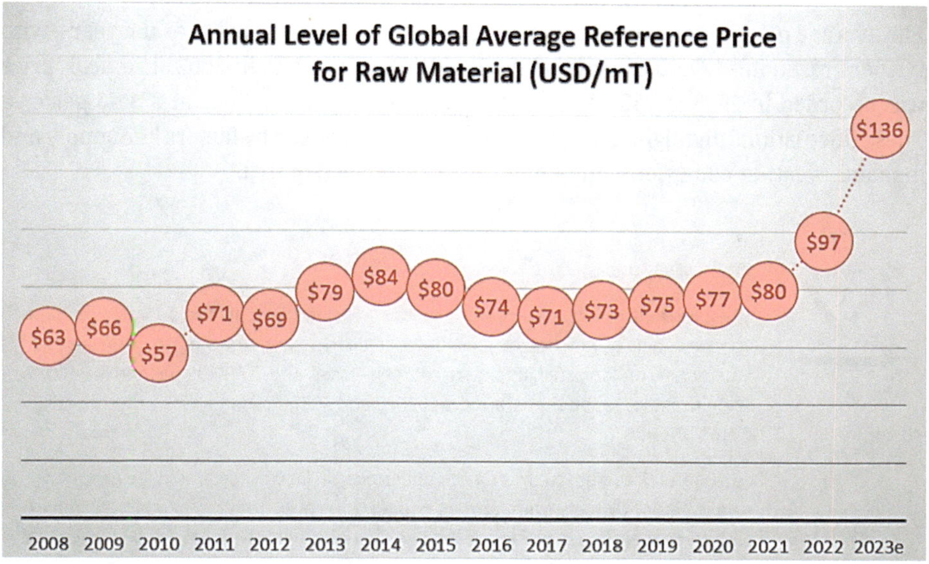

Figure 5: Global averge prices.

from approximately $30.7 per cwt in 2000 to $40.7 per cwt in 2016 [396]. This demonstrates that tomato prices can fluctuate over time due to multiple influencing factors (eq. (1)):

$$y = 0.6396x + 14.167 \tag{1}$$

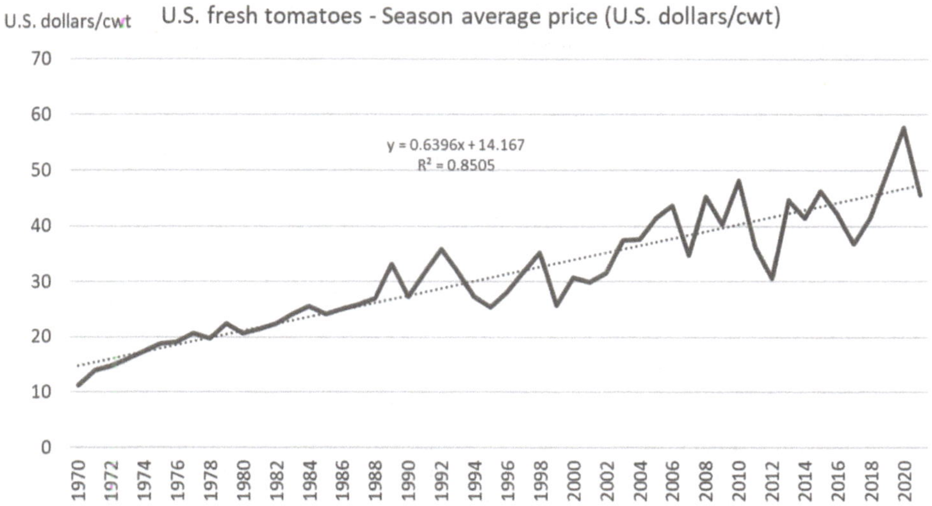

Figure 6: US fresh tomatoes average prices.

The average price of tomatoes per hundredweight (cwt) has varied over the years, with farmers receiving $27.40 per cwt in 1990 and $31.40 per cwt in 2002. The peak price was recorded in 1998 at $35.20 per cwt, with another peak in 2020 at $31.40 per cwt. These fluctuations highlight that tomato prices are influenced by factors like supply and demand, weather conditions, and import/export trends (Figure 6).

Throwaway prices!

Despite registering a bumper yield this year, farmers in Asia's largest tomato-growing belt of Annamayya and Chittoor districts are choosing to leave acres of their crops unharvested, hoping to cut their losses. The COVID-19 pandemic inflicted significant losses on these farmers in 2020 and 2021, making financial sustainability a top priority.

In June 2022, tomato cultivation was undertaken in 20,000 hectares in the Annamayya and Chittoor districts, with farmers hoping to recover from the pandemic's impact. However, their hopes quickly dashed as they observed the bleak market prospects for their produce. Other states were also poised for bumper yields, leaving local growers with few potential buyers in other parts of the country [395].

This unfortunate situation highlights the challenges faced by smallholder farmers and the need for effective risk management strategies, such as accurate price forecasting and diversification of crops, to ensure financial sustainability. By prioritizing these measures, farmers can weather the impact of market fluctuations and continue to produce high-quality fresh produce that meets the demands of consumers and markets worldwide.

The US tomato market is subject to significant price fluctuations (figure 7), both within a season and across years. While weather effects on production cause most of the price dissimilarity within a season, changes in acreage and weather are responsible for the price variations observed over the years [392].

Despite slight changes in demand from year to year, the downward trend in tomato prices was consistent in the years following the highest average retail price recorded in the first quarter of 2018. However, 2018, 2019, and 2022 proved to be exceptional years, with increased prices resulting from the suspension of the tomato agreement with Mexico [397]. In contrast, tomato prices remained relatively stable in 2022, despite higher inflation [397].

For price forecast modeling, the years 1996 and 2018 are essential as government intervention significantly impacted the overall prices of tomatoes. In 2022 year end, optimum cost of approximately $2.22 for each pound was noted, with changes observed from month over month and year over year due to the quantity produced and imported, particularly from Canada and Mexico [392]. These fluctuations highlight the need for effective risk management strategies and accurate price forecasting to ensure the financial sustainability of the industry.

Machine learning variables

The years 1996 and 2018 hold immense significance for price forecast modeling in the tomato industry, given the substantial government intervention that occurred during this time. These pivotal years continue to shape the industry and provide critical reference points for accurate price forecasting and effective risk management strategies.

By incorporating data from these years into pricing models, stakeholders are able to profit a more comprehensive interpretation of market dynamics and take learned judgments that optimize profitability and reduce risk. This approach is particularly important given the volatility of agricultural markets and the need to balance supply and demand while maintaining high-quality produce that meets the expectations of discerning consumers.

Moreover, prioritizing effective risk management strategies is vital for the industry's long-term sustainability and growth. By identifying and mitigating potential risks, growers and processors can protect their investments and ensure a stable supply of high-quality produce that meets the evolving needs of global markets.

Author
Chandrasekar Vuppalapati

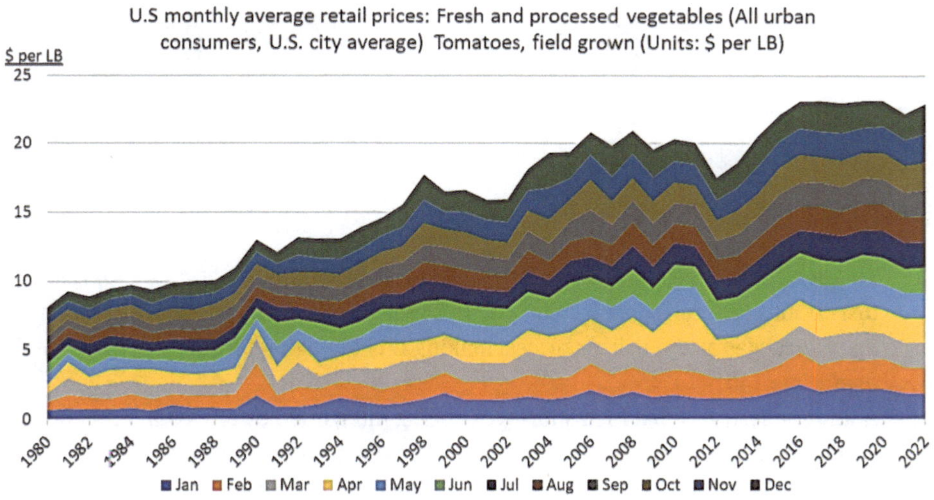

Figure 7: US monthly average prices.

In 2022, Americans experienced significant price increases and widespread shortages of tomatoes and their derivatives such as ketchup and tomato sauce. These issues were exacerbated by a severe drought in California, which produces over 90% of the country's tomatoes, alongside the lingering effects of the pandemic [398, 399]. Both consumers and farmers felt the impact, with many struggling due to low inventory and the high demand for takeaway food [400].

Given the circumstances that transpired in 2021, the trend for 2022 is increased prices of tomatoes at the retail level. This serves as a reminder of the importance of effective risk management strategies and accurate price forecasting to ensure the financial sustainability of the industry. By prioritizing these measures, the industry can continue to produce high-quality fresh produce that meets the demands of consumers and markets worldwide (Figure 8). The price increase in 2022 was due to two facts (retail prices – trade and prices by category data):

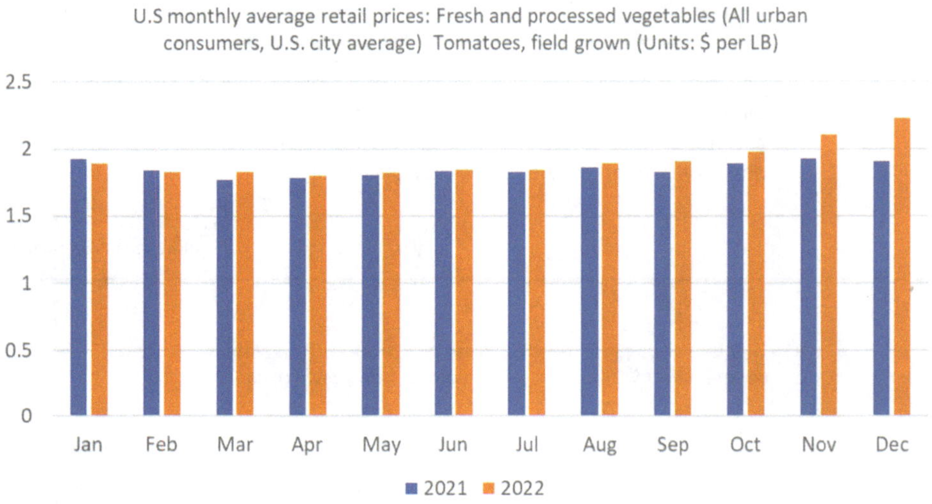

Figure 8: US monthly average retail prices.

1. The agriculture sector is grappling with soaring energy costs and supply chain disruptions, exacerbated by the Russian invasion of Ukraine, which has driven up natural gas and fertilizer prices, making it challenging for farmers to maintain operations [401].
2. Additionally, the global food shortage is being intensified by environmental factors and lead to fewer tomatoes being planted or replaced by more profitable alternatives [402]. Warmer winters are also allowing pests and diseases to spread further into tomato-growing regions, delaying harvests and causing significant losses [402].

These challenges facing the agriculture sector underscore the importance of effective risk management strategies and accurate price forecasting to ensure the financial sustainability of the industry. By prioritizing these measures, farmers can continue to produce high-quality fresh produce that fulfills the requests of patrons and markets worldwide despite the various challenges posed by energy costs, supply chain disruptions, and environmental factors.

In 2021, farmers received a smaller share of the retail price (Figure 9) for fresh, field-grown tomatoes, which dropped from 43% in 2020 to 36% [404]. Despite a decrease in the average retail price of tomatoes from $1.96 to $1.85 per pound, the price farmers received also fell from $0.72 to $0.56 per pound. This decline is partly due to a 1.3% increase in US domestic tomato production, even as overall fresh vegetable production decreased by 4% due to extreme heat [405].

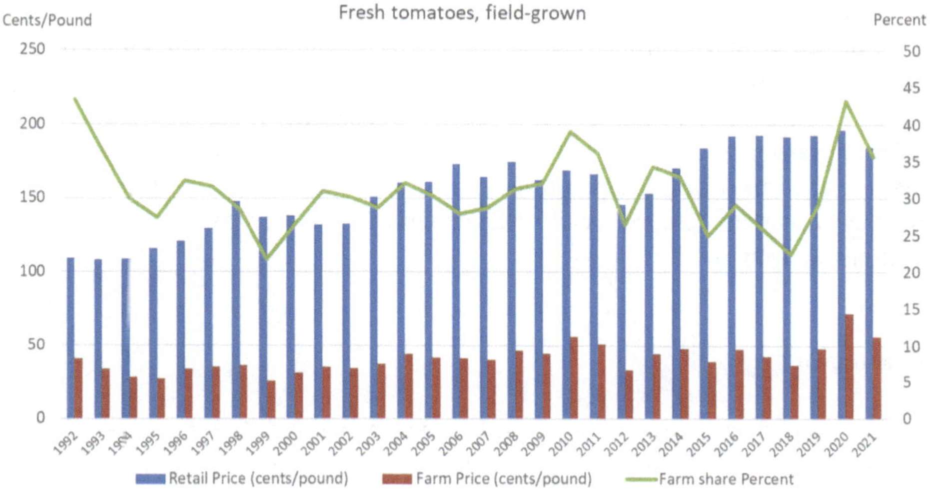

Figure 9: Fresh tomatoes – imports.

- Retail prices
- Farm prices
- Farm share [406]

California – atmospheric rivers

In March 2023, approximately a dozen atmospheric rivers brought immense storms to California, releasing trillions of gallons of water. The resulting floods left countryside extremely watery for setting, causing significant delays in tomato cultivation. As a result, consumers may find their favorite tomato-based products missing from store shelves and increased prices for ketchup, salsa, and other tomato products may be observed [398].

This situation highlights the impact of environmental factors on the agriculture sector and the need for effective risk management strategies to mitigate these effects. By prioritizing accurate price forecasting and diversification of crops, farmers can weather the impact of market fluctuations and environmental factors to continue producing high-quality fresh produce that meets the demands of consumers and markets worldwide.

Author
Chandrasekar Vuppalapati

The UK's largest tomato supplier has sounded the alarm, warning that soaring gas prices have made it prohibitively expensive to heat greenhouses, thus threatening production. The resulting uncertainty, driven by high global gas prices and rising fertilizer costs, has created significant challenges around the availability of fertilizers in the UK [399]. Despite these challenges, the supplier remains committed to working with the government to ensure a steady supply of these vital resources.

After addressing immediate supply concerns, the supplier plans to concentrate on enhancing the resilience of CO_2 production to safeguard the food and beverage supply chain. This highlights the crucial role of robust risk management strategies and precise price forecasting in maintaining the industry's financial stability. By prioritizing these measures, farmers can continue to produce high-quality fresh produce that meets worldwide markets despite various challenges posed by energy costs, supply chain disruptions, and environmental factors.

Field grown

Average consumer prices for household fuel, motor fuel, and food items are collected for the consumer price index (CPI), which includes both organic and nonorganic field-grown tomatoes. While average prices can reflect the price level in a specific month, they are not suitable for measuring price changes over time. For a more accurate assessment of price changes, it is better to use CPI index values for specific item categories. The CPI measures the average change in prices over time for a fixed basket of goods and services by comparing costs across different periods. This allows economists and policymakers to track changes in the cost of living and understand how economic performance and policy changes affect consumers [400].

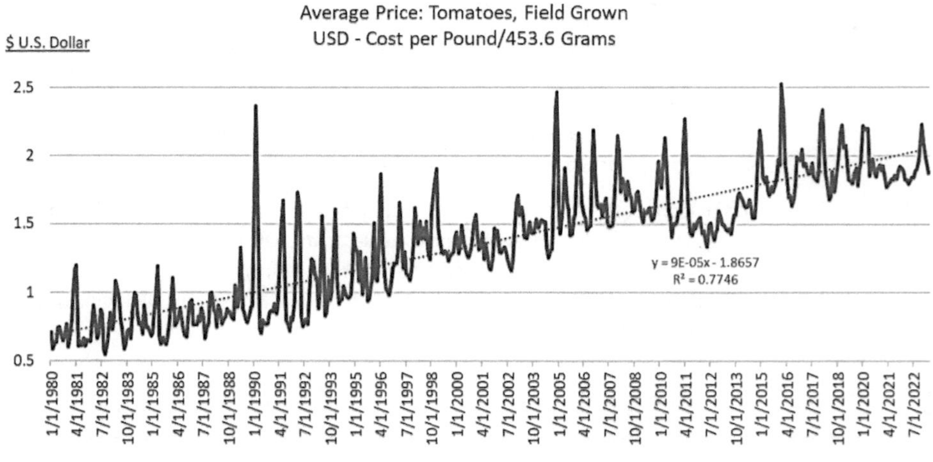

Figure 10: Average price of tomatoes.

You can find retail prices for vegetables and pulses (Figure 10), including fresh and processed products, from Trade and Prices by Category. This provides data on different classifications and categories of products. Two key indicators to look out for are the Consumer Price Index and Retail Prices. From 1980 to 2022, the average price of field-grown tomatoes in the United States has exhibited a general upward trend, reflecting an increase over time. The graph shows frequent fluctuations with several notable peaks, particularly around 1990, 2004, and 2014, where prices exceeded $2 per pound. These peaks suggest periods of significant price hikes possibly due to market, environmental, or economic factors. The latter decade shows a continued rise in prices with a more consistent upward trend, indicating sustained demand or increasing production costs. The trend line and (R^2 = 77.46%) value signify a moderate to strong relationship between the years and the rising prices, underscoring a general increase in the cost of field-grown tomatoes over the period analyzed.

Tomatoes for processing

To find US prices for processed tomatoes, you can use the Year Tables and navigate to Table 59-Tomatoes, which provides average prices for this particular product (Figure 11). Throughout 2008, input costs for agricultural growers experienced significant increases, with the most notable spikes occurring during the peak usage months indicated in gray (May through September). Potash and phosphate prices saw the steepest rise, peaking at around 175% above the January 2008 baseline in mid-2008, before sharply declining toward the end of the year. Mixed fertilizer costs followed a similar trend, reaching over 100% above the baseline and then decreasing to near-original levels by early 2009. Nitrogen, herbicides, and diesel prices also increased, albeit less dramatically, peaking around 50–75% above January 2008 levels, and subsequently fell, with diesel showing a notable drop. The shaded period aligns with the peak usage months for these inputs, highlighting the correlation between increased demand and rising costs.

In 2008, the export demand for US tomatoes increased by nearly 200% due to factors such as a weak USD, reduced tomato crops in Mediterranean countries, and irregular production in China [401]. This led to higher tomato prices and increased input costs during peak usage, which later declined after the harvest [402]. Additionally, there was growing demand from nonconventional markets like Italy, Africa, and Latin America, while imports into the US remained low amid rising demand for tomato products [401]. Overall, the data illustrates the significant volatility in input costs throughout 2008 and early 2009, driven by seasonal demand and subsequent market adjustments.

Another reason for the increased prices was the impact of water shortages, as shown in Figure 11. In 2009, acreage for tomato cultivation was lower due to the lowest water levels in California's reservoirs since 1977. Planters were thoughtfully alarmed about their water resources for year 2009, and any water they received was allocated

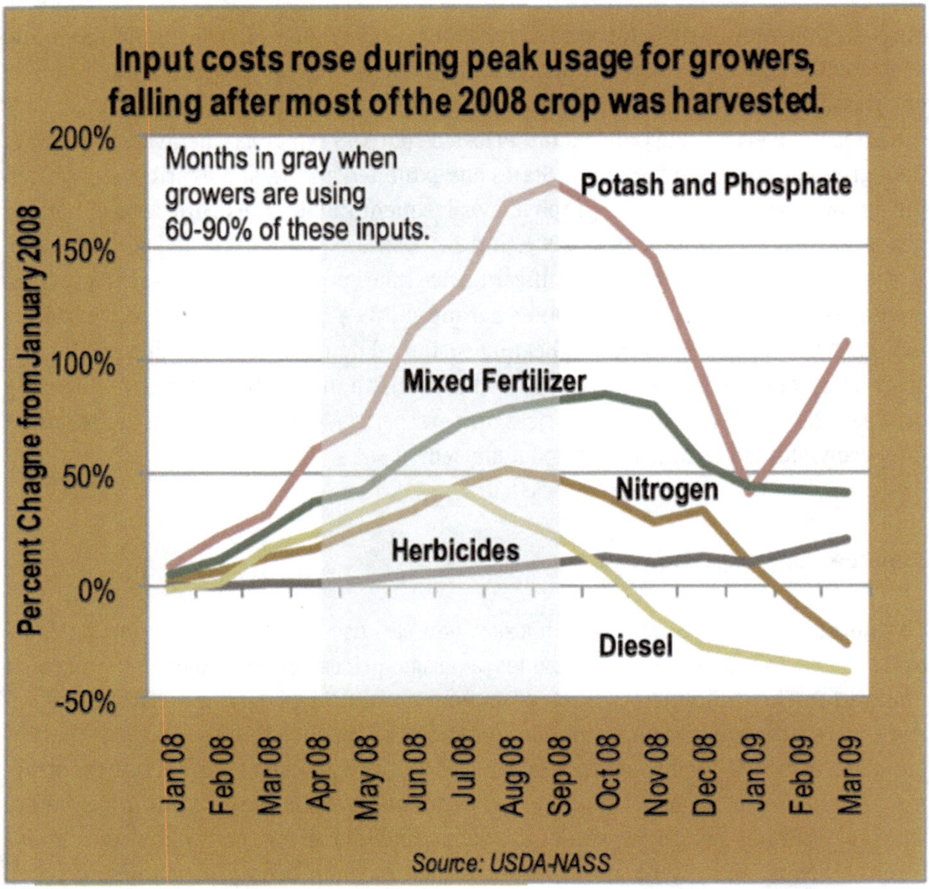

Figure 11: Input costs.

to permanent crops first [401]. Please kindly note that for both long seasoned crops and agricultural in general, farmers consider planted acreage based on realistic early season water supply projections [401].

These trends highlight the importance of accurate price forecasting and effective risk management strategies to ensure the financial sustainability of the industry. By prioritizing these measures, farmers can continue to produce high-quality fresh produce that meets demands of worldwide despite various challenges posed by market fluctuations, environmental factors, and supply chain disruptions.

In Figure 12, from 1970 to 2020, the season average prices for US tomatoes for processing have shown an overall increasing trend. In the early period from 1970 to 1980, prices rose significantly from about $30–$60 per ton. The mid-period from 1980 to 2000 was characterized by fluctuations between $50 and $70 per ton, reflecting periods of both increases and decreases but maintaining a relatively stable average. In the more recent period from 2000 to 2020, prices experienced more significant increases, reach-

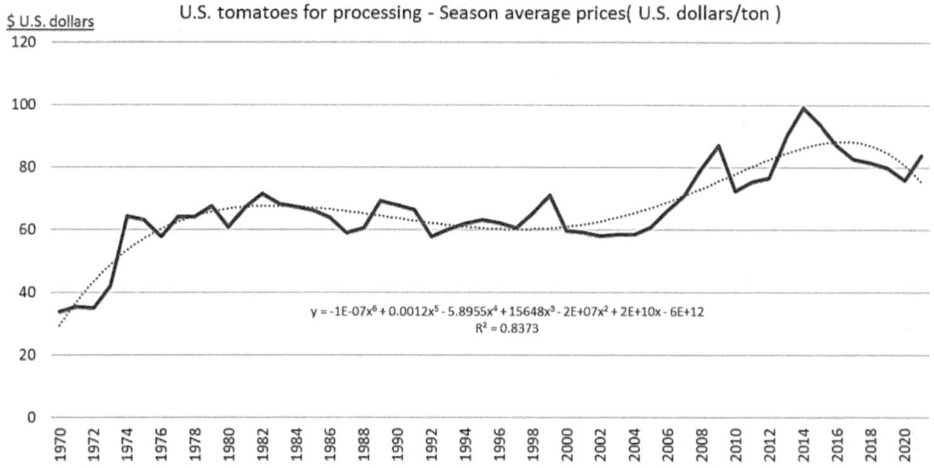

Figure 12: US tomatoes for processing.

ing a peak of around $100 per ton in 2015, before a slight decline and a small recovery toward 2020. In 2009, growers and processors finally reached an agreement after a prolonged negotiation, settling on a price of $80 per ton [401]. The polynomial trend line and the (R^2) value of 0.8373 indicate a strong correlation, suggesting a consistent upward trend in prices over the 50-year span.

These developments underscore the importance of effective risk management strategies and accurate price forecasting to ensure the financial sustainability of the industry. By prioritizing these measures, farmers can continue to produce high-quality fresh produce that meets worldwide demands despite the various challenges posed by market fluctuations, environmental factors, and supply chain disruptions.

Price of tomato for processing: machine learning features [401]

- US dollar strength
- Crop size of Mediterranean countries
- China's production
- Exchange rate
  - CADD
  - Mexico
- Abundant sunshine and significant temperature variation between day and night [403]
- Fertilizer cost
  - Potash and phosphate
  - Mixed fertilizer
  - Nitrogen
  - Herbicides

- Diesel–diesel price also plays a foremost role in deciding retail prices of the agricultural commodity, diesel price changes every day due to changes in international crude oil price and policies [381]
- Labor
- Equipment
- Repairs

The future of California's processing tomato industry looks promising, provided it secures sufficient water supplies and offers growers competitive prices [398].

California atmospheric rivers [398]

Record-breaking rainfall has left California farms waterlogged, thereby potentially driving up prices for canned tomato products.

China

This chart (Figure 13) presents a comparison of tomato prices in California and China over the past 12 years. Although tomato prices in China have increased 21% in 2020–2022, we remain highly competitive in price compared to California. The chief reason for the price increase is free of renting fields, which accounts for approximately 30% of the cost of planting tomatoes. As of 2022, the rental cost of fields has risen to about 50% of planting costs, while other costs, such as water, pesticides, and energy, have only increased by 2 or 3% [375].

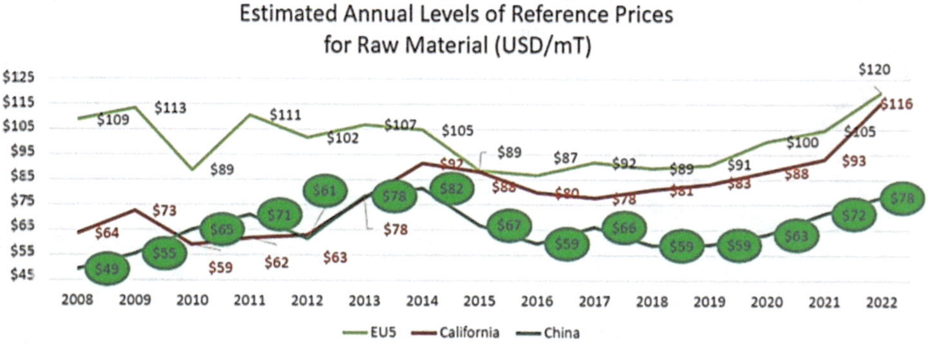

Figure 13: Reference prices [375].

Thanks to advancements in planting techniques, farmers have significantly increased their yields. Before 2015, the yield was below 90 mT per hectare, but in the last 3 years

(2019–2021), and even in 2022, the yield has increased to an average of 120–130 mT per hectare. The highest recorded yields have reached up to 195 mT per hectare [375].

The Chinese government has implemented various rules to protect farmers, and many processors have received collateral from local governments to borrow money from financial institutions to ensure that all farmers who deliver tomatoes to processors are paid. From 2014 until now, no farmers have lost money, which has helped to maintain good relationships between farmers and processors, encouraging farmers to plant more tomatoes and making their relationships more sustainable [375].

In terms of the international tomato market and pricing, ocean freight plays a critical role, as China exports about 80% of its products. In 2021, the maximum freight index was 3,500, and as of November 2021, the peak period, the freight going to Europe was around 9,000 USD per container. However, this figure has significantly dropped, and it is now at 7,000 USD, which is an excellent advantage for China's exports of tomato paste this year [375].

The currency conversion rate between yuan (¥) and USD ($) is another factor that benefits Chinese processors. The exchange rate has increased by over 30% in the past 6 months, providing an additional margin of about 15% for China's processors. The current government and financial situation are expected to maintain the exchange rate between 7.1 and 7.3 for the next 6–8 months [375].

Rising prices for tomato products are driving the expansion of acreage and increased use of inputs like fertilizer and labor. This will ultimately result in higher yields, fostering a mutually beneficial cycle of yield enhancement and expansion [404].

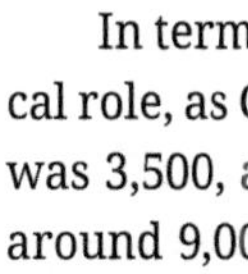

Yield improvement symbiotic cycle

The anticipated increase in prices is expected to foster expansion synergies and promote a symbiotic cycle of yield improvement in the agricultural industry. The higher prices are encouraging farmers to expand their acreage and invest, which will ultimately lead to increased yields.

This positive feedback loop is poised to enhance the industry's financial sustainability by improving the efficiency and productivity of farming operations. The resulting increase in yields will not only meet the growing demands of consumers and markets worldwide but also create opportunities for farmers to achieve greater profitability and reinvest in their operations.

Moreover, the expansion synergies generated by higher prices will enable farmers to leverage cutting-edge technologies and innovative practices that optimize crop growth. This will guarantee that industry remains competitive, sustainable, and responsive to the evolving needs of global markets.

Author
Chandrasekar Vuppalapati

Influencers

The global prices of raw tomatoes have experienced a significant increase in 2021–2022, as growers continue to grapple with bullish drivers. Limited water supply for irrigating fields, adverse weather conditions, rising input costs (fertilizers, labor), and energy costs are exerting unbearable pressure on fresh tomato production [398]. From a machine learning perspective, the following variables have been identified as major influencers:

- Extreme weather conditions such as Hurricane Ian
- Imports from Mexico and Canada [405]
- Domestic production, particularly in greenhouses [405]
- Yield reduction due to disease pressure and viruses, including the Brown Rugose Virus, which has plagued the industry for several years
- Rising energy costs, driven by the distant conflict in Ukraine, have significantly increased winter production expenses, directly impacting growers' profitability.

These factors underscore the importance of effective risk management strategies and accurate price forecasting to ensure the financial sustainability of the industry. By prioritizing these measures, farmers can continue to produce high-quality fresh produce that meets worldwide demands, despite various challenges posed by market fluctuations, environmental factors, and supply chain disruptions [402, 403].

Tomato prices and energy correlation

In general, fertilizers are a significant factor influencing crop input costs, and they are also subject to energy costs. When it comes to tomatoes cultivation, the cost of lighting is a significant consideration, given that most greenhouses in the United States are furnished with high-pressure sodium or light-emitting diode grow lights. These lighting systems can significantly impact the costs of tomato production, in addition to fertilizer costs.

Understanding the various factors that influence input costs is critical to effective risk management and accurate price forecasting. By prioritizing these measures, farmers can continue to produce high-quality fresh produce that meets worldwide demand despite the challenges posed by market fluctuations, environmental factors, and supply chain disruptions.

Chandrasekar Vuppalapati

US tomatoes

Machine learning model: tomatoes pricing models

Developed tomato forecast pricing model. The pricing model involves various components of fresh produce markets that include macroeconomic variables, infrastructure, crop price behavior, climate change models, energy, and market access and value chain (Figure 14).

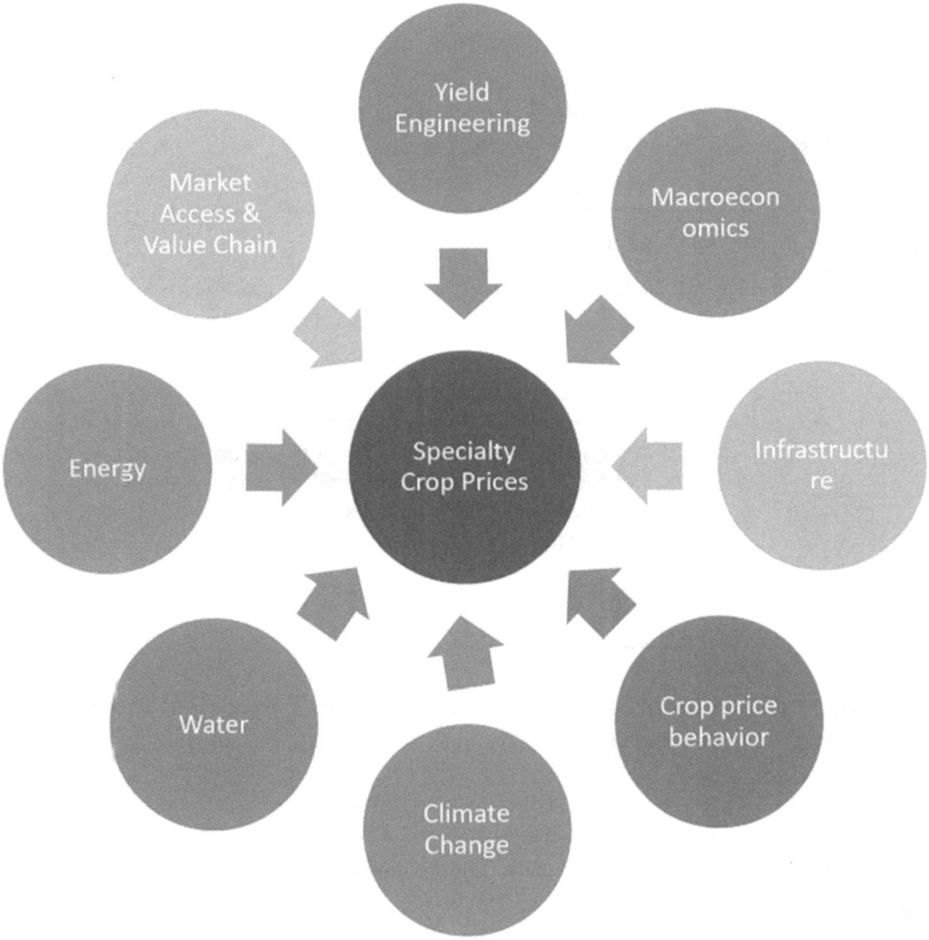

Figure 14: Tomatoes pricing components.

The proposed approach is generally applicable to issue forward-looking market guidance as part of the commodities price updates. Forward-looking market guidance refers to information provided by companies or organizations that offer insight into future market conditions or potential trends that may impact the industry. This guidance typically includes forecasts and predictions on factors such as sales, revenue, and overall market performance.

Companies may provide forward-looking market guidance to investors, analysts, and market in general to help them drive more advised conclusions about their investments or business strategies. This guidance can be based on a variety of factors or macroeconomic trends. It is important to note that forward-looking market guidance is not a guarantee of future performance and may be subject to change. It is intended to provide insight into potential future market conditions and trends, but actual results may vary depending on a range of factors that cannot be predicted with certainty.

For analyzing pricing models, a traditional approach would apply historical data and link to macroeconomic view. However, in the proposed model, many interwove parameters are considered to model price forecast.

NAFTA-infused ML variables: CAD and MXN

NAFTA was implemented on January 1, 1994 [393]. Since then, exports from both Mexico and Canada have significantly increased, having a considerable impact on domestic prices.

Two variables that greatly influence the retail pricing of fresh tomatoes in domestic markets are the US dollar to Canadian dollar exchange rate (USD/CAD) and USD to MXN (Mexican Peso) conversion rate. Understanding the impact of these variables is crucial to effective risk management and accurate price forecasting. By prioritizing these measures, farmers can continue to produce high-quality fresh produce that meets the needs of worldwide markets despite the challenges posed by market fluctuations, environmental factors, and supply chain disruptions.

Author
Chandrasekar Vuppalapati

Succinctly, the price forecast developed is based on the proposed framework that links causative factors of many different fields on the price of tomato (Figure 15). Let's build model for US tomatoes:

Final release USA Fresno tomato price econometric weather notebook code

---

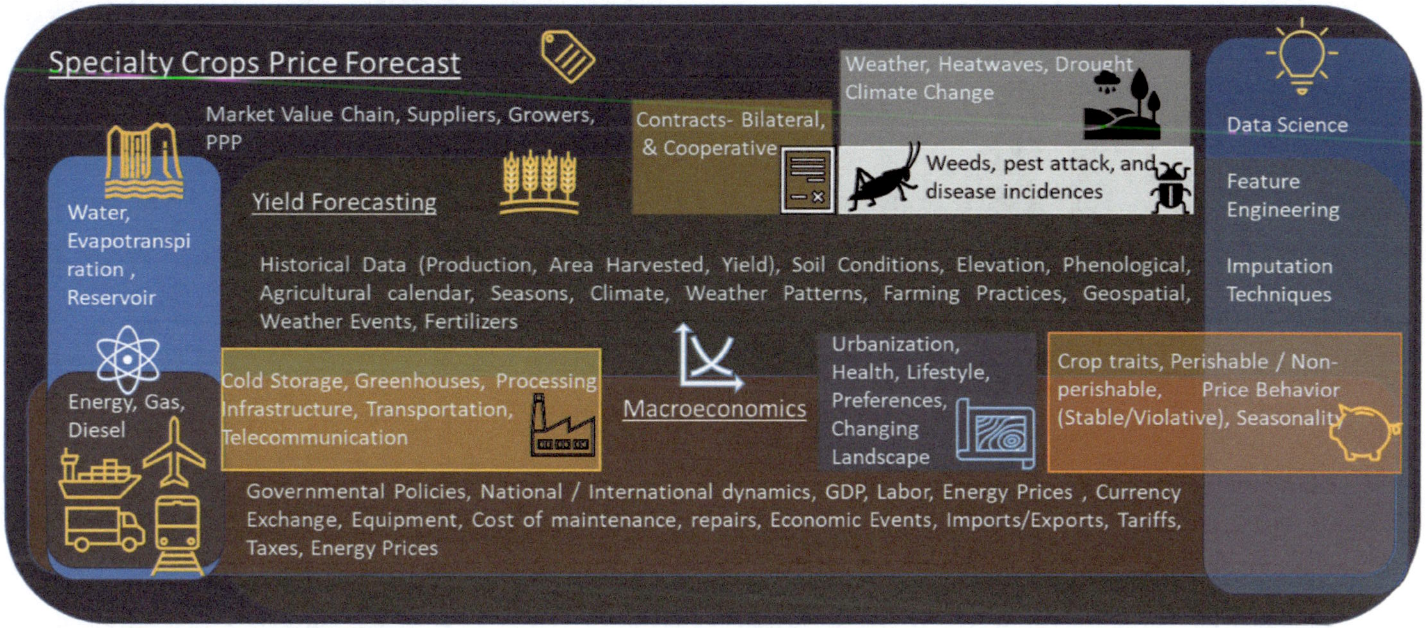

Figure 15: Specialty crops price forecast components.

Data sources

The following table has the list of major attributes and data source details.

Data source	Name
USDA	Retail prices of fresh and processed vegetables for tomatoes under trade and prices by category.
FRED	Average price: APU0000711415[1] US diesel sales price (GASDESM): diesel prices CPIAUCSL and maintenance[2]
World Bank	Pink Sheet data
NOAA	Maine and New Hampshire weather data

Pricing model framework: variable list

Price forecasting is Following data sources are used as part of the model:

Independent feature time series name	Frequency	Description	Source
Fresno weather	Monthly	MaxTemperature(C)', 'MeanTemperature(C)', 'MinTemperature(C)', rain or precipitation,	NOAA GSOM
GASREGCOVM	Monthly	Gas prices	Gas price
Consumer price index (CPI)	Monthly	CPIAUCSL	CPIAUCSL

1 APU0000711415 - https://fred.stlouisfed.org/series/APU0000711415

2 Commercial Machinery Repair and Maintenance- https://fred.stlouisfed.org/series/PCU8113108113105

(continued)

Independent feature time series name	Frequency	Description	Source
Fertilizer	Monthly	PhosphateRock($/mt)', 'Dap($/mt)', 'Tsp($/mt)', 'Urea($/mt)', 'PotassiumChloride($/mt)',	World Bank commodity markets
GDP	Quarterly	gross domestic product (GDP)	GDP
GEPUCURRENT	Monthly	Current Price Adjusted (GEPUCURRENT)	GEPUCURRENT
S&P 500 Dividend by Month	Monthly	S&P Dividends	Dividend by month
Industrial Production Index (INDPRO)	Monthly	INDPRO	INDPRO
Rail car loadings	Monthly	Rail freight carloads	Rail freight carloads (RAILFRTCARLOADSD11)
EmpInAgri (1000sOfPersons)			Number of agricultural practitioners
UnEmpRate	Monthly	Unemployment rate (UNRATE)	Unemployment rate (UNRATE)
Rail Freight Carloads (RAILFRTCARLOADSD11)	Monthly		Rail freight Carloads (RAILFRTCARLOADSD11)
SP500	Daily	The standard and poor's 500 index	SP500

Step 1: Load agricultural farm-input data: fertilizer data from World Bank Pink Sheet data

The fertilizer industry experienced a significant price spike that lasted for almost a year, starting in October 2007. This abrupt price increase stemmed from a convergence of numerous factors. Fertilizer costs escalated due to a disparity between supply and the swiftly expanding demand.

The rising demand for fertilizers in the USA, Brazil, and Europe to produce biofuels and support livestock production has significantly driven up fertilizer prices. During the 2007–2008 price hike, the situation was exacerbated by China's high tariffs on fertilizer exports and the devaluation of the US dollar, making imports more costly. Additionally, soaring energy prices increased the cost of natural gas, essential for nitrogen fertilizer production, and heightened demand for sulfur drove up phosphate fertilizer prices, leading to a tight supply of quality phosphate rock. Various factors influencing fertilizer prices include governmental regulations, delays in permits, financial assurance requirements, and adverse weather conditions. Understanding these elements is crucial for farmers, policymakers, and consumers to make informed decisions and mitigate adverse effects on agriculture and food supply [407].

The ripple effects of fertilizer price variations

The surge in fertilizer prices during 2007–2008 led to unintended consequences, such as "demand destruction," where high costs significantly reduced fertilizer demand. This issue was further compounded by the global credit market collapse, trade recession, and economic slowdown, forcing manufacturers to cut production and severely impacting the agriculture sector. Potash prices, however, have remained high due to shortages and transportation issues from Russia, exacerbated by a growing sinkhole near the Silvinit mines. Phosphate rock, crucial for soil fertility and crop yields, saw prices peak at 266 US dollars per metric ton in 2022, with a moderate decline to $240 per ton expected by 2024. This situation underscores the complex dynamics of supply and demand and their wide-reaching impacts on various industries and markets.

Understanding the various factors that influence fertilizer prices is critical to effective risk management and accurate price forecasting. By prioritizing these measures, farmers can continue to produce high-quality crops that meet the needs of consumers and markets worldwide despite the challenges posed by market fluctuations, environmental factors, and supply chain disruptions.

Future data imputation strategy

Forecast of DAP is difficult as no trend provides a higher acuracires in estimating. The most potential would be polynomial regressors (eqs. (2) and (3)):

$$y = -3E{-}20x^6 + 7E{-}15x^5 - 7E{-}10x^4 + 4E{-}05x^3 - 1.2007x^2 + 19616x - 1E{+}08 \quad (2)$$
$$R^2 = 0.4935$$

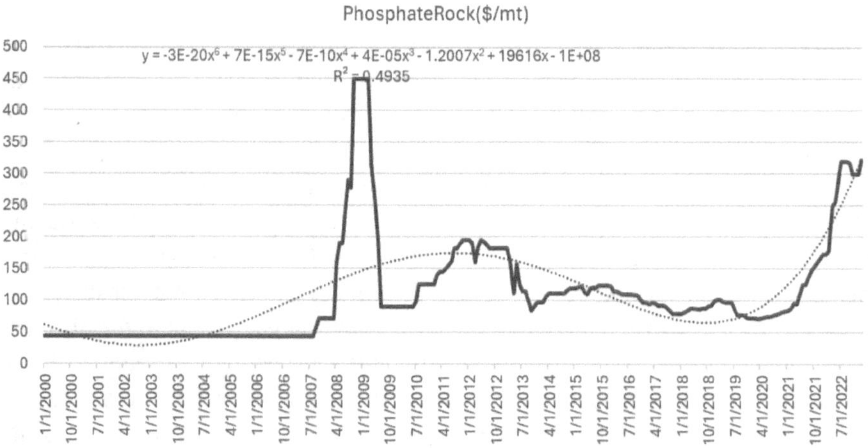

Urea prices have similiar price movements (eq. (3)):

$$y = -9\text{E}{-20}x^6 + 2\text{E}{-14}x^5 - 2\text{E}{-09}x^4 + 0.0001x^3 - 3.7747x^2 + 60899x - 4\text{E}{+08} \quad (3)$$
$$R^2 = 0.6292$$

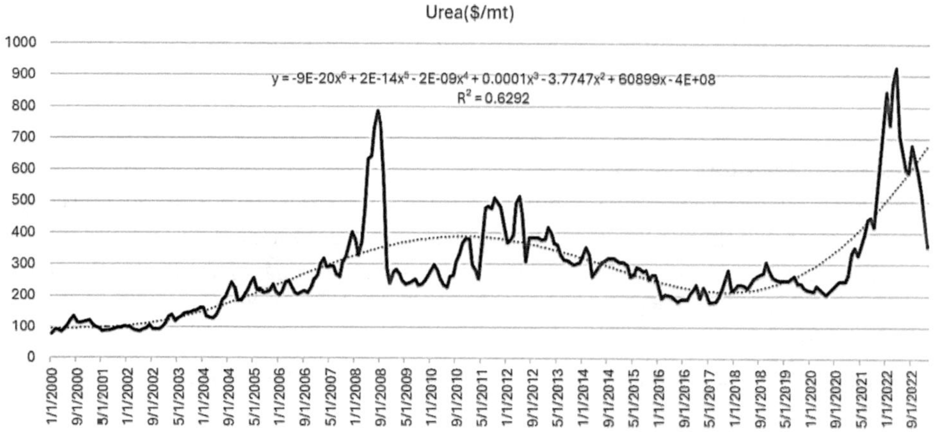

Step 2: Load agricultural input data: energy costs, average price – gasoline (APU000074714)

The World Bank collects data on household fuel, motor fuel, and food items to calculate average consumer prices using the CPI. While these averages are useful for assessing price levels in a specific month, the CPI index values should be used to track price changes over time.

Output:

	Date	CrudeOilBrent($/bbl)	NaturalGasUs($/mmbtu)
0	01-01-1960	1.63	0.1400
1	02-01-1960	1.63	0.1400
2	03-01-1960	1.63	0.1400
3	04-01-1960	1.63	0.1400
4	05-01-1960	1.63	0.1400
...	...	...	...
750	07-01-2022	108.92	7.2561
751	08-01-2022	98.60	8.7854
752	09-01-2022	90.16	7.7629
753	10-01-2022	93.13	5.6195
754	11-01-2022	91.07	5.2769

755 rows × 3 columns

Step 3: Load macroeconomic data: uncertainty index (GEPUCURRENT)

The Global Economic Policy Uncertainty Index looks at how uncertain economic policies are in 20 different countries including the United States, Japan, and China. The index is calculated by taking an average of national indices for each country and weighting them based on their gross domestic product (GDP). This can give you an idea of how much uncertainty there is in the global economy, which can affect demand for products and, in turn, their pricing.

Future data imputation strategy

The Global Economic Policy Uncertainty Index (GEPUCURRENT) has a curved line called a polynomial trendline with six bends in it. This line is used to analyze changes in data over time, and the fitline is not perfect but better than other types of trendlines like linear, power, exponential, or logarithmic. A polynomial trendline with six bends is useful for analyzing gains and losses in large data sets. In addition, there is an equation (eq. (4)) that fits a polynomial trendline to the RepairMaintenanceProducerPriceInd data:

$$y = -4E{-}20x^6 + 1E{-}14x^5 - 1E{-}09x^4 + 5E{-}05x^3 - 1.594x^2 + 25437x - 2E{+}08 \quad (4)$$

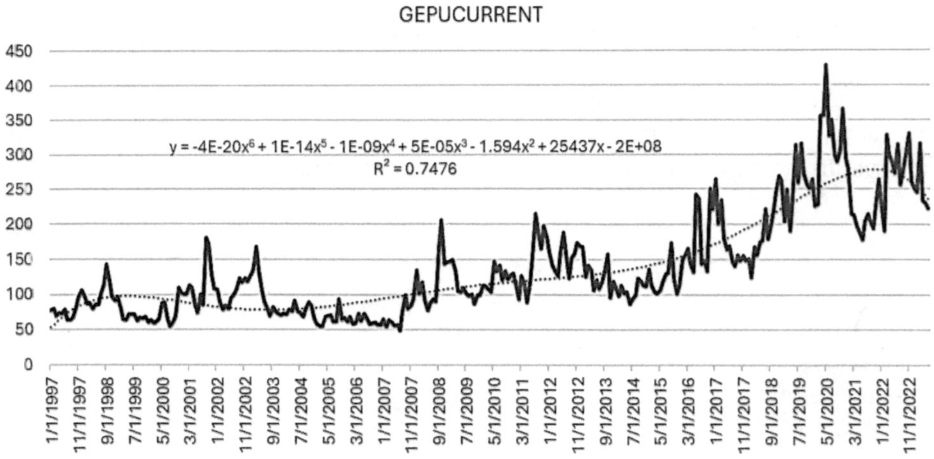

Step 4: Load agricultural input data: repair maintenanceProducerPriceInd

California's agricultural workforce, consisting of around 400,000 individuals, is essential but often lacks proper safety measures and guaranteed benefits. In Ventura County, these workers hand-pick strawberries and pack them for supermarkets [406] despite advancements in agricultural technology that have yet to be widely adopted. Consequently, nearly all of the 27 billion pounds of strawberries harvested in 2021 were picked manually, requiring significant labor. The industry also faces challenges related to the availability of local labor and the seasonal nature of harvesting. Rural areas where farming takes place often lack a large or skilled enough labor force, and narrow harvest windows leave workers with limited local job opportunities once the picking season ends.

Understanding the various challenges faced by agricultural workers is essential to developing effective solutions for improving working conditions and increasing productivity. By prioritizing measures such as worker safety, fair compensation, and access to benefits, farmers can attract and retain the skilled labor needed to harvest their crops successfully. These efforts are critical to ensuring the continued success of the industry, despite the challenges posed by market fluctuations, environmental factors, and supply chain disruptions.

Future data imputation strategy

The repair maintenance producer price index has a curved line called a polynomial trendline with six bends in it. This line is used to analyze changes in data over time. This line is fitted to the RepairMaintenanceProducerPriceInd data to help understand changes in the index over time.

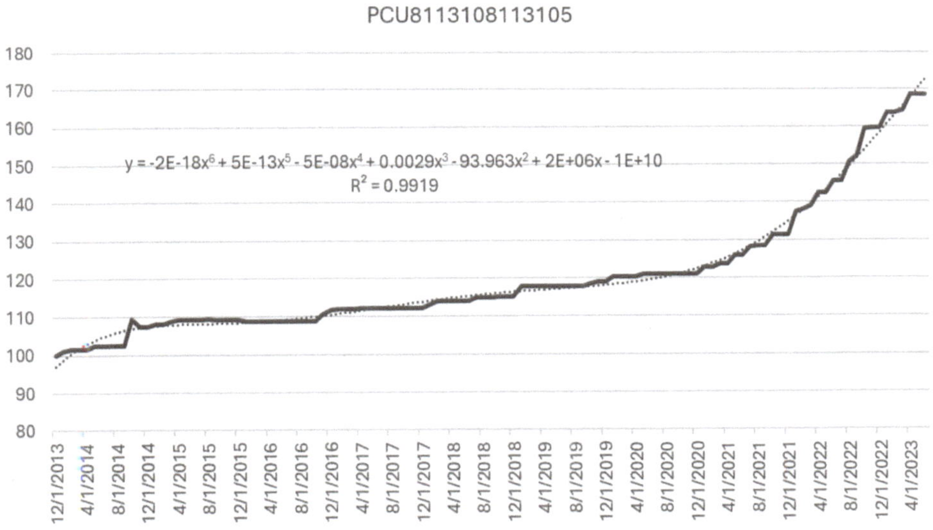

Step 5: Load macroeconomic data: inflation (CPIAUCSL)

To predict future changes in the consumer price index, a power trendline (eq. (5)) is used. This is a curved line that works best when comparing measurements that increase at a specific rate. The power trendline can help us understand how the index is likely to change in the future based on past trends:

$$y = 1\text{E}{-}12x^{3.0997} \qquad (5)$$
$$R^2 = 0.983$$

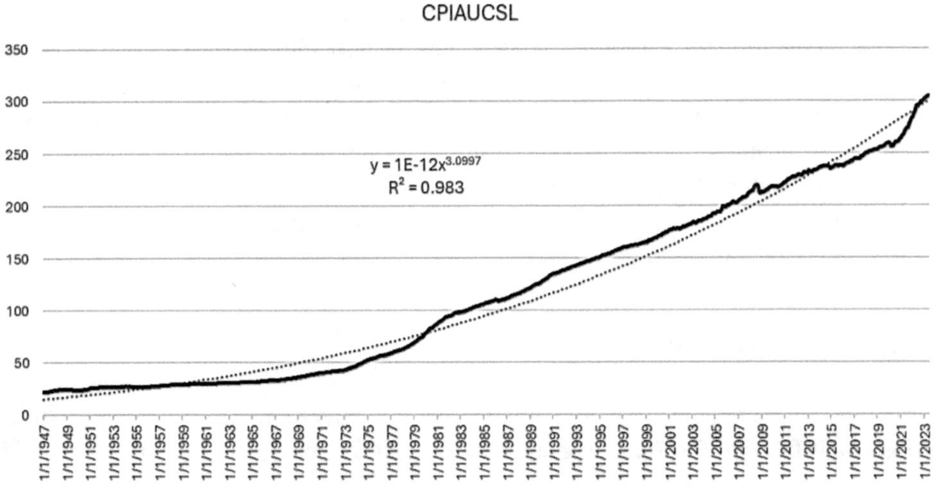

Step 6: US diesel sales price (GASDESW)

Diesel prices are very critical to tomato prices as farm operations such as tractor and equipment need diesel to operate.

Future data imputation strategy: US diesel sales price exhibits polynomial trend with order 6 with $R^2 = 0.8309$

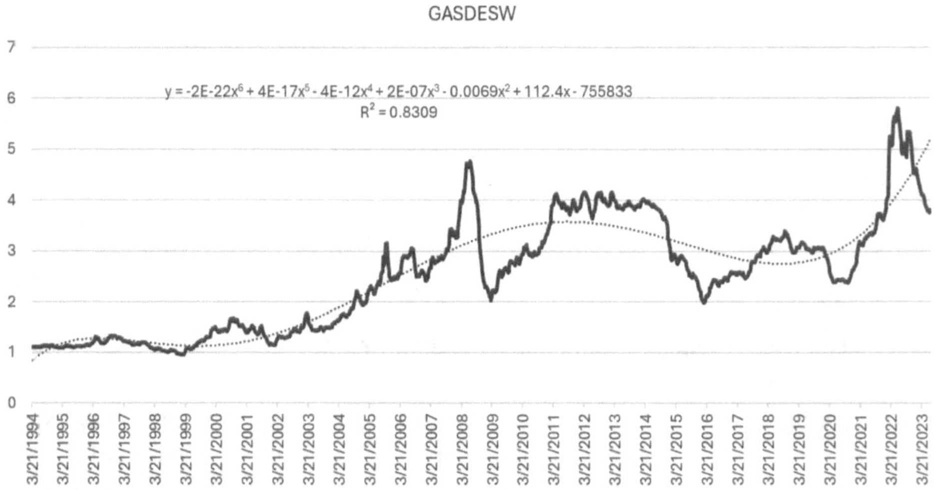

Step 7: Rail freight carloads (RAILFRTCARLOADS)

Rail road data is relevant to tomato prices as tomatoes are tranportation is a major cost factor.

Future data imputation strategy: Rail freight carloads exhibit polynomial trend with order 6:

$$y = 2E{-}16x^6 - 5E{-}11x^5 + 5E{-}06x^4 - 0.2707x^3 + 8235.2x^2 - 1E{+}08x + 9E{+}11$$
$$R^2 = 0.8085$$

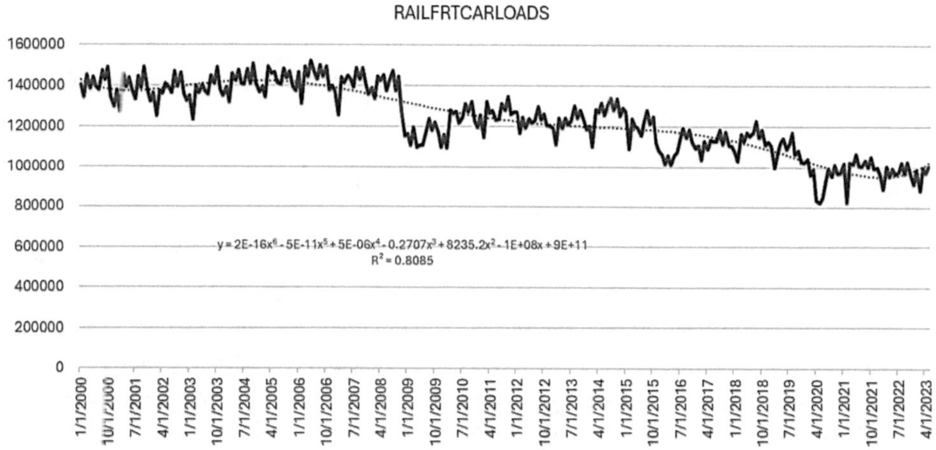

Step 8: Load unemployment rate (UNRATE)

To predict future changes in the unemployment rate, a polynomial trendline with six bends is used. This line is fitted to the unemployment rate data to help understand changes in the rate over time.

Future data imputation strategy: Unemployment rate exhibits polynomial trend with order 6:

$$y = -3E{-}24x^6 + 6E{-}19x^5 - 4E{-}14x^4 + 2E{-}09x^3 - 3E{-}05x^2 + 0.3811x - 1712.3$$
$$R^2 = 0.2733$$

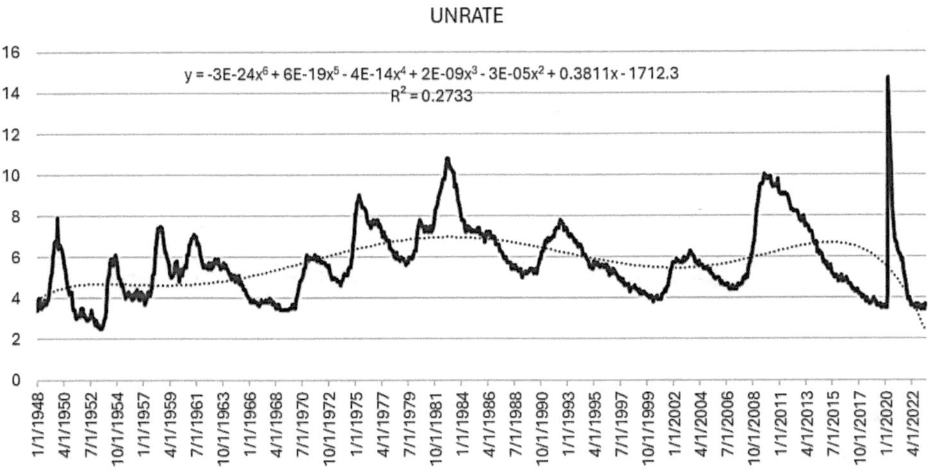

Step 9: Load industrial production: total index (INDPRO)

INDPRO assesses goods produced by businesses in the United States, regardless of who owns them. This index does not include businesses located in US territories. To predict future changes in the industrial production index, a polynomial regression model is used. This model takes into account the historical trends in the index over a period of time from 2000 to 2023 and can help predict future changes in the index based on those trends. Recently, the trend has shifted and can be partly explained by a polynomial regression model:

$$y = 2E{-}20x^6 - 4E{-}15x^5 + 4E{-}10x^4 - 2E{-}05x^3 + 0.6551x^2 - 10632x + 7E{+}07$$
$$R^2 = 0.5765$$

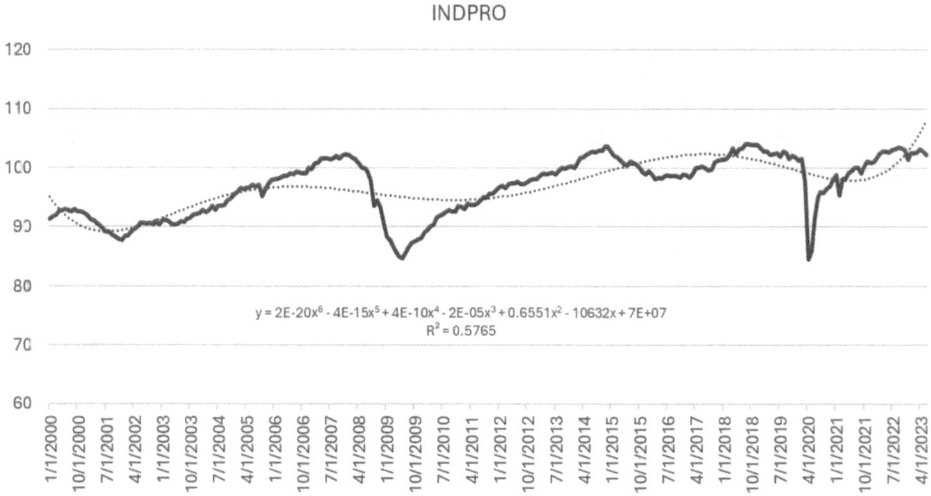

Step 10: Load data tomatoes prices data and feature data

The code imports several Python libraries that are commonly used in data analysis and machine learning. The “pandas” library is used for data manipulation and analysis, while “numpy” is used for numerical operations. “functools” provides tools for working with functions, and “datetime” is used for working with dates and times.

```
import pandas as pd
import numpy as np
import functools as ft
from datetime import date
import plotly.graph_objects as go
import seaborn as sns; sns.set()
import statsmodels.api as sm
from statsmodels.tsa.arima_process import ArmaProcess
from scipy import stats
from scipy.stats import pearsonr
import matplotlib.pyplot as plt
import plotly.express as px
from sklearn.preprocessing import MinMaxScaler
from sklearn.model_selection import train_test_split
from sklearn.linear_model import LinearRegression
from sklearn.metrics import r2_score
from sklearn import metrics
from sklearn.impute import SimpleImputer
from sklearn.metrics import mean_absolute_error
from prophet import Prophet
import eli5
```

And load data pricing model data

```
finaldf_Original= pd.read_csv(r"./USA_Fresno_TomatoPrice_Finaldf_Release.csv")
finaldf_Original
```

Output:

	Date	TomatoPrice(USD/Pound)	TomatoPPIndex	IndustrialProductionIndex	RAILFRTCARLOADS	CPIndex
0	1/1/2000	1.443	69.900	91.4251	1422012	169.300
1	2/1/2000	1.286	95.500	91.7357	1420123	170.000
2	3/1/2000	1.364	108.700	92.0933	1409969	171.000
3	4/1/2000	1.487	144.900	92.6838	1400406	170.900
4	5/1/2000	1.366	110.400	92.9376	1405395	171.200
...	...	...	...	...	...	...
243	10/1/2022	1.974	507.243	103.4114	1014120	297.987
244	11/1/2022	2.107	638.990	103.0707	1004493	298.598
245	12/1/2022	2.228	638.990	101.4741	997887	298.990
246	1/1/2023	2.110	305.112	102.4963	998018	300.536
247	2/1/2023	1.990	233.320	102.5007	979817	301.648

248 rows × 21 columns

Create Prophet time series mandatory columns: y and ds.

```
finaldf = finaldf_Original.copy()
```

```
finaldf['ds'] = pd.to_datetime(finaldf['Date'])
finaldf.drop(columns={'Date'}, inlpace=True)
finaldf.rename(columns={'TomatoPrice(USD/Pound) ': 'y'}, inplace=True)
finaldf.head()
```

```
finaldf.columns
```

Output:

```
Index(['y', 'TomatoPPIndex', 'IndustrialProductionIndex', 'RAILFRTCARLOADS',
   'CPIndex', 'GDPIndex', 'UnEmpRate(%)', 'EmpInAgri(1000sOfPersons)',
   'USAGasPrice(USD/Gallon)', 'SP500', 'PhosphateRock($/mt)', 'Dap($/mt)',
   'Tsp($/mt)', 'Urea($/mt)', 'PotassiumChloride($/mt)', 'CLDD', 'TMAX',
   'TMIN', 'PRCP', 'HTDD', 'ds'],
   dtype='object')
```

Step 11: Weather data: NOAA GSOM – FRESNO YOSEMITE INTERNATIONAL, CA US

Load weather data from FRESNO YOSEMITE INTERNATIONAL, CA US to see influence of weather on the prices.

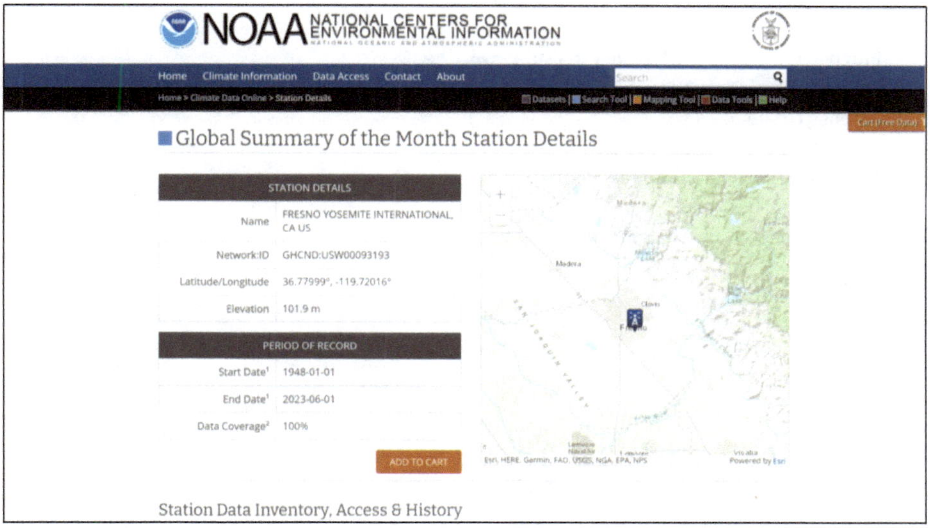

STATSTATION DETAILS	
Name	FRESNO YOSEMITE INTERNATIONAL, CA US
Network:ID	GHCND:USW00093193
Latitude/Longitude	36.77999°, -119.72016°
Elevation	101.9 m
PERIOD OF RECORD	
Start Date[1]	1948-01-01
End Date[1]	2023-06-01
Data Coverage[2]	100%

Step 12: Prepare prophet model

Create Prophet model. Add feature variables.

```
Prophetdf_train, Prophetdf_test = Prophetdf[0:n_obs],Prophetdf[n_obs:]
  multi_model = Prophet(interval_width = 0.95)
  Prophet_cols = Prophetdf.columns.tolist()
  Prophet_cols.remove('ds')
  Prophet_cols.remove('y')
  print(Prophetdf_train.columns)
  # adding all columns in add regressor
  for col in Prophet_cols:
    multi_model.add_regressor(col)
```

Fit the model.

```
multi_model.fit(Prophetdf_train)
  print('Prophetdf_test.shape[0]')
  print(Prophetdf_test.shape[0])
  # make furture frame
```

Make future DataFrame. The code is creating a new DataFrame that extends beyond the end of the original DataFrame, which can be used for making predictions based on the trained model.

```
future = multi_model.make_future_dataframe(periods = Prophetdf_test.shape[0],freq='MS',
include_history=True)
  for col in Prophet_cols:
    future[col] =Prophetdf[col]
```

The code is using a trained time series forecasting model to generate predictions for a future time period, and then combining those predictions with the original data to create a new DataFrame for further analysis.

```
print('future')
   print(future)
   #predict future
   forecastProphet= multi_model.predict(future)
   combined_df = pd.merge(Prophetdf_test[['ds', 'y']], forecastProphet[['ds', 'yhat', 'yhat_lower',
'yhat_upper']], on='ds')
   print(forecastProphet[['ds', 'yhat', 'yhat_lower', 'yhat_upper']].tail())
   fig1= multi_model.plot(forecastProphet)
   Prophetdf.plot(x ='ds', y= 'y')
   multi_model.plot_components(forecastProphet);

   combined_df = pd.merge(Prophetdf_test[['ds', 'y']], forecastProphet[['ds', 'yhat',
'yhat_lower', 'yhat_upper']][-13:], on='ds')
```

Output:

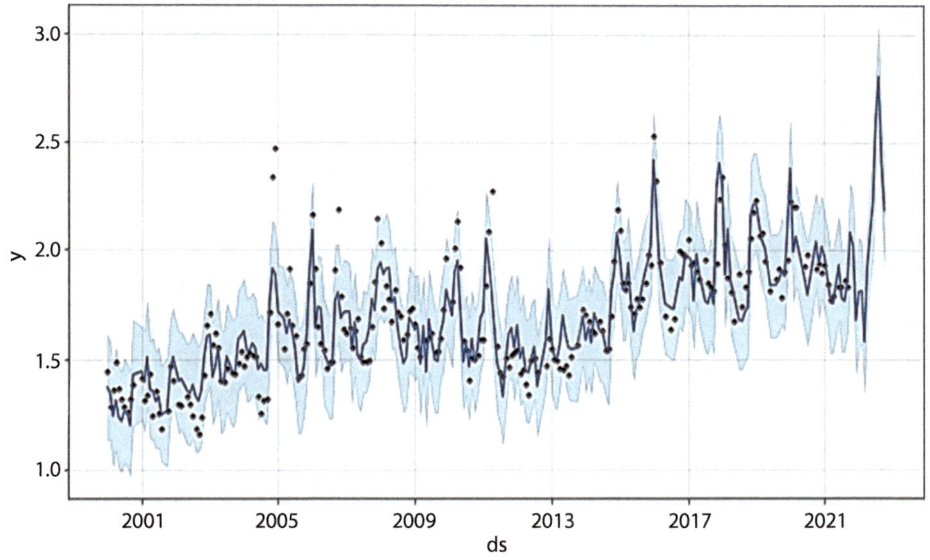

The black dots represent historical data.

The components of Prophet model:

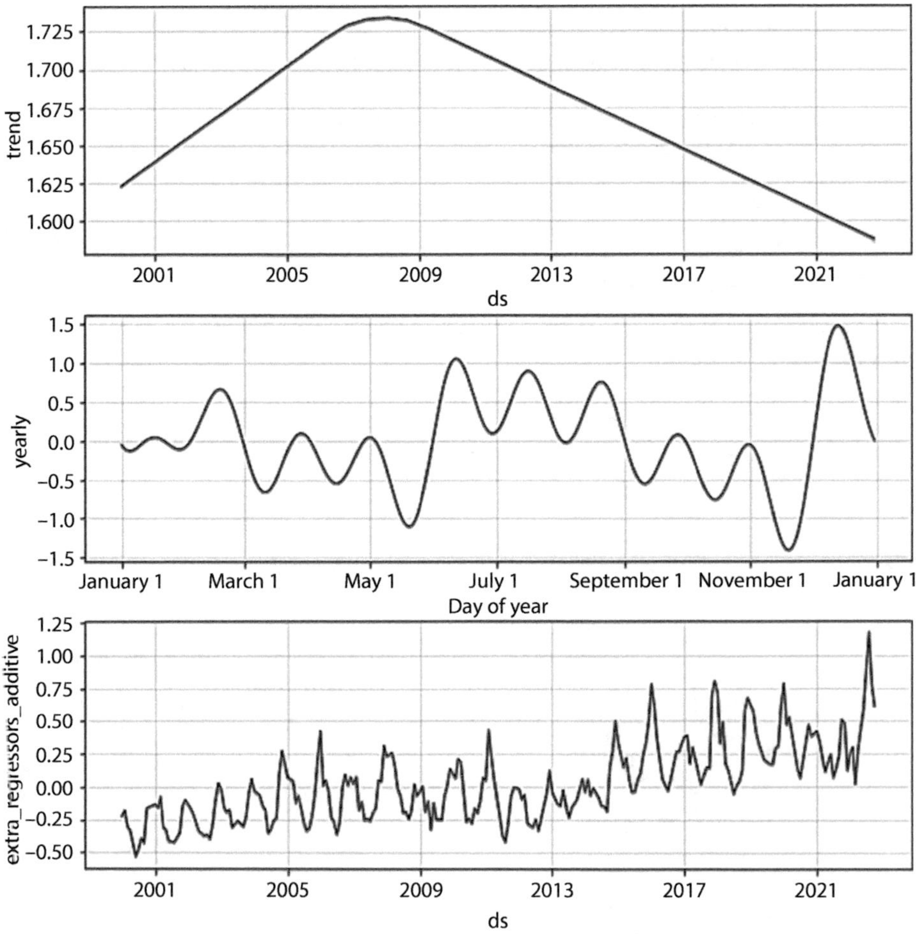

Finally, compute MAE.

```
#Check MAE value
  MAE = mean_absolute_error(combined_df['y'], combined_df['yhat'])
  print('MAE')
  print(MAE)

  import seaborn as sns
  import matplotlib.pyplot as plt
  plt.rcParams.update({'figure.figsize': (15, 3), 'figure.dpi' : 300})
  fig, ax = plt.subplots()
```

```
sns.lineplot(data= Prophetdf, x = 'ds', y = 'y', label = 'Original')
sns.lineplot(data= forecastProphet, x = 'ds', y = 'yhat', label = 'Forecast')
plt.grid(linestyle = '-', linewidth = 0.3)

plt.legend(["Original", "forecast"])
```

Output:

```
[248 rows × 20 columns]
        ds          yhat        yhat_lower   yhat_upper
243 2022-06-01   2.222499    1.988000     2.454735
244 2022-07-01   2.592528    2.356150     2.803044
245 2022-08-01   2.804100    2.556949     3.032141
246 2022-09-01   2.410229    2.183641     2.630955
247 2022-10-01   2.184239    1.948893     2.400303
MAE
0.346458795271778
```

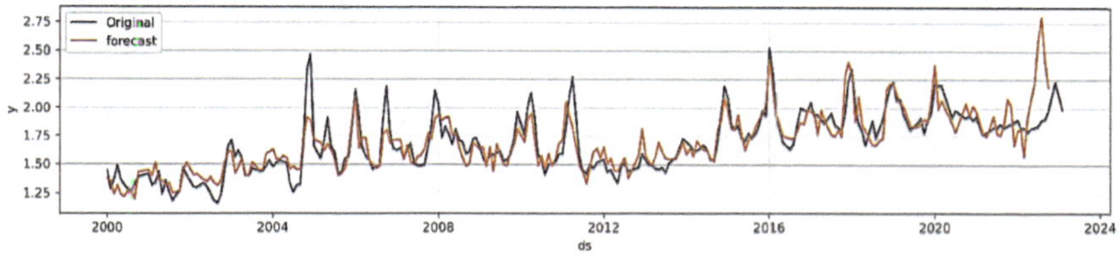

Check model evaluation.

```
plt.rcParams.update({'figure.figsize': (15, 3), 'figure.dpi' : 300})
fig, ax = plt.subplots()
sns.lineplot(data= Prophetdf[-13:] , x = 'ds', y = 'y', label = 'Original')
sns.lineplot(data= forecastProphet[-13:] , x = 'ds', y = 'yhat', label = 'Forecast')
plt.grid(linestyle = '-', linewidth = 0.3)
plt.legend(["Original", "forecast"])
```

Output:

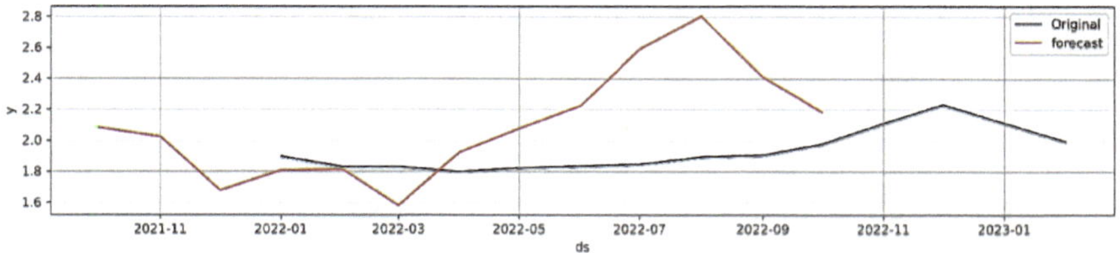

The following code has full code for invoking Prophet model.

```
def model_prophet(Prophetdf,n_obs= 235):

  Prophetdf_train, Prophetdf_test = Prophetdf[0:n_obs],Prophetdf[n_obs:]
  multi_model = Prophet(interval_width = 0.95)
  Prophet_cols = Prophetdf.columns.tolist()
  Prophet_cols.remove('ds')
  Prophet_cols.remove('y')
  print(Prophetdf_train.columns)
  # adding all columns in add regressor
  for col in Prophet_cols:
    multi_model.add_regressor(col)

  multi_model.fit(Prophetdf_train)
  print('Prophetdf_test.shape[0]')
  print(Prophetdf_test.shape[0])
  # make furture frame
  future = multi_model.make_future_dataframe(periods = Prophetdf_test.shape[0],freq='MS',
include_history=True)
  for col in Prophet_cols:
    future[col] =Prophetdf[col]

  print('future')
  print(future)

  # predict future
  forecastProphet =  multi_model.predict(future)

    combined_df = pd.merge(Prophetdf_test[['ds','y']], forecastProphet[['ds', 'yhat', 'yhat_lower',
    'yhat_upper']], on='ds')

      print(forecastProphet[['ds', 'yhat', 'yhat_lower', 'yhat_upper']].tail())

  fig1 = multi_model.plot(forecastProphet)

  Prophetdf.plot(x = 'ds', y = 'y')

  multi_model.plot_components(forecastProphet);

  #Check MAE value
  MAE = mean_absolute_error(combined_df['y'], combined_df['yhat'])
  print('MAE')
  print(MAE)
```

```
import seaborn as sns
import matplotlib.pyplot as plt
plt.rcParams.update({'figure.figsize': (15, 3), 'figure.dpi' : 300})
fig, ax = plt.subplots()

sns.lineplot(data= Prophetdf , x = 'ds', y = 'y', label = 'Original')
sns.lineplot(data= forecastProphet, x = 'ds', y = 'yhat', label = 'Forecast')
plt.grid(linestyle = '-', linewidth = 0.3)

plt.legend(["Original", "forecast"])

import seaborn as sns
import matplotlib.pyplot as plt

plt.rcParams.update({'figure.figsize': (15, 3), 'figure.dpi' : 300})
fig, ax = plt.subplots()
sns.lineplot(data= Prophetdf[-13:] , x = 'ds', y = 'y', label = 'Original')
sns.lineplot(data= forecastProphet[-13:] , x = 'ds', y = 'yhat', label = 'Forecast')
plt.grid(linestyle = '-', linewidth = 0.3)
plt.legend(["Original", "forecast"])

return MAE
```

Step 13: Invoke prophet model

Load data and modify the columns to meet Prophet model needs – column names “y” and “ds”.

```
df = pd.read_csv(r"./USA_Fresno_TomatoPrice_Finaldf_Release.csv")
df
```

```
df["Date"] = pd.to_ datetime(df["Date"])
```

```
df.rename(columns={'TomatoPrice(USD/Pound) ': 'y'}, inplace=True)
df.rename(columns={'Date': 'ds'}, inlpace=True)
```

```
MAE_Prophet = model_prophet(df)
MAE_Prophet
```

Step 14: Fine-tune data features and reinvoke prophet model

Given California employed mechanized tomatoes farming with most of the work performed by machines, re-optimize the model by dropping features: UnEmpRate(%), EmpInAgri(1000sOfPersons), USAGasPrice(USD/Gallon), PotassiumChloride($/mt), PotassiumChloride($/mt), CLDD, and HTDD.

```
df.drop(['TomatoPPIndex', 'UnEmpRate(%)',
'EmpInAgri(1000sOfPersons)','USAGasPrice(USD/Gallon)',
    'PotassiumChloride($/mt)','PotassiumChloride($/mt)',
    'CLDD','HTDD'
    ], axis=1, inplace=True)
```

```
df.columns
```

Output:

```
Index(['ds', 'y', 'IndustrialProductionIndex', 'RAILFRTCARLOADS', 'CPIndex',
       'GDPIndex', 'SP500', 'PhosphateRock($/mt)', 'Dap($/mt)', 'Tsp($/mt)',
       'Urea($/mt)', 'TMAX', 'TMIN', 'PRCP'],
       dtype='object')
```

Call the model:

```
MAE_Prophet = model_prophet(df)
MAE_Prophet
```

Output:

MAE: 0.21913522641692343

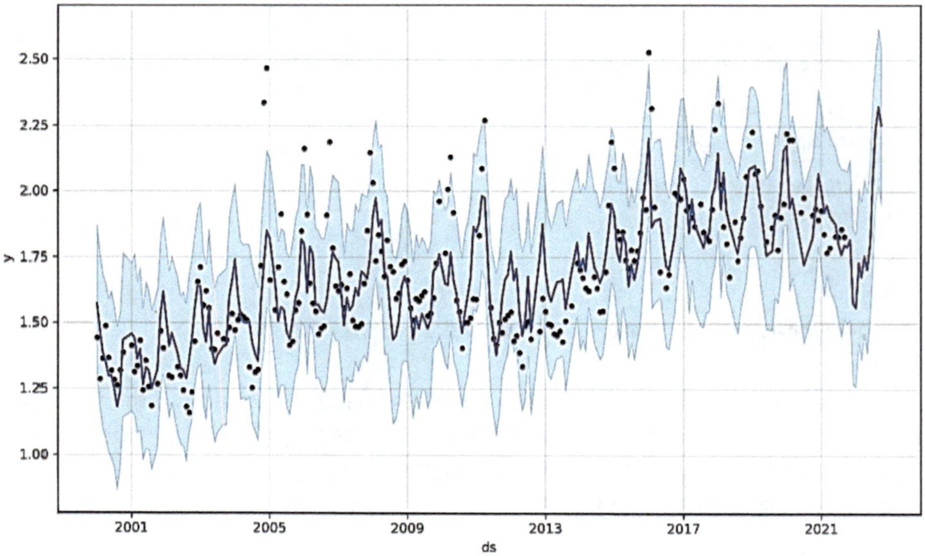

Prophet time series components:

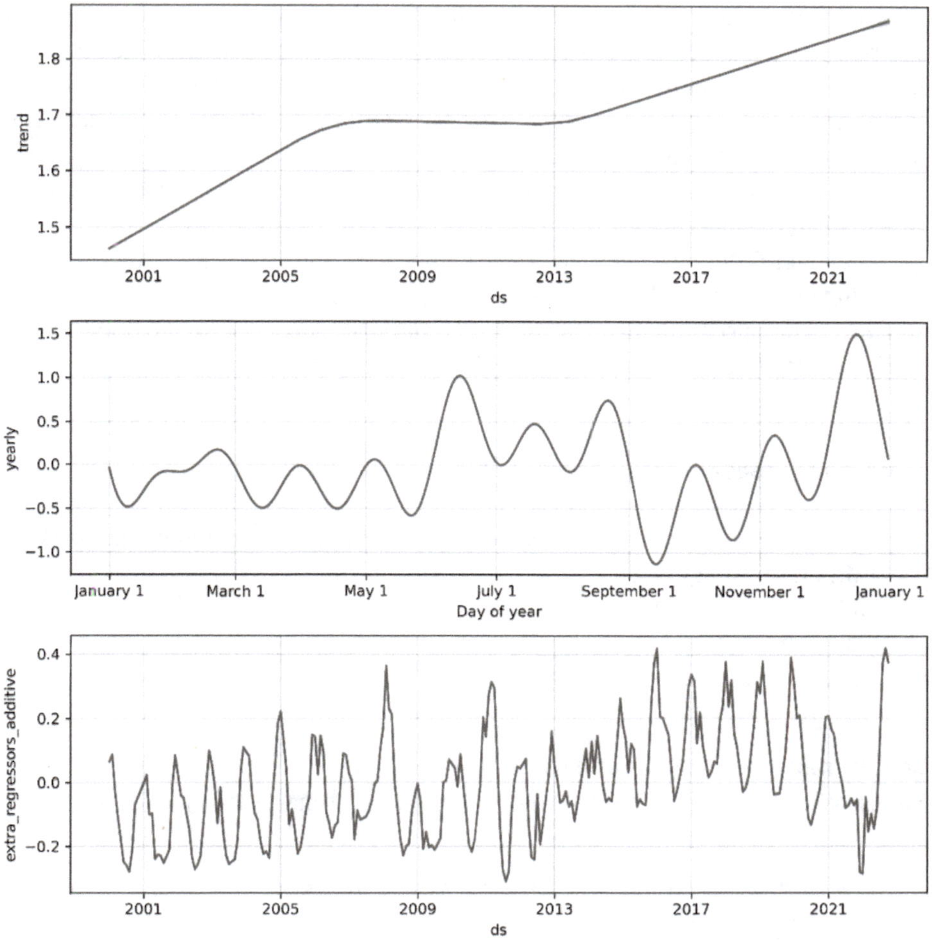

Please note by dropping UnEmpRate(%), EmpInAgri(1000sOfPersons), USAGasPrice(USD/Gallon), PotassiumChloride($/mt), PotassiumChloride($/mt), CLDD, and HTDD. the model has improved by 38%.

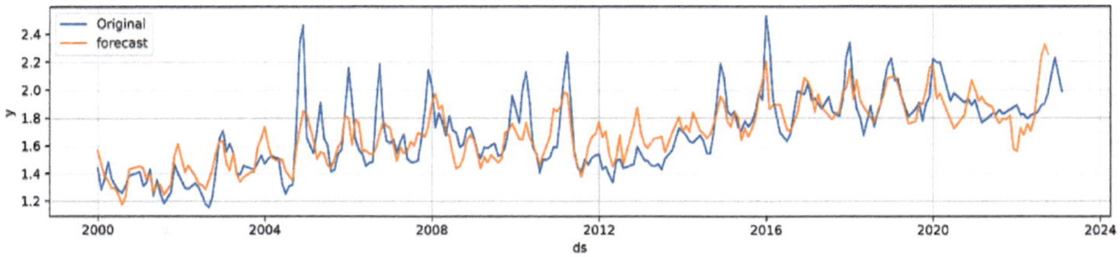

Forecasting: what-if modeling

After creating a time series forecasting model, the next step is to prepare datasets for future predictions. One important step in this process is imputation, which involves filling in missing data in the dataset. One approach to imputation is called "scenario modeling," which involves using hypothetical scenarios to fill in missing data. This approach is often driven by business users or subject matter experts. Another approach is called "heuristics," which involves using domain knowledge or tacit details of the use case to fill in missing data.

The main difference between scenario modeling and heuristics is that scenario modeling relies more on business outcomes, while heuristics requires a deeper understanding of the specific domain. In either case, the goal is to create a dataset that can be used to make accurate predictions using the forecasting model.

What-if: tomatoes prices due to crop failures

Let's check how prices of tomatoes when following macroeconomic conditions prevail:
- TMAX from 16.71 to 30.44
- TMIN from 2.13 to 20.22
- PRCP from 79,8 to 10.02
- HTDD from 214 to 400

Step 1: Prepare and load what-if dataset

First, let's load what-if dataset. This data is completely scenario driven data:

```
futurewhatifdf = pd.read_csv(r" Tomatoes_Fresno_Whatif_CropFilures.csv",index_col=0)
print(futurewhatifdf.shape)
```

```
futurewhatifdf=futurewhatifdf.reset_index()
```

```
futurewhatifdf
```

Output:

```
(2, 19)
          TomatoPPIndex  IndustrialProductionIndex  RAILFRTCARLOADS  CPIndex  \
Date
3/1/2023         233.32                   102.5007           979817  301.648
4/1/2023         233.32                   102.5007           979817  301.648

            GDPIndex  UnEmpRate(%)  EmpInAgri(1000sOfPersons)  \
Date
3/1/2023  249.168683           3.6                       2346
4/1/2023  249.168683           3.6                       2346

          USAGasPrice(USD/Gallon)    SP500  PhosphateRock($/mt)  Dap($/mt)  \
Date
3/1/2023                    3.304  3970.15                322.5      612.5
4/1/2023                    3.304  3970.15                322.5      612.5

          Tsp($/mt)  Urea($/mt)  PotassiumChloride($/mt)  CLDD   TMAX   TMIN  \
Date
3/1/2023      547.5       357.5                   496.88     0  30.44  20.22
4/1/2023      547.5       357.5                   496.88     0  30.44  20.22

          PRCP  HTDD
Date
3/1/2023  79.8   214
4/1/2023  79.8   214
```

Step 2: Setup time column

Convery date to reqyured ds coikunb.

```
futurewhatifdf.rename(columns = {"date": "ds" }, inplace = True)
futurewhatifdf.info()
futurewhatifdf["ds"] = pd.to_datetime(futurewhatifdf["ds"])
```

Output:

```
<class 'pandas.core.frame.DataFrame'>
RangeIndex: 2 entries, 0 to 1
Data columns (total 20 columns):
 #   Column                       Non-Null Count  Dtype
---  ------                       --------------  -----
 0   ds                           2 non-null      datetime64[ns]
 1   TomatoPPIndex                2 non-null      float64
 2   IndustrialProductionIndex    2 non-null      float64
 3   RAILFRTCARLOADS              2 non-null      int64
 4   CPIndex                      2 non-null      float64
 5   GDPIndex                     2 non-null      float64
 6   UnEmpRate(%)                 2 non-null      float64
 7   EmpInAgri(1000sOfPersons)    2 non-null      int64
 8   USAGasPrice(USD/Gallon)      2 non-null      float64
 9   SP500                        2 non-null      float64
 10  PhosphateRock($/mt)          2 non-null      float64
 11  Dap($/mt)                    2 non-null      float64
 12  Tsp($/mt)                    2 non-null      float64
 13  Urea($/mt)                   2 non-null      float64
 14  PotassiumChloride($/mt)      2 non-null      float64
 15  CLDD                         2 non-null      int64
 16  TMAX                         2 non-null      float64
 17  TMIN                         2 non-null      float64
 18  PRCP                         2 non-null      float64
 19  HTDD                         2 non-null      int64
dtypes: datetime64[ns](1), float64(15), int64(4)
memory usage: 448.0 bytes
```

Step 3: Predict

Call predict on what-if data.

```
#forecastProphet = multi_model.predict(futurewhatifdf)
forecastProphet = multi_model.predict(futurewhatifdf)
```

Output:

	ds	yhat	yhat_lower	yhat_upper
0	2023-03-01	1.815777	1.584318	2.057021
1	2023-04-01	1.874070	1.646724	2.105782

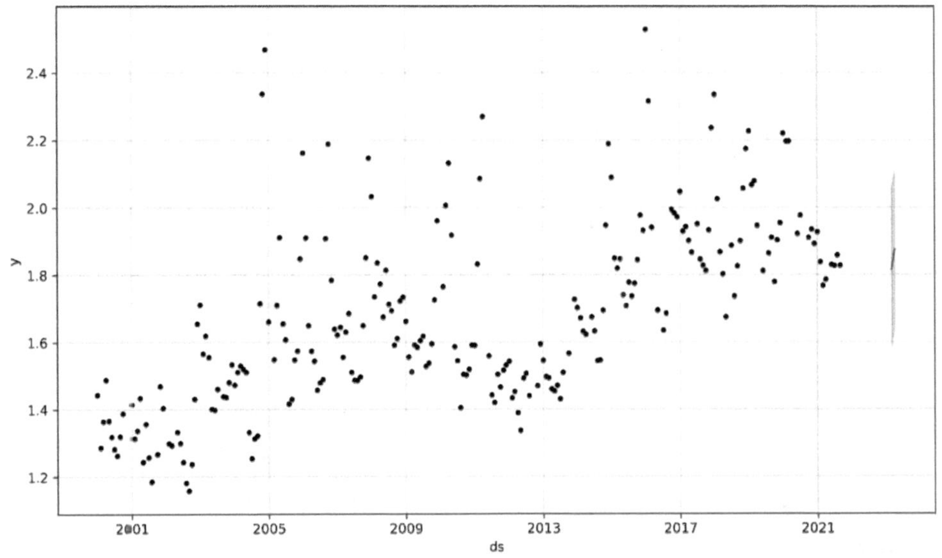

What-if: tomatoes prices due to sustained CPI and lower GDP modeling

We want to see how the price of tomatoes changes when certain macroeconomic conditions occur. For example, if there is a drop in economic activity and GDP uncertainty index increases from 249.16 to 400.34, we want to see how that affects the price of tomatoes.

Similarly, we want to see how the price of tomatoes is affected by an increase in unemployment rate from 3.6% to 5.6%, an increase in the price of gas (USAGasPrice) from 3.304 to 5.8, and a drop in the S&P Index from 3970.15 to 2999.34.

By analyzing how the price of tomatoes changes in response to these macroeconomic conditions, the impact of broader economic trends can be studied on tomato market. This information can be used to inform decisions about pricing, supply chain management, and other aspects of the tomato industry.

Step 1: Prepare and load what-if dataset

First, let's load what-if dataset. This data is completely scenario driven data:

```
futurewhatifdf = pd.read_csv(r" Tomatoes_Fresno_Whatif_Economic.csv",index_col=0)
print(futurewhatifdf.shape)
```

```
futurewhatifdf=futurewhatifdf.reset_index()
```

```
futurewhatifdf
```

Output:

```
(2, 19)
          TomatoPPIndex  IndustrialProductionIndex  RAILFRTCARLOADS  CPIndex  \
Date
3/1/2023         233.32                   102.5007           979817  301.648
4/1/2023         233.32                   102.5007           979817  301.648

            GDPIndex  UnEmpRate(%)  EmpInAgri(1000sOfPersons)  \
Date
3/1/2023  249.168683           3.6                       2346
4/1/2023  249.168683           3.6                       2346

          USAGasPrice(USD/Gallon)    SP500  PhosphateRock($/mt)  Dap($/mt)  \
Date
3/1/2023                    3.304  3970.15                322.5      612.5
4/1/2023                    3.304  3970.15                322.5      612.5

          Tsp($/mt)  Urea($/mt)  PotassiumChloride($/mt)  CLDD   TMAX   TMIN  \
Date
3/1/2023      547.5       357.5                   496.88     0  30.44  20.22
4/1/2023      547.5       357.5                   496.88     0  30.44  20.22

          PRCP  HTDD
Date
3/1/2023  79.8   214
4/1/2023  79.8   214
```

Step 2: Setup time column

Convery date to reqyured ds coikunb.

```
futurewhatifdf.rename(columns = {"date": "ds" }, inplace = True)
futurewhatifdf.info()
```

Output:

```
<class 'pandas.core.frame.DataFrame'>
RangeIndex: 2 entries, 0 to 1
Data columns (total 20 columns):
 #   Column                      Non-Null Count  Dtype
---  ------                      --------------  -----
 0   ds                          2 non-null      datetime64[ns]
 1   TomatoPPIndex               2 non-null      float64
 2   IndustrialProductionIndex   2 non-null      float64
 3   RAILFRTCARLOADS             2 non-null      int64
 4   CPIndex                     2 non-null      float64
 5   GDPIndex                    2 non-null      float64
 6   UnEmpRate(%)                2 non-null      float64
 7   EmpInAgri(1000sOfPersons)   2 non-null      int64
 8   USAGasPrice(USD/Gallon)     2 non-null      float64
 9   SP500                       2 non-null      float64
 10  PhosphateRock($/mt)         2 non-null      float64
 11  Dap($/mt)                   2 non-null      float64
 12  Tsp($/mt)                   2 non-null      float64
 13  Urea($/mt)                  2 non-null      float64
 14  PotassiumChloride($/mt)     2 non-null      float64
 15  CLDD                        2 non-null      int64
 16  TMAX                        2 non-null      float64
 17  TMIN                        2 non-null      float64
 18  PRCP                        2 non-null      float64
 19  HTDD                        2 non-null      int64
dtypes: datetime64[ns](1), float64(15), int64(4)
memory usage: 448.0 bytes
```

Step 3: Predict

Call predict on what-if data.

```
#forecastProphet = multi_model.predict(futurewhatifdf)
forecastProphet = multi_model.predict(futurewhatifdf)
```

```
forecastProphet[['ds', 'yhat', 'yhat_lower', 'yhat_upper']].tail()
```

Result:

	ds	yhat	yhat_lower	yhat_upper
0	2023-03-01	0.266603	0.029218	0.487184
1	2023-04-01	0.324897	0.103113	0.560082
2	2023-05-01	0.314397	0.088883	0.553985

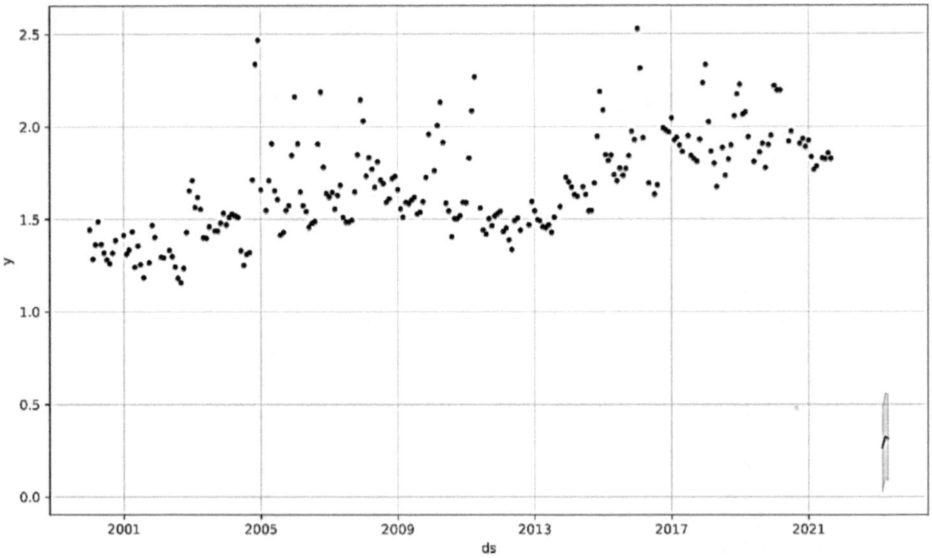

What-if modeling is a technique used to explore different scenarios and their potential outcomes. It is less focused on the scientific principles underlying a model and more driven by intuition and business expertise. What-if modeling involves creating hypothetical situations and using the model to predict how those situations might play out. A more reliable method for preparing datasets for time series forecasting is to perform trend engineering of independent features. This involves using mathematical techniques like linear interpolation, spline interpolation, and trend engineering to fill in missing data and smooth out any irregularities in the data. Trend engineering is a scientific approach to data preparation that involves analyzing and manipulating the data to detect arrangements and movements. By engineering the data in this way, we can create a more accurate and reliable dataset for time series forecasting.

Data preparation: trend-based future data imputation and forecast modeling

Trend-based forecasting considers each independent feature inherent trends and based on these trends prepares future data for forecasting purposes. For trend based forecasting, it's instrumental to understand data behavior to prepare future dataset for the horizon.

Software code for this model:
Final_California_Tomatoes_Pricing_Future_Dataset_PolynomialRegression.ipynb

Step 1: Load price forecast train dataset

Create DataFrame of Fresno Tomato Price Forecast train dataset.

```
FresnoTomatoPricedf =
pd.read_csv("USA_Fresno_TomatoPrice_Finaldf_Release_PolyRegressor.csv")
FresnoTomatoPricedf
```

Output:

TomatoPrice(USD/Pound)	TomatoPPIndex	IndustrialProductionIndex	RAILFRTCARLOADS	CPIndex	GDPIndex
1.443	69.900	91.4251	1422012	169.300	63.603339
1.286	95.500	91.7357	1420123	170.000	58.702278
1.364	108.700	92.0933	1409969	171.000	61.315947
1.487	144.900	92.6838	1400406	170.900	64.554142
1.366	110.400	92.9376	1405395	171.200	87.116317
...	...	...	...	...	...
1.974	507.243	103.4114	1014120	297.987	299.774458
2.107	638.990	103.0707	1004493	298.598	331.335811
2.228	638.990	101.4741	997887	298.990	260.434961
2.110	305.112	102.4963	998018	300.536	251.893250
1.990	233.320	102.5007	979817	301.648	249.168683

```
FresnoTomatoPricedf.info()
```

Output:

```
RangeIndex: 248 entries, 0 to 247
Data columns (total 22 columns):
 #   Column                      Non-Null Count  Dtype
---  ------                      --------------  -----
 0   SequenceNumber              248 non-null    int64
 1   Date                        248 non-null    object
 2   TomatoPrice(USD/Pound)      248 non-null    float64
 3   TomatoPPIndex               248 non-null    float64
 4   IndustrialProductionIndex   248 non-null    float64
 5   RAILFRTCARLOADS             248 non-null    int64
 6   CPIndex                     248 non-null    float64
 7   GDPIndex                    248 non-null    float64
 8   UnEmpRate(%)                248 non-null    float64
 9   EmpInAgri(1000sOfPersons)   248 non-null    int64
 10  USAGasPrice(USD/Gallon)     248 non-null    float64
 11  SP500                       248 non-null    float64
 12  PhosphateRock($/mt)         248 non-null    float64
 13  Dap($/mt)                   248 non-null    float64
 14  Tsp($/mt)                   248 non-null    float64
 15  Urea($/mt)                  248 non-null    float64
 16  PotassiumChloride($/mt)     248 non-null    float64
 17  CLDD                        248 non-null    float64
 18  TMAX                        248 non-null    float64
 19  TMIN                        248 non-null    float64
 20  PRCP                        248 non-null    float64
 21  HTDD                        248 non-null    float64
dtypes: float64(18), int64(3), object(1)
memory usage: 42.8+ KB
```

Step 2: Perform data analysis and check for nulls

Perform explicit casting of Date column to DataTime type. Second, check any NULL rows.

```
FresnoTomatoPricedf["Date"] = pd.to_datetime(FresnoTomatoPricedf["Date"])
```

```
FresnoTomatoPricedf[FresnoTomatoPricedf.isna().any(axis=1)]
```

Output: No null rows 0 rows × 22 columns

Step 3: Impute each feature variable with built-in trend

Start each varialbe and impute its value based onn inherent prevaling trend

```
X_areaharvest = FresnoTomatoPricedf.iloc[:,0:1].values
y_areaharvest = FresnoTomatoPricedf.iloc[:,13].values
```

```
#Fitting Linear Regression to the dataset
from sklearn.linear_model import LinearRegression
lin = LinearRegression()

lin.fit(X_areaharvest,y_areaharvest)
```

```
#Fitting Polynomial Regression to the dataset
from sklearn.preprocessing import PolynomialFeatures

polyareaharvest = polynomialFeatures(degree = 6)
X_polyareaharvest = polyareaharvest.fit_transform(X_areaharvest)

polyareaharvest.fit(X_polyareaharvest,y_areaharvest)
lin2 = LinearRegression()
lin2.fit(X_polyareaharvest,y_areaharvest)
```

```
plt.scatter(X_areaharvest,y_areaharvest,color='blue')

plt.plot(X_areaharvest, lin.predict(X_areaharvest), color = 'red')
plt.title('Linear Regression')
plt.xlabel('Date')
plt.ylabel('Dap($/mt)')
```

Output:

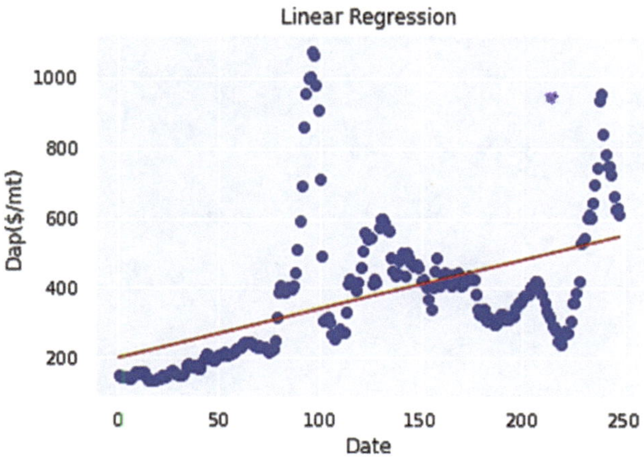

Step 4: Linear regressor: metrics

Check metrics for Linear regresdsor.

```
from sklearn.metrics import mean_squared_error,r2_score
mse = mean_squared_error(y_areaharvest, lin.predict(X_areaharvest))
print("MSE:", mse)
rmse = np.sqrt(mse)
print("RMSE:", rmse)
r2 = r2_score(y_areaharvest,lin.predict(X_areaharvest))
print("R2:", r2)
```

Result:

```
MSE: 27632.05372734053
RMSE: 166.22891964799786
R2: 0.2700864687870589
```

As it can be seen, the data cannot be fited with linear regressor.

Step 5: Impute with poly regressor

Let's impute woith poly regressor.

```
plt.scatter(X_areaharvest,y_areaharvest,color='blue')
plt.plot(X_areaharvest,lin2.predict(polyareaharvest.fit_transform(X_areaharvest)),
color = 'red')
plt.title('Polynomial Regression')
plt.xlabel('SequenceNumber')
plt.ylabel('Dap($/mt)')
plt.show()
```

Output:

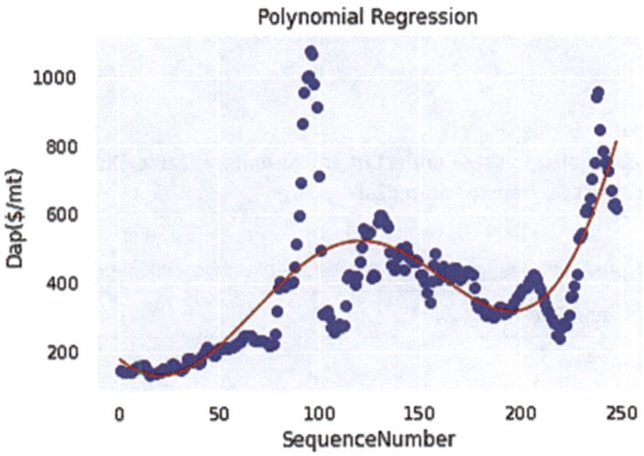


```
from sklearn.metrics import mean_squared_error,r2_score
mse = mean_squared_error(y_areaharvest, lin2.predict(polyareaharvest.fit_transform(X_areaharvest)))
print("MSE:", mse)
rmse = np.sqrt(mse)
print("RMSE:", rmse)
r2 = r2_score(y_areaharvest,lin2.predict(polyareaharvest.fit_transform(X_areaharvest)))
print("R2:",r2)
```

Result:

MSE: 15902.716822003078
RMSE: 126.105974569023
R2: 0.5799223501095555

As it can be seen, the polynomial regressor performed well over linear regressor.

Step 6: Create future dataset with one year time horizon

Create time series and future prediction values.

```
seqnumber = [i+0 for i in range(284)]
print(seqnumber)
predictions_value=[]
prediction_SequenceNumber=[]
for x in seqnumber:
    pred2array = np.array([[x]])
    prediction_SequenceNumber.append([x][0])
    predictions_value.append(line2.predict(polyareaharvest.fit_transfrom(pred2array))[0])
    print(x,lin2.predict(polyareaharvest.fit_transform(pred2array))[0])
```

```
newployNextValueDF =
pd.DataFrame({'SequenceNumber':prediction_SequenceNumber,'Dap($/mt)':predictions_value})
```

```
newployNextValueDF=newployNextValueDF.iloc[248:340]
```

```
newployNextValueDF
```

Output:

	SequenceNumber	Dap($/mt)
248	248	807.682024
249	249	827.780287
250	250	848.241781
251	251	869.058375
252	252	890.221379
253	253	911.721536
254	254	933.549011
255	255	955.693375
256	256	978.143599

Perform similar future imputation for all other feature variables. The following summary table contains all the values and metrics:

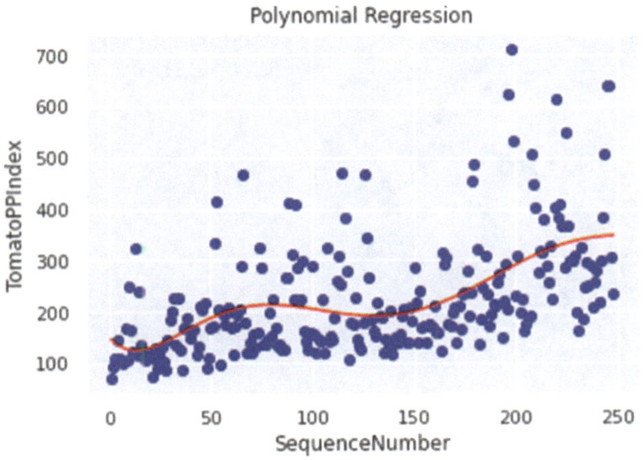

MSE: 8779.06768058733
RMSE: 93.69667913318662
R2: 0.30292772062811746

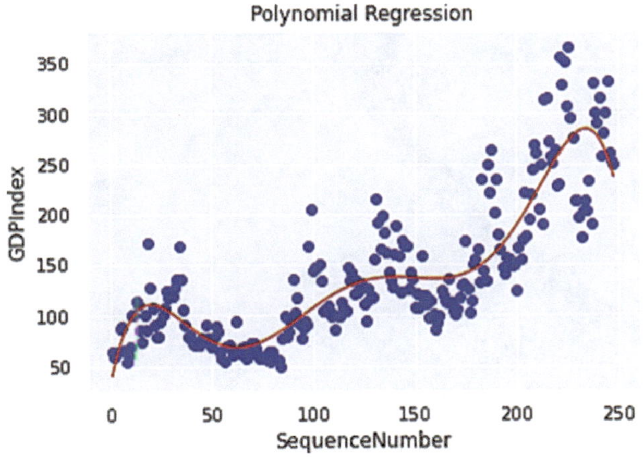

MSE: 1150.0970751706789
RMSE: 33.91308118072846
R2: 0.7740805968862469

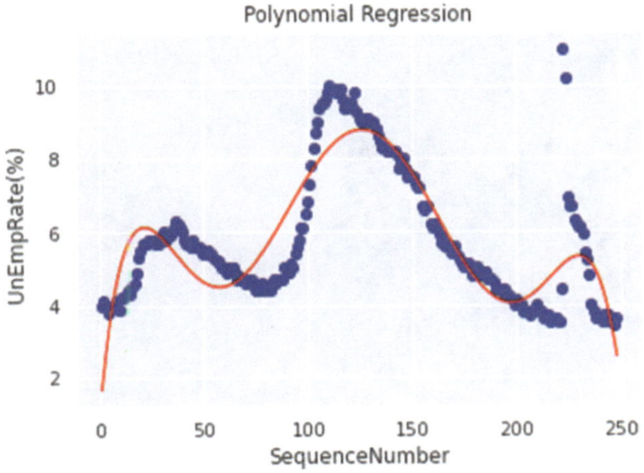

MSE: 0.8965994064413336
RMSE: 0.9468893316757422
R2: 0.7376138418809515

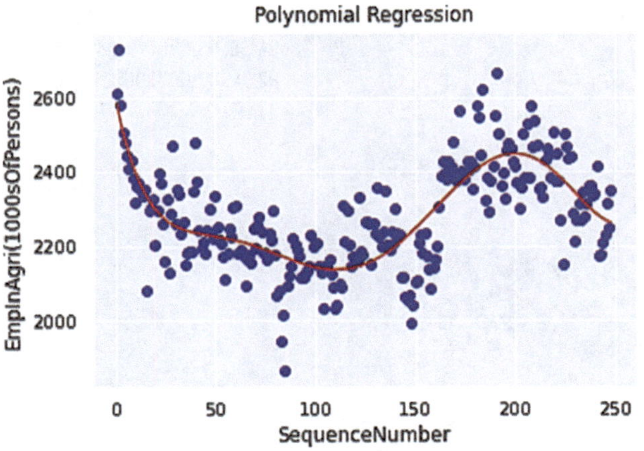

MSE: 7985.5215406741445
RMSE: 89.36174539854369
R2: 0.5912143823709626

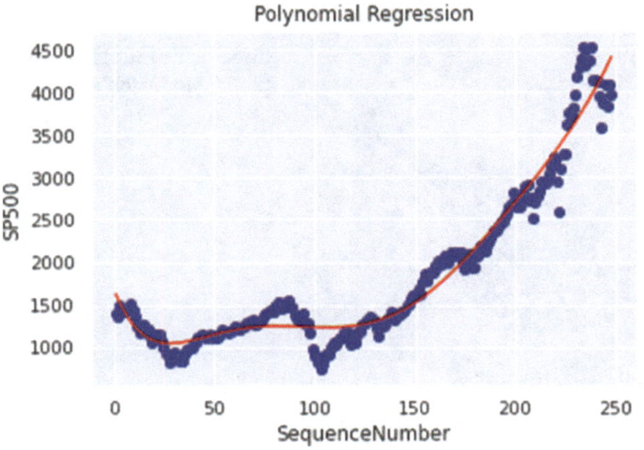

MSE: 40244.51265478185
RMSE: 200.61035031817738
R2: 0.9542642642054482

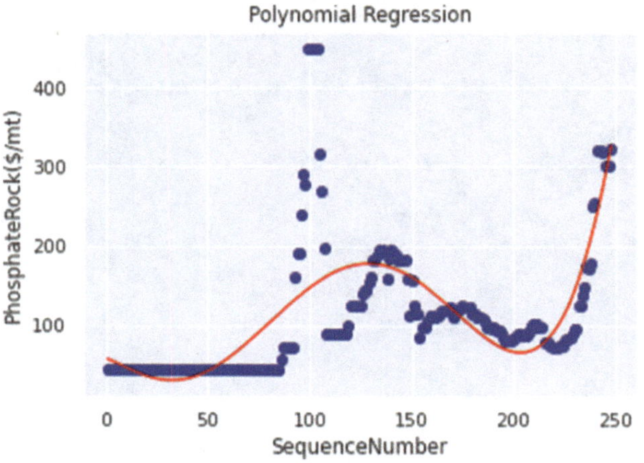

MSE: 3618.135966333727
RMSE: 60.15094318739921
R2: 0.4952419591779118

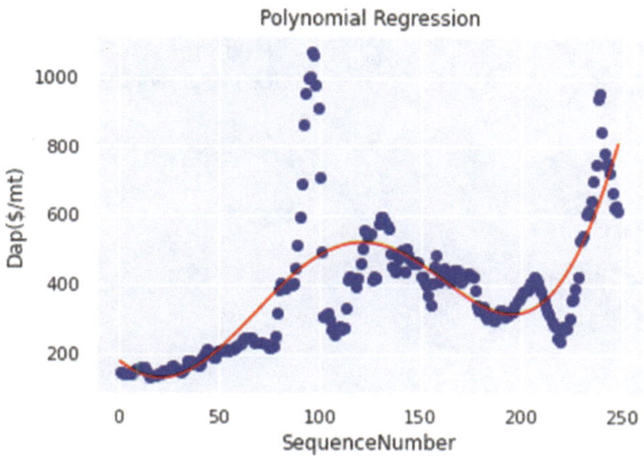

MSE: 15902.716822003078
RMSE: 126.105974569023
R2: 0.5799223501095555

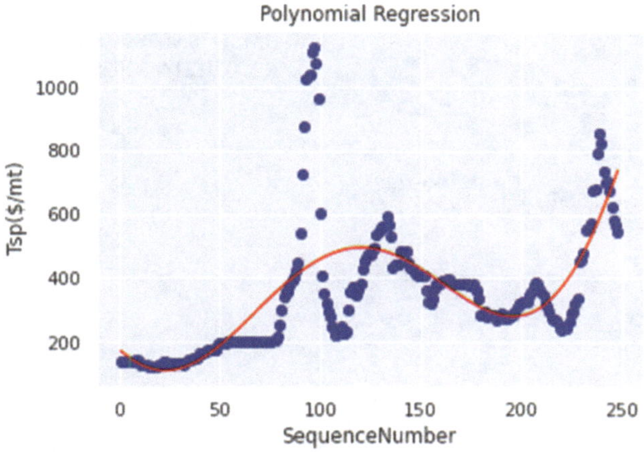

MSE: 18801.77233796731
RMSE: 137.1195549072681
R2: 0.5149817696628016

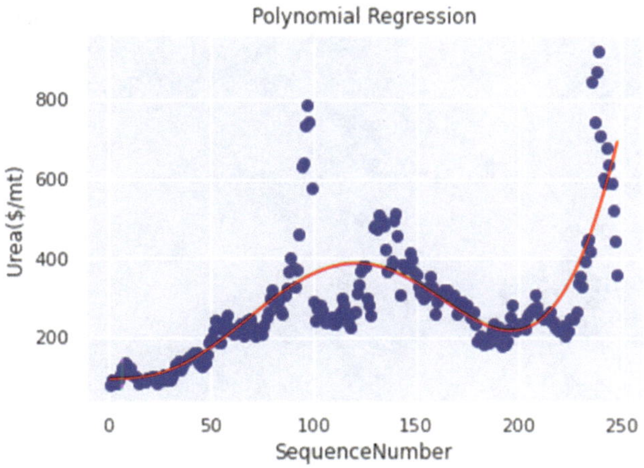

MSE: 8765.07528117752
RMSE: 93.62198075867397
R2: 0.6137050887774084

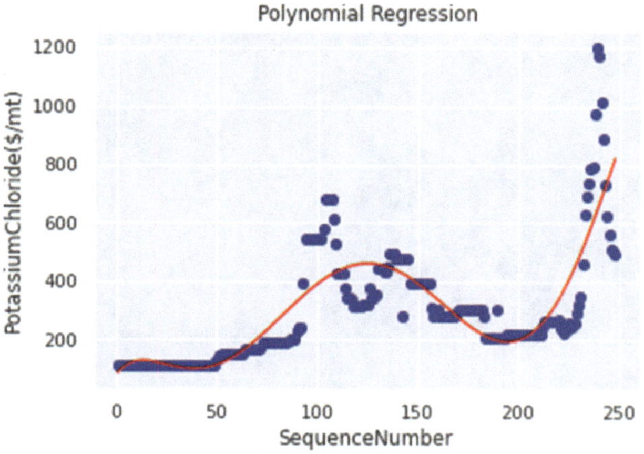

MSE: 11097.76595659028
RMSE: 105.34593469417925
R2: 0.6928380029439966

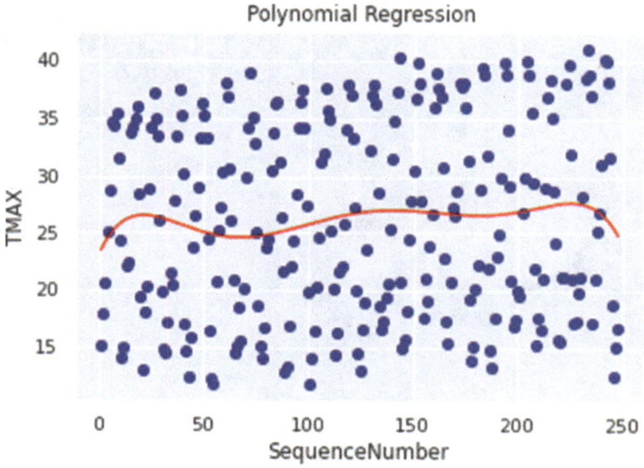

MSE: 70.62543553552739
RMSE: 8.403894069746917
R2: 0.012146320590713189

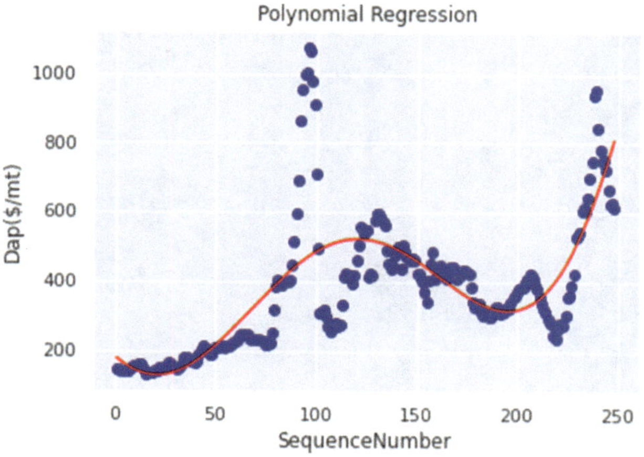

MSE: 15902.716822003078
RMSE: 126.105974569023
R2: 0.5799223501095555

Save all feature variable horizon forecasts into USA_Tomato_Prices_forecastTendValuesr CSV file.

Trend-based forecasting

In this step, let's prepare data based on prevailing data trend and forecast based on the future trend dataset preparation.

Step 1: Prepare and load trend dataset dataset

First, let's load what-if dataset. This data is completely scenario driven data:

```
futureTrenddf
pd.read_csv(r"USA_Tomato_Prices_forecastTendValuesr.csv",index_col=0)
#summarize shape
print(futureTrenddf.shape)
#show first few rows
print(futureTrenddf.head())
```

```
futureTrenddf = futureTrenddf.reset_index()
```

```
futurewhatifdf
```

Output:

```
(18, 19)
          TomatoPPIndex  IndustrialProductionIndex  RAILFRTCARLOADS  \
Date
2/1/2023     233.320000                 102.500700         979817.0
3/1/2023     346.937791                 106.187400        1036481.0
4/1/2023     347.212473                 107.217532        1047326.0
5/1/2023     347.481355                 108.339584        1059377.0
6/1/2023     347.748826                 109.558305        1072698.0

            CPIndex    GDPIndex  UnEmpRate(%)  EmpInAgri(1000sOfPersons)  \
Date
2/1/2023  301.648000  249.168683      3.600000                2346.000000
3/1/2023  306.365481  236.446255      2.542393                2261.026465
4/1/2023  309.301546  228.007932      2.137772                2259.765853
5/1/2023  312.355483  218.693265      1.694872                2259.124534
6/1/2023  315.531190  208.459163      1.211606                2259.151538

          USAGasPrice(USD/Gallon)         SP500  PhosphateRock($/mt)  \
Date
2/1/2023                 3.304000  3970.150000           322.500000
3/1/2023                 4.028312  4407.711597           326.208054
4/1/2023                 4.132226  4460.532860           340.510371
5/1/2023                 4.240192  4514.865539           355.296471
6/1/2023                 4.352298  4570.787461           370.573436
```

Step 2: Setup time column

Convery date to reqyured ds coikunb.

```
futurewhatifdf.rename(columns = {"date": "ds" }, inplace = True)
futurewhatifdf.info()
futurewhatifdf["ds"] = pd.to_datetime(futurewhatifdf["ds"])
futureTrenddf=futureTrenddf.dropna()
```

Output:

```
<class 'pandas.core.frame.DataFrame'>
RangeIndex: 2 entries, 0 to 1
Data columns (total 20 columns):
 #   Column                       Non-Null Count  Dtype
---  ------                       --------------  -----
 0   ds                           2 non-null      datetime64[ns]
 1   TomatoPPIndex                2 non-null      float64
 2   IndustrialProductionIndex    2 non-null      float64
 3   RAILFRTCARLOADS              2 non-null      int64
 4   CPIndex                      2 non-null      float64
 5   GDPIndex                     2 non-null      float64
 6   UnEmpRate(%)                 2 non-null      float64
 7   EmpInAgri(1000sOfPersons)    2 non-null      int64
 8   USAGasPrice(USD/Gallon)      2 non-null      float64
 9   SP500                        2 non-null      float64
 10  PhosphateRock($/mt)          2 non-null      float64
 11  Dap($/mt)                    2 non-null      float64
 12  Tsp($/mt)                    2 non-null      float64
 13  Urea($/mt)                   2 non-null      float64
 14  PotassiumChloride($/mt)      2 non-null      float64
 15  CLDD                         2 non-null      int64
 16  TMAX                         2 non-null      float64
 17  TMIN                         2 non-null      float64
 18  PRCP                         2 non-null      float64
 19  HTDD                         2 non-null      int64
dtypes: datetime64[ns](1), float64(15), int64(4)
memory usage: 448.0 bytes
```

Step 3: Predict

Call predict on what-if data.

```
#print('future')
print(future)
#predict future
forecastProphet = multi_model.predict(futureTrenddf)
print(forecastProphet[['ds', 'yhat', 'yhat_lower','yhat_upper']].tail())
fig1 = multi_model.plot(forecastProphet)
multi_model.plot_components(forecastProphet);
```

Output:

	ds	yhat	yhat_lower	yhat_upper
9	2023-11-01	2.508922	2.279238	2.756682
10	2023-12-01	2.459934	2.229996	2.688226
11	2024-01-01	2.613239	2.393625	2.845321
12	2024-02-01	2.587306	2.366214	2.832855
13	2024-03-01	2.647250	2.406510	2.883337

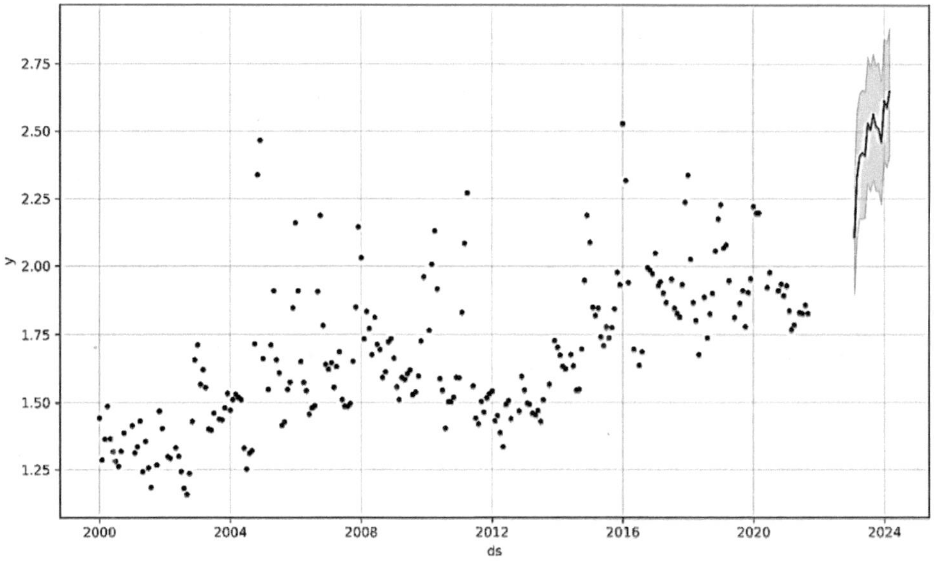

```
import seaborn as sns
import matplotlib.pyplot as plt
sns.lineplot(data= forecastProphet,x = 'ds', y = 'yhat', label = 'Forecast')
plt.grid(linestyle = '-', linewidth = 0.3)

plt.legend(["forecast"])
```

Plot future prices of tomatoes:

Output:

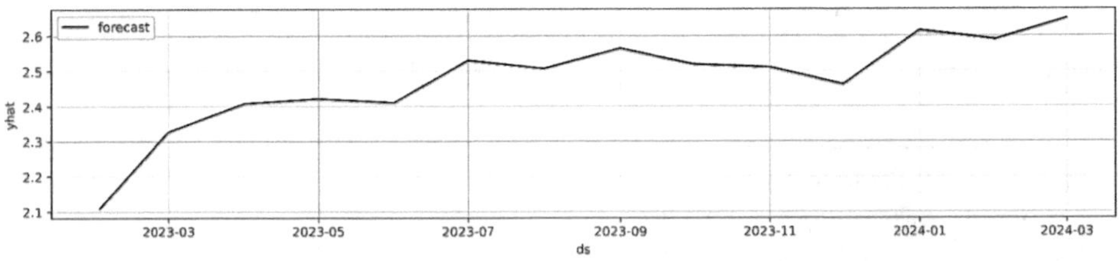

Models have shown that climate change is causing crop failures that are becoming more severe over time. This is a major problem because it affects both food security and the financial stability of farmers. It is urgent that we take measures to ease the impact of weather shift on agriculture and increase more environmental farming practices.

The way address is to invest in research and development to find new ways to adapt to changing climatic conditions. For example, scientists are developing drought-resistant crops that can thrive in areas with less water. By adopting sustainable farming practices, farmers can also amend moderate the impact of environment alter. This might include using more efficient irrigation systems, reducing the use of chemical fertilizers, and adopting regenerative agriculture practices.

Addressing the effects of climate change on agriculture is essential to ensure sustainable food sources for future generations and the continued livelihoods of farmers.

Author
Chandrasekar Vuppalapati

Use cases: volatility of tomato prices in India and food security [407]

Central banks [408] note that in agriculture-dependent countries like India and Pakistan, fluctuations in tomato prices have historically influenced overall inflation levels.

Urgent need for sustainable farming practices in the face of climate change

Tomatoes are mainly grown in Andhra Pradesh, Madhya Pradesh, Karnataka, Odisha, and Gujarat states. These regions produce almost half of India's total tomato production, while including more states brings the total to around 90%. It's important to understand these regional concentrations of production to manage the supply chain and ensure that high-quality tomatoes can be delivered to markets all over the country.

Tomatoes are grown twice a year in India, and different regions have different growing seasons. Despite the importance of tomatoes as a crop, production in India has been decreasing since 2019–2020. Understanding the dynamics of tomato production and consumption is important to increase production and ensure high-quality tomatoes are available in markets all over the country.

In June 2023, the price of tomatoes in retail markets doubled in just one day, which is a big increase. Prices went up by 200%, which is probably the highest increase in a single day.

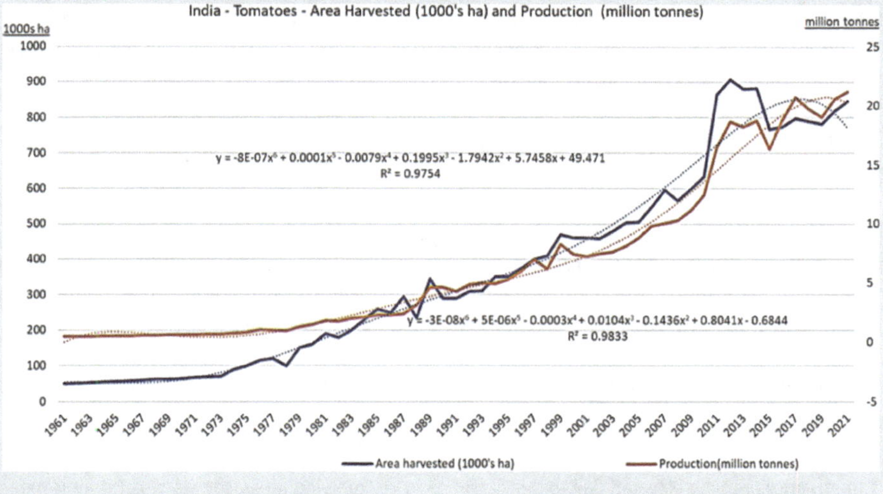

The impact of extreme weather conditions and low prices on tomato farmers

There are many reasons why there is a decrease in tomato production this year. One reason is the extreme weather conditions. In April/May of 2023, heatwaves, delayed monsoon showers, and pest attacks affected tomato crops, resulting in lower quality produce and lower prices for farmers. Incessant rains also made transportation difficult.

According to a report from the Agriculture Ministry, there was a fall in tomato cultivation in producing states, which further affected tomato supplies. Additionally, the lean production period for tomatoes in July–August compounded the problem. Many farmers in Karnataka have shifted to growing beans because they could make more money.

It's important to understand the different factors affecting tomato production to device effective policies to reduce uncertainty and market fluctuations on food industry. By prioritizing these measures, farmers can continue to produce high-quality tomatoes that meet the needs of consumers and markets worldwide despite the challenges posed by environmental factors, market fluctuations, and supply chain disruptions.

The high volatility of tomato prices and its impacts

The price of tomatoes has suddenly risen sharply, but the government says it's a seasonal and temporary issue. Experts are worried about the high volatility of tomato prices and how it affects the overall Consumer Price Index. A study by NABARD found that tomatoes are the highest unstable of the three Tomato-Onion-Potato agri-commodities.

Although vegetables account for a small part of food basket of inflation, tomato has the largest role among 299 commodities in the basket, at 8.9%. The perishability of tomatoes and supply chain issues make the problem worse.

Tomato prices follow a recurring pattern, meaning price patterns repeat itself. In the year 2021, prices dropped so low that many farmers switched to other crops, leading to a glut. Understanding the factors contributing to price volatility is important to develop effective strategies to mitigate market fluctuations and ensure high-quality tomatoes for consumers and markets worldwide.

Controlling tomato market volatility

Experts suggest that the high volatility of the tomato market can be controlled by implementing some improvements. Data science and machine learning is safer of tomatoes cultivators. Tomato yields in India are lower than the global average. Encouraging cultivation in polyhouses and greenhouses can help control pest attacks and boost tomato yields. By implementing these measures, farmers can reduce market volatility, ensuring a stable and sustainable industry for years to come.

Boosting tomato production in India: overcoming market fluctuations, environmental

Tomato prices remain elevated due to heavy rainfall in key growing areas, though relief is anticipated with the new crop in August or September. To mitigate the issue, the government is selling tomatoes at a subsidized rate and plans to further reduce the price. However, extreme weather and low market returns have led to decreased production, emphasizing the need for strategies to boost output and ensure timely delivery of high-quality tomatoes.

Additional machine learning experiments

Q1. Mexico imports

Imports from Mexico have huge influence on pricing of fresh tomatoes in USA. Please add fresh tomatoes imports from Mexico and see the influence of pricing? The import from Mexico has polynomial regression trend (R^2 = 0.9754). The data is from FAOSTAT (2023):

$$Y_{\text{imports from mexico}} = 0.0435x^6 - 5.2772x^5 + 244.26x^4 - 5399.2x^3 + 59184x^2 - 265811x + 706319$$

Year	Import quantity (tonnes)	Year	Import quantity (tonnes)
1986	430,924	2006	844,343
1987	406,783	2007	949,486
1988	362,725	2008	987,914
1989	385,941	2009	1,046,869
1990	352,312	2010	1,380,108
1991	353,544	2011	1,327,312
1992	183,116	2012	1,380,080
1993	400,494	2013	1,381,261
1994	376,031	2014	1,389,334
1995	593,080	2015	1,427,920
1996	685,678	2016	1,619,717
1997	660,609	2017	1,612,337
1998	734,053	2018	1,691,902
1999	615,064	2019	1,696,477
2000	589,954	2020	1,668,601
2001	679,187	2021	1,754,006
2002	724,016		
2003	784,988		
2004	779,020		
2005	801,408		

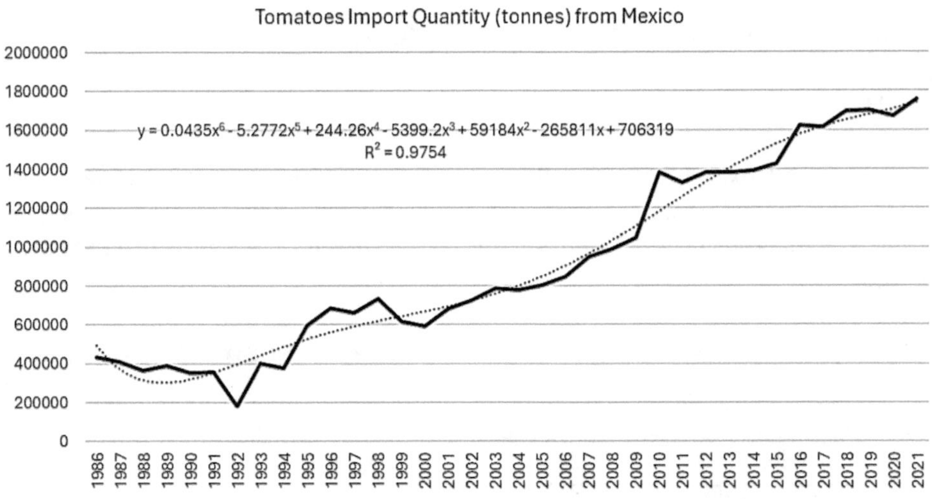

Tomatoes and Mexico pesos

Q2: Tomato production in Mexico is forecasted to recover slightly from the year 2022 due to stable weather and sufficient rainfall in Sinaloa despite the uncertainty brought by ongoing drought conditions. Increased planting is encouraged by the reopening of the restaurant and hotel sectors, favorable export prices, and the US-Mexico Tomato Suspension Agreement, with protected agriculture systems further boosting yields and quality.

What is the influence of Mexican Pesos-US dollar-conversion rate on overall prices in USA?

$$y = -7\text{E}{-}22x^6 + 2\text{E}{-}16x^5 - 2\text{E}{-}11x^4 + 8\text{E}{-}07x^3 - 0.0248x^2 + 387.63x - 3\text{E}{+}06$$

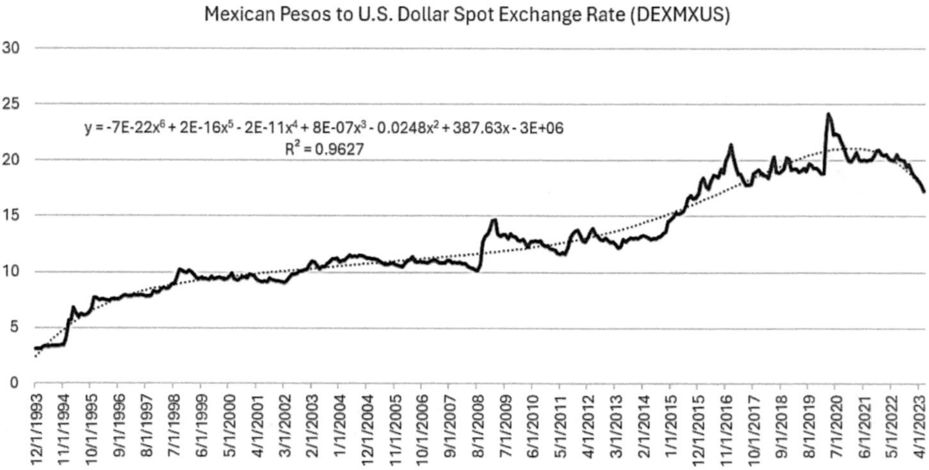

In this chapter, you will learn about the economics of tomato production in main cultivating nations – USA, India, and Türkiye. You will understand how the prices of tomatoes are determined in these countries. Furthermore, you will be able to create pricing models that can help farmers make better pricing decisions. You will also learn about a better framework for analyzing tomato yields in different countries. By the end of this chapter, you will have a comprehensive understanding of the global tomato industry and the various factors influencing tomato prices and yields.

References

[1] Goedde, L., Katz, J., Ménard, A., Revellat, J. (October 9, 2020). "Agriculture's connected future: How technology can yield new growth", https://www.mckinsey.com/industries/agriculture/our-insights/agricultures-connected-future-how-technology-can-yield-new-growth, Access Date: 09/18/2020

[2] Goedde, L., Katz, J., Ménard, A., Revellat, J. (October 9, 2020). "Agriculture's connected future: How technology can yield new growth", https://www.mckinsey.com/industries/agriculture/our-insights/agricultures-connected-future-how-technology-can-yield-new-growth, Access Date: 09/18/2020

[3] Walch, K. (Jul 5, 2019). "How AI Is Transforming Agriculture", 08:00am EDT, https://www.forbes.com/sites/cognitiveworld/2019/07/05/how-ai-is-transforming-agriculture/?sh=7ce84c004ad1, Access Date: 01/08/2021

[4] Brennan, E. (October 2018). "Agricultural Intelligence: What AI Can Do for Smallholder Farmers", https://foodtank.com/news/2018/10/agricultural-intelligence-what-ai-can-do-for-smallholder-farmers/, 01/20/2021

[5] Columbus, L. (Feb 17, 2021). "10 Ways AI Has The Potential To Improve Agriculture In 2021", 12:20pm EST, https://www.forbes.com/sites/louiscolumbus/2021/02/17/10-ways-ai-has-the-potential-to-improve-agriculture-in-2021/?sh=7f611e297f3b, Access Date: March 10, 2021

[6] Medeiros, M. (April 2018) "Artificial intelligence and the future", https://www.nortonrosefulbright.com/en-br/knowledge/publications/6400e1ea/artificial-intelligence-and-the-future%20The%20World%20Bank%20-%20Agriculture,%20forestry, Access Date: February 14, 2021

[7] Kumar, D. P. (August 17 2019). Artificial Intelligence: Reshaping Life and Business, Chapter 2 (1 edition), BPB Publications, ISBN-10: 9388511077.

[8] West, D. M. (Thursday, October 4, 2018). "What is artificial intelligence?" https://www.brookings.edu/research/what-is-artificial-intelligence/, Access Date: November 22, 2020

[9] Faggella, D. (December 21, 2018). "What is Artificial Intelligence? An Informed Definition", https://emerj.com/ai-glossary-terms/what-is-artificial-intelligence-an-informed-definition/#:~:text=In%20%E2%80%9CArtificial%20Intelligence%3A%20A%20Modern,many%20different%20splintered%20fields%20%E2%80%93%20speech, Access Date: October 2020

[10] Stuart, R., Norvig, P. (December 11, 2009). Artificial Intelligence: A Modern Approach (3rd edition), 3 edition, Pearson: Publisher.

[11] Nandi, J. (Dec 03, 2021). India needs additional $1 trillion to achieve its climate goals: Govt to Rajya Sabha, 12:45 AM IST, https://www.hindustantimes.com/india-news/india-needs-additional-1-trillion-to-achieve-its-climate-goals-govt-to-rajya-sabha-101638472545191.html, Access Date: May 03, 2023

[12] Pulakkat, H. Adaptations by India towards climate change likely to cost as much as $360 billion a year by 2030, Last Updated: Dec 02, 2015, 11:45 AM IST, https://economictimes.indiatimes.com/adaptations-by-india-towards-climate-change-likely-to-cost-as-much-as-360-billion-a-year-by-2030/articleshow/49990031.cms?from=mdr, Access Date: May 03, 2023

[13] British Petroleum, Country Insight India. (2022) https://www.bp.com/content/dam/bp/business-sites/en/global/corporate/xlsx/energy-economics/statistical-review/bp-stats-review-2022-all-data.xlsx, Access Date: May 04, 2023

[14] THE HINDU BUREAU. 'Adapting to climate change to cost India ₹85.6 lakh crore by 2030', May 03, 2023 09:51 pm | Updated 10:05 pm IST – MUMBAI, https://www.thehindu.com/business/adapting-to-climate-change-to-cost-india-856-lakh-crore-by-2030/article66808787.ece, Access Date: May 03, 2023

[15] Luedeling, E., Zhang, M., Girvetz, E. H. Climatic Changes Lead to Declining Winter Chill for Fruit and Nut Trees in California during 1950–2099, Published: July 22, 2009, https://journals.plos.org/plosone/article?id=10.1371/journal.pone.0006166, Access Date: May 06, 2023

[16] Rogers, P. Massive snowpack's summer bonus: Clean, cheap electricity for California. PUBLISHED: May 9, 2023 at 5:45 a.m. | UPDATED: May 9, 2023 at 3:54 p.m., https://www.mercurynews.

com/2023/05/09/massive-california-snowpacks-summer-bonus-more-clean-cheap-electricity/, Access Date: May 10, 2023
[17] Vuppalapati, C. (2019 December 17). Building Enterprise IoT Applications (1st edition, CRC Press, ISBN-13‏: 978-0367173852.
[18] Yang, X.-S., Sherratt, S., Dey, N., Joshi, A., ICICT. (eds) (2019). “Fourth International Congress on Information and Communication Technology”, London, Volume 2, eBook ISBN 978-981-329-343-4 and Softcover ISBN 978-981-329-342-7
[19] Croke, D. (March 30, 2023). The Impact of Produce Season on Carrier Availability and Rates, https://www.foodlogistics.com/transportation/cold-chain/article/22780083/dat-solutions-the-impact-of-produce-season-on-carrier-availability-and-rates, Access date; July 11, 2023
[20] Cassidy, W. B. Late US produce season boosting spot reefer truckload rates, May 22 2023 – 5:30 PM EDT, https://www.joc.com/article/late-us-produce-season-boosting-spot-reefer-truckload-rates_20230522.html, Access date; July 11, 2023
[21] Li, S. “Building A Logistic Regression in Python, Step by Step”, Publication Date: Sep 28, 2017, URL: https://towardsdatascience.com/building-a-logistic-regression-in-python-step-by-step-becd4d56c9c8, Access Date: Nov 22, 2019
[22] Morde, V. “XGBoost Algorithm: Long May She Reign”, Publication Date: Apr 7, 2019, URL: https://towardsdatascience.com/https-medium-com-vishalmorde-xgboost-algorithm-long-she-may-rein-edd9f99be63d, Access Date: Sep 18, 2019
[23] Parikh, A. (1982). An econometric model of the agricultural sector of the Indian economy. Journal of Policy Modeling, 4(3), 395–411. ISSN 0161-8938. https://doi.org/10.1016/0161-8938(82)90027-8.
[24] Han, J., Kamber, M., Pei, J. (June 15, 2011). Data Mining: Concepts and Techniques (3 edition), Publisher: Morgan Kaufmann, ISBN-10: 9780123814791.
[25] Vuppalapati, C. Machine Learning and Artificial Intelligence for Agricultural Economics Prognostic Data Analytics to Serve Small Scale Farmers Worldwide, Edition, ISBN-13: 978-3-030-77484-4, https://link.springer.com/book/10.1007/978-3-030-77485-1, Access Date: December 15, 2022
[26] Vuppalapati, C. (January 18, 2021). Democratization of Artificial Intelligence for the Future of Humanity (1st edition), CRC Press, ISBN-13: 978-0367524128.
[27] Vuppalapati, C. (September 17, 2022). Artificial Intelligence and Heuristics for Enhanced Food Security (1st ed. 2022 edition), Springer, ISBN-13: 978-3031087424, Access Date: December 03, 2022.
[28] Binieli, M. Machine learning: An introduction to mean squared error and regression lines, examples and documentation, https://medium.com/free-code-camp/machine-learning-mean-squared-error-regression-line-c7dde9a26b93, Access Date: December 07, 2022
[29] Pedregosa, F., Varoquaux, G., Gramfort, A., Michel, V., Thirion, B., Grisel, O., Blondel, M., Prettenhofer, P., Weiss, R., Dubourg, V., Vanderplas, J., Passos, A., Cournapeau, D., Brucher, M., Perrot, M., Duchesnay, É. (2011). Journal of Machine Learning Research, 12, 2825–2830. 12(85), 2825–2830. Access Date: December 05, 2022.
[30] What is logistic regression? https://www.ibm.com/topics/logistic-regression, Access Date: December 05, 2022 What is logistic regression? https://www.ibm.com/topics/logistic-regression
[31] What is Regression? https://www.nvidia.com/en-us/glossary/data-science/linear-regression-logistic-regression/, Access Date: December 05, 2022
[32] Truckload, A. Florida Tomato Shipping by the Truckload, Last Modified: May 5, 2023, https://usatruckloadshipping.com/florida-tomato-shipping-by-the-truckload/, Access date; July 14, 2023
[33] Alexander, L., Grierson, D. (1 October 2002). Ethylene biosynthesis and action in tomato: A model for climacteric fruit ripening. Journal of Experimental Botany, 53(377), 2039–2055. https://doi.org/10.1093/jxb/erf072.
[34] USDA. (July 12 2023). SPECIALTY CROPS NATIONAL TRUCK RATE REPORT, https://www.ams.usda.gov/mnreports/fvwtrk.pdf, Access date; July 14, 2023

[35] Sargent, S. Associate Professor, Department of Horticultural Sciences, Cooperative Extension Service, Institute of Food and Agricultural Sciences, University of Florida, Gainesville, 32611, Access date; July 14, 2023

[36] Cantwell, M. (Sept 2008). Impact of Ripening & Storage Conditions on Ripe Tomato Quantity, https://ucanr.edu/sites/Postharvest_Technology_Center_/files/235436.pdf, Access date; July 14, 2023

[37] The Chef's garden. (2018). Flavorful fresh tomatoes vs. Ethylene-gassed ones: you decide, https://www.chefs-garden.com/blog/june-2018/flavorful-fresh-tomatoes-vs-ethylene-gassed-ones, Access date; July 15, 2023

[38] Nath, A., Bagchi, B., Verma, V. K., Rymbai, H., Jha, A. K., Deka, B. C. (2015). Extension of Shelf Life of Tomato Using KMnO4 as Ethylene Absorbent. Indian Journal of Hill Farming, 28(1), Retrieved from. https://epubs.icar.org.in/index.php/IJHF/article/view/51201. Access date; July 15, 2023.

[39] Mariah, M. A. A., Vonnie, J. M., Erna, K. H., Nur'Aqilah, N. M., Huda, N., Abdul Wahab, R., Rovina, K. (Jan 20 2022). The Emergence and Impact of Ethylene Scavengers Techniques in Delaying the Ripening of Fruits and Vegetables. Membranes (Basel), 12(2), 117. doi. 10.3390/membranes12020117. PMID: 35207039; PMCID. PMC8877706. Access date; July 15, 2023.

[40] Tilahun, S., Lee, Y. M., Choi, H. R., Baek, M. W., Lee, J.-S., Park, D. S., Kang, H.-M., Jeong, C. S. (2021). Modified atmosphere packaging combined with CO2 and 1-methylcyclopropene prolong the storability and maintain antioxidant properties of cherry tomato. Scientia Horticulturae, 288, 110401. ISSN 0304-4238. https://doi.org/10.1016/j.scienta.2021.110401. https://www.sciencedirect.com/science/article/pii/S0304423821005082.

[41] Green, W. (11 October 2021) Price fixed for CO2 to maintain production, https://www.cips.org/supply-management/news/2021/october/price-fixed-for-co2-to-maintain-production/, Access date; July 15, 2023

[42] Estabrook, B. (Author). Tomatoland: How Modern Industrial Agriculture Destroyed Our Most Alluring Fruit Paperback, Publisher: Andrews McMeel Publishing; Reprint edition (April 24, 2012), ISBN-13:978-1449423452

[43] Chanda, S., Bhat, M., Shetty, K. G., Jayachandran, K. (May, 2021). Technology, Policy, and Market Adaptation Mechanisms for Sustainable Fresh Produce Industry: The Case of Tomato Production In, Florida, USA, https://www.researchgate.net/publication/351841169_Technology_Policy_and_Market_Adaptation_Mechanisms_for_Sustainable_Fresh_Produce_Industry_The_Case_of_Tomato_Production_in_Florida_USA, Access date, July 15, 2023.

[44] bhigyan. (Aug 1, 2020). Understanding Polynomial Regression!!!, https://medium.com/analytics-vidhya/understanding-polynomial-regression-5ac25b970e18, Access Date: December 12, 2022

[45] Medium, Python | Implementation of Polynomial Regression, Last Updated: 24 Aug, 2022, https://www.geeksforgeeks.org/python-implementation-of-polynomial-regression/, Access Date: December 11, 2022

[46] Baker, G. CMPT 353 Lecture Notes, 2022, https://ggbaker.ca/data-science/, Access Date: December 11, 2022 ML – https://ggbaker.ca/data-science/content/ml.html

[47] Weber, C., Kramer, J. Imports play dominant role as U.S. demand for avocados climbs, Last updated: Monday, May 02, 2022, https://www.ers.usda.gov/data-products/chart-gallery/gallery/chart-detail/?chartId=103810, Access date; July 16, 2023

[48] Vuppalapati, C. (July 17, 2023). Artificial Intelligence and Advanced Analytics for Food Security (1st edition), Publisher: CRC Press, ISBN-13: 978-1032346182, Access Date: June 03, 2023.

[49] Kantor, J. (2016 January 29). Atlas of Suturing Techniques: Approaches to Surgical Wound, Laceration, and Cosmetic Repair (1st edition), McGraw-Hill Education / Medical: Publisher, ISBN-13 : 978-0071836579.

[50] Vuppalapati, C., Ilapakurti, A., Kedari, S., Vuppalapati, R., Vuppalapati, J., Kedari, S. "The Role of Combinatorial Mathematical Optimization and Heuristics to improve Small Farmers to Veterinarian

access and to create a Sustainable Food Future for the World," 2020 Fourth World Conference on Smart Trends in Systems, Security and

[51] Rasmussen, S. E. (2021). Severe Drought Adds to Afghanistan's Woes, Endangering Millions as Economy Collapses. Publication: Oct, 10(9:35 am ET), https://www.wsj.com/articles/severe-drought-adds-to-afghanistans-woes-endangering-millions-as-economy-collapses-11633872935?page=1. Access Date: December 18, 2021.

[52] Karthe. Introductory guide on Linear Programming for (aspiring) data scientists, Publication Date: February 28, 2017, https://www.analyticsvidhya.com/blog/2017/02/lintroductory-guide-on-linear-programming-explained-in-simple-english/, Access Date: 12/12/2021

[53] Suresha, H. P., Uppaladinni, M., Tiwari, K. K. (22 December 2021). Indian Commodity Market Price Comparative Study of Forecasting Methods – A Case Study on Onion, Potato and Tomato, https://www.researchgate.net/profile/Suresh-Hp-2/publication/358037089_Indian_Commodity_Market_Price_Comparative_Study_of_Forecasting_Methods_-_A_Case_Study_on_Onion_Potato_and_Tomato/links/622a067484ce8e5b4d163012/Indian-Commodity-Market-Price-Comparative-Study-of-Forecasting-Methods-A-Case-Study-on-Onion-Potato-and-Tomato.pdf, Access Date: June 06, 2023

[54] Bart Kenner, U. S. (2020). Fruit Imports Grew By $8.9 Billion Over the Last Decade to Meet Rising Demand, September 01, https://www.ers.usda.gov/amber-waves/2020/september/us-fruit-imports-grew-by-89-billion-over-the-last-decade-to-meet-rising-demand/, Access date; July 16, 2023

[55] Rural Migration News, US Imports of Fresh Fruit and Vegetable, February 24, 2021, https://migration.ucdavis.edu/rmn/blog/post/?id=2569 Access date; July 16, 2023

[56] Bernal, R. Mexican avocado imports booming during pandemic, 12/02/20 4:40 PM ET, https://thehill.com/latino/528452-mexican-avocado-imports-booming-during-pandemic/, Access date; July 16, 2023

[57] Davidson, M. Fresh Avocado Imports from Mexico Resume, 2022, https://www.aphis.usda.gov/aphis/newsroom/stakeholder-info/SA_By_Date/SA-2022/avocado-imports-mexico, Access date; July 16, 2023

[58] Webb, R. E.; Bruce, W. M. Redesigning the Tomato for Mechanized Production, https://naldc.nal.usda.gov/download/IND43895151/PDF, Access date; July 10, 2023

[59] Edwards, W. Farm Machinery Selection, Updated January 2017 File A3-28, https://www.extension.iastate.edu/agdm/crops/html/a3-28.html, Access date; July 10, 2023

[60] Vuppalapati, C. (May 31 2024). Assessing Policy Effectiveness using AI and Language Models: Applications for Economic and Social Sustainability (2024th edition), Publisher: Springer, ISBN-13: 978-3031560965.

[61] Vuppalapati, C. (2023). Specialty Crops for Climate Change Adaptation. Strategies for Enhanced Food Security by Using Machine Learning and Artificial Intelligence (STEAM-H: . . . Agriculture, Mathematics & Health) (1st ed), 1st ed, 2023 edition, Publisher: Springer. (October 24, 2023), ISBN-13: 978-3031383984.

[62] Zhao, C., Stöckle, C. O., Kruse, J., Gustafson, D., Xiao, L., Hoogenboom, G., Karimi, T., Nelson, R. L., Rosenbohm, M., Intarapapong, W., Li, Y., Guan, K., Parajuli, R., Asseng, S. (October 1 2018). Fruit & Vegetable Supply Chains Climate Adaptation & Mitigation Opportunities, https://foodsystems.org/wp-content/uploads/2021/01/ProtocolforUSFruitandVegetableSimulations-Version-3.pdf, Access Date: May 22 2023

[63] Tsiboe, F., Turner, D. Federal Crop Insurance Program cost, Last updated: Wednesday, May 03, 2023, https://www.ers.usda.gov/topics/farm-practices-management/risk-management/crop-insurance-at-a-glance/#fcipcost, Access Date: July 01, 2023

[64] USDA. FCIC/RMA's Fiscal Years 2022 and 2021 Financial Statements – AUDIT REPORT 50401-0020-11, November 2022, https://www.oversight.gov/sites/default/files/oig-reports/USDAOIG/05401-0014-11508FOIA.pdf, Access Date: July 02, 2023

[65] FAO. (07 May 2020). Land use in agriculture by the numbers, https://www.fao.org/sustainability/news/detail/en/c/1274219/, Access Date: November 30, 2022

[66] Aubrey, A. If We All Ate Enough Fruits And Vegetables, There'd Be Big Shortages, July 17, 20196:30 PM ET, https://www.npr.org/sections/thesalt/2019/07/17/742670701/if-we-all-ate-enough-fruits-and-vegetables-thered-be-big-shortages, Access Date: December 16, 2022

[67] Greenaway, T. Eight foods you're about to lose due to climate change, Wed 29 Oct 2014 09.00 EDT, https://www.theguardian.com/vital-signs/2014/oct/29/diet-climate-maple-syrup-coffee-global-warming, Access Date: May 21, 2023

[68] USDA, Vegetables Usual Planting and Harvesting Dates. (May 2007). https://naldc.nal.usda.gov/download/CAT30992961/PDF, Access Date: May 21, 2023

[69] Agriculture & Food System Institute. Helping to Ensure a Nutritious Food Supply in the Face of Climate Change, 2023, https://foodsystems.org/what-we-do/nutrition/fruit-vegetable-supply-chains/#, Access Date: May 31, 2023

[70] Guan, Z., Hee Suh, D., Wu, F. Tomato Suspension Agreements and The Effects On Market Prices and Farm Revenue, 4/23/2018, https://edis.ifas.ufl.edu/publication/FE1025, Access Date: May 26, 2023

[71] USDA Agricultural Projections to (2032). Office of the Chief Economist, World Agricultural Outlook Board, U.S. Department of Agriculture. Prepared by the Interagency Agricultural Projections Committee. Long-Term Projections Report OCE-2023-1, 119 pp, https://www.usda.gov/sites/default/files/documents/USDA-Agricultural-Projections-to-2032.pdf, Access Date: June 06, 2023

[72] Kassel, K. (March 14, 2023). Farming and Farm Income, Last updated: Tuesday, https://www.nass.usda.gov/Publications/Highlights/2021/census-typology.pdf, Access Date: July 03, 2023

[73] The California Department and Food and Agriculture. CALIFORNIA AGRICULTURAL STATISTICS REVIEW 2020-2021, 2022, https://www.cdfa.ca.gov/Statistics/PDFs/2021_Ag_Stats_Review.pdf, Access Date: December 18, 2022

[74] Munch, D. (Nov, 30 2022). Specialty Crop Considerations for the Farm Bill, https://www.fb.org/market-intel/specialty-crop-considerations-for-the-farm-bill#. Access Date: June 30, 2023.

[75] ICIMOD. (2023). Water, Ice, Society, and Ecosystems in the Hindu Kush Himalaya: An Outlook, Wester, P., Chaudhary, S., Chettri, N., Jackson, M., Maharjan, A., Nepal, S., Steiner, J. F. (eds.), ICIMOD, https://doi.org/10.53055/ICIMOD.1028.

[76] Armanini, K., Sennott, A. May frost brings severe damage to spring harvest in New England, Updated June 3, 2023, 5:24 p.m., https://www.bostonglobe.com/2023/05/25/metro/frost-nearly-destroys-blueberry-crop-at-farm/, Access Date: June 25, 2023

[77] Calderwood, L., Yarborough, D. E., Ph.D. Maine Wild Blueberry Production Statistics, Updated May 2023, https://extension.umaine.edu/blueberries/factsheets/statistics-2/crop-production-statistics-2019/, Access Date: June 25, 2023

[78] Neufeldpress, K. A. Y. Maine's wild blueberry crop fell 26% in size, 30% in value last year, Posted May 9 2023 Updated May 9 2023, https://www.pressherald.com/2023/05/09/maines-blueberry-crop-fell-26-in-size-30-in-value-last-year/, Access Date: June 25, 2023

[79] Gunes, E. Agribusiness and Contract Farming: The Case of Tomato Production In Turkey, Published: 2007, https://www.ishs.org/ishs-article/758_37, Access Date: May 23 2023

[80] Colvine, S. A partial overview of the Turkish industry, Date Posted: 08/10/2018, https://www.tomatonews.com/en/a-partial-overview-of-the-turkish-industry_2_513.html, Access Date: May 28, 2023

[81] Carlson, B. (Apr 25, 2022). Idaho potato processors agree to pay more to growers, https://www.capitalpress.com/ag_sectors/smallfarm/idaho-potato-processors-agree-to-pay-more-to-growers/article_47230116-c4c6-11ec-83a2-c7fa095386e7.html, Access Date: June 09, 2023

[82] Lathim, D. (January 4, 2021). Potato Growers of Washington, https://potatocountry.com/2021/01/04/navigating-the-negotiation-process/, Access Date: June 09, 2023

[83] Gulati, A., Wardhan, H., Sharma, P. (2022). Tomato, Onion and Potato (TOP) Value Chains. In: Gulati, A., Ganguly, K., Wardhan, H. (eds), Agricultural Value Chains in India. India Studies in Business and Economics, Springer, Singapore, https://doi.org/10.1007/978-981-33-4268-2_3.

[84] Chengappa, P. G., Manjunatha, A. V., Shah, V. D. K. (2012). Competitive Assessment of Onion Markets in India, Agricultural Development and Rural Transformation Centre, Institute for Social and Economic Change, https://www.wsj.com/public/resources/documents/onionstudy.pdf, Access Date: December 21, 2022.

[85] Amand, R., Gummagolmath, K. C. (March 2019). Temporal Analysis of Onion Prices in major Markets in India, https://www.manage.gov.in/publications/resArticles/kcg/Onion%20price%20analysis-SMDr%20KCG.pdf, Access Date: December 23, 2022

[86] Suresha, H. P., Uppaladinni, M., Tiwari, K. K. (22 December 2021). Indian Commodity Market Price Comparative Study of Forecasting Methods – A Case Study on Onion, Potato and Tomato, https://www.researchgate.net/profile/Suresh-Hp-2/publication/358037089_Indian_Commodity_Market_Price_Comparative_Study_of_Forecasting_Methods_-_A_Case_Study_on_Onion_Potato_and_Tomato/links/622a067484ce8e5b4d163012/Indian-Commodity-Market-Price-Comparative-Study-of-Forecasting-Methods-A-Case-Study-on-Onion-Potato-and-Tomato.pdf, Access Date: June 06, 2023

[87] Agarwal, P., Singh, R., Singh, O. P. (2018). Dynamics of Prices and Arrivals of Major Vegetables: A Case of Haldwani and Dehradun Markets, Uttarakhand, http://isadp.in/publication/Dynamicd%20of%20prices%201-11.pdf, Access Date: June 02, 2023.

[88] Kumar1, V., Sharma2, H. R., Singh, K. (2005). Behaviour of Market Arrivals and Prices of Selected Vegetable Crops: A Study of Four Metropolitan Markets, https://ageconsearch.umn.edu/record/58477/files/art-10.pdf?ln=en&withWatermark=1, Access Date: June 02, 2023

[89] Reyes, J., Elias, E. (2019). Spatio-temporal variation of crop loss in the United States from 2001 to 2016. Environmental Research Letters, 14(7), https://doi.org/10.1088/1748-9326/ab1ac9,. Access Date: July 02, 2023.

[90] Solman, P., Estes, D. L. The major factors driving up the cost of food, Oct 11, 2022 6:40 PM EDT, https://www.pbs.org/newshour/show/the-major-factors-driving-up-the-cost-of-food, Access date; July 13, 2023

[91] Bailey, D., Diepenbrock, D., Earles, D., Jin, D., Kong, D., Pourreza, D., Vougioukas, D., Arias, D., Mäkiharju, D., Mosalam, D., Mueller, D., Zohdi, D. (2018). AI-Enabled Yield Sensing and Forecasting for Agricultural Production, https://food-manufacturing.berkeley.edu/yield-sensing-and-forecasting/, Access Date: June 02, 2023

[92] Gabhane Srushti, N., Shaikh Naushinnaaz, H., Sadavarte Shivani., M., Khan Huda., A., Waghmare, A. I. (2020). Crop Yield Prediction To Maximize Profit Using Machine Learning, https://www.irjmets.com/uploadedfiles/paper/volume2/issue_6_june_2020/1499/1628083038.pdf, Access date; July 14, 2023

[93] Ndubiwa, M. Tomato Processors Set to Pay Unprecedented Prices for Raw Tomatoes in 2022, Updated Apr 29, 2022, https://www.tridge.com/stories/tomato-processors-set-to-pay-unprecedented-prices-for-raw-tomatoes-in-2022, Access Date: May 24, 2023.

[94] Williams, J. US: Stronger field tomato availability puts pressure on hothouse tomato pricing, Publication date: Thu 5 Jan 2023, https://www.hortidaily.com/article/9490938/us-stronger-field-tomato-availability-puts-pressure-on-hothouse-tomato-pricing/, Access Date: May 23, 2023.

[95] PTI. Rise in food prices confined to tomato, potato, onion: Report, Last Updated: Jul 20, 2016, 10:39 PM IST, https://economictimes.indiatimes.com/news/economy/indicators/rise-in-food-prices-confined-to-tomato-potato-onion-report/articleshow/53307210.cms?from=mdr, Access Date: June 03, 2023

[96] Vuppalapati, C. (July 17, 2023). Artificial Intelligence and Advanced Analytics for Food Security (1st edition), Publisher: CRC Press, ISBN-13: 978-1032346182, Access Date: June 03, 2023.

[97] Durisin, M. UK Worker Shortage Leaves £60 Million of Food to Rot in Fieldss, August 15, 2022 at 5:56 AM PDT, https://www.bloomberg.com/news/articles/2022-08-15/uk-worker-shortage-leaves-60-million-of-food-to-rot-in-fields?leadSource=uverify%20wall, Access Date: December 16, 2022

[98] Dewey, R. L., Nelson, J. C. (1940). The Transportation Problem of Agriculture, https://naldc.nal.usda.gov/download/IND43893743/PDF, Access Date: December 15, 2022

[99] Millard, C. (Summer 2019). From Farm to Table, https://highways.dot.gov/public-roads/summer-2019/farm-table, Access Date: December 1g5, 2022

[100] FAO. Seeking end to loss and waste of food along production chain, 2022, https://www.fao.org/in-action/seeking-end-to-loss-and-waste-of-food-along-production-chain/en/, Access Date: December 17, 2022

[101] Sharma, S. India wastes up to 16% of its agricultural produce; fruits, vegetables squandered the most, July 31, 2019, 2:27:24 pm, https://www.financialexpress.com/economy/india-wastes-up-to-16-of-its-agricultural-produce-fruits-vegetables-squandered-the-most/1661671/, Access Date: December 17, 2022

[102] Kibiti, B., Strubenhoff, H. (October 16, 2019). How off-grid cold storage systems can help farmers reduce post-harvest losses,Wednesday, https://www.brookings.edu/blog/future-development/2019/10/16/how-off-grid-cold-storage-systems-can-help-farmers-reduce-post-harvest-losses/, Access Date: December 17, 2022

[103] Nassar, L., Saad, M., Okwuchi, I. E., Chaudhary, M., Karray, F., Ponnambalam, K. (2020). "Imputation Impact on Strawberry Yield and Farm Price Prediction Using Deep Learning," 2020 IEEE International Conference on Systems, Man, and Cybernetics (SMC), Toronto, ON, Canada, pp. 3599–3605, doi: 10.1109/SMC42975.2020.9283383.

[104] Jafari, F., Mousavi, J., Ponnambalam, K., Karray, F., Nassar, L. (2020). "Machine Learning Tools for the Prediction of Fresh Produce Procurement Price," 2020 IEEE International Conference on Systems, Man, and Cybernetics (SMC), Toronto, ON, Canada, pp. 3091–3095, doi: 10.1109/SMC42975.2020.9282887.

[105] Handley, D. T. (2022). Bulletin #2067, Growing Strawberries, https://extension.umaine.edu/publications/2067e/, Access date; July 20, 2023

[106] Karst, T. O. M. (June 22 2023). Strawberry consumption grows while imports surge, https://www.thepacker.com/news/produce-crops/strawberry-consumption-grows-while-imports-surge, Access date; July 19, 2023

[107] Purohit, M., Chandak, A. India inflation likely rose to 4.58% in June on higher food prices: Reuters poll, July 10, 20232:58 AM PDT, https://www.reuters.com/world/india/india-inflation-likely-rose-458-june-higher-food-prices-2023-07-10/, Access date; July 13, 2023

[108] Baker, S. R., Bloom, N., Davis, S. J. (10 March 2016). Measuring Economic Policy Uncertainty, https://www.policyuncertainty.com/media/EPU_BBD_Mar2016.pdf, Access Date: December 17, 2022

[109] Federal Reserve Bank of St. Louis. Spot Crude Oil Price: West Texas Intermediate (WTI) [WTISPLC], retrieved from FRED, Federal Reserve Bank of St. Louis; https://fred.stlouisfed.org/series/WTISPLC, December 17, 2022.

[110] U.S. Bureau of Labor Statistics. Consumer Price Index for All Urban Consumers: Fruits and Vegetables in U.S. City Average [CUSR0000SAF113], retrieved from FRED, Federal Reserve Bank of St. Louis; https://fred.stlouisfed.org/series/CUSR0000SAF113, December 18, 2022.

[111] U.S. Bureau of Labor Statistics. Producer Price Index by Industry: Pesticide, Fertilizer, and Other Agricultural Chemical Manufacturing [PCU32533253], retrieved from FRED, Federal Reserve Bank of St. Louis; https://fred.stlouisfed.org/series/PCU32533253, December 18, 2022.

[112] Board of Governors of the Federal Reserve System (US), Nominal Broad U.S. Dollar Index [TWEXBGSMTH], retrieved from FRED, Federal Reserve Bank of St. Louis; https://fred.stlouisfed.org/series/TWEXBGSMTH, December 18, 2022.

[113] Niyogi, D. (December 15, 2009). Irrigation decreases, urbanization increases monsoon rains, https://www.purdue.edu/uns/x/2009b/091215NiyogiIrrigation.html, Access Date: December 17, 2022
[114] Smith, H. California drought pits farmers vs. cities. But neither is the biggest water victim, OCT. 3, 2022 UPDATED 6:59 AM PT, https://www.latimes.com/california/story/2022-10-03/californias-environment-takes-biggest-hit-during-drought, Access Date: December 17, 2022
[115] The World Bank. (2016). High and Dry: Climate Change, Water, and the Economy, https://openknowledge.worldbank.org/bitstream/handle/10986/23665/K8517.pdf?sequence=3&isAllowed=y, Access Date: December 16, 2022
[116] Keck, A. (Aug 19, 2021). Evapotranspiration: Watching Over Water Use, Last Updated, https://www.nasa.gov/feature/evapotranspiration-watching-over-water-use, Access Date: May 30, 2023
[117] Bajaj, V. (Sept 3, 2012). Crops in India Wilt in a Weak Monsoon Season, https://www.nytimes.com/2012/09/04/business/global/drought-in-india-devastates-crops-and-farmers.html, Access Date: December 20, 2022
[118] Moole, M. J. (5 October 2019). India's onion crisis: Why rising prices make politicians cry, https://www.bbc.com/news/world-asia-india-49933613, Access Date: December 23, 2022
[119] Ariong, R., Ilukor, J., Bonabana-Wabbi, J., Birachi, E., Ugen, M. (2018). Returns to Market Coordination Mechanisms and Implications for Partial Bilateral Contracts for Commodity Exchange in Central Uganda, https://ageconsearch.umn.edu/record/276010?ln=en, Access Date: June 16, 2023
[120] Pinol, E. M. (December 18 2018. Philippine Banana Industry Roadmap 2019–2022, https://www.da.gov.ph/wp-content/uploads/2019/06/Philippine-Banana-Industry-Roadmap-2019-2022.pdf, Access Date: November 16, 2022
[121] HLPE. (2017). Nutrition and Food Systems. A Report by the High Level Panel of Experts on Food Security and Nutrition of the Committee on World Food Security, Rome, www.fao.org/fileadmin/user_upload/hlpe/hlpe_documents/HLPE_Reports/HLPE-Report-12_EN.pdf.
[122] Panda, A. (2022). Climate Change and Agricultural Insurance in the Asia and the Pacific Region, https://www.adb.org/sites/default/files/institutional-document/731791/adou2021bp-climate-change-agri-insurance-asia-pacific.pdf, Access Date:July 09, 2023
[123] ET Online. Tomato Thefts Continue: After Bengaluru, thieves steal 150 kg tomatoes in Jaipur
[124] 4. Last Updated: Jul 11, 2023, 12:38 PM IST, https://economictimes.indiatimes.com/news/india/tomato-thefts-continue-after-bengaluru-thieves-steal-150-kg-tomatoes-in-jaipur/articleshow/101660187.cms?from=mdr Access date; July 14, 2023
[125] Timesofindia.Com. (July 6 2023). Amid soaring prices, thieves flee with tomatoes worth Rs 2.5 lakh in Karnataka, https://timesofindia.indiatimes.com/city/bengaluru/amid-soaring-prices-thieves-flee-with-tomatoes-worth-rs-2-5-lakh-in-karnataka/articleshow/101536485.cms, Access date; July 14, 2023
[126] Executive Office of the President of the United States. (Apr 26, 2022). Climate Risk Exposure – White Paper, https://www.whitehouse.gov/wp-content/uploads/2022/04/OMB_Climate_Risk_Exposure_2022.pdf, Access Date: July 01, 2023
[127] Kamisher, E., Reyes, M., Carson, B. It's not just State Farm. Allstate no longer sells new home insurance policies in California, JUNE 2, 2023 12:20 PM PT, https://www.latimes.com/business/story/2023-06-02/allstate-state-farm-stop-selling-new-home-insurance-in-california#, Access Date: June 07, 2023
[128] Schumacher, Y, Ford, A, Douglas, E. Climate change has sent temperatures soaring in Texas, JUNE 27, 20233 PM CENTRAL, https://www.texastribune.org/2023/06/27/texas-climate-change-heat/, Access Date: June 29, 2023
[129] Garcia-Salazar, C. (June 01, 2023). Michigan State University Extension; Rufus Isaacs and Jenna Walters, Protecting blueberry blooms from extreme heat injury using overhead irrigation, https://www.canr.msu.edu/news/protecting-blueberry-blooms-from-extreme-heat-injury-using-overhead-irrigation, Access Date: June 25, 2023

[130] AFP. El Nino arrives, raising extreme weather fears, Thu, June 8, 2023 at 7:50 AM PDT, https://www.yahoo.com/news/us-says-el-nino-arrives-135713065.html, Access Date: June 08, 2023

[131] Jadhav, R., Bhardwaj, M. India monsoon reaches Kerala after longest delay in four years, June 8, 2023 6:14 AM PDT, https://www.reuters.com/world/india/india-monsoon-onsets-over-kerala-after-delay-week-2023-06-08/, Access Date: June 08, 2023

[132] Moore, J. (June 8, 2023). Expected to be moderate-to-strong by late fall/early winter, https://www.weather.gov/news/230706-ElNino, Access Date: June 08, 2023

[133] Diamond, A., Tropp, D., Barham, J., Muldoon, M. F., Kiraly, S., Cantrell, P. (May 2014). Food Value Chains: Creating Shared Value to Enhance Marketing Success. U.S. Dept. of Agriculture, Agricultural Marketing Service. Web. http://dx.doi.org/10.9752/MS141.05-2014, Access Date: December 02, 2022

[134] Subba Rao, G. V. R. Banana farmers reaping it rich, March 13, 2021 09:55 am IST, https://www.thehindu.com/news/national/andhra-pradesh/banana-farmers-reaping-it-rich/article34055852.ece, Access Date: November 14, 2022

[135] Australian Almond Board. (August 2021). Australian Almonds – 2020–21 Insights, https://australianalmonds.com.au/wp-content/uploads/2021/08/2021_Almond_Insights_soft_copy.pdf, Access Date: November 24, 2022

[136] RRHHpress. (2013). In Spain, the nuts and snacks sector employs 6,100 workers distributed in 470 companies, http://jimspanishalmonds.com/el-sector-de-frutos-secos-y-snacks-emplea-en-espana-a-6-100-trabajadores-distribuidos-en-470-empresas/, Access Date: November 24, 2022

[137] Almond Board of California. (2016). The Economic Impacts of the California Almond Industry, https://aic.ucdavis.edu/almonds/Economic%20Impacts%20of%20California%20Almond%20Industry_Full%20Report_FinalPDF_v2.pdf, Access Date: November 22, 2022

[138] Asian Development Bank (Rana, A. S.). Nepal: Support for Value Chain Development Under the Nepal Agriculture Development Strategy, https://www.adb.org/projects/48218-007/main#project-pds, Access Date: December 02, 2022

[139] Executive Office of the President of the United States. Climate Change: The Fiscal Risks Facing The Federal Government – A Preliminary Assessment, November 2016, https://obamawhitehouse.archives.gov/sites/default/files/omb/reports/omb_climate_change_fiscal_risk_report.pdf, Access Date: July 02, 2023

[140] Emsden, C. Production growth to slow in step with population, while geopolitical tensions, climate change, animal and plant diseases and price volatility of critical farming inputs pose long-term uncertainty, 06/07/2023, https://www.oecd.org/newsroom/production-growth-to-slow-in-step-with-population-while-geopolitical-tensions-climate-change-animal-and-plant-diseases-and-price-volatility-of-critical-farming-inputs-pose-long-term-uncertainty.htm, Access date; July 10, 2023

[141] Deressa, T., Hassan, R., Ringler, C. (2011). Perception of and adaptation to climate change by farmers in the Nile basin of Ethiopia. The Journal of Agricultural Science, 149(1), 23–31. doi: 10.1017/S0021859610000687.

[142] Hassan, R. M., Nhemachena, C. (2008). Determinants of African farmers' strategies for adapting to climate change. Multinomial Choice Analysis, 02(1), 22. https://econpapers.repec.org/article/agsafjare/56969.htm. Access Date:July 08, 2023.

[143] Alam, M. M., Toriman, M. E. B., Siwar, C., Molla, R. I., Talib, B. (2011). The Impacts of Agricultural Supports for Climate Change Adaptation: Farm Level Assessment Study on Paddy Farmers. American Journal of Environmental Sciences, 7(2), 178–182. https://doi.org/10.3844/ajessp.2011.178.182.

[144] Chaukhande, P., Kharumnuid, P., Sanjay Rawal, V. K. D., Kumar, S., Kumar, A., Sharma, J., Rama Rao, C. A., Chakrabarti, S. K. Perceptions of Potato Growers on Climate Change And Their Adaptation Strategies: Evidence of Field Level Study In Agra District of Uttar Pradesh, 2021-02-11 – Updated on 2022-10-06, https://epubs.icar.org.in/index.php/PotatoJ/article/view/101064, Access Date: July 08, 2023

[145] Reyes, J., Elias, E. (2019). Spatio-temporal variation of crop loss in the United States from 2001 to 2016. Environmental Research Letters, 14(7), https://doi.org/10.1088/1748-9326/ab1ac9.

[146] Shields, D. (2015). Federal Crop Insurance: Background (No. R40532), Washington, DC: Congressional Research Service.

[147] USDA. FCIC/RMA's Fiscal Years 2022 and 2021 Financial Statements – AUDIT REPORT 50401-0020-11, November 2022, https://www.oversight.gov/sites/default/files/oig-reports/USDAOIG/05401-0014-11508FOIA.pdf, Access Date: July 02, 2023

[148] Crane-Droesch, A., Marshall, E., Rosch, S., Wallander, S. Climate Change Projected To Increase Cost of the Federal Crop Insurance Program due to Greater Insured Value and Yield Variability, Last updated: Wednesday, May 03, 2023, https://www.ers.usda.gov/topics/farm-practices-management/risk-management/crop-insurance-at-a-glance/#fcipcost, Access Date: July 01, 2023

[149] Kassel, K. Farming and Farm Income, Last updated: Tuesday, March 14, 2023, https://www.nass.usda.gov/Publications/Highlights/2021/census-typology.pdf, Access Date: July 03, 2023

[150] Munch, D. (NOV, 30 2022). Specialty Crop Considerations for the Farm Bill. https://www.fb.org/market-intel/specialty-crop-considerations-for-the-farm-bill#, Access Date: June 30, 2023.

[151] Reyes, J. J., Elias, E. Spatio-temporal variation of crop loss in the United States from 2001 to 2016 – Supplementary Material, https://cfn-live-content-bucket-iop-org.s3.amazonaws.com/journals/1748-9326/14/7/074017/revision2/erlab1ac9f2_hr.jpg?AWSAccessKeyId=AKIAYDKQL6LTV7YY2HIK&Expires=1689174162&Signature=93vuRCXowGTw6KGA74%2B%2BSE04z6E%3D, Access Date: July 05, 2023

[152] Maples, W. E., Coble, K. H. (August 18, 2022). Crop Insurance Loss Ratio Trends Over Time. Southern Ag Today, 2(34.4), Permalink, Access Date: June 30, 2023.

[153] Coble, K. H., Knight, T. O., Goodwin, B. K., Miller, M. F., Rejesus, R. M., Duffield, G. (2010). A comprehensive review of the rma aph and combo rating methodology: Final report. Prepared by Sumaria systems for the risk Management agency.

[154] Olen, B., Auld, S. Oregon State University, Farming: Weather is Leading Cause of U.S. Crop Loss – How Do You Assess the Risk? January 25, 2019, https://www.agfax.com/2019/01/25/farming-weather-is-leading-cause-of-u-s-crop-loss-how-do-you-assess-the-risk/, Access Date: June 30, 2023

[155] Tsiboe, F., Turner, D. Federal Crop Insurance Program cost, Last updated: Wednesday, May 03, 2023, https://www.ers.usda.gov/topics/farm-practices-management/risk-management/crop-insurance-at-a-glance/#fcipcost, Access Date: July 01, 2023

[156] Hooker, B., Wyant, S. Crop insurance losses from water shortages continue to mount, 10/13/21 7:25 AM, https://www.agri-pulse.com/articles/16620-crop-insurance-losses-from-water-shortages-continue-to-mount, Access Date: July 02, 2023

[157] Bjerga, A., Cohen, D., Hoffman, C. California Almonds Are Back After Four Years of Brutal Drought, March 14, 2018, https://www.bloomberg.com/graphics/2018-thirst-for-almonds/, Access Date: July 02, 2023

[158] Nidever, S. Staff Reporter, Rain and cold could impact almonds

[159] Lucrative industry weathering obstacles in 2015, Feb 25, 2015 Updated May 18, 2021, https://hanfordsentinel.com/news/local/rain-and-cold-could-impact-almonds/article_519983bd-1788-5921-a70c-235a2edd5f99.html, Access Date: July 02, 2023

[160] Crane-Droesch, A., Marshall, E. Climate change projected to increase cost of the Federal Crop Insurance Program, Last updated: Wednesday, August 07, 2019, https://www.ers.usda.gov/data-products/chart-gallery/gallery/chart-detail/?chartId=93634, Access Date: July 02, 2023

[161] Meinshausen, M., Nicholls, Z. R. J., Lewis, J., Gidden, M. J., Vogel, E., Freund, M., Beyerle, U., Gessner, C., Nauels, A., Bauer, N., Canadell, J. G., Daniel, J. S., John, A., Krummel, P. B., Luderer, G., Meinshausen, N., Montzka, S. A., Rayner, P. J., Reimann, S., Smith, S. J., van den Berg, M., Velders, G. J. M., Vollmer, M. K., Wang, R. H. J. (2020). The shared socio-economic pathway (SSP) greenhouse gas

concentrations and their extensions to 2500, Geosci. Model Development, 13, 3571–3605. https://doi.org/10.5194/gmd-13-3571-2020,, Access Date, July 02, 2023.

[162] Western Fire Chiefs Association History of California Wildfires, November 17 2022, https://wfca.com/articles/history-of-california-wildfires/#, Access Date: July 02, 2023

[163] USDA, Crop Insurance Program Models, 1995, https://www.rma.usda.gov/ftp/publications/handbooks/CROPMODL.PDF, Access Date: July 01, 2023

[164] Pulakkat, H. Adaptations by India towards climate change likely to cost as much as $360 billion a year by 2030, Last Updated: Dec 02, 2015, 11:45 AM IST, https://economictimes.indiatimes.com/adaptations-by-india-towards-climate-change-likely-to-cost-as-much-as-360-billion-a-year-by-2030/articleshow/49990031.cms?from=mdr, Access Date: June 07, 2023

[165] Calderwood, L., Yarborough, D. E. Maine Wild Blueberry Production Statistics, Updated May 2023, https://extension.umaine.edu/blueberries/factsheets/statistics-2/crop-production-statistics-2019/, Access Date: June 25, 2023

[166] Whittle, P. (September 4, 2018). With industry in decline, Maine wild blueberries sing the blues, https://www.boston.com/food/local-news/2018/09/04/with-industry-in-decline-maine-wild-blueberries-sing-the-blues/, Access Date: June 25, 2023

[167] Romero, E. D. New Map Exposes Critical Gaps in Bay Area's Readiness for Sea Level Rise, May 2023, https://www.kqed.org/science/1982800/new-map-exposes-critical-gaps-in-bay-areas-readiness-for-sea-level-rise, Access Date: May 26, 2023

[168] Weir, B. Thousands of acres are underwater in California, and the flood could triple in size this summer, Updated 9:47 AM EDT, Sat April 15, 2023, https://www.cnn.com/2023/04/15/us/tulare-lake-california-flood-climate/index.html, Access Date: June 22, 2023

[169] Baker, D. R., Chipman, K., Chediak, M., Sullivan, B. K. Battered California faces billions in storm damage to crops, homes and roads, PUBLISHED: March 23, 2023 at 11:27 a.m. | UPDATED: March 23, 2023 at 11:39 a.m., https://www.mercurynews.com/2023/03/23/battered-california-faces-billions-in-storm-damage-to-crops-homes-and-roads/, Access Date: June 22, 2023

[170] ICIMOD. (2023). Water, Ice, Society, and Ecosystems in the Hindu Kush Himalaya: An Outlook, Wester, P., Chaudhary, S., Chettri, N., Jackson, M., Maharjan, A., Nepal, S., Steiner, J. F. eds., ICIMOD, https://doi.org/10.53055/ICIMOD.1028.

[171] Mahul, O., Stutley, C. J. (2010). Government Support to Agricultural Insurance: Challenges and Options for Developing Countries, © World Bank, http://hdl.handle.net/10986/2432, License: CC BY 3.0 IGO.

[172] Baskaran, G., Maher, B. Agricultural insurance: The antidote to many economic illnesses, May 26, 2021, https://www.brookings.edu/articles/agricultural-insurance-the-antidote-to-many-economic-illnesses/, Access Date:July 08, 2023

[173] Alam, M. M., Toriman, M. E. B., Siwar, C., Molla, R. I., Talib, B. (2011). The Impacts of Agricultural Supports for Climate Change Adaptation: Farm Level Assessment Study on Paddy Farmers. American Journal of Environmental Sciences, 7(2), 178–182. https://doi.org/10.3844/ajessp.2011.178.182.

[174] Biswal, D., Bahinipati, C. S. (2022). Why are farmers not insuring crops against risks in India? A review. Progress in Disaster Science, 15, 100241. ISSN, 2590–0617, https://doi.org/10.1016/j.pdisas.2022.100241,, Access Date:July 09, 2023.

[175] Gulati, A., Wardhan, H., Sharma, P. 2022. Tomato, Onion and Potato (TOP) Value Chains. In: Gulati, A., Ganguly, K., Wardhan, H. (eds). Agricultural Value Chains in India. India Studies in Business and Economics, Springer, Singapore. https://doi.org/10.1007/978-981-33-4268-2_3.

[176] L. C.Corbett, T. (1905). https://naldc.nal.usda.gov/download/ORC00000144/pdf, Access Date: July 10, 2023.

[177] U.S. Bureau of Labor Statistics, Consumer Price Index for All Urban Consumers: All Items in U.S. City Average [CPIAUCSL], retrieved from FRED, Federal Reserve Bank of St. Louis; https://fred.stlouisfed.org/series/CPIAUCSL, July 9, 2023.

[178] Lawrence, K. The cost of tomato products has doubled, Publication date: Tue 22 Nov 2022, https://www.freshplaza.com/asia/article/9480184/the-cost-of-tomato-products-has-doubled/, Access date; July 10, 2023

[179] Bureau of Labor Statistics, U.S. Department of Labor. The Economics Daily, Steep increase in energy prices again in 2000 at https://www.bls.gov/opub/ted/2001/may/wk3/art04.htm (visited July 10, 2023).

[180] Wells, J. Natural Gas Factors Affecting Prices and Potential Impacts on Consumers, Monday, February 13, 2006, https://www.gao.gov/assets/gao-06-420t.pdf, Access date; July 9, 2023.

[181] Lawrence, K. (2023). Average cost of wholesale U.S. natural gas in 2022 highest since 2008. January, 9, https://www.eia.gov/todayinenergy/detail.php?id=55119, Access date; July 10, 2023.

[182] Webb, R., Bruce, W. M. Redesigning the Tomato for Mechanized Production, https://naldc.nal.usda.gov/download/IND43895151/PDF, Access date; July 10, 2023

[183] Edwards, W. Farm Machinery Selection, Updated January, 2017 File A3-28, https://www.extension.iastate.edu/agdm/crops/html/a3-28.html, Access date; July 10, 2023

[184] Brownlee, J. Time Series Forecasting With Prophet in Python, August 26 2020, https://machinelearningmastery.com/time-series-forecasting-with-prophet-in-python/, Access date; July 10, 2023

[185] Vuppalapati, C. (2023). Artificial Intelligence and Advanced Analytics for Food Security 1st edition, Publisher: CRC Press, July 17, ISBN-13: 978-1032346182.

[186] Ferguson, L., Polito, V., Kallsen, C. The Pistachio Tree; Botany and Physiology and Factors That Affect Yield, October 03, 2022, https://ucanr.edu/sites/fruitandnut/files/73683.pdf, Access Date: May 17, 2023

[187] Ferguson, L. Botany and Physiology of the Pistachio Tree, January 03, 2013, https://www.pgai.com.au/wp-content/uploads/2013/01/MIldura_Botany-and-Physiology-Nov.pdf, Access Date: May 17, 2023

[188] Eddy, D. How Much Is the Pistachio Industry's Economic Impact? Try $10,000 a Minute, June 15 2021, https://www.growingproduce.com/nuts/what-is-the-pistachio-industrys-economic-impact-try-10000-a-minute/, Access Date: July 03, 2023

[189] Mike Pomranz. Why the Government Is Buying $40M Worth of Pistachios, Published on May 18, 2021, https://www.foodandwine.com/news/usda-buys-pistachios-seafood-surplus, Access Date: May 05, 2023

[190] Laguaite, M. Health Benefits of Pistachios, August 08, 2022, https://www.webmd.com/food-recipes/benefits-pistachios, Access Date: May 05, 2023

[191] Nosowitz, D. Why is the USDA Buying $40 Million Worth of Pistachios? May 17, 2021, https://modernfarmer.com/2021/05/why-is-the-usda-buying-40-million-worth-of-pistachios/, Access Date: May 05, 2023

[192] Thomas, Z. The US and Iranian battle over the pistachio nut trade, https://www.bbc.com/news/business-41640066, Access Date: May 08, 2023

[193] Connor, W. Global Pistachio Production Hits New Records in 2020/21, February 28, 2021, https://www.producereport.com/article/global-pistachio-production-hits-new-records-202021, Access Date: May 05, 2023

[194] Yoo, S. Iranian Pistachios Face Tough Competition from the US, Oct 23 2019, https://www.tridge.com/stories/iranian-pistachios-face-tough-competition-from-the-us, Access Date: May 08, 2023

[195] Pomranz, M. Why the Government Is Buying $40M Worth of Pistachios, Published on May 18, 2021, https://www.foodandwine.com/news/usda-buys-pistachios-seafood-surplus, Access Date: May 05, 2023

[196] Nosowitz, D. Why is the USDA Buying $40 Million Worth of Pistachios? MAY 17, 2021, https://modernfarmer.com/2021/05/why-is-the-usda-buying-40-million-worth-of-pistachios/, Access Date: May 05, 2023

[197] Parsons, C. 2019 'Off' Year Pistachio Crop Looks Above Average, September 11, 2019, https://www.wcngg.com/2019/09/11/2019-off-year-pistachio-crop-looks-above-average/, Access Date: May 05, 2023

[198] Jolly, D., Norris, K. (1992). To anticipate the future, models simulate US. pistachio prices. California Agriculture, 46(3), 14–16.

[199] Zaleski, A. 6 incredible facts about the pistachio: A super nut with a rich history, April 15 2021. https://www.visaliatimesdelta.com/story/sponsor-story/setton-farms/2021/04/15/6-incredible-facts-pistachio-super-nut-rich-history/7212106002/, Access Date: May 15, 2023

[200] Solo, D. American Pistachio Industry: Born from a Single Iranian Seed, 2020, https://ratinkhosh.com/american-pistachios/, Access Date: May 05, 2023

[201] Geisseler, D., Horwath, W. R. Pistachio Production in California, June 2016, https://apps1.cdfa.ca.gov/FertilizerResearch/docs/Pistachio_Production_CA.pdf, Access Date: May 14, 2023

[202] Cone, M. Sept. 21, 2019, In a Race Against Warming, Growers Try to Outsmart Climate Change, https://www.nytimes.com/2019/09/21/climate/agriculture-climate-change.html?auth=login-google1tap&login=google1tap

[203] Duginski, P., What causes dangerous tule fog in California's Central Valley, and why is it becoming less common? Jan. 11, 2020 3:18 PM PT, https://www.latimes.com/california/story/2020-01-11/what-causes-dangerous-tule-fog-in-californias-central-valley-and-why-is-it-becoming-less-common, Access Date: May 10, 2023

[204] Perez, A., Ferreira, G. (2016). Fruit and Tree Nuts Outlook. Sept, 30, https://www.ers.usda.gov/webdocs/outlooks/79884/fts-363.pdf?v=9421, Access Date: May 08, 2023.

[205] Lawrimore, J. H., Ray, R., Applequist, S., Korzeniewski, B., Menne, M. J. (2016). Global Summary of the Month (GSOM), Version 1.0.3 [Indicate Subset Used], NOAA National Centers for Environmental Information, https://doi.org/10.7289/V5QV3JJ5, Access Date July 06, 2023.

[206] Erdogan, C., Conlon, M. (October 03, 2022). Report Name: Tree Nuts Annual, https://apps.fas.usda.gov/newgainapi/api/Report/DownloadReportByFileName?fileName=Tree%20Nuts%20Annual_Ankara_Turkey_TU2022-0041.pdf, Access Date: May 16, 2023

[207] Solo, D. Turkish Pistachios Industry: A slow rising star, 2019, https://ratinkhosh.com/turkish-pistachios, Access Date: May 15, 2023

[208] Aşkan, E. (2019). Economic analysis and marketing margin of pistachios in Turkey. Bulletin of the National Research Centre, 43, 177. https://doi.org/10.1186/s42269-019-0216-5,, Access Date: May 15, 2023.

[209] Talaie, A., Panahi, B. (2002). Pistachio Growing In Iran. Acta Horticulturae, 591, 133–138. 10.17660/ActaHortic.2002.591.17. https://doi.org/10.17660/ActaHortic.2002.591.17.

[210] Kallsen, C. E., Parfitt, D. E. (2017). Famoso', a New Male Pistachio Cultivar to Replace 'Peters. HortScience, 52(12), 1829–1831. Retrieved May 15. 2023. from. https://doi.org/10.21273/HORTSCI12218-17.

[211] Wilson, A., Rezendes, A., Gonzales, G. 2023. Growing And Harvesting American Pistachios, https://americanpistachios.org/growing-and-harvesting, Access Date: May 14, 2023

[212] Geisel, P., Beede, R. (2004). Pistachio: Calendar of Operations for Home Gardeners, https://anrcatalog.ucanr.edu/Details.aspx?itemNo=8147, Access Date: May 14, 2023

[213] Farms, K. (2023). "Growing & Harvesting", https://keenanfarms.com/about-our-pistachios/growing-harvesting, Access Date: May 14, 2023

[214] Bland, A., Oh, N. Why California's Pistachio Trees Are Shooting Blanks, September 11, 20154:28 PM ET, https://www.npr.org/sections/thesalt/2015/09/11/439509278/oh-nuts-why-california-s-pistachio-trees-are-shooting-blanks, Access Date: July 03, 2023

[215] Ferguson, L., Haviland, D. R. (December 2, 2016). Pistachio Production Manual, Publisher: Univ of California – Agriculture & Natural Resources, ISBN-13: 978-1601078773

[216] Kallsen, C. (2008). Pistachio Climate & Cultivars, https://fruitsandnuts.ucdavis.edu/climate-cultivars, Access Date: May 15, 20

[217] Rosenstock, T. S., Rosa, U. A., Plant, R. E., Brown, P. H. (2010). A reevaluation of alternate bearing in pistachio. Scientia Horticulturae, 124, 149–152. Access Date: May 14, 2023.

[218] Farms, P. Growing and Harvesting American Pistachios, Last update: March 31 2022, https://americanpistachios.org/growing-and-harvesting, Access Date: July 03, 2023

[219] Kallsen, C. E., Parfitt, D. E., Maranto, J., Holtz, B. A. (2009). New pistachio varieties show promise for California cultivation. California Agriculture, 63(1), 18–23. Access Date: May 14, 2023.

[220] Der AUDITOR. Pistachios: Summer heat takes its toll, September 23, 2021 at 9:23 AM, https://www.mundus-agri.eu/news/pistachios-summer-heat-takes-toll.n26999.html, Access date; July 14, 2023

[221] Jakobs, J. W. "March Miracle 1991" – Where were you and what do you remember? March 21 2018, https://abc30.com/weather/march-miracle-1991–where-were-you-and-what-do-you-remember/3242859/, Access Date: May 14, 2023

[222] Shields, D. (2015). Federal Crop Insurance: Background No. R40532, Washington, DC: Congressional Research Service).

[223] Reyes, J., Elias, E. (2019). Spatio-temporal variation of crop loss in the United States from 2001 to 2016. Environmental Research Letters, 14(7), https://doi.org/10.1088/1748-9326/ab1ac9.

[224] Romero, E. D. January 25, 20172:38 PM ET, If These Trees Don't Get Time To Chill, Farmers Will Be Out On A Limb, Access Date: May 01, 2023 https://www.npr.org/sections/thesalt/2017/01/25/510571835/if-these-trees-dont-get-time-to-chill-farmers-will-be-out-on-a-limb

[225] Shahbandeh, M. Global harvested area of pistachios 2021, by leading country, Jan 23 2023, https://www.statista.com/statistics/960737/harvested-area-of-pistachios-by-leading-country-worldwide/, Access Date: July 06, 2023

[226] Der Auditor. Pistachios: Production in Turkey declines by 70%, November 18, 2021 at 11:38 AM, https://www.mundus-agri.eu/news/pistachios-production-turkey-declines-70.n27427.html, Access Date: July 06, 2023

[227] Kaska, N. (1995). Pistachio Nut Growing in Turkey. Acta Horticulturae, 419, 161–164. 10.17660/ActaHortic.1995.419.26,. https://doi.org/10.17660/ActaHortic.1995.419.26. Access Date: May 15. 2023.

[228] Ferguson, L., Polito, V., Kallsen, C. The Pistachio Tree; Botany and Physiology and Factors That Affect Yield, October 03, 2022, https://ucanr.edu/sites/fruitandnut/files/73683.pdf, Access Date: May 17, 2023

[229] Ferguson, L. Botany and Physiology of the Pistachio Tree, January 03, 2013, https://www.pgai.com.au/wp-content/uploads/2013/01/MIldura_Botany-and-Physiology-Nov.pdf, Access Date: May 17, 2023

[230] Laguaite, M. Health Benefits of Pistachios, August 08, 2022, https://www.webmd.com/food-recipes/benefits-pistachios, Access Date: May 05, 2023

[231] Nosowitz, D. Why is the USDA Buying $40 Million Worth of Pistachios? May 17, 2021, https://modernfarmer.com/2021/05/why-is-the-usda-buying-40-million-worth-of-pistachios/, Access Date: May 05, 2023

[232] Chaukhande, P., Kharumnuid, P., Rawal, S., Dua, V. K., Kumar, S., Kumar, A., Sharma, J., Rama Rao, C. A., Chakrabarti, S. K. Perceptions of Potato Growers on Climate Change and Their Adaptation Strategies: Evidence of Field Level Study In Agra District of Uttar Pradesh, 2021-02-11 – Updated on 2022-10-06, https://epubs.icar.org.in/index.php/PotatoJ/article/view/101064, Access Date: July 08, 2023

[233] Munch, D. (NOV, 30 2022). Specialty Crop Considerations for the Farm Bill. https://www.fb.org/market-intel/specialty-crop-considerations-for-the-farm-bill#, Access Date: June 30, 2023.

[234] Reyes, J., Elias, E. (2019). Spatio-temporal variation of crop loss in the United States from 2001 to 2016. Environmental Research Letters, 14(7), https://doi.org/10.1088/1748-9326/ab1ac9,. Access Date: July 02, 2023.

[235] Parker, L. E., McElrone, A. J., Ostoja, S. M., Forrestel, E. J. (2020 Jun). Extreme heat effects on perennial crops and strategies for sustaining future production. Plant Science, 295, 110397. 10.1016/j.plantsci.2019.110397 Epub 2020 Jan 18. PMID: 32534613, Access Date: July 02, 2023.

[236] Hooker, B., Wyant, S. Crop insurance losses from water shortages continue to mount. 10/13/21 7:25 AM, https://www.agri-pulse.com/articles/16620-crop-insurance-losses-from-water-shortages-continue-to-mount, Access Date, July 02 2023.

[237] USDA, Crop Insurance Program Models. 1995, https://www.rma.usda.gov/ftp/publications/handbooks/CROPMODL.PDF, Access Date: July 01, 2023

[238] Romero, E. D. Collab. Oh, Nuts! U.S. Pistachio Growers Worry About Competition From Iran, February 19, 201612:56 PM ET, https://www.npr.org/sections/thesalt/2016/02/19/467266572/oh-nuts-u-s-pistachio-growers-worry-about-competition-from-iran, Access Date: May 20, 2023

[239] Bland, A. Oh, Nuts! Why California's Pistachio Trees Are Shooting Blanks, September 11, 20154:28 PM ET, https://www.npr.org/sections/thesalt/2015/09/11/439509278/oh-nuts-why-california-s-pistachio-trees-are-shooting-blanks, Access Date: July 03, 2023

[240] Ferguson, L., Haviland, D. R. Pistachio Production Manual. Publisher: Univ of California – Agriculture & Natural Resources, December 2, 2016 ISBN-13: 978-1601078773.

[241] Farms, P. GROWING AND HARVESTING AMERICAN PISTACHIOS, Last update: March 31 2022, https://americanpistachios.org/growing-and-harvesting, Access Date: July 03, 2023

[242] Greenaway, T. Eight foods you're about to lose due to climate change Wed 29 Oct 2014 09.00 EDT, https://www.theguardian.com/vital-signs/2014/oct/29/diet-climate-maple-syrup-coffee-global-warming, Access Date: May 21, 2023

[243] Artificial Intelligence and Heuristics for Enhanced Food Security by Chandrasekar Vuppalapati. Publisher: Springer; 1st ed. 2022 edition (September 17, 2022), ISBN-13: 978-3031087424

[244] USDA. Climate Vulnerabilities to California Specialty Crops, 2023, https://www.climatehubs.usda.gov/hubs/california/topic/climate-vulnerabilities-california-specialty-crops, Access Date: May 21, 2023

[245] Kallsen, C. Fall Juvenile Pistachio Freeze Damage, April 2017, https://cekern.ucanr.edu/files/261139.pdf, Access Date: May 21, 2023

[246] Greenaway, T. Eight foods you're about to lose due to climate change, Wed 29 Oct 2014 09.00 EDT, https://www.theguardian.com/vital-signs/2014/oct/29/diet-climate-maple-syrup-coffee-global-warming, Access Date: May 21, 2023

[247] Specialty Crops for Climate Change Adaptation. (2023). Strategies for Enhanced Food Security by Using Machine Learning and Artificial Intelligence (STEAM-H: . . . Agriculture, Mathematics & Health) 1st Ed, Edition, Chandrasekar Vuppalapati (Author), Publisher: Springer, 1st ed. 2023 edition (October 24, 2023)ISBN-13: 978-3031383984.

[248] Cone, M. (Sept. 21, 2019), In a Race Against Warming, Growers Try to Outsmart Climate Change, https://www.nytimes.com/2019/09/21/climate/agriculture-climate-change.html?auth=login-google1tap&login=google1tap

[249] Wheeler, T., Von Braun, J. (2013). Climate Change Impacts on Global Food Security. Science, 341, 508–513. doi: 10.1126/science.1239402.

[250] BBC. (May 07, 2023). Climate change: Vietnam records highest-ever temperature of 44.1C, https://www.bbc.com/news/world-asia-65518528, Access Date: May 08, 2023

[251] Assessing Policy Effectiveness using AI and Language Models: Applications for Economic and Social Sustainability. (2024th edition 2024). Chandrasekar Vuppalapati, Publisher: Springer, May 31, ISBN-13: 978-3031560965.

[252] Ferguson, L., Polito, V., Kallsen, C. (October 03, 2022). The Pistachio Tree; Botany and Physiology and Factors That Affect Yield, https://ucanr.edu/sites/fruitandnut/files/73683.pdf, Access Date: May 17, 2023
[253] Ferguson, L. Botany and Physiology of the Pistachio Tree, January 03, 2013, https://www.pgai.com.au/wp-content/uploads/2013/01/MIldura_Botany-and-Physiology-Nov.pdf, Access Date: May 17, 2023
[254] Laguaite, M. Health Benefits of Pistachios, August 08, 2022, https://www.webmd.com/food-recipes/benefits-pistachios, Access Date: May 05, 2023
[255] Nosowitz, D. Why is the USDA Buying $40 Million Worth of Pistachios? MAY 17, 2021, https://modernfarmer.com/2021/05/why-is-the-usda-buying-40-million-worth-of-pistachios/, Access Date: May 05, 2023
[256] Thomas, Z. The US and Iranian battle over the pistachio nut trade, https://www.bbc.com/news/business-41640066, Access Date: May 08, 2023
[257] Connor, W. Global Pistachio Production Hits New Records in 2020/21, February 28, 2021, https://www.producereport.com/article/global-pistachio-production-hits-new-records-202021, Access Date: May 05, 2023
[258] Yoo, S. Iranian Pistachios Face Tough Competition from the US, Oct 23 2019, https://www.tridge.com/stories/iranian-pistachios-face-tough-competition-from-the-us, Access Date: May 08, 2023
[259] Connor, W. Global Pistachio Production Hits New Records in 2020/21, February 28, 2021, https://www.producereport.com/article/global-pistachio-production-hits-new-records-202021, Access Date: May 05, 2023
[260] Laguaite, M. Health Benefits of Pistachios, August 08, 2022, https://www.webmd.com/food-recipes/benefits-pistachios, Access Date: May 05, 2023
[261] Mike Pomranz, Why the Government Is Buying $40M Worth of Pistachios, Published on May 18, 2021, https://www.foodandwine.com/news/usda-buys-pistachios-seafood-surplus, Access Date: May 05, 2023
[262] Parsons, C. 2019 'Off' Year Pistachio Crop Looks Above Average, September 11, 2019, https://www.wcngg.com/2019/09/11/2019-off-year-pistachio-crop-looks-above-average/, Access Date: May 05, 2023
[263] Klonsky, K., Blank, S. C. Economic Considerations In Pistachio Production, 1981, https://ucanr.edu/sites/fruitandnut/files/73681.pdf, Access Date: May 18, 2023
[264] Karli, B., Cakmakli, M. (2001). A Study on the Economic Analysis of Pistachio Farms in San Liurfa Province. In: Ak, B. E. (ed). XI GREMPA Seminar on Pistachios and Almonds, Zaragoza: CIHEAM, 289–294 (Cah iers Option s Méditerran éen n es; n . 56).
[265] California Department of Food and Agriculture. Pistachios bring more than $5 billion in economic impact – From Western Farm Press, April 16 2021, https://plantingseedsblog.cdfa.ca.gov/wordpress/?p=22650, Access Date: May 08, 2023
[266] Fitchette, T. Pistachios infuse over $5 billion in economic activity, April 16 2021, https://www.farmprogress.com/tree-nuts/pistachios-infuse-over-5-billion-in-economic-activity, Access Date: May 08, 2023
[267] Hirigoyen, J. California Pistachio Growers and Processors Create $5.2 Billion Impact on State's Economy, Wednesday, March 31, 2021, https://americanpistachios.org/about-us/pistachio-power-unshelled/press-releases/california-economic-impact, Access Date: May 15, 2023
[268] Tootelian, D. H., Ph.D., The Economic Impact of Pistachio Growing And Processing In The State Of California, February 2021, https://americanpistachios.org/sites/default/files/2021-03/APG%20ECONOMIC%20IMPACT%20REPORT%20FOR%20CALIFORNIA%2002-26-2021%20%20Final.pdf, Access Date: May 15, 2023

[269] Goodhue, R. E., Martin, P. L., Simon, L. K. Chapter 7. California's Fruits and Tree Nuts, 2020, https://s.giannini.ucop.edu/uploads/pub/2021/01/21/chapter_7_fruits__nuts_2020.pdf, Access Date: May 31, 2023

[270] Eddy, D. How Much Is the Pistachio Industry's Economic Impact? Try $10,000 a Minute, June 15 2021, https://www.growingproduce.com/nuts/what-is-the-pistachio-industrys-economic-impact-try-10000-a-minute/, Access Date: July 03, 2023

[271] Erdogan, C., Conlon, M. Report Name: Tree Nuts Annual, September 10 2021, https://apps.fas.usda.gov/newgainapi/api/Report/DownloadReportByFileName?fileName=Tree%20Nuts%20Annual_Ankara_Turkey_09-15-2021.pdf, Access Date: May 15, 2023

[272] Odası, Z. M. Antepfıstığı Raporu 2015 2016. https://www.zmo.org.tr/genel/bizden_detay.php?kod=25199&tipi=38&sube=0 (accessed May 15, 2023).

[273] Akhavan, A., Gonçalves, P. Managing the trade-off between groundwater resources and large-scale agriculture: The case of pistachio production in Iran, 29 September 2021, https://doi.org/10.1002/sdr.1689, Access Date: May 19, 2023

[274] Talaie, A., Panahi, B. (2002). Pistachio Growing In Iran. Acta Horticulturae, 591, 133–138. 10.17660/ActaHortic.2002.591.17. https://doi.org/10.17660/ActaHortic.2002.591.17.

[275] Thomas, Z. The US and Iranian battle over the pistachio nut trade, https://www.bbc.com/news/business-41640066, Access Date: May 08, 2023

[276] Jolly, D., Norris, K. (1992). To anticipate the future, models simulate US. pistachio prices. California Agriculture, 46(3), 14–16.

[277] Romero, E. D., Oh, N. U.S. Pistachio Growers Worry About Competition From Iran, February 19, 201612:56 PM ET, https://www.npr.org/sections/thesalt/2016/02/19/467266572/oh-nuts-u-s-pistachio-growers-worry-about-competition-from-iran, Access Date: May 20, 2023

[278] Tolomeo, V., Rutz, J. California Agricultural Statistics 2004, October 2005 – Revised January 2006, https://www.nass.usda.gov/Statistics_by_State/California/Publications/Annual_Statistical_Reviews/2004/2004cas-all.pdf, Access Date: May 31, 2023

[279] Peters, N. Turkey restricts tomato exports to keep domestic prices low,Publication date: Mon 6 Mar 2023, https://www.hortidaily.com/article/9508958/turkey-restricts-tomato-exports-to-keep-domestic-prices-low/, Access Date: June 01, 202

[280] Assessing Policy Effectiveness Using AI and Language Models. (May 31 2024). Applications for Economic and Social Sustainability, Chandrasekar Vuppalapati (2024th, edition), Publisher : Springer, ISBN-13: 978-3031560965.

[281] Zaraska, M. The tomatoes at the forefront of a food revolution, 8th December 2021, https://www.bbc.com/future/article/20211207-the-tomatoes-at-the-forefront-of-a-food-revolution, Access Date: May 29, 2023

[282] FAO (2023). Tomato, https://www.fao.org/land-water/databases-and-software/crop-information/tomato/en/#c236455, Access Date: May 30, 2023

[283] Chipman, K. Spaghetti Sauce Is Under Threat as Water Crisis Slams Tomatoes, Aug. 13, 2022, 5:45 AM, https://news.bloomberglaw.com/environment-and-energy/spaghetti-sauce-is-under-threat-as-water-crisis-slams-tomatoes, Access Date: May 23 2023

[284] Coolong, T., Boyhan, G. E. Commercial Tomato Production Handbook,Published with Full Review on Jan 30, 2017, https://extension.uga.edu/publications/detail.html?number=B1312&title=commercial-tomato-production-handbook, Access Date: May 26, 2023

[285] Dillion, D. Determinante vs Indeterminante Tomatoes, Updated on Apr 14, 2020, https://union.ces.ncsu.edu/2020/04/determinante-vs-indeterminante-tomatoes/, Access Date: May 26, 2023

[286] Guan, Z., Biswas, T., Feng, W. The US Tomato Industry: An Overview of Production and Trade, Publication #FE1027 Date: 4/24/2018, https://edis.ifas.ufl.edu/publication/FE1027, Access Date: May 22 2023

[287] Siqi, J. Why has the US ban on Xinjiang's tomato exports had such limited effect? Published: 8:00am, 9 Oct, 2022, https://www.scmp.com/economy/article/3195195/why-has-us-ban-xinjiangs-tomato-exports-had-such-limited-effect?module=perpetual_scroll_0&pgtype=article&campaign=3195195, Access Date: May 23 2023

[288] Gunes, E. Agribusiness And Contract Farming: The Case of Tomato Production In Turkey, Published: 2007, https://www.ishs.org/ishs-article/758_37, Access Date: May 23 2023

[289] Brownne, B. (Oct 1999). Record tomato harvest may stretch into November, https://www.recordnet.com/story/business/1999/10/16/record-tomato-harvest-may-stretch/50804771007/, Access Date: May 28, 2023

[290] Tomato. A Covert "Gold-Mine" of Recent Times, Date Posted: 2022-08-23 16:54:39, https://tradekaiju.com/blog/view/tomato-a-covert-gold-mine-of-recent-times-11, Access Date: May 28, 2023

[291] Benbrook, C., Promoting Global Food Security One Crop of Tomatoes at a Time, October 23, 2014, https://csanr.wsu.edu/promoting-global-food-security-tomatoes/, Access Date: May 26, 2023

[292] Zaleski, A., 6 incredible facts about the pistachio: A super nut with a rich history, April 15 2021. https://www.visaliatimesdelta.com/story/sponsor-story/setton-farms/2021/04/15/6-incredible-facts-pistachio-super-nut-rich-history/7212106002/, Access Date: May 15, 2023

[293] Adanacioglu, H., Yercan, M., An analysis of tomato prices at wholesale level in Turkey: an application of SARIMA model, September 2012, http://www.custoseagronegocioonline.com.br/numero4v8/Tomato%20english.pdf, Access Date: May 26, 2023

[294] Latner, K., Lei, Z., China,, Peoples Republic of Tomatoes and Products Annual 2006, May 15 2006, https://apps.fas.usda.gov/gainfiles/200605/146187753.pdf, Access Date: May 26, 2023

[295] Dalwai, A. (Production Enhancement through Productivity Gains, December 2017). Report of the Committee for Doubling Farmers. Income –, VIII, https://agricoop.nic.in/Documents/DFI%20Vol-8C.pdf, Access Date: May 29, 2023.

[296] Department of Agriculture – India, Annual Report 2020–2021, 2021, hhttps://agricoop.nic.in/Documents/annual-report-2020-21.pdf, Access Date: May 27, 2023

[297] Amarender Reddy, A. (2018). Price Forecasting of Tomatoes. International Journal of Vegetable Science. doi: 10.1080/19315260.2018.1495674.

[298] Department of Consumer Affairs. Tomato Grand Challenge, June 2023, https://doca.gov.in/gtc/#, Access date; July 14, 2023

[299] Shan, L. Y. India's tomato prices surge over 300%, sparking theft and turmoil, Published Wed, Jul 12 20239:46 PM EDT, https://www.cnbc.com/2023/07/13/indias-tomato-prices-surge-over-300percent-prompting-thieves-and-turmoil.html, Access date; July 13, 2023

[300] FAO. Tomato- production and marketing in Turkey and North Eastern Anatolia Region, https://agris.fao.org/agris-search/search.do?recordID=TR2015000321, Access Date: May 28, 2023

[301] Colvine, S. A partial overview of the Turkish industry, Date Posted: 08/10/2018, https://www.tomatonews.com/en/a-partial-overview-of-the-turkish-industry_2_513.html, Access Date: May 28, 2023

[302] USDA. (May 2007). Vegetables Usual Planting and Harvesting Dates, https://naldc.nal.usda.gov/download/CAT30992961/PDF, Access Date: May 21, 2023

[303] Ndubiwa, M. (2022). Tomato Processors Set to Pay Unprecedented Prices for Raw Tomatoes in 2022. Updated Apr, 29, https://www.tridge.com/stories/tomato-processors-set-to-pay-unprecedented-prices-for-raw-tomatoes-in-2022, Access Date: May 24, 2023.

[304] Davidson, K. (February 06 2023). Record high canning tomato prices reported in California, https://thegrower.org/news/record-high-canning-tomato-prices-reported-california, Access Date: May 24, 2023

[305] Osteen, C. (April 01 2003). Methyl Bromide Phaseout Proceeds: Users Request Exemptions, https://www.ers.usda.gov/amber-waves/2003/april/methyl-bromide-phaseout-proceeds/, Access Date: July 04, 2023

[306] Cline, H. (December 20, 2008). Processing tomato costs to rise in 2009, https://www.farmprogress.com/vegetables/processing-tomato-costs-to-rise-in-2009, Access Date: May 24, 2023

[307] Baskins, S., Bond, J., Minor, T. (March 2019). Unpacking the Growth in Per Capita Availability of Fresh Market Tomatoes, https://www.ers.usda.gov/webdocs/outlooks/92442/vgs-19c-01.pdf?v=8360.4, Access Date: May 22 2023

[308] Estabrook, B. (Author). Tomatoland: How Modern Industrial Agriculture Destroyed Our Most Alluring Fruit Paperback, Publisher: Andrews McMeel Publishing; Reprint edition (April 24, 2012), ISBN-13: 978-1449423452

[309] Talk of the Nation. The Unsavory Story Of Industrially, August 26, 20111:00 PM ET, https://www.npr.org/2011/08/26/139972669/the-unsavory-story-of-industrially-grown-tomatoes, Access date; July 15, 2023

[310] Chanda, S., Bhat, M., Shetty, K. G., Jayachandran, K. (May 2021). Technology, Policy, and Market Adaptation Mechanisms for Sustainable Fresh Produce Industry: The Case of Tomato Production In, Florida, USA, https://www.researchgate.net/publication/351841169_Technology_Policy_and_Market_Adaptation_Mechanisms_for_Sustainable_Fresh_Produce_Industry_The_Case_of_Tomato_Production_in_Florida_USA, Access date; July 15, 2023.

[311] Nair, A. Recommended Tomato Varieties for Commercial Production in Iowa., March 2015, https://store.extension.iastate.edu/Product/hort3024-pdf, Access Date: May 26, 2023

[312] CNBCTV18.com. Severe heatwave hits tomato, mango production; prices surge to over Rs 100 a kilo, May 28, 2022 7:28:03 PM IST (Published), https://www.cnbctv18.com/agriculture/severe-heatwave-hits-tomato-mango-production-prices-surge-to-over-rs-100-a-kilo-13648102.htm, Access Date: May 24, 2023

[313] Toms, L. Record wet winter, planting delays may impact California's tomato crop, UPDATED ON: APRIL 13, 2023 / 4:30 PM / CBS SAN FRANCISCO, https://www.cbsnews.com/sanfrancisco/news/record-wet-winter-planting-delays-california-tomato-crop/, Access Date: May 29, 2023

[314] Keck, A. Evapotranspiration: Watching Over Water Use, Last Updated: Aug 19, 2021, https://www.nasa.gov/feature/evapotranspiration-watching-over-water-use, Access Date: May 30, 2023

[315] Kallsen, C. E., Parfitt, D. E. (2017). Famoso', a New Male Pistachio Cultivar to Replace 'Peters. HortScience, 52(12), 1829–1831. Retrieved May 15, 2023, from, https://doi.org/10.21273/HORTSCI12218-17.

[316] Branthôme, F.-X. The 2022 Tomato News Conference: The 2022 Crop in China, 04/01/2023, https://www.tomatonews.com/en/the-2022-tomato-news-conference-the-2022-crop-in-china_2_1864.html, Access Date: May 25, 2023

[317] Horticulture Statistics Division. (April 2020). Monthly Report Tomato, hhttps://agricoop.nic.in/sites/default/files/Monthly%20Report%20on%20Tomato%20for%20April%2C%202020.pdf, Access Date: May 24, 2024

[318] Jadhav, R., Bhardwaj, M. India monsoon reaches Kerala after longest delay in four years, June 8, 20236:14 AM PDT, https://www.reuters.com/world/india/india-monsoon-onsets-over-kerala-after-delay-week-2023-06-08/, Access Date: June 08, 2023

[319] Marantos, J. 10 secrets to growing the tastiest tomatoes, JUNE 11, 2016 6:30 AM PT, https://www.latimes.com/home/la-hm-0611-tomatoes-20160606-snap-story.html#, Access Date: May 29, 2023

[320] Pittenger, D. R. (ed) (2002). California Master Gardener Handbook [UNABRIDGED] Paperback – January 1, Publisher: Univ of California Agriculture & Natural Resources; Third Printing Used edition, (January 1, 2002), ISBN-13: 978-1879906549.

[321] McClure, J. Garden Notes (GN 154), August 2017, https://sacmg.ucanr.edu/files/164220.pdf, Access Date: May 29, 2023

[322] Cammarano, D., Jamshidi, S., Hoogenboom, G., et al. (2022). Processing tomato production is expected to decrease by 2050 due to the projected increase in temperature. Nature Food, 3, 437–444. https://doi.org/10.1038/s43016-022-00521-y.

[323] Geisel, P., Beede, R. (2004). Pistachio: Calendar of Operations for Home Gardeners, https://anrcatalog.ucanr.edu/Details.aspx?itemNo=8147, Access Date: May 14, 2023
[324] Lombardo, I. Tomatoes: China's Role, November 2021, https://www.producebluebook.com/2021/12/15/tomatoes-chinas-role/, Access Date: May 28, 2023
[325] Suresha, H. P., Uppaladinni, M., Tiwari, K. K. Indian Commodity Market Price Comparative Study of Forecasting Methods – A Case Study on Onion, Potato and Tomato, 22 December 2021, https://www.researchgate.net/profile/Suresh-Hp-2/publication/358037089_Indian_Commodity_Market_Price_Comparative_Study_of_Forecasting_Methods_-_A_Case_Study_on_Onion_Potato_and_Tomato/links/622a067484ce8e5b4d163012/Indian-Commodity-Market-Price-Comparative-Study-of-Forecasting-Methods-A-Case-Study-on-Onion-Potato-and-Tomato.pdf, Access Date: June 06, 2023
[326] Gulati, A., Wardhan, H., Sharma, P. (2022). Tomato, Onion and Potato (TOP) Value Chains. In: Gulati, A., Ganguly, K., Wardhan, H. (eds), Agricultural Value Chains in India. India Studies in Business and Economics, Singapore: Springer, https://doi.org/10.1007/978-981-33-4268-2_3.
[327] Kaska, N. (1995). Pistachio Nut Growing in Turkey. Acta **Horticulturae**, 419, 161–164, 10.17660/ActaHortic.1995.419.26, https://doi.org/10.17660/ActaHortic.1995.419.26, Access Date: May 15, 2023.
[328] Guan, Z., Suh, D. H., Feng, W. Tomato Suspension Agreements and the Effects On Market Prices and Farm Revenue, 4/23/2018, https://edis.ifas.ufl.edu/publication/FE1025, Access Date: May 26, 2023
[329] Yamamoto, K., Seida, K., Nishiyama, J., Hayashi, K., Daishi, S., Tanaka, M. S. "Predicting System of Harvest Time and Yield of Tomato," 2018 IEEE 7th Global Conference on Consumer Electronics (GCCE), Nara, Japan, 2018, pp. 437–439, doi: 10.1109/GCCE.2018.8574865.
[330] Sakunrasrisuay, C., Musikawan, P., Nguyen, A.-N., Kongsorot, Y., Aimtongkham, P. and C. So-In "Tomato Maturity Classification: A Transfer Learning Approach," 2021 25th International Computer Science and Engineering Conference (ICSEC), Chiang Rai, Thailand, 2021, pp. 411–416, doi: 10.1109/ICSEC53205.2021.9684584.
[331] Birkett, D. C. Water Monitor Lakes and Reservoirs, 2023, https://blueice.gsfc.nasa.gov/gwm/lake/Index, Access Date: July 22, 2023
[332] Ruess, P. J., Konar, M., Wanders, N., Bierkens, M. Irrigation by Crop in the Continental United States From 2008 to 2020, First published: 29 December 2022, https://agupubs.onlinelibrary.wiley.com/doi/10.1029/2022WR032804#wrcr26385-bib-0047, Access Date: July 22, 2023
[333] Withlacoochee Rive Basin Board. Friday, February 23, 2007 9:00 a.m., https://www.swfwmd.state.fl.us/sites/default/files/calendar/notebooks/withla02-23-0
[334] Caputo, A., Kortsha, M. (2022). Climate Change is Coming for Your Ketchup. June, 15, https://www.jsg.utexas.edu/news/2022/06/climate-change-is-coming-for-your-ketchup/, Access Date: May 24, 2023.
[335] Zaraska, M. The tomatoes at the forefront of a food revolution, 8th December 2021, https://www.bbc.com/future/article/20211207-the-tomatoes-at-the-forefront-of-a-food-revolution, Access Date: May 29, 2023
[336] IANS. Tomato is changing the fortunes of Himachal farmers in Solar. Sirmaur and Kullu, Jul 4, 2022, 09:44 IST, https://www.businessinsider.in/business/news/tomato-is-changing-the-fortunes-of-himachal-farmers-in-solar-sirmaur-and-kullu/articleshow/92644004.cms, Access Date: May 27, 2023.
[337] Munch, D. (2022). Specialty Crop Considerations for the Farm Bill. Nov, 30, https://www.fb.org/market-intel/specialty-crop-considerations-for-the-farm-bill#, Access Date: June 30, 2023.
[338] Reyes, J., Elias, E. (2019). Spatio-temporal variation of crop loss in the United States from 2001 to 2016. Environmental Research Letters, 14(7), https://doi.org/10.1088/1748-9326/ab1ac9,, Access Date: July 02, 2023.
[339] USDA, Crop Insurance Program Models. 1995, https://www.rma.usda.gov/ftp/publications/handbooks/CROPMODL.PDF, Access Date: July 01, 2023

[340] Romero, E. D. Oh, Nuts! U.S. Pistachio Growers Worry About Competition From Iran, February 19, 201612:56 PM ET, https://www.npr.org/sections/thesalt/2016/02/19/467266572/oh-nuts-u-s-pistachio-growers-worry-about-competition-from-iran, Access Date: May 20, 2023

[341] Air, F. How Industrial Farming 'Destroyed' The Tasty Tomato, June 28, 201111:44 AM ET, https://www.npr.org/2011/06/28/137371975/how-industrial-farming-destroyed-the-tasty-tomato, Access Date: July 03, 2023

[342] Estabrook, B. (Author 2012). Reprint edition Tomatoland: How Modern Industrial Agriculture Destroyed Our Most Alluring Fruit Paperback, Publisher: Andrews McMeel Publishing(April 24) ISBN-13: 978-1449423452

[343] Guan, Z., Biswas, T., Feng, W. The Us Tomato Industry: An Overview Of Production and Trade, PUBLICATION #FE1027 Date: 4/24/2018, https://edis.ifas.ufl.edu/publication/FE1027, Access Date: May 22 2023

[344] Osteen, C. Methyl Bromide Phaseout Proceeds: Users Request Exemptions, April 01 2003, https://www.ers.usda.gov/amber-waves/2003/april/methyl-bromide-phaseout-proceeds/, Access Date: July 04, 2023

[345] McAvoy, G., Ozores-Hampton, M. Unique Challenges For Florida Growers In Tomato And Pepper Production, 2/11/2018, https://edis.ifas.ufl.edu/publication/IN733, Access Date: July 03, 2023

[346] Cao, X., Guan, Z., Vallad, G. E., Feng, W. Economics of fumigation in tomato production: The impact of methyl bromide phase-out on the Florida tomato industry, 2019, https://ageconsearch.umn.edu/record/290388/?ln=en, Access Date: July 04, 2023

[347] Brahambhatt, R. Climate change is threatening ketchup, salsa, and California, August 19 2022, https://www.zmescience.com/science/news-science/climate-change-is-threatening-ketchup-salsa-and-california/, Access Date: July 04, 2023

[348] Branthôme, F.-X. Climate change is already shocking our industry, 04/11/2021, https://www.tomatonews.com/en/climate-change-is-already-shocking-our-industry_2_1499.html, Access Date: July 04, 2023

[349] DiFeliciantonio, C. Higher prices for ketchup and spaghetti sauce? California's drought is hurting tomato farmers, Oct. 23, 2022 Updated: Oct. 24, 2022 7:51 p.m., https://www.sfchronicle.com/california/article/tomato-price-farming-drought-17526327.php, Access Date: July 04, 2023

[350] USDA. (2019). California Processing Tomato Report, Released: August 28, 2019 – 12:00 p.m. PDT, https://www.nass.usda.gov/Statistics_by_State/California/Publications/Specialty_and_Other_Releases/Tomatoes/2019/201908ptom.pdf, Access Date: July 04, 2023

[351] Dillon, A. California Experiences a Turbulent 2020 Season, November 25th, 2020, https://www.morningstarco.com/california-experiences-a-turbulent-2020-season/, Access Date: July 04, 2023

[352] Reed Fujii, S. J. tomato crop damaged by pest, Updated: August 9 2013, https://www.recordnet.com/story/business/agricultural/2013/08/10/s-j-tomato-crop-damaged/44373179007/, Access Date: July 04, 2023

[353] tfitchette Virus slams 2013 California tomato yields, February 12 2014, https://www.farmprogress.com/vegetables/virus-slams-2013-california-tomato-yields, Access Date: July 04, 2023

[354] Greenaway, T. Eight foods you're about to lose due to climate change, Wed 29 Oct 2014 09.00 EDT, https://www.theguardian.com/vital-signs/2014/oct/29/diet-climate-maple-syrup-coffee-global-warming, Access Date: May 21, 2023

[355] Ndubiwa, M. (2022). Tomato Processors Set to Pay Unprecedented Prices for Raw Tomatoes in 2022. Updated Apr, 29, https://www.tridge.com/stories/tomato-processors-set-to-pay-unprecedented-prices-for-raw-tomatoes-in-2022, Access Date: May 24, 2023

[356] Artificial. (2022). Intelligence and Heuristics for Enhanced Food Security by Chandrasekar Vuppalapati (1st edition), Publisher: Springer, (September 17, 2022), ISBN-13: 978-3031087424.

[357] Shan, L. Y. India's tomato prices surge over 300%, sparking theft and turmoil, PUBLISHED WED, JUL 12 20239:46 PM EDT, https://www.cnbc.com/2023/07/13/indias-tomato-prices-surge-over-300percent-prompting-thieves-and-turmoil.html, Access date; July 13, 2023

[358] USDA. Climate Vulnerabilities to California Specialty Crops, 2023, https://www.climatehubs.usda.gov/hubs/california/topic/climate-vulnerabilities-california-specialty-crops, Access Date: May 21, 2023

[359] Farms, P. Growing and Harvesting American Pistachios, Last update: March 31 2022, https://americanpistachios.org/growing-and-harvesting, Access Date: July 03, 2023

[360] Kallsen, C. Fall Juvenile Pistachio Freeze Damage, April 2017, https://cekern.ucanr.edu/files/261139.pdf, Access Date: May 21, 2023

[361] Cone, M. (Sept. 21, 2019), In a Race Against Warming, Growers Try to Outsmart Climate Change, https://www.nytimes.com/2019/09/21/climate/agriculture-climate-change.html?auth=login-google1tap&login=google1tap

[362] Gerald (Jerry) Brust. Viruses Turning Up in High Tunnel Tomatoes, Updated: May 22, 2023, https://extension.umd.edu/resource/viruses-turning-high-tunnel-tomatoes, Access date; July 13, 2023

[363] Bhat, M., Chanda, S. Florida's tomato and strawberry farmers look to future amid market, climate challenges, December 6 2021, https://casenews.fiu.edu/2021/12/06/floridas-tomato-and-strawberry-farmers-look-to-future-amid-market-climate-challenges/, Access date; July 15, 2023

[364] Wheeler, T., Braun, J. V. (2013). Climate Change Impacts on Global Food Security. Science, 341, 508–513. 10.1126/science.1239402.

[365] Coolong, T., Boyhan, G. E. (2017). Commercial Tomato Production Handbook. Published with Full Review on Jan, 30, https://extension.uga.edu/publications/detail.html?number=B1312&title=commercial-tomato-production-handbook, Access Date: May 26, 2023.

[366] Rubin, B. Why tomato sauce is spreading thin: How the tomato industry is responding to the climate, economy, and the American appetite, 2023, https://global.wf.com/hub_article/tomato-sauce-spreading-thin-tomato-industry-responding-climate-economy-american-appetite/, Access Date: May 24, 2023

[367] BBC. Climate change: Vietnam records highest-ever temperature of 44.1C, May 07 2023, https://www.bbc.com/news/world-asia-65518528, Access Date: May 08, 2023

[368] Specialty Crops for Climate Change Adaptation. (2023). Strategies for Enhanced Food Security by Using Machine Learning and Artificial Intelligence (STEAM-H: . . . Agriculture, Mathematics & Health) (1st ed. 2023 edition). Edition, Chandrasekar Vuppalapati (Author), Publisher: Springer, (October 24, 2023), ISBN-13: 978-3031383984.

[369] Assessing Policy Effectiveness using AI and Language Models. (May 31 2024). Applications for Economic and Social Sustainability, Chandrasekar Vuppalapati 2024th, Publisher: Springer, ISBN-13: 978-3031560965.

[370] Rubin, B. Why tomato sauce is spreading thin: How the tomato industry is responding to the climate, economy, and the American appetite, 2023, https://global.wf.com/hub_article/tomato-sauce-spreading-thin-tomato-industry-responding-climate-economy-american-appetite/, Access Date: May 24, 2023

[371] Adanacioglu, H., Yercan, M. An analysis of tomato prices at wholesale level in Turkey: An application of SARIMA model, September 2012, http://www.custoseagronegocioonline.com.br/numero4v8/Tomato%20english.pdf, Access Date: May 26, 2023

[372] Brownne, B. Record tomato harvest may stretch into November, Oct 1999, https://www.recordnet.com/story/business/1999/10/16/record-tomato-harvest-may-stretch/50804771007/, Access Date: May 28, 2023

[373] Adanacioglu, H., Yercan, M. An analysis of tomato prices at wholesale level in Turkey: an application of SARIMA model, September 2012, http://www.custoseagronegocioonline.com.br/numero4v8/Tomato%20english.pdf, Access Date: May 26, 2023

[374] Bhardwaj, M. R., Pawar, J., Bhat, A., Deepanshu, I. E., Kartik Sagar, Y. N. An innovative Deep Learning Based Approach for Accurate Agricultural Crop Price Prediction, 15 April 2023, https://arxiv.org/abs/2304.09761, Access Date: May 25, 2023

[375] Branthôme, F.-X. The 2022 Tomato News Conference: The 2022 Crop in China, 04/01/2023, https://www.tomatonews.com/en/the-2022-tomato-news-conference-the-2022-crop-in-china_2_1864.html, Access Date: May 25, 2023

[376] Tomato. A Covert "Gold-Mine" of Recent Times, Date Posted: 2022-08-23 16:54:39, https://tradekaiju.com/blog/view/tomato-a-covert-gold-mine-of-recent-times-11, Access Date: May 28, 2023

[377] Simnitt, S., Martin, P. U.S. Fruit and Vegetable Industries Try To Cope With Rising Labor Costs, December 28, 2022, https://www.ers.usda.gov/amber-waves/2022/december/u-s-fruit-and-vegetable-industries-try-to-cope-with-rising-labor-costs/, Access Date: May 27, 2023

[378] Kumar1, V., Sharma2, H. R., Singh, K. Behaviour of Market Arrivals and Prices of Selected Vegetable Crops: A Study of Four Metropolitan Markets, 2005, https://ageconsearch.umn.edu/record/58477/files/art-10.pdf?ln=en&withWatermark=1, Access Date: June 02, 2023

[379] Emsden, C. Almost half the world's population lives in households linked to agrifood systems, 03/04/2023, https://www.fao.org/newsroom/detail/almost-half-the-world-s-population-lives-in-households-linked-to-agrifood-systems/, Access Date: May 29, 2023

[380] Ohri, N. India cenbank chief says inflation has moderated, but no room for complacency, May 24, 2023 – 02:33 am EDT, https://www.nasdaq.com/articles/india-cenbank-chief-says-inflation-has-moderated-but-no-room-for-complacency, Access Date: May 24, 2023

[381] Suresha, H. P., Uppaladinni, M., Tiwari, K. K. Indian Commodity Market Price Comparative Study of Forecasting Methods – A Case Study on Onion, Potato and Tomato, 22 December 2021, https://www.researchgate.net/profile/Suresh-Hp-2/publication/358037089_Indian_Commodity_Market_Price_Comparative_Study_of_Forecasting_Methods_-_A_Case_Study_on_Onion_Potato_and_Tomato/links/622a067484ce8e5b4d163012/Indian-Commodity-Market-Price-Comparative-Study-of-Forecasting-Methods-A-Case-Study-on-Onion-Potato-and-Tomato.pdf, Access Date: June 06, 2023

[382] U.S. Embassy Ankara, Turkey – Country Commercial Guide, Last published date: 2022-07-26, https://www.trade.gov/country-commercial-guides/turkey-agriculture, Access Date: June 01, 2023

[383] Ziraat Mühendisleri Odası. Antepfıstığı Raporu 2015 2016. https://www.zmo.org.tr/genel/bizden_detay.php?kod=25199&tipi=38&sube=0 (accessed May 15, 2023).

[384] Truckload, A. Florida Tomato Shipping by the Truckload, Last Modified: May 5, 2023, https://usatruckloadshipping.com/florida-tomato-shipping-by-the-truckload/, Access date; July 14, 2023

[385] Alexander, L., Grierson, D. (Issue 2002). Ethylene biosynthesis and action in tomato: A model for climacteric fruit ripening. Journal of Experimental Botany, 531 October(377), Pages, 2039–2055. https://doi.org/10.1093/jxb/erf072.

[386] Sargent, S., Associate Professor, Department of Horticultural Sciences, Cooperative Extension Service, Institute of Food and Agricultural Sciences, University of Florida, Gainesville, 32611, Access date; July 14, 2023

[387] Cantwell, M. Impact of Ripening & Storage Conditions on Ripe Tomato Quantity, Sept 2008, https://ucanr.edu/sites/Postharvest_Technology_Center_/files/235436.pdf, Access date; July 14, 2023

[388] Hickman, K. 20 Foods You Should Never Store Near Each Other, Published on March 13, 2022 | 7:30 AM, https://www.eatthis.com/foods-ethylene-never-store-together/, Access date; July 15, 2023

[389] The Chef's garden. Flavorful fresh tomatoes vs. Ethylene-gassed ones: you decide, 2018,https://www.chefs-garden.com/blog/june-2018/flavorful-fresh-tomatoes-vs-ethylene-gassed-ones, Access date; July 15, 2023

[390] Nath, A., Bagchi, B., Verma, V. K., Rymbai, H., Jha, A. K., Deka, B. C. (2015). Extension of Shelf Life of Tomato Using KMnO4 as Ethylene Absorbent. Indian Journal of Hill Farming, 28(1), Retrieved from, https://epubs.icar.org.in/index.php/IJHF/article/view/51201, Access date; July 15, 2023.

[391] Mariah, M. A. A., Vonnie, J. M., Erna, K. H., Nur'Aqilah, N. M., Huda, N., Abdul Wahab, R., Rovina, K. (2022 Jan 20). The Emergence and Impact of Ethylene Scavengers Techniques in Delaying the Ripening of Fruits and Vegetables. Membranes (Basel), 12(2), 117, 10.3390/membranes12020117, PMID: 35207039; PMCID, PMC8877706., Access date; July 15, 2023.

[392] Coolong, T., Boyhan, G. E. Commercial Tomato Production Handbook,Published with Full Review on Jan 30, 2017,https://extension.uga.edu/publications/detail.html?number=B1312&title=commercial-tomato-production-handbook, Access Date: May 26, 2023

[393] Chanda, S., Bhat, M., Shetty, K. G., Jayachandran, K. (May 2021). Technology, Policy, and Market Adaptation Mechanisms for Sustainable Fresh Produce Industry: The Case of Tomato Production In, Florida, USA, https://www.researchgate.net/publication/351841169_Technology_Policy_and_Market_Adaptation_Mechanisms_for_Sustainable_Fresh_Produce_Industry_The_Case_of_Tomato_Production_in_Florida_USA, Access date; July 15, 2023.

[394] Morgan, K. L., Cui, X., Guan, Z. Trends in Florida Tomato Production and Markets, November 10, 2022, https://specialtycropindustry.com/trends-in-florida-tomato-production-and-markets/, Access Date: July 22, 2023

[395] Umashanker, K. Acres of crop to be deserted in Asia's largest tomato belt in Andhra Pradesh, December 04, 2022 07:53 pm | Updated 07:53 pm IST – RAYACHOTI/CHITTOOR, https://www.thehindu.com/news/national/andhra-pradesh/acres-of-crop-to-be-deserted-in-asias-largest-tomato-belt-in-andhra-pradesh/article66222524.ece, Access Date: May 27, 2023

[396] Guan, Z., Biswas, T., Wu, F. The US Tomato Industry: An Overview Of Production and Trade, PUBLICATION #FE1027 Date: 4/24/2018, https://edis.ifas.ufl.edu/publication/FE1027, Access Date: May 22 2023

[397] Hopper, B. Impacting Global Food Security Through Improved Tomato Varieties, August 1, 2022, https://cals.ncsu.edu/horticultural-science/news/impacting-global-food-security-through-improved-tomato-varieties/, Access Date: May 26, 2023

[398] Ndubiwa, M. (2022). Tomato Processors Set to Pay Unprecedented Prices for Raw Tomatoes in 2022. Updated Apr, 29, https://www.tridge.com/stories/tomato-processors-set-to-pay-unprecedented-prices-for-raw-tomatoes-in-2022, Access Date: May 24, 2023.

[399] Rowsell, J. Biggest tomato supplier shuts greenhouses due to gas price, 12 October 2021, https://www.cips.org/supply-management/news/2021/october/biggest-tomato-supplier-shuts-greenhouses-due-to-gas-price/, Access date; July 15, 2023

[400] U.S. Bureau of Labor Statistics. Average Price: Tomatoes, Field Grown (Cost per Pound/453.6 Grams) in U.S. City Average [APU0000712311], retrieved from FRED, Federal Reserve Bank of St. Louis; https://fred.stlouisfed.org/series/APU0000712311, May 23, 2023.

[401] Cline, H. Processing tomato costs to rise in 2009, December 20, 2008, https://www.farmprogress.com/vegetables/processing-tomato-costs-to-rise-in-2009, Access Date: May 24, 2023

[402] Woodward, M. Domestic Crop: Records for Tomato Price and Crop Outlook, April 9th, 2009, https://www.morningstarco.com/domestic-crop-records-for-tomato-price-and-crop-outlook/, Access Date: May 24, 2023

[403] Siqi, J. (2022). Why has the US ban on Xinjiang's tomato exports had such limited effect? Published: 8:00am, https://www.scmp.com/economy/article/3195195/why-has-us-ban-xinjiangs-tomato-exports-had-such-limited-effect?module=perpetual_scroll_0&pgtype=article&campaign=3195195, Access Date: May 23 2023.

[404] Latner, K., Lei, Z. (2006). China, Peoples Republic of Tomatoes and Products Annual, May 15 2006, https://apps.fas.usda.gov/gainfiles/200605/146187753.pdf, Access Date: May 26, 2023

[405] Williams, J. US: Stronger field tomato availability puts pressure on hothouse tomato pricing, Publication date: Thu 5 Jan 2023, https://www.hortidaily.com/article/9490938/us-stronger-field-tomato-availability-puts-pressure-on-hothouse-tomato-pricing/, Access Date: May 23, 2023.

[406] Cagle, S. California's farm workers pick America's essential produce – Unprotected from coronavirus, Tue 31 Mar 2020 11.00 BST, https://www.theguardian.com/world/2020/mar/31/us-coronavirus-outbreak-california-farm-workers, Access date; July 19, 2023

[407] Munjal, D., Explained | Why are tomato prices still high? July 19, 2023 10:58 pm | Updated July 21, 2023 01:58 pm IST https://www.thehindu.com/business/Economy/explained-what-is-behind-the-soaring-tomato-prices/article67099213.ece, Access Date: July 22, 2023

[408] Assessing Policy Effectiveness Using AI and Language Models. (May 31 2024). Applications for Economic and Social Sustainability, Chandrasekar Vuppalapati. (2024th, edition), Publisher: Springer, ISBN-13: 978-3031560965.

Index